GREEN STAR OVER WEST BENGAL

GREEN STAR OVER WEST BENGAL

Study of Mamata Banerjee

Surajit Kumar Dasgupta

KALPAZ

Green Star Over West Bengal : Study of Mamata Banerjee

ISBN: 978-81-7835-933-5

Published in 2012 in India by
Kalpaz Publications
C - 30 Satyawati Nagar
Delhi - 110052
E-mail: kalpaz@hotmail.com
Phone : 9212729499

Leser Type setting : Lucky Graphic, Delhi
Printed at : Chawla Offset Printer, Delhi

CONTENTS

PREFACE

The highly spirited and dynamic lady Mamata Banerjee was born in Calcutta on 5th January 1955. She is the daughter of Promileswar Banerjee, a government contractor and freedom-fighter whose brief life oscillated between periodic spells of affluence and penury and it was terminated at the age of fortyone. Her mother Gayatri Devi had instilled in her mind at an early age the spirit of justice and fairplay, deep feeling for all human beings and the courage to stand for the downtrodden.

Simplicity and austerity and uprightness are the hallmarks of her turbulent political career and dynamic moral character. Not unlike America's Clara Jetkin, Europe's Joan of Arc, Orissa's Nandini Satpathi and India's illustrious Indira Gandhi from her early childhood days, she had been an intrepid and intelligent lady who believes in the equality of sexes and displayed pronounced leadership qualities and organising abilities. All along she had been an uncompromising crusader against all sorts of social and political injustices and oppressions. Her life-history is a consistent account of immaculate altruism, self-abnegation and high idealism, coupled with indomitable elan and will power to bring about transformation in an unjust and obsolete polity economy and society.

In the last 34 years what did she not have to tolerate in the 'hell of crimes' the leftist West Bengal? Everything, from personal character assassination to physical aggression is the answer. In 1991 at the Hazra crossing the rod of a Lalu Alam a C P(M) miscreant almost snatched away her life. In 1994 when she was herself a minister in the national government the barbarous police forces of the left front chief minister Jyotl Basu of West Bengal literally caught hold of her by hairs and threw her out of Writers Building by force.

This was in fact an act of gross misbehaviour and vandalism

and violation of all norms of civilized conduct and sobriety. It was highly unbecoming of an old man like Jyoti Basu. Nonetheless the Central Government remained unconcerned and Jyoti Basu was not brought to book. The seemingly incurable reluctance to use the security forces on the part of Mamata Banerjee was also partly responsible for this disaster. The 'mulish' and uncultured gesture of then Minister for Cultural Affairs Buddhadev Bhattacharya and the obnoxious and pejorative utterances of senior leaders of CPM like Benoy Konar and Anil Basu constitute a dark chapter in the discredited history of the left front rule in west Bengal.

Ultimately out of disgust Mamata Banerjee came out of Congress and formed her own party Trinamool Congress in 1997. Today she has turned out to be victorious in her struggle against her arch enemy CPM.

All these years she has continued her struggle against the injustices and oppressions of CPM in an uncompromising manner. In the final analysis she has succeded in her noble mission of winning the hearts of the masses. Her crusade in favour of the 'mother, earth and man' (MA-MATI-MANUSH) has at last been crowned with success. She has acquired the magical powers to attract the ordinary masses to her own viewpoint.

Today, she is not only a highly popular woman leader of the region but also the first woman chief minister of West Bengal. In the electoral warfare in 1984, in the leftist bastion of Jadavpur the veteran CP(M) leader Somnath Chatterjee was defeated at her hands. The entire left front turned turtle in the lands of the 'giant killer' who later converted the 'winds of change' into a cyclone.

She never indulged in opportunist politics. By virtue of her charismatic image she has ascended today the pinnacle of political powers in West Bengal. She was determined to drive out the left front from the political arena in West Bengal but that government has left for the government of the 'fire daughter' (agnikanya) the burden of a debt of two lakh crores of rupees. Now the big question before her is how Mamata Banerjee will solve the problem of rescuing West Bengal from this insolvent situation. Not only that this victory has significantly enlarged her image in national politics. There are many interesting stories behind this dramatic ascent and upheaval of Mamata Banerjee.

She holds Bachelors Degrees in Arts (Hons. in History), Education (B.Ed.), Law (L.LB) and Master's Degree (in Islamic History) from Calcutta University. She was a student of Jogamaya Devi College of South Calcutta, Shri Shikshyatan and Jogesh Chandra Chaudhuri College. She was inducted to the West Bengal Chhatra Parishad while a student of Jogamaya Devi College and worked as a member of the working Committee of Chhatra Parishad during 1977-1983. She held the position of General Secretary West Bengal Congress (Indira) from 1979-1980 and Secretary, West Bengal Provincial Trade Union Congress. During the period 1983-1988 she was the Secretary of the Women's wing of the Indian National Trade Union Congress and Secretary, South Calcutta District Congress (Indira) for the period 1980-1985. In 1984 she was elected as a Member of Parliament from Jadavpur Constituency and held the post of General Secretary of the Youth Congress (Indira) and became a member of the National Council in 1987 and a member of the Executive Committee in the Congress Parliamentary Party in 1988. She has got re-elected as a Member of Parliament in 1991, 1996, 1998, 1999, 2004 and 2009 from the South Kolkata Parliamentary Constituency making her one of India's most experienced Parliamentarians. She has been a member of several Parliamentary Committees.

Mamata Banerjee served as a Minister of Railways twice (1999 and 2009), Minister of Coal and Mines in 2004 and Minister of State for Human Resource Development, Department of Youth Affairs and Sports and Women and Child Development once in the cabinet of the Government of India.

She opposed forceful land acquisition for industrialization by the then Communist Government in West Bengal at Singur and Nandigram for Special Economic Zones (SEZ) at the cost of the agriculturists and farmers.

In 2011, All India Trinamool Congress registered a landslide victory defeating the world's longest serving democratically elected Communist government, the Communist Party Of India (Marxist) led Left Front government, bringing to an end a 34 year - old regime. On May 20, 2011 Mamata Banerjee took over as the first lady to be the chief minister of West Bengal.

She is the 11th chief minister and first woman chief minister of the region. The highlight of the election was that only four ministers out of the 28 of the outgoing regime were able to retain their seats. Even the outgoing chief minister Buddhadev Bhattacharya lost in his own constituency.

In spite of her very busy work schedule she has authored over 20 books and created over 5,000 oil paintings quite a few of which have been auctioned. The proceeds of such auctions have been donated by her to various social activities. Throughout her political life she maintained an austere lifestyle and never spent money on costly clothes, cosmetics and jewellery and slung a cotton bag on her shoulder. She has remained single throughout her life.

She is a widely travelled lady who represented the country in (i) U.N. General Assembly (ii) as a woman parliamentarian at World Women's Round Table Conference, Russia and (iii) World Youth Conference, Vietnam, (iv) attended the Working Women's Conference of ILO and ICFTU at Kualalumpur. She observed *dhama* in 1995 for 21 days to restore Human Rights and protested against atrocities on women and lock-up deaths in the country specially in West Bengal.

Kolkata - 700004 **SURAJIT KUMAR DAS GUPTA**

Acknowledgements

I am thankful to Subhrajyoti Barat for the careful typing of the entire manuscript and to my sister Sumitra, wife Gayatri and brothers-in-law Santosh Kumar Dasgupta and Prabir Roy for their unstinted help and co-operation during the writing of the book.

INTRODUCTION

In the Assembly election of 2001 Buddhadev Bhattacharya won in 199 seats and became the chief minister of West Bengal and gave three assurances. First, the 'Do it now' slogan to bring back work culture to the government departments. In other words, work should not be kept unfinished. Secondly, administration will be sensitive. In other words, the government will stand by the side of common man in their times of trials and tribulations. Thirdly, one of the objectives of the government will be to bring back 'transparency' to administration. People will be aware of everything. Taken all things together, a populist image of CP(M) was sought to be built up by the chief minister.

For understandable reasons, the question was raised then Jyoti Basu, who had been chief minister for 23 years and in whose ministry Buddhadev Bhattacharya remained from the very beginning, was doing what for this long period? From the relevant papers it was seen that after coming to power in 1977 Jyoti Basu also uttered almost similar words which Buddhadev Bhattacharya said after coming to power in 2001.

After becoming chief minister Buddhadev Bhattacharya made it clear that Jyoti Basu's left front government did not keep its promises. At the same time he also gave the assurance that performance will match the words during his administration which was given the highsounding title 'improved left front government'. In other words, the assurances of a change were given. In this year's election Trinamool Congress gave the same assurance of change in its manifesto in which are implicit those three declarations of Buddhadev Bhattacharya.

Today while taking stock of events, it is seen that Buddhadev Bhattaeharya was the fittest successor of Jyoti Basu, that is, a total failure. But the matter should not be concluded here. Rather, the government of 'mother-earth-and-man' can take lessons from the failure of its predecessor.

Today in order to draw its graph of success the story of the failure of Buddhadev Bhattacharya is most pertinent. He promised that he would not step into the shoes of Jyoti Basu. His failure in keeping that promise is directly proportional to the success in achieving the targets by Mamata Banerjee.

In 2005 Mamata Banerjee protested against the forceful land acquisition and the atrocities on local farmers in the name of industrial development policy of the Left front Government in West Bengal. Benny Santosa, CEO of the Indonesia-based Salim Group had pledged a large investment to West Bengal and the West Bengal Government had given him farmland in Howrah, sparking protest.

Mamata Banerjee suffered further setbacks in 2005 when her party lost control of the Kolkata Municipal Corporation and the sitting Mayor defected from her party. In 2006 the Trinamool Congress was defeated in West Bengal's Assembly elections losing more than half of its sitting members.

In 2006 the Tata Nano Singur controversy took place. It was generated by the Nano factory of Tata Motors at Singur in the Hooghly district. Singur gained international media attention since Tata Motors started constructing a factory to manufacture their $2500 car, the Tata Nano at Singur. The small car was scheduled to roll out of the factory by 2008. The regional government of West Bengal facilitated the controversy by using an old rule of 1897 to conduct an eminent domain takeover of 997 acres of farmland to have Tata build its factory. The rule is meant for public improvement projects and the West Bengal government wanted Tata to build its factory in its own region. Opponents included displaced farmers and Land-rights people.

The choice of Singur was made by the company among six sites offered by the regional government. The project faced massive opposition from displaced farmers. The unwilling farmers were given political support by West Bengal's opposition leader Mamata Banerjee. whose 'Save Farmland' movement was supported by environmental activists and intellectuals like Medha Patkar, Anuradha Talwar and Arundhuti Roy. Mamata's movement against displacement of farmers was also supported by several kolkata based celebrities like Aparna Sen, Kaushik Sen, Shaonli Mitra and Suva Prasanna. Ultra left activists also shared the platform with Mamata Banerjee's Trinamool Party.

In the 1950s West Bengal was one of the most industrialized regions in the country. Bidhan Roy its first chief minister founded large industrial plants in Durgapur, Asansol, Kalyani and Howrah and Calcutta proper. In the 1960s and 1970s disruptions by the Bangladesh war, the Naxal movement and militant trade unionism by leftist parties led by Jyoti Basu slowed down industrial development.

Consequently, other regions such as Maharashtra, Gujarat, Punjab, Tamil Nadu and Karnataka attracted industrial investment and experienced job growth. The rapid rise in the population of West Bengal has not been accompained by significant economic growth. Key indicators such as unemployment rates, poverty rates, infant mortality rates, job growth rates, per capita income, mobile phone penetration rates lag behind the more industrialized regions of India.

Local politicians gained power by promising agricultural land to landless farmers, but given West Bengal's population density, the land-holdings are small and the yields are insufficient to sustaion poor families. While the shift from agricultural to industrial jobs require retraining given its economic growth *it* provides an opportunity for earning higher income.

The people staying in the proposed land were forced to evacuate by the government.The compensation given was considered inadequate and the new housing facilities were delayed. This led to the protest of the peasants backed by opposition political parties who thought it would be a good opportunity to end the Communist rule.

The company has made substantial promises. According to their claims Singur would become a mini-auto city and approximately 70 vendors would set up shops along with the factory. The total investment planned is to the tune of Rs.1000 crores. The project had however generated controversy right from the start particularly on the question of government acquisition of fertile agricultural land for private enterprise.

The Nobel Laureate Amartya Sen defended the decision to set up the factory. The protesters have been trenchantly attacked, verbally by the CP(M) leaders and physically by the party's succesors. However in the 2011 Assembly elections while the sitting Trinamool Congress MLA Rabindranath Bhattacharya retained the Singur seat, Becharam Manna, the convener of Krishi Jami Raksha Samiti won the adjoining Haripal seat.

While the ruling party went all out for acquisition of 997 acres (404 ha) of multicrop land required for the car factory, questions were raised about the party's forcible acquisition which was made under the Colonial Land Acquisition Act of 1894.

Some said that the provisions of this Act were allegedly not met. The Law had provisions for government taking over privately held land for public purposes but not for development of private business. The illegality of the acquisition was substantially conceded by the Kolkata High Court. The Tata Motors site is the most fertile one in the whole of Singur and the Singur Block, in turn, is among the most highly fertile in West Bengal. Consequently, almost the entire local populace depends on agriculture with approximately 15,000 making their livelihood directly from it. With the number of direct jobs to be created no more than about 1,000, many of which were expected to go to outsiders, the local populace felt understandably threatened for their livelihood. Environmental degradation was also feared. Chief protesters included the opposition parties spearheaded by the Trinamool Congress under Mamata Banerjee and Socialist Unity Centre of India.

The land earmarked for the project was taken control of by the government administration amidst protests and fencing off commenced on December 1,2006. Mamata Banerjee who was prevented from entering Singur by the police called a state wide bandh in protest. Later she went on a 25-day hunger strike. The fenced off area was regularly guarded by cadres of the CP(M) party besides large contingents of policemen. They were accused of the multiple rape followed by turning to death of teenage villager Tapasi Malik who was active in the protests, on December 18, 2006. Negligence and political interference in the probe into her death were alleged. Later CP(M) activist Debu Malik and based on his statement CP(M) Zonal Committee Secretary Suhrid Datta were arrested by the Central Bureau of Investigation in connection with the crime.

Other aspects of the process of setting up the factory that came under severe criticism were the government's secrecy on the details of the deal and the chief minister's furnishing of false information in the Bidhan Sabha. In particular, the concessions being given to Tata Motors have not been publicly revealed.

The falsehoods of the chief minister pertain to claims made by him of having acquired 912 acres (3.69 km^2) through voluntary consent of the owners without the use of force. In 2007, the government admitted that 30 percent of the land was acquired from farmers without consent. It remained unclear whether the lack of consent was based on insufficiency of compensation or refusal to sell altogether.

Tatas ceremonially initiated the construction of the plant on 21 January, 2007. They announced on October 3, 2008 that they are pulling off Singur due to the political agitation and unrest by the Trinamool Congress against the construction of the plant. On 7th October, 2008 the Tatas announced that they would be setting up the Tata Nano Plant in Sanand, Gujarat.

While going to follow the 'Do-it-now' principle people like Buddhadev Bhattacharya and Nirupam Sen etc. ignored the government regulations and went to acquire land to build a chemical hub (SEZ) at Nandigram in East Midnapore district, resulting in the killing of 14 villagers in police firing. Trinamool Congress staged blockade, protests and strikes. The left front government shelved the proposed chemical hub project.

The Bengalees understood that Buddhadev Bhattacharya was not only a crafty political leader but also an expert actor. After the killing incident in Nandigram he admitted that he was alone responsible for the whole thing but he did not give up power. Nor did he punish the guilty police officers. And again in the last lap of the electoral propaganda he claimed that 'I did not give the order of firing. Nor did I know that the police will open fire.

But from the flow of events it is clear that firing was done to smash the Nandigram movement at the clearcut directives of the authorities of Writers's Building and Alimuddin Street. In the following period Buddhadev's administration has ignored the directives of the High Court and the Human Rights Commission and day after day neglected to pay compensation to the families of the dead and the wounded persons. It indicates that 'sensitivity' was never a strong point of his administration. Shamelessly he converted Writers Building into his party office and supported the armed attacks of his party activists on the unarmed villagers and reoccupying Nandigram. Shamelessly he declared that 'they have been paid back in their own coins'.

During the last lap of his ministership Benoy Chowdhury said that the government was being conducted by the contractors in the interest of the contractors. Benoy babu was a symbol of honesty and the second person in Jyoti Basu's ministry Benoy babu's words are more applicable to the ten years of administration of Buddhadev Bhattacharya. All the government offices including the Writers Buildings have become converted into the heavens of the contractors, promoters and the brokers of the industrialists. The direction of administration was towards the affluent section of the society and Buddhadev's role in this matter was significant. On the one hand he has instigated his officers to procure land for the Tatas, Salims and Jindals and on the other hand owing to unavailability of land hundreds of crores of rupees alloted by the Centre for the building of houses of poor people in Indira Avas yojana and Ambedkar Yojana have been returned to the national government.

As regards transparency as well, Buddhadev's administration was a sad failure. He never disclosed the government's contracts with the Tatas about Singur, with the Salims about the chemical hubs at Nandigram and with the Jindals about the Shalbani Steel Plant. Secrecy was the hard malady of his government.

Despite great failures Buddhadev Bhattacharya continued to be the chief minister for 10 years, Mamata Banerjee has no comparable party organisation. But this very fact may be the keystick of her success. She does not have to think of the party at every step.

Because hers is the last word in her party. If she can utilise this seemingly undemocratic organization for the purpose of public welfare, it will indeed create a new chapter in the history of West Bengal.

PART-I

(MAY - SEPTEMBER 2011)

1

GREEN STAR OVER WEST BENGAL

In the month of April 1975 the Special Branch of Calcutta Police first opened a file in the name of the youngest politician in West Bengal and commented in her name: 'the most aggressive political leader'. Her name was Mamata Banerjee. In the previous years she had been the Unit Secretary of the Student's Union of Jogamaya Devi College. Since then she was regarded as a frontranking Congress leader of South Calcutta. However at that time very few people believed that the young lady who had just then become the convenor of the South Calcutta Mahila Congress in 1976 will turn out to be a giant-killer within only eight years and ultimately become a Member of Parliament. Thereafter in 1997 she left the Congress and formed her own new party. Everybody had the impression that she would end in becoming a total failure. In 2004 and 2006 the election results were miserable. But she was undaunted and did not give up all hopes.

Mamata Banerjee, the Cinderella of Indian politics had been continuously humiliated by being marginalised within her own party but did not totally break down. In the Loksabha election of 2004 she was victorious only in her own seat and day after day she sat totally alone as a single member party in the Parliament. The leftist MPs hurled ridicules at her and excited her by uttering ugly words. She was hindered at every step in delivering her own speech. With her own eyes she had witnessed the camaraderie between CP(M) and the Congress. Wiping the tears of her eyes she had left the parliament House but never gave up all hopes.

This transition in the life of Mamata Banerjee is today the inspiration for many people. Through sheer talent and tenacity or hard labour she has demolished the red bastion of 34 years' rule of

CP(M) and become the green star in the political firmament of West Bengal almost by her single-handed efforts. The allegory which started by selling Haringhata milk in a roadside depot of Kalighat ended at the assumption of political powers as the chief minister in the Writers Building.

Many of us have read the book entitled 'From Log-cabin to White House' which is concerned with the life of President Abraham Lincoln of America. The political upheaval of Mamata Banerjee is in many ways comparable to this meteoric rise of the American President. She belongs to a lower middle class Bengali family and lacks the political or educational pedigrees of any of her predecessors.

Two of her most memorable political achievements are: in the first place she came out of the Congress, built up her own party almost single handed, rose to the apex of the regional politics and established her party in the second position in the arena of New Delhi politics. Secondly, she smashed down almost single handed a cadre-based political machinery like CP(M). It was she who proved in the last 34 years to the residents of West Bengal that CP(M) was not invincible and that it can also be defeated.

How could Mamata Banerjee achieve these two extraordinary political successes? Mamata Banerjee succeeded in these two objectives by virtue of her personal integrity, her sincere and unflinching efforts in an uncompromising struggle against CP(M) and her facile ability to mix with and move among the ordinary citizens. It is these ordinary citizens who remain throughout at the very centre of all her political activities. That is why she received in return the unstinted and inexhaustible support of the common men. Undoubtedly, her qualities are admirable and rare in contemporary Indian politics.

Not that Mamata Banerjee was the first person to rebel against the Congress and form a party of her own. Many people before her did it and will also do the same in future. But how many among them could achieve such spectacular and historic success? Let us first have a look at regional politics. In 1967, Ajoy Mukherjee severed all connections with Congress and fought the election after constituting his own Bangla Congress. By holding the hands of the leftists it was possible for him to receive instantaneous success. Mukherjee's personal integrity, past political tradition and his role in the freedom struggle were above all suspicions and possible criticism. But not unlike a comet his Bangla Congress all on a sudden appeared and disappeared in the political firmament of West Bengal. In 1977 the veteran Gandhian leader Prafulla Chandra Sen who was the ex-chief minister of West Bengal left Congress and became a leader of the Janata Party in West Bengal but failed to estabilish that party on a strong foothold in the regional politics. By their centrifugal movement outside the mainstream of Congress both the leaders faced the end of their political careers. The political pedigree of Mamata Banerjee cannot certainly be compared with those of Ajoy Mukherjee and Prafulla Chandra Sen.

Pranab Mukherjee once left Congress and formed his own Rashtriya Samajbadi Congress. Along with him there was Gundu Rao of Karnataka. In the Assembly vote of 1987 the deposits of all the candidates of that party of Pranabbabu were confiscated by going out of the Congress Party. Nobody among Ajoy Mukherjee, Prafulla Sen or Pranab Mukherjee could establish their own parties on a strong foothold, not to say anything about rising at the vertex of popularity in the regional politics and dislodging the ruling CP(M) from the pedestal of political power unlike Mamata Banerjee.

At the first half of the seventies at the all-India level leaders like Morarji Desai and Jagjivan Ram came out of Congress and formed the Congress (Organization) but failed to give it or its successor Janata Party a long span of life. Although they suceeded in dislodging Indira Gandhi from power, it was only a temporary occurrence. At the end of the seventies in the year 1978-1979, men like Devraj Urs, K. Brahmananda Reddy, Y.B. Chavan, A.K. Anthony, Sharad Pawar, Priyaranjan Dasmunshi, Sharat Chandra Sinha etc. broke away from the Congress (I) and at first formed Congress (Urs) and thereafter Congress (S) or Congress (Socialist) but all these were totally transient happenings. In course of time with the exception of Saratbabu all the other persons eventually returned to the mainstream of Congress. In 1987-1988 keeping V.P. Singh in the forefront Arun Nehru, Ashok Sen, Arif Mohammed Khan etc. left the Congress of Rajiv Gandhi and at first formed the Jan Morcha and thereafter Janata Dal but failed to lengthen its life span.

Very recently in 1998 i.e. within one year of the formation of

Trinamool Congress by Mamata Banerjee men like Sharad Pawar and Purna Sangma came out of Congress and formed in 1999 the Nationalist Congress Party (NCP). Within thirteen years Mamata Banerjee succeeded in uprooting a so-called organized party like CP(M) from power and established her own party Trinamool Congress in power in West Bengal almost by her lone efforts. But this is what Sharad Pawar failed to do in Maharashtra. Also in the arena of national politics Sharad Pawar's NCP is lagging much behind Trinamool Congress of Mamata Banerjee.

This is where Mamata Banerjee is superior to all the others. Because they left the Congress owing to a fight of ego over personal image. Ajoy Mukherjee had troubles with Prafulla Chandra Sen. And starting from Prafulla Chandra Sen, Morarji Desai, V.P. Singh and very recently Sharad Pawar and Purna Sangma had either conflict of ego with Indira Gandhi or personal differences with Rajiv Gandhi or sought to serve their own narrow personal political interests in the grab of fighting on the sham excuse of foreign citizenship of Sonia Gandhi by birth and left Congress on that account. On the other hand Mamata Banerjee left Congress solely for the sake of conducting an uncompromising crusade against CP(M). Because her allegation was that the West Bengal Pradesh Congress was not sincere in their fight against CP(M). Like melons they are green outside but red inside. She called them 'tarmuz congress' who have sold themselves to the CP(M). Mamata forsook the company of Congress (I) and formed her own party Trinamool Congress because she was convinced that even the Congress High Comm and was not sincerely interested in fighting an uncompromising battle against CP(M) in West Bengal. Even today she is confirmed in that conviction and conflict. Her personal integrity is above anybody's suspicion.

Mamata Banerjee has held ministerial positions in the national government in more than one phases. She was also the Railways Minister once before. But taking advantage of the Ministry in the national government she did not become another A.Raja or Sukhram. Even today we can see that she does not believe in the blind allegiance to the party. Her vision is not befogged by a division between 'We and They' and she feels comfortable in the midst of the crowds of men. It was Mao Ze-Dong who used to aver that Communists must always remain among the people just as fishes abound in water. In a like manner Mamata Banerjee is seen to be comfortable in the midst of human crowds. CP(M) and CP(I) however do not behave in a like manner. Wearing a pair of hawai chappals Mamata Banerjee can walk miles after miles in a procession. On the other hand the CP(M) and CP(I) leaders can not walk even a single furlong.

This is the second keystick of the political success of Mamata Banerjee. She demolished CP(M) in West Bengal. She closed down the shutters of Buddhadev Bhattacharya & Co. in West Bengal.

The CP(M) activists are free to heap their ridicules over her as the 'fire-daughter' (Agnikanya) of Patuapara but the miserable defeat of this large party in her hands is an undeniable fact of history.

The familiar socio-economic circumstances of the lower middle class Bengalee tinshed which was the nursing home of the cadres of the Communist Party and the origin of the political support and the votebank of the undivided CPI at first and CP(M) thereafter also gave birth to Mamata Banerjee. She was not born with a silver spoon in her mouth. Unlike Dr. Bidhan Chandra Roy, Siddharthashankar Roy or Jyoti Basu she had no familial political or educational pedigree. She is not the niece of any famous poet. She was never a student of Presidency College. She never went to U.K. to become a barrister. She did not have higher education unlike the first chief minister of West Bengal, Dr. Prafulla Chandra Ghosh. Unlike Prafulla Chandra Sen or Ajoy Mukherjee she did not have any firsthand experience of working as an apprentice of Gandhian politics. On the contrary she had once the hard life of working as an ordinary employee of Haringhata milk depot. Such a person could easily become a cadre of the Communist Party. But the irony of fate is that incourse of time she proved to be the nemesis of the biggest political party in West Bengal CP(M).

No one knows for certain what Mamata Banerjee will become in the future years. For the simple reason that there is no last word in politics. Already the international opinion is highly optimistic about her probable future career. However if she persists in her humanist conduct like today, if she remains unflinching in her own political convictions and determination, if she is not over-whelmed with the intoxication of chief ministership in the Writers Building, if she also does not, like her adversaries, go to acquire farming lands on the pretext of industrial development, if she can expedite the progress of her own region, at least to some extent her name will ultimately be inscribed in letters of gold in the hearts of the umpteen millions of this region for ever and her image will continue to shine as the green star over the political horizons of West Bengal.

2

STRATEGY OF DEVELOPMENT - 1

The 'package' which the chief minister Mamata Banerjee announced in Jangalmahal has demonstrated a holistic approach to development. Employment, vocational training, improvement of the educational system at all levels, improvement of the standard of health services and improvement of the transport system-all these facets have been emphasised in her declaration. There is little doubt that for the rapid development of any area these matters are essential and over and above that, for the sake of establishment of social justice such efforts are indispensable. The increase in the number of old age allowances, rice at a subsidised rate, conveyance of medical treatment to the remote villages through the bike-driving health activists-all these initiatives will help the poorest people to live with dignity.

The question may of course be raised how all such matters may be arranged within a short period? Jangalmahal is neglected for long and by taking advantage of this phenomenon, the Maoist movement had broken out in this area. An adequate environment is needed for constructing colleges, health centres and factories and to keep them in an on-going position. How can new institutions be started where many schools had been remaining closed for long? Then again what will be the gain by building a centre for cultural exercise within a climate of terrorism? When the public treasury of the region has been exhausted, it is also difficult to provide the finance for these huge development activities. Then again how can one ignore the likelihood that the finance for development after coming to Jangalmahal will be squandered amidst various channels of corrupt activities?

All these are important misgivings but not the most important questions. In her visit to Nayagram and Jhargram the new chief minister has explained to the people at large how she desires to solve the problems of Jangalmahal and what are her designs and strategy. After her declaration it has been evident that she is looking upon socio-economic development as the foremost weapon for tackling terroristic activities. This area can be released from the clutches of terrorism only if the allegation of neglect and a change can be brought about in the behaviour of police-administration to the poor and indigent people. Because only transparent and dynamic administration can reduce the weight and appeal of the arguments of the Maoists. It is that path which Mamata Banerjee has adopted.

There can be no doubt that this will cause much uneasiness in the minds of the Maoists. As a result of identifying development and social justice as the guiding principles of the new government and as a result of opposition to CP(M) which is marked as the opponent party of the Maoists, the later have lost all the arguments against sitting in a conference with Mamata Banerjee. On the other hand the chief minister has shown administrative firmness against the demands of the Maoists for the removal of the CRP. She is firm in her resolution that the CRP will not be removed before the surrender of arms by the Maoists.

Under the circumstances the Maoists will have to ponder over the question why sitting in a conference is not the best solution for the sake of the greater interest of the poor people. Over and above that by giving the local people services in the police and by calling upon them to hold weapons in the interest of the country will undoubtedly put pressure on the Maoists.

In Bihar by way of allocating finance for the development of the Naxal-infested areas and bringing about development in the system of law and order Nitish Kumar obtained good dividends. His return in the election has been interpreted as an index of popular support to his policy of development. Therefore there is good likelihood that Mamata Banerjee also by way of bringing about development of education, health and nutrition will be able to check the advance of the Maoists and increase the support to her own party. Possibly this apprehension is at the root of the fact that the Maoists have prevented the villagers from attending the meetings of Mamata Banerjee. There is little doubt that Mamata Banerjee has succeeded in pressurising the Maoists and in this way given well-pronounced evidence of her political and administrative acumen.

3

STATE IS GOOD, MARKET EVIL

Market prices are rising in West Bengal and all the other regions of India and also China. The official authorities as well as the experts in Economics in different regions and different nations are anxious how the skyrocketing market prices can be brought under control. A certain and reliable remedy for controlling the prices has not been discovered by anybody in any country, otherwise prise-rise can never remain a nerve-racking problem-everybody from Wen Jia-Bao to Manmohan Singh would heave a sigh of relief. But an infallible remedy of this malady is ready at hand. It is a purely Bengali medicine made in Alimuddin Street.

A few days ago in a public meeting at Dharmatala the earlier chief minister Buddhadev Bhattacharya has proudly announced the secret of that medicine. He has declared that the commodities should be brought within the purview of the rationing system. The problem will be mitigated if the absolute necessaries like rice, pulses, wheat and oil can be sold at cheap prices through the fair price shops. But how the extra expenditure which are necessary for this purpose will be provided? Buddhadevbabu's easy prescription is that the government should give subsidies. It is from time immemorial that CP(M) had been distributing this good advice for public benefit but the national government has the incurable habit of paying no heed. The inevitable consequence is that the people had been burning at the fire of uncomfortable price-rise.

Before accusing Buddhadev Bhattacharya and his party let us consider another pertinent point. By defeating CP(M) powers have been captured by Trinamool Congress. The adverse attitude of the new chief minister Mamata Banerjee to Alimuddin is well known to everybody. But what about its principle and attitude to economic problems? Is Mamata Banerjee opposed to this principle? Let us make an analysis. No detailed analysis is necessary, an overall study is sufficient. As a result of the rise in price of diesel the cost of running the transport has increased. The regional government has announced that transport fares cannot be increased. Why? Because if transport fares are hiked the expenditures of the passengers will be increased. In other words the government's objective is to keep the fares at a low level. Whether the equilibrium between revenue and expenditure in the transport business is maintained as a consequence need not be taken into account.

It should be noticed that both the former chief minister and the present chief minister are unmindful of the market. Both of them believe in the principle of forcibly reducing the prices of rice, pulses, wheat and oil and the fares of buses, minibuses and taxis. Buddhadevbabu has in his speech indulged in the familiar Marxist condemnation of the market system. And his successor is attuning also her utterances easily with that strain.

It is unfortunate, but not strange. Whatever be the name of the party or whatever be the colour of the flag everybody in West Bengal is opposed to the market and is a votary of the control by the state.The leftist mind of this region is unwilling to subscribe to the primary principle of economics that the prices of goods and services in the market should be fixed in the open market by the free play of market forces of demand and supply. Hence the subsidisation of the prices of rice, pulses, wheat and oil and the fares of the buses, minibuses and taxis.If subsidies are not given what will happen to the poor?

The argument for giving subsidies to those who are truly poor is of course rational. But wholesale rationing or introduction of cheap fares at wholesale rates would only mean that the advantages will be mainly enjoyed by the middle class people in the short run. It is they who normally attend the meetings at Dharmatala, are passengers in the minibuses, are vocal, able and unified. And they also lack farsightedness. It is they who have ultimately to bear the brunt of the subsidies because these are provided finally from the public treasury.

But this is in fact a long-run affair. For the time being it is of course desirable that bus fares are kept at a low level and that food is available through fair price shops at subsidised rates. The whole thing is in fact the politics of appeasing the middle classes behind an ideal which is in favour of the control by the state and opposed to the operations of the market.

4

STRATEGY OF DEVELOPMENT - 2

A high level conference was held on June 15, 2011 at the Writer's Building with chief minister Mamata Banerjee for the purpose of discussing developmental activities at Jangalmahal. She has issued directions for making a package on an emergency basis for providing employment, supply of food and drinking water as well as medical services for the inhabitants of Jangalmahal. Among those who attended the meeting there were the chief secretary Samar Ghosh, Home Secretary GD Goutam and the Director General of Police Naparajit Mukherjee.

It has been decided that the government will take greater initiatives for giving to the young residents of Jangalmahal greater number of services in the police where at present there are quite a few thousands of vacant positions. The government is under the impression that by giving the young people of Jangalmahal services in the police the Maoist problem in the area can be mitigated. In case of necessity a seperate battalion of the police may be set up with the young people of Jangalmahal. In this way employment of the local people will ensure economic development of the area.

The chief minister previously declared that more people of Jangalmahal should be provided with rice at Rs. 2 per kg. She has issued direction to implement the project at a rapid pace. Her government has taken initiative so that in order that a single person in Jangalmahal does not remain in starvation rice should be provided free of cost. On this very day the chief minister visited the Food Department and issued instructions to the officers that rice and wheat should be distributed among the poor people before these are invaded by the insects.

The water Resources Development Department has already submitted a project of Rs. 22 crores for increasing the supply of drinking and irrigation water at Jangalmahal. Apart from accumulating ground water the Department has also emphasised the holding of rain water for this purpose.

The chief minister has also issued instructions to the Health Department so that satisfactory medical services are available at the health centres at Jangalmahal. The Health Department is giving special attention to the fact that there are no problems, relating to the availability of physicians and medicines in the health centres.

The chief minister has alerted all the departments to remain conscious so that the minimum requirements of living of the people of Jangalmahal do not remain unsatisfied.

5

FINANCE TANGLES

From the last month of May there was strong speculation that from the month of April, the government employees and the teachers will not receive their salaries. This was announced in different newspapers and TV channels and was discussed in the corridors of the government offices and even in the school and college compounds. Among the ministers also some were heard to express the apprehension of this financial crisis. And the then Finance Minister Asim Dasgupta had to visit New Delhi repeatedly in order to sit in conference with the Central Finance Minister Pranab Mukherjee so that a moribund regional economy can be kept enlivened for one or one and a half month till the election. Thereafter took place the popular mandate through the election of the Assembly. The disastrous defeat of the left front government after its continuous rule for thirty four years was followed by the installation of a new government under Trinmool Congress. This is the first time that after assuming the charge of ruling the region, the government received direct evidence of the fact of the bankruptcy of the treasury. Moreover, the predecessors have imposed upon the new government a huge burden of debt. Of course for the last few months the previous government had been repeatedly alerting the citizens of this region about this bankruptcy. This fact was also pointed out in their electoral manifesto and publicity campaign.

Under such critical conditions, the newly elected Finance Minister Amit Mitra was entrusted with the responsibility of managing the financial affairs of the regions. His ministerial career started through a serious crisis and the challenge to overcome it. No sooner than a single month was over, he had to submit the new budget. But this is not a full-fledged budget. In financial terms it is called 'Vote-on-Account Budget'.

It may be remembered in this context that since the election was due to be held in the month of May, the outgoing Finance Minister Asim Dasgupta also submitted a Vote-on-Account budget for the first four months of the new financial year (April 2011 - March 2012).

In fact, whenever a general election is held at the beginning of a financial year or whenever towards the end of a financial year, there occurs unexpectedly a natural or man-made disaster or, whenever due to some unavoidable reason there is not enough time for preparing a full-fledged budget a 'vote-on-account budget' is submitted. In case it is a regional budget, it has got to be submitted in the Legislative Assembly and recommended through a majority vote. If it is a central budget, it has to be passed in the Loksabha. The tenure of this budget is usually two months to six months.

Amit Mitra did not receive the minimum time of the few months necessary for preparing a full fledged budget. That apart he alleged that while submitting the vote-on-Account budget, his predecessor declared in the Annual Economic Report that the expected rate of increase of revenue will be 39 P.c. At the same time he showed the estimated amount of probable expenditure at a very low level. Amit Mitra complained that this statement was not only exaggerated, it was actually an unrealistic myth. And the ordinary citizens of the region have in this way been deliberately confused. This was another reason why he had to submit a fresh 'Vote-on-Account Budget.'

Amit Mitra has submitted a budget for two months only August and September. The allotment is to the extent of Rs. 11,165 crores 62 lakhs 22 thousand only. The subjects to which has been paid special notice and additional importance are rural health and drinking water project, universal education or secondary education and the midday meal project, constitution of 17 clusters of small and medium industries (and additional job creation through this process), development of Jangalmahal, Sunderban and development of hill areas etc.

In short, emphasis has been laid on the development of social and physical infrastructures, development of human resources and development of the neglected backward areas of the region. These matters were given importance in the pre-electoral publicity campaigns as well as the manifesto of Trinamool Congress. It is remarkable that although the 'Vote-on-Account' is only a temporary and partial budget the Finance Minister has remembered their earlier promises to the people.

For the purpose of getting the necessary finance to this end, he has to put greatest reliance on grants from the central government. Already along with the Chief Minister, he has attended fruitful conferences with the central Finance Minister, Prime Minister and the Deputy Chairman of the Planning Commission.

Apart from relying on grants from the centre Mr. Mitra has also mentioned the need for making wholehearted efforts by the region for boosting the total internal production. If this can be successfully materialised in the short run, the credibility of the regional government will be enhanced.

The disappointing circumstances which are created in both the fields of internal production and revenue collection during the years of the last leftist regime were responsible for the questionable credibility of the region. In the recent years Reserve Bank of India alerted many times the erstwhile government on account of the financial distress of the region and also for taking too much credit in overdraft. There are instances of meeting official expenditures by taking credit from DFID which is an organisation under the British government.

The upper limit of the credit to be received from the centre in the present financial year was Rs. 17,800 crores. From this amount Rs. 5,000 crores are withdrawn in the last two months before the election by the leftist government. The new government after installation in power has withdrawn another Rs. 3,000 crores of rupees as emergency credit with a view to paying the salaries of the government employees and the teachers and also meeting the routine expenses of paying the pensions of the retired people and the widow allowances. Because it has inherited from the last government an empty treasury. Therefore almost half the amount of the total credit limit has already been withdrawn within three months of the current financial year While mentioning this pathetic situation Amit Mitra has also alerted that the burden of debt of this region is 2 lakh 3 thousand 867 crores of rupees or, in other words our per capita credit is 22 thousand 638 crores of rupees at the present moment.

But following the FRBM Act, West Bengal government could much earlier put a check on financial indiscipline. In that case the region could be saved from the current debacle. In fact with the exception of Sikkim, West Bengal is the only region within the nation which defied this Act and did not implement it till the middle of 2010.

It was argued then that in case of implementation of this law, the expenditure for various activities in the social sphere as well as many public welfare activities have to be severely curtailed. The real truth, however, was that in the garb of this rationale indulgence was being given to many kinds of financial irregularities which had been continuing for a pretty long time.

As per the FRBM Act, the deficit in different accounts of the government are to be regularly reduced at predetermined rates, the amounts of credit from the Reserve Bank as well as the open market are to be restricted and transparency was to be maintained in the official financial matters. From the information received from RBI, it is learnt that West Bengal happens to be one of those regions where the proportion of credit in relation to the total internal production were highest. This proportion was 47.0% on an average in 2005-08 and the positions of Bihar and Uttar Pradesh were very near this figure. In the year 2008-09 this figure was reduced somewhat to 42.5%. But in that year all the other regions except U.P. improved their circumstances from good to better conditions. Even Bihar also registered much improvement in their unenviable circumstances and reached a higher position. But West Bengal was a failure. It does not appear that the other regions incurred any loss by following the FRBM Act.

Amit Mitra has observed that this year's Annual Economic Report was based on the CAG calculations for 2010-11 and not on the basis of fictitious statistics.

It has already been mentioned that the 'vote-on-Account Budget' is not a detailed full-fledged budget. This is merely a short-term makeshift budget. In this budget only the broad outlines of the allotments are given. Unlike the Interim Budget the detailed sources of income or the accounts of both revenue and expenditure are not required to be presented. Because very often this budget is prepared within a short period for short term purposes. Apart from that it is the headache of the new government to determine how financing for two or four months will be carried out. That is why 'Vote on Account Budget' is usually passed without any detailed debates. And whenever it is submitted by a new government, it is expected that the opposition will normally consider it with democratic decency.

Nonetheless the opposition leader was very vocal about why the sources of revenue were not mentioned in detail in Amit Mitra's budget. This fact was also mentioned at large in their party organ. Aspersions have also been made over the pronunciation difficulties of the Finance Minister during his budget speech. All this indicates the lack of courtesy of the oppositionists in the Assembly.

But more discourteous and contrary to democratic ideas was the empty treasury left for the successor by the previous Finance Minister and the huge burden of debt.

Because the chief ideal of democracy is to give due respect as well as ample facilities to the opposition, it is regrettable that Amit Mitra did not receive this facility although their government is in its infancy now and they have now 'many miles to go' in the matter of administration.

It is not improper to raise the question why despite 35 years' continuous dominance the leftist government failed to build up a strong and stable economy. Why the previous Finance Minister after staying in the government at a stretch for twenty years made the regional economy sick and bankrupt although he gave for many years the stunt of a Zero-deficit budget and an alternative development model. Will they even now accuse for this failure 'the deprivation by the Centre', 'limited power of the region' and 'the problem of globalisation"?

6

DEVELOPMENT IN COUNTRY-SIDE

The regional government is making due arrangements for the rehabilitation of those inhabitants of Marichjhampi who espcaped to save their lives from the carnage committed by the onslaught of the police as well as the militant activists of the Communist Party of India (Marxist). That attempt has started under the initiative of the Refugee Rehabilitation Department. The work of registering the names of the previous residents of Marichjhampi has been going on in the Kareya area in Barasat since 30th June, 2011. About one and a half year ago, the refugees of Marichjhampi themselves set up an organisation. It is that organisation which has started the work of identifying the earlier residents of Marichjhampi. They are desirous of rehabilitation in Marichjhampi once again. The members of the organization have already met the Chief Minister Mamata Banerjee and apprised her of their problems. The organisation informed that apart from rehabilitation the Chief Minister has also given the assurance of an inquiry into the entire Marichjhampi episode.

The Minister of state of the Refugee Rehabilitation Department, Manjul Krishna Thakur has wanted a list of names of the victims from them. As soon as the names are registered that list will be handed over to the Minister. It is a lamented fact that after the Marichjhampi massacre, many refugees were displaced from their original habitat. Although the government of Jyoti Basu sent them back once again to Dandakaranya, many of them went underground in this very region. Presently they are living in different regions of India. Till now they have no lands of their own. The leftist government paid no heed to any of their appeals. On the contrary they were given the threat to send them back to Dandakaranya.

Quite a few thousands of refugees of Marichjhampi are living in Barasat, Deganga, Madhyamgram, Gobardanga, Gosaba, Kumirmari and Ranaghat. Although many refugees of Bangladesh received rehabilitation in West Bengal, the refugees of Marichjhampi were so unfortunate that they received nothing other than deprivation.

Manjul Krishna Babu informed that he had discussed this problem with the Chief Minister who was highly sincere in the matter of solving this problem. Adequate arrangements of rehabilitation of these hapless people will be undertaken. A form has already been prepared on behalf of the Refugee Rehabilitation Committee in which the names of all the members of the families, their present addresses and the respective experiences of the victims of the Marichjhampi episode will be included.

The Chief Minister Mamata Banerjee is well aware that the solution of the Jangalmahal problem is a big challenge to her government. Even before the election Mamata has repeatedly asserted that if they ever come to power they will leave no stones unturned in solving the Jangalmahal problem. Her government will pay adequate attention to the all sided development of Jangalmahal which is totally deprived from the light of development. Utmost importance has been laid on the problem of lack of development in the electoral manifesto of the Trinamool Congress.

Mamata Banerjee did not ultimately forget her electoral assurances. The very next day of assuming the changes of the Chief Minister, she started discussions in different circles regarding her duties in respect of the indigent people of Jangalmahal. On Sunday Mamata declared that the district magistrates and the district Superintendents of police should act with wartime alacrity so that each of the poor persons in Jangalmahal can get at least two square meals a day. Without caring for governmental formalities of redtapism, the new Chief Minister has issued directives to the district magistrates and district superintendents of police to provide food for the starving people in the first instance and think of the official formalities thereafter. In other words, the Chief Minister has asked her subordinates to see to it that bureaucratic bunglings are avoided so that food reaches the hungry people without delay.

Following the directives of the Chief Minister the Food Minister

Jyotipriya Mallik is going very soon to visit West Medinipur. Before that he has already informed that the regional government will start a 'Food for all' programme in order to reach food for each of the indigent persons of Jangalmahal. In case any family remains hungry and that information reaches the administration, reasures should be adopted to reach rice to that family within two hours. The additional expenses incurred for this purpose should be subsidised from the Food Department.

It is all too evident that through all these declarations, the Chief Minister is trying to present a human face of her administration. And she is careful that this human face does not obliterate as a result of any bureaucratic complexity. That is why, sidetracking many unnecessary bureaucratic restrictions, she is talking of putting emphasis on public interest. This attitude and initiative of the Chief Minister are welcome for many reasons. So long the bureaucratic complexties were given undue importance. It is a fact that questions of public interest have very often been neglected as a result of redtapism and governmental indifference.

These bureaucratic mindset and the official indifference were responsible for the most part for the lack of development in this long period after the independence. During the previous left front government five bureacrats were sent to Jangalmahal by a helicopter. Returning from that place, they submitted a few proposals regarding the development of Jangalmahal to the regional government. But as a result of the bureaucratic complexities none of those proposals were ultimately implemented. It is really thanksworthy that the new Chief Minister by demolishing that obsolete structure is laying stress on the building of a humane administration.

But, at the same time one important matter should be kept in mind. In order to remove the poverty of Jangalmahal a correct blueprint for the development of this area has to be drawn up. This problem cannot be solved only by distributing rice through subsidies through the rationing system. If the whole system becomes solely dependent on subsidies, the government will itself find it difficult to continue the system for long. It is well and good that the government is arranging to supply rice at Rs. 2 per kg to the starving people. But at the same time, it should adopt arrangements so that all the inhabitants of that area can receive work throughout the entire year. Adequate planning has to be undertaken by the government for this purpose. Mamata Banerjee has already announced that all the young men of this area will be given employment in the police force.

The handicrafts of the Adivasis of Jangalmahal should be placed in the world market by numerous little self-help groups and their income opportunities should be ensured in this way. The forest areas of Jangalmahal should be utilised for the purpose of expansion of the tourism industry. The government will have to frame plans so that the income opportunities of the local people can expand depending on the tourism industry. By means of utilising in a befitting manner, the forest areas of Jangalmahal in the field of herbal treatment income opportunties of the local residents may be further expanded.

For the conservation of rain water and ground water for drinking purposes, adequate arrangements have to be made. Apart from drinking water medical treatment and education should be made available to the deprived people of Jangalmahal. In other words, the government must of necessity cultivate a far-reaching outlook beside which they must posses a sincere political will to work for the common masses. Only a little ray of development is sufficient to enlighten the entire area of Jangalmahal.

Just where the shoe pinches in Jangalmahal is nothing new to Mamata Banerjee. At least two decades ago she witnessed with her own eyes how the people of Jangalmahal pass their days. If in the light of that experience, she now wisely draws up a blueprint for the development of the area the local people will reap ample dividends.

7

MORE ABOUT JANGALMAHAL

The Chief Minister Mamata Banerjee has taken initiatives for a political solution of the Jangalmahal tangle. Very recently the bigwigs of her government met the representatives of the civil society in a long conference at the end of which the Chief Minister apprised that she was determined to establish peace in Jangalmahal at any cost. She also informed that very soon she would visit the area with a special package of economic and social development. At the same time the Chief Minister has also appealed to the Maoists to hold their weapons. She has assured them that the Allied Forces will be withdrawn from Jangalmahal on the return of peace.

Without naming the Maoists she has assured them that the government is willing to sit in conference with them over the return of peace, in Jangalmahal. In order to create suitable atmosphere for that meeting, she has also entrusted a few representatives of the civil society with that responsibility. This interest of the Chief Minister for solving the Jangalmahal problem through discussion in this way has only expressed the sincerity of the new government.

The difference between this initiative of the new government with the line of action of the previous government is that the previous government showed no interest at all in the creation of a suitable climate for mutual discussion. On the contrary the previous government chose the path of state-controlled violence and oppression. The left front government failed to realise that police atrocities can never suppress totally the movement which broke out as a reaction against deprivation and lack of development. They also failed to understand that perhaps police action can temporarily suppress a mass movement but the grievances of the people still did not vanish. Rather the fire of grievances continue to simmer and whenever there is time and opportunity, it again breaks out into a conflagration. Just this has happened in Jangalmahal. To the extent the leftist government has advanced in the path of state-governed violence and oppression suspicion and aversion about the government have thickened in the minds of the Adivasi people. The climate of Jangalmahal has also become proportionately hot.

Another matter which the previous leftist government failed to realise was that a major reason of the grievances of the Adivasi community was the lack of their respect and honour from the Administration. When in the name of controlling the militants, the police perpetrated atrocities on the tribal women in the Adivasi villages of Jangalmahal. The demand was raised from the Adivasi community that suitable punishment should be given to the guilty police personnel and the district superintendent of police must offer apologies.

The previous leftist government out of their own egotism attached no importance to this demand. In the following period this incident led the people to build up their committee against police terrorism. But the punishment of the guilty police officials and offering of apologies by them would definitely improve the circumstances. However the previous government instead of doing that chose to continue the police campaign even after that incident, and this was done only in the political interest of the foremost political party CPI(M). That is why in the previous regime, the tribal community had all along the impression that the question of their respect and honour is at stake.

The new Chief Minister has recently declared that judicial inquiries will be made very soon into the incidents of injustices and oppressions committed on the peaceful tribals in Jangalmahal. If the Chief Minister really succeeds in this mission and punishing the offenders, the inhabitants of Jangalmahal will find back their faith and confidence in the government.

The Chief Minister has talked about solving the problems of Jangalmahal through discussion. The Maoists should also give positive response to this question. If by giving a positive response to this question Maoists restrain their weapons and come to the table of discussion, it will be understood that they are really interested in the development of Jangalmahal. However, if on the contrary they are disinterested in coming to the conference table, it will be understood that they are not interested in the development of Jangalmahal and their political purpose is different.

On their part the Maoists will have to appreciate that only by killing persons and remaining in the path of terrorism and violence, they will fail to gain support of the people at large to their demands however justifiable they may be. And not unlike the Naxalite movement of the seventies their movement will turn into misguided romanticism and consequently many innocent people will lose their lives. On the other hand, if they resort to the path of democratic methods and compel the government to adopt active measures in the development of Jangalmahal their action will be admired everywhere. Keeping this fact in mind, it would be a wise political step if the Maoists today agree to the proposal of coming to the conference table with Mamata Banerjee.

But only the government and the Maoists do not constitute the whole picture. All the political groups, nonpolitical corners and the civil society should immediately take adequate initiatives in the solution of the problems of Jangalmahal. Everybody concerned will have to realise that a suitable climate for free discourse should be built up above narrow politics. At the same time all concerned should be made alert about another matter. There should be circumspection that while attempting to create a congenial atmosphere for the free discussion no pressure groups of vested interests should make a misconceived attempt to nullify it. The civil society who has been entrusted by Mamata Banerjee with the responsibility of creating a suitable atmosphere should remember that not only those citizens who reside in the urban areas should be exclusively included within the periphery of these discussions. On the contrary the marginal people of Jangalmahal should also be included because it is these people whose honour and respect are at stake.

8

NEW ERA IN THE HILLS

The residents of the Hills have marked the day July 18, 2011 as a historic day. In all the senses the day is really historic. With a view to restoring peace in the Hills the Gorkha Territorial Administration Treaty has been signed on this day at the initiatives of the national Home Minister Palaniappan Chidambaram and the regional chief minister Mamata Banerjee. A new era has started in the Hills. The residents of the Hills have also been overwhelmed with joy at this Treaty. They have got the impression that many of their demands have been considered by the chief minister of the new government with adequate sympathy. The ovations of the residents of the Hills have almost overflooded the chief minister. After taking oath as the chief minister Mamata Banerjee declared that establishment of peace in the Hills is her immediate objective. She also gave the assurance that within one hundred days she will perform this task. Looked at from that point of view she has progressed a lot towards the objective of establishing peace much before the scheduled time limit of one hundred days.

Previously on August 22,1982 a treaty was signed about the Hills in the Rajbhavan. By virtue of that treaty the Darjeeling Gorkha Hill Council was constituted. Subas Ghishing signed in that treaty in the presence of the then chief minister Jyoti Basu and the national Home Minister Buta Singh. The difference between the present treaty and the earlier one is that the Gorkhaland Territorial Administration received more than before. Previously the representation of the government in the Hill Council was much greater. Among the total number of 42 members, 14 were the re-presentatives of the government. This time the representation of the government is much less. Among a total number of 50 members only five are the representatives of the government. Apart from that this time there are many more departments in the hands of the Gorkhaland Territorial Administration, the power of liberally using the finances of the national and regional governments remaining in its hands, in comparison to the Gorkha Hill Council the number of seats has increased much in the Territorial Administration. What is most important is that a probable road remains open of the probability to bring some portion of Terai and Dooars within the jurisdiction of the Territorial Administration.

After receiving all these concessions from the new government the chief of the Gorkha Janamukti Morcha Bimal Gurung and his followers are naturally quite happy. It can reasonably be expected that after the signing of the treaty they will give up their earlier demands for a separate Gorkhaland and pay greater attention to the development of the Hills and cooperate with the government by all means to establish peace and harmony in the Hills.

Both the national Home Minister Chidambaram and the regional chief minister made it clear on the day of signing the treaty that both of them are sincere on the question of development of the Hills. And this is the reason why they have handed over greater powers to the new Territorial Administration. But they have also made it clear that they are not supporting the demand for a seperate Gorkhaland and that Darjeeling should not be isolated from West Bengal.

In his speech Chidambaram emphasised that India is unity in diversity. The area whose responsibility is being handed over to the Territorial Administration consists of many religions, castes, languages and cultures. The Territorial Administration must remain equally respectful to everybody. And the chief minister Mamata Banerjee has spoken in more clearcut terms that Darjeeling is not outside West Bengal which is not going to be divided. The leaders of the Gorkha Janamukti Morcha will have to understand the import of the speeches of the home minister and the chief minister. Bimal Gurung and all the other leaders of the Gorkha Janamukti Morcha must be careful so that they never have to face the allegation of breach of trust against the home minister and the chief minister.

All the parties involved must concern themselves with the question of establishing peace in the Hills and expedite the process of development of these areas. During the eighties the Hills have burnt for long in the fire of unrest. Of course, after the signing of Gorkha Hill Council Treaty in 1988 the Hills were peaceful for quite some time. But that peace was of a very short duration. As a result of the movement of the Gorkha Janamukti Morcha and the driving away of Ghishing, the Hills became heated once again. This unrest has repeatedly provoked disorder in the public life of the Hills.

The tourism industry of the Hills on which most of the local residents are dependent have suffered severely. Other lines of trade and Commerce in the Hills were also not exempted. As a whole the path of progress in the Hills was blocked. Repetition of turmoil in the Hills cannot be desirable. It is urgently necessary to evolve a durable solution of the problems of the Hills. It is now desirable that through the constitution of the new Territorial Administration a durable solution of the Hills problem must be enacted and the Hills will once again return to their natural rhythm.

Every year the national government will grant the new Territorial Administration an amount of Rs. 200 crores. This financial year help will continue for the first three years after the constitution of the autonomous Administration.

The responsibility of those who are being empowered with this objective in view is the greatest. They will have to remember that the power which is vested in them must be *Properly* utilised. They must have a steadfast attitude towards the development of the Hills. They will have to remember that their commitments to the people of all religions and all cultures living in the Hills are equal. And above all they must be in a position to appreciate the truth that the Hills are an inalienable part of West Bengal, not a seperate territory outside the borders of the region.

9

AGONY OF AGRICULTURE

The initiative that the new government of West Bengal has adopted with a view to returning the lands of the unwilling peasants at Singur has recently fallen in a much more complex vortex. On June 28, 2011 as a result of the efforts of the Chief Minister Mamata Banerjee the administration started the work of returning the lands of the unwilling peasants. In the evening on that day 12 peasants were shown the plots of land fixed for them. It was decided that in the morning on the very next day the papers relating to the ownership of those lands will be handed over to them. But on the previous day the Tatas appealed to the Supreme Court for an injunction over the land distribution process at Singur. Consequently, owing to the complexities of the legal system, the whole process has become more complicated. It is not clear even now how this tie of complication will be simplified. What is explicit is that the Tatas will not very easily agree to give up the ownership of the land at Singur.

In such a perspective the Chief Minister Mamata Banerjee has also advanced an important demand. She has claimed that in all those places throughout the country where land has been acquired in the name of building up industries but left unutilised such lands should be immediately returned to the original owners. In this context she has pleaded for returning the land by amending the Act of 1894.

A little observation will indicate that as things stand today in different corners of the country, unrest has been intensified around the question of land acquisition. Direct conflicts have broken out between the regional governments on the one hand and those peasants and sons of the soil who have lost their lands on the other. It is not unoften that these conflicts are causing much bloodshed and loss of lives. Nor are such land skirmishes confined to Singur alone. Land movement has now broken out in various important places in the political landscape. In the Jagatsinghpur district in Orissa, a conflict is going on between the Orissa government and the sons of the soil over land acquisition for the proposed Poscoe factory. The residents of Jagatsinghpur has come down to the streets to build up direct resistance movement against land acquisition. In the Greater Noida area of Uttar Pradesh the local peasants have built up mass movement in protest against urbanisation by means of acquisition of fertile agricultural lands. This movement has become the headache of the Supreme Court who has observed that they do not want the happening of another Nandigram. It has also alerted the U.P. Government that in case of necessity it is prepared to intervene in the matter. The peasants movement in Singur and the effort of the new government in the following period to return the lands of the peasants by way of legislation- all these will leave their impact on the land movements elsewhere. It goes without saying that Singur will become the model in land movements throughout the nation.

Under the circumstances the national government will have to consider the matter with great importance. In the first place the government will have to realise that the Land Acquisition Act which was passed by the British government in 1894 cannot remain in force even to this day. Following the demands of time and circumstances this law should have been amended much earlier which however, the government failed to do. Of course, the national government is now saying that this law will be amended in the coming session of the Loksabha. Right now the government should start speculation regarding how lands should be returned to the peasants by amending this law. What the Chief Minister Mamata Banerjee opined in this matter is appropriate.

At the time of amending this law, the government should keep in mind one important matter. It is that a law is enacted chiefly with the purpose of safeguarding the interests of the citizens. If ever by evading the restrictions imposed by the law anybody wants to hurt the interest of the citizens, it is the government's duty to resist such misconceived attempts. That is why the Act of 1894 should be amended in such wise that everywhere the interests of the sons of the soil are safeguarded. Constant vigil should be maintained so that the sons of the soil are not deprived of, their natural rights are not downtrodden and any land shark cannot receive the opportunity to engulf the lands of any poor peasant. A piece of land not only ensures the life and livelihood of a peasant family throughout generations, but also it becomes the determinant of the social identity of a son of the soil. The government will have to understand in the light of sociology the probable impact on the society if this condition is destroyed. The more delay is done by the government in this matter the feeling of deprivation in the minds of the sons of soil will become greater and greater. The feeling of grievance will continue to simmer in the public psyche in different corners and that is why the government should take adequate steps before that fire engulfs the entire social superstructure.

10

TURMOIL OVER ACQUISITION

The vitriolic comment which the Supreme Court recently passed in connexion with a case relating to land acquisition while rebuking the Mayabati government in Uttar Pradesh is considerably significant in the contemporary perspective. Supreme Court has commented that taking advantage of a colonial law, the poor people's lands are snatched away from their hands in order to build up shopping malls and residential complexes. In this way ordinary people are being marginalised in the name of 'globalisation'. Numerous incidents of suicide which are taking place as a result have only one reason at their roots. People are gradually being sent to the end of a precipice.

However, at the same time on the same day in the Kolkata city the new Chief Minister of West Bengal Mamata Banerjee has adopted a few important decisions regarding the landed properties of the rural peasants. The Chief Minister has decided that her government will not apply special powers in the case of acquisition of land. Even if a single square yard of land is to be acquired, the concerned department will have to submit a proposal to that effect to the Ministry. The Ministry will adopt a decision only after considering such questions as to why the land is required, how much land is required, what is the character of land and what are the likely social consequences of the acquisition.

A little speculation will reveal that there is a close nexus between the verdict of the Supreme Court and the decision of Mamata Banerjee. The thought processes of both the parties are flowing along the same channel.

There is little gain in denying the fact that during the last few years, there has appeared unrest in different corners of the nation over the land acquisition question. Everywhere there is the allegation against the regional government over the issue of acquisition of land of the poor villagers. There is the allegation that taking advantage of the Land Acquisition Act of 1894 and in the interest of multinational industrial organisations attempts are going on in different regions to capture the lands of the poor people. Nor can it be asserted that such allegations are totally fabricated. It is over the question of forcible land acquisition that the grievances of the rural masses against the leftist government were crystallised as a consequence of which the left front had to bid adieu from power. It can not also be denied that the lands of the poor masses were snatched away for building the luxury palaces of the upper classes." At least Rajarhat is an instance of this occurrence in our region. The land movement is now gradually gathering momentum and assuming the form of a main stream movement. Already the demand for amending the Land Acquisition Act of 1894 has been advanced. The national government is also now thinking about amending this law in the coming session of the Parliament.

The Supreme Court is now realizing that the land movement is gradually becoming more and more violent in the countryside and ordinary people are being exploited by taking resort to the colonial law of 1894. Because also in the past in this case relating to land acquisition in Uttar Pradesh, Supreme Court issued a warning that another Nandigram was not necessary. And this time the appeal of the U.P. government has been rejected by the Supreme Court.

It is as a result of movement against the forcible acquisition of land that the present Chief Minister Mamata Banerjee has come to power. She is well aware that a piece of land does not ensure only economic security but it also indicates a person's proper identity in the social-political milieu or social ambience. Mamata understands well the agonies of the landless persons and that is why she is eager to avoid the mistaken steps of the earlier government in the case of land acquisition. She has already issued a directive that so long as an account of the unutilized land in the hands of the government is not prepared, no further acquisition will take place. At the same time the Chief Minister has also emphasised in detail the necessity of examining in advance the possible social impact of such forcible acquisition.

Neither in the case of Singur or Nandigram this social impact was kept in mind by the previous government and they had also to suffer the inevitable consequences on this account.

Two honourable judges of the Supreme Court G.S. Singhbhi and Ashoke Gangopadhyaya rebuked the U.P. Government in the following terms: 'Do you think that we the judges live in a 'paradise of fools'? By way of misusing a largely outdated colonial law, you are jeopardising the interests of the ordinary citizens, If those two judges knew that on that very day the Chief Minister of West Bengal has adopted this populist and responsible decision, they would certainly have eulogised her abundantly. Perhaps they would have advised other regions to follow the West Bengal model. The honourable judges of the Supreme Court would very certainly remind the governments of all the other regions to learn from Mamata Banerjee that it is the government which is entrusted with the duty of protecting the fundamental rights of the umpteen millions of the nation as well as the respective regions.

11

RETURNING LANDS OF UNWILLING PEASANTS

The intiative taken by the new Government to return the lands of the unwilling peasants at Singur was stumbled on 29th June, 2011. On the previous day as a result of the efforts of the Chief Minister Mamata Banerjee the administration started the work of returning the lands of the unwilling peasants. In the evening of that day 12 peasants were shown the plots of land specified for them. It was decided that in the morning on the next day the documents regarding the ownership of those plots of lands would be transferred to their hands. But on Tuesday, i.e., the previous day, the TATAs approached the Supreme Court with an appeal for the stay order on the land allotment process. On next day morning the Supreme Court issued an injunction in the perspective of this appeal of the TATAs. Consequently as a result of the legal complexities the whole process has became complicated. It is not clear when these complications will become simplified. What is obvious is that the TATAs will not easily agree to give up the ownership of the land at Singur. In these circumstances the Chief Minister Mamata Banerjee has advanced an important claim. She has demanded that wherever land has been acquired in the name of industry and development throughout the regions and kept unutilised should be returned forthwith to the original owners. In this context she pleaded for amending the Land Acquisition Act of 1894 and returning the lands without delay.

A little scrutiny will reveal that unrest has appeared in different corners of the country over the question of acquisition. Landless peasants and sons of the soil are coming in direct conflict with the regional governments. Occasionally these conflicts are assuming the appearances of bloody carnages. Nor is this land movement confined to Singur alone the land movement has appeared in important hotbeds in the political map throughout the length and breadth of the entire nation. In the Jagatsingpur District of Orissa a conflict is going on between the Orissa Government and the sons of the soil over the issue of the acquisition of land for the proposed Poscoe factory. The residents of Jagatsingpur have come down to the streets and directly built up mass resistance against the government. In Greater Noida of Uttar Pradesh the local peasants have waged up movements in protest against urbanisation through the acquisition of fertile agricultural lands. This movement has provoked the Supreme Court in arguing that they are not interested in witnessing another Nandigram carnage. It has also alerted the U.P. Government that it will intervene in these matters if need be. The peasant's movement in Singur and the effort to return the lands of the peasants by enacting law by the new government in the following period will also cast their shadow on land movements elsewhere. It can be safely asserted that Singur will this time become the model in the matter of land movement throughout the entire nation.

Under these circumstances the national government will like to attach adequate importance to this matter. In the first place it has got to be understood that the Land Acquisition Act (1894) of the British Government can no longer be valid under the present circumstances. This law should have been amended much earlier as per the requirements of the time and the circumstances. The government however failed to do that. Although the national government is now giving the assurance that in the coming session of the Loksabha the law will be amended. The Government will have to immediately start speculation as to how the law may be amended and the lands may be returned to the dispossessed peasants.

While amending this law the Government will have to remember another matter. It is that law is enacted principally with the purpose of protecting the interests of the citizens. If any power bypasses that law and attaches the interest of the citizens of the nations the Government should come forward to resist that power. That is why the Act of 1894 should be amended in such a way that the rights of the sons of the soil are protected everywhere. It should be ensured that the sons of the soil are not deprived of their natural rights and the landowners are not enabled to grab the lands of peasants with the assistance or connivance of law. A piece of land not only ensures the life and livelihood of a peasant family through generations, it also becomes the determinant of the social identity of a peasant family who are the children of the soil. The Government has to perceive in the light of sociology the impact of this iedntity in the society. If the government makes undue delay in understanding this simple truth the sons of the soil will suffer from greater feeling of exploitation and deprivation. The fire of grievance will engulf the entire countryside. The government should therefore remain alert on this account.

12

SINGUR ORDINANCE

The regional government has recently imposed an Ordinance to return to the peasants the lands forcibly acquired for the purpose of building an automobile factory at Singur. Many debates and controversies may appear on this score. Particularly CPI(M) has already declared this step as unconstitutional. Their upshot is that when the Assembly is continuing this sort of Ordinance which bypasses it is equivalent to violating the constitution. But the whip of that party in the Assembly Rejjak Molla has made no bones about welcoming this decision of the Chief Minister, Mamata Banerjee. No wonder that this sudden decision of the new government has confounded the CPM. This is obvious from the internal dissension of the party.

Through this Ordinance, within 21 days of coming into power, Mamata Banerjee lived upto the number one electoral assurance of Trinamools Congress. Her victory started from the very first day of embarking in the movement against the snatching away of the lands of the peasants of Singur. From the very first day that it was known that she has stood by the side of the poor, downtrodden peasants in the rural areas of Bengal, CPM has become paralysed. In all the elections in Panchayat, Loksabha and Vidhansabha Mamata Banerjee gave the assurance of remaining by the side of the poor and indigent people of rural Bengal and the highest priority was laid during the Assembly election on returning the lands to the peasants of Singur. This Ordinance of the new government is an indication that those assurances were not mere eyewash is also clear from this Ordinance. If the assurance to return the lands to the peasants was a mere eyewash the government could take time in an unjustified manner by giving excuse of the legislation of the British period. Because the Land Acquisition Act of 1894 could not be easily amended for the asking of the government. Much efforts would have been required for that purpose. Other regions of the Indian nation have also to suffer on account of the British Land Act because the legal complications are extremely complex. If Mamata believed that the assurances given in the manifesto were merely a few electoral stunts she could very easily sidetrack the issue. But she did not do that. Rather with the understanding that much time will be required for amending the law, she has rapidly declared the Ordinance in order that the peasants are not deprived. In other words she has given a definite proof of the proposition that where there is a will there is a way. Perhaps this particular measure of the West Bengal government will show the other regions the necessary direction for solving their respective problems.

When the Tatas took the decision to shift their operations from Singur to Gujarat as a result of the dharna movement of the local peasants under the leadership of Mamata Banerjee, the then ruling party CPI(M) and the so called votaries of industrialisation began to cry wolf. The question that they raised was what will be the next happenings. Now that the Tatas have left West Bengal industry will in this region go to rack and ruin. The hopes of the peasants that they will get back their lands are unfounded. They will never receive back the lands which they have already lost. Such happenings are impossible under the present legal system. And for all these debacles is responsible the obstincy of Mamata Banerjee.

But today after the declaration of this Ordinance CPI(M) has realised that no such comments can be made. It has therefore only raised questions about the constitutional legitimacy of the Ordinance. But the thing to regret is that in this case also there is lack of understanding in the midst of the opposition. That is why on behalf of the party Suryakanta Misra is saying one thing while the ex-Land and Land Reform Minister Rejjak Molla who calls himself a 'peasant's son' is arguing in a different channel. The latter has openly supported this measure of the new government. What, now, will be the course of action of the legislators of CPI(M) in the opposition bench when the Chief Minister-cum-Land Minister Mamata Banerjee will submit the bill in the House during the next Assembly Election? Will they attune their utterings to the opposition leader or will they welcome the decision of the Chief Minister by following the instance of the whip of the party ?

Controversy over this Ordinance is not unlikely. Nonetheless the peasant community of not only Singur but also the entire rural Bengal is delighted at this instance of taking bold steps and rapid decisions of Mamata Banerjee i.e. the Alliance government by taking into consideration the happiness or otherwise of the peasant community. Time was when the peasant community of undivided Bengal regarded Fazlul Haqtue as a person of their own. The down-to-earth politics of Fazlul Haque kindled among them new hopes of living. When the left government was installed in power in 1977 the poverty-stricken agriculturists wrongly presupposed that their happy days have returned once again. But there was little delay in belying their hopes. It was the party leaders who were responsible for exploiting this expectation of theirs. Probably the Singur Ordinance will raise new hopes in the minds of the peasants. We can only expect that Mamata Banerjee's new government will attach due importance to this optimism.

13

CONFISCATING LANDS OF TATAS

Many leftist leaders and activists have been started at the way the Chief Minister Mamata Banerjee has confiscated the lands of the Tata Project at Singur by declaring an Ordinance. Although a few leaders of CP(M) have opposed the Ordinance by raising a few technical questions, many leftwing people have welcomed the decision of Mamata Banerjee. They cherish the impression that there is no precedent in our country of the vehement struggle that the Trinamool supremo has waged for the last five years against a big industrial organisation like the Tatas. It is doubtful whether any other regional government or even the powerful national government could show the courage to deliver such a big blow to a mighty organization like the TATAs.

It was in 1968 that the youth wing of CPI(M) DYF held a convention in Howrah. In that convention not unlike the other Marxists the regional Secretary of DYF Buddhadeva Bhattacharya raised the battle cry of confiscating the properties of Tatas and Birlas. There was a time when all the communists of this country always used to mouth the slogans of confiscating the properties of the capitalists like the Tatas and Birlas. But in the long run they have all detracted from their earlier paths. To speak the truth, Buddhadeva Bhattacharya has undergone a somersault. During the last five years in his capacity as the Chief Minister he has been converted into a lackey of the Tatas and the Birlas. His government has handed over lands worth crores of rupees to the Tatas and Birlas.

For example, in order to acquire the land at Singur at least 150 crores of rupees were spent from the public exchequer. Tatas were given lease of 600 acres of land on such easy terms that in five years the government earnings will amount to only 5 crores of rupees. If the land was given lease by following proper regulations, the Tatas would have to pay at least Rs. 100 crores in the very first year. Apart from that the huge advantages which the left front government gave to the Tatas ensure that the Nano cars would be manufactured in West Bengal at government expenses.

The left front government has given away lands for long not only to the Tatas but also to the Birlas, Batas and Salims. All the necessary regulations were bypassed and in the name of renovation of the factory, they gave the permission for selling surplus land to the extent of 314 acres to the Hind Motor Factory of the Birlas in Uttarpara, Hooghly. That land was transferred to the Hind Motor authorities in exchange for only Rs. 10 crores. It was argued that Rs. 84 crores which will be obtained by selling the land will be spent for the purpose of renovating the factory. Ultimately it was known that by selling the land, the Hind Motor authorities have amassed Rs. 284 crores.

The same thing has happened in the case of Bata in South 24 Parganas. In this case also the surplus 262 acres of land of the factory were handed over by the left front government to the Bata company in exchange for Rs. 12 crores only. There also the owner of the land was the government. In both the two areas of Hind Motor and Bata it was proposed that townships, shopping malls, schools and hospitals for the rich should be built up. The land scandal of Bidhannagar is under the consideration of the industrial Committee. On the other hand much turmoil is going on in Bata over this issue for long.

No less obeisance was paid by Buddhadeva Bhattacharya and Nirupam Sen to the Salims. They handed over the Nayachar island of 45 square kilometers in exchange for Rs. 25 crores only to Salim and his company, for the purpose of building a chemical hub. As per the opinion of the Land Department of the region the market price of that land is Rs. 1268 crores only. The new government should scrutinise whether anybody's personal interest is hidden behind these land deals. At the same time all these lands should be confiscated and taken into the custody of the governments

Owing to the scarcity of land the housing projects of the poor people like Indira Abasan Prakalpa and Ambedkar Yojana are suffering. Crores of rupees granted by the national government are being returned. It is the duty of the new government to confiscate these land deals and scrutinise all the relevant matters. If land has to be allotted such conditions should be imposed that ensure the construction of residential complexes, schools, colleges and hospitals principally for the benefit of the poor for the simple reason that it is the poor and weaker section of the people from whom this government receives its principal support.

14

VICTORY OF THE PEASANTS

The movement for preserving the agricultural lands in Singur gave political reestablishment to the Trinamool Congress supremo Mamata Banerjee. Following the disaster in the Assembly election of 2006 when everybody had the impression that the political future of Mamata Banerjee was totally bleak, right at that moment the movements of Singur and Nandigram supplied oxygen to Trinamool Congress. The strength of that movement was so great that within five years Mamata tornado totally destroyed the last remnants of CPI(M). The political pundits had dubious ideas regarding the political future of Mamata Banerjee in 2006 but in 2011, she has been installed in the position of the Chief Minister of West Bengal. The Singur episode which gave her the opportunity to turn around once again in politics was not forgotten by Mamata Banerjee. Even before the election she has repeatedly asserted that if she is returned to power, she will definitely return the lands of the unwilling peasants of Singur. On the twenty fourth day of being returned to power with the objective of returning the lands of the unwilling peasants of Singur on June 14, 2011 she passed the historic. 'Singur Land Rehabilitation and Development Bill 2011.' In a sense on this day the Chief Minister of the new government gave official recognition to the landless peasants of Singur and their demands.

It was as a consequence of going to acquire agricultural lands by brute force that the previous leftist government ensured their own downfall. Following the Singur episode the peasant community of rural Bengal turned away their face from the leftist government. The Singur episode made it as clear as daylight that instead of safeguarding the interest of the peasants, the government of Buddhadeva Bhattacharya was more interested in protecting the interests of the big capitalists and industrialists. Of course, the highest leaders of CPI(M) are now admitting that the Singur and Nandigram episodes use at the root of the fall of the leftist government. In the recently held Central Committee Conference of CPI(M) in Hyderabad, the all-India General Secretary of CPI(M) Prakash Karat has also confessed that it had been highly improper to acquire lands in Singur and Nandigram in a forcible manner. Much earlier, the Singur and Nandigram incidents snatched away the earth from under the feet of the left front i.e., chiefly the CPI(M). This time by passing the bill for returning the lands of the unwilling peasants Mamata Banerjee politically drove CPI(M) to the corner. CPI(M) is now realising that in case they decide to oppose the bill they will be far more isolated from the masses. This is the reason why ethically they failed to oppose this bill inside the Assembly. This is also the reason why the previous Land Minister of the region Abdur Rejjak Molla has been compelled to comment in the Assembly that 'I am congratulating the Trinamool Chief Minister for taking this initiative.' The leader of the Opposition Suryakanta Misra has also observed that from the moral point of view, we are also not opposing, the Bill. It is in this question that people have given their verdict against us. The Forward Block MLA Akshay Thakur has also confessed that it is because we turned a deaf ear to the weepings of the peasants that we are today in the opposition bench. The political success of Mamata Banerjee consists in the fact that standing on the floor of the Assembly she has succeeded in making the opposition legislators including the opposition leader to admit their political mistakes.

In her Assembly speech Mamata Banerjee informed the House that in Tamil Nadu, by way of amending the law, the peasants have been given lease of the land. But the present alliance government of the region is desirous to give the peasants not land on lease but the ownership of land. This assurance of the Chief Minister has infinite importance. By giving ownership of lands to the peasants she is actually trying to establish the rights of the peasants in the agricultural lands. At the same time she has also informed that very soon a package will also be declared for the agricultural workers in Singur. This declaration of the Chief Minister is also very momentous. Only the life and livelihood of the owners of the land do not depend on the agricultural land, but it is connected with the future of numerous agricultural workers.

As a result of the acquisition of agricultural lands in Singur not only the future of the owners of land became uncertain but also thousands of agricultural workers were faced with a crisis. While acquiring the lands, the previous left front government did not take into consideration the plight of these impoverished agricultural workers. Mamata Banerjee has to be thanked not only for the reason that she was concerned with the interest of the owners of land alone but she has also attached due importance to the circumstances of the hapless agricultural workers as well.

Of course the MLA of Singur Rabindra Nath Bhattacharya has raised an important question. He said that adequate importance should be attached separately to the cases of those unwilling peasants who were pressurised to accept the cheques of compensation. Rabindranath Babu is quite justified in making this observation. It may be reasonably expected that the new government would pay due consideration to the fact that such peasants are not deprived in any way.

This historic Bill of Singur is not only the victory of the peasants of Singur, but also it is the victory of the peasant community in all the corners of the country. It is the victory of the peasant movement.

This victory will be recorded in letters of gold in the history of the peasant movement of the nation.

15

SPOTLIGHT ON JUDICIARY

In all the regions of India including West Bengal three crores of cases have already been accumulated in all the legal institutions. These statistics were recently quoted by the Chief Minister Mamata Banerjee who observed that in cases of necessity the 'Shift System' may be introduced in the different courts of the region. At the same time she has laid stress on the need for infrastructural development in the legal institutions.

Inaugurating a meeting in the Kolkata High Court in order to implement the project for reducing the number of cases pending in the entire legal system the Chief Minister opined that the infrastructural circumstances in different courts in the region are deplorable. There is acute shortage of space. Many of the judges do not receive vehicular facilities. True, there are ample men for operating the computers, but the thing to deplore is that there is an acute scarcity in the number of computers. A few days ago the Law Minister went on a business to the Bankshall Court and he has submitted a report regarding the mismanagement prevailing there. The Chief Minister commented that very soon e-governance has to be introduced in the courts. She informed that she has already issued the necessary instruction in this regard.

In another function on the occasion of the 150th Year of the High Court, the Chief Minister commented that the regional government is desirous of drawing up a housing project for the lawyers and the members of the judiciary. The Law Minister Malay Ghatak who was also present on the occasion was given the necessary instruction to this effect.

She made the further comment that we must also keep in mind

the very vital question of the security of the lawyers. They have no post-retirement security. All the government employees enjoy the benefits of pension, P.F. and gratuity. But the lawyers have no such benefits. Something should be done for these people and the members of their families. So many years have elapsed since the attainment of independence but it is strange that even today there is acute scarcity of toilet facilities in the court premises.

It is also strange that so far nobody bothered himself over all such matters. The new government will however pay adequate attention to these problems. If we can cooperate with the Kolkata High Court, it will raise its head further and show the proper direction to the region. 'Own your Own Housing' scheme will be introduced for the benefit of the lawyers. She observed that not much land is required in such projects. It is the government who will procure the land and also assume the responsibility of building the houses. There will be three or four categories of houses. So that the persons concerned will be enabled to purchase houses according to his or her financial capabilities.

Commenting on the question of insurance and other projects, she observed that the main problem in this matter was that accurate statistics in this respect were unavailable and nobody knows for certain how many lawyers are there in the region, She advised the Law Minister Malay Ghatak to make the necessary inquiries in this matter.

Commenting on the problem of so many cases pending in the courts, she observed that if three or four judges are accommodated in a police vehicle, their efficiency and work-capacity are bound to suffer. Of course there is scarcity of financial resources but we must try our level best to solve the problems. She informed that 151 fast track courts of the region were closed down. But from the month of March necessary directions have been given to reopen them for at least 1 year.

The Central Law Minister Birappa Moili inaugurated the project for reducing the pending cases and commented that "Within six months i.e. within December 31 attempts will be made to reduce pending cases in the *lower* courts to the extent of 40%. The task is difficult but we are optismistic if everything goes well, 2/3rds of the undertrial prisoners w*ill* be released", Moili informed that the number of undertrial prisoners in the entire country is 8 lakh. For the infrastructural development of the lower courts, Rs. 21,000 crores had been granted. In case more finance was required, appeal should be made to the Central Finance Minister. He informed that it was a matter for hope that the Chief Justices of 21 High Courts of the country have taken initiatives in implementing these projects. As things stand today only 5% of the total number of persons desirous of availing themselves of the legal facilities can go to the courts. The door of judicial facilities should be opened to more and more people.

16

RATIONALE OF SECOND CHAMBER

Mamata Banerjee's Government wants to revive the Legislative Council in West Bengal which was closed down by Jatin Chakravarti in the Period of Jyoti Basu. This, however, is not a new decision. The programme to revive the Legislative Council was included in the list of electoral assurances of the Trinamool Congress. That is why the new Chief Minister will perhaps aver that she is only desirous of fulfilling her earlier promises.

But the problem involved in this connexion cannot be overlooked. This assurance was in reality the outcome of a misguided mindset. If this decision is actually translated into action West Bengal will be confronted with a disaster. If on the contrary it is judiciously given the go-bye, the region will derive ample benefits in the long run. A section of the ruling party or the critics of the party chief will explain that the sole purpose behind reviving this already defunct institution is to please the favourite persons of the chief minister. It is however not known for certain whether this impression is true or false. But the tendency to find out a motive behind all activities is actually a kind of meanness. This malady should be avoided like a poison. The objection against the revival of Legislative Council comes not from a mean attitude of mind. It is actually an ethical issue in character. In a pluralistic political setup the upper chamber is superfluous precisely because it involves unnecessary financial burdens which should punctiliously be curtailed in a poverty-ridden regional economy of a developing subcontinent.

The model of representative plurality which is prevalent in our country presupposes the existence of a legislative Assembly at the regional level and the Loksabha at the national level. These institutions are entrusted with the function of Legislature. In case there is a Second Chamber in the Legislature it reduces the status of this institution. It is due to this reason that not only the Legislative Council of a region but also the Rajya Sabha at the national level is considered as detrimental and also inessential. What is actually the purpose of these institutions and what is their rationale ? Whom do the members of these bodies really represent ? Whatever be the actual mode of their election they will have to be indirectly worked upon as people's representative. In a democracy there cannot be any other mode of moral sanction behind becoming a member of the Legislative Assembly. But the direct representatives of the people are the members of the Loksabha and Vidhansabha. And by virtue of what moral right will the indirectly elected popular representatives attenuate the gravity of the directly elected representatives.

The answer to this question is familiar. It is pleaded that the members of the Rajya Sabha or the Vidhan Parishad are comparatively speaking wiser, shrewd and senior in thoughts. They will definitely enrich the legislative process through their intellectual abilities. But this is a fallacious argument. In the first place both in the Loksabha and Vidhansabha there exist committees for different purposes which consider various legal proposals. These committees are constituted with veteran popular representatives or at least that should be the case. That is why there is no necessity for setting up an additional chamber for the purpose of monitoring and review. Secondly, there is little necessity for accomodating experts or intellectuals in different matters for knowing their opinions in the Rajya Sabha or the Vidhan Parishad. The Government or the legislature can always adorably adopt their advices. In cases of necessity specific committees can be set up with their associates. The new Government in West Bengal has already considerable experience in this respect. A possible argument in favour of the Rajya Sabha would be advanced if there was the provision of equal numbers of reprosentives for each of the component regions of the Indian federation in the pattern of the American Senate or, in other words if the importance of Uttar Pradesh and Mizoram in the Rajya Sabha were equal to each other. In that case the Rajya Sabha would really become the representative of the component regions.

In U.S.A. the Senate has its own logic. But it did not happen in the case of India. Like the Lok Sabha in the Rajya Sabha as well the number of members of the component regions has been fixed in proportion to the population. Consequently the Rajya Sabha has been reduced to a replica of the Lok Sabha. This also is not enough. Mamata Banerjee will not be able to advance this theoretical and probable argument in favour of the Vidhan Parishad if of course she does not intend to view the Vidhan Parishad as a representative of the districts. That is why she should immediately desist from her attempt to revive the Legislative Council. On the contrary she should concentrate her efforts to convert the Legislative Assembly in an arena of ideal democratic debates. Such efforts will not only initiate a process of transformation in West Bengal but will also lead the remaining nation on the path of democracy i.e. a Government by debate discussion and dialogue as opposed to an autocratie type of Government.

17

FINANCIAL SQUABBLES : DIFFICULT CHALLENGE AHEAD

So long the outgoing Finance Minister of West Bengal - Asim Dasgupta was unwilling to admit the truth that they have drained off the public exchequer. Even the other day the outgoing Chief Minister was uttering words of hollow assurance that 'everything was in right order'. The real truth however was that people like Buddhadeva Babu and Asim Babu had the wrong notion that all along they would succeed in befooling the citizens of the region by sitting on a mountain of falsehoods and hiding all the truth from public view. But an unpalatable truth is that one hardly enjoys happy days forever. A person who was at the peak of affluence yesterday may today become a discarded person in public estimation. After Buddhadeva Babu and Asim Babu have been dislodged from their pedestals of power in the Writers Building as a result of the blast of winds of change, it is understood that they have made the region totally bankrupt. It is a matter of wonder that these misdeeds of the earlier ministers have been made public by the very bureaucrats of the previous government. The Economic Report which these bureaucrats have submitted to the new government indicates that the administration left behind by Buddhadeva Bhattacharya and Asim Dasgupta etc. is literally bankrupt.

In order to review the present financial circumstances of the regional government, the Finance Secretary Chanchalmal Bachhawat recently convened a conference. The picture of financial impoverishment of the region is clear from that conference. Already a debt of 2 lakh crores of rupees has been incurred by the regional government. Over and above that an amount of about Rs. 2800 crores will have to be procured by it at the beginning of June as the salaries and pensions for the month of May. Money has got to be collected for the payment of arrears of the government creditors. The quantum of this money exceeds Rs. 5000 crores. Over and above that there are no accounts of Rs. 480 crores taken as advances from different government treasuries. On the eve of the election this acute financial crisis prompted Asim Dasgupta to stop the works of different developmental projects. Payments of the bills of the contractors employed in these projects were stopped. Consequently the activities relating to East-West Metro, Jawaharlal Nehru all-India Urban Development, Ganga Action Plan and the construction of the different roads and bridges were faced with a deep crisis.

In order to reactivate these developmental projects the new government will have first to make the payment of the bills of the contractors. Taken all things together men like Asim Babu have gifted a difficult situation to the new government.

This financial crisis of the region did not happen overnight. The unwise decision that had been followed by the regional government is responsible for this miserable plight of West Bengal. For quite a few number of years Asim Babu tried to hide this bankruptcy from public gaze by giving sheer bluff in the name of submitting a zero-deficit budget. But even in this way he failed to hide the poverty of West Bengal. Rather the more this destitution became self-evident, the more vocal had become the Finance Minister in his misconceived efforts in denying the real circumstances. Sometimes he accused the deprivation of the Centre. Sometimes he described the situation as make-believe propaganda of the Opposition. But what is true can not be concealed forever. The cat that men like Asim Babu kept hidden so far has at last come out of the bag.

Men like Asim Babu wholly neglected the question of development of this region for all these thirty four or thirty five years. No holistic programme was adopted for enhancing the income of the region. It was the official statistics which disclosed that in West Bengal debts have mounted more in comparison to the hike in annual internal productions. It is for a pretty long time that West Bengal had been suffering from a pathetic disequilibrium between public revenue and expenditure. The real truth was that in the name of giving services men like Asim Babu spent up the entire government finance in the act of maintaining the party cadres. It was as a result of expenditure in the unproductive account that the public treasury has been emptied. No positive programmes were ever adopted by them for increasing the public revenue. And this is the reason for the anemia of the regional government. This destitution is therefore all too evident at present.

Under such circumstances the new government under the leadership of Mamata Banerjee has assumed the charges of administration. After it is installed in power the first challenge before the new government will be to free the region from this economic crisis. It is impossible for even the Almighty to alter overnight the economic circumstances of the region which is gasping under the burden of a debt of Rs. 2 lakh crores. There can be no gainsaying the fact that the new government will have to undertake inhuman efforts to remove this burden and fill up once again the public exchequer. Much circumspection and much discretion will be necessary for tackling this hazardous situation. From the very beginning the new government will have to make wise endeavours for meeting the huge burden left behind by the people like Buddhadeva Babu and Asim Babu.

18

ROAD TO SOLUTION

On 7th June, 2011 within three weeks of sitting in the chair of the chief minister in Writers Building Mamata Banerjee entered into a treaty with the leaders of Janamukti Morcha and declared that the problems of the Hills have been solved. This was certainly an exaggeration. Because a treaty and a solution are hardly synonymous, a treaty is in fact only a step, towards a solution. If the bipartite treaty of the month of June was the first step the tripartite treaty of July 18,2011 which took place between the national government, the regional government and the Morcha is of course the second step. The Gorkhaland Territorial Administration (GTA) may not be the last answer to the problems of the Hills but if we advance in quest of a solution in this path its importance in the history of solution of a long undecided problem is undeniable.

Apparently the conflict between the regional government and Janamukti Morcha during the period of the leftist government reached an 'insoluble' stage. It appeared that the distance between the two sides can never be bridged up. In order to overcome such distance in political affairs each side has to concede some grounds to the demands of the other. It can also be described as an act of compromise but in a positive sense. The GTA treaty of course consists of such a compromise. The regional government has acceded to the demands of Morcha to a considerable extent, allowed the right of autonomy or self-administration and even raised no objection to the inclusion of the word 'Gorkhaland'. The Morcha also remained inhibited from the repitition of the demand for a seperate region. This is indeed a good augury.

But there is of course some apprehension between the treaty

and the consequence. For the time being Bimal Gurung is positive, considerate and in the middle position. So far so good. But it is difficult to ascertain whether he will remain stable in this position. Because the politics which he practises is usually adverse to the middle position and has a normal tendency to move towards an extreme position.

The rise of Bimal Gurung in the place of Subash Ghishing has partially proved this proposition. If in the future the Morcha leaves the middle path and once again raises the demand for a separate region the whole process of establishment of peace will be at stake. And its impact will be felt in the Plains. The Plains are already full of unrest, simmering with discontent and in this fire fuel is being provided by party politics. Such a situation will continue for long.

In the first phase Mamata Banerjee has shown discretion to tackle this conflict, particularly in the signature ceremony of this Tripartite Treaty she has sat by the side of Bimal Gurung and Roshan Giri to emphasise the existence of undivided West Bengal and the good relation between the Hills and the Plains. We can only expect that this wisdom will be victorious in the long run.

But wisdom alone, though necessary, is not sufficient. It must be accompanied by development. In the tripartite treaty the outline of development is well defined and substantial. Not only is there a programme of allotment of finance, the liberty to utlise that finance has also been proposed. If this liberty is utilised properly, if unlike in their past the greater part of this allotted finance is not strayed through corrupt practices, if the rate of socio-economic development of the people of the Hills is actually accelerated, then that will be the real long term strategy of the development of the Hills. If the leaders of the Hills and the Plains irrespective of their factional differences can forget their small and short-run differences and become partners of that develoment Darjeeing need not be converted into Switzerland; it can automatically become a symbol of peace and stability and it is only then that the problems of the Hills will be solved in the truest sense.

19

RESOLUTIONS OF NEW MINISTRY

On May 19, 20th the new Ministry under the leadership of Mamata Banerjee took oath in the Rajbhavan and immediately thereafter in the first conference of the Ministry the following resolutions were adopted. For example, (l) the contents of the agreement with the Tatas over the lands at Singur will be made public, (2) the report of the Sachar committee for the development of the Muslim Community will be implemented, (3) the direction for recovering all kinds of illegal armaments will be declared, (4) impartiality in administration will be brought back instead of blind allegiance to the party, (5) accurate identity cards will be arranged for the persons living below the poverty line and the deficiencies will be corrected in the matter of allocating hundred days' work, (6) review committee will be constituted for releasing the political prisoners, (7) collective efforts will be undertaken with the Home Ministry in the matter of disaster management, (8) a separate secretariat will be constituted for the development of North Bengal (9) attempts will be made to solve the problems of the Hills as well as Jangalmahal within three months, (10) the press corner before the chamber of the Chief Minister in the Writers Building which was broken down in the leftist regime will be reconstructed. There is little doubt that most of these decisions are related with the interests of the impoverished working people of West Bengal. The point to note at present is whether the new government is really sincere about their implementation.

It is of course true that there are many difficult challenges before the new regional government. In the first place it is not easy to reactivate the administrative machinery, which was converted into a static and blind lackey of the ruling party during the last thirty three or thirty four years. For about three and a half decades in this region all the governmental activities were conducted effectively by the direction of CPI (M). It was the leaders of CPI (M) who treated the district magistrates, subdivisional officers and the administrators and police officials of all levels as the lackeys of their own party. In every activity the permission of the party activists rather than the recommendations of the government has served as the green signal. The matter has assumed an uglier shape at the civic and panchayat levels. Lakhs of rupees from the public treasury have been squandered there in a planned manner. Decade after decade this menace has vitiated the administration in West Bengal and also caused a rot in the entire social system, starting from health and education in all the departments relating to public interest there has taken place the interference of the party activists. It is really difficult to move forward by breaking this deadlock or vicious circle.

For a long time the people of this region yearned for a really unrestricted and transparent election. This demand became far stronger than earlier after the panchayat, Loksabha and the civic elections. In this year's Assembly polls Qureshi's Election Commission tried to fulfil this demand of the citizens of West Bengal to the best of its ability. After many years the ordinary voters in the district areas are happy to cast their own votes. Many year later there has occurred a mass uprising in the voting machine. And in that connection a new government has come into power - a government which is truly elected by the verdict of the majority of the voters.

But it should not be forgotten that who had been continuously in power in the region since 1977 were not wholly lonely. Impelled by the urge to hold power in their hands for year after year, they created numerous pressure groups at different levels of the social and governmental system. They have themselves relished the taste of power and nourished these pressure groups with fertilizers and water. It is true that in comparison with the lakhs of crores of people of the region the people of these quarters are less numerous. But by virtue of their movement for long at different levels of the governmental and administrative structures they are quite familiar with the nuances of the governmental activities. When they will find that the impartial activities of the new government are proving to be a stumbing block to their long-drawn-out habits of serving their own interests, they will make utmost efforts to hinder all these activities. The new ministry will have to take into account all these possible hazards in a cool brain.

Ordinary citizens are aware that the CPI(M) government of the last regime has drained off the life-bloods of the region. They are aware of the burden of 2 lakh crores of rupees of the region. The vehicle in which the new ministry has ascended is totally ramshackle. Even the optimism of the crores of the citizens of the region is not sufficient to provide motion to this car. But people will be happy if it observes that the new government is at least repairing its obsolescent machinery and making efforts to put new life into it. Its sincere efforts will convince the citizens that the new government is at least not lacking in political good will. Unlike the previous government the new authorities are not intent upon making scapegoats of the ordinary citizens.

20

NOT JUST BLIND ALLEGIANCE

On the very second day of taking oath as the Chief Minister Mamata Banerjee has declared that not blind allegiance to the party but competence will be taken by her administration as the criterion of efficiency. She will admire the efficiency and dexterity of the public workers as well as the officers and will not go into the analysis of the question of a person's political allegiance. At the same time the new Chief Minister has issued a directive to the government officers, she has said that within seven days the government officers will have to inform which department is in which stage. Within seven days a blueprint of action should be drawn up. There is no doubt that this declaration on the very second day of being installed into power will create hopes among the citizens at large. Everybody will extend thanks to the sincerity of the new government. If the image of the unbiased and transparent administration which disappeared from the region can be made to return by the new Chief Minister her slogan of bringing about a 'change' will be fruitful in all manners. The people who entrusted Mamata Banerjee with the changes of the Chief Minister and installed her in the Writers Building are desirous to see that 'change' should come not only in the colour of the government but also in its modus operand. This declaration of Mamata Banerjee has given due honour to that demand of the populace.

During the last thirty four years the citizens of this region were totally oblivious of the transparent and dynamic image of the administration which is above the cult of party allegiance. During the leftist regime of this long period the government used to be controlled by Alimuddin street. No trace of an impartial government could be observed anywhere. The promotion of the officers took place not on the basis of efficiency or competence but the extent of intimacy of an official with Alimuddin street. Consequently the government officers gained the impression that salvation is possible only by lubricating the authorities of the Alimuddin street. And that is why accountability to Alimuddin instead of the people at large came to assume prime importance. Not only the officrs of the Writers Building but also the question of putting the officers in important positions was determined by Alimuddin street. It was Alimuddin Street which decided who will become the vice-chancellor of which university. The direction of Alimuddin Street was indispensable for deciding which particular person will be selected for becoming the chairman of a committee or a commission. In this way blind party allegiance came to permeate the administration from top to bottom. Naturally the question of efficiency and competence was pushed to the background. For the simple reason of being intimate to the party unworthy mediocre people became important at all the levels of the administration. Its inevitable impact in the administration was also conspicuous.

The citizens of the region observed an one-eyed incapable administration. In reality CPI(M) never gifted a people's government to the inhabitants of the region, What CPI(M) gave the region was a biased CPI(M) government.

It is this scandalous situation in the administion which Mamata Banerjee has taken the initiative to remedy. Mamata is well aware that the tasks which were left untouched by the perfunctory performance of the Left Front government will have to be completed by her. It is with that expectation that the people of West Bengal have sent her to the Writers' Building. In order to fulfil that expectation she needs first of all a dynamic transparent and capable administration which will work in the interest of the people. With that end in view the government officers should be accorded responsibility in terms of efficiency and competence. So long as this is not performed the government cannot be made dynamic and workworthy. This is the reason why the new Chief Minister has laid emphasis on the question of administrative reform by giving recognition to the factors of efficiency and dexterity.

The predecessor of Mamata Banerjee, Buddhadeva Bhattacharya raised the slogan 'Do it now'. But his slogan was reduced to a farce. He failed to transform even an iota of the work culture of the government officers. The misbehaviour that was meted out to ordinary people in government offices was continued in the period of Buddhadeva Bhattacharya. The dillydallying modus operandi of the government offices of the previous period were repeated in the period of Buddhadeva Babu. The truth is that Buddhadeva Babu failed to release his government from the clutches of the party. That is why he did not have the courage to give due recognition to questions of efficiency and competence. In fact he had to give leadership to an unworthy and inept government.' On the contrary Mamata Banerjee did not raise any catchy slogan. But she has made it clear that she will take stern steps in gifting the people a dynamic and workworthy government. This firm and liberal outlook is her hallmark. If she really succeeds in breaking the deadlock of 34 years and brings in West Bengal the flood of a new work culture the people of this region will remain grateful to her for all times to come.

21

TIMELY WARNING

On July 21, 2011 in the vast mass meeting of the party in the Brigade Parade Ground the Trinamool Congress supremo Mamata Banerjee has unleashed a warning against her opponent CPI (M) and also alerted the activists and supporters of her own party. In this meeting of July 21 the TMC supremo has announced that instances of corruption and bossing in her party will never be tolerated. Any kinds of factional politics in her party will also not be tolerated. All such instances will be suitably punished.

Mamata Banerjee has also made it clear that she dislikes the ideal that the leaders of the party will unnecessarily poke their noses in the business of the government. She has reminded everybody that no one should rake up any disorder in the hospitals or health centres. In case there is uncleanliness the party activists should themselves put their hands in cleaning them up. The TMC supremo has also warned the party activists not to get embroiled in the politics of retribution. She has said that no one should create disorder or kill the CPI (M) activists. They have already been adequately punished by the citiezens of the region in the electoral warfare. Instead of running after money TMC activists should learn to stand by the side of the ordinary citizens. In her own characteristic style in the Brigade Parade Ground she has made her party people take oath that unlike CPI (M) Trinamool Congress will never steal nor commit murder. The very words which were expected from her as a responsible leader were uttered by Mamata Banerjee in the Brigade Parade Ground. These words will give solace to the citizens of the region. In fact Mamata Banerjee is aware that after assuming administrative power of the region her responsibility has much enhanced.

She has realised that the citizens of the region did not only yearn for a change in the outward form of the government. A change was sought in the political culture which struck root in this region for the last decades. It is this yearning which has impelled the citizens of this region to give unstinted support to her party and her party in this year's Assembly election. Mamata Banerjee knows how to honour this demand of the populace.

The deficiencies about which Mamata Banerjee alerted her party activists in the Brigade Parade Ground meeting were responsible for this sorry plight of CPI(M). She has warned the Trinamool Congress not to run after money. In the last three decades CPI(M) went away from the side of the people and was converted into a party whose chief objective became earning money by hook or by crook. This observation applies to all sorts of CPI(M) leaders, big, small or middle. Conse quently they are submerged in corruption and gave encouragement to corruption at all levels. Mamata Banerjee has warned that bossing by the party activists will not be tolerated any more. Every where beginning from the local clubs or school committees to government offices or educational institutions the CPI(M) leaders have exercised their authority. And in cases of lack of allegiance to the CPI(M) leaders hard punishments were awarded.

The citizens of the region failed to tolerate this unbridled corruption and authoritarian attitude of the CPI(M) leaders and that is why with the revival of 'free and fair'voting system they have thrown away the yoke of this corrupt regime. With the expectation and of the conclusion of corruption and authoritarianism that men have given unstinted support to Trinamool Congress.

People have witnessed the failure of the CP(M) leadership to stop the prevalence of corruption and authoritarianism.They correctly understood that outwardly CP(M) speaks of purification campaigns but in actual fact gives indulgence to instances of corruption and authoritarianism. That is why the electorate refused to be led along the gardenpath in this year's election. Rather they turned a deaf ear to the slogan of 'purification'and have given abundant support Mamata Banerjee understands well that at the end of the leftist regime of three decades her first and foremost duty is to present a transparent and uncorrupt administration and to stop the authoritarian activities of the ruling party in different areas.

At the Brigade Parade Ground meeting she has given indication of this determination. Mamata is also aware that in Trinamol Congress she happens to be the first person and she also happens to be the last. The rest are only her shadows. She alone is responsible for all the successes of Trinamool Congress. Similarly, if there is the slightest disorder in this party people will point an accusing finger at Mamata Banerjee. That is why she will have to remain alert always and hold the reins of the party with capable hands, If she really succeeds in this difficult task she will be marked as an exceptional ruler in regional politics and she will never have to look back.

22

A TRULY WISE STEP: NOT JUST ANOTHER GIMMICK

During the last few days after assuming the charge of the chief minister of West Bengal Mamata Banerjee has taken a few most important administrative decisions. Among these decisions are : arranging payment of monthly salary to the teachers and the non-teaching staff on the first day of the month, payment of salary and allowances to the government servants through the banks, increase of budget allowances to the North Bengal Development Board, allotment of Rs. 40 crores as food subsidies to backward areas and BPL consumers, taking the advices of the experts for saving the region from incidence of flood and drought etc. All these administrative decissions adopted by the new chief minister are undoubtedly highly populist. Over and above that, all these decisions are fruits of deep and far-reaching reflection. All these decisions are giving the impression that Mamata Banerjee instead of being concerned with instantaneous profits is far more eager to derive future benefits.

Another such constructive decision has also been recently announced by Mamata Banerjee. She has announced that without the collective decision of the regional ministry the Municipality or the Municipality Department is not entitled to allot any land. In other words, Mamata has brought the right to allot lands into the hands of the ministry.The Municipal and Urban Development Minister Firhad Hakim has informed the people of this decision of the chief minister and said that nobody could allot the lands the Municipalities of the region including Salt Lake according to their own free will. Before allotting the lands the matter should be recommended by the regional cabinet. Neither the Municipality Department nor the Municipalities will any longer have the right to distribute lands in their own hands.

There are two possible consequences of this decision. Firstly, as a result of this decision it would be possible to resist unplanned urban development. It would also be possible to know where and how much land is there in the hands of the government. Secondly, speculative activities and corrupt practices around lands can be resisted to a great extent.

There can be no gainsaying the fact that so far as a result of retaining unrestricted rights of land distribution in the hands of the Municipalities and the Municipality Department hindrances were created in the road to planned urban development. In many cases different municipalities allocated lands according to their sweet will. In many cases in times of necessity private lands were not available. What is more, no clear account of where and how much land was in the hands of the government was available. As a result of the new decision it would be possible for the government to understand where and how much land is in its hand. The government would also realise how that land can be utilised according to plan. By utilising these lands properly in a planned manner the government can instil discipline into urban development.

Along with planned urban development as a result of this governmental decision speculative activities and corrupt practices around land would also be resisted to a greatest extent. During the leftist regime a dishonest circle of speculators around land grew up throughout the region. Many bigwigs of the ruling party also were involved in that circle. The left front minister took the decision that unutilised government khasland should be distributed among the shelterless at Re. 1 only. Apparently this decision of the last government seemed to be a populist move. Actually, however, this was a secret ploy to manipulate the vote bank. More than that, as a result of that decision of the government the circle of people who found indulgence of the party in land speculation in different areas, instead of the poor people derived extra benefits.

On the one hand, these people deprived the really indigent persons and obtained vast tracts of land under false names. On the other hand they have deprived the real patta-recievers and kept the government documents in their own possessions and earnt lakhs of rupees by selling that same lands to others at high prices. Since during the last regime there were no regulations in the allocation of lands these speculators and their dapendent mastans (ruffians) uttered the last words. Murders and incidents of violence around lands were rife. And throughout the region almost everywhere above their heads there was the umbrella of the ruling party CP (M).

Apparently, the present decision of the new government may not appear to be a populist decision. But a little reflection will convince anybody that a constructive outlook is working behind this decision. Constructive activity means very often avoidance of the path of cheap popularity. The present government of course deserves our thanks for deviating from the cheap and popular path of land allocation of the left front government. The circle of dishonest speculators which has grown up around land distributors throughout the length and breadth of the region should be broken up for ensuring proper utilisation of land and this will open up the path of genuine development.

23

VISIT TO HOSPITAL

On Saturday, July 2, 2011, Mamata Banerjee paid a surprise visit to the B.C. Roy Children's Hospital and this has solved many longstanding problems. Following her advice in order to resist the sudden "referring" of the sick children, the system of 'teleconferencing' of the B.C. Roy Hospital to the hospitals at the district, sub division and block levels is being introduced. At a particular time of the day, the teachers and the physicians of the Roy Children's Hospital will talk through this teleconferencing system with the pediatricians of these hospitals and give them necessary advice.

Apart from that in order to restore the work culture in the hospital, necessary directions have been issued this day for timely attendance of the physicians and health workers. It has been declared that in case of misbehaviour with the guardians of the children, the physicians and nurses may be given hard punishment.

The scarcity of ambulance in this largest hospital for children's treatment is a longstanding problem. There was no police stations in the vicinity in order to resist any problem of law and order. After the surprise visit of the Chief Minister, two ambulances have been allotted for the hospital as per the direction of the Chief Minister. New officers have been appointed for the police outpost on this very day.

Apart from that responding to the appeal of the hospital authorities, the Chief Minister also gave the green signal for purchasing machinery worth Rs. 1 crore 36 lakhs for the sick new born care unit under construction. Among these instruments are USG machine, pulse oximeter infusion pump, monitor etc. The parents of children were panic-stricken for the death of 19 children in two days. They all heaved a sigh of relief at the arrival of the Chief Minister.

The Principal, Dr. Mrinalkanti Chatterjee observed that as a result of sudden visit of the C.M. there would be much advantages in adopting adequate measures against the derelict physicians and the health workers. He added that in order that the new mothers could learn to cook nutritious food at less cost, we were starting a nutritious rehabilitation centre at Beliaghata B.C. Roy Polio Hospital for the purpose of giving training.

On this day the Chief Minister remained in the B.C. Roy Hospital for 20-25 minutes. She asked the physicians many questions relating to the outdoor, emergency step down ward, different wards in the first floor, the newly born babies in the second floor and the measures adopted to save the seriously sick new born children. She inspected the neonatal and pediatric intensive care unit.

She was extremely amazed to learn that the weights of 30 newly born babies were 700-800 gms only. She observed that the weights of these children were half of those of the normal children. She commented that the real reason was that their mothers also lacked adequate nutrition. She advised the officers to adopt necessary steps for this matter.

Receiving complaints from the parents, she expressed her grievance to the journalists that there were no free beds in the hospital. In case BPL certificates could not be available within 3 days, daily bed fees had to be given to the extent of Rs. 30/. Many children have to stay in the hospital for 20 or 30 days. It is difficult for the indigent parents to procure so much money.

The Chief Minister said that there was much pressure in the hospital. Two or three children have to be kept in a bed. Most of the children were in serious condition and brought from far away areas. In certain areas of the hospital there are shortages of infrastructural facilities. Such facilities have to be expanded further. She was amazed to learn that every year 40,000 newly born babies die in this region despite the best efforts of the physicians to save them. She commented that no politicking should be made over this matter and our best wishes should be reserved in favour of these children.

24

IRON DUST SCANDAL

Another scandal which was suppressed during the leftist regime is now coming to the limelight. The chief Minister Mamata Banerjee has ordered a CID inquiry into the iron dust scandal of more than 350 crores of rupees. As per the directive of the Chief Minister, the Food Minister Jyotipriya Mallik has already prepared the necessary papers relating to that scandal. It was known that during the Beijing Olympic in 2008 India received the huge order of supplying iron dust for construction purposes. West Bengal was entrusted with the duty of supplying iron dust worth Rs. 358 crores.

In the name of supplying iron dust the Essential Commodities Supply Corporation paid this amount of money to 24 private organisations. Subsequently after consulting the necessary papers, it was discovered that not a single kilogram of iron dust was sent to China. But various organizations received payments. The managers of the organizations among whom this huge amount of money was distributed all rub shoulders with the leaders of CPM or Forward Block.

The story does not end here. The Home Department of the previous government did not give the necessary permission to the Essential Commodities Supply Corporation to submit the chargesheet against an IAS officer involved in this scandal of Rs. 350 crores. It was learnt from the Home Department itself that much hindrances used to put up in order to suppress the whole matter and protect the big shots of the previous left government from the tentacles of law.

However, this iron dust scandal is a minute fragment of the scandal relating to thousands of crores of rupees in the period of the left front. Many other such scandals are perpetrated by the previous leftist rule. And all these scandals have been suppressed in this manner. The way the previous leftist rulers sought to suppress this scandal of 350 crores of rupees indicates that in case of an inquiry many big shots will be implicated. Many dishonest activities of many people will be revealed. At the same time it will also be revealed that all these mischiefs were done in the knowledge of the government and by the encouragement of the government.

It should be remembered that the organisations which were paid Rs. 350 crores, but supplied not a single grain of iron dust simply as a result of their intimacy with the earlier ruling coterie were actually paid the money of the people. During the last three and a half years, the previous leftist government has in this way squandered vast amounts of public money. This incident is the proof that the previous leftist government in West Bengal was not innocent in comparison to the corrupt performances of the Lalu Prasad government in Bihar or the Mayabati government in Uttar Pradesh.

It is welcome that the new government in West Bengal has taken initiatives to inquire into the scandal relating to this vast amount of money. No one can give moral support to this sort of squandering of public money. It is in public interest that an inquiry must immediately be made into this scandal. At the same time hard punishments should be awarded to those who will be found guilty in the inquiry. The government will have to keep strict vigil so that any guilty bigwig cannot escape the clutches of the legal machinery.

At the same time it should be remembered that the duties of the new government will not be finished by making an inquiry into this single scandal. All the cases of corruption perpetrated during the leftist regime have to be inquired into one by one. Because it is the expectation of the people that the new government will make due inquiry into all the misdeeds of the earlier government, identify the guilty people and give them adequate punishment. The new government must of necessity remedy the injustices. It may be logically expected that in case the new government makes inquiry into all the scandals of the previous leftist regime, many bigwigs will be implicated and many secret stories of squandering the public money will come to the limelight.

25

HEALTH SERVICES IN THE BALANCE

On 31st May, 2011 the Chief Minister Mamata Banerjee announced a few measures for the development of the health infrastructure of the region. She has informed that in Jangalmahal four super speciality hospitals will be set up, a programme for setting up a modern hospital at Rajarhat has been adopted for neurological treatment, at Bhowanipore a 300-bed orthopaedic hospital will be set up, the programme for setting up a separate hospital for women is considered and along with these all the district hospitals and primary health centres will be modernised.

The chief minister has kept the charge of the Health Department in her own hands. In the mean time she has made an on-the-spot inspection of four hospitals of Kolkata. She is trying to find out exactly where the shoe pinches in the Health Department. It may be presumed that after assuring the responsibility of the new government she is certainly realising that the health infrastructure of the region is totally deficient. Bringing back this deficient health system to the proper position on a wartime footing should occupy the foremost position in the list of priorities of the regional government.

The imbalance in the health circumtances of the region has been discussed many times earlier. No body has expressed satisfaction on that score. As in other spheres of social services the earlier leftist rulers have irrationally injected party politics into the health services too for the last three and a half decades and thus inflicted infinite damage on the entire system.

In other regions the governments always give a high prority to the sphere of health and medicine. But in the left front regime in West Bengal no Health Minister was found to concern himself with the health services. Consequently there has been continuous deterioration in the government hospitals and health centres. The business of private hospitals and nursing homes has flourished. Gradually the health services have gone out of the reach of the economically weaker section and the lower middle classes of the people. People have lost confidence in the system of health and medicine of this region and started depending upon the southern regions. The new chief minister has raised the question why the helpless people of this region should go to Vellore for medical treatment? This question is quite justified. Not that such questions were never raised during the last 34 years, but the left front government paid no heed to it. The authorities of the left front government never perceived that if the citizens of this region, in want of adequate health services, set out for a different region it is an object of shame for the regional government. In fact the feelings of the authorities of the left front were totally distorted.

It is really a good indication that the new chief minister-cum-health minister has taken initiatives to alter the health circumstances. If she suceeds in this task the inhabitants of this region will derive ample benefits. They will no longer have to start for other regions for good treatment. If the conditions prevailing in the government hospitals and health centres really improve, the indigent and lower middle classes of people will no longer feel helpless in case of illness.

But at the same time the new chief minister will also have to remember that the mere introduction of a few new hospitals will not be able to improve the standard of health services in the region. In order to perform this task successfully the state of work culture of all those persons who are connected with the health services must be altered. The spirit of public service must be aroused in their minds. It is the misfortune of this region that involvement in political activities in hospitals and health centres was responsible for the vanishing of this spirit from the minds of the health activists.

Under the indulgence of the party bosses of CP(M) the hospitals and health centres were converted into the centres of reckless hullabaloo of a kind of health activists and of various corrupt practices. Whenever the ordinary citizens visit the government hospitals for availing medical treatment they used to be degraded, humiliated and defrauded at the hands of the former.

In order to alter these circumstances the chief minister will have first of all to remedy this situation. Undoubtedly this is a very serious task. It is also certain that this will compel the chief minister to face different kinds of hazards. Still this-task has of course to be performed. Otherwise truly efficient health services will remain for ever a distant dream to the citizens of this region. At the same time another task which the government should perform is to improve the standards of performance of primary health centres and district hospitals so that the pressures on the government hospitals of the Kolkata city may be reduced.

No one can deny that the health circumstances prevailing in this region cannot be improved overnight. This is indeed a matter of longrun programming. If such planning is kept at the top of the iist of priorities and the long term planning is successfully implemented, the sorry plight of the inhabitants of this region can be mitigated to a considerable extent.

26

MORE ON HEALTH SERVICES

Every step of the Chief Minister Mamata Banerjee indicates that she is much concerned about the health services of the region and she is constant by thinking about how this disorderly health system can be put to order at the earliest convenience. Chief Minister Mamata Banerjee has kept the Health Department in her own hands. During the last 34 years in the left front regime the health services of the region were in total shambles - the new chief minister knows that it is not possible to repair the system overnight. And she is also aware that however impossible she will have to make it possible. It may not be done in one day but gradually the circumstances have to be improved. Active steps for this purpose should start being taken from right now. The new chief minister is well aware that among the foremost demands of the citizens of West Bengal is to bring about improvement in the deficient health services and provide really satisfactory medical treatment to the umpteen millions of the citizens of West Bengal.

Because of this awareness right after assuming the resposiblity of Chief Ministership Mamata Banerjee has girded up her loins to improve the state of the health services. Already she has paid sudden visits to quite a few government hospitals. With her own eyes she has observed the condition of those hospitals and listened to the allegations of the ordinary citizens. It is learnt now that after these visits of the chief minister the state of those hospitals have improved atleast to some extent. But this is hardly sufficient. In order to improve the circumstances of the health services many other things remain to be done. Along with brining about improvement in infrastructures of the hospitals change has got to be brought about in the mindsets of the physicians. They are engaged in great services in public interest has to be generated in their minds. Their devotion to duty was to be aroused and they should be pursuaded to become more human.

After visiting a few government hospitals, on June 7, 2011, Mamata Banerjee suddenly appeared in Swasthyabhaban. There she inspected all the activities in a detailed manner and entered into meetings with the officers. In such conference in Swasthyabhaban Mamata Banerjee told an important thing. She said that in government hospitals, out of temptation for commissions a few physicians ask the patients to go to outside laboratories for examining their blood and disease. What impertinance! This 40% commission system should be stopped. The chief minister's allegation about this sort of dishonest practices of certain physicians cannot be dismissed as insubstantial. Rather there is considerable truth in such allegation Many of the common men who usually come to government hospitals have the bitter experience of becoming victims of similar inhuman behaviour at the hands of certain physicians. Such people have resorted to the ignoble practice of the cut money and commission system which has inducted corrupt practices in the entire body politic. These physicians usually forget the Hippocratic oath which they have to take on the eve of entering their profession and become more concerned with looking after their business interest by exploiting the indigent and the low-income group of people. Through collusion with private nursing homes and laboratories they compel the patients to spend more for medical treatment. Consequently, it goes without saying the pockets of these physicians are inflated with the money earnt from commissions.

If we are at all determined to bring about an improvement of the health services the Administration must adopt strict measures against these dishonest physicians. The government must ensure that whenever the low-income-group and indigent people visit government hospitals for medical treatment they are not victimised by the circle of brokers or agents and their diagnosis and treatment are done inside the hospital itself. If any case of detection of a physician of a government hospital of enjoying 'commission' comes to the notice of the appropriate authorities punitive measures against him should be adopted instantaneously.

It was for a long time that this system of 'Commission Raj' was being practised by a class of doctors and health activists in the government hospitals. The earlier left front government used to connive at them. Because so long they had continued to conduct their illegal business through unwritten licences by showing political allegiance to the left front. The new government will have to remedy this menace in the government hospitals. The words uttered by the chief minister in the Swasthya Bhaban contains a kind of warning as well as a kind of threatening. This warning as well as threatening was really necessary for the dishonest circle of the medical people. If this warning as well as threatening does not bear fruit the chief minister must adopt far more stringent measures against them. Then only she will receive the heartiest thanks of the rank and file.

27

RIGHT MESSAGE FOR INDUSTRY

On July 30, 2011 the Industries Minister of the region Partha Chatterjeee has issued a clear message to the industrialists. It is that if land is taken for the purpose of industry it cannot be kept unutilised. Immediately industries have got to build up If land is taken for industry and yet industry is not built up I within the scheduled period the government will take back the land. The Industries Minister has also made it clear that housing complexes cannot be built up in the land taken for industrialisation.

After taking oath as the Chief Minister Mamata Banerjee also said the same words which were later uttered by Partha Chatterjee in his capacity as the Industries Minister. Already Mamata Banejee clearly said that after taking land for industry it should neither be kept unutilised nor utilised for residential purposes, her government will never tolerate this sort of speculative activities.

On July 30, 2011 the Industries Minister visited three industrial estates of the Howrah district and realised that it was the practice of many industrialists to take land for industrial purposes but keep it unutilised for many years. It was for this speculative attitude of these people that new lands are difficult to find for industries. After scrutinising the matter by making an on-the-spot study the Industries Minister has been annoyed and issued this clear message to the industrialists. This message of the Industries Minister is quite correct as well as timely. This message was really necessary for those industrialists who were keeping lands unutilised in this manner for speculative purposes.

During the last left front government much speculation and dishonest trades around lands have taken place. Beginning from giving pattas to indigent people and land acquisition for industrial purposes-everything was done by way of unbridled speculative activities by a kind of dishonest industrialists and land brokers in co-operation with a few leaders and ministers of CP(M). Knowing everything during the the last three decades the leaders of the left front government kept its eyes and ears closed. Mistaking this silence as indirect support these dishonest circles have continued their operations without any resistance. Administrative support has come in this manner. In order to give various advantages to this dishonest circle a quarter of the administration has rendered different illegal cooperations. After becoming the chief minister Mamata Bankerjee has paid attention to the large scandal relating to lands in this region. An inquiry into the land scandals will definitely throw light on many bigwigs. During the regime of the left front government a section of traders and industrialists have misutilised the government and misappropriated lands one after another. The earlier government had the pratice of indiscriminately distributing lands to them in the name of industry. In exchange these traders and industrialists who were close to the ruling coterie rendered different kinds of assistance to the ruling party. In reality it was seen that although land was taken in *the* name of industry nothing actually was done in this respect. Rather keeping that land unutilised they have tried to engage themselves into speculative activities. Many of them have tried to derive large profits by building up residential complexes by taking lands in the name of industry. Not only that, many of them have misappropriated the lands of closed factories for the purpose of promoting business. And in all theses matters they have received government help. We must welcome the initiative of the Industries Minister to stop this speculation around lands. At the same time the new Industries Minister must pay attention to another matter. No attempts to build up residential complexes in the lands of closed factories should be tolerated. Other rather new industries should be built up in those lands. The government should draw up a list of those industries who have taken land during the previous government in this manner but kept them unutilised. At the same time if they are unable to build industries adequate measures should be adopted to take away those lands immediately from them.

If the government can immediately resist this speculation around land two benefits will be received. In the first place, the government will no longer have to rack its brains to find out lands for industry. Secondly, if this speculation in land is really stopped in the interest of building industry employment opponities in the region will expand very much. It is expected that Mamata Baneriee's government is proceeding in that very direction.

28

REFLECTIONS ON POLICE FORCES

During the leftist regime in his capacity as the chief minister of West Bengal Buddhadev Bhattacharya demanded that so far as the question of law and discipline was concerned his region was a veritable 'oasis' among the entire nation. The proof of this proposition was, however, bitter to the citizens of this region. For a pretty long time West Bengal remained in the front rank of those regions where the decline of law and order took place to the maximum extent. For this was resposible the administrative inefficiency as well as the shamelessly obeisant mentality and the activities of a portion of the police forces who virtually lost their honour and respects and became converted into sycophants of the ruling party. They acted like lackeys of the ruling party and following the directives of their leaders used to file false cases agaist the activists and the supporters of the opponent party, harassed them without reason, kept their eyes closed to the torments of the CP(M) activists and whenever the ordinary citizens went to the police stations to lodge complaints they were humiliated and driven out. For years in succession this was the experience of the rural masses. If in any rare case, a police officer did show the mettle to stand agaist the officious behaviour of the ruling party he was either transferred elsewhere or his life was in peril.

Day after day, night after night people have forborne much tortures and atrocities and have at last turned back and this fact has been reflected in this year's Assembly election. Lakhs of people have pressed the buttons of the voting machines and expressed their refusal to tolerate these circumstances any longer and their yearnings for an immediate change. Now the change has arrived at last. Throughout the sprawling West Bengal one after another red bastions have broken down like houses of cards. In the face of this change in the political scenario the apprehension was frequently expressed that such a change will inevitably be followed by retribution and there will be a blood-bath all around. Law and order circumstances will further deteriorate. It cannot be said that these apprehensions were totally unfounded. That is why after the election results were published many bigwigs of CP(M) in different areas went undergound for fear of retributive activities on the part of the common masses. Actually, however such things did not happen. The slogan of Trinamool 'We want change, not retribution' certainly touched the minds of the ordinary masses. The result was that the conflagration that was apprehended turned out to be false, only a few sparks were splattered here and there.

But that hardly means that within these few days the region has been converted into a Ramrajya. Starting from political murders incidents like murders of promoters, manhandling, application of force, damaging houses, dacoity etc., are happening ceaselessly. There is no indication of a decline in the incidence of the type of criminal offences. In the different district areas just as Trinamool activists are being murdered and facing assaults by the desperate CP(M) activists, CP(M) are also not being spared.

It is true that the way the incidents of CP(M) activists being attacked are publicised in the party organ gives many the impression that the region has become overnight a 'jungle-raj! 'The communists are unparalleled in exaggerated publicities of such matters. Nonetheless it is true that such matters are happening. It is not a fact that in all cases people of one party are killing the people of the other party. Behind many such cases there may be incidents of old time enmity over which political colour has been applied. The continuous experience of staying in power for thirty four years at a stretch has led to the cultivation of mutual recrimination, acrimony and enmity among the cadres of CP(M) themselves. The outbreak of such rancour and ill feelings is happening in many cases. Even in many cases of recovery of weapons, police is being informed not by outside people but by the insiders of CP(M). Taking all things together disorder and unrest are continuing to reign supreme in the district areas. This is more so in the rural areas than in the urban areas.

Therefore in tackling the law and discipline circumstances the new government will have to adopt really firm steps. Owing to the obeisant mentality of a long period the rusting of the police administration cannot be removed in the short period. But the citizens of the region will be primarily happy if they see that police is no longer judging the political colours of the offenders and promptly dealing with the complaints received.

29

REFLECTIONS ON POLICE FORCES-2

It is urgently necessary to alter the image of the police forces in West Bèngal. This is the opinion of Kolkata's civil society. This opinion has been expressed on June 18, 2011 at the meeting of the civic committee which has been constituted at the initiative of Mamata Bannerjee by the police, popular representatives and distinguished citizens. Everybody has opined in that meeting that the image which police has projected before the people is not acceptable. Rather the very word 'police' generates in people's mind a peculiar feeling of panic and aversion. The participants did not forget to attract niotice to the fact that the activities of a certain section of the police is responsible for the building up of this unsavoury image.

It is in this conference that the distinguished artist Samir Aich has commented that the word 'police' is frightening to everybody. The actor and legislator Chiranjit has observed that by way of acting in the role of a police activist in the Bengali movies he has become converted into a villain in the public's eyes. It is in the presence of the bigwigs of Kolkata Police that this feeling of disaffection was expressed by the distinguished citizens.

When the idea of the distinguished persons regarding police forces is of the above character the general people's impression in this respect need not be elabrated upon. If during the last three decades somebody has to be primarily accused for this decline in the image of the police forces in the region the earlier left front government has to be held responsible. During the last three decades the police forces were never allowed to act in an impartial manner. The police was controlled by the CP(M) party office. Which police official will be entrusted with which responsibility was determined by the authorities of the Alimuddin

Street. Like other professions party allegiance was being given predominance. Consequently it was found that many worthless and unskilled police officers were installed in important positions by virtue of their intimacy with the party higher-ups. That apart the abominable action of injecting politics in the police service was also performed by the left front.

A kind of police officials took advantage of this narrow outlook of the left front government. They have simply appeased the party leaders and carried on their own illegal activities. The police have turned out to be the drawing rooms of the local party offices. The mastans who received indulgence from the party became the comrades-at-arms with the police. Not unlike the party cadres police has been utilised in political activities. Police also behaved like the party cadres. This corruption and politicisation of the police forces were opposed by honest and upright IPS officers like Najrul Islam who were consequently harassed and humiliated by the previous government.

Besides this politicisation there is the unbridled corruption of a class of police officials. Raising money like the tolabajs, taking bribes here and there - such malpractices have become their habits. Particularly when indigent people fall in distress and go to police stations for redress these dishonest police officials mulct money from them as rewards for insignificant services. For all these reasons people's confidence in police has gradually eroded. Day by day police has assumed the role of villains in the eyes of the ordinary citizens.

In the conference of June 8 the demand raised by the distinguished persons for altering the image of the police forces is highly justified. In the last three decades the image of the police almost reached the bottom; the immediate duty of the present government is to raise it up from that crevice. For this purpose the first thing that the government will have to do is to stop the politicisation of the police forces.

Outside the periphery of party obeisance police forces will have to operate impartially. Ordinary citizens will have to be convinced that the police forces will from now on take steps against the offenders without taking into account their polical pigment and the higher officers of Kolkata Police and regional police officers will have to mark out the corrupt officers and officials and arrange for their hard punishment.

It must be ensured that whenever the ordinary persons had occasions to visit the police stations they will receive appropriate remedies. The attitude to harass the poor and indigent visitors in an unjustified manner must be dispelled from the minds of the police officials. The officers and the officials must be taught the lesson of not surrendering before any poltical pressure. The mud which was slung in the uniform of the police during the last 30 years must be washed away at any cost.

30

IN THE CONTEXT OF EDUCATIONAL REFORM

After coming to power the new government has taken special initiatives in the matter of educational reform. There are two aspects of this reform: the all-round development of the standard of education in the region and recovery of the lost glory of Presidency College by turning it into a University. A few specialist committees have already been formed for this purpose and a special 'mentor group' has been set up with the internationally reputed educationists like the Nobel-wining economist Amartya Sen and Professor Sugata Basu of Harvard University.

What is more important is that the Chief Minister Mamata Banerjee is herself monitoring the whole matter of educational reform amidst her diverse administrative and political assignments. Naturally therefore in different circles this initiative of educational reform has generated ample inspiration. At the same time she has also created sufficient enthusiasm in the concerned circles by announcing payment of salaries of the teachers and the non-teaching staff on the first day of the month, provisional pension, assurance of the rapid payment of the arrears and announcements of different exemptions in the studies of the pupils and movements to schools and colleges. Witnessing this personal initiatives and efficiency of the chief minister Mamata Banerjee many ordinary people have got the impressions that something will happen this time. Like industry and health a big change will certainly come over the educational system of the country. The educational climate in schools, colleges and universities which has been vitiated so long by different kinds of politicking and the preponderance of mediocre elements will improve and students will not be cheated any longer after spending thousands of rupees, adequate recognition of talents will be received and taking all aspects into account the moribund circumtances in education will be enlivened once again.

Such hopes in today's West Bengal are not totally unfounded. The strongly positive outlook which Is noticed on behalf of the government in the matter of development of the standard of education is in fact generating such hopes in our minds. But the region is West Bengal and our Bengali nature is unalterable— That is why already in certain quarters questions have started being asked about some persons in the educational reform committee and their political identities. It is being said that most of her announcements will remain unimplemented. Everything is actually a kind of political gimmick. In the name of emancipating education from party dominance the ruling party Trinamool Congress is actually positing its own patrons in various places and committees. The purpose it is alleged is obvious. It is of course to replace the dominance of one party by that of another. What the leftists taught us throughout their 34 year's misrules that if you are a supporter of the leftists you are actually 'impartial' and an 'expert' in all matters while if, on the contrary, you are a supporter of Mamata Banerjee you are not only an enemy but also a 'polluted politician' from whom nothing can be expected. Singur, Darjeeling or the educational programmes of the Mamata Banerjee government- all are poohpoohed by the leftists in this manner.

But what is the benefit? Everyone knows that all these problems have been inherited from the previous government and each of them is extremely hard and complex which cannot be solved overnight. But Mamata Bannerjee and the members of her ministry have tried to tackle the problems on a wartime footing and progressed very much. Peace has returned to Darjeeling and deep expectations have been aroused in the minds of the Gorkhas regarding the development of the standard of living in the Hills. The peasants of Singur have been overwhelmed with joy at the prospects of return of their lands. Even in the static educational world of the region the movement of change has been noticed. Time alone can say that will happen ultimately and Mamata has succeeded or not in what matter. The earlier government could do nothing in the 34 years. Now when Mamata has started showing some achievements they have started politicking in the opposition bench. What the Education Committeee doing is not important in their eyes. They are more concerned with the question as to who among them are Trinamool and who are Naxals. But the real truth is that the comprehensive development of the standard of education is a multi dimensional issue for which is needed multi level planning and far reaching understanding and faith. The question of politics in this perspective is secondary. And then again the big question is whether that politics is positive or negative, whether it is an outcome of good will or whether it is controlled by the party directives?

During the 34 years of the CP(M) regime the sphere of education was converted in that negative politics controlled by the party directives. That is why they could perform nothing significant.

In the last lap of their regime they built up two incomplete Universities (Refound University at Barasat and the Gourbanga University) and declared a few startling pacakages for the candidates of the minorities and the Pichhre Barg. But there was a lack of well coordinated planning and experienced educationists for implementing those plans and programmes.

The inevitable effect was domination of CP(M), in schools, colleges and Universities. The major consideration was how many students were members of SFI, how many teachers and teaching activists registered their names in ABTA or WEBCUTA, how many CP(M) activists and how many oppositionists are there in the school committies and governing bodies. What should be the strategy to keep those opponets in control. Whether the principal was abiding by the instruction of the council or Alimuddin Street. All these became the chief concerns of studies and teaching. In every school or college there were appointed some activists of CP(M) through whom the information of the institution reached the local party office, the education cell and Alimuddin street in that order. In many cases the regular attendance of the principals in the party office became compulsory.

It is from this contagion of party politics that Mamata Banerjee has sought to save education at all levels. Certainly she is aware that the task is extremely difficult and for that is necessary a well thought out and integrated education policy. At the same time it is necessary that a meticulous blue print for the implementation of that policy is drawn up. This realisation has worked behind assembling the internationally reputed educationists behind the formation of the expert committee.

In the development of the standard of education the instructions of the advisors are as important as it is necesarry to see how far the actual realities are in keeping with those instructions. This is true not only in case of education but in all other programmes. Chief minister Mamata Banerjee is not taking a single step without first taking into consideration these material circumstances. To speak the truth, CP(M) has been defeated by this strong sense of realism of the chief minister. This realism has enabled her to arrange recovery of the lands at Singur and return those to the peasants, and find out solutions of the Darjeeling tangle. I firmly believe that this sense of realism will also enable her to emancipate education from the eclipse by political rambles and lead it to developed standards and traditions.

31

RAMBLES ON PRESIDENCY UNIVERSITY-I

For last two years much deliberations have been going on about the Presidency College in the newspapers, civil society, government departments, inside and outside the country. Previously, It was a college but presently it is a university. Previously there were the principal and the lecturers, presently there is a vice-chancellor and a registrar. Besides that there are a committee and a mentor group etc., set up by Mamata Banerjee. Those who are included in the mentor group are scholars of international eminence who have given evidence of uncommon talents in their own fields of study. The advisor is Amartya Sen himself. Scholars of high competence are thinking about the future of Presidency college. It is expected from their discussions that the college will ultimately arrive at the destination where it is presumed to reach. In this context Amartya Sen, a Nobel laureate has made a pertinent comment. He has spoken of civil initiatives behind the establishment of Hindu college. Right now another kind of civil initiative is noticeable which will certainly be 'light-bearing' as well as 'fruit-bearing'. However, in this connection one can remember the tragic history of Derozio who continued his process of human construction for altogether four or five years after which he was removed from the college. That history of humiliation still now generates a feeling of anguish and remorse in our hearts. Then there is the history of the illustrious ancestor of Professor Sugata Bose whose courage and bravery were umparalleled. But viewed in the perspective of the present day market economy he was ultimately a total failure. Far from being the Prime Minister of the nation he could never even become chief minister of a component region.

The whole history of Presidency College turns around its achievement as an undergraduate college. A few extraordinary teachers had been there. Their names are frequently heard in the lips of the intelligentsia who were the alumni of this institution. But the performance of Presidency College in the postgraduate level was not very remarkable. Because there had been a few unexceptionable teachers at the graduation level and because they had great commitment in the matter of teaching. The students of the Presidency College mastered their subjects thoroughly at the graduation level. In later days for postgraduate education they either went to the Science College or to the College Street campus of Calcutta University. Many students after graduating from Presidency College went to Delhi, Mumbai, Kanpur. Many students also went abroad. This was the culture of Presidency College.

At the graduation level a special tradition of the college was built up. A climate of teaching and learning was built up around a few teachers. These teachers have created a few generations. All these people have become successful in life. But unlike the illustrious ancestor of Prof. Sugata Basu no one has made so much sacrifices in the interest of the nation. In order to reconstruct Bengal and the place of Bengali institution in the world perspective that 'commitment' will be deemed absolutely necessary.

Derozio about whom I was talking a little earlier always used to enthuse his pupils to take part in debates with him. Not only that, he encouraged his students to argue against the side on which he was talking himself. In this way Derozio induced his students to form their own independent opinions and they also began to raise questions about their own household operations and that proved to be his own nemesis. By giving excuse of India's traditional ideals the man was driven out from history of the Presidency College.

The mindset of the Bengalees throws light on this history. But in order to construct something some other things have to be destroyed.

Futile egotism has to be dispensed with. Unless this is done man's internal strength cannot be awakened. Tolerance of the viewpoints of others has to be acquired. This is also a kind of self-exercise. Study of books can not give us this education. It has to be developed from one's own self. It has to be understood that a well-educated person is also a self-educated person. And an institution cannot also be built up if this ideal of self-education is done away with.

No institution can grow up overnight. The same law applies in the case of an educational institution. People of Britain, Europe and America know how to grow it up. We Indians are deficient in this. Bengalis are more inept in this respect. We are only interested in services which we have learnt from our European masters. But we did not learn from them the art of building up institutions. Just think for once how many institutions of international standard have been set up in independent India. Apart from that after the attainment of independence Presidency College retained its earlier glory till 1980 or 1985 or, in other words, for 30 to 40 years since 1947. This is only a consequence of the so called 'inertia of motion'. A wheel is moving it does not suddenly come to a stop. Its original motion keeps it moving for some time. Thereafter it slowly loses its motion.

In the sixties or seventies of the last century which type of students got admitted in Presidency College? Remember the rat race for studying medicine or engineering did not start as yet. Consequently the best students came to Presidency College with the intention of studying Physics or English or Economics. That picture began being totally altered since the eighties when the subjects of preference for the best students appeared to be medicine or eneineering.

The quality of raw materials has its inevitable impact on industry. If there is adulteration in raw materials an industrial establishment is compelled to increase its cost of production if the quality of the product is to be maintained at a high level. The same law is applicable to the sphere of education as well. An exceptionally good student can do well in the examination with little help from the college. But that is not possible for a less meritorious student. Therefore even for an exceptional teacher it is difficult to uphold the earlier standard of Presidency College. It would be an over-simplification if politics alone is accused for this phenomenon. An in-depth analysis and understanding will be called for on this account.

I have already commented that the Indians are not very adept in building institutions. In order to set up an institution self-interest has got to be sacrificed. Men who are prepared to undertake such sacrifices are extremely rare in our society. Although a few such men were noticed earlier as things stand today all those people have vanished altogether from the picture. Today's society runs after success and establishment. But the commitment or determination which is necessary for getting established or setting up institutions is normally absent. But we have to keep it in mind that without 'commitment' no solid achievement is ever possible.

The period when there were no such plethora of conferences witnessed researches of exceptionally high calibres in the city of Kolkata. But now everthing appear to be shallow and superficial. A few air travels, meetings with native and foreign guests and mutual back patting the foremost aim of the educational world seems to be to find out the 'summum bonum' of life among such events. This is the current craze and the index of intelligance lies in acting like so many veritable 'weather cocks'. Of course Derozio made a futile attempt to stand against the current craze and build up a new culture which, however did not fit in with our temperment. And that is why we tried every means fair and foul to drive him out from the precincts of the academic world.

32

RAMBLES ON PRESIDENCY UNIVERSITY-II

In the present perspective we have Presidency University. In the present age a university is known by the standards of its researches. The American universities are known by how many Nobel-winners are found to move about in their corridors. The recovery of the lost glory of Presidency College means nothing. Because all the grandeur of Presidency College was due to the extra ordinary standard of teaching of a few teachers at the undergraduate level. It would not be perhaps proper to say that although a few research centres were there those were actually centres of excellence.

As things stand today, Presidency College has started its journey as Presidency University. New paths and new objectives are necessary. In order to establish the institution on a novel basis' a totally novel attitude is necessary. The University has to be established with sincere efforts of highly expert students and teachers. This is an altogether different game.

The Presidency College of the undergraduate level and today's Presidency University are qualitatively different. An exceptionally good teacher may not necessarily be a good researcher. A famous researcher may not necessarily become a good teacher. In America a teacher who lost his job as a result of the judgement of the students was awarded Nobel Prize the next year of losing his job.

Presidency University has started its journey. People belonging to all the levels of the society, all the other universities of the region and the nation will have to come forward to its assistance. A university is not set up in a day. A university is the outcome of the efforts of many people. The Bengali i.e. Indian habit usually smacks of an escapist bent of mind. At the slighest difficulty we take to our heels. In order to set up an institution we must be brave enough to face all hazards and provide leadership. The mentor group will give the necessary directives and we the ordinary mortals will have to translate those directives into action.

The light of modern education came to India through the Hindu College which was then the pathbreaker. Today the perspective is different. 121 crores of people live today in India. Here only a few 'pockets of excellence' or 'Islands of excellence' will not serve the purpose.

Unless the supreme virtues of all persons are unified together it would not be possible to reach the apex of development. America has introduced such a system through which the paths for florination of the capabilities of even very ordinary persons have been opened. Of course we may have differences with the political system of America. But their dexterity in the matter of setting up institutions must be emulated by us. The ordinary students of our country go to America and attain excellence by virtue of these institutions. That knowledge of running an institution has to be mastered by us. The fittest persons must be given enough latitude, help and support and we must have confidence in their ability. An institution can be built up only in this way.

A question that automatically a rises in this context is whether there is a very serious difference between the academice qualifications of the authorities of the American universities and those in our countries? I do not think so. But successs is more conspicuous in those countries and less in our country. Where is the difference? My own idea is that the difference lies in the mind set. In those countries men have a dogged determination - inflexible decision, unflinching devotion to duty and the attitude of never escaping from the field of action. On the other hand we always have an escapist atttude. The sincerity that is urgently called for in the setting up of an institution is lacking in us.

The government has much responsibility in this context. The available human resources have to be utilised. Everybody must be involved in the matter. Along with the Presidency University all other universities should also be taken care of.

In a poverty-stricken country it is difficult to pay equal attention to all the matters. But if there is tenacity with honesty, if cleverness is replaced by intelligence there will of course be progress in the Bengali society. Unique human resources inside and lawns of green grasses outside, glittering coffee shops, the person engaged in clearing the road, the health of the swans swimming in the lakes putting our people to shame - these all constitute the surroundings of the universities of the foreign countries. Much time will be required to raise Presidency University to that standard. In the meanwhile we will have to keep faith in the mentor group. At the same time we must rightly perform our own respective duties. The vice-chancellor and his team should be given adequate time. The professors should be given their due respect. Let us make a united effort based on mutual trust and respect.

33

TECHNICAL EDUCATION IN THE SHAMBLES

Entrance examination and merely by securing 50% marks on an average in physics, chemistry and mathematics in the Higher Secondary Examination, one will be entitled to go in for studying engineering in this region. The new government which has been installed in power recently has adopted this novel decision. The Director of Technical Education under the Department of Higher Education, Sajal Dasgupta has disclosed this information. Sajal Babu's moot point is that for the last two years many seats have been remaining vacant in the private engineering colleges of this region. Last year about 650 seats remained vacant in 80 non-government colleges in the region. It is with a view to filling up these vacant seats that the new government has taken this decision. Of course Siddhartha Datta who is the chairman of the Central Selection Committee of the Joint Board of Engineering is wholly unaware of this 'novel' decision of the regional government. Nonetheless in the field of technical education this decision has assumed the form of the centre of gravity of a controversy inside the ruling party Trinamool Congress itself 'the criticism of this decision can be heard. The question that has arisen in this context is' how much this decision of the regional government is relevant and expedient?

What the regional government pleads is that since there are vacant seats in the non-governmental engineering colleges, this decision has been adopted. If this is the only reason for taking this decision by the government one must be forced to opine that this decision hardly helps in improving the standard of higher education. The standard of education can never be improved by somehow or other filling up the vacant seats in the private colleges. Rather the question that has arisen is what really is the purpose of the government-to improve the standard of education or fulfilling the business interest of the non-governmental colleges.

In the developed countries, however, the door of higher education is not open for everybody. In those countries higher education is available only on the basis of merit. Only those students who are above average get the opportunity for studying in colleges or universities. On the contrary in our case the door of higher education is open to everybody irrespective of the merit of the candidate. College or university degrees in our country are available to anybody and everybody. Consequently in our country the number of jobless people with degrees is also high. In developed countries it is difficult to topple the barriers of engineering and medical degrees.

In those countries in order to enter these specialised courses of study the students have to go through many screening processes. Previously in our country too there were many restrictions in getting the facility for studying medicine or engineering. Opportunities for studying these subjects were obtained only in cases of proven merit.

During the period of the left government, however, the door for higher education was opened to everybody especially in the sphere of engineering. The left front government opened numerous private engineering colleges in a misconceived effort to create a machinery for generating engineers in every household. This has led to an indiscriminate attitude towards quality. In many cases the judgment of merit is deficient. There has been a consequent decline in the standards of teaching and studying as well as the level of merits.

This time the decision of the new government leads to the apprehension that this will lead to further devaluation of standards. In the first place as a result of this decision the Joint entrance education will be bereft of all its earlier importance. The mediocre students who scored 50% marks on an average in physics, chemistry and mathematics in the Higher Secondary Education will be easily entitled to get admission in the engineering colleges. No one will go to judge whether they have the necessary talent for studying engineering. There will be an indiscriminate decline in the relative merits of the students in the colleges.

What is more important is that the number of jobless engineers in this region will be more inflated. The Director of Technical Education has observed that already the governments of Tamil Nadu, Karnataka and Orissa have legislated in order to facilitate the studies of engineering on the basis of the marks obtained in H.S. or equivalent examination. But only a little scrutiny will reveal that in those regions the thousands of students who pass out every year do not get any importance in the sphere of the job market.

The Technical Education Minister from this region Rabiranjan Chatterjee is a distinguished educationist who had also been the Dean of a university. It is expected that he has the ability to understand the harm that is done by allowing without adequate scrutiny all the mediocre students to study a course like engineering. Instead of being infatuated by the demands of the owners of the non-governmental engineering colleges if he really intends to improve the standard of technical education in the region, he will have to attach importance to the merits of the students aspiring to study engineering. Consequently he will have to desist from the step initiated by the regional government.

34

RIGMAROLE ON SCHOOL EDUCATION

Side by side with higher education, the regional government has taken initiative to improve the standard of school education in West Bengal. Already nine task forces have been constituted for the purpose of improving the standard of school education. In the list of priorities of these task forces there is the arrangement of training of the teachers of primary and secondary levels as per the direction of the centre, drawing up the syllabus in keeping with the national level and changing the text books, improvement of the school infrastructure, special monitoring in the midday meal project etc. It has also been decided that the chairman in charge of the task forces will sit in conference with the School Education Minister or the Departmental Secretary on the last Wednesdays of every month. It is no use denying the fact that the topics included in the list of priorities of the task forces are highly momentous. In order to improve the standard of school education adequate importance should be attached to all these matters. Looked at from this point of view the official decision for constituting nine task forces is of course thanksworthy.

It is not true that the picture of education in the region will improve only through the Presidency University or the development of the standard of higher education in West Bengal. In order to bring about a total improvement of the educational system in the region, work has to be started from the grassroot level of the educational system. If the grassroot level is defective, it will naturally have its impact on the sphere of higher education. In order to improve the talents and the standard of studies, attempts should be made from the school level. In case the roots of the tree are strong, it will naturally proliferate its branches. The educational field can be easily compared with it. If the school education is neglected, the thought of improving the higher education is an idle dream. It is a good angury that the new government is determined to avoid this pitfall. They have taken action to improve the standard of education right from the grassroot level. It may legitimately be expected that the benefits of this effort will be available in not too distant future.

During the last thirty years in this region side by side with higher education, much deterioration took place in school education. In the all India perspective in statistical terms this region went back to the last row. Like higher education in school education also the earlier leftist rulers went to the path of total politicisation The chief reason for the decline of school education was politicisation. During the leftist regime of the last three decades the service of a teacher would not be available unless one was a supporter or an activist of the ruling party. Instead of ability, party allegiance had become the chief point at issue.

School committees were organised by the stalwarts of CPI(M). The textbooks written by the authors who were close to the ruling party were prescribed in the schools. The teachers who remained under the umbrella of the ruling party paid greater attention to politics than the teaching of students. That apart by taking the injudicious step of abolishing English from the primary stage, the leftist rulers have totally destroyed the future of more than one generation. Throughout the last thirty years, the government was seen to adopt no effective initiative for the improvement of standard of school education. Rather as the inevitable result of the dilly dallying attitude of the government gradual decline has taken place in school education.

Very recently Bratya Basu has taken the charge of the Department of School Education along with his earlier charge of the Higher Education Department. In the improvement of the standard of school education, he should immediately pay attention to bringing about the improvement of school infrastructure. There are many schools in the region where the laboratories are deficient or the conditions of the libraries are unenviable. In many schools there are inadequate arrangements of the lavatories or the school buildings are dilapidated. The new school minister will have at least to make the schools fit for study purposes. He will have to keep watch that while coming to study in the schools the students do not have to face any hazards. At the same time attention should be paid to the adequate training of the teachers. Importance should be attached to the problem of making the teachers aware of the world standard of teaching and practising those principles in their own life. The Education Minister should also take the initiative to bring about a change in the mindsets of the teachers. He must also be alert that the school teachers are freed from the mentality of half-hearted teaching in the school and private tuition outside. Before all these attempts should be made to stop the conversion of the schools into political training centres. Whichever party attempts to indulge in such malpractices, should be ruthlessly suppressed. Attention should be paid to the fact that the service of the school teacher must be based on worthiness and merit. No political identity should be given importance in this mattter.

The way the standard of school education has declined during the last thirty years indicate that it is not possible to rescue school education within one or two months. The task is difficult as well as time-consuming. Nor is it a fact that this will not involve direct confrontation with many vested interests. Nonetheless the government and the school education minister will have to tackle these obstacles in a determined manner. If these tasks are performed with adequate sincerity, benefits will definitely be available in future.

35

EDUCATIONAL CONUNDRUM

What is the means to bring about excellence in education? This question is being occasionally heard here and there in 'altered' West Bengal. The preparation for newly building the Presidency University is patently visible. A special committee has been constituted to bring about reforms in higher education. Different projects or proposals for bringing about changes in secondary or higher secondary education are also floating in air. Of course primary education is outside the periphery of discussion even now, perhaps somewhat forgotten. Nonetheless, the discussion about education as in such a stagnant society like West Bengal is not significant. The talent resources of this region is historical-perhaps the foremost ability of this region. but during the last few decades there has been a terrible decline in such resources. Therefore if we really wait to turn round, our first duty will be to bring about improvement in education which means education at all levels. If we want to improve the economic condition of West Bengal rapid reform of higher education is really necessary. Looked at from that point of view the importance accorded to colleges and universities is highly important. But an unpleasant truth should be remembered at the very beginning.

It would have been nice if all the colleges and universities could be upgraded to a sufficiently high level but actually it is difficult, practically impossible. At the very initial stage of the Presidency University one truth has come out in bold relief. Without the arrangememt for special financial grants, it would be difficult to attract teachers or researchers of sufficiently high levels to this university.

Just as it is true that finance is not the only attraction to them it is also no less true that it is difficult to attract them without a minimum financial incentive. Just because only teachers of international levels are relevant here the yardstick of international levels of salaries and allowances cannot be forgotten within the conventional structure of government colleges and universities. That is why special arrangements are necessary. It is for this reason that the project for improving all the educational institutions in unison is unrealistic. The theory of 'communistic' equality is invalid in higher education.

The same words are applicable in the case of education at the secondary levels. In comparison to higher education a greater number of 'centres of excellence' is necessary to build up at the school level and it is also possible. But this is a question of numbers, the real truth remains unaltered thereby. All the schools cannot be developed to the same extent. Not that finance is the only scarce factor. Even if adequate finance is available an adequate number of teachers of high standard are not available.Therefore in this sphere also a few ideal educational institutions need be set up.

In the British period the district schools were built up for this purpose. In many cases those were recognised as 'centres of excellence'. Ethically we can very well think of bringing about this structure. If possible in large districts more than one ideal school can be built up and if the number of districts are increased naturally the number of schools can be increased. In many cases for the district schools houses and primary infrastructures need not be built up afresh.

In quite a few schools these are already there and certain schools are really developed so far as standard of teaching is concerned. In other words, improvement in education need not start from zero.

What is necessary is to keep excellence as the target. Once the target is fixed finding out the route becomes easy.

36

REMOVING HURDLES FROM INDUSTRY

Chief Minister Mamata Banerjee knows it well that only help from the national government will not mitigate the economic problems of West Bengal. That is why she reminded a few days ago that the region must be financially self-reliant. It must draw up the guidelines for standing on its own feet. With that purpose in view collection of fiscal revenues must be increased and large capital and heavy industries must be brought to the region at an early date. In order to facilitate the path of industrialisation she has given direction to the Industries Minister Partha Chatterjee that as early as possible the unfinished industrial projects should be disentangled. Or, in other words, these should be freed from the regulations of red-tapism. When Manmohan Singh visited Kolkata Mamata took his advice regarding the manner in which economic revitalisation of West Bengal can be brought about and which are the fields where industrial development can take place.

A lawsuit is hanging on over the Singur problem. The position of the new government regarding acquisition can not be violated. Violation of the interests of the peasants should not be allowed. This does not mean that Mamata does not want industry. Actually, however, she is in favour of industrialisation and her objective is to facilitate the path of establishment of new industries in this region.

Following the directions of the chief minister attempts have been made to overcome complexities in the case of applications for new industries and very soon 'one window system' is going to be introduced. Said the Industries Minister, 'Previously, for the purpose of getting recommendations of new industries 99 forms were required to be filled up. Indian Chamber of Commerce was given the responsibility for simplifying this process. Thereafter the number of forms was reduced to 35. But the chief minister was not pleased even then. Right now the number of forms has been reduced to 15. From this fact it is obvious that Mamata is now giving priority to the matter of industrialisation.

Quite a few new decisions are being adopted by her so that the aspect of industrialisation is not neglected.

The Managing Director of West Bengal Industrial Development Corporation, Nandini Chakravarti opined that we are not asking the entrepreneurs to invest in industry only because a new government has taken over in West Bengal. Rather such an infrastructure is being sought to be built up by the government, so that an industrialist may be enthused to undertake investment. If years after years were required to get licences for industries, if in order to submit the application it was seen the same information was required to be written for pages after pages the investor will naturally become disheartened. The 15-page application form which has been drawn up at present includes the value-added tax also. If that portion is ommitted total number of pages in the letter of intent will be 13.

From the Industries Department sources, it has been known that this letter of intent can be submitted on-line. After one week it will be known in what position it is lying.

Although new acquisition of land is postponed for the time being the government is paying attention to the fact that there is no scarcity of land for new industry. There are 35 industrial parks under the WBIDC for each of which the Industries Department has already prepared a database. How much land is unused even now and what are the infrastructural facilities- evey such thing is clear now. Consequently those who will come to build up industries will get the facilities for selecting the lands according to their own choice.

So that licences for industry can be issued promptly the Industries Department has built up a core committee with the representatives of Departments of Finance, Urban Development, Agriculture, Irrigation, Small Industries, Power, Environment and Fisheries. Frequent meetings of this committee are held. Consequently the opinions of different departments regarding a project are promptly being known at present.

In certain cases the approval of the national government is also known for the industrial projects of the region. In quite a few cases that licence is given on-line by the Centre. Attempts are being made so that different projects of the region can get the letters of approval of different departments of the Centre within seven days. The chief minister has informed that for this purpose she will herself consult the national government. Apart from that the national Commerce ministry has adopted a new project to facilitate the application process of the entrepreneurs with INFOSIS. This attempt is called 'Pay One, Apply One'. In a particular line of industry application fee will be given only for once. On that basis the letters of approval of all the departments will be available.

As per the directives of the chief minister, on the one hand, investment process is being simplified and on the other new investments are showing rays of hopes.

The chief minister, Mamata Bannerjee has recently inaugurated the Bengal Intelligence Park of Purnendu Chatterjee in Sector-5 of Salt Lake. For that ITI knowledge based project conceived by Purnendubabu 200 workers will be given training. There had been a discussion between Purnendubabu and Mamata Banerjee. The Industries Minister Partha Chatterjee has informed that with a view to building up the Poly Park in Haldia Purnendu Chatterjee and Associates have already invested one thousand crores of rupees. In future further 4,500 crores of rupees will be invested.

Previosly there was some complexity regarding the industrial corporation at Shalbani of Sajjan Jindal. Because there permission was not taken regarding the ceiling of land. Of course Mamata has explained that not that the project will not be implemented because it was started in the regime of Buddhadev Bhattacharya. She wants to rectify the deficiencies in the case of those projects which were not implemented earlier due to administrative failures. Right now the project of the Jindals are free from all complexities. Prathababu wants to emphasise that instead of judging the political colour of the entrepreneurs all the projects have been examined impartially. Care is taken of the fact so that the projects do not go against the interests of the peasants.

Its effects are already at hand. Y.K. Modi has already invested one thousand crores of rupees. In Barasat Rs. 500 crores have been invested in a cloth factory. In Domjir golden ornaments and diamond hub has been set up. In Kharagpur Tractor India is engaged in setting up a corporation for manufacturing machinery and component parts. In Sankrail a foundry hub is being set up. Foundry Park Assocition is also setting up a hub at Howrah's Panihati. Prasun Mukherjee of Universal Success submitted a few projects for Nayachar and recently he had a conference with Partha Chatterjee over those projects.

Mamata Bannerjee has given the green signal to those projects, because these projects are ecofriendly (just what Mamata wanted). Following the demands of the regional government Pasunbabu's organisation has submitted the Financial Disclosure Report. Parthababu is very much pleased at the receipt of this report. In the meanwhile Partha Chatterjee had a meeting with Mukesh Ambani. The latter has shown interest in building up a food processing industry park. Anil Ambani also is investing capital in animation industry in this region. Mukesh Ambani, Anil Ambani and Sajjan Jindal are interesed in having meetings with chief minister Mamata Bannerjee. A schedule has also been prepared for this purpose. Mamata wants to be elected to the Vidhan Sabha. Besides that, the chief minister is also giving priority on generation of power so that there may not be any deficit 'of power in industry. Every Friday she is meeting in conference with the Industries Minister, Finance Minister and the Power Minister where each of the projects are being reviewed in detail.

PART- II

(SEPTEMBER-DECEMBER 2011)

37

HAVEN OF INVESTMENT IS WEST BENGAL

The regional government claims that West Bengal is going to be the new haven for investment. Using the international trade fair in New Delhi this message was given by the chief minister Mamata Banerjee.

This is the first time that in the current trade fair West Bengal has become a partner 'region'. Utilising that opportunity she explained the current circumstances of the region before the circle of industrialists and the dignitaries of different nations and gave the assurance for setting up industries. She also threw light before the industrialists on the successes of her own government during the last six months and demarcated the specific spheres of investment. Development of food processing, agricultural marketing, health education and tourism were specifically stressed in a seminar at Pragati Maidan entitled 'Rising Bengal' and Mamata commented that in our region there are various spheres where there are opportunities for investment. We earnestly desire that captains of industry should come forward to invest in these areas. Already durng the last six months the region has received the assuraance of 56,000 crores of rupees.

The Finance Minister of the region Amit Mitra commented that the fruits of the initiatives of the regional government have already started being available. Quite a few foreign organisations, like Mitsubishi have shown interest in investment. Already they have come forward to set up a manufacturing unit in the region.

The chief minister has also issued a few declarations necessary for industrial development. The non-resident industrialist Prasun

Mukherjee appealed to her that for the puroose of development project in Nayachar island it is extremely necessary to establish communication with the maintanance through the building of a bridge. In reply Mamata assured that this communication will be set up through the railways. Recently the regional Industries Minister Partha Chatterjee had a discussion with the national minister Jayanti Natarajan regarding the licences relating to Nayachar. Jayanti informed that the matter would be settled very soon.

Mamata has all along highlighted the negative attitude of the industrial circles which have been created in West Bengal during the leftist rule of 34 years. She now opined that there is now a sincere effort on the part of the regional government to come out of this negative mindset. In her words we are imploring all the countries like America, Britain, Germany, China to invest capital in West Bengal. We have cheap labour here. An auxiliary atmosphere for industrial development has been created here.

It has to be remembered that West Bengal is the gateway to Bangladesh, Nepal and Bhutan. We have common boundaries with many regions in the north-east. Consequently in case of investment in our region the markets for so many nations can be captured. She also informed that in order to attract investment Rising Bengal Summit will be held on 6-11 January in the regions adjacent to New Delhi. Industrialists like Prasun Mukherjee, Sanjay Budhia and Y.K. Modi admitted that the climate of investment i.e. the overall circumstances in the region are gradually changing. The national Commerce Minister Ananda Sharma advised that the infrastructural development in the region should be given topmost priority. He informed that in the near future ASEAN Industrial Summit will be held in West Bengal.

In the case of the region land acquisition is a highly sensitive matter. That is why Mamata recently assured the industrialists to the effect that the region has set up land banks. There are also land-maps. If the industrialists so desire they can also themselves acquire land. In case industry is required to be set up availability of land will be no problem. At the same time the chief minister informed the industrialists that in order to avoid all kinds of red-tapism the government has introduced 'single window' arrangement for the industrial system.

38

WHO ARE THE GREATER LEFTISTS?

Who are the greater leftists? CP(M) - CPI or, the Trinamool Congress? In the question of national approval in foreign investment in retail trade the equivalent opposition of the two warring rivals recently highlighted this vital question. After petrol came the question of foreign investment in retail trade and there was the paradoxical situation that TMC criticised the national government by attuning their utterances with the opponents. And going to do that the TMC MPs actually embarked in a competition with the leftists.

On November 22, in the meeting of the national cabinet the MPs of the four leftist parties became vocal in the Parliament in protest against foreign direct investment of 51% in retail trade. On November 25, TMC joined in that protest. In the recent past probably this type of reaction was noticed for the first time. Of course the Trinamool MPs did not raise a hue and cry by coming down to the well unlike the leftists. Since they were the partners of the leftist government they showed restraint in this manner. But there was no difference in their language of opposition to the national government.

Side by side with the leftists as well as TMC all the opposition parties including BJP and even the other partner of the national government DMK also became vocal in the Parliament. In both the chambers of the Parliament along with the opponents the two partners of the government raised a hue and cry and the proceedings of the meeting were obstructed. In the Rajyasabha a few leftists and BJP MPs tore down the statement of the national Commerce Minister Ananda Sharma over the decision of the national cabinet.

The sessions of both the chambers of the Parliament were progressed. Consequently for four days at a stretch both the chambers of the Parliament remained virtually paralysed.

But the matter did not end here. The leftist, TMC and BJP leaders gave the indication that in future also much unrest may be created in the Parliarent. BJP and the leftists wanted to bring prorogue proposal in this matter in the Parliament. But in the Loksabha the leader of TMC, the state Minister of Health. Sudip Banerjee said, since we are partners of the national government, owing to the parliamentary obligations we cannot bring prorogue proposals. But strategically we will oppose it. He made reference to the question of the rise in oil price and commented that TMC has already shown in the recent past to what extent opposition can be drawn to the national government.

The leftist parties have all along opposed the entry of foreign investment in retail trade. Their rationale is that this will result in the exploitation of the country's peasants, agricultural labourers and small traders. Now the TMC is also raising their voice of protest in the same strain and arguing that the national government can hardly adopt any such policy which can cast a negative influence on the livelihoods of the peasants, small traders and agricultural labourers. Recently TMC raised this issue in the Loksabha as well. Their contention is that this decision of the Centre will engulf the small peasants and the small shopkeepers. Apart from that the foreign investors will at first purchase commodities from the peasants with extra money and keep it in storage.

The peasants will be enthused to produce more but in the next year the situation will become such that they will be unable to sell their produce. Whereupon they will be compelled to sell their produce at lower prices. In this way, TMC apprehends, new avenues of peasant suicides will be opened up. This is the reason of their objection. DMK is also opposing the decision of the national government in the same strain.

The CP(M) leader Basudev Acharya commented that all the opponent parties along with the partners of UPA like TMC and DMK were opposing the decision of the national government. Basudev and the CPI leader Gurudas Dasgupta informed that they would bring prorogue proposal against the decision of the national government. Gurudas recently talked with Sudip in this matter. But Sudip explained to him the limitations of the TMC.

BJP also threatened to bring prorogue proposal against this issue. Later a leader of the party Murali Manohar Joshi informed that the regions under the administration of BJP are advised that they should not implement this policy of the national government. The regions under Congress administration should also walk along the same avenue.

But the Parliamentry Affairs Minister Paban Banshal commented that a prorogue proposal of BJP regarding the recovery of black money had already been adopted. In the same session of the Parliament prorogue proposals cannot be raised more than once.

When asked to comment about the opposition of TMC - DMK he said that all the political parties have the right to express their own opinion.

Written objections were submitted by TMC and DMK. Questions were raised by Congress leaders like the Ministers like Jairam Ramesh and A.K. Anthony. The TMC leader and the Railways Minister Dinesh Trivedi walked out on this occasion from the meeting of the cabinet. Nonetheless the Manmohan Ministry disregarded that opposition and managed to secure the reco ommendation for foreign investment in retail trade of more than one brand of commodities. It is presumed that owing to quite a few economic and political obligations the national cabinet had to ignore the opinions of the partner parties.

The principal reason is of course to alter the total image of the national government. The Prime Minister Manmohan Singh and the Finance Minister Pranab Mukherjee had the responsibility to change the impression that the national government had moved away from the path of economic reform while going to tackle the problem of corruption in public life. They had also the resposibility to restore the confidence of the investors and the industrial circles. When on the one hand the external value of rupee is descending at a terrific rate and there is a crash in the stock market that resposibility has been much more magnified. Yesterday's decision had its impact on today's stock market. The sensex has come down as a whole this day also. But the share prices in the organisations of retail trade of the merchandise of more than one brand like Shoppers Stop, Pantaloons, Bishal and Trent have gone up.

The Manmohan Government is presupposing that the way foreign investment is mostly being attracted to America owing to the European crisis a few portions of it will of course this time be diverted to India. Those foreign investors who were so far withdrawing their capital from the Indian market will regain their confidence after watching the positive outlook of the national government. The Finance Ministry has the impression that this will revitalise the 'real estate' sector. Because those organisations who in view of the recession held up their programmes for building maills or shopping complexes will again be interested in launching new programmes.

It is understood that Pranababu explained to the Railways Minister that West Bengal had little chances of any harm at this occurrence. Because the West Bengal Government has already taken into account the interests of the small traders and peasants and consequently has the likelihood of imposing restrictions on the retail organisations in the region. That condition has already been retained. But TMC cannot obstruct the process if others regions presume that they will be benefited as a result. Congress leaders are saying that TMC did not extend this time their resistance to the same extent which they did at the time of enacting the land bill or hiking the prices of petrol products. They did not this time totally obstruct the path of taking decisions.

The Governor of the Reserve Bank,. D.Subbarao today expressed the hope that this decision of the national cabinet will result in controlling the rise in prices. Because there will be improvement in the system of supply of the agricultural products. So long among the farmers and the buyers the middle men derived the greatest benefit. The peasants received less prices for the agricultural products and the buyers used to pay higher prices. In the organised retail trade the peasants also will receive higher prices than previously, the buyers also will receive products at less prices. What is more important is that investment will be made in the country in the correct method.

As per the estimate of the national Commerce Minister, Ananda Sharma in case of foreign investment in retail trade one crore of new jobs will be created in 3 years. As per the government estimates 40 lakhs of jobs will be created in the retail trade centres and the rest in the supplies and transport sectors.

The industries and Commerce Minister Ananda Sharma recently

informed the journalists that in case any region wants that, it can withhold the permission of retail trade to any multinational corporation. Taking into consideration the probable objection of Mamata Banerjee's West Bengal as well as other regions, this matter has been kept in the national - regional concurrent list. But Ananda Sharma expected that any progressive region will definitely welcome foreign investment in retail trade in its own area. Previously in Kolkata and recently in the trade fair Ananda Sharma discussed this issue with Mamata Banerjee.

The topmost level of the Manmohan Government points out that in future the national government wants to invite foreign investment also in the sphere of civil aviation.

Before that it was necessary to give the information that the Manmohan Government is committed in the reform programme of the second phase.

39

KISHENJI'S DEATH AND THEREAFTER

The topmost Maoist leader, Mallajula Koteshwar Rao alias Kishenji has been killed recently in a conflict with the Cobra forces in the Burishole forest in the Jambani area of West Medinipur. Recently the curtain has dropped over the dramatic life of this character enshrouded in mystery who remained hidden from public sight for thirty years. For this long period Kishenji had been the reason for head ache to the police and administration in Andhra Pradesh, Chhattisgarh, M.P., Orissa, Jharkhand, West Bengal and Bihar.

In the past also even by conducting repeated enquiries the police and the allied forces found no traces of Kishenji. Every time in the last moment he threw dust in the eyes of the police and allied forces. On behalf of the administration the price of this Maoist leader was fixed at Rs. 35 Lakhs. At last Kishenji failed to escape from the clutches of the Cobra forces and his bullet-shot body was recovered in the Burishole forest.

Another Maoist guerilla leader Suchitra Mahato was known to be wounded in conflict with the Cobra forces. Undoubtedly this incident was a great success for the allied forces. Such a great success against the Maoists was never achieved in any previous campaign.

Although in the meanwhile some allegations were levelled from some quarters around the death of Kishenji. It has been alleged that this death did not occur as a result of military action. He was actually captured by the Cobra forces. He was later killed in a mock conflict.

Kishenji's mother herself brought this allegation. The real

circumstances however should be subject to further inquiry. But there is little doubt that Kishenji's death will somewhat dishearten the Maiosts. Not only Jangalmahal of this region, but all over the country the death of Kishenji will give a terriflc jolt to the Maoists.

Naturally a question has appeared in an enlarged manner. Will the regional administration succeed in wholly suppressing Maoist activities in Jangalmahal after the death of Kishenji?

Will this incident also lead to a stoppage in the Maoist movement?

Although the death of Kishenji is a great shock to the Maoists, the administration has little reason to be elated over the matter right now. Although the Maoist activities will be retarded for the time being the administration has little reason to get the impression that these will be stopped wholly. The administration should remember that the Maoist organisation does not centre around any particular organisation. Here in the absence of one leader another leader occupies his position. Although the function of extending the organisation is somewhat impeded the Maoists continue the same function sub rosa.

All though the death of Kishenji has for the time being created a vacuum in the Maoist leadership some other person will be positioned in his place. What is a matter for greater apprehension is that as a retaliation for the killing of Kishenji the Maoists can deal a big blow. Before this incident after the killing of Cherukurhi Rajkumar alias Azad in Andhra Pradesh, the Maoists dealt a big blow. That possibility cannot be totally wished away after the death of Kishenji.

At the same time the administrators should remember that so far seven top most Maoist leaders including Kishenji have lost their lives in direct confrontation. Five topmost Maoist leaders are confined in the jail. Nonetheless Maoist activities have not been retarded. That is why there is little reason for complacence that Jangalmahal will be quietened after the death of Kishenji. On the contrary the administration will have to remain alert always for the reason that although for the time being. Maoist activities in Jangalmahal can be retarded some what these will probably raise their ugly heads again in the future.

But with Kishenji's death the whole process of discussion of the Maoists with the regional government has been nullified. It does not appear to be possible that in response to the proposal of the regional government the Maoists will agree to come to a discussion. And if there is no liklihood of resuming the discussion process the field of conflict and controversy will be expanded further. In such a perspective the administration will have to ponder over the manner in which peace can be restored in Jangalmahal. Because the primary duty of restoring peace rests with the administration.

Even the Maoists have some lessons to take from the death of Kishenji. It is that since the path of their movement is mistake they are gradually being dissociated from the public at large. And their movement also is gradually approaching towards a miserable consequence. If the Maoists dispense with the politics of murder, terrorism and violence and return to the mainstream of democratic movement they will succeed much in securing popular support.

After the death of Kishenji the Maoists should at least realise the truth that the politics of violence does not lead to any other consequence apart from the loss of a few lives.

40

GREATER EMPHASIS SHOULD BE PAID TO POWER SECTOR

The music of Durgapuja was still ringing in the air when the citizens of the region fell in the clutches of severe loadshedding. During the last few days, the amount of shortfalls in both the WBSEB and CESC areas have been abnormally increased. Of course two days ago since the demand for power in the region was much less, the amount of loadshedding was somewhat less. Nonetheless the authorities of the regional Power Department could not utter any words of hopes regarding the improvement of the circumstances. Rather the words they have uttered caused sufficient apprehension. The authorities of the Power Department are saying that on the occasion of Dipavali, the entire region of West Bengal may suffer from a power crisis. For this unbalanced position of power the Power Department is accusing the scarcity of coal as the chief reason. The amount of coal stored in the unit of Power Development Corporation has reached the rockbottom level. Coal for one or two days have been stored in Kolaghat, Bakreswar, Bandel and Sagardighi. It is obvious that on the working days if the demand for power is increased the region will again face disaster.

Under the circumstances neither the Power Minister Manish Gupta nor the authorities of the Power Department could utter any words of hopes. It has been announced in newspapers that due to the fact that a large amount of finance remaining unpaid by the regional government coal supplying organisations are refusing to supply coal. As a result, the stock of coal has dwindled and a critical situation has arisen.

Of course the power Minister Manish Gupta has four days ago gave the assurance of 60 crores of rupees to Eastern Coalfields Limited. Even after two days, it was announced in newspapers that finance was not paid so far. The authorities of the Power Development Corporation presume that even if that finance is deposited within one or two days, there will be little improvement in the circumstances. They are saying that 3 days ago the Power Development Corporation received 16 rakes of coal according to demand. But on the next day it was again reduced. Simultaneously with it, problems have been multiplied for the reason that power generating centres have not been modernised in due period at Kolaghat, Bakreswar and Bandel.

The power sector has a special role in the development and industrialisation of the region. Particularly there is an intimate nexus between Power and industrialisation. That is why in cases the government wants to doncern itself with development and industrialisation, it must also speculate separately about the sphere of power with special emphasis on it. With a view to developing the sphere of power, careful steps have to be taken on the basis of an emergency.

Although after being installed into the saddle, the new government started thinking deeply with various other sectors. No special consideration has still now been made about the power sector. It has also not been known whether the government has any special programme about the power sector. After the new government came to the saddle for the first three months, the Power Department was in the hands of the chief Minister Ms. Mamata Banerjee. Thereafter the charge of that department was given to Manish Gupta. After assuming the charge of the Power Department, Manish Gupta has been confronted with this severe problem of loadshedding.

At the root of the present power crisis, the chief reason is the dwindling of the supply of coal and its stock. The supply and stock of coal did not take place in one day. For a pretty long time, the crisis was deepening. Since that has taken the final shape everybody has now become alerted. After coming to the saddle, the new government attached adequate importance to the power sector from the very beginning, identified the specific problems in different areas in a detailed manner. This problem originating from the supply of coal could never escape their notice and they also could find adequate time for tackling the problems in a befitting manner. And the Power Minister also could not have to behave in a directionless manner after the problem assumed an acute shape.

Apart from that there is also the problem of lack of timely modernisation of the power generating centres in Kolaghat, Bakreswar and Bandel. The responsibility for not modernising these plants mostly belongs to the previous leftist government organised by CPI(M). It was they who damaged the power generating centres by accepting cutmoney and placing orders for installing machinery of poor qualities. It was in their period that the burden of debt increased due to failure in timely payment of money to coal supplying agencies.

Still then the present government will have to understand that in the circumstances, they should not wash their hands only after criticizing and accusing their predecessors. It should appreciate which sector should receive priority and which action should he performed first with utmost urgency. The government would have to draw up its programmes accordingly. In case there is no improvement in the power sector, no industrial organisation will ever look up at the face of this region. After realising this truth, priority should be accorded by the Power Minister and the top leaders of the regional government to the power sector. Right steps should be adopted in the matter of development of the standards of the power generating centres.

41

MORE ABOUT POWER SECTOR

The power Department of the region has made an understanding for receiving coal from Eastern Coalfields Limited (ECL) on the condition of not repaying the cess in an attempt to tackle the power crisis of the region. In a meeting with the ECL authorities, the Power Minister of the region Manish Gupta himself has entered into this understanding. It has been known from the Chief Minister's secretariat that before about seven days, the Power Minister Manish Babu sat in a conference with the Managing Director of ECL regarding the supply of coal. The Managing Director of ECL proposed to the Power Minister that since the regional government is failing to meet the price of coal, it should give up the claim to the money to be obtained as cess from the ECL. In exchange for that money, ECL will keep the supply of coal at the normal level. The Power Minister eagerly welcomed this proposal of ECL. He informed the ECL that on the basis of this understanding, they should continue to send coal to the regional government. It was then that the principle of receiving coal in exchange for cess was finalised.

Before allowing the cess to remain unpaid, the Power Minister never previously had any discussion with either the Finance Minister or any senior Officer of the Power Department. Even in the meeting where the Power Minister adopted this decision, no representative of the Finance Minister was present. It was by keeping the Finance Minister in the dark that the Power Minister took a unilateral decision in such an important matter. Naturally a controversy has been created over this decision of the Power Minister. The question has arisen whether the Power Minister can unilaterally adopt such a decision by actually sidetracking the Finance Department?

The question of collecting the cess is connected with the principle of collecting the revenues of the region. It is the jurisdiction of only the Finance Department to adopt any decision regarding the collection of revenues. In case the other departments have any pertinent point to suggest in this matter, they can inform the Finance Minister. But no decision can be independently adopted by any department. Looking at that point of view, the unilateral decision that the Finance Minister has adopted regarding the non-payment of cess by ECL contravenes the official regulations. Of course there is plausibility in the argument of the Power Department that there is no finance in their hands. The purpose of allowing the ECL not to pay the cess is that they will enable the Power Department to receive coal. There is no way to deny the fact that in this region crisis has appeared in the power sector due to the shortfall in the supply of coal.

In this case, owing to lack of finance, the Power Department is hamstrung. Consequently the Power Department could send the proposal for cancelling the cess to the Finance Department. Instead this unilateral decision by the Finance Department will strike at the root of coordination inside the government. If by taking the Power Department as a precedent, other departments *also* continue to take similar decisions the coordination between the government will be destroyed and consequently the government *will* have to face further financial difficulties.

This decision of the Power Department will result in a financial crisis of great magnitude for the regional government. The annual earning of the regional government on account of cess of coal is Rs. 110 crores. Cancelling the cess means that this huge income will be cut down.

Naturally the question will arise as to how the regional government will make up this deficit. The estimate received from the Chief Minister's secretariat reveals that this decision will make the financial crisis of the region more complex.

It has been known that right now the total monthly loss of the power generation and distribution company is Rs.225 crores. As a result of increase of contingency expenditures, very *soon* it will exceed the figure of Rs. 260 crores. At the same time Rs. 110 crores to be received as cess from the ECL will have to be adjusted with the price of coal. With that will be added the monthly payment of power tariff of Rs. 40 crores by the power department to the regional government and Rs. 40 crores as the interest of the credit taken from the government. Even if this Rs. 190 crores is kept aside, every month the deficit amounts to Rs. 70 crores. Apart from that the amount of finance which used to be deposited in the exchequer as being the cess from ECL will also be cut down. The result is that the quantum of liquid finance which will be daily required for running the government will fall short.

Of course, the power minister did not take into account the future possibilities before adopting this unilateral decision. In case he did premeditate on such vital matters, he would certainly be inhibited from making hurry in taking such a crucial decision. Now he is required to preview the future possibilities and enter into a conference with the finance department in order to find out a feasible solution of the likely future pitfalls. Otherwise the entire region will have to bear the brunt of his indiscretionary and myopic decision.

42

MORE ON SCHOOL EDUCATION

The regional government has taken the decision that following the Right to Education Act, upto Class VIll no student should be detained in the same class. Two days ago in the conference of the regional cabinet, this decision has been unanimously adopted. After the meeting of the cabinet, this decision of the regional government has been announced by the Industries and Commerce Minister Partha Chatterjee. It was clear from the declaration of Partha Chattarjee that upto class VIII in secondary schools, the matter of success or failure will not remain any further.

It was in the period of the left front that the system of success or failure at the primary stage was given the go-bye. It was from the educational year 1983-84 that decision to abolish the system of success or failure was made effective at the primary stage. Recently going to announce the new decision at the meeting of the regional cabinet, the Industries Minister has declared that in order to assess the learning of the students in the classes, the system of evaluation will be introduced. Otherwise the weaknesses of the students could not be identified.

There was a time when by abolishing the system of success or failure at the primary stage, the left front government was in the throes of a severe criticism. A section of the distinguished educationists of the region still holds the opinion that by abolishing the system of success or failure at the primary stage, the earlier government under the leadership of CPI(M) has actually spoiled the future of the boys and girls. It can be easily presupposed that the new government by adopting the decision of abolishing the system of success or failure upto class VIII in secondary schools, a controversy will again appear. Not unlike the former left front government, the new government will have to face adverse criticism from many quarters.

Two days ago after declaring this decision in the meeting of the regional cabinet, a controversy has started. No matter how emphatically the Industries Minister asserted that in order to assess the learning of the students in the classes, there will be a system of evaluation most of the teachers' organisations do not agree to accept the new decision. Their moot point is that if upto class VIII the system of success or failure is replaced by the grading system this will ultimately cause harm to education at the secondary school. Even Professor Sunanda sanyal who has been appointed as the chairman of the syllabus committee constituted by the School Education Department has disagreed to see eye to eye with this decision of the new government, in this context the observation of the regional Education Minister Bratya Basu is noteworthy. When asked to comment on the why this decision was adopted by the regional cabinet the Education Minister replied: Ask the Chief Minister. In other words the Education Minister was reluctant to enter into any such debate or discussion.

It cannot be totally denied that there are a few practical disadvantages in abolishing the method of success or failure till class VIII in secondary schools. In the first place the students of class VIII have to appear in the secondary examination after two years. Looked at from this point of view, if there is no longer the method of success or failure till class VIII, the necessary mindset for appearing in the secondary examination lord not grow up among the students. That apart, whether the students have been fit for studies in the secondary level, cannot be known through the process of winnowing any further. At the same time the teachers' organisations are also telling of another possible bad effect of abolishing the system of success or failure upto class VIII. They are saying that as a result of this questionable decision, the students themselves will fail to be in a position to appreciate what the exact level of depth of their learning is. Guardians also will fail to gauge the exact extent of the learning of their children. Right before the secondary examination when they will be confronted with this issue they will simply have no time to rectify the drawbacks of their children. None of these arguments can in fact be refuted easily.

Education in fact is a highly sensitive issue. On the adoption of a correct decision depends the future of the next few generations. If in the sphere of education a sudden decision is adopted without considering the pros and cons, it may result in considerable harm to the next generations.

The previous left front government abolished the system of learning English in the primary stage and thus caused harm to the future of quite a number of generations. If not unlike the last leftist government, the new government also fails to consider the pros and cons before taking an unwise decision, it will be a reason for apprehension from the point of view of the following generations.

Before adopting the momentous decision of abolishing the system of success and failure, this government ought to have entered into discussions with different teachers organisations and educationists. But the present government did not care to do that. Just as during the regime of the left front there was a noticeable tendency to impose a decision from above, the new government also displayed a comparable tendency at the time of introducting the decision to abolish the system of success or failure till class VIII in secondary schools.

Education Minister Bratya Basu said in Delhi that there is no truth in any such possibility. After the Education Minister said such words, it would be perfectly justified if the regional government was wise enough to enter into a discussion with the distinguished teachers and teaching organisations before taking a praiseworthy and pragmatic decision in this matter. The regional government can ill afford to forget that the future of a few following generations is inextricably intertwined with this single decision. That is why any puerile shortsightedness or indiscretion does not fit in well with its honest intentions.

43

AGRICULTURAL CRISIS CONTINUES

The Food Minister of West Bengal Jyoti Priya Mallik has claimed after the change of government that paddy worth one hundred crores of rupees has been purchased. This claim of his is likely to generate the hope in the public psyche that the peasants have been really benefited as a result of this official initiative. But the real truth is otherwise. Whatever be the claim of the government, the peasants have not yet received relief from the hands of the middlemen. They are in fact remaining in the same darkness they had been in the previous regime. But the middlemen are making huge profits like in the earlier days. In the previous leftist regime there was acute grievance among the peasants about the purchase of paddy at support prices. During the regime of the leftist government, paddy used to be purchased through cooperatives at the head of which there were mostly the CPI(M) leaders. In collusion with the owners of mills, little quantities of paddy used to be purchased from the peasants and the rest amount used to be purchased from the middlemen. Consequently the market of paddy could never be revived in an effective manner. Instead of going through the cooperatives, the new government has embarked in directly purchasing paddy through owners of mills at support prices. But paradoxically, this decision of the new government has resulted in deepening further the crisis of the government.

The bands of middlemen who are appointed by the mill-owners and by taking advantage of the poverty of the peasants they are purchasing paddy at the rate of Rs. 530/- to Rs. 540/-. When that paddy enters the mills, its price becomes Rs. 648/- per sack. It is actually the owners of the mills who are enjoying the major portion of the profits. The peasants observe that just in the same way in which potato used to be purchased at support prices in the leftist regime through the middlemen, the new government is also throttling the peasants in almost the same manner.

At the same time in a different news item, it was seen that in Hooghly district middlemen are purchasing vegetables from the peasants at lower prices and selling those at exorbitant prices. In other words not only paddy but also in the cases of all agricultural products, it is the peasants who are deprived by the middlemen. During the regime of any government, the domestic wants of the peasants have not been mitigated. Incidentally during all the regimes, the middlemen and agents are being considerably benefited.

It may be remembered here that sometime also due to the abnormal rise of the prices of vegetables, the Chief Minister Mamata Banerjee herself came down to the streets in visiting the market places in the Kolkata City. Following her laudable instance, other leaders and ministers in different districts also visited the market places in their respective areas for a few days. The administrative big shots also dispensed with their inertia of rest. But in reality the total situation remained unaltered. The middlemen are throwing dust in everybody's eyes and continuing their evil practices as usual. The administrative authorities are continuing to stick to their usual indifferent attitude or simply continuing to connive at the middlemen. The Chief Minister also along with the other members of the cabinets is being busy with other involvements. Nobody seems to have any time to concern himself with the problem of investagating how the middlemen are exploiting the poor and helpless peasants without any hindrance from any quarters.

The Food Minister Jyotipriya Mallik has observed : We simply lack an adequate infrastructure for directly purchasing paddy from the peasants. Therefore, we took help from the mill-owners. In other words, the government has knowingly left the fortune of the peasants in the hands of the middlemen.

Two questions may arise here. In the first place, what is the reason that the infrastructure for directly purchasing paddy from the peasants cannot be built up. Where actually is the shoe pinching? If in this matter the earlier government is a total failure, is then the new government taking new initiatives?

Secondly, even if we assume that for the time being there is no official infrastructure, why should not the present government have control and monitoring authority over the mill-owners.

Why should not the government gather adequate information about the way millowners are exploiting the hapless peasants in this way? And if such information does reach the government, why will it not immediately take adequate steps for remedying this miserable situation?

The government can ill afford to sit idle under such circumstances by putting the responsibility on anybody else's shoulder. The government will have to remember that instead of constituting ten or twenty committees with the members of the intelligentsia the priority in its programme of assistance is to maintain the interest of the peasants in travail. It will have to develop awareness about this priority. The previous government failed to understand this priority. If the present government also fails to appreciate this responsibility the citizens of the region will be utterly frustrated.

The Food Minister demands the new government has already spent Rs. 100 crores in purchasing paddy at support prices. But why Rs. 100 crores? The Food Minister can spend Rs. 500 crores on this account but if as a result of this public expenditure, the depressed peasant community is not benefited and on the contrary the middlemen and agents are the undesirable gainers, the real target of the government remains unfulfilled. In the present instance the target is really unfulfilled.

The last leftist government could not or rather did not remove this unholy dominance of the middlemen and agents. Rather these middlemen extended their hands even to the administrative machinery. No remarkable initiative to stop the mischievous activities of the middlemen is noticeable even now on the part of the new government.

All that has been done to stop these mischief-makers from their blood-sucking operations seems to be mere lip-service and there is no remarkable practical initiative. If like in the previous regime the middlemen again extend their dirty hands of interference in the administration of the new regime that will be an extremely unfortunate happening. Therefore by throwing a wet blanket on the evil designs of the blood-sucking middlemen, the new government will have to prove its sincerity in protecting the interests of the impoverished peasants.

44

OFFENDERS AT NANDIGRAM SHOULD BE SQUARELY PUNISHED

The criminal Investigation Department (CID) has in the montl of October 2011 started inquiry about those hapless people who los their habitats as a result of the joint operation of the CPI (M)'s cadre and the police during the land movement of Nandigram.

Very recently the CID officers visited and inspected differen areas of Nandigram including Sonachura and enquired from th eyewitnesses about the day on which the carnage happened under th instructions of the previous Chief Minister-cum-Police Ministe Buddhadev Bhattacharya.

Naturally the people of Nandigram are jubilant at this role of th CID after the change of government in the political scenario. The da of judgment which they were so long expecting has at last arrived a their door. This seems to be the impression of the aggrieved resident of Nandigram. Nothing new can be said about the infernal carnag committed at Nandigram in 2007 by the CPI(M) activists in allianc with the police. Not only mass massacre and massrape exactly, hov many people were killed and kidnapped in that hullabalo are nc accurately known even to this day. The relatives and family membe of those missing persons are even now unaware what consequenc ultimately befell in their fates.

The last left front government had made continuous efforts t cover up this nightmarish mass massacre from public attention. was strange that this inhuman incident was elogised by the Region secretary of CPI(M) Biman Basu who gave it a testimonial saying 'new sunrise has taken place in Nandigram.' The residents (

Nandigram and various mass organisations have repeatedly been vocal in the demand of an impartial inquiry of this infernal incident. From different sources the demand for punitive measures has been raised against the culprits in Nandigram. But unfortunately even today the guilty persons involved in the tragic happenings of Nandigram have not been brought to book.

Not only West Bengal but the entire nation was embittered and enraged at the tragic massacre of Nandigram. Even outside the borders of India the Nandigram incident attracted the wrathful notice of umpteen millions. Distinguished persons with both national and international reputation condemned this incident in an indubious voice. But it is regrettable that the then leftist government were not ashamed at that matter. Rather they made an attempt to suppress the weeping residents of Nandigram under the boots of the police.

These oppressed people of Nandigram were so far waiting for receiving social justice. In the history of the land movement of the country, the incidents of Nandigram and Singur will be mentioned for ever with adequate importance. To speak the truth, the initiation of a political change in this region has started from the movements of singur and Nandigram. The sparks of protest was lit up in Singur and at Nandigram that spark was converted into a flame. It was that flame which in later days spread all over the region and burnt the CPI(M) regime to rack and ruin. It is by keeping that history of Nandigram and Singur moments in mind that the new government will have to pay respect and obeisance to the sentinels of these two movements. The new government has done the right thing by calling upon the CID in the inquiry about the missing persons of Nandigram.

During the regime of the left front government quite a few mass massacres took place with the joint villainy of police and the party cadres. Our hairs will stand on edge if we hear an account of these mass massacres at Marichjhampi, Chhota Angaria, Bijan Setu, Nandigram - the accounts of all these incidents are bloodcurdling. No proper inquiry was made in any of these carnages which happened during the left front government. Those who were responsible for or connected with the mass massacres were not punished in any manner. They moved about in open air with full security and are still now moving about in a fearless manner. Some of them are occupying high positions inside CPI(M). Some of them were posted in important official positions during the leftist government.

During the leftist regime the families of the victims who died in mass massacres went from door to door or from pillar to post but found no justice. Rather instead of justice, they were subjected to threatening by the party and the government. But to speak the truth those who were connected with these mass massacres were in a real sense enemies of civilization. They are averse to humanism. It is in the interest of humanism that they should be meted out adequate punishment.

Now the government has been altered. The new government has started once again a new inquiry by the CID in the Nandigram episode. We can only cherish the hope that that enquiry will result in giving proper punishment to the guilty persons involved in the Nandigram incident. At the same time we will also demand that fresh inquiries should be made into other episodes by the new government. This government should this time arrange for adequate punishment to all those persons who are remaining outside the clutches of law and order even after committing atrocious killing of innocent citizens.

45

FOCUS ON INNER CONFLICT

Almost six months have elapsed since the residents of West Bengal have received the taste of political change. This change has at last come at the conclusion of the nightmarish misrule of 34 years on the 8 crores of citizens of this region. The very clear popular mandate in this year's election was that -whatever be the means CPI(M) should be defeated. There was no clear idea regarding the exact shape of the change to be brought about. But what was certain was that the people earnestly yearned for freedom from the hands of CPI(M) which was dominanted by promoters, free footers armed cadres, fake industrialists and ill-reputed leaders like Lakshman Seth, Sushanta Ghosh, Anil Basu and Majid. Master etc. The ordinary citizens did not want to listen any further to the rodomontades of the day dreaming Chief Minister Buddhadev Bhattacharya who was at the helm of the hellish episodes of Nandigram and Netai. They did not wish to witness any further the gesticulations of Biman Basu or Goutam Dev. Such was the attitude prevalent among the common masses. That is why despite thousand macabre manipulations there appeared fissures on the red bastions of CPI(M) at Buddhadev Bhattacharya's Jadavpur, Goutam Dev's Dum Dum, Ashoke Bhattacharya's Siliguri, Asim Dasgupta's Khardaha, Nirupam Sen's Burdwan (south). Actually these infamous CPI(M) leaders became the eyesores of the ordinary citizens of West Bengal.

In the election of change the citizens have given their verdict against the evil practice of bossing against forcible collection of money, against the dominance of promoters, against the ruthless killing of the local residents in Jangalmahal, against the breakdown of law and discipline, against the joblessness of government offices, against the hospitals where medical services were unavailable, against restlessness and to cap it all, against a rotten and monotonous administrative system of 34 years. There was the universal expectation that only Mamata Banerjee is capable of appearing in the role of the saviour of the region from the misrule of CPI(M). It is the Trinamool Congress (TMC) which alone is an effective alternative to CPI(M) which for a long period appeared to have no viable alternative. That is why a change in the political scenario was urgently called for.

The much-yearned-for change actually arrived at last. But at the same time the Tsunami of change also appeared inside the new ruling party TMC as well and consequently the entire backbone of the party underwent a change. Those who were the earlier activists of TMC remained even now but they did not receive the taste of power. They are only bearing the happy memory of being the associates of Mamata Banerjee for a long period. They did not receive any official advantage. They are the majority in number. All these TMC activists really loved the party. Despite mental and physical persecution at the hands of CPI(M), they never thought of deserting the company of Mamata Banerjee. But after the party came to power in the region within these few months, most of them have lost their earlier authority. Inside the party they are the green TMC. On the other hand following the familiar rule of alteration of the government, the ruling party has now come to be dominated by the new entrants.

From the cabinet to administration in every branch of the party the new entrants have gained in influence and publicity. Most of them enjoyed the blessings of power during the CPI(M) regime to the fullest extent. Most of them have joined the TMC after the Lok Sabha election in 2009. The farsightedness of many such leaders or semi-leaders is admirable. About three years ago, they could very well preconceive that the days were altering. It will no longer pay to remain in CPI(M), rather it would be much more profitable to join TMC. In many cases lots of expenditure were incurred by many of them in the pursuit of winning the favours of many present leaders and ministers. Needless to say, by virtue of their own competence they have now been placed in suitable positions in the ruling party. Men who were earlier subordinate officers of CPI(M) have now become MLAs or ministers. Again a small trader who was a mastan in the favour of the earlier chief minister is now seen to accompany the present chief minister in her rural visits. The people of this category have been registered as

Red TMC inside the party. After the political change which came about in 2011 there is now a conflict between these two factions; Green TMC and Red TMC. To explain it further the conflict is between the old agencies and the presently discredited members of TMC and the new entrants and opportunists in TMC. The more their infighting inside the party will intensify the TMC after gaining the experience of winning numerous battles against CPI(M) will be faced with prospects of decline and downfall.

A few examples will clarify the issue of infighting *between* green TMC and red TMC to a greater extent.

Let us turn our attention to the Coochbehar district. In this district of North Bengal the fight between these two factions has assumed an acute shape. The leadership of the red TMC is in the hands of Hiten Barman who has become a minister in TMC after leaving *his* earlier party Forward Block. And the leadership of green TMC is in the hands of the old Trinamool leader Rabindranath Ghosh. Hitendra Babu has become the Forest Minister. He is entrusted with supervising everything from smuggled timber to seesaw mills. The opportunity of both enjoying and demonstrating power is plenty in this department. On the other hand Rabindranath Babu has received the charge of somehow operating the North Bengal Transport with subsidies. His days are busy with the task of making appeal for finance to the Transport Minister. At this opportunity the leaders who came recently from Forward block to TMC has taken over the charge of running the party in the district. At the present moment there is going on a skirmish between green TMC and Red TMC in different *blocks* of the Coochbehar district.

Let us now turn to Nanur. Rana Sinha, who was the terror of Nanur and the confidential assistant of five Forward Block Ministers is now in TMC. After the change in government, the district Chairman of TMC, Anubrata Mondal has given him the charge of running the party in the district. Witnessing this, those who have been fighting for long in Nanur are dismayed like anything. They are thinking that this is indeed a strange phenomenon. All their lives they have been fighting a bitter struggle against those who have now become their leaders after the transfer of power. This is a fact with which they cannot agree.

A direct confrontation has already started between the MLA of Nanur Gadadhar Hazra and the district chairman Anubrata Mandal (Keshta). It is learnt that in Birbhum everybody belonging to green TMC is now a supporter of the MLA of Nanur. However the leaders of the red TMC are also not ready to admit defeat. Because most of the important areas of the party have already been brought under their manipulation and domain. As a consequence of the conflict between red TMC and green TMC a half-leader has been sent to jail in Bardhaman's Mangalkote on charges of forcible multing of money. It is alleged that the police and administration are at the beck and call of the red TMC leaders. Consequently green TMC has now been confronted with acute danger. In case of the slightest disorder the green TMC leaders are being imprisoned. Thus, the situation is much like the condition prevailing during the earlier regime.

But there are also many opposite events. In North 24 Parganas right before the eyes of the national minister Mukul Roy the green TMC leader and activists have hit with a broomstick the local M.P, Nurul Islam. Mr. Islam is a votary of the red TMC.

His offence was that he took the strategy of taking into the party an illreputed person called Babu Master. The thrashing that was given to him of course made him alter his mind.

Again in Rajarhat-New Town the scenario are like this. The stalwarts of red TMC are building up different syndicates in the name of MA-MATI-MANUSH and indulging in forcible collection of money from different peoples in an unrestrained manner. Only yesterday these people were in the shelter of CPI(M). In Mandirbazar of South 24 Parganas the situation is far more critical. A few leaders and supporters of CPI(M) after committing murder have taken shelter in TMC in order to get protection from the clutches of law. The family of the murdered person (belonging to green TMC) is moving from post to pillar, but everywhere the red TMC people are so strong that the murderers who have recently altered their political career are safely moving about in the public for the 'offence' of being vocal against the misdeeds of the red TMC people. The green TMC leader Tapan Datta of Bally has been assassinated.

At Singur a red TMC legislator is up and doing in the matter of removing a green TMC minister. At Nandigram in order to protest against the whimsical activities of a red TMC leader the workers and officers of the East Medinipur Zilla parishad undertook a ceasework. The red TMC has spread its influence not only over the party but also over the branch organisations of TMC.

For example in the TMC organization of the doctors in Barasat there is one guilty ENT specialist who was only the other day a leader of the doctors' organisation of CPI(M). The woman leader of the Trinamool Trade Union is a red TMC. As a matter of fact from the Trinamool trade union the green TMCs have all been driven away by the red TMCs. Consequently wherever there is a labour union the mudsling between the green TMC and the red TMC is assuming an ugly shape.

Not only inside the party but also inside the government as well the division between the green TMC and red TMC is very much conspicous now. In the matter of running the government also the clout of red TMC is comparatively greater. Mamata has kept her old compatriots with befitting honour in the regional cabinet but she has failed to do adequate winnowing in reshuffling her bureaucracy. Involuntarily there has occurred a division between the Bengalees and the non-Bengalees among the IPS Officers.

It is true that during the left front regime CPI(M) did not attach much importance to the Bengalee IPS officers. But going to give importance to the Bengalees how could a gram panchayat Pradhan, Bardhaman of CPI(M) Madan Ghosh became the superintendent of Police in a district like Howrah. How does a person like Tanmoy Roy Choudhury even now manage to remain the Superintendent of Police in the Hooghly district with the notorious record of firing on innocent villagers in Nandigram. If only the jersey is changed, a heinous offence cannot certainly be washed away. If the new Chief Minister makes a little inquiry she will come to have the impression that those who are enjoying the support of the red TMC activists are giving indulgence to such guilty officers in the administration.

The Chief Minister Mamata Banerjee is of course aware of the unseemly contest between the green TMC and the red TMC inside the party. Greater knowledge about this matter can be expected from the two leaders Mukul Roy and Subrata Baxi. Because these two gentlemen even now regularly sit in the Trinamool Bhavan and give a patient hearing to the grievances of the party leaders. Perhaps in view of this terrible tendency Mamata has hastily called election in the party. The purpose is to bring the really capable persons in running the party to the forefront. At this critical moment the TMC leadership will have to remember that if the party somehow goes into the grip of the red TMC, the circumstances will go out of control.

Because about the red TMC people, CPI(M)'s opinion is that they were merely floodwater which earlier brought about a rot in their earlier organisation. It is a great relief that they have shifted their allegiance to TMC. These red TMC people who were the back bone of CPI(M) are now the epicentre of power inside the TMC. In case an earthquake breaks out the entire party will break down. Because the other contestant the green TMC, although they are more numerous, have not yet tasted power. Most of them belong to the grassroot level of TMC. Of course the leaders of the ruling party are certainly aware of all these matters. The matter to watch is whether they can take any remedial measures in the organisational election. Those ordinary citizens who have elected the party to victory want to see that at the forefront should remain leaders who are cultured, considerate, transparent, honest and capable to win the admiration of the common masses.

46

PRICE-RISE AND ALL THAT

The price-rise of food articles has exceeded 10% in the week which ended on October 8. The price-rise of food articles in the country has increased to the extent of 10.60%. Consequently the prices of food articles like spices, fruits, vegetables, milk, fish, meat, eggs etc. have increased by leaps and bounds. This information has been revealed by the national government.

At the same time from the statistics submitted by the national government in the week ended on the last August 20, the rise in prices of food articles exceeded the limit of 10% in a similar manner. From the statistics submitted by the national government it is known that in the annual account on the week ended on 8th October, the prices have increased most in the case of spices and vegetables. The amount of this price-rise is 17.59%. In one year vegetable prices have increased 18%. The prices of eggs, fish and meat have increased 14.10%. The prices of fruits have increased by 12.39 per cent. The price of milk has risen by 10.60%. The prices of pulses have risen by 7.42%. In this annual account it is seen that in the week ended on 8th October, it is seen that the price of rice has increased by 4.42%.

The crisis does not end here. It has been known that in response to this inflationary price-rise Reserve Bank may very soon raise the Repo rate of interest. Consequently it was apprehended that the real or reverse repo rates of interest of the commercial banks in the cases of cars and houses and personal credits may be hiked further.

In order to combat inflationary price-rise from the month of March 2010 uptil now, the RBI has increased its money rate or repo rate of interest at least twelve times. If the RBI once again raises this rate of interest, those middle class service holders who took loan from commercial banks for purchasing houses and cars will be in jeopardy. Taking all things together, it may be presumed that the circumstances are gradually becoming straitened,

When there was a crash in the American economy and consequently there was a worldwide great depression, many people opined that in the case of India owing to the farsightedness of Manmohan Singh that recession has been resisted at least to some extent. This assertion has some partial validity. The blast of worldwide recession hit India to some extent, but the Indian economy was not affected in the same manner as the economies of the western nations like the U.S.A. After resisting that blast of depression, India has now been affected by the current inflation. And whatever the public opinion about it, it is a fact that during the last one year all the efforts of the UPA government in resisting inflation and price-rise have been virtually frustrated. During the last year the present government could not at all bring inflation under control.

In the case of India one of the causes of this infltionary price-rise is the parallel economy of black money. The RBI has repeatedly emphasised the recovery of this hidden volume of black money in the nation in combating inflation. UPA government also repeatedly issued the threatening of recovering the black money hidden in the national economy. Reference has also been made occasionally to the need for recovering the total volume of black money of the Indians accumulated in foreign countries.

But apart from enlivening the media and keeping it warm the national government failed to show any remarkable initiative in recovering the black money. The impact of the worldwide depression could not certainly be avoided by India and it will be definitely felt in this country sooner or later.

But if at the sametime the national government could take at least some active steps in recovering black money, if it could actually succeed in breaking down the parallel economy of black money price-rise could not be skyrocketing. Middle classes and lower classes could not have fallen in such great crises. But no initiatives of the national government in the matter of breaking *down* the black *economy* were noticed so far.

During the last one year the UPA government has failed in many instances. Among them the failures of the UPA government in existing inflation and price-rise are most glaring. No such possibility is visible in the near future that the national government could succeed in adopting any immediately effective step. Although the national Finance Minister Pranab Mukherjee expressed the hope that near about the month of March 2012 inflation may come down to the level of 7%.

Even if this expectation continues to be true the citizens of the nation will have to carry out the burden of inflation for the coming four months. Already Congress is bewildered by the critical problem of inflationary price-rise. The other partners of UPA like TMC and DMK are unwilling to share this responsibility with the major partner.

Another partner of UPA is NCP whose leader is the national Agriculture Minister Sharad Pawar who has declared in no uncertain terms that this is not one of his responsibilities. It is clear that he has blamed the Congress for the entire matter.

In case the UPA government under the leadership of Congress Party fails to imprison the evil spirit of inflationary price-rise in the bottle at an early period, no one can foretell with certainty their probable future in the coming election. No one can indicate with emphasis that in the ultimate analysis the current inflation will not turn out to be the principal reason of crackdown of UPA in the next election.

47

RESERVE BANK'S ADVICE TO REGIONAL GOVERNMENT

In the context of the current financial crisis of West Bengal the Governor of Reserve Bank, D. Subba Rao has recently given it some advices. A few days ago he has commented in Kolkata that there is only one way to come out of the crisis through which the region is currently passing, that is, the government will have to increase its own earnings and cut down its expenditures. About reducing its expenditure two matters should be taken into account. Essential expenditures should of course be incurred but at the same time alertness must be maintained so that inessential expenditures are brought down. Although the Governor of the Reserve Bank did not utter it explicitly the message that it has given to the regional government is that the government cannot be run by depending only on loans and grants. If the government is to be managed in a really efficient manner the illusions of cheap popularity should be dispelled and the positive thoughts of increasing the fiscal revenues should be concentrated upon. There is of course the possibility that this sort of advice from the RBI may not please many higher-ups of the regional government. But those who have strong sense of realism will admit that the Governor of RBI has actually prescribed a correct remedy. Previously the national Finance Minister Pranab Mukherjee also gave the same advice to the regional government.

The majority of the politicians in our country cannot succeed in winning freedom from the illusion of cheap popularity. They always suffer from the apprehension that in case firm steps are adopted with a view to ensuring economic reform, popularity in electoral politics will perhaps be at stake. From this apprehension derives the politics of making things available. This politics thereafter becomes a burden on the shoulders of the government as an inevitable consequence of which the government bows down. The greatest instance in this matter is West Bengal. During the last 34 years in pursuance of the politics of cheap popularity the left front government has drained off the public treasury of the region. They have bowed out from the political pulpit after imposing a huge burden of public debt on the shoulders of the regional government.

No doubt a new government has come to power. But they are puzzled to understand how this huge burden of public debt of the previous government will be squarely dealt with. The authorities of the new government are simply bewildered to find out the way of redemption of this huge public debt and carry on the developments activities of the government.

Without trying to find out means for increasing the fiscal finance the previous government was unwisely offered with the illusory pursuits of cheap popularity and left the public treasury into shambles from which the authorities of the new government could uptil now find no way out.

Nobody expects that from this miserable economic crisis the region can be recovered overnight. In actual reality, this matter is a time-consuming process. But in order to come out from this imbroglio the government will have to take initiatives from right now. It should take careful lessons from the ways suggested by the Governor of the RBI and reduce the inessential expenditures with increasing the fiscal revenues. The government will have to practise abstinence and carefully think out the ways in which revenues must be increased.

It is a matter for regret that the new government is also failing to win freedom from the illusion of cheap expensive popularity among the masses. Consequently just as there are blemishes in the list of priorities of the government, there is also a hike in the official expenditure in the unproductive account. The proof of this proposition has been obtained in the recent hike of the allowances of the ministers and legislators and the official decision to give 10% dearness allowance to the government employees. It was the Chief Minister Mamata Banerjee who herself commented previously that within Rs. 1.00,96 paise are spent for repaying the debts and giving salaries to the government employees. Nonetheless it was she again who herself increased the expenditure on this account at this period of acute financial crisis. As a result of this declaration additional 3 thousand crores of rupees will be annually spent from the public treasury and not unlike the previous government, the new government will also feel called upon to raise finance from the market by issuing bonds. Just as in the past, the left front government advanced in the path of paying salaries by borrowing finance from the market the new government is also actually following the same precedent.

If the government is really determined to enhance the fiscal finance, it is necessary to impose taxes in certain spheres. But the Chief Minister of the region and TMC leader Mamata Banerjee is not in this case willing to move away from the path of popularity although new government has not yet found any alternative avenue for enhancing incomes.

The Governor of RBI has commented that it is easy to talk about enhancing income by cutting down inessential expenditures. But this is actually a hard nut to crack. And if West Bengal is determined to come out of this shell of financial crisis, it is urgently necessary to perform that difficult task. This is really a monstrous challenge before the Chief Minister of the new government.

48

PLIGHT OF RURAL HOSPITALS

An extensive crisis of oxygen has appeared in the government hospitals of the rural areas of Hooghli and South 24 Parganas. In different blocks like Hooghli's Khanakool Haripal and Dhaniakhali, the rural hospitals of the highest lands have either 2 or 1 oxygen cylinders in their hands. From the official statistics it is known that in the rural hospitals of the block levels in Hooghly and South 24 Parganas the stocks of oxygen cylinders are like this: Khanakool 2, Dhaniakhali-2; in Raidighi only 4 among the 34 cylinders are full, in Sagar almost all the 19 cylinders are empty; in Mandir Bazar there are only 2 cylinders. But in the Khanakool rural hospital of Hooghli there is the responsibility of the treatment of 2 lakhs 43 thousands of people of that Block, in the Dhaniakhali rural hospital rests the responsibility of treatment of 3.5 lakh people. In the Purshura Block Primary Health Centre rests the charge of treatment of 1 lakh 73 thousand local residents. The physicians there are compelled to bring oxygen cylinders from outside.

Under the circumstances the two block medical officers raised an important question. They have made the comment that in the winter numerous patients will require oxygen. But we are not getting oxygen. If therefore there is any scandal in the hospital for not providing oxygen, will the responsibility for that devolve on us? These doctors have spoken out absolute truth. If due to the want of necessary medical treatment, the local residents raise protest in those hospitals, who will bear the responsibility? The local residents or the physicians of the hospital or the regional Health Department ?

It has been known that this crisis of oxygen started even before the Pujas. Presently it has assumed a more acute shape. In other words in these district hospitals despite the fact that oxygen cylinders were unavailable in these hospitals from before the Pujas the Health authorities remained inactive. It is clear now that so long they remained silent and took no necessary steps. The Special Secretary of the Health Department Sanjoy Mitra has observed : 'I have heard the matter. The direction to adopt the necessary measures has been issued.' Needless to say that he has talked in the familiar method of the bureaucrats. Oxygen cylinders are unavailable in the rural hospitals. But the Special Secretary of the Health Department is completely silent about the reason why attempts to solve the crisis were not made, or when the necessary measures will be adopted? This attitude of the Health authorities give the impression that the rural hospitals and health centres have only secondary importance. It is not necessary to pay much attention towards this direction.

There can be no hesitation in commenting that the rural hospitals and health centres have all along received the neglect and disaffection of the health authorities. After the new government came to power, the Chief Minister Mamata Banerjee has made many sudden visits to the government hospitals of Kolkata. Consequently the standard of services in those hospitals has improved to some extent. But the rural hospitals and health centres escaped the notices of everybody. They are staying in the same darkness in which they had been remaining earlier.

Even now rural hospitals mean places without adequate infrastructures where cattle move about without any restriction and where visits for adequate medical treatment are almost always infructuous since there is lack of adequate infrastructures. Many doctors are unwilling to be posted in rural hospitals and health centres. The left front government did not take initiatives to improve their state of management notwithstanding their continuance in power for 34 years. Yet if adequate infrastructure could be provided their standards of services could have been much improved and the extra pressure on the urban hospitals could have been much relieved.

It is principally the indigent families of lower class who come for medical treatment to these rural hospitals. They do not have the finance to come for medical treatment to the cities. But they have also the inconvertible right to get government health services. Keeping this fact in mind the government health authorities will have to take adequate initiatives for improving the standards of the rural hospitals. Otherwise the state of the health circumstances in the total perspective will remain unaltered.

49

JANPATH -VERSUS-KALIGHAT

7 Race Course Road, 8th November, 2011, 5:35 P.M., Prime Minister Manmohan Singh was speaking, 'I won't be able to bring down petrol prices. Do not ask me to do what is not possible. I respect Mamataji. I request all of you to desist from the decision to go out from the national government. We understand that amid inflation if the price of petrol goes up there is a severe pressure on the ordinary citizens. But in the international market as a result of the causing impacts of price-rise and devaluation of rupee, oil prices are causing heavy losses. That is why if the price of petrol is not hiked, the domestic economy will be faced with further crisis. There should be a limit to subsidisation. We can very well witness in different countries of the world what happens when that limit is crossed. We can ill afford to drive our own nation to that kind of jeopardy.

At this point Manmohan Singh became silent for some time. Possibly he was waiting for the reaction of the 24 TMC MPs sitting in front. In this occasion, Sudip Banerjee, Sougata Roy and Kalyan Banerjee etc. made an attempt to impress upon the Prime Minister that price of petrol has increased 11 times in 12 months. Just as if in the international market price of a commodity goes up the government also hikes its domestic price, similarly the government should also bring down its domestic price if international price is lowered. But that is not happening. The Prime Minister was ready. He corrected the mistake by saying, the government does not raise or lower the price, it is the oil-producing organisations who take the relevant decision. Right now there is no official control over the price of petrol.

The MPs raised the question: Will then the price of petrol not go up any further? After remaining quiet for some time, Manmohan Singh replied : I cannot give any such guarantee. If the barrel-wise price goes up in the international market, the domestic price of petrol will of course be hiked.

The TMC MPs asked the Prime Minister : But where will this process be concluded? A meeting has already been called on 26 November over the hike in the prices of cooking gas, diesel and kerosene. Apprehension will be expressed there about further hikes in prices.

The Trinamool MPs expressed anxiety and opined that in this way pressure is being continuously mounted on the ordinary citizens. The Prime Minister disregarded this anxious question and looked straight at the face of the Railways Minister Dinesh Trivedi and commented in a cold voice. 'You are a member of the Cabinet. It has not been proper on your part to disclose in this way the secret message of the cabinet.' In great uneasiness Dinesh Tribedi shook his head and tried to protest that he did not disclose any official secret. But before he could speak anything Kalyan Banerjee intervened and said: He did not tell anything. It is actually the Petroleum Minister, Jaipal Reddy who gave this information to the media. In fact we have come to know this information from the newspaper titled Economic Times. This time the Prime Minister on his part fell in great uneasiness and murmured, God alone knows what is the rule truth. At least I did not have any such information in advance!

The Prime Minister remained silent for sometime and then commented : Much capital has to be invested in the social sector. Different social projects are going on. I am asking you to comment yourself how this can be possible if fiscal finances are not increased. No, no. There cannot be any argument about lowering the price of petrol. Trinamool MPs raised the question : Then you should suggest some other way of bringing down the price of petrol. Manmohan singh shook his head and replied : It is better if you yourselves could advise the regional government to cut somewhat the fixed expenditure. This will definitely result in much benefits!

Sudip Banerjee et al argued that we are the second largest partner in the UPA-2 alliance. But none of its decisions is available to us. This is not good for the politics of alliance. The Prime Minister seemed to concur somewhat with this grievance and said : Yes, in future days we should of course pay attention to adequate discussion with all the partners. But it appears to me that the coordination committee about which you are so anxious is unnecessary. Everybody remains present in the Cabinet meetings. That is why.....".

It is obvious that the UPA-2 government has suddenly taken a strict position regarding its principal partner. The TMC MPs have also admitted that so much stiff attitude was never before noticed in the case of Manmohan Singh. They were all really perplexed. Very naturally Mamata Banerjee after hearing this information from Mukul Roy was highly enraged. Because just when the Prime Minister was taking this stiff attitude to the TMC MPs in New Delhi at that time in Kolkata the national Finance Minister Pranab Mukherjee and Mamata Banerjee met in a conference. And in that conference also Mukherjee did not give any hopeful information to Mamata Banerjee. Far from giving any assurance of providing finance according to need Mukherjee gave her the unpalatable advice to procure their own finance by their own efforts. He has opined in unmistakable terms that there has occurred no reason for providing a greater quantum of finance to West Bengal in comparison to other regions precisely because in the perspective of the federal structure this happening is impossible.

The question that is uppermost in the minds of everybody is what might be the possible reason for the indifence of the UPA government about its principal partner. A lot of theories have emerged at the time of analysing this strange attitude.

Congress has already been marginalised by instances of corruption and scandals and consequently it is not desirous to drag the present government till 2014. It is planned that the election should be held much earlier. That is why if TMC withdraws its support and consequently the national government collapses, Congress just does not care. Rather amidst a thousand infamies the status of a martyr party will provide some additional advantage.

The protagonists of this theory believe that the level of mercury in the barometer of ambition regarding Rahul Gandhi inside the national government and the Congress Party has come down to a great extent. In other words the confidence with which it was presumed that he will come and conquer in the arena of politics was actually not noticed. Even now so far as political wisdom and clout are concerned, Rahul Gandhi is still now remaining in the average scoring ground. The probability that in the scheduled election of 2014 the popularity of Congress Party i.e. the UPA government will suddenly be skyrocketing is still now not noticeable. Rather there are indications that in the coming days more scandals will come to light.

Indications are also available that many other big shots are involved in the 2G Spectrum incident of corruption. That is why if the UPA government does break down and thereafter the Congress Alliance fails to come to power then for a pretty long time Rahul Gandhi will receive the advantages of becoming the opponent party leader. It is much more acceptable to gain popularity by becoming leader of the opposition party than to become a flop by making efforts to come to power as the leader of the government. Because no matter which government comes to power, this inflationary trend and the price-rise of petrol will not be easily resisted. Thousand other issues will accompany this incident. In this way by staying out of government for a few years the government will accumulate strength and power. It is certain that during that period there will be some 'Khichri' government in the centre. That government will of course not be able to continue for five years. Therefore after its fall Congress will return to power in its own glory. That strong government will be piloted in a capable manner by Rahul Gandhi himself.

Another view point is that all this is nothing. It is presumed that even if TMC withdraws its support the national government will not collapse. Mulayam Singh Yadav, Mayabati and even the leftists will of their own accord come forward to save it from breaking down. Because if an election in case of a possible breakdown of the national government is held none of the presently existing parties has the necessary strength to face that election. None of them is actually certain about its real strength. There are also misgivings about the fact whether even the foremost opponent party BJP at all wants interim election, because a regionwise analysis will reveal that just as Congress will perform miserably in many regions and fail to reach the figure 207. Similarly notwithstanding good performance in some regions BJP will face disaster in many other regions. Among the *second group* Karnataka is one. Apart from that BJP also lacks adequate partners for its alliance. Only the Sanjukta Janata Dal of Nitish Kumar is capable of winning 20 to 30 seats. It can be foretold right now that in the next election Shiromoni Akali Dal will cut a sorry figure and even if the number of MPS of Shiv Sena remains more or less the same, what will be its impact on the total situation. On the other hand if the NDA attempts to form the government at the centre by way of increasing the strength of its alliance, *will* that attempt be appreciated by the leftists or Mulayam Singh Yadav or Mayabati? Therefore notwithstanding the existence of a thousand *crises* Congress has presupposed that the government at the national level is not *going* to fall. That is why the programme has been taken to poohpooh for the time being the harangues of TMC.

The question that may be raised now is regional, Congress has made alliance with TMC at both the national and levels. Can *anybody* in that party from the topmost leadership to the grassroot level - workers sincerely desire that the West Bengal government under the leadership of Mamata Banerjee should be considered as a totally successful regional government? The Congress party which has been reduced to a signboard and the anti-left support has been monopolised by Mamata Banerjee from the headquarters at her Kalighat residence can certainly ill afford to forget that humiliation. Uptil now neither Ajoy Mukherjee nor Pranab Mukherjee nor Priyaranjan Dasmunshi could turn it into an insignificant entity after coming out of its predominant position. But Mamata has succeeded in this feat by her lone efforts. It is difficult for Congress to forget that humiliation and anger. Therefore it can be certainly foretold that the national Congress government will never take a liberal attitude to render all kinds of help to her in order to assist her government to ascend to the vertex of success. Rather the opposite attitude is likely in the Indian politics. In other words, in order to recover its own lost glory by slow or quick means Congress will have no stones unturned in causing obstacles to Mamata Banerjee's government at each and every step. There can be little doubt that the more faux pas will be taken by this government the more elated Congress will become not unlike the leftists.

And this fact is not unknown to Mamata Banerjee and she is also not unaware that this mischievous design is engineered by Sonia Gandhi herself.

It is quite likely that she has already realised that the national government in New Delhi with a view to discrediting her regional government *will* indirectly use the weapon of economic deprivation in this manner. When no additional help can be expected this sham friendship of UPA government through outward support is simply meaningless.

Therefore Mamata also has taken the decision that she should loterate this far and no farther and get prepared for witnessing the coming contest in panchayat election: CPI(M) versus TMC versus Congress. In comparison to the earlier elections it will become a much more interesting chapter in West Bengal's regional parties: 10 Janpath Road vs 30B Harish Chatterjee Street.

50

WEST BENGAL, BANGLADESH AND THE TISTA TREATY

West Bengal will cooperate with Bangladesh as much as possible regarding the distribution of water of the Tista river. In the month of November the Chief Minister Mamata Banerjee has given this assurance to the Foreign Minister of Bangladesh, Dipu Mani. In a conference with the Foreign Minister Mamata has said that in the matter of distribution of water of the Tista, West Bengal will render all kinds of assistance to Bangladesh. But which Bengal will receive how much water will he determined not at the political level but by the experts. The Chief Minister has informed that recently a Commission has been formed by keeping the river specialist Kalyan Rudra in mind. After this discussion with the Chief Minister, the two countries have come to believe that they will be enabled to proceed along a positive path about the Tista treaty.

In the month of September during the visit of Prime Minister Manmohan Singh to Bangladesh, the Tista Treaty was scheduled to be drawn up. But at the last moment Mamata Banerjee raised objection about the treaty and refused to accompany the Prime Minister in his visit to Bangladesh. Ultimately the treaty was not signed in the absence of Mamata Banerjee. The government of Bangladesh also was aggrieved at this fact of not signing this treaty. The heads of the two governments could perceive that unless Mamata Banerjee was appeased the future of that treaty was totally dark. From that period the government of Bangladesh had been trying to arrange a confidential meeting of Mamata Banerjee with the Prime Minister of Bangladesh Sheikh Hasina.

Bangladesh believes that such a meeting will to a great extent help in unfastening the gordian knot. To speak the truth, with this purpose in view the Foreign Minister of Bangladesh after attending a programme at Bengaluru rushed to Kolkata. Dipu Mani's objective was that a bridge should be built up for arranging a meeting between Sheikh Hasina and Mamata Banerjee. From that point of view this visit of the Foreign Minister of Bangladesh is quite successful. Because a few days later Prime Minister Sheikh Hasina will visit Kolkata. It is then that the Hasina-Mamata meeting will take place.

Altogether 54 rivers are flowing through India and Bangladesh among which there are the Ganga, the Tista, the Feni, the Ichhamati etc. Previously there was a long conflict between India and the erstwhile East Pakistan over the treaty regarding the distribution of water of the Ganga river. After the then Chief Minister of West Bengal entered into a treaty of distribution of water in 1996 that dispute came to be solved. But over the distribution of the Tista and the Feni, India still now has difference of opinion with Bangladesh. As the fall out of the Tista treaty, India will have to give more water to Bangladesh but it will become the gainer as the consequence of the Feni treaty. As the Tista treaty was not signed during the Dacca visit of India's Prime Minister as a protest, Bangladesh refused to sign the Feni treaty.

Consequently the future prospects of both the treaties are uncertain. It is true that around the Tista treaty not only West Bengal, Sikkim has also some objections. In case the Tista treaty is drawn up, it is alleged that there will be a crisis of irrigation water in the hilly areas including north Bengal. Similarly again Tripura will gain much in case of the Feni treaty.

Chief Minister Mamata Banerjee has asserted that the quantum of water to be received by a country will not be decided at the political level. On the contrary it will be settled by the experts. In this respect she has uttered the exactly right words. Till now no bipartite settlement has been arrived at regarding the distribution of water of the Tista. Both Bangladesh and India have respectively advanced their own view points, as a result of there being no joint survey, the controversy over the distribution of waters of the Tista continues to persist even to this day. That is why the proposal advanced by the Chief Minister is acceptable even now. But the expert committee that has to be constituted in this respect should ideally accommodate the impartial persons of both the countries.

At the same time at the time of drawing up the treaties regarding the Tista or the Feni, the Heads of the governments of both India and Bangladesh should remember the relevant lessons of history in the sub-continent between India and Bangladesh. The length of this frontier is 2 thousand 979 kilometers. Right from the time of the independence India had conflict with East Pakistan over this frontier. Even after the birth of Bangladesh that conflict has not been resolved as yet.

In 1975 the then Head of the state Sheikh Mujibar Rehman wanted to solve the border conflict by an agreement. Those who have conducted researches on the assassination of Mujib assert that Pakistan and its friend China did not want that this treaty should be materialised. That is why Mujib was assassinated with the help of the Pakistani agents. Both India and Bangladesh should remember that Pakistan and China do not want that a friendly relation should grow up between them. If the India-Bangladesh disagreement over the Tista and Feni continues there will be reason for elation of both Pakistan and China. Without allowing them the scope for elation if both Bangladesh and India sacrifice somewhat their respective interests and come to a common understanding, both of them will be benefited in the long run to a great extent.

51

PROBLEMS OF TOURISM IN NORTH BENGAL

Those who usually denounce the authorities are condemning the new Tourism Minister for the reason that uptil now he could not manage to pay a visit to North Bengal. Already many ministers of small, medium and big statures had occasions to pay visit to this area. Some of them came here more than once, some accompanied the Chief Minister, some of them came in connexion with the business of their own departments, some visited for their personal purposes or by virtue of some relations. But the Tourism Minister happens to be the only exception.

But we are all aware that both in the national and international arenas tourism in West Bengal means the hills and forests of this region. But without a separate department for north Bengal or the special thoughts of the new Chief Minister has lightened the responsibility or importance of the new minister can only be friendly the critics who are in the habit of denouncing the government. Those who are the traders of tourism can also explain whether the expansion of tourism can very well proceed without even the personal presence of the Tourism Minister. But those who have even very slight connection with this service can assert that the little development which has taken place in the sphere of tourism in north Bengal so far was never very extensive. Not only that its spread and intensity till today have been so little that they failed to serve the purpose of tourism of ordinary citizens.

Those people who are seen everyday to travel in congested buses inside the city or trains in the downtown areas under pressure of heavy crowds whenever they get the occasion rush to the side of hills, fountains or tea gardens or to the gates of the forest conservatories. Uptil now no government of either colour concerned themselves with their unshackled madness or limited financial capabilities.

Let us think of the experience of the people fifteen years earlier. When the tourism service has reached the international level in Rajasthan, Kerala or Madhya Pradesh, in West Bengal the tourist lodges meant ramshackle bedsteads, the nuisance of rats running helter skelter, windows with broken glasses and prehistoric airconditioning machines etc.

Thereafter a change was noticed in the situation. Reforms and changes in the circumstances of the tourist lodges began to appear. Popularity started increasing but at the same time service charges also went on being hiked, so much so that very soon these charges went outside the capacities of the Bengalee tourists with poor monthly incomes. How much per cent of the total number of tourists can bear the expenses of food and lodging with the entire family for two nights in Jaldapara tourist lodge today ? In the restaurant of Kurseong Tourist Lodge on the road to Darjeeling if a team of eight to ten persons enter for lunch or breakfast, their per capital expenses can never be cut below Rs. 100/. But 75% of the tourists who come to visit the hilly areas of Dooars have a daily per capital budget of not more than Rs. 750/. Hence the idea is gradually being deeprooted in the public psyche that government visits are invariably highly costly. The lodges of the Forest Development Corporation are comparatively less costly but their number also is limited. Profits from these circumstances are being made by non-governmental package tour at whose hands are victimised the low-budget tourists.

Not only the ordinary tourists but also those who derive their income from employment in tourism also should be considered in this context. Today all of us are more or less aware that the new name of tourism now is 'eco-tourism' which includes tourists, environment and the local aboriginals, and everybody's interest is preserved. But once a distinguished leader raised the question that 'It is very well understood that 'eco-tourism' means 'ecological' or 'ecofriendly' but can it at all be 'economical'? It is strange that in this question is hidden its positive answer. As a result of the initiatives of the divisional forest department of north Bengal thoughts of eco-tourism have been implemented in reality. But here also the development of the tribals of the forest has been taken into account and the ordinary tourists have been neglected. The Ghatakpur eco-camp of Sinchal Forest Conservancy or Ramsai Chino camp of Gorumara National Garden are in a word, unique but these are outside the capabilities of the lovers of tourism afflicted with wanderlust.

Very naturally, here arises the question of 'community tourism'. Ethically in this rural tourism based on communities both pleasure and profits can be derived by both the ordinary tourists as well as the ordinary local indigent people. But what has been noticed so far in the name of 'community tourism' although there are a few isolated attempts are actually a 'kind of exploitation'- the "cunning efforts" of a few urban traders under the garb of 'welfare', year after year have passed. In any of the villages of north Bengal, no remarkable socio-economic development came to the notice of anybody through the medium of community development. Because there was not the slightest effort or good will for participation or intervention or policy determination.

Under the circumstances we can raise a very easy question. The only region in India is West Bengal where the coexistence of the Himalaya sea-mangrove is not the only word, this is the only region in the country which can be self-reliant in the matter of its own tourist potential. Why then is it difficult to make tourism a populist programme here. Let the question of the mountains forests and ocean remain apart, but tourism can be made popular by an easy medium - the holy places. In the north Bengal there are very ancient Shivaratri festival of Jalpesh or Baneshwar or the Srabani Purnima fair or the Rasmela of Madanmohan Bari of Coochbehar on which occasion there take place unimaginable congregrations of people. But it is strange that the tourism Department has not yet assumed any significant role.

Similarly the flow of tourists can easily be catalysed by the schools or colleges receiving government grants, with official directions. Summer camps and nature observation can be made compulsory in the syllabus. Can there be misgivings or scepticism in anybody's mind that this will lead to the spiritual development of the future generation as well as enlargement of the total volume of tourism throughout the length and breadth of north Bengal.

Farming is not possible in the sprawling areas of the Dooars due to the disturbances caused by the elephants. Is it a very difficult task to please the low-budget tourists with arrangements for earning alternative incomes at the panchayat level by erecting cottages with bamboos, straws and tins, or building up cooperatives of the local jobless young men and women and cultivating vegetables in the gardens, fishes in the tanks, hatching the eggs of ducks or raising the poultry of the gardens?

After the new government came to power the unrest in the hills has disappeared. The wind of peace and tranquillity has started blowing throughout north Bengal. After a long time has returned an ideal climate for development of tourism. The voice of a populist development of tourism has been heard in the new decision of North Bengal Regional Transport corporation. Every morning matching time with the trains arriving from Kolkata one after another buses are starting from New Jalpaiguri station for Darjeeling, Kalimpong and Gangtok. In the evening they are returning in order that the train for Darjeeling can be caught. Similarly at Malbazar tourist transport hub is being constructed very soon. Other buses going to the Dooars and various ends of the mountain will be ready, in other words the expenses of ordinary people to visit Dooars and the mountains will be cut down. The higher is the number of buses and the more regular they become, both the aspects of reliance and economy will be ensured.

But what thereafter? In the tourism map of the world the presence of this region resembles a fossil. Bringing about its development calls for much time and patience. Before that are needed some populist activities. For example tourism will not increase if only tents are fixed at the Baxa Fort, for reading there will be needed a hanging bridge on which people will walk on feet, repair of broken roadways upto the Sadar or chief town and light and sound show at the fort compounds. Citizens aged 60 or 70 will be enabled to visit the place at least for once in their life to recount the memories of the freedom struggle and the new generation will receive the opportunity to inquire about its roots of ancestry.

And the responsibility for its preservation will be entrusted on the local residents. They will eagerly guard their noble possessions. If tents are fixed only red scorpions and indigenous dogs will abound there. Profits will only be appropriated by tent contractors and consultants, who succeeded in earning lots of finance in the early regime and after changing their colours are now moving around the ministers of the new government. Much caution will be required to get relief from the evil influences of these selfseekers.

On the contrary we must find out and get in touch with those persons who are ignoring the light of publicity in the remote corners of forests and mountains in a painstaking effort to explain to the poor and indigent local residents the matter of community tourism, the acute necessity of giving up the terrilbly harmful addiction to wines and narcotics, the need for sports and a developed way of life.

52

ANATOMY OF KOLKATA MUNICIPAL CORPORATION

In order to resist any kind of construction in the city along with hospitals the Kolkata Municipal Act of 1980 is sufficient. This has been admitted by the senior officers of the KMC themselves. They are saying that in the civic legislation it is the KMC which has been invested with full powers to resist illegal constructions. Apart from that there is the Municipal Buildings Rule. It is mandatory to abide by the Municipal Buildings Rule in the field of constructing houses in the Kolkata civic area and this rule has been erected on the basis of the National Building Code. Consequently without enacting a new rule the corporation can break down any illegal construction by virtue of the correct regulations.

Just a glance at the civic law can give one the idea regarding what sort of strict measures can be adopted by the Municipal Corporation on receipt of an allegation of illegal construction. In sections 400(1) and 400(8) of the Municipal Act, it has been clearly mentioned that if an inquiry reveals that there is an apprehension of major danger or that there is a violation of the law the Corporation can decide to adopt suitable measures. In this case it can without giving the owner of the house any opportunity for hearing, demolish the building. In case of necessity it can also issue instruction to break down only the illegal portion of a house. If this law is examined in depth, it can never be asserted that the Corporation has been given no power to resist illegal construction. Rather it should be understood that by virtue of the power which rests in the hands of the Corporation it can pull down at any time any kinds of illegal construction.

The matter to regret is that although there is so much legal power in the hands of KMC, illegal construction is not being stopped. Nor is the KMC taking adequate measures to break down illegal constructions. Moreover taking advantage of the inactivity of the KMC illegal constructions are going on in full speed.

Even in the earlier days after big fire accidents in the city the indifference and dereliction on the part of the KMC came to the notice of the citizens. Such incidents are coming to our notice ever after the fire accident of the AMRI hospital. The KMC cannot deny the responsibility for such fire accidents. Now the question that may be raised here is, why notwithstanding the existence of sufficient law in its hands KMC is not taking adequate initiatives to resist illegal construction.

The lawyers of the Kolkata Municipal Building Tribunal are saying that the indifferent attitudes of the officers of the Building Department are the principal hindrances in the matter of pulling down the illegal constructions. The files relating to many illegal buildings have been deliberately destroyed. Behind this activity is operating a vicious circle. Although files are being asked for by the Tribunal, the officers of the Building Department are dilly-dallying in this matter. Quite a few officers of CMC are also saying that there is indifference in the matter of implementing the laws.

It is quite clear that due to the tendency of indulging in dereliction on the part of a section of workers and officers of KMC initiatives are not conspicuous in the matter of checking illegal constructions. When Subrata Mukherjee was the Mayor of Kolkata, he succeeded to a great extent in restoring the work culture of KMC. The opportunist circle in the KMC was brought under control at that time.

After Subrata Mukherjee bowed out from KMC, it has returned to its earlier practice of dereliction and inactivity. At the sametime the present Mayor of CMC Shobhan Chatterjee in an attempt to cover up this failure of the CMC has advanced a ridiculous argument. He has said that in many cases illegal constructions cannot be pulled down for reasons of human interest. The question that may be raised here is why cannot illegal constructions be prevented before these are actually started.

According to the civil laws before the construction of any building the blueprint of the building has to be sent to the Municipal Building Committee. It is only when their approval is received the Building Department gives the necessary permission for construction. If despite all these safeguards illegal constructions are erected. we can safely conclude that there are blemishes at the very beginning where some dishonest circle is active.

That apart, despite the existence of much power in the hands of KMC for resisting illegal constructions, the perpetrators of such constructions are escaping from the clutching of the law due to a ludicrous directive of the civic authorities. In this directive it has been observed that these portions of the construction which fall outside the main blueprint can be made legal by paying fines to the KMC. By virtue of this instruction many people are being enthused for legalising their illegal constructions after these are actually erected. Hospitals like AMRI wanted to avail themselves of this opportunity. And the KMC gave them the necessary permission without first enquiring whether the security arrangements of that illegal portions were proper or improper.

After the fire accident of the AMRI hospital, both the Mayor and the regional government should become alert. The work culture in the KMC must be brought back and that ludicrous directive must be cancelled so that arrangements may be made to grant sanction to the blueprints of houses in consonance with the prevalent law in this respect.

POSITIONS HELD BY MAMATA BANERJEE

01.01.1970 : General-Secretary, Mahila Congress (I), West Bengal, (P.M. Indira Gandhi, President-Sarvepalli Radhakrishnan). Bengal Chief Minister 1.1.1970. Ajoy Kumar Mukherjee Bangla Congress in United Front, Governor - Shanti Swaroop Dhavan.

01.01.1978 : Secretary, District Congress Committee (Indira) [D.C.C. (I)], Calcutta South (P.M. Morarji Desai, President Basappa Danappa Jatti (Acting) Bengal Chief Minister 01.01.1978 Jyoti Basu Communist Party of India (Marxist) in Left Front, Governor - Anthony Lancelot Dias.

01.01.1984 : Elected to 8th Lok Sabha (P.M. Indira Gandhi, President - Neelam Sanjiva Reddy).

General-Secretary, All India Youth Congress (I). (P.M. Indira Gandhi, President - Neelam Sanjiva Reddy).

01.01.1985 : Member, Committee on the Welfare of Scheduled Castes And Scheduled Tribes (P.M. Rajiv Gandhi, President -Zail Singh).

01.01.1987 : Member, National Council, All India Youth Congress (I) (P.M. Rajiv Gandhi, President - Zail Singh).

01.02.1987 : Member, Consultative Committee, Ministry of Home Affairs (P.M. Rajiv Gandhi, President - Zail Singh).

01.03.1987 : Member, Consultative Committee, Ministry of Human Resource Development (P.M. Rajiv Gandhi, President -Zail Singh).

01.01.1989 : Member, Executive Committee, Congress Parliamentary Party [C.P.P. (I)] (P.M. Rajiv Gandhi, President - Zail Singh).

01.01.1990 : Member, Executive Committee, Pradesh Congress Committee [P.C.C. (I)], West Bengal (P.M. Rajiv Gandhi, President - Zail Singh).

01.01.1991 : President, Youth Congress, West Bengal (P.M. Vishwanath Pratap Singh, President - Ramaswamy Venkataraman).

01.01.1991 : Re-elected To 10th Lok Sabha (2nd Term) (P.M. Chandrashekar, President - Ramaswamy Venkataraman).

Union Minister of State, Human Resource Development, Department of Youth Affairs and Sports; and Women and Child Development (P.M. Chandrashekar, President - Ramaswamy Venkataraman).

01.01.1993: Member, Committee on Home Affairs (P.M. Pamulapartienkata Narasimha Rao, President -Ramaswamy Venkataraman).

01.01.1996 : Member, Consultative Committee, Ministry of Home Affairs (P.M. Pamulaparti Venkata Narasimha Rao, President-Ramaswamy Venkataraman).

01.01.1996 : Member, Committee on Public Accounts (P.M. Pamulaparti Venkata Narasimha Rao, President- Ramaswamy Venkataraman).

01.02.1996 : Re-elected to 11th Lok Sabha (3rd Term) (P.m. 1/2/1996 Pamulaparti Venkata Narasimha Rao, President-Ramaswamy Venkataraman).

01.03.1996 : Member, Committee on Home Affairs (P.M. Pamulaparti Venkata Narasimha Rao, President- Ramaswamy Venkataraman).

01.04.1996 : Member, Consultative Committee, Ministry of Home Affairs (P.M. Pamulaparti Venkata Narasimha Rao, President-Ramaswamy Venkataraman).

Founded All India Trinamool Congress, and elected Chairperson,

All India Trinamool Congress. (Haradanahalli Dodde Gowda Deve Gowda, President - Shankar Dayal Sharma).

1/1/1998 : Re-elected to 12th Lok Sabha (4th term) (P.M. Inder Kumar Gujral, President - Shankar Dayal Sharma).

1/2/1998 : Chairman, Committee on Railways (P.M. Inder Kumar Gujral, President - Shankar Dayal Sharma).

01.03.1998 Member, General Purposes Committee (P.M. Inder Kumar Gujral, President - Shankar Dayal Sharma).

01.04.1998 : Member, Consultative Committee, Ministry of Home Affairs (P.M. Atal Bihari Vajpayee, President - K.R. Narayanan).

1/1/1999 : Re-elected To 13th Lok Sabha (5th Term) (P.M. Atal Bihari Vajpayee, President - K.R. Narayanan).

1/2/1999 : Leader, All India Trinamool Congress Parliamentary Party Lok Sabha (P.M. Atal Bihari Vajpayee, President - K.R. Narayanan).

1/3/1999 : Member, General Purpose Committee (P.M. Atal Bihari Vajpayee, President - K.R. Narayanan) 01.04.1999

Union Cabinet Minister, Railways (P.M. Atal Bihari Vajpayee, President - K.R. Narayanan) 01.01.2002 Member, Consultative Committee, Ministry of IndustrIes (P.M. Atal Bihari Vajpayee, President - K.R. Narayanan).

01.01.2003 : Union Cabinet Minister (without any portfolio) (P.m. Atal Bihari Vajpayee, President - K.R. Narayanan).

1/9/2004 : Union Cabinet Minister, Coal and Mines (P.M. Atal Bihari Vajpayee, President - K.R. Narayanan).

5/14/2004 : Re-elected to 14th Lok Sabha (6th term) (P.M. Atal Bihari Vajpayee, President - K.R. Narayanan).

05.15.2004 : Member, Committee on Personnel, Public Grievances, Law and Justice (P.M. Atal Bihari Vajpayee, President - K.R. Narayanan).

1/1/2006 : Member, Committee on Home Affairs (P.M. Manmohan Singh, President, Abdul Kalam).

06.06.2006 : Member, Committee on Home Affairs (P.M. Manmohan Singh, President Abdul Kalam).

1/1/2009 : Re-elected to 15th Lok Sabha (7th term) (P.M. Manmohan Singh, President Abdul Kalam).

2/1 /2009 : Union Cabinet Minister, Railways (P.M. Manmohan Singh, President Abdul Kalam).

03.01.2009 : Leader, All India Trinamool Congress Parliamentary Party, Lok Sabha (P.M. Manmohan Singh, President Abdul Kalam).

20/5/2011 The First Woman Chief Minister of West Bengal after a Landslide Victory of Trinamool Congress over the Left Front (P.M. Manmohan Singh, President Pratibha Patil).

Social and Cultural Activities : Connected with different social and human rights organisations to promote the welfare of poor, children and women; providing free legal aid to the poor and working for the protection of human rights; organised various health camps for mothers and children.

Special Interest : Protecting human rights.

Favourite Pastimes : Writing books and songs; painting and music.

INDEX

SYNCRETISM IN INDIA

RELIGIOUS AND CULTURAL DIMENSIONS

SYNCRETISM IN INDIA
RELIGIOUS AND CULTURAL DIMENSIONS

Edited

G. Lazar SVD
Sarit K. Chaudhuri
K. Jose SVD

First Published, 2019

Published by

Gyan Publishing House
5, Ansari Road
Daryaganj, New Delhi-110002
Phone: 011-47034999, 9811692060
www.gyanbooks.com
E-mail: books@gyanbooks.com

Printed at: G. Print Process, Delhi.

Cataloging in Publication Data—DK
Courtesy: D.K. Agencies (P) Ltd. <docinfo@dkagencies.com>

Syncretism in India : religious and cultural dimensions / edited, G. Lazar (SVD), Sarit K. Chaudhuri, K. Jose (SVD).
pages cm
Includes bibliographical references.
ISBN 9788121214179

1. Syncretism (Religion)—India, Northeastern. 2. Syncretism (Religion)—India. 3. Tribes—India, Northeastern. 4. Tribes—India. 5. India, Northeastern—Social life and customs. 6. India—Social life and customs. 7. India, Northeastern—Religious life and customs. 8. India—Religious life and customs. I. Lazar, G. (Gyanpragasam), editor. II. Chaudhuri, S. K. (Sarit Kumar), editor. III. Jose, K., 1963- editor.

LCC HN683.5.S96 2017 | DDC 306.0954 23

Contents

List of Contributors

Agnik Bhattacharya, Post Graduate Department of History, Presidency University Kolkata, India; E-mail: agnik8393@gmail.com; Ph: (0)8017433238

Ankit Kumar Gaur is Life Member, Sanskriti-NEICR, Guwahati & Ph. D. Research Scholar, Assam Don Bosco University, Azara, Guwahati, Assam, E-mail: ankit.anthro@gmail.com

Anupma Bharadwaj, A Freelance Anthropologist, New Delhi, E-mail: anupma22c@gmail.com

Arifur Zaman, Assistant Professor, Department of Anthropology, Dibrugarh University 786004, Assam, E-mail: arifurzaman@gmail.com, Mobile: 9435145920

Aritra Ghosh, Research Scholar, Department of Sociology, University of Kalyani, Kalyani, Nadia, W.B. E-mail: ritrasocio1987@gmail.com

Avijit Sahay, Junior Research Fellow (UGC), Department of Geography, University of Allahabad, Allahabad-211002 E-mail- avijitsahay@gmail.com

D. Sun, Anthropological Survey of India, NERC, Shillong. E-mail: dei07sunn@gmail.com; Mobile: (0) 9436732425

Daili Neli, is asst. professor, New Delhi. E-mail: neli.daili@gmail.com

G. Lazar SVD, Founder Director, Sanskruti-Institute of Dravidian Culture and Research, Hyderabad, Telangana State.

Gautam Kumar Bera, Upanishadam 147/1, Jaigirghat Road Thakurpukur Kolkata 700 063

Geetika Ranjan, Associate Professor, Department of Anthropology, North Eastern Hill University, Shillong. E-mail: geetikaranjan19@gmail.com

Kuntala Dowarah, Research Scholar, Department of Sociology, Tezpur University. E-mail: kuntaladowarah@gmail.com

Naorem Naokhomba Singh, Department of Anthropology, NEHU, Shillong, Meghalaya - 793022. E-mail: naokhombanaorem@gm ail.com

Neha Singh is currently a senior research fellow in the department of Anthropology in University of Allahabad, U.P.

Onkar Prasad, Former Professor, Dept. of Anthropology, Visva-Bharati, Santiniketan-731235 E-mail: opanthropos@gmail.com

Pinky Barua, Research Scholar, Sociology Department, Tezpur University, Tezpur, Assam

R. P. Athparia, North Eastern Social Research Centre, Guwahati. E-mail: rpathparia@yahoo.co.in

Rajib Chatterjee, Research Associate, Tribal Research Institute, Kolkata.

Ranga Ranjan Das, Director [i/c], Law Research Institute, Eastern Region, Gauhati High Court, Guwahati; E-mail: ranga_das@rediffmail.com

Ravi Khangai, Assistant Professor, Department of History, RTM Nagpur University, Nagpur, E-mail: ravikhangai@gmail.com

Reshmi Chakraborty, Research Scholars, Department of Sociology, University of Kalyani, Kalyani, Nadia, W.B.

Rimi Sarkar, Research Scholar, Department of Sociology, University of Kalyani, Kalyani, Nadia, W.B.

Samita Manna, Professor, Department of Sociology, University of Kalyani, Kalyani, Nadia, West Bengal. E-Mail: samitamanna@ gmai.com

Sampa Taraphdar, Research Associate (Contractual), Cultural Research Institute, Govt. of West Bengal Add. Q-11, Panchasayar, Kolkata-700094, W.B.

Shajymon M.L., Research Scholar, Assam Don Bosco University, Guwahati, Life Member: Sanskriti, Guwahati, E-mail: shajimlcsc@gmail.com. Ph: 09774539437/09436123514

Srija Mandal, Doctoral Scholar, Department of Anthropology, University of Kolkata. E-mail: srija.nov17@gmail.com

Sumitabha Chakraborty, Anthropological Survey of India, Kolkata; E:mail: chakru4_su@yahoo.com

Sunumi Changmi, Research Scholar, North Eastern Social Research Centre, Guwahati; E-mail: sunumichangmii@gmail.com

Supratim Bhattacharya & Pushpita Purkayastha, Anthropological Survey of India North Eastern Regional Centre, Shillong E-mail: supratimanthropology@gmail.com / pushpitapurkayastha@yahoo.co.in

Surojit Sen Gupta, Assistant Professor. Department of Sociology, Maharaja Bir Bikram College, Agartala – 799004, West Tripura. E-mail: meghaboy@yahoo.com

Vijoy S. Sahay, Professor, University of Allahabad, Allahabad, U.P. Email: vijoysahay@gmail.com

1

Introduction

— G. Lazar, Sarit K. Choudhury and K. Jose

1. Understanding Indian civilization has been an arduous task on many counts. Many well meaning people or scholars have taken multi-dimensional perspectives to unearth the rich diversity of this land, but have met with partial success in spite of their passionate enquiry and long term commitment. Can this country of ours be discovered in a more holistic way? A research journey yet again undertaken through the vantage point of syncretistic religious and cultural traditions of this vast expanse of land and people is hoped to bring more optimism in this regard. We are aware that many Indian communities have a long history of migration and a mixed ancestry, and it is today impossible to separate their roots. All received the regional ethos of the area that they settled in, and contributed substantially to its local traditions. Thus, Indian culture has enormously enriched itself by adopting elements from diverse sources.

In common parlance Syncretism indicates blending on even merging of diverse religious or cultural elements or tradition or even belief systems. The logical expression of this notion leads to convergence, coexistence and even unification of cultural ethos or worldviews or traditions of diverse communities or ethnic groups.

2. The term 'syncretism' has often been perceived in multifarious ways by scholars of different disciplines in social science, including anthropology. A number of articles could be found in anthropology relating to syncretism that interprets the term as mere borrowing of cultural traits among two or more than two groups; more specifically, between Hindus and Muslims, or Hindus and Christian, or even between tribal and non-tribals etc. It may be

fitting for us to ask, why this is so happen in spite of the ever expanding knowledge base of the academic fraternity. Sometimes, such interpretations may create a sense of deviations from the root-meaning of the term which discussed above.

3. According to Das (2003:1) "Syncretism as an important constituent of multi-cultural mainstream offers an opportunity to reinforce greater cultural amalgam and multi-confessional harmony. The vast region of south Asia in general and India in particular symbolizes a remarkable confluence of cultural strands and cross-fertilization of religious ideas and ethnic/linguistic intermingling. The sociologists and socio anthropologists have thrown much light on the variety of religious forms through their studies of belief systems, rituals, symbols and meanings all over the world but they have not paid adequate attention to the phenomenon of syncretism, which represents a blend of multiple religious beliefs, in variegated degrees. The concept of syncretism uncovers a remarkable dimension in the exploration of cultural reciprocation. It is unfortunate that this important dimension of contemporary culture has been dismissed as passing and trivial". According to Lindstrom (2003: 539-540), "Syncretism refers to the hybridization or amalgamation of two or more cultural traditions. It makes best sense in the context of *functionalist theories of integrated social systems, or doctrines of cultural holism, that presuppose unified and bounded social or cultural units that, under certain conditions, can be conceived as merging to produce some novel syncretic formation… New terminology to describe the cultural admixtures occasioned by expanding global economic, communicative and political systems, however, is replacing an earlier language of syncretism".

4. Under this backdrop Sanskriti- an institute engaged in anthropological research and documentation, thinking and pulse of the national scene hope to contribute substantially by involving ourselves in this two day national seminar on Syncretism in India: Cultural and religious dimensions from 21st to 22nd November, 2015 at our Institute in Guwahati. We are contemplating to organize a National Seminar on 'Syncretism' in order to provide a platform to the social scientists at large comprising anthropologists, sociologists, linguists, activists, tribal leaders, social workers and others to ventilate their cognition and empirical observation on various issues to build up a critical discourse on the notion of Syncretism in the context of our nation state.

The editors of this comprehensive volume are pleased to be part of the team who were invited to put together the proceedings of the 9th annual seminar titled Syncretism in India: Cultural and Religious Dimensions. It has been a learning process for us as we sat to fine tune the proceedings of the seminar. As we place this volume in your hands we hope that you will have a wonderful time reading through the myriad perspectives contributed by a large array of scholars.

Vijoy S Sahay in his B. N. Saraswati Memorial Lecture titled **Syncretism in India: A Reality or a Utopia?** makes it clear that the term 'syncretism' has often been misinterpreted by scholars of different disciplines in social science, including anthropology. A number of articles could be found in anthropology relating to syncretism that interprets the term as mere borrowing of cultural traits among two or more than two groups; more specifically, between Hindus and Muslims, or Hindus and Christian, or even between tribals and non-tribals, or tribals and Christianity. Such interpretations are gross deviations from the root-meaning of the term. The essential components of syncretism are; first, that it emerges only when two incompatible groups unite together as a front to face a common crisis or a common foe, and secondly, that it is a temporary phenomena. The paper deals with a number of examples of mistakenly suggested syncretistic phenomena put forward by anthropologists, and concludes with this remark that syncretism hardly exists in the daily life and culture of India. It is a myth, a utopia.

Rajib Chatterjee's paper **Syncretism among the Muslims of Darjeeling Himalaya** argues that Islam has a distinct presence in the Himalayas particularly in the Himalayan region of Darjeeling hills and the blending of diverse religious systems is an example of syncretism here. People of the region would not think it unusual to offer worship to the coreligionists. Since historical periods Muslims actively interact with other segments of the greater hill society rather than presenting themselves as a minority. Their existence is noticed at various levels in the society though their numerical strength is low. Their peculiarities in cultural tradition never make a barrier in relationship and thus remain an integral part of the greater society, which has become a cultural mosaic. The present paper deals with the multidimensional processes of the Muslims adaptation and integration in their habitat. It also explains some of their determinants like socio-economic adaptation, social integration and their participation in inter-ethnic associations.

Ravi Khangai observes in his paper titled **Hindu Symbolism In Rahim's Poetry** that the coming of Islam in India in medieval period brought phenomenal changes in the Indian society. With the initial fury of the victorious invaders mellowed down, a background was prepared for interaction at different levels. Architecture, food and dress habits underwent changes and religious life also did not remain untouched. Many Hindus became disciples of the Sufis without converting to Islam and there are number of Muslims who were also influenced by the ongoing wave of the Bhakti movement. One such person was Rahim. (A.D.1556-1626). Though Muslim, he used many Hindu symbolism like allegory of Radha and Krishna, and the pinning of the individual soul for the divine soul. Orthodox interpretation of the Koran, do not accept anybody other than Allha as God. But Rahim's praise of Hindu gods like Krishna, Rama and Shiva proves that during his time, there was an atmosphere of tolerance, which provided space for Rahim to give free expression to his mystic experience. From his poetry it is obvious that he had good understanding of the Hindu mythology. He refers to the stories from the *Puranas*. His thoughts are also influenced by traditional *Advita* philosophy as he says that we are not sure in which form we may meet God. Proposed paper is an attempt to understand the influence of Bhakti movement on Rahim's poetry.

Naorem Naokhomba Singh in his paper **Religious Syncretism among the Meiteis of Manipur** argues that in this present era of interculturalism and transculturation syncretism is a significant prevailing event. Religious syncretism is one of the most interesting events in a country like India where various different ethnic groups with their own culture, tradition, religion, language and different origin live together as a nation of 'unity with diversity'. The present study deals with religious syncretism among the Meitei peoples of Manipur. The state lies at the most eastern side of the Indian union and it can be seen as the meeting point between the east and west, i.e. south-east Asia and south Asia in terms of culture. This population is more close to Southeast Asia in terms of somatic characters. In the early period of 18th century this state witnessed the influence of Hinduism. Thenceforth the state has been a melting pot of cultural traits of Hinduism and traditional religion. This syncretism of Hinduism and traditional religion gave rise to a new and unique form of culture among these people. Anthropological field work has been conducted to collect primary data for this study using interviews (structured and non-structured), observation, case study methods, etc. From this study it was ascertained that religious syncretism of traditional primordial religion and Hinduism among these people gave rise to a new and unique essence to their culture. In fact, it gives a unique and aesthetic feature to the culture of Meitei people which is different from the rest of the Hindu population of other regions. The syncretism of the Meitei indigenous religion with its gods and goddesses, its myths and rituals, its legends and traditions, its beliefs and practices, its rites and ceremonies, the brahmanical faith and Vaishnava Hinduism constitute the essence of present day Hinduism in Manipur. Present day Hinduism of this population exhibits aesthetic cultural products of religious syncretism.

Onkar Prasad in his paper **Musical Syncretism: The Indian Context** discuss on the Indian *raga* (modal) music stands for a particular type of musical presentation following the strict rules governed by the four basic concepts of *vadi* (dominant), *samvadi* (sub-dominant), *anuvadi* (assonant) and *vivadi* (dissonant) notes. Despite some melodic modes of foreign origin have been introduced to the North Indian classical music, this complex form of music is considered to have been developed from the simple primitive musical base but is differentiated from the latter or any other form in its exclusive measured mode of presentation. In fact, any alien melodic motif when moulded and presented in the North Indian classical musical format loses its individuality totally. However, the recent experiment with the Santal music gives an altogether a different picture which is the main objective of presenting this paper.

Neha Singh in her paper **Anthropo-Historic Discussion on Syncretism in Language and Dressing Pattern among People of Central India** affirms that Indian society is full of diversity. Different groups of people live together in unity and harmony without any conflict. The ethnic diversity of the people of India is revealed through their multiple colours, languages, faces, religions, customs, festivals, dresses and food habits. They also project the cultural diversity of the people. The cultural diversity could be seen in the past, starting from the arrival of Aryan invaders. In the course of time The Portuguese, Dutch, Parsi, Arabs, English and many more had come and brought changes through market exchange, export and import of goods in this country. It was an interaction with conflict and co-operation. There was a synthesis of different cultures and religious streams. We know that culture is not frozen but is constantly changing time and again and gets modified according to the need of people. The Indian civilizational dimension of cultural pluralism and syncretism encompasses ethnic diversity, linguistic heterogeneity and fusion, as well as synthesis in customs, behavioral patterns, rituals and beliefs. This paper is, primarily an attempt to bring to light the concept of syncretism in language and dressing pattern.

Ankit Kumar Gaur in his paper **Assam: A Socio-Religious Syncretistic Entity Of North East India** observes that the Socio-religious syncretism stands for the merging or union of different socio-cultural institutions, religious and theological beliefs. This paper is an attempt to clarify the concept of Syncretism, by taking Assam as an example of Socio-Religious Syncretism in North East India. Assam has geographical region that flourished in relative cultural isolation for thousands of years but during the course of time, the kings who came across and ruled this land, made an impact of their existence as colonization and expansion in this geographical locality. In this way, Assam became one of the most socio-religiously syncretistic regions in North East India. In the contemporary Assam, new religious practices are arising by the interaction between Assamese culture, Neo-Vaishanavism and impact of Christianity that offers syncretistic process, which projects Assam as an entity of Socio-religious syncretism.

Kuntala Dowarah in her paper **Syncretism Among the Tribes of North East India: A Socio-Historical Perspective** arguest that diversity and heterogeneity has been the hallmark of the Indian society. Therefore, the ethnic identities and cultural traits of the tribal population of India have been in a state of flux. Different scholars have thus conceptualised the processes of social change in different terms as like 'sanskritisation' and 'hinduisation' and so on. A section of tribes moves to a new pattern of life, so to say Christianity, Hinduism and Islam. The tribes of India had often borrowed cultural traits and religious practices of various sects and major religions such as Buddhism, Hinduism and Christianity. It was J.H. Hutton who reconstructed tribal religion as an integrated whole, having liberated from 'animism' and identified some of the parameters of its linkage to Hindusim. But K.S. Singh opines that many elements of tribal religion are as alive, even vibrant as ever. As studies have recently shown tribal religion has not lost its distinct identity in spite of its long years of interaction with Hinduism and Christianity. Thus the paper attempts to highlight some of the tribes in terms of cultural adoption and adaptation of linguistic, religious, and cultural traits in the region from the socio historical perspective. It will also analyse the processes through which the tribes have mingled with the mainstream culture, religion and language.

D. Sun in her paper **Syncretism: Religious Dimensions Among the Khasi of Meghalaya** makes an attempt has been made to discuss the pattern and process of syncretism in the wider context, as pursued by the Khasi of Meghalaya, along with the status of the tribal religion which is very complex in nature. The trend of religious revivalism and the impact of Christianity, in the ultimate analysis, seems to have minimal effect in the life of these highly conservative people.

Daili Neli in his paper **Syncretism: Christianity and Traditional Belief System among the Nagas in Northeast India** affirms that one of the basic institutions in every human society is Religion. It is a system of beliefs usually involving the worship of supernatural forces or beings which continues to have major influence in the life and events of humankind. The traditional religion of the Naga is nature centered. All things are understood within the framework of nature. The Naga religion has no founder and thus no historical personality is central in the Naga religion apart from nature. It is community oriented belief system, which sprung up from the people and practiced in the community. Today, Christianity has taken root in many Naga communities however it has not eclipsed the traditional religious beliefs. Although they embraced Christianity, the traditional beliefs system, symbols, values, etc continue to be major part of their culture. This paper is an attempt to examine the development of religious syncretism in Naga communities highlighting the patterns and processes through which both Christianity and traditional belief system have been creatively blended.

Supratim Bhattacharya & Pushpita Purkayastha in their paper **Language Shift and Maintenance: A Process of Linguistic Syncretism among the War Khasi of Meghalaya** writes that the undivided Khasi Hills district of Meghalaya is chiefly populated by the Khasi tribal group and a number of its sub-groups who are distributed and confined territory wise. The eastern side is the belt of the major Khasi tribe while the southern end is the homeland of the War Khasi, the south-central is the abode of the Bhoi Khasi, the north-western side is the abode of the Lyngngam Khasi, and so on. The present study highlights the process of language shift or maintenance as the case may be of the War Khasi tribe living in the rural set up of southern Meghalaya that is coterminous with the border regions of the neighbouring country of Bangladesh. It also ventures to see under what socio-cultural circumstances a linguistic community shifts its linguistic identity towards another linguistic community dealing there by extra-linguistic factors responsible for either maintenance or shift of language behaviour as a process of syncretic language behaviour. To understand the above situation, an empirical study was conducted among the War Khasi of Sohra sub-division in the East Khasi Hills District of Meghalaya.

Sumitabha Chakraborty in his paper **Syncretism in Kinnaurese Religion, Custom, and Belief** says that Syncretism is as old as Plutarch, who seems to have coined the term as an act or system of blending or reconciling heterogeneous elements. After Plutarch the term has extended its application in the field of cultural, philosophical and ecclesiastical situations and a number of definitions and views of this term have been added in due course. Syncretism is a process following acculturation, assimilation and fusion of both heterogeneous elements and would create a new type after synthesis, where both the original element persists (Hastings, 1980). Religious syncretism exhibits blending of two or more religious belief systems into a new system, or the incorporation into a religious tradition of beliefs from unrelated traditions. In religion, blending of different supernatural forces or the blending of magic, witchcraft with beliefs may give birth to the concept of syncretism. Religious syncretism is the product of contact and interpretation of people's mind. Syncretism takes place when new beliefs and techniques are introduced and blended in the existing native belief system. The new religion that emerges is heterogeneous in nature and acquires a new identity. The traditional religion of the Kinnaurese of the Kinnaur Himalayas is principally based on spiritual beliefs anthropomorphized into different deities. Each of the deities have its own identity, area of jurisdiction, prescription and prohibition. This paper is an attempt to highlight how the traditional spiritual beliefs blended with the Hindu fold of deity worship on the one hand and Buddhist fold of lama performances on the other.

Avijit Sahay in his paper Regional Variation In Syncretic Cultures Across India observes that India is an incredibly diverse and plural society. In the last five millenniums, many different races and many different cultures have come and found their home here. These constant influxes of new arrivals have given India a syncretism that is reflected in India's art, architecture, literature, language, culture and tradition. However, not all parts of India have been affected in the same way by the coming of new people. If the Malabar

Coast of Kerala has been influenced by the coming of Saint Thomas and the Syrian Orthodox Christianity, then the Northern Indian Plains have seen the influence of Islamic conquest in all walks of life. This different mixing of cultures has partly become responsible for India's much acclaimed diversity. Thus, different regions of India could be classified on the basis of not one linguistic or ethnic group, but on syncretic values and iconography of major cultural groups. The present study is an attempt to find the spatial variations in India caused by the cultural influences of a foreign culture on the original population.

Pinky Barua in her paper **Religious Syncretism And Culture Among Amri Karbi Of Karup District, Assam** writes that Religious syncretism exhibits blending of two or more religious belief systems into a new system, or the incorporation into a religious tradition of beliefs from unrelated traditions. This can occur for many reasons and sometimes it happens in areas where multiple religious traditions exist in proximity and function actively in the culture. Karbis have been converted into Hinduism and Vaishnavism especially those who reside in the plains of Nagaon and Kamrup and still they are following their tradition simultaneously. Karbis, some subsequently become Koch a caste of the Hindus. Conversion into Vaishnavism started by Srimanta Sankardeva himself the founder of Vaishnavism movement in Assam. The Karbi Christians are to be found mainly in the Karbi Along District and are divided into several denominations, such as (i) American Baptist, (ii) Welsh Mission, (iii) Church of God, (iv) Baptist Fedaration (v) Baptist Mild Mission, (vi) Seventh Day Adventist (vii) Catholic (Phangcho, 2003:62). In Kamrup area also Amris are slowly getting converted to Christianity in recent times. With the changing of religion, they become a part of a new belief and a new social system.

Samita Manna, Reshmi & Aritra Ghosh in their study on **Cultural Syncretism: An Empirical Study on Hindu-Christian Community of Kalyani** reiterate that Indian civilization has a pluralistic nature from its very birth. The pluralistic and composite ethos of Indian civilization is celebrated with its variegated religious thoughts, languages, cultural beliefs and philosophies of different cultural groups. Cultural and religious diversity are two basic components of Indian society. Religion is a form of culture having specific beliefs and practices. Religion is understandable only in its own terms, as a phenomenon which is *sui generis*. It is a critical construct for understanding contemporary social life and it plays a vital role in culture construction and social change. Every culture has some definite features. But now, globalization creates multi-cultural dimensions all over the world. Consequently, syncretism is a process by which the cultural assimilation is very rampant. It is the combining or fusion of different, often contradictory beliefs, thoughts, religions and cultures. This paper shows the cultural syncretism of Hindu-Christian community in Raghunathpur, Kalyani. It is noticed that this community sustains with a mixed religiosity of both the communities: the Hindu and the Christian. In their day to day interaction, they come in contact with various Hindu people as their locality is within the Hindu *'paras'*. Most of the families of this Christian *'para'* migrated from different places and settled here after 1970s are becoming Christian. Before that, most of them were Hindus and earlier this Christian *'para'* was dominated by the Muslim people. In the course of time, their socio-economic and cultural lives are deeply influenced with the Hindu society. This paper attempts to find out the nature of socio-cultural interaction pattern of the Christian families with the Hindu families and also the nature of assimilation between the two.

R. P. Athparia in his paper **Syncretism In Religious And Cultural Dimension: A Study Of The Jaintia Of Meghalaya** wirtes that syncretism means "in religion, the adoption of elements of one religion into the fabric of another; used by anthropologists to refer to analogous cultural processes, sometimes in preference to acculturation". In this paper an attempt has been made to examine the adoption of Hinduism and Christianity into the traditional religion of *Ki Hynniew Tre* among the Jaintias. The Jaintias inhabit in the Jaintia Hills District of Meghalaya. They were known in the beginning as *Ki Hynniew Trep*. Sen (2002:89-90) states that the progeny of 'seven huts' of the mythic narrative of '*Ki Hynniew Trep*' include Khasi and Jaintia can be said to have the same myth of origin. The most widely spread version mention of a place of habitation of *Ki Hynniew Trep* called *Sophetbneng*, a hill top in Khasi Hills. In all narratives, one element is common i.e., the seven families and the Khasis (and perhaps including the Jaintias) are the progeny of these seven families and are known as the children of *Ka Hynniew Trep*. The mythic narrative of *Ka Hynniew Trep* is repeatedly referred to enhance the identity consciousness. To sum up, it can be said that their traditional beliefs and practices have been in vogue till they came into contact with the Christianity. The whole of the Jaintia life of an individual is very dependent upon the good will of various deities to whom he/she must offer appropriate propitiation in some way or the other in his/her life time. Christianity appears to have an appreciable impact on the traditional religion of the Jaintias in recent years. Since before Independence, Christianity penetrated into the Jaintia land through a process. It was rather a systematic process of acculturation among them especially in cultural and religious field.

Aritra Ghosh, Rimi Sarkar & Samita Manna in their paper **Cultural Diversity And Religious Syncretism: A Sociological Interpretation On Santal In Kalyani, Nadia, West Bengal** discus on Ethnic origins, religions, and languages are the major sources of cultural diversity. India is a country incredible for its diversity: biological and cultural. However, the process of synthesis and integration has been extensively at work in most parts of India.

Indeed ethnic identities and even the cultural traits of Indian people have never been frozen in time or in space, they have been in state of flux. Though each group or community has a distinctive identity and ethos of its own, it does not exist in a social vacuum. Syncretism denotes the combination or alliance of opposing religious or philosophical doctrines, often with political undertones, that result in public and private rituals and commonly accepted local practices which appear to the observer to link orientations that are normally disparate, if not disjunctive (Claus and Mills, 2003). Kalyani is a planned urban sector. In this urban area, some Santal population (Kalyani Rathtala, 20 No. Ward) stay here. Being a people of this urban area some cultural assimilation has been perceived among them. In recent days, some changes have also been noticed in the sphere of social, economic and cultural life of these Santal people. The effect of such changes can be seen in their changing cultural values, social and religious institutions and role perceptions. They have adopted and also assimilated with the Hindu culture, beliefs and practices. Despite maintaining distinct identities of their own communities, they have been interacting with the other segments of the population. This paper has tried to find out how the Santals have accepted the different forms of the modern urban culture together with their changing life-style. This paper also deals with their changing nature of religious and cultural practices, establishing syncretistic nature of socio-religious and cultural tradition across the world.

Agnik Bhattacharya in his papr **Syncretism in Early Indian Society: A Case Study of Buddhism** says that this research paper establishes that the notion of syncretism did exist in early Indian context, which can be substantially felt after the rise and evolution of a new philosophical order known as *Buddhism*, in 6th BCE. The article will revolve around different socio-economic trends of early Indian multi-lingual society. It will also examine different cultural heterogeneities that took place due to the political and religious supremacy performed by a particular caste (*considered to be superior to others*); mainly against the people who can be referred to as subaltern in the context of early Indian historical paradigm. The article will also trace cultural homogeneity in early Indian society, the evidences of which can be seen strongly, right from 6th BCE till the Islamic period. The article will focus on a critical case study of Buddhist order and its attempt to promulgate the ideas of syncretism, by disbanding the ideas of discrimination on the basis of caste, creed, gender, etc. Hence, the article will be a critical analysis of the different political trends that influenced the social compositions of early India, the teachings of Buddha and the cultural legacy of the Buddhist doctrines, through which an attempt will be made to recreate a cultural homogeneous society.

Anupma Bharadwaj in her paper **An Empirical Study on the Syncretistic Values among the Indian Population** argues that Syncretism is the process by which two or more independent cultural systems, or elements thereof, conjoin together at a given time and space to form altogether a new and distinct system. The process of syncretism occurs largely due to long time and continued interaction of different cultural systems; howsoever they may be opposed to each other, theoretically and conceptually. In India, due to age-old interaction of the Hindus with the Muslims and the Christians, a number of syncretistic phenomena can be observed in the cultural systems of the respective populations. It should be very clearly noted that syncretism is much more than mere borrowing of cultural traits among two groups, which often takes place when two cultural systems meet together. The paper furnishes a number of significant instances of beliefs and rituals that are observed among the Hindus, Muslims and Christians that have syncretistic value.

Srija Mandal in her paper **Syncretism - A Religious Harmony In India** affirms that India is a country incredible for its cultural diversity. It is the natural resources that attract people belonging to different cultures and traditions from different directions bringing together under a common canopy of syncretism. However, there have been a differential rate of the degree of acceptance in different societies, if observed individually, but the uniqueness of this mythical spread is that it lies at the cognitive dimension of the people. The sharing of space, regional ethos and cultural traits cut across ethnic and sectarian differences and bind the people together. Thus, we have found a firm balancing between cultural diversity and syncretism across India. The present paper discusses about the concept of syncretism as a whole and it also explores, by discussing ethnographic examples from different parts of India, mainly in West Bengal, the multi-dimensional and many layered contexts of reciprocally shared cultural realms and inter-religious and synthesized cultural formations, including common religious observances. This paper is an attempt at building a broad perspective of diversity, convergence and dissemination of cultural practices and religious beliefs, highlighting the patterns and processes through which religions and cultures on both sides have been creatively blended.

Shajymon M.L, in his paper **Syncretic Cultural Practices among the Halam of Tripura** studies on one of the communities of Tripura. The population of Tripura is blessed with unique social scenario and multifaceted expressions of religious, social, cultural and linguistic blends. It is a land of forest and envious natural resources. The flora and fauna of the state is conducive for human habitation, agriculture and blessed with natural wealth such as Natural Gas. One of the major tribes of Tripura is Halam and there are as many as 11 sub-groups/clans in this community. According to the Census of India 2001 the Halam population is 47,245 published by Directorate of Census Operations, Tripura. The population has risen to 53,549 in 2008 according to a field survey. The endeavour over here is to identify and portray such syncretic cultural practices among the Halam of Tripura. In other words this paper is an attempt to elucidate the commonality among the different groups of Halam practicing different religions showing their cultural characteristics. As we know, religion provides a unique and universal identity and different social status. However, it is significant to admit that in spite of the attractions of the new or foreign/local religions, cultures and their influence, for certain, there are a few sociological and anthropological elements which are unique and equally and powerfully nurtured in terms of esteemed identity among the Halam community of Tripura.

Samita Manna, Reshmi Chakraborty & Aritra Ghosh in their paper **Cultural Syncretism: An Empirical Study On Tribal-Christian Community of Kalyani** debate on Indian civilization which has a pluralistic nature from its very birth. The pluralistic and composite ethos of Indian civilization is celebrated with its variegated religious thoughts, languages, cultural beliefs and philosophies of different cultural groups. Cultural and religious diversity are two basic components of India. Religion is a form of culture having specific beliefs and practices. This paper shows the cultural syncretism of Tribal-Christian community in Raghunathpur, Kalyani. It is noticed that this community sustains with a mixed religiosity of both the communities: the Tribal and the Christian. In their day to day interaction, the tribals come in contact with various Hindu people as their locality is within the Hindu *'paras'*. Most of the tribal families of this Christian *'para'* migrated from different places and settled here after 1970s, becoming Christian. Before that, most of them were Christians when they lived in Jharkhand, Odisha and Ranchi. Earlier this Christian *'para'* was dominated by the Muslim people. In course of time, their socio-economic and cultural lives are deeply influenced with the dominating Hindu-Bengali culture associated with Christianity. This paper has tried to find out the cultural syncretism of the Christian Oraon tribal with the Bengali-Hindu culture of the locality. The study also focuses on the changing nature of interaction pattern of the Oraon families especially during the time of ceremonial functions and festivals.

Geetika Ranjan in her paper **Influence Of Different Religions On A Particularly Vulnerable Tribal Group: An Anthropological Exploration** attempts to bring forth the picture of Bhoksa religion – an amalgamation of beliefs and practices representing different religions. Bhoksa is a tribe in the state of Uttarakhand. It falls under the constitutional category of Particularly Vulnerable Tribal Group (earlier known as the Primitive Tribal Group). Bhoksa trace their roots to the royal family of Raja Jagatdeo of Rajasthan. The Bhoksa have a distinct impact of Hinduism on their religious beliefs. Yet they continue to have deep faith in the essential ingredients of their Bhoksa specific tribal religion. Among the Bhoksa there are a large number of their tribal gods and goddesses who also command respect from the neighbouring Hindus. There are some deities which can be said to be exclusive Bhoksa deities, those who are not worshipped by the Hindus such as the village deity – Bhumia and the protector of the village-Bhumsen. The present research emphasizes that religious notion of a people can be adequately garnered when understood against their history. Further allegiance to diverse religious beliefs is also determined by the kind of relationship a group shares with the adherents of those beliefs.

Surojit Sen Gupta in his paper **Synthesis Of Cultural Modernization With Western Impact- A Sociological Review On Indian Society.** Westernization refers to the process of change brought about in non-western countries as a result of the adoption of western cultural elements on their part. It refers to the process of diffusion of western values and ideologies like liberalism, egalitarianism, humanism, rationalism and individual freedom. The process of westernization has spread like a socio-cultural movement to the different parts of the World and has brought about wide spectrum of changes in economy and polity of the human society. It is under the influence of the Britishers that the real process of westernization started in India. They have left such long lasting influences on Indian culture that even after many decades of the end of British rule, Indian culture is still under the heavy influence of the western culture of the British. Thus, this paper will focus on the westernization process and cultural modernization of Indian society theoretically and from a sociological angle.

Arifur Zaman in his paper **Indigenous Beliefs and Practices of The Deoris of Assam** studies on the Deoris who are one of the indigenous scheduled tribes of Assam inhabiting mostly in the plain areas of Upper Assam. The entire Deori tribe is divided into four broad divisions or khel on the basis of their places of origin. They are – Dibangiyas, Tengapania, Borgoyan and Patorgoyan. Of all the four divisions of the Deoris, the Dibangiyas have preserved their socio religious organisations almost along with their indigenous dialect known as Duan. The Dibangiya Deoris observe various rites and rituals in connection with the principal events of life as well as for the welfare of the community as a whole and to propitiate their different pristine God and Goddesses. But at contemporary times due to the influences of other religious beliefs, specially the influence of great traditional Hinduism of neighbouring caste Hindus, some impinging factors have been percolated in their indigenous belief system. In this present endeavour an attempt to know the traditional belief system of the aforesaid ethnic group in a rural context.

Sunumi Changmi in her paper **Culture, Religious Change and Identity a Case Study of the Muklom (Tangsa) of Arunachal Pradesh** argues that loss of culture is loss of identity. From this it follows that a community must preserve its culture in order to maintain its identity. It is well known that religion is a basic feature of culture because it provides a world view, a value system and a set of norms for behaviour. However, there are innumerable cases of communities changing their religion. In fact, in North East India itself many tribal communities in the past accepted Buddhism. In recent times a large number have accepted Christianity. Some have even given a new orientation to their so called "traditional" religion. This situation of change in religion raises some interesting questions: what happens to their culture? Does their culture change? If their culture changes, what happens to their identity? This paper intends to study the case of the Muklom (Tangsa) of Arunachal Pradesh to find out how they have dealt with these questions as followers of Rang-frah (a traditional religion) or as Christians.

Ranga Ranjan Das in his paper **Syncretism in an Urban Context of Assam: Cultural and Religious Dimensions** writes that in contemporary times, the term 'syncretism' is often used in both social and religious discourse as well. According to Oxford English Dictionary, 'syncretism' means an 'attempt to sink differences and affect union between sects or philosophical schools' and New Oxford Advanced Learner's Dictionary defines it as 'the mixing of different religions, philosophies and ideas'. The Assamese equivalent is '*samanvay*'. Scholars of anthropology and history have utilized the term 'syncretism' as a descriptive term referring to the 'borrowing, affirmation, or integration of concepts, symbols or practices of one religious tradition into another by a process of selection and reconciliation'. In religious discourse, the term refers to a process of religious amalgamation, of blending heterogeneous beliefs and practices. India is rich in diversity in terms of ethnic origins, religions, languages and right from the arrival of the Aryans, there are interaction with conflict, cooperation and synthesis of different cultural and religious streams. However, tolerance and communal harmony is intact in spite of insurmountable differences in religious and cultural identities. Assam, the premier north eastern states has shown good examples of assimilation, synthesis and syncretism. This paper is a modest attempt to understand, the process of 'samanvay' when it comes under the banner of 'Greater Birubari' (Brihattar Birubari) as well as while performing certain religious occasions, socio-cultural occasions, neighbourhood relationships at family or personal level, common social cause, that reflect syncretism.

In Sampa Basu paper **Looking in to Indian Civilisation through religious Syncretism** she tries to explore the patterns and processes through which religious and cultures on both sides have been creatively blended.

References

1. Das, N.K.: (Page No.1, Ref: Culture, Religion and Philosophy Critical studies in Syncretism and Inter-Faith Harmony by Shri N.K. Das, published by Rawat Publications Jaipur and New Delhi in 2003)

2. Barnard Alan and Jonathan Spencer: 2003, Ref: Encyclopedia of Social and Cultural Anthropology, Routledge, London.

2

Concept of Syncretism analysed from Cultural and Religious Perspectives

— *G. Lazar SVD*

Syncretism is a process where the fusion of cultures, religions, and philosophies produce both new faiths and cultures or the destruction of older faiths. One definition from www.britannica.com states:

Religious syncretism is the fusion of diverse religious beliefs and practices. Instances of religious syncretism-as, for example, Gnosticism (a religious dualistic system that incorporated elements from the Oriental mystery religions), Judaism, Christianity, and Greek religious philosophical concepts-were particularly prevalent during the Hellenistic period (c. 300 BC. ad 300). Indeed, all of the world religions, that is, Hinduism, Buddhism, Christianity, Judaism, Islam and Confucianism are to a fair extent syncretistic. But the process occurs whenever previously independent belief systems come into sustained contact, no matter what their respective levels of sophistication may be.

Thus, Syncretism is a combination of separate concepts into one new, unique idea. Cultural syncretism is when an aspect of two or more distinct cultures blend together to create a new custom, idea, practice, or philosophy.

L. Bouyer (614) derives ***"syncretism"*** from the Greek etymology **synkratein,** meaning «pouring together». It is like pouring one type of liquid into another; for instance water into wine, and thereby obtaining a totally different substance which is neither purely water nor purely unadulterated or undiluted wine. From this etymological meaning, syncretism designated "a system or rather a tendency of Hellenistic thought which tended to mix and to confuse most diversified cults". It is "a fusion of rituals and doctrines". The concept finds place in almost all modern religions as syncretism is a "blending," a tampering, a mixing together, and a "bringing together of conflicting ideologies into a unity of thought and/or into a cooperating, harmonious social relationship."

Angeles (286). The word syncretism is used to refer to the practice of harmonizing two or more distinct sets of beliefs to create an entirely new one. Syncretism normally refers to merging beliefs of two or more religious systems in order to come up with a new one, which sometimes demonstrates the traits of the systems involved. This may also include the fusion of two contradictory schools of thought.

From the **sociological point of view**, syncretism is necessary for the smooth functioning of a society with different backgrounds, as its absence can disturb the balance of such a society. The fact that this concept can bring together two contradictory thoughts may sound confusing and rightly so. However, that is a fact. Syncretism is predominant when it comes to religions and cultures. As far as religion is concerned, it is a well-known fact that most of the modern religions evolved from various ancients beliefs; hence the tendency to carry-over and blend with the former creedal milieu. From the religious perspective then, it is in this blending that is found the adulterating character of syncretism. This makes syncretism an inauthentic tenet gotten by combining bits of various creeds, ideologies and views – even contradictory ones – resulting in a formulation of a doctrine that is completely new and sometimes unidentifiable with any of its original stuffs.

From **religious point of view**, a religion can readily accommodate to the worldviews of its age. Such accommodation is called religious syncretism. It is the reshaping of religious beliefs and practices through cultural accommodation so that they consciously or unconsciously blend with those of the dominant culture. It is blending of one religious belief and practices with those of the dominant culture so that that particular religion loses its distinctive nature and speaks with a voice reflective of its culture. Syncretism occurs when one religion opts into the major cultural assumptions of its society (Van Rheenen 1997).

Speaking from **anthropology**, "syncretism" has recently re-emerged as a valuable tool for understanding the complex dynamics of ethnicity, interconnectedness and post-modernism. In the present era of increasing cultural condensation, syncretism is a prevailing event. The sociologists and social anthropologists have thrown much light on the variety of religious forms through their studies of belief systems, rituals, symbols and meaning all over the world but they have not paid adequate attention to the phenomenon of syncretism, though we find a few exceptions (Firth 1970:87). In anthropological literature the Cargo cult has been described as a form of syncretism. Cargo cults are essentially syncretistic, blending the "Christian doctrine" with "aboriginal beliefs" (Worsley 1990). Anthropologists have also included the blend of African, Native American, and Roman Catholic saints and deities in Caribbean "voodoo" cults as instances of syncretism. Though the process of syncretism provides an independent field of study, it was nevertheless ignored by the anthropologists and when discussed it was imperfectly included within "the study of acculturation" (Kottak 1991:407).

Shaw and Stewart (1994), have observed that within anthropology, where notions of the 'purity' of traditions have not had much credibility for some time, syncretism has been ascribed a neutral, and often positive, significance. Recently, there has been criticism of concepts such as 'cultural purity', wholeness or 'authenticity'. In post-modern-anthropology in which syncretic processes are considered basic not only to religion and ritual but to 'the predicament of culture' identities no longer presuppose continuous cultures or traditions. Everywhere groups improvise local performances from (re-) collected pasts. Organic culture (is indeed) reconceived as inventive process or creolised 'interculture' (Clifford 1988: 14-15).

Sociologically, syncretism has always been part of the negotiation of identities and hegemonies in situations such as conquest, trade, migration, religious dissemination and intermarriage. The growth of a western-dominated world economic system, however, was accompanied by the growth of a Western-dominated world cultural system (Hannerz 1987, 1992), in which processes of capitalism and cultural hegemony transformed not only relations of power and production but also experiences of personhood, of the body, gender, time, space and religion. The appropriation of totalizing and globally spread processes such as capitalism, commodity consumption and 'rationalist' models of development is often inseparable from the appropriation of totalizing and globally spread religions… (Shaw and Stewart 1994). Van der Veer argues that there are debates over syncretism in societies in which identities are defined through religion. **Since India combines these by being a secular state in which religious affiliation partially defines cultural identity, it makes sense that syncretism and multiculturalism are often equated in Hindu political discourse** (1994).

Hendry (1999: 12) has observed that in complex societies, people have come to live with apparently conflicting worldviews increasingly. In Japan a sick person simultaneously consults a diviner as well as a doctor, and may also visit a shrine or temple to pray for recovery (Ohnuki-Tierney 1984). **Religious movements and plethora of religious ideas, in varied historical phases, motivated the people and brought them closer towards numerous religious cults, sects, reform movements and diverse belief systems** (Das 2003). The underlying assumption seems to be that people need solace and assurance about fulfilment of all their wishes ultimately; hence they solicit refuge and sanctification of their expectations through their trust on varied religious and sectarian dogmas. Syncretism is a matter of degree, some societies have blended prominent aspects of two religious dogmas, in others only certain aspects of the original or adopted religion/sect has been retained and internalised. It is shown that syncretism pertains to a commingled religious sequence whose ill-defined frontier shapes its fundamental collective character (Das 2003a). Mingling of exterior religious beliefs with pre-existing religious belief of people may not be regarded as an aberration. It is also not a system within system but the survival and situationally determined growth of multifaceted religious beliefs systems existing as a rational order.

Rosalind Shaw and Charles Stewart (1994), the editors of the volume, *Syncretism and Anti-Syncretism*, have observed that within anthropology, where notions of the 'purity' of traditions have not had much credibility for some time, syncretism has been ascribed a neutral, and often positive, significance. In anthropology as a matter of fact now the essentialising of culture is generally dismissed. What is more there has been increasing criticism of concepts such as cultural purity, wholeness or 'authenticity'. In post-modern-anthropology in which syncretic processes are considered basic not only to religion and ritual but to 'the predicament of culture' (Clifford 1988: 14-15) identities no longer presuppose continuous cultures or traditions. Everywhere groups improvise local performances from (re) collected pasts. Organic culture reconceived as inventive process or creolised 'interculture' (Clifford 1988: 14-15). These scholars feel that although syncretic processes currently loom large in new writings, there seems to be an uneasiness about the term in post-modern anthropology: we hear far less about culture as syncretic than about culture as collage, as creolised, as fragmented, as 'interculture', as subversive hybrid invention (Shaw and Stewart 1994: 2). If we recast the study of syncretism as the politics of religious synthesis, one of the first issues which needs to be confronted is what 'anti-syncretism': the antagonism to religious synthesis shown by agents concerned with the defence of religious boundaries. 'Authenticity' or 'originality' do not necessarily depend on purity both pure and mixed traditions can be unique. Van der Veer argues that there are debates over syncretism in societies in which identities are defined through religion. Since India combines these by being a secular state in which religious affiliation partially defines cultural identity, it makes sense that syncretism and multiculturalism are often equated in Hindu political discourse (see Shaw and Stewart 1994). Shaw and Stewart (1994) agree with Richard Werbner who, argued that the term 'syncretism' should be limited to the domain of religious or ritual phenomena where elements of two different historical 'traditions' interact or combine.

Nadel (1954:7-8) has rightly observed that however the sphere of 'things religious' is defined; there will always remain an area or border zone of uncertainty making it difficult to portray the dividing line between religion and non-religion. This statement seems truer for Indian context where pluralistic cultural religious traditions provide solid syncretistic coherence. In dealing with religion one deals with many different things. Religion is an affair of the community and anthropologists indeed are more competent to do empirical study of religion in its social context. The fact remains that the notion of 'community' has itself been subjected to analytical deconstruction (Haim Hazan 1995; see also David Morley and Kevin Robins 1995). Cohen (1985) has reduced 'community' to its symbolic boundaries. Here it may not be out of place to restate that cultural practices are integrated in religious practices and vice-versa. Throughout in our above account we have tried to elucidate in a broad anthropological-historical perspective mingling and fusion of religious/ culture practices and traits as observable in day to day life.

Gauri Viswanathan in an article titled "Beyond Orientalism: Syncretism and the politics of knowledge" (SEHR, volume 5, issue 1: 1996) has reviewed the issue of syncretism from a broad historical –sociological angle. Beginning the arguments around "In an Antique Land", by Amitav Ghosh, Viswanathan finds it disturbing to see Ghosh's twist to a culturally and religiously hybrid medieval past and its engagement with the romance of syncretism, as a solution to sectarianism, nationalism, ethnocentrism, and religious intolerance. Does syncretism offer truly global possibilities for a merging of religious difference, or is it a code word for the incorporation and assimilation of "minority" cultures? Is syncretism indeed the language in which, as Ghosh claims, people "once discussed their differences". Peter Van der Veer has established that the historical roots of syncretism's semantic association with trans denominational universalism lie in the rise of Protestantism and the decline of the absolute authority of Catholicism; and he further argues that syncretism's subsequent identification with cultural relativism accompanied the spread of colonialism and the politically charged contact with alien religious cultures that colonial expansion promoted (1994). Viswanathan while putting the 'state' and 'law' above other considerations, argues that this syncretism gets transferred to the secular plane of plural identities, (thus) allowing for the creation of a homogeneous national identity, mediated by law.

This point indeed may require valid data based evidences and justification, particularly in reference to India. Viswanathan is particularly insensitive to any official data, such as Nandy's use of 1911 Census wherein the Muslims of Gujarat identified themselves as "Mohammedan Hindus". Contrary to what Viswanathan and many sociologists believe, Nandy rightly concludes from this example that there existed "a prior state of harmony" between Muslims and Hindus which was disrupted by the colonial state (1990). While equating the syncretism of Ghosh's narrative voice as analogous to Matthew Arnold's culture, Viswanathan suggests that both culture and syncretism have been able to deal with difference by amalgamating difference to a totalizing, homogeneous whole. Syncretism in the review presented by Viswanathan is closely seen from certain basic 'difference' perspective, viewed at larger macro -national level. This approach will eventually lead us to miss the core of very process of coming together of practices and beliefs of people (in cultural – religious sphere) which result in multiple levels of syncretic traditions to be seen in unique manner in places like south Asia. Christophe Jaffrelot has recently advanced the concept of "strategic syncretism" as a sub-category of the invention of Hindu tradition and Hindu ideology. Such an ideology is syncretic, argues Jaffrelot, because its content is supplied by material taken from the cultural values of groups who are seen as hostile to the Hindu community (1993). Christ no longer is a threatening alien religious figure, but made into an Indian god.

There is probably more diversity of religions in India than anywhere on the earth. Apart from having representations from almost all the major religions of the world, India was also the birthplace of Hinduism, Buddhism, Jainism and Sikhism. It was also the home to one of the oldest religions of the world, Zoroastrianism. While India is the cradle of Hinduism, Buddhism, Jainism and Sikhism, Islam too has a long tradition of existence. So also Judaism, Christianity and Baha'ism have their followers in India. As early as by the 12th century, India began to have Islamic bases as wave after wave of Islamic groups came down to India. And the confluence of the two religions gradually produced a cultural syncretism, which is exemplified by the Urdu language – an amalgam of Persian and Hindi. Out of the fusion of the two cultures arose new religious denominations characterizing the Hindu-Islamic interface. The best example of this synthesis is the Ahmediyas – a sect that abides by the Koran and the Prophet, yet practicing idolatry, which is a decidedly Hindu custom. Ahmediyas in some areas are not recognised as "proper Muslims" because of their syncretic traditions. Christianity came to India with St. Thomas who came to India in 50 A.D. and brought the teachings of Jesus along with him – even before the Messiah was adopted by Europe. Contacts between India and other cultures have led to the spread of Indian religions throughout the world, resulting in the extensive influence of Indian thought and practice on Southeast and East Asia in ancient times and, more recently, in the diffusion of Indian religions to Europe and North America.

In the anthropological study of religions in India, the major emphasis has been on descriptive account of religious customs and their association with ethnic groups, including the tribes, the themes of purity/pollution in relation to caste system, descriptive concepts relating to religious phenomena and the modernisation processes. Milton Singer, who along with Robert Redfield and Surajit Sinha, studied the 'anthropology of Indian civilisation', states that the Great Tradition of Indian civilisation may be identified with what Srinivas calls "Sanskritic Hinduism" which has an all-India 'spread' and to which Monier-Williams called "Brahmanism" . Singer also used Srinivas's concepts of "All-India Hinduism", "Peninsular Hinduism", "Regional Hinduism" and "Local Hinduism" in his various studies. Srinivas' "Sanskritisation" model through which lower castes and tribal groups are brought into the Hindu fold with elements from the Sanskritic tradition of Hinduism (Srinivas 1952: 1968), is clubbed together by Singer with model of "Hindu method of tribal absorption" (Bose 1953). Singer uses the term "popular Hinduism", to include within it numerous beliefs and religious practices observed among tribal people, including the worship of numerous godlings, animal sacrifice, witchcraft and magic (Singer 1972: 45). 'Tribal religions' indeed remained essential element of Hinduism in the writings of American and Indian anthropologists belonging to Chicago school, and this tendency largely survives. Singer as per his own admission is indeed not sure about the basis and persistence of "Lower Level" popular Hinduism. Singer quotes Surajit Sinha (1959) who says that "the culture of tribal India represents a "folk" dimension of the "Little Tradition" of Hinduism, while the culture of Hindu peasantry represents "a mixture of folk elements with elements from the greater and Sanskritic tradition of Hinduism" (Emphasis added, Singer 1972:46). With new data that are with us now it is felt that this whole perspective indeed calls for a reappraisal.

In a recent review, K.S. Singh (2003) discards the views of the Orientalists and anthropologists, who described 'tribal religion' in terms of a set of 'primitive values' surviving in Hindu religion, and the sureness of tribal religion being swallowed up by major religions, a claim equally made by colonial scholars and Indian anthropologists alike. In his view nothing has happened. It was indeed J. H. Hutton, an administrator-anthropologist, who was the first to have reconstructed tribal religion as an integrated whole. He is credited rightly with having liberated tribal religion from the waste paper basket of 'animism', identified the parameters of its autonomy and the range of its linkages with Hinduism. But like most census officials he too was prone to describe tribal religion as the "surplus material not yet built into the temple of Hinduism"(Hutton 1931: 399).

Societies in various parts of India have evolved through dialogue and interactions at many levels. The multi-cultural, multi-ethnic, multi-lingual and multi-religious society like India could survive because of dialogue and exchange of ideas. Scholars agree that the great heritage of Indian civilisation spanning over 5000 years is sustained broadly through its pre-dominant agricultural and rural character of its population. Appadurai finds the use of traditional techniques and folk knowledge as critical for survival of Indian farmers. Similarly, playwright Girish Karnad sees continuity in indigenous Indian dramatic forms and finds a sense of energy in folk theatre. For Girish Karnad, the past coexists with the present in a parallel form. Similarly, Muslim painter, Gulam Mohammad Sekh revealed a close convergence of Hindu and Muslim rituals in family custom and ceremonies.

Conclusion

The reality, however, is that every culture has, in fact, ingested foreign elements from exogenous sources, with the various elements gradually becoming 'naturalised' within it. As Said (1979) argues 'the notion that there are geographical spaces with indigenous, radically "different" inhabitants who can be defined on the basis of some religion, culture or racial essence, proper to that geographical space is a highly debatable idea' (quoted in Clifford, 1988: 274). As many authors have noted (for example, Appadurai, 1990; Bhabha, 1987; Hall, 1987), cultural hybridity is, increasingly, the normal state of affairs in the world, and in this context any attempt to defend the integrity of indigenous or authentic cultures easily slips into the conservative defence of a nostalgic vision of the past which can be also described as an 'absolutism of the pure' (Rushdie 1982).

References

Appadurai, A., (1990). 'Disjuncture and difference in the global cultural economy' in M. Featherstone, ed. *Global Culture*, London: Sage.

Bhabha, H. (1987). 'Interrogating Identity' in L. Appignanesi, ed. *Postmodernism and the Question of Identity*, London: Institute of Contemporary Arts.

Bose, N. K. (1953).*Cultural Anthropology and Other Essays*, Calcutta: Indian Associated Publishing Co.

Bose N.K, Ed. (1961).*Peasant Life in India: A Study in Indian Unity and Diversity*, Calcutta; Anthropological Survey of India.

Cohen, A.P. (1985).*Symbolic construction of Community*, London; Tavistock.

Clifford, J. 1988. *The Predicament of Culture: Twentieth Century Ethnography, Literature and Art,* Cambridge, MA: Harvard University Press.

Das, N.K and P. Gupta. (1982).*The Ahom Movement in Tribal Movements in India*. Vol.1 Ed. K. S. Singh, Delhi: Manohar.

Das, N.K.(1988).Tribal Priesthood and Shamanism in Chattisgarh, *Journal of Indian Anthropological Society.23:223-231.*

Das, N. K. (1989). *Ethnic Identity, Ethnicity and Social Stratification in North East India.* New Delhi: Inter-India Publication.

Das, N.K and C. L. Imchen, Eds.(1994). *Nagaland, People of India*. Calcutta: Anthropological Survey of India.

Das, N.K. (1998). *The Chick Badaiks of Orissa*. People of India. Mimeographed.

Das, N.K. (2000). *The Satnamis of Chhattisgarh*. Mimeographed. Calcutta: Anthropological Survey of India.

Das, N.K. (2001). Ethnic Character and Regional Identity of Chhattisgarh. *The Journal of the Anthropological Survey of India* (2001)50:45-55.

Das N.K. (Ed.) (2003a). Culture, Religion and Philosophy: Critical Studies in *Syncretism and Inter-Faith Harmony*. Jaipur: Rawat Publications.

Das N.K. (2003b). "Introduction: An outline of Syncretism" In *Culture, Religion and Philosophy: Critical Studies in Syncretism and Inter-Faith Harmony*. pp 11-36, Jaipur :Rawat Publications.

Das N.K. (2003c). "Religious syncretism and cultural Homonisation in North East India" In *Culture, Religion and Philosophy: Critical Studies in Syncretism and Inter-Faith Harmony*. pp 295 - 324, Jaipur: Rawat Publications.

Datta, B. (1993). Rama Katha among the Tribal communities of the North East in Rama-Katha in *Tribal and Folk traditions of India*. Eds. K.S.Singh and B.Datta. Calcutta : Seagull Books.

Dube, S.C.(1990). Indian Society.New Delhi: National Book Trust.Pluralism& civil society,www.islam21.net/pages/keyissues/key3-21.htm.

Eschmann, Annacharlotte, "Hinduisation of Tribal Deities in Orissa: The Shakti Typology". In *The Cult: of Jagannath and Regional Tradition of Orissa*, edited by A Eschmann, Herman Kulke, and Gaya CharanTripathi, Manohar, 1986.

Firth, Raymond. (1996).*Religion: A Humanist Interpretation*. London: Rutledge.

Gadgil, M. and Guha, R. (1992). This Fissured Land: An Ecological History of India.

Oxford University Press, New Delhi and University of California Press, Berkeley.

Gnanambal, K. (1970). "The Study of Mattas and seats of Sanskritic Learning" in Research Programmes on Cultural anthropology and allied disciplines. Ed. Surajit Chandra Sinha. Calcutta : Anthropological Survey of India.

Gauri Viswanathan (1996). "Beyond "Orientalism: Syncretism and the Politics of knowledge" SEHR, volume 5, issue 1: Contested Polities Updated February 26, 1996.

Ghosh, Amitav, (1992).In an Antique Land London: Granta.

Hall, S. (1987). 'Minimal selves' in L. Appignanesi, Ed. *Postmodernism and the Question of Identity, London: Institute of Contemporary Arts.*

Hannerz, U. (1987). *The World in Creolisation*, Africa 57: 546-59.

Hannerz, U.(1992). *Cultural Complexity: Studies in the Social Organisation of Meaning*. New York: Columbia University Press.

Hazan, Haim, (1995). Lost Horizons Regained: Old Age and the Anthropology of Contemporary Society in *The Future of Anthropology*. Eds. Akbar Ahmed and Cris Shore, London: The Athlone Press.

Hendry, Joy (1999).*An Introduction to Social Anthropology*. London: Macmillan Press.

Hutton, J. H. (1931).*Census of India*, Vol. I, p. 399 (also see K S. Singh. Foreword Census of India, 1931), Vol. I, Gyan Publication (reprint), 1936.

Jaffrelot, Christophe. "Hindu Nationalism: Strategic Syncretism in Ideology Building," *Economic and Political Weekly* 20-27 March 1993: 517-524.

Jordan, J.T.F. (1975). Medieval Hindu Devotionalism. In *A Cultural history of India,* Ed.A.L.Basham,Delhi: Oxford University Press.

Hutton, J. H. (1931), *Census of India*, Vol. I, p. 399 (also see K S. Singh. Foreword census of India, 1931), Vol. I, Gyan Publication (reprint), 1936.

Lyall, Alfred. (1899). *Asiatic Studies*, Vol.ii. Royal Asiatic Society.

Matthew Arnold, (1869).*Culture and Anarchy*, ed. J. Dover Wilson Cambridge: Cambridge UP, 1981.

Momin (1996). Cultural Pluralism, National Identity and Development: The Indian Case. In *Interface of cultural identity development*. Ed. BaidyanathSaraswati. New Delhi: IGNCA.

Nadel, S.F. (1954m).*Nupe Religion*. London: Rutledge and Kegan Paul.

Nandy, Ashish "The Politics of Secularism and the Recovery of Religious Tolerance" in *Mirrors of Violence*, ed. Veena Das (Delhi: Oxford UP, 1990) 70.

Ohnuki-Tierney, Emiko (1984)*Illness and Culture in Contemporary Japan*. London: Cambridge University Press.

Peter Van der Veer, "Syncretism, Multiculturalism, and the Discourse of Tolerance," in *Syncretism/Anti-Syncretism: The Politics of Religious Synthesis*, eds. Charles Stewart and Rosalind Shaw London: Routledge, 1994.

Redfield, R., R. Linton and M.J.Herskovits(1936).*A Memorandum on Acculturation American Anthropologist* 38: 149-152.

Risley, H. H. 1915 [1969, 1973] *The People of India*, New Edition by W. Crooke New Delhi: Oriental Books.

Roy Burman, B.K.(1958). The Ramayana as related by a Mech Elder. *Folklore* October-December 1958.

Roy, Shibani and S. H. M Rizvi.(2003).Monotheistic Islam and Pluralistic Islamic Traditions of India in N. K. Das (Ed.) *Religion and Philosophy: Critical Studies in Syncretism and Inter-Faith Harmony*. Jaipur: Rawat Publications.

Rushdie, Salman, (1982). 'Imaginary homelands', *London Review of Books*, October: 18-19.

Said, E., (1979).*Orientalism*, Harmondsworth: Penguin.

Sarkar RM (1990).*TheBauls of Bengal.* New Delhi: Gyan Publishers.

Saraswati, Baidyanath(2000). The New Anthropology, In *Contributions to Holistic Traditions: Anthropology in India*. R.K.Bhattacharya (Ed.) Calcutta: Anthropological Survey of India.

Shaw, Rosalind and Charles Stewart, (Ed.) (1994).*Introduction: problematizing Syncretism. Syncretism? Anti-Syncretism: The Politics of Religious Synthesis* London: Rutledge.

Shyam, N. (1993). A note on the Tai Ramayana. In Rama-Katha in *Tribal and Folk traditions of India*. Eds. K.S.Singh and B.Datta. Calcutta: Seagull Books.

Singh K.S.(1985). *Tribal Society in India*. New Delhi: Manohar.

Singh K.S. 1992 [2002] *People of India: Introduction*. Calcutta: Anthropological Survey of India.

Singh, K.S. (1993). *Introduction, Rama-Katha in Tribal and Folk traditions of India*. Eds. K.S.Singh and B.Datta. Calcutta: Seagull Books.

Singh K.S.(1995).*The Scheduled Castes*, Calcutta: ASI.

Singh K.S.(1996).*Identity, Ecology, Social Organisatrion, Economy, Linkages and Development Process: A Quantitative Profile*. New Delhi: Oxford University Press and ASI.

Singh, K.S. (2003). Hinduism and Tribal Religion In*Culture, Religion and Philosophy: Critical Studies in Syncretism and Inter-Faith Harmony*. Jaipur: Rawat Publications.

Sinha, Surajit, (1959). 'Tribal Cultures of Peninsular India as a dimension of Little Tradition in the Study of Indian civilisation: A Preliminary Statement' in Milton Singer (ed.), *Traditional India: Structure and Change*. Philadelphia: The American folklore society, 298-312.

Srinivas, M. N.(1952).*Religion and Society among the Coorgs of South India*. Oxford: Clarendon Press.

Singh, Yogendra. (2000). *Culture Change in India: Identity and Globalisation*. Jaipur: Rawat Publication.

Smith, Donald Eugene, (1963). *India as a Secular State*, London: Princeton University Press.

Smith, W.C., (1946). *Modern Islam in India*, London: Princeton University Press.

Smith, William Roy, (1938). *Nationalism and Reform in India*, London: Yale University Press.

Stewart, Charles and Rosalind Shaw (Ed.) (1994).*Syncretism? Anti-Syncretism: The Politics of Religious Synthesis*. London: Rutledge.

Tamo, Mibang. (1991).*Indigenous faiths and Practices of the Minyongs in Religion and Society in the Himalayas* Eds. T.B.Subba and K.Datta. New Delhi: Gyan Publications.

Thio, A. (1989).*Sociology*. New York, Harper and Row – Publishers.

Troisi, J. *Tribal Religious Beliefs and Practices among the Santals*, New Delhi: Manohar, 1979, pp. 272-274.

Tylor, E.B.(1958) (1913) *Primitive Culture*. New York: Harper Torch Books. (London: John Murray).

Worsley, Peter M. (1990). "Cargo Cults" in *Anthropology: Contemporary Perspective* Ed. Whitten, P. and D.E.K

3

Syncretism in India: A Reality or a Utopia?

— *Vijoy S Sahay*

The term 'syncretism' has often been misinterpreted by scholars of different disciplines in social science, including anthropology. A number of articles could be found in anthropology relating to syncretism that interprets the term as mere borrowing of cultural traits among two or more than two groups; more specifically, between Hindus and Muslims, or Hindus and Christian, or even between tribals and non-tribals, or tribals and Christianity. Such interpretations are gross deviations from the root-meaning of the term. The essential components of syncretism are; first, that it emerges only when two incompatible groups unite together as a front to face a common crisis or a common foe, and secondly, that it is a temporary phenomena. The paper deals with a number of examples of mistakenly suggested syncretistic phenomena put forward by anthropologists, and concludes with this remark that syncretism hardly exists in the daily life and culture of India. It is a myth, a utopia.

In terms of variety of cultural traditions, India is perhaps next only to the continent of Africa that consists of more than fifty nations; and in terms of antiquity, she stands next to none. Very obviously, a nation, which has such a cultural antiquity and diversity; a nation, which became home of most of the ethnicities that entered into India at different periods of its checkered history; a nation, which has been victim of unaccountable number of physical, cultural, and religious onslaughts; a nation, which has been repeatedly ravaged by wars and plunders; a nation which has been ruled by foreign powers for about 800 years, it is but natural that the people of that nation must have borrowed and even assimilated a number of cultural and religious elements from the alien cultures and religions. And in turn, the aliens also who came and settled here, and made India their homes, must have adopted a number of social, cultural, and religious elements of the host people and culture. Anthropologically speaking, borrowing of such cultural traits has been a perennial feature of mankind. Ever since man's appearance on earth, human culture has spread from one place to another through migration and diffusion. And such a borrowing of cultural elements is not a one-way phenomenon; but it is always reciprocal. However, should we call such mutual borrowing and even assimilation of social, cultural, and religious elements of one culture by the other as 'syncretism'? And above all, could syncretism be a perennial phenomenon in any society? I differ.

Without having a peep into the history of India of at least one thousand years, any attempt to understand and discuss 'syncretism in India' would be misnomer; rather, I would call it, futile. Therefore, let's have for a moment, in brief, a peep into the past of the sub-continent. We should also be aware that one could neither deny history, nor could one undo it.

In India, the world religions that flourish today are: Hinduism, Buddhism, Jainism, Sikhism, Islam, Christianity, and Zoroastrian. Out of these, the first four are the products of the Indian soil i.e., Hinduism, Buddhism, Jainism, and Sikhism. The latter three, i.e., Islam, Christianity, and Zoroastrian entered into India at different times and in different phases. However, the followers of the Zoroastrianism are in such a minuscule that they have made little impact on any of the indigenous religions. Moreover, the Parsees, who are the followers of Zoroaster, never ruled over India at any time of Indian history; therefore, their presence also made little impact on the religious life of the country. The everlasting impact on the Indian social, cultural, and religious life has been made by Islam and Christianity. Let's, in brief, examine the advent of these two world religions and of course great civilisations, in India. Both entered into India at different times and phases. This is also very much understandable that both, Islam and Christianity, made everlasting impact on the traditional Indian life and culture, sheer because the followers of both the religions ruled over the country for over 800 years, and proselytized the people by one means or another.

Though the advent of Islam in the Indian sub-continent began with the invasion by the Arabs on Sind in 712 A.D., but the actual Muslim rule in India began several hundred years thereafter. With the establishment of the Slave Dynasty in 1206 that lasted till 1290, the Turko-Afghan Period in India began. Without going into the details of this period, it is sufficient to conclude that the Turko-Afghan Period in India lasted till 1526. In between this period, a number of dynasties, such as, the Khaljis (from c. 1290- 1320 A.D.), the Tughlaks (from 1320- 1414), the Sayyads (from 1414- 1451), and the Lodis (from 1451- 1526), ruled the country. The Battle of Panipat in 1526 between Ibrahim Lodi and Babar laid down the foundation of Moghal dynasty in the sub-continent. The Moghal rule, according to historians, is said to have lasted till the death of Aurangjabe in 1707. Thereafter, the Moghal power weakened. However, by this time, the Europeans, particularly, the Portuguese, the Dutch, the French and the British, had already made inroads into different parts of the country, and there had begun a scramble for power among them. Finally, in this race for supremacy of power, the British proved to be the most tactical, and the Battle of Palassy in 1757 proved for them to be turning point. Lord Clive easily and overnight won the battle without any casualty on his side. Immediately thereafter, the Battle of Buxar in 1764 took place that gave a final blow to the Muslim rule in India; and the solid foundation of British Raj was laid down through the East India Company that finally handed over the reign to the British Crown in 1858, soon after the First War of Independence in 1857. Thereafter, India became a part of the British Empire till independence of the country on 15th of August 1947.

It's true that barring a few exception, such as Mohammad Ghori, Mohammad Ghazani, Ahmad Shah Abdali, and Timur, who came to India just for plunder and loot, and after accomplishing their task of loot and organised massacre, returned to their respective lands with the booty. However, one of the plunderers, Mohammed Ghori, who is said to have invaded India for no less than seventeen times, once appointed his slave Kutub buddin Aibak as the Sultan of Delhi, and thus began to rule the country indirectly; the Muslim rule as such in India thus began.

It is axiomatic that such a long rule by the Muslims in India would bring everlasting impact on Indian society and culture. And this could be observed in many walks of life of an Indian even today. The impact of Islam in India could be seen not only in Indian social life, but it could also be discovered in art and architecture, in literature, in language, in philosophical thoughts, in dress, in food habit, and in many such domains. Unaccountable number of mutual borrowing and even assimilation of social and cultural elements have taken place among the Hindus and Muslims. A Hindu seldom hesitates to visit a Muslim *Dargah* to seek blessings of the holy *Sufi* saint of the *Dargah*, especially when facing physical or mental crises. Perhaps unaccountable number of such *Dargah* could be found in different nooks and corners of the country. A number of Hindu marriage rituals have been adopted in Muslim marriages. A number of Muslim women could be found using vermillion after their marriage on their forehead. On the other hand, a number of Hindu women, and sometimes men also, carrying their infants on their laps could be found standing anxiously in queue, waiting outside a mosque during the period of *Ramzan*, so that the *namazis* i.e., those who observe fast during this holy period, come out of the mosque after evening prayer, and would blow air from their mouth on the head and face of the ailing child. These men and women believe that since such *namazis* live the most pious life during this period, therefore, their blessings would cure the ailing child. Even if the child has been the victim of any black magic or 'bad eye' of any sorcerer, or possessed by any malevolent spirit, such blessings would ward off the spirit; and the child would be cured.

Let us also examine in brief the advent, and the impact of British rule and simultaneous impact of Christianity in India. The advent Christianity in India is even older than the Islam. By tradition, Christianity is said to have arrived in India with St. Thomas in the very first Century, one of the apostles of Jesus Christ, who spent some years in South India and possibly died there. However, others believe that the first missionary to arrive in the country around the same time was St. Bartholomew. Impact of the arrival of both the apostles of the Jesus could be observed even today in the states of Kerala and Tamilnadu.

However, for all practical purposes, Christian missionary activities started in India with the advent of St. Francis Xavier in 1544. He was followed by Portuguese missionaries at first; and eventually by missionaries from other countries like Denmark, Holland, Germany and Great Britain. Throughout the 18th and 19th centuries Catholic as well as Protestant missionaries preached Christian doctrines in India and also made important contributions to social improvement and education in the country. Much of the modern influences in the Indian society can be attributed to the role of Christianity in India. Christian missionaries helped in setting up schools and colleges all over India and also spread the message of their faith and goodwill in the country. Christianity and its teachings also influenced a number of intellectuals and thinkers in India, including Mahatma Gandhi.

In the preceding paragraphs, I have made an attempt to delineate in the briefest possible way the circumstances under which the Muslim and the British rules were established in India. There are a number of dates, a number of personalities, a number of events that have played their respective roles in the shaping of over a thousand year destiny of the Indian sub-continent, which I have deliberately avoided to refer; because those have little relevance with the theme of this paper and the seminar. My sole purpose in the preceding paragraphs is to suggest that during such a long period of Muslim and the British rule, and in the process of proselytisation to Islam and Christianity, it is very natural that mutual borrowing of social and cultural elements between the Hindus on the one hand, and the Muslims and Christians on the other, was inevitable. This is the fact of the history; and as I have earlier said that neither we can deny history, not could we undo it.

One of the significant consequences of the advent of Islam and Christianity in India was the emergence of Urdu language and introduction of English in the Indian soil, respectively. Language is the most effective means and carrier of transmission of cultural elements and behavior. It also serves as one of the most effective tools of cultural diffusion. When, culture-contact between two distinct cultures takes place, borrowing of cultural traits is an inevitable result. Through language, such borrowing of cultural traits between two cultures becomes more expedited, more reciprocal and spontaneous. Let us examine the status of Urdu and the English languages, and their respective roles in transmission of Islamic and European socio-cultural elements in India.

Urdu language is the product of the Indian sub-continent. It is to be noted that Urdu developed under the influence of the Persian and Arabic languages, and both of which have though contributed a significant amount of vocabulary to it; however, it is more important to note that around 99% of Urdu verbs have their roots either in Sanskrit or in *Prakrit* languages. It is the national language and *lingua franca* of Pakistan, and an official language of six states of India. It is also recognised as one of the 22 official languages by the Constitution of India. During the Muslim rule, Persian was the official language. However, after the establishment of the British, it was replaced by Urdu, which was then popularly called Hindustani dialect/language.

With the arrival of the missionaries in India, entire educational system received a turning point. Wherever the missionaries arrived, as their usual practice, they first opened a school there; and thus, English education was introduced in the Indian soil. It made a far reaching impact in the mind as well as life style of both, the Hindus and Muslims alike. It would not be an exaggeration to say that to a great extent, credit goes to English education in the country that our leaders and social reformers of the 19th and 20th centuries learnt the value of freedom, liberty, democratic values etc, of the west that sowed the seeds of national awakening in India. Also, the educated Hindus and Muslims both began to adopt the life style of an English gentleman, their dress, their food habits, and even their mannerism. However, this did not mean that they absolutely quit their own cultural and religious traditions. Despite adopting a number of traits of British culture, a Hindu continued to remain a staunch Hindu, except, if not proselytized; and a Muslim remained a hard core Muslim. Likewise, even during the long period of Muslim rule in India, despite adopting a lot of Islamic cultural tradition, a Hindu then also remained a staunch Hindu, except, if not converted to Islam, either by the force of sword or at his will voluntarily. *It is for this reason I assert that mere adoption of some aspects of life style, or in anthropological term borrowing and even assimilation of some isolated or even complex cultural traits by one culture from a different culture could not be called 'syncretism.'*

Today, 'syncretism' has become a buzzword, even in anthropological discourse. The concept of 'syncretism' has made a complete departure from its root meaning. A particular genre of scholars and intellectuals (including anthropologists) attempt to depict syncretism as a 'value-loaded ideal model' that exists in different places and different facets of society; and as if, it is ubiquitous and perennial feature that exists in Indian society. They even assert that if a Hindu woman or a man visits a *Dargah* in any distress, it is syncretism; if some Hindu marriage rituals are maintained or followed by any Muslim family or a Christian in their marriages, it is syncretism; if a Hindu writes a poem in Urdu, it is syncretism; if a Muslim writes and recites a song in praise of Lord Rama or Krishna or any of the Hindu deity, it is syncretism, and likewise. According to N. K. Das (2003), even 'Cargo Cult' is an example of syncretism. I think it is misnomer to consider such isolated examples of borrowing, or observing, even assimilating and integrating some culture traits of another culture, as syncretism.

The term syncretism emerged in Greece, more particularly in Crete. Greece and Crete were the centers of ancient civilisations. In Greece, Athens and Sparta were city nations. These centers of great civilisations, thereby, were also centers of trade and commerce. People belonging to different ethnicities and from different places and regions lived there; and they all contributed to the growth of the civilisation. However, the following points are to be noted:

1. That the original inhabitants of Greece and Crete considered themselves as nobles.
2. That the non-Greeks and non-Cretans, which lived there, were looked down by the nobles, and were considered as outsiders, uncivilised, savage, etc.
3. War between the city nations was a perennial feature.

Whenever war broke in Crete or any of the city nations, the nobles and all the other ethnicities including the outsiders, united together to face and defended themselves and their city from their common foe as a unified front, who otherwise though remained quite against and opposed to one another. This was considered 'syncretistic' attempt of the Cretans or the Greeks to defend themselves from their foes, and the phenomena was known as 'syncretism.' After the war was over, the contradictions among them surfaced again

Irina A. Levinskaya (1993), a Russian scholar, in her article "Syncretism-Term and Phenomenon", published in Tyndale Bulletin has very succinctly examined the definitions of syncretism furnished by different scholars at different centuries. She observes that in centuries, the term has acquired altogether new connotations, which has made its use very vague. *The Oxford English Dictionary* defines syncretism as 'attempted union or reconciliation of diverse and opposite tenets or practices, esp. in philosophy and religion'. However, according to her, Plutarch was perhaps the first to define syncretism. He very clearly said, syncretism is "to be united like Cretans at the time of danger from outside enemies". Erasmus also supported Plutarch and suggested syncretism as "to come to concord and fight mutual enemies together, despite the differences of opinions".

If we analyze the definitions of syncretism, the common elements that emerge out of it are as follows:

1. That the phenomena of syncretism emerge in times of crises only, whether individual or group crisis, no matter.
2. That it does not become a permanent feature of any society.
3. That it is a compromise between two or even more than two opposite and absolutely contradictory groups, forces, doctrines, religions or religious philosophies, ideologies, customs, traditions, or any material or non-material cultural element at a given time and space.

On the contrary, today, it has acquired a very vague meaning. Some consider it, as I have earlier said a 'value-loaded-and-ideally-desired model' of a society. Such scholars erroneously fail to demarcate the boundary line between 'syncretism' on the one hand, and 'secularism' on the other. Some scholars interpret mere borrowing and assimilation of certain cultural elements by another culture as syncretism, and likewise.

However, if we cling to the root meaning of the term, as earlier explained, syncretism is neither a permanent phenomena, nor spontaneous. Though culture contact, borrowing of cultural traits, and in some cases assimilation of such traits are necessary components in a case of syncretism; however, all cases of borrowing of cultural traits cannot be called syncretism. For example, most Indians today wear pants, shirts, suits, neck ties etc., just like the British or the Europeans do. Could this be called syncretism? Certainly not!

Let's examine Cargo cult also. Cargo cult is merely borrowing of some material and non-material cultural elements by the indigenous Melanesians from the Europeans; such as, European goods manufactured in factories, plus because of the efforts of missionaries some knowledge of the world-view of Christian world. The fact of the matter is that Cargo Cult, instead of being any example of syncretism; ***it is the result of culture contact and manifestation of culture conflict.*** During the days of exploration of the South Seas, the Europeans, who were then at the highest level of technological advancement, came in contact with the indigenous Melanesians, who were at the lowest level of technology. The Melanesians had become so habituated of European goods and liquor that on the one hand they could not afford to abstain from its use; on the other hand they very well realised that they were most disproportionately exploited by the Europeans. This was the cause of their anguish, frustration, and depression. They could not encounter the strength of gun-powdered arms and ammunitions of the Europeans with their primitive bows, arrows, and spears. In helplessness, they psychologically reacted very often, as if to break the shackles of their subjugation by the Europeans. At such moments, one of their shamans assumed the role of a Messiah and announced that the 'dooms day' had arrived; the earth will be soon inundated with flood, therefore, there was no need to protect the gardens; they destroyed all their gardens, and killed all their pigs; they believed that there would be a new beginning; and in that beginning, they would become very prosperous; the blacks will become white and the whites will become black. They also believed the goods that they obtained from the Europeans were, in fact, sent by their ancestors from heaven, but the shrewd Europeans intercepted them mid-way and same goods they supplied to them at higher costs. Thus, they were outrageously exploited by the Europeans. The Europeans first considered such occurrences as uprisings against them, hence suppressed such movements by force.

In anthropology, such phenomena are to be found in plenty, especially in tribal societies, who live comparatively at low technological level. Whenever they encounter with any society of higher technological level, despite mutual borrowing of certain cultural elements, a feeling of being exploited by the technologically higher society gradually develops among them that often take the shape of psychological depression in the group. They know that they cannot physically overthrow the superior power. Such helplessness and anger in them sometimes make the entire group psychologically depressed. At such a juncture, they find a Messiah in their shaman, who attempts to unite and revitalize the group, sometimes even by reviving obsolete customs and traditions of the tribe. A number of tribal movements during the British Raj in India, such as that of Birsa Munda movement, Jatra Bhagat's *Tana* Movement, Siddhu Kanu's movement, and yet another movement launched by the Orans of Chotanagpur under the leadership of Bhikh Ram Bhagat, during mid-1960s for the revival of '*Dhumkuria*' i.e., youth dormitory in the present state of Jharkhand are the examples of such phenomena. But how could such a phenomenon be called syncretistic? *Such phenomena in anthropology are called 'revitalisation movements' or a 'revival movements'; and not syncretism.*

I have earlier referred to the so called syncretism to be found in art and architecture, in literature, in language, in philosophical thoughts, in dress, in food habit, and in many such domains. We can also add one more type of such syncretism today; it is 'political syncretism' in India. Very often two political parties totally opposed to each other in political ideologies and practice have been often found united as a front to defeat their political foe. And after the task of winning the election, they again clash because of opposite political doctrines; and within a very short time split into pieces. After independence, Indian politics has witnessed such political syncretism a number of times, and that is one good reason of the 'criminalisation of politics' and 'political bankruptcy' of the country today.

Nevertheless, with certain reservations, I agree that syncretism does exist. I also agree that 'syncretism' is a value loaded term. Syncretistic values are very much desirable also. To recognize, accept, and follow the ideals, and good religious thoughts and practices, even if they are of alien people and culture, is very much desirable. After all, every religion preaches us to be humane. There have been individuals, who can be said to have epitomized in them the syncretistic values during their life time, for example, Kabir, Guru Nanak, Rahim, Mullick Mohammad Jaisi, Raskhan, Dara Shikoh, and many others in the past. In recent time also Sufi singers Hussain Brothers, Shabina Abid, Kunwar Javed, Munnawar Rana, etc, are such individuals, who are true examples of the carriers of syncretistic values. However, to assume that society as whole becomes all time syncretistic is, I would say, an unreality. Because society is not guided by the values of any individual, but every individual has his own value by which he is guided, every ethnic group, religion, philosophy, doctrine has its own value. It is but natural that in such a multiplicity of values in a pluralistic society like India, there would be clash of values between individuals and groups both, especially, those diametrically opposed and contradictory to each other in many respects. May be in times of crisis, the individuals or the groups forget their contradictions for some time, and face the crises individually or unitedly. But it only remains for some moments only. No sooner than the crisis is over, the contradictions again raise its head, and the conflict surfaces. This is what has happened in India for over a thousand year; and this is what has been happening even today. Indian society is though pluralistic, but had there been 'Syncretism in India' a permanent feature, the 'Common Civil Code' would have long been passed by both the houses of Parliament and made constitutional. Therefore, Syncretism in India, as a permanent feature and an ideal model, is, not a reality but a utopia, as good as the utopia of *Ram Rajya* of Mahatma Gandhi.

Note: The paper presented as B. N. Saraswati Memorial Lecture at Guwahati in November 2015 in the National Seminar organised by SANSKRITI- North Eastern Institute of Cultural Research (NEICR), Guwahati.

References

Das, N. K. (2003). *Culture, Religion, and Philosophy: Critical Studies in Syncretism and Inter-faith Harmony* (eds.), Rawat Publications, Jaipur

Levinskaya, I.A. (1993). 'Syncretism-The Term and Phenomenon' in *Tyndale Bulletin* 44 (1): 117-128

Rizvi, S. A. A. (2005) The Wonder That Was India, Vol. 2: *A Survey of the History and Culture of the Indian Subcontinent from the Coming of the Muslims to the British*, Pan Macmillan, New Delhi

4

Syncretism among the Muslims of Darjeeling Himalaya

— *Rajib Chatterjee*

(I)

Theologically or textually Islam as a religion is non syncretic. Its beliefs and practices are completely divinely revealed. It does not stand in need of any borrowing from other faiths but the ground reality is totally different from the text. The popular Islam practiced by Indian Muslims in diverse regions of the country may be described as a product of indigenisation. Islam in Darjeeling Himalaya is the 'contextualised' or 'localised' form of Islam. Here Islam has been confronted with well integrated indigenous societies, but it accommodates itself to the realities of the cultural reciprocity of the popular hill society. They are borrowing and striking parallels with local hill customs and traditions. Thus, syncretistic beliefs and practices have manifested themselves in different ways and forms among themselves without affecting the basic principles of Islam. They do not see anything wrong in mixing some beliefs and practices with those of the coreligionists of Hindu and Buddhist traditions. Being a Muslim does not prevent them from seeking assistance from gods and goddesses of other traditions.

Islam has a distinct presence in the Himalayas particularly in the Himalayan region of Darjeeling hills and the blending of diverse religious systems is an example of syncretism here. People of the region would not think it unusual to offer worship to their coreligionists. Since historical periods Muslims are actively interact with other segments of the greater hill society rather than presenting themselves as a minority. Their existence is noticed at various levels in the society though their numerical strength is low. Their peculiarities in cultural tradition never make barrier in relationship and thus remain an integral part of the greater society, which has become a cultural mosaic. The social and cultural life of the Muslims in the poly-ethnic environment of Himalayas shows a very distinctive character as it bears both the Islamic great tradition as well as the local or little traditions (Mondal 1997; 2000; 2001). The formation of the Muslim population in Darjeeling hills is the result of historical process and the majority of Muslims consists of second and third generation migrants from the plains. The region has an inadequate history of Muslims and was exposed to the outer world only after the annexation of the tract by the British East India Company during middle of the nineteenth century. The history reveals the fact that the development of Darjeeling town as a sanatorium and health resort by the colonial administers during 1835 to 1850 attracted many Muslim marginal communities to migrate here to serve the increasing urban necessities of the dwellers. Among them most non familial male individuals settled permanently after marriage with the native girls and some settled with their families gradually in later.

There is a popular myth regarding the origin of the Muslim habitation in Darjeeling town. The Muslim inhabitants of the town believed that they are decedents of the Muslim invaders to Tibet during the early sultanate and Mughal regime. But this above said story has no authentic historical evidences. The migratory history of the Muslims in Darjeeling town only can traceable from the colonial periods and we can only speculate that the political intrusion of Mirju-Mullah and Hussain Shah into the terai and dooars region might brought some Muslim subedars, faujdars, lascars, officials, intellectuals, artisans and other occupational groups to migrate the hill regions of present day Darjeeling district (Mondal 1997). In the colonial past, Muslims were viewed as the most necessary group in an urban life as of their specialised services. They were considered as a part and parcel of the urban social life. Muslim communities of Darjeeling are all from various occupational categories. Their genealogical diagrams authenticate the fact. As a gradually developed urban centre during the colonial era, the town Darjeeling along needs a large number of special services. To fill this shortage, a large number of various skilled and semi skilled occupational groups were encouraged to migrate. Their migration was beneficial to both. It allows the Muslims to accommodate a major centre of European interests in one hand and systematic expansion of their trade and business network on the other. The rich cultural traditions of the Muslims are also accommodate within the greater hill society and the Muslims became a dynamic and efficient minority of the hills.

(II)

Muslims in Darjeeling town are of diverse caste and ethnic backgrounds. The interaction within community often plays a vital role in contributing the overall integration towards the greater society or the habitat. Stratification within community or sects and sub sects often creates barrier in collective unity. Notwithstanding as a distinct religious group they interact with each other through the common bond Islamic brotherhood. Religious organisations, mosques and Anjuman-E-Islamia have a good role in integration of diverse Muslim groups nevertheless a distinct community identity is being maintained through the little traditions exclusive for them.

On the question of assimilation, a plurality of Darjeeling Muslims believe that Muslims should adopt the customs and ways of life of the hills, though a significant minority thinks they should try to remain distinct. Muslim population in Darjeeling Himalaya is ethnically and linguistically diverse. There are various groups within them. Some were come much earlier in comparison to other group and their inclination towards the wider integration is much more noticed in their life ways activities. The new comers are always struggling to find a balance between two different cultural traditions. The Muslims born and brought up in Darjeeling Himalaya particularly the early migrant families are assimilating fully with the hill life. Majority of the early migrant families have and had marital alliance with the native Nepali families as they believe that there is nothing significant wrong with interfaith marriages.

Due to close association with the hill society and culture, the Muslims share many cultural traits of their neighbours. The Muslim society and culture of Darjeeling hills has been shaped by the interacting forces of several set of traditions viz. Islamic, Nepali caste and tribe, Tibetan and etc. which led to propagate a meaningful coexistence of Muslims and non Muslims in the town. The major concentrations of the Muslims in Darjeeling are in butcher basti which is a multi ethnic in character. Nepalis and Bhutias are the next door neighbours presently. Though they are different in religious faith, yet the participation of Muslims in their socio-religious programme and vice versa are very usual. Marriage alliance is often occurred. Some members of these non Muslim families recent past embraced Islam. But communal harmony never breaks in their locality for the occurrences. This harmonial coexistence has often enriched the secular environment which helped the Muslims in adaptation to the social environment of their habitat.

Muslims are not much different from their ethnic Nepali and Tibetan or Bhutia neighbours in respect to language, food, dress pattern, occupation, material culture, family organisation, habits and customs. Their morphological similarities often made other confused in physical identification. Due to constant mixing and breeding with the ethnic Nepalis, these paharia Muslims are almost identical with their non Muslim neighbours. Any one can't distinguish the Tibetan Buddhists and Tibetan Muslims in respect to language, food, traditions, habits and customs. Even the Muslims often observe the major festivals of popular hill culture. Except some basic principles of Islam, the life cycle rituals have a great similarity with the Nepalis and Bhutias. Many Muslim families respect the local deities and pay devotional respect along with their next door Nepali neighbours. Due to this close association with the dominant hill culture, the Muslims in Darjeeling hills are gradually inclined towards the popular local traditions.

Majority of the Muslims in Darjeeling town are self employed and hereditary occupation. They are either in their traditional occupation or engaged in small business entrepreneurship. Still there are some sections in which Muslims are dominated or rather expert since colonial times. Examples from Muslim occupational groups (Kureshi or butcher, Mansuri or dhunia, Dorji or tailor etc.) may authenticate the fact. Peoples are exclusively dependent over them for their particular services and they have a monopolistic control over this occupation. Say for example, the supply of meat (beef and goat) to the town is circulated by the *kureshi* brethren since the British time and this tradition is still maintained by this Muslim group. Muslims are expert in skilled or semi-skilled works like mechanical works, masonry work, colouring, plumbing, repairing etc.

A large number of services are rendered exclusively by the Muslims in the town. Mechanical and semi mechanical works are largely monopolised by the Muslim occupations. Substantial numbers are engaged in food production and supply. Several specialised items of beautification and ornaments are manufactured or sold by some Muslim occupations. Their pioneering knowledge and experience in bakery and confectionary industry by some Muslim families placed the town Darjeeling in a place of excellence. They are considered experts in such job.

Muslims of the town are integrated greatly to the society by the very necessity of their services. Very often their specialised services are required to maintain the daily life way activities. From the very formation of the town, a particular Muslim occupational category or rather say birathari is being supplying the regular meat and fish to the town dwellers. Since colonial past meat and fish trade is being maintained by them. Meat is almost a regular item in the daily menu of the hill people irrespective of their caste and creed. Beef is edible to all of them except of some Nepali upper castes. Since colonial times, Kureshi families are exclusively the seller of beef and goat. A slaughter house was established by the Darjeeling Municipality after 1850 for regular slaughter of cow and goat. A formal fish market was also established in the year 1936. All the labours and beef sellers are from kureshi family who migrated much earlier and integrated with the local culture by establishing marital alliance with Nepali girls. These Muslims later formed a separate cultural identity within their own social group. And the families later treated as a son of the soil by their ethnic neighbours and gradually established their right over their habitation. Thus these Muslim families act as stabilizer in conflict minimisation of the resource utilisation between two creeds.

Bakery industry of the town is also maintained by the Muslims since colonial past. During the developing phase of this town, the British administrators encouraged Muslims to established bakery as they are skilled in such industry. H S Guramia was the first Muslim man who started a bakery at the town though the famous European bakery shop Glanery's was established much earlier but the confectionary items was manufactured and supplied by small Muslim bakery owners. And during the Christmas, these small bakery owners and suppliers circulated printed pamphlets to the dwellers as advertisement. Gradually, bakery products are preferred other that Europeans and now cake, biscuit, pastry and bakery bread is almost a regular dietary item of the Darjeeling town people. Almost all the confectionary shops are owned by Muslims. The famous shop Walis has their own bakery. And the other small bakery owners are all Muslims. The Muslim association with this particular industry later encouraged many non Muslims to open shops for selling confectionary and bakery products which ultimately an opportunity of self employment to the hill people. This is a typical example of building trade entrepreneurship which authenticates the necessity of Muslim occupations.

The fruit trade of the town was previously in the hand of Muslims exclusively. But after partition the trade was transferred in the hand of Nepalis. But this fruit trade of the Muslims opened an opportunity to the other hill people a method of self employment. Darjeeling is a land of orange and presently orange trade is an important business of the Nepalis during the winter times.

A hill dweller must have the need of a man who knows the technique of repairing utensils of their daily life. The most striking features of the Darjeeling Muslim occupation is that a relatively high share of the Muslims of the town are engaged in the activity of repairing utensils though a bulk of them are not the permanent settler of Darjeeling. Yet they are continuing their services. The repairing shops at chackbazar and old bus stand area are all owned by Muslims. Their services have a great need to the people of the town. All the spectacles shops are also owned by Muslims. Watch repairing shops at the two sides of chackbazar are all owned by Muslims. But these families are not a domiciled permanently at the town though some of these families are being here since colonial times. They served the town from two to three generations.

Garments industry is also monopolised by the Muslim tailors. The regular dress requirements are fulfilled by the Muslim tailors as Muslims are skilled in tailoring cloths since colonial past. Some emotions are wrapped in peoples mind regarding tailoring. Families of some famous tailor masters even now maintaining their traditions and keep supplying the garments as per required. The most tailoring shops are at Daroga bazar region and Muslim tailors from

Bihar and UP are employed as tailor masters. These shops are all owned by Muslim families domiciled permanently at Darjeeling.

Muslims have a great role in tourism industry of Darjeeling. Tourism has long been viewed as a tool for economic development not only for the people but also for the region or locality. As one of the most important hill station of the country, Darjeeling has always been attracted by the tourists from within and without India. Hotels owned by Tibetan Muslims and curio shops owned by both Tibetan and kashmiri Muslims influenced a lot in developing tourism in Darjeeling town. The famous Habib Mallik shop at Darjeeling mall attracted a bulk of European and American tourists to visit Darjeeling. Darjeeling and Habib Mallik's shop almost synonymous to them. The major tourist's attractions are all covered by the chain of curio shops. Foreign tourists are really fond of Tibetan art and culture objects, James, jewelry and precious stones. And Darjeeling curio shops are very famous for these objects. Hence, directly Muslims has a major role in the tourism industry of Darjeeling. And the economy of the town is also primarily dependent on tourism. The tourists seasons are the only peak season of selling garments and commodities. Because there is no other alternative way of acquiring money as there is any other industry except tea.

(III)

Darjeeling Himalayan town is a blend of diverse ethnic and cultural elements. Integration between diverse groups would never be possible without the spirit of socio-cultural accommodation between such diverse communities which ultimately helped them to live together in harmoniously under harsh environmental condition of the mountain. The people of Himalayan region are an amalgamation of animism, lamaist Buddhism, Hinduism and Islam (Dastidar 1995 & 2010; Siddiqui 1991). And Darjeeling has no exception to this. As a matter of this social-cultural amalgamation, the Muslims of the town exhibit a unique cultural matrix which reflected at the various levels of their cultural practices. There have been diverse perceptions of social relations in the context of inter-ethnic or inter-religious interaction in Darjeeling town. Some may perceive this situation as the face of tension and conflict, while the others believe it as the process of assimilation or integration. The most important manifestation of intercommunity and inter-religious interaction is the attribute of syncretism which is an old social fact among the Muslims living in Darjeeling town. It refers to the hybridisation of two or more cultural or religious traditions over time. It's a result of acculturation or culture contact. It is a social mechanism to create protective defense around communities in a place and also incorporate the ideas and behaviours from different societies living around them. Members of different communities like Bhutias, Sherpas, Marwaris, Bhojpuris, Lepchas etc. frequently participate the festivals of the Muslims with joy.

The Muslim society of the town is habituated with the customs and traditions of Nepalis. They have adapted themselves gradually to the dominant social environment of their habitat. Nepali is a common lingua franca of all the communities residing in the Darjeeling hills. Muslims also acquired Nepali as a medium of communication. Even a majority of them talked in Nepali at their home. Though there is no significant leadership among the Muslims, nevertheless the participation of Muslims in the present political matter of separate statehood as a consensus citizen of hills is very remarkable. They believe that the ultimate demand of state will not fulfill the development aspiration of the Muslims as a backward community. But irrespective of this they firmly support the demand of a separate as because of their integration or inclination towards the dominant hill community. Muslims raised separate wings along with other minority community of the town to strongly support the state hood demand of Gorkha Jana Mukti Morcha. They closed their shops and business along with their coreligionists as a symbol of demonstration. The unique situation of this communal harmony is thereby differing from other places of India which enriched the secular environment in polity and society of Darjeeling Himalaya.

Being one of the major centres of European interest during the colonial days, Darjeeling encouraged a good number Muslims to migrate from various parts of inside and outside India whose specialised services had an urgent necessity to the urban dwellers of Darjeeling town. Within a couple of years of the development of the town Muslims were considered as an integral part of the larger urban complex of the Darjeeling Hill society. Even today, quite a number of services rendered to the dwellers are mainly by the Muslim groups. The presence of a Dhunia (cotton carder), baker, watch repair and very often of a butcher is a necessity of the every days life of the town. The tailors of daroga bazaar, bakery shop at chowck bazaar, utensils repairing shops, fish market etc., have all largely been occupied by the diverse Muslim groups though considerable changes have recently occurred which affecting the virtual monopoly of the Muslims in these occupations. The functions of a few Muslim groups like the Tibetan Muslims and Kashmiri Muslims deserve special consideration as their traditional occupations of curio, Hotel and handicrafts trade linked the development of tourism industry of Darjeeling.

The Muslims of Darjeeling as because of their diverse traditional occupations and ethnic backgrounds exhibits a mosaic of diverse cultural traditions of both Islamic and local traditions where to some extend local influences are strong. Local culture or traditions have effects a great in their food habit and other social and cultural practices of birth, marriage and death rituals which are considered to some extent against the text though the primary or basic rituals are identical with the greater Muslim ummah. The cordial relationship with neighbouring hill communities helped the subsequent generations of the Darjeeling Muslims adjust better with their habitat in contemporary times but varies across the Muslim communities living permanently in Darjeeling town. Due to the enculturation across their physical and social background, the children of some Muslim group have the larger scope of adjustment which is reflected in their cultural life like wearing or offering khada in all social or cultural ceremonies, preparation of typical hill food items of momo and thukpa.

Despite the religious and ethnic differences with the ethnic Nepalis and other hill dwellers, a sense of belonging and functional interdependence has emerged due to acculturation and vice versa. The Muslim are now habituated with the customs and traditions of the dominant Nepalis and other hill communities. Even the Nepali is considered as mother tongue to some Muslim families exclusively in case of Nepali Muslims and in many Muslim occasions or festivals a functional interdependence between Hindu-Buddhist-Christian ethnic groups and Muslims are seen which is an example of social-cultural integration.

References

Dastider, Mollica. (1995). *Religious Minorities in Nepal: An Analysis of the State of the Buddhists and Muslims in the Himalayan Kingdom*. New Delhi: Nirala Publication.

Dastider, Mollica. (2010). *Understanding Nepal: Muslims in a Plural Society*. New Delhi: Har-anand Publications Pvt. Ltd.

Mondal, Sekh.Rahim. (1997). Muslims of Siliguri: Aspects of Their Society, Culture and Relationship with the Metropolis. New Delhi: Institute of Objective Studies.

Mondal, Sekh.Rahim. (2000). "Muslims of Sikkim" in *Islam and the Modern Age*, Vol. XXXI No.1. Jamia Millia Islamia. New Delhi. pp. 101-116

Mondal, Sekh Rahim. (2001). "Tibetan Muslim Refugees in India: The Problem and the Prospects" in S.C.Roy (ed.) *Refugees and Human Rights*. Jaipur: Rawat Publications. pp. 236-255.

Mondal, Sekh Rahim. (2001). "The Muslim Minority in the Buddhist Kingdom of Bhutan: A Socio-cultural Perspective" *in Islam and the Modern Age*, Vol. XXXII. No. 2. Jamia Millia Islamia. New Delhi. pp. 113-125.

Siddiqui, Ataullah. (1991). "Muslims of Tibet," in *Tibet Journal*, Vol. 16. No. 4. pp. 71-85.

5

Hindu Symbolism in Rahim's Poetry

— *Ravi Khangai*

Introduction

Medieval Bhakti movement had provided a platform for the process of acculturation. It represents a liberal face of Hinduism and thus it opens its doors to all including Muslims. Akbar's liberal rule (1556-1605 A.D.) also facilitated the growth of syncretism. Disillusioned with orthodox Islam and perhaps hoping to bring about religious unity within his empire, Akbar promulgated Din-i-Ilahi, a creed derived from Islam, Hinduism, Zoroastrianism, and Christianity.

The poet Rahim, (A.D.1556-1627) whose work is a subject of this paper was a member of Royal family. His biological father was Bairam Khan, who was regent to young Akbar. But later on differences developed between them and Bairam Khan revolted against Akbar. His revolt was crushed, but taking into consideration his earlier service Akbar spared his life and asked him to proceed to Macca. On the way towards Macca, Bairam Khan was murdered in Gujrat by Afghan Mubrak Khan, who had some earlier grievances to settle.

Rahim was very young when his father was murdered. Akbar married the widow of Bairam Khan(Step mother of Rahim) and brought up Rahim as his own son. Due his talentand hard work Rahim reached high position in the Mughal court. After the death of Akbar in A.D. 1605, Rahim had to put up with discomfort as he was not trusted by Jahangir (Mishra 2010:14).

The liberal sprit of Akbar's time is reflected in Rahim's poetry. His compositions give an indication that he is well versed in the Hindu mythology like he says,

"Bhaj Narhari Narayan, Taji Bakwad

Pragati Khamb te Rakhyo, Jin Prahalad" (Prakash 7)

(Worship Narhari Narayana and do not waste your time in useless talks Narayan had emerged from the pillar and protected Prahalad)

This refers to the story form Bhagavad Purana, when God Vishnu appears from the pillar to save his devotee Prahalada from his own father Hiranykashpu. (*Srimad Bhagavat Mahapurana*, Book VII)

Among the Hindus there is a belief '*Sarva Bhuteshu Bhagavant'* (God exists in each and everything). Same sentiments are echoed by Rahim when he says,

"Rahiman Yahi Sansaar Me, Sab So Miliye Dhai,

Na Jane Kehi Rup Me, Narayan Mili Jayi" (Prakash 10)

(Rahim says that one should not disregard anyone, as we are not sure in which form we may find Narayana)

Narayana is one of the important trinity of the Hindu Gods. Concept of *Allaha* in the Quran is that he is a separate entity than his worshippers, sitting in the high heaven, rewarding and punishing the people for their deeds. The God being present in each and everything is a belief in the Indian religious tradition. The *Advita*School believes that there is only one soul, which is present in each and everything.

"*Adirup ki Param Duti, Ghat Ghat Rahi Samai*" (Prakash 22)

(The God is present in each and everything.)

Advita reflect at number of places in Rahim's compositions, like he says,

"Rahiman Gali Hai Sankari, Dujo Na Thaharai

Ap Hai To Hari Nahi, Hari Hai to Ap Nahi" (Prakash 44)

(The way towards divine is narrow, two people can not pass through it. If you remain aware of your individual separate existence, you will not find Hari and if You get Hari, you will loose your separate existence)

Rahim's thorough knowledge about the Hindu mythology is obvious as he says,

"Man Sahit Vish Khayke, Sambhu Bhaye Jagdish

*Bina Man Amrit Piye, Rahu Katayo Sis" (*Prakash 11).

(Shambhu, the God Shiva became the savior of the world by drinking the poison with honour Demon Rahu drank ambrosia without honour i.e. invitation and got his head cut)

This is mythological story of churning of sea. When the poison named *Halahala* came out as a result of the churning and the world was about to be destroyed, Shiva came forward and drank the poison to save the world. The demon named Rahu tried to secretly drink the ambrosia which was meant for the Gods, his head was cut by Vishnu (Pandeya 85).

Rahim also simplifies the *Karmayoga* of the Gita as he says,

"Nij Kar Kriya Rahim Kahi, Sudhi Bhavi Ke Hath

Pase Apne Hath Me, Dav Na Apne Hath" (Prakash 12).

(O Rahim, do your work, the result is in the hands of destiny

We have only the dice in our hands, but how they fall is not in our hands)

The divinity can not be explained, says the Indian tradition. Echoing the same sentiments, Rahim says,

"Rahiman Bat Agaymaki,Kahan Sunan Ki Nahi

Jai Janat Te Kahat Nahi, Kahat Te Janat Nahi" (Prakash 19).

(O Rahim, the divinity can not be explained, nor it can be heard, people who knows it do not speak and who speak do not know)

Rahim was well versed with the *Mahâbhârata* and he uses the episodes from the epic to draw the moral lesson.

"Samay Par Oche Bachan, Sab ke Sahe Rahim

Sabha Dushasan Pat Gahe, Gada Liye Rahe Bhim" (Prakash 23).

When the situation is against you, one has to put up with the insulting words, In the assembly hall, Dushasana was misbehaving and mighty Bhima with his club could not do anything. Similarly, when faced with the adverse situation the Pandavas had to live under disguise and Nala, the king had to become a charioteer. (Prakash 31)

The belief that everything is predetermined is explained by Rahim by giving an example from the epic. He says mighty Bhima had to cook food in the kitchen. (Prakash p.60) This is reference to the *Virata Parva* in the Mahâbhârata when the Pandavas had to spent a year incognito.

He also says that if a person is truly great, he do not mind of being called small. Krishna though he was *Giridhar* (He had lifted the mountain), will not mind of being called *Murlidhar* (The holder of the flute) (Mishra 19).

While expressing the intensity of love also he uses the symbolism drawn from the Hindu mythology.

"Kaha Karo Vaikuntha Le, Kalp Vriksha Ki Chah

Rahiman Dakh Suhavano, Gal Pritam Ki Bah" (Prakash 29)

O Rahim what you will do of *Vaikuntha*[1] and shade of *Kalpvriksha*[2].

If the arms of the beloved are around me, the *Dakh*tree is also pleasant.

Indian religious traditions have a remarkable influence of the philosophy of renunciation. Buddha also said that it is the desire which is the main cause of misery. Rahim says,

"Chah Gai Chinta Miti Mauva Beparvaha,

Jinko Kachu Na Chahiye, Ve Sahan Ke Sah" (Mishra 19)

(Your mind will become free, if you discard desires and you will be without worries. People who do not want anything, they are the king of the kings.)

The humility and surrender to the supreme that we find in the Bhakti is also reflected in Rahim's poetry. Making reference to the Ramayana, he says that Rama had emancipated a woman of stone (Ahilaya), Monkeys and lower caste like Guha. Accepting humility he says that as if all these three were part of his body (Prakash 31).

Rahim feels piety that the human being do not cherish Ram in their heart, but remain engrossed in pleasure. (Prakash 32)

Indian tradition also believed that everything is predetermined and one cannot change what is destined. Neither we know about what is going to happen. Had Rama knew that what is likely to happen probably he would have never gone behind the deer, nor Sita would have been kidnapped. (Prakash 47).

Madhura Bhakti, where the God is considered as a lover and devotee as beloved forms a very prominent part of the Medieval Bhakti literature. In Krishna Bhakti, many times the individual soul is allegorised as Radha and the divine soul is allegorised as Krishna. The desire of a devotee to meet God is mentioned as strong desire of beloved to meet the lover. Rahim portrays Radha as telling her friend that she repeatedly raises her hills to look at the door to see if Krishna had come. Though Krishna had promised her that he will come in Mansoon, he did not come and her soul is in pain. (Prakash 56)

Radha's pinning for Krishna is described in her own words,

"Jab Te Bichare Mohan, Bhukh Na Pyas

Beri Beri Bhadhat Avat, Bade Usas" (Prakash 106).

(Since the time Mohan had gone away from me, I am filling neither hunger nor thirst I am repeatedly sighing for him)

Many times the superstitious in Bhakti is carried too far. For example,

"Rahiman Dhokhe Bhav Se, Mukh Se Nikle Ram

Pavan Puran Param Gati, Kamadik Ko Dham" (Prakash 58)

(Even if the word Ram is uttered by mistake

The Person even if he is addicted to sensual pleasure will be liberated)

Though belonging to nobility, Rahim had an empathy for the downtrodden and this is reflected in his poetry as he says the truly great people are those who work for the welfare of the poor and he gives an example of Krishna who helped his friend Sudama. (Prakash p.67) It is said about Rahim that he himself was a great donor and used to spend lot of money on donation (Mishra 2010: 42-43).

Expecting something from someone makes you small. To explain this also he gives and example from the Puranic story of the *Vamana* (the dwarf) incarnation of Vishnu and says that the God Narayana had to become small in order to demand something from the king Bali (Prakash 70).

With mind devoted and filled with the divine, Rahim sees divinity in every act. Like he says an elephant throws soil on his own head because he is searching for the soil which was touched by Rama's feet and emancipated Ahilya. (Prakash 73)

The people who embark on the spiritual path are sometimes filled with the doubt. Rahim says if he speaks truth, he will not be successful in the world and if he tells lies he will not get the God (Prakash 74).

Rahim's thorough awareness about the Hindu mythology is obvious at many places as he makes reference to the Purnic story of king Shibi, who gave his own flesh to save the pigeon and the sage Dadhichi gave his bones to make weapon for God Indra (Prakash 116).

Conclusion

The interaction between the Hindus and Muslims forms an important feature of the medieval India. However this process of mutual enrichment did not achieve a significant proportion and remained a very weak link across the two communities. But nevertheless it does give hope to the word torn apart by the hatred and violence. Acceptance of the different viewpoint is one of the hallmarks of the Indian society which is personified in people like Rahim and Kabir.

Explanatory Notes

1. *Vaikuntha*- Supposed to be an abode of God Vishnu, where *Vaishnavas*, the devotees of Vishnu aspire to go.
2. *Kalpvriksha*- A mythical tree which is supposed to fulfill all wishes.

References

1. Gosawami C.L. & Shastri M.A., '*Srimad Bhagavad Mahapurana*, Part-I' Gita Press, Gorakhpur, 2008.
2. Mishra V. & Rajnish G., '*Rahim, Granthavali*', (Hindi) Vani Prakashna, N. Delhi, 2010.

3. Pandeya R.S. '*Mahabharata, Pratham Khand*'(Hindi), Gita Press, Gorakhpur.
4. Prakash P., '*Rahim Ke Lokpriya Dohe*', (Hindi) Manoj Pocket Books, Buradi, Delhi. (YEAR?)

6

Religious Syncretism among the Meiteis of Manipur

— *Naorem Naokhomba Singh*

Introduction

The term syncretism was originally used by Plutarch for 'fusion of religious cults' which occurred in the Graeco-Roman world, 300BC-200BC (Das, N.K. 2003, 15). It is derived from the two Greek words; syn meaning 'with' and krasis- 'mixture' which means the mixing together of two or more elements. The Oxford English Dictionary defines syncretism as attempted union or reconciliation of diverse and opposite tenets or practices, especially in Philosophy and religion. Encyclopaedia of Social and Cultural Anthropology defines it as hybridisation or amalgamation of two or more cultural traditions. Thus, syncretism is blending of ideas and practices, by means of which either one set adopts more or less thoroughly the principles of another or both are amalgamated in a more pluralistic shape.

Religion is one of the most important aspect of culture. It is generally understood as a system of beliefs in something which we the humans consider to be beyond ourselves and which binds us together as to organise our lives into some kind of group or community. It is indeed one of the most significant attribute of culture as well as one of the most studied area in many disciplines. Different scholars from various disciplines give different definitions of religion. Frazer (1890) defined religion as a propitiation or conciliation of powers superior to man which are believed to direct and control the course of nature and human life. Emile Durkheim (1915) defined it as a unified system of belief and practices relative to sacred things. Paul Radin (1957) defined religion in two parts, the first an easily definable, if not precisely specific feeling; and the second includes certain acts, customs, beliefs and conceptions associated with this feeling. For E.B.Tylor (1958) religion is the belief in spiritual beings. Yinger (1970) define it as a system of beliefs and practices by means of which a group of people struggles with the ultimate problems of human life. Clifford Geertz (1973) defined religion as a system of symbols. It is an organised system of beliefs, attitudes, emotions, behaviour and a set of beliefs concerning the cause, nature and purpose of the universe.

Materials and Methods

The present study is based on the data from an Anthropological fieldwork conducted among the Meiteis of Manipur. Primary data collection was done with the help of observation, interviews and case study methods. Observation, both participant and non-participant had been use to collect data on various rituals and festivals. Interviews were conducted with the help of schedule with *Maibas* (priest), *Maibis* (priestess) and local peoples who have a good knowledge about Meitei religion and life cycle rituals. Necessary aids have been taken for secondary data collection from the earlier monographs, books, journals, ancient Meitei texts and chronicles.

LAND AND PEOPLE

Study Area and Community

Manipur is situated at the North-eastern corner of the Indian sub-continent. It is one of the seven (eight, including Sikkim) north-eastern states commonly known as seven sister states of Indian union. The state lies between the $93^{0}03^{/}$ to $94^{0}78^{/}$ east longitudes and $23^{0}83^{/}$ to $25^{0}68^{/}$ north latitude covering a geographical area of 22,327 square kilometres. The state is bound by Myanmar (Burma) in the east, Nagaland in the north, Assam in the west and Mizoram in the south. Geographically the state can be divided into two; the oval shaped valley at the centre and its surrounding parallel hill ranges. The surrounding hill ranges constitutes more than 90 per cent (3/4th) of the total geographical area of the state. The oval shaped valley in the centre is of approximately 2000 square kilometres. This is the area where the Meiteis inhabit predominantly.

According to census 2011 data the total population of the state is 25,70,390 out of which 12,90,171 are male and 12,80,219 are females. Sex ratio of the state is 992. 67.5 per cent of the total population lives in the rural areas and 32.5 per cent is of urban population. Literacy rate of the state is 79.21 per cent in which 86.06 per cent is of male and 71.73 per cent is of female population. Population density of the state is 115 persons per square kilometres. Out of nine districts Imphal west being the state capital has the highest population density (998 per sq.km) and Tamenglong has the least population density

(32 per sq.km). The state has nine districts out of which four districts belong to the valley and 5 to the surrounding hills. They are; Imphal east, Imphal west, Thoubal, Bishnupur, Chandel, Tamenglong, Churachandpur, Ukhrul and Senapati district. Manipur observes a moderate climate. Summer prevails from the month of March to May. Monsoons arrive in the month of June and extend the rainy season up to September. The state receives an average annual rainfall of 1467.5 mm. The winter season extends from December to February. The maximum temperature during summer is recorded up to 32^{0}C while in the winter season the temperature often falls below 5^{0}C and sometimes up to 0^{0}C.

The history of the Meitei people goes back to a very early stage despite the fact that its recorded history came to existence at much later phase. Manipur was inhabited since Stone Age which has wide cultural affinity in Asia, particularly with the Stone Age cultures of south-east Asia (O. K. Singh 1988, 69). The recorded history of Manipur begins from the second quarter of the first century of Christian era when Pakhangba became the king of Meiteis (Manikchand, 1988, 49). The state was an ancient sovereign civilisation ruled by independent rulers (clan leaders) in their respective areas. This kingdom (Manipur) had been known to different nations of that period and they had trade relations between them as well. It had trade relations with the countries like Myanmar (Burma), China, Indian mainland, Arab and Greek world. Indian trade routes to China and south-east Asia also lay through Manipur (Acharya, 1988, 57). Manipur was known by various names to different countries and states in the past. In the past the name of the kingdom was 'Poirei Meitei Leipak' or 'Kangleipak' (Sanajaoba 1988, (i). The name Manipur came into existence only after the adoption of Hinduism in the eighteenth century. Before that there is not a single word Manipur referring as the name of this kingdom in ancient manuscripts or the royal chronicle. In the first recorded treaty between East India Company and Jai Singh (then king of Manipur) in 1762 the kingdom was recorded as 'Meeckley' (Kabui, 1988, 3). To the Shans the kingdom was known as 'Kase' and to the Burmese as 'Kathe', a corruption of the same word. The Ahoms called it 'Makeli' and the Cacharis 'Magli'; while the old Assamese name for it is 'Moglan'. There are differences of opinion whether the name Manipur is associated with this land from very ancient time or in recent period. Whatever it may be, in view of the old manuscripts it can be safely asserted that the name Manipur of this land became popular only in the modern age (Roy, 1973).

There are different opinions on the origin of Meitei people. According to Dr. S.K. Chatterji the Meiteis or Manipuris are the most advanced section of the Kuki Chin people (Chatterji, 1967). Brian H. Hodgson in a footnote to a contribution to the Asiatic Society of Bengal in 1853 expressed the view that in the Moitay of Manipur we have the combined appellations of the Siamese Tai and the Kochin Chinese Moi. In other words, the Manipurian tribe belongs to the Moi section of the great tribe called Tai by themselves. Sir James Johnstone writes the early history of Manipur is lost in obscurity but there can be no doubt it has existed as an independent kingdom from a very early period. In the days when Indian branch of the Aryan was still in progressive and colonising stage this district was repeatedly passed over by one wave after another of invaders intent on penetrating into the remotest part of Burma. The fertile valley of Manipur witnessed the invasions of different tribes from time immemorial. At different periods the Nagas, the Kukis, the Shans and the Chinese came and settled in this land and merged themselves into the Manipuri community. Some Aryans and Dravidian features are also found in them (Roy 1973).

From the archaeological perspective it seems highly probable that a group of people from the regions of south China equipped with fully ground and polished stone tools and corded tripod wares entered into Manipur following the courses of Irrawaddy River and its tributaries (Roy, 1973). This valley with its great fertility and favourable topography had always attracted peoples from different parts of the world; likewise the ancestors of the different clans of Meiteis came from many different directions and built up a settled civilisation and evolved into a remarkable nationality with unique national character and pristine national heritage long before the Aryan migration in this belt. Thus, ethnologically and linguistically the Meiteis are Tibeto-Burman Mongoloid with Australoid, Aryan and Thai admixture (including some Negrito and Dravidian elements). Sociologically Meiteis have absorbed these foreign elements and completed integration in their social structure (Kabui, 1988, 3). On the archaeological findings- before the coming of the Tibeto-Burmese speaking proto-Meitei tribes, there were Mon-Khmer speaking Australoid-Mongoloid people who were later on absorbed by the Tibeto-Burmans.

The dominantly Mongoloid somatic features of these people, their Tibeto-Burman linguistic affinity and the oriental base structure of their cultural system-all however may also be considered together pointing to an association with early Chinese history (Budhi, 1988, 79). On the other hand, the Hinduised Meiteis of Manipur strongly believe that they are of western and Hindu descent. This Aryan connection was an outcome of the adoption of Hinduism by the ruling family and the people of the valley in early eighteenth century and resultant claim of the descent of the ruling dynasty from Babrubhahana, a scion of the Pandava hero, Arjuna of the Mahabharatta (Kabui, 1988).

Meitei-leipak (Kangleipak) which has been known in the sanskritised nomenclature as Manipur during the last three centuries had been the cradle of the autochthones which evolved the Stone Age culture, the earliest settlers and the other ethnoses in the early period of history. This process of assimilation of the ethnoses was completed in the pre-Christian era with the integration of seven major principalities, which ultimately emerged into a confederate nationality- the Meiteis (Sanajaoba, 1991, 23). The ethnic group of Meitei as we find it today was formed by the amalgamation of seven different but closely knit and allied principalities, once settled in different parts of Manipur, each independent of each other. The components of Meitei confederacy were; the Meitei also known as Ningthoujas, Khaba-Nganba, Chenglei, Angom, Khuman, Luwang and Moirang. Besides these there existed several other tribes such as Mangang, Manding, Chairen, Khende, Heirem Khunja etc., all of whom were in course of time, merged into one or the other of the seven major principalities. The seven principalities again went underwent an age long struggle amongst themselves till the Meiteis (Ningthoujas) finally established supremacy over the rest and absorbed them one by one in a period that covered several centuries. After this association, the name Meitei became the common nomenclature for all of them (Manikchand, 1988, 147).

It is well known that historically, the word Meitei was used during the period of the establishment of Ningthouja dynasty by Pakhangba to mean this clan or dynasty and those ethnic and social groups who were politically and socially integrated within the suzerainty of the Ningthouja (Kabui, 1988, 12). Thus, after amalgamation of those principalities the Meitei became their common name. Perhaps it may be pertinent to mention here that different scholars are found using two names, Meitei and Meetei while describing this same ethnic group. But the scuffle among the people over their ethnic name as to whether it is Meitei or Meetei need not linger on; Meitei or Meetei carries the same historical meaning. They are simply free variations of this language like any other language so permits (Budhi, 1988, 80).

Manipur continued to exist as the sovereign kingdom of its own till the year 1891 despite ever increasing British influence in this region. After the Anglo-Manipuri conflict of 1891 which was caused by a strained relationship developed between the British and the Manipuris on account of the murder of five British officers; Chief Commissioner of the erstwhile British province Mr JW Quinton, the Political Agent of Manipur, Mr Grimwood, Colosel Skene, Lieutenant Simpson and Mr Crossins by a unruly mob at the Manipur's palace, Kangla on 24 March 1891. Manipur lost her independence to the British India on 27th April 1891. From 1892 onwards the state became a princely native state under British India. The British Paramountcy continued till 1947. According to a merger agreement signed on 21st September 1949 between Maharaja Budhachandra, the then king of Manipur and the Government of India, the state was merged to India as a part 'C' state on the 15th October 1949. On 1st November 1956 Manipur became a union territory. It became a full-fledged state of the Indian union on 21st January 1972.

Syncretism among the Meiteis

The Meiteis have their own primordial religion which has its own myths and legends, gods and goddesses, priests and priestesses, rituals and festivals, etc. This religion centres around their belief in a supreme being, *Taibang Mapu Sidaba* who is a formless divinity having myriad manifestations and also his two progenies-God Sanamahi and God Pakhangba (Manikchand, 1988, 145-146). This primal religion of ancient Manipuris known as Sanamahi, not only thrived but also reached its zenith as a state religion during the reign of King Khagemba (1597-1652) (Nibir, 2009, 239). This ancient kingdom however, came within the fold of Hinduism since the beginning of the eighteenth century. Charairongba who ascended the Manipuri throne in 1697 was the first Manipuri king initiated into Hinduism. His initiation to Hinduism was done in 1704 and he was given the first Sanskrit name, Pitambar Singh among the Meitei Kings (Kulachandra, 2009, 239). After the death of Charairongba, his son Pamheiba also known as Garib Niwaz ascended the throne in 1709. In the year 1717 he was initiated into Hinduism by Gopal Das. Some time afterwards, in 1729 he was again initiated into the fold of Ramanandi Hinduism on the advice of his spiritual guru Santa Das. Since his initiation onto Ramanandi he became much more spirited and endowed with much greater valour, prowess and inspiration hence used with significant end result in his aggrandizement policy and wartime pursuits to achieve 'Greater Manipur'. On that dimension Lord Ram of the Ramayana seems to have had much greater religious sway and impact on the faithful Garib Niwaz than the Shri Krishna focused-Bhakti cult earlier initiated by Gopal Das (Kulachandra, 2009, 449).

Garib Niwaz made Hinduism state religion of then Meitei kingdom and tried his best to propagate among his subjects. His methods of proselytisation were far more direct and punitive. Religious dissent was treated with the same ruthless severity as was to meted out to political opponents, and wholesale banishments and executions drove the people into acceptance of the tenets of Hinduism (Hodson, 1908, 95). Those methods includes destruction of certain indigenous worship places (Laiphams), burning of all the ancient Meitei texts (Puya Mei-Thaba) and punishment of those who did not accept Hinduism. But in spite of all possible attempts of Garib Niwaz to establish supremacy of Hinduism over the traditional religion, the worship of traditional deities continued along with that of the Hindu gods. In fact, the root of traditional religion was so firmly embedded in the soil of Manipur that it was well-nigh impossible for him to stamp it out completely (G. P. Singh, 2013, 2).

Both the religious system - a system based on the Vaishnava doctrines of Hinduism and traditional religious doctrines and also the cultural pattern based on the Hindu culture and the traditional culture, as followed by the king Charairongba since his initiation into Hinduism in 1704 constitute the earliest evidence of religio-cultural syncretism in Manipur (Bhagyachandra, 2008, 4). Even though the Meiteis have pronounced Hindus and passed through the golden period of Hindu orthodoxy they never ceased to worship their native deities or follow indigenous cultural practices and creeds. They have rather been adhering to an amalgamated or a composite code of religious practices. Each and every Meitei household worship the prime and primary deities of both the religious beliefs in ordinary daily life. An apparent process of amalgamation can be seen at the instance of the Meitei king Garib Niwaz as well. The king himself would accompany an image of his devine Lainingthou Sanamahi on any armed expedition even though he had accepted the Nimandi cult of Hinduism (Kulachandra, 2009, 449).

After conversion into Hinduism, the old kingdom of the Meiteis was renamed as Manipur and identified as the Manipur of Mahabharata, once ruled by Babrubahana, son of Arjuna. But till the end of the seventeenth century in the Royal Chronicle Cheitharol Kumbaba the word 'Manipur'was never used. It clearly show that the name Manipur is of recent origin and came only after the period of Hinduism in this kingdom.

Manipur Hinduism gradually became a synthesis of the primordial Meitei religion with its gods and goddesses, with its myths, legends and traditions, its social customs and usages; its priests and ceremonials and of Brahmanical Hinduism with its special worship of Radha and Krishna. As usual, approximation of the old Meitei religion to the Hindu Brahmanical one began with the identification of the gods of two religions. A syncretism of the old pre-Hindu Meitei religion, mythology and ritual with the Hindu Brahmanical religion started (Chatterji, 1950, 288). The spread of Vaishnavism was achieved only by a compromise with the ancient faith. Traditional Lais (gods) were brought into the Hindu pantheon. Hindu deities were absorbed into the Meitei culture. As a consequence of this process of assimilation Manipur exhibits today a remarkable synthesis of the indigenous faith of the Meiteis and Vaishnavism. Vaishnava form of Hinduism flourished side by side with the traditional religion during that time. The worship of Panthiobi-the greatest goddess in the Meitei pantheon continued concurrently with that of the Hindu deities. The identification of the local deities with the divinities of the Hindu pantheon also began. Goddess Panthoibi was identified with goddess Kali. Nongpok Ningthou of the Koubru hill become god Shiva and Lairembi (goddess) of Hiyangthang hillock become goddess Kamakhya during the reign of Bhagyachandra 1759-98) (G. P. Singh, 2013, 2). During the brief reign of Labanyachandra (1798- 1801) the traditional and Hindu deities received an equal amount of attention from the king. The traditional deities were worshipped even by the followers of Hinduism and Hindu rituals were also adopted in worshipping the traditional deities.

On the advice of preceptor Santa Das, Garib Niwaz, then king of Manipur introduced the Hindu Gotra system and identified traditional seven yeks/Salais (Clans) of Meitei into respective Gotras as follows;

Yek/Salai (Clan) – Hindu Gotras

(i) Ningthouja/Mangang – Shandilya

(ii) Luwang – Kashyap

(iii) Khuman – Madhugalya

(iv) Angom – Kaukhika

(v) Moirang – Aitereya

(vi) Khaba-Nganba – Gautam

(vii) Sarang Leisangthem – Bhardwaj.

During his reign the king also modified or identified a number of Manipuri traditional festivals with concurrent Hindu festivals.

(a) The annual boat race festivals then traditionally known as Heigru Hidongba was renamed as Jala Yatra.

(b) The festival of Waira Tenkap was redesignated as Kirtan of Lord Ram.

(c) The traditional festival of Kongba Leithong Phatpa was reidentified with Vishnu Sankranti.

(d) The festival of Ahong Khongching was modified as Dol Yatra.

(e) The ancient festival of offering feast to the ancestors known as Tara Chanou Katpa became known as Priti Lok Iratpa.

(f) The worship of Nung-goibi was substituted by Dusserah.

(g) Festival of testing newly harvested rice known as Chanou Huichintu in the month of October was replaced by Govardhan Puja (Nilbir, 2009).

The introduction of Hinduism marked the synthesis of the old and new elements and consequently it led to the evolution of a syncretised form of Hinduism which is still practised here in Manipur, and that the harmonisation which has been going on in India since ancient times forming a single culture was also seen at work in Manipur and it can be seen from the syncretisation of old and new faiths or tenets.

In the later period, since 1930 the traditional cult has undergone a crusade for revival through a process of renovation, reinstatement, reformation etc. As a result, the amalgamated/ composite religious motto began to wane. But these amalgamated beliefs and practices had very deep roots in the lives of the people and it is not easily possible to separate them completely. So there are many aspects that show the result of amalgamated beliefs and practices. In fact, it gives a unique and aesthetic feature to the culture of Meitei people which is different from the rest of the Hindu population of other regions. These syncretised features can be seen in day to day life activities, life cycle rituals, ceremonies and festivals. Perhaps, we can see these syncretised elements in every aspect of Meitei way of life if we observe carefully.

Here in this study the researcher pick out life cycle rituals to describe those syncretised features. Life cycle rituals are the events or ceremonies which marks the important stages of an individual's life. These rituals mark the passage of an individual's life course from one stage to the next. These events mark important transitional stages in an individual's life such as birth, puberty, marriage and dead. Birth, marriage and dead rituals are the most pivotal life cycle rituals in Meitei culture. They are important aspects of Meitei socio-cultural life. In fact they are very significant parts of Meitei culture. Through these rituals an individual passes from one stage to the next stage of life and finally reunites with the nature again; whence it originates after its time.

Meitei birth rituals are very elaborate in nature. Religion plays a vital role in these rituals. These rituals started even before the birth of a child. The first ritual is performed when the expecting mother attains third month of pregnancy. Then the next one is performed on the fifth month and next on seventh month of pregnancy. By the time she attains ninth month of pregnancy an elaborate ritual known as "*Kokthok-Chamthokpa*" is performed. It is a ritual performed to avoid any unwanted complications at the time of child birth. It is firmly believed among the people that if these rituals are properly performed than no unwanted incidents can happen to the child and mother during childbirth. But nowadays these rituals are becoming very uncommon and most of the households skip these prenatal rituals. Postnatal rituals are still prevalent among the Meiteis, be it in the urban or rural areas of Manipur.

In birth rituals we observe the synthesised elements in different stages. In *Heisoi Eepan Thaba* (Swasti Puja), which is held on the sixth day of birth there are composite activities of traditional religion and Hinduism. Rituals perform in the morning of this day are traditional practices and in the evening Hinduised forms of puja is conducted along with the indigenous ritual of arrow shooting; in the view of protecting the child from evil spirits by the maternal uncle.

Marriage is one of the most important life cycle rituals of every human society. It has been prevalent in every known human society since ancient times in one form or another. And Meitei society is not an exception. In Meitei society it is called Luhongba. This term is derived from the two words, Lu and Hongba. Here, Lu means head (of our body) and Hongba is to inaugurate or initiate. So the etymological meaning of the term Luhongba is ritualistic inauguration of human mind and body. Inauguration in this context is like those inauguration of temples, house, market etc. For instance, in Meitei tradition a pond can be used by the people only after the proper inauguration of it. Likewise, Luhongba is the inauguration of the boy and girl. It is a sacred bond between them forming a single mind and body. In Meitei philosophy, until their marriage a boy or a girl's mentality is consider as that of a child. It is only after their marriage that they are consider as adults and their thoughts (mental dignity) is consider valid by the society. After this ritual (marriage) the married couple gets their mental status to the society. It is worth mentioning here that there is no tradition of child marriage in Meitei society. It is also believe that a married couple has learnt the rules and regulations (principles) of the society. From this day onwards the girl change her head (mind) to another family i.e. the boy's family. This ceremony marks the entering of boy and girl's life to a new stage; from youth to matured adulthood both physically and mentally. Generally marriage is forbidden between those of the same Yek/ Salai (clan). There are some exceptions but it is a strong belief of the people that same Yek/Salai marriage is always followed by unwanted consequences in their lifetime or in their siblings.

Present day Meitei marriage incorporate elements from both the religions (traditional and Hinduism) in its system, process and procedures. Meitei Hindus do not arrange yajna (sacrifice) for marriage, but hold Sankeertan (a form of ritual singing, drumming and dancing). They have also modified the satpathi (seven steps) in the form of circumambulation of the groom seven times by the bride. They have also redefined that the nuptial garland be necessarily made of Kundo, a specific white flower (Jasminum multiflorum).

According to Meitei philosophy human body (*Hakchang*) is made up of five elements; Mei, Esing, Nungsit, Leipak and Atiya (fire, water, air, earth, and sky) and a living principle called Thawai (the soul). Death is the separation of Thawai from its dwelling place, Hakchang. It is called Nongkaba meaning going up to the Nong (heaven) or Lairamlen (abode of the gods). When a person dies, her /his soul gets reunite as scent of flower in the garden of supreme almighty. Human body is left by the soul as it is no longer fit to stay. Then the body goes back to its original abode, to where it comes from, to the place where it originate from. It is now buried in the earth (Leipak). This is called Leitaiba; Lei-mother earth and Taiba-union. Thus, when an individual die all the elements that constitute the mortal body get united with the mother earth again and the soul goes up to its original abode where the supreme almighty dwells.

The Meiteis believe in the immortality and transmigration of soul. Death is regarded as the separation of the soul from the body with a view to transmigrate into a new body. (Kulachandra, 1967). After a person die her/his soul stay with the ancestors in the land of death where the supreme almighty lives. It is called Lairamlen, heaven or abode of the gods. So the Meiteis perform death rituals in order to give a right path to the Lairamlen and for its deliverance to the departed soul. Meiteis also perform death rituals in order that the departed soul gets a new body in a human birth in the case of natural deaths and rituals to avoid reoccurring in the case of unnatural deaths such as suicides, children died in infancy, women died in childbirth etc.

Present day death rituals of the Meiteis is different from those ancient practices. The chronicles and other ancient texts mention existence of four different forms of disposal of the dead. They are, (i) Nungsitki Potloi (disposal of death in the air), (ii) Eshinggi Potloi (disposal in the water), (iii) Leipakki Potloi (burial) and (iv) Meigi Potloi (cremation). (Birachandra, 2006, 119-120). The disposal of death in the air was oldest of all. During the ancient time of king Kangba the dead body was thrown out to a particular place to be taken over by Kakyen Meengamba, a divinely bird who take the dead body to the land of death. Then came the days of throwing into water. The Kangbalon puya says that dead bodies were thrown into the river near the sacred place, Heibokching. Then from the time of Tongkonba funeral of dead bodies in a specific place began to practice. Upto the advent of Hinduism this practice was prevailing. (Bhagyachandra, 1991, 119-121). Cheitharol Kumbaba, the royal chronicle reports, on the 20th day of the month of Hiyangkei, the king took all the bones of the ancestors to Ningthi for cremation. (Cheitharol Kumbaba, 1967, 73).

It is well known that up to the advent of Hinduism, the death were buried and chronicles mention the enactment by Khagemba of a rule that the death were to be buried outside the enclosures of the houses. Garib Niwaz, then Manipuri king ordered the Manipuris to exhume the bodies of their ancestors, which they formerly use to bury inside their compounds. At a later date in his reign, in the year 1724, Garib Niwaz exhumed the bones of his ancestors and cremated them on the bank of the Engthee River and from that time ordered his subjects to burn their dead. (Hodson, 1908, 116-117). The body is even today place in a coffin before cremation, which supports the contention that burial was practiced in pre-Hindu times in Manipur. (Parratt, 1980, 85).

In the ancient pre-Hindu Meitei society there were two rituals to be performed on the death of an individual. They are, Nimtki Mathou Yangkempa (ritual according to the days) and Thaki Mathou Yangkempa (rituals according to the months). The ritual according to the days is called Chupsa Moithem. It is observed on the seventh day of the death. It is a ritual perform by the family and relatives of the death in order that the departed soul gets a body in a human birth. All the male members of the clan participate in this ritual. The Piba, chief of the clan writes off the name of the dead individual from the clan chronicle. Appropriate prayers and offerings are make to the supreme almighty (Tengbanba Mapu) and other dieties, Salailel Sidaba (supreme clan ancestor), Leimarel Sidabi and Lainingthou Sanamahi for peace and happiness of the departed soul. Due prayers and offerings are also make to the supreme almighty to give a new body to the departed soul in a new birth.

The ritual according to the month is called Kumon Phiroi. It is the last rite for the death of an individual. This ritual is perform on the completion of 12 months (a year) from the death. According to traditional Meitei beliefs life starts from the father. The ultimate life source stays two months in the father's body and then it pass on to the mother who bears the child for 10 months. Altogether a period of 12 months, a year is consider to be require for a departed one to get a new birth. The ritual of Phiroi is thus perform on the completion of 12 months from the death by assuming the departed one would get a rebirth after the completion of a year by offering a grand feast in honour of Taibang Mapu, Salailel Sidaba and Salai ancestors.

Present day death rituals of the Meiteis are the composite practices which are synthesised from traditional Meitei religion and Hinduism. There are slight variations in the components, procedures and style of the rituals among the peoples who follow Hinduism and traditional religion. But, by and large in both the systems we can observe syncretised elements.

In the funeral ritual there is traditional rituals accompanied by the Hindu practices like walking around the funeral pyre seven times etc. In death ritual, on the fifth or sixth day after death the Asti-Sanchaya or mangani Leihun is arranged as per traditional Meitei rites in addition to the Hinduized Shraddha occasion on the 13th day.

Unlike in other regions, after conversion to Hinduism all the converted Meiteis, including members of the king's own family and other royal dynasty were declared to belong to the Kshatriya caste. It is one of the unique feature of Manipuri Hinduism where only two caste viz. Kshatriya and Brahmin coexists; descendants of immigrant Brahmins belonging to the Brahmin caste and the rest Meitei population belonging to the Kshatriya caste, in particular, Surya Vamsa of Shri Ramchandraji of the Ramayana.

Another significant aspect of syncretised Manipuri Hinduism can be seen in Ras Lila, a dance drama. The Ras Lila also known as Manipuri Ras is one of the few classical dance forms of India. It was introduced by Rajarshi Baghyachandra, then king of Manipur during his reign (1759-98). It is based on Srimad Bhagavatam but enacted with indigenous dance forms, in particular Lai Haraoba dance. The fundamentals of the Ras dance are based on the various forms of Lai Haraoba dance (a traditional form of dance). When Bhagyachandra invented the Ras Lila, he presented its dance forms out of the ancient Lai Haraoba dance making some modifications. The main aspect of the Ras Lila; Bhangi pareng are the modified versions of the Laibou Jagoi and Panthoibi Jagoi of ancient Lai Haraoba dance (Manikchand, 2009, 288). From this dance drama we can clearly see how an indigenous dance form transformed into one the few classical dances of this nation through syncretism.

Hinduism as we see now among the Meiteis in Manipur is a fusion of the two religious traditions, one represented by classical Hinduism and the other by the primordial religion of the Meiteis. The syncretism of the Meitei indigenous religion with its gods and goddesses, its myths and rituals, its legends and traditions, its beliefs and practices and its rites and ceremonies and the Brahmanical faith and Vaishnava Hinduism constitutes the essence of present day Hinduism in Manipur. The religious system prevailing today in Manipur valley can be taken as a legacy of syncretised form of Hinduism that evolved during eighteenth century Manipur.

Conclusion

Manipur lies in the meeting point of south and Southeast Asia. From the very early period of human history this region had been a connecting link between east and west (southeast and south Asian countries). This can be observed from its varied cultural affinity with Southeast Asian countries. Linguistic affinity, food habits, dressing pattern, traditional religion, performing arts, martial arts, mythology and folk lore are some of the cultural traits that shows close connection with southeast Asian nations. For instance, eating with chopsticks, one of the most significant trademarks of Southeast Asian culture prevails till Moreh (an Indo-Myanmar border town) of Manipur. This population is more close to Southeast Asia in terms of somatic characters and cultural traits. In the early period of eighteenth century this state witnessed the influence of Hinduism. Thenceforth the state has been a melting pot of cultural traits of Hinduism and traditional religion. This syncretism of Hinduism and traditional religion gave rise to a new unique form of culture among these people.

Acknowledgment

I wish to express my gratitude to the Department of Anthropology, NEHU, Shillong for continuously supporting me throughout my work.

References

Acharyya, N. N. 1988. Manipur in the Eye of Foreign Historians. In *Manipur Past and Present.* Vol. I. Ed. N. Sanajaoba. New Delhi: Mittal Publications.

Bhagyachandra, Singh L. 1991. A Critical Study of religious Philosophy of the Meiteis before the advent of Vaishnavism in Manipur. Imphal: L. Momon Devi.

Birachandra, N. 2006. The Meitei Society: A study of Traditional Life Circle Ceremony. New Delhi: Akansha Publishing House.

Budhi, Chongtham. 1988. The Ethonym "Meitei". In *Manipur Past and Present.* Vol. I. Ed. N. Sanajaoba. New Delhi: Mittal Publications.

Census of Manipur. 2011. Imphal: Directorate of Census, Government of Manipur.

Chatterji, S. K. 1950. Kirata-Jana-Kriti: Journal of the Royal Asiatic Society of Bengal. 16(2). Calcutta.

Chatterji, S. K. 1967. Religious and Cultural Integration of India. Imphal: Atombapu Research Centre.

Cheitharol Kumbaba. 1967. By: Ibungohal, Singh L and N. Khelchandra Singh. Imphal: Manipur Sahitya Parishad.

Das, N.K. (Ed). 2003. Culture, Religion and Philosophy: Critical Studies in Syncretism and Inter-Faith Harmony. Jaipur: Rawat Publications.

Durkheim, E. 1912. The Elementary Forms of Religious Life. New York: The Free Press.

Frazer, J. 1976. The Golden Bough: A study in Magic and Religion. Part 1. Vol. 1. London: Macmillan.

Geertz, J. C. 1973. The Interpretation of Cultures. New York: Basic Books.

G. P. Singh. 2013. Religious and Cultural Syncretisation of the 18th century Manipur: H. Dwijashekhar (Ed) The Other Manipur. Vol. I. History, Ethnicity, Bio-Recources and Environment. Part I. New Delhi: Akansha Publishing House.

Grimwood, E. 1982. My three Years in Manipur. New Delhi: Gyan Publishing House.

Hodson, T. C. 1908/2008. The Meitheis. New Delhi: Low Price Publications.

Johnstone, Sir J. 1896. My Experience in the Naga Hills and Manipur. London: S. Low, Marston and Company, Limited.

Kabui, G. 1988. Glimpse of Land and People of Ancient Manipur. In *Manipur Past and Present.* Vol. I. Ed. N. Sanajaoba. New Delhi: Mittal Publications.

Kamei, G. 2006. On History and Histography of Manipur. New Delhi: Akansha Publishing House.

Kulachandra, Singh Ng. 1967. Apokpa Thounirol. Imphal: Unique Printing Works. Kulachandra, B. 2009. Similarities Between Sanamahi and Vaishnavsm. In *New Insights into the Glorious Heritage of Manipur.* Ed. H. Dwijasekhar Sharma. New Delhi: Akansha Publishing House.

Manikchand, K. 1988. The Evolution of Meitei State (A Confederacy through the Last Two Millennia). In *Manipur Past and Present.* Vol. I. Ed. N. Sanajaoba. New Delhi: Mittal Publications.

Manikchand, K. 2009. Rajarshi Bhagyachandra- The Royal Saint and Patriot. In *New Insights into the Glorious Heritage of Manipur.* Ed. H. Dwijasekhar Sharma. New Delhi: Akansha Publishing House.

McCulloch, W. 1859. An Account of the Valley of Manipur and Hill Tribes. Calcutta: Bengal Printing Company.

Moffat, J. 1921. Syncretism. In *Encyclopaedia of Religion and Ethics.* Ed. James Hastings. Vol. xii. Edinburg: T &T Clark.

Nilbir, S. 2009. Sanskritisation process of Manipur under King Garib Niwaz. In *New Insights into the Glorious Heritage of Manipur.* Ed. H. Dwijasekhar Sharma. New Delhi: Akansha Publishing House.

Parratt, S. N. 1980. The Religion of Manipur. Calcutta: Firma KLM Pvt. Limited.

Parrat, J. S.N. Arambam Parrat. 1992. Queen Empress vs Tikendrajit Prince of Manipur. The Anglo-Manipur conflict of 1891. New Delhi: Vikas Publishing House.

Radin, P. 1957. Primitive Religion: Its Nature and Origin. New York: Dover Publications.

Roy, J. 1973. History of Manipur. Calcutta: Eastlight Book House.

Sanajaoba, N. (Ed). 1988. Manipur: Past and Present. (The Heritage and Ordeals of a Civilisation). Vol.I. History, Polity and Law. New Delhi: Mittal Publications.

Sanajaoba, N. (Ed). 1991. Manipur: Past and Present. Vol.2. Philosophy, Culture and Literature. New Delhi: Mittal Publications.

Sanajaoba, N. (Ed). 1993. Manipur Treaties and Documents (1110-1971). Vol.I. New Delhi: Mittal Publications.

Sharma, H.D. (Ed). 2009. New Insights Into the Glorious Heritage of Manipur. Vol. II. New Delhi: Akansha Publishing House.

Sharma, H.D. (Ed). 2012. The Other Manipur. Vol.I. Historicity, Ethnicity, Bio-Recources and Environment. Part-I. New Delhi: Akansha Publishing House.

Singh, G. P. 2012. Hinduism in Manipur. New Delhi: Gyan Publishing House.

Singh, L. J.1995. The Lost Kingdom (Royal Chronicle of Manipur). Imphal: Prajatantra Publishing House.

Singh, M. K. 1980. Religious Development in Manipur in the 18th and 19th Century. Imphal: Manipur State Kala Akademy.

Singh, M. K. 1988. Religion and Culture of Manipur. Delhi: Manas Publications.

Singh, O. K. 1983. Archaelogy in Manipur, series-I. Napachik: A Stone Age site in the Manipur valley. Imphal: State Archaeology, Government of Manipur.

Singh, O. K. 1988. Aspects of Archaeology in Manipur. In *Manipur Past and Present.* Vol. I. Ed. N. Sanajaoba. New Delhi: Mittal Publications.

Tylor, E. B. 1958. Religion in Primitive Culture. New York: Harper and Row.

Yinger, J. M. 1970. The Scientific Study of Religion. New York: Macmillan.

7

Musical Syncretism: The Indian Context

— *Onkar Prasad*

Introduction

Syncretism is a cosmic principle of bringing together two or more things of either different nature, character or origin, thereby, forming a functioning and continuing whole but at the same time retaining their individual identity. The electron and the proton, the former a negatively charged particle and the latter a positively charged particle of all atomic particles of which the whole universe is constituted is a glaring example of syncretism, a cosmic principle as established in physical science. Forming alloys by mingling different metals in desired proportion is basic to the development of metallurgy and so on.

Syncretism involves the merger and analogizing of several originally discrete traditions, especially in theology and mythology, thus asserting an underlying unity and allowing for an inclusive approach to other faiths. Syncretism also occurs commonly in expressions of arts and culture (known as eclecticism) as well as politics (syncretic politics). But it implies compromising by mixing its own with not just with a culture but another thing. It becomes effective when concurred with established cultural traditions and interface a thing into a fundamentally particular synthesis. In contrast to what happens in nature, for man it is a conscious level strategy to cope with the controversy for survival, spread, acceptance of certain values and development in various fields of natural or other sciences. (See Wikipedia for detail). As evident from my topic I would limit my demonstration and discussion to the two experiments of musical syncretism in the North Indian classical music.

The first experiment has been conducted by Sri Mohan Singh Khangura, Professor of North Indian classical music at Visva-Bharati. He composed the *raga* Santali Durga by blending the characteristic melodic movement like RMR (-RS) of the Sohrae song in the melodic structure of the *raga* Durga (SRMPDS/SDPMRS) of the Bilawal *That* in descending order, again and again. In addition, he also introduces the note G to a minimum to the *raga* structure in descending order. The second experiment has been done by the author himself. He composed the *raga* Bihu Dhani by introducing the characteristic musical piece MmMg of the Bihu, a folk song and dance of Assam into the melodic structure of the *raga* Dhani(SgMPnS/SnPMgS) of the Kafi *That*. These two examples along with word texts and musical notations are given below:

Example No. 1

Raga Santali Durga

(Composer: Sri Mohan Singh Khangura, Professor of the North Indian Classical Music, Visva-Bharati, Santiniketan, a disciple of Pandit Dhruv Tara Joshi).

Composition in Trital (Madhya Laya)

Sthayi:

Ankhiyon Ke Noor Sarur Hamare I
Bali Bali Jaun Kanta Hamare II

Antara:

Shyamranga Mori Baat Ye Mano,
Dijo Daras Hamare I
Taras Rahin Sab Sakhiyan II

English Translation:

O you an exhilarating radiance of our eyes,
We bestow upon you.
O Shyamrang, listen to us,
Give us your glimpse.
Your all female friends are longing (for you).

Musical Notation:

Sthayi:

X

1 2 3 4 5 6 7 8 9 10 11 12 13 14 15 16
// R M R - / S S S S / R .D S S / S R M R //
//A khi yon s / ke nu s ra / sa ru s r / ha ma s re//
// S R M R / M - M - / M - P P / P R R S //
// Ba li ba li / ja s un s / kan s ta s / ha ma s re //

Antara:

X

1 2 3 4 5 6 7 8 9 10 11 12 13 14 15 16

// M - P D / S S S S / S - S D / R - S - //

// Shya - m ran/s ga mo ri / ba s ta ye / ma s no s //

// S - D - / M M P P/ MP MP MP DP/ R - - - //

// Di s jo - / da ra sa ha/mas s s ss ss / re - - - //

// D D S S / G R S D / P M R

// Ta ra sa ra / hi - sa b / sa khi yan Ankhiyon ke noor

Example No-2

Raga Bihu Dhani

(Composer: Dr. Onkar Prasad, a disciple of Sri Mohan Singh Khangura, Santiniketan and Pandit Rajeshwar Acharya, Bhadaini,Banaras).

Composition in Ektal (Vilambit)

Sthayi:

Ab Mori Man Le Kahanma Pyare Kanhaiya I

Antara: Dhith Langarava Chandon Ancharva More Manaharva I

English Translation:

O dear Kanhaiya, now keep our words.

You stubborn and dissolute, leave the border of my body- cloth

O my enchanting boy.

Musical Notation:

Sthayi:

X

1 2 3 4 5 6 7 8 9 10 11 12

// S g / Mm Mg /g S / P n / S - / S g //

// A ba / mos sri /ma na / le s / s s / ka ha //

// M P / P n / S - / S np / Mg gM / mM gS //

// na ma / pya s / re s / ka nha / ss ss / ss ya //

Antara:

X

// gM Pn / Sn S / S Sn / gg S / nP gM / PS - //

// Dhi s thalan/gara va / chan roan / chara va / mo re / mana //

// n p / g M / mM g / n S /

// ha ra / va s / ss s / s s / Aba mori

Composition in Dhamar (Madhya laya)

Sthayi:

Tumare Guna Gayun I

Tu Hi Data, Tu HI Vidhata II

Antara:

Sab Jag Dekhat Tumri Or I

Kijo Daya Drishti Payun II

English Translation:

I sing in praise of you.

You are the benefactor. You are the ordainer.

All people of the world are looking at you.

Give your glimpse to have your blessing.

Musical Notation:

Sthayi:

X

1 2 3 / 4 5 / 6 7 / 8 9 10 / 11 12 13 14

// g n S / M M / M M / M g M / m M g S //

// Tu s m / ro s / s s / s s gu / n ga s un //

// S - S / n g / - S / S - S / n g - S //

// Tu s hi / s da / s ta / tu s hi / vi dha - ta //

Antara:

X

// g g g / M P / - n / n S S / n S - S //

// Sa ba ja / ga de / s kha / t tu ma / ri o s r //

// S - n / P P / g M / m M g / S

// Ki s jo / da ya / dri s / ti pa s / un Tuma

Some Observations

I have cited above two examples of musical syncretism only but it happens at various levels. As we know there are seven categorical (SRGMPDN) and five sub- notes (rgmdn) in an octave of the North Indian classical music and each note is different from the other. It is by mingling at least five musical notes or more, several *ragas* have been formed. Again two different *ragas* are mingled to form several *ragas*. In addition, the melodic motifs of the tribal/ folk origin as demonstrated above, are mixed to form some other *ragas* (See Chaitanyadev 1974, Sanyal 1959, Vasant 1970 for detail). From these examples it is observed that apart from having its constructive role in other spheres viz. religion and politics as discussed before, the syncretism in the sphere of music has helped in enriching the repository of thc North Indian classical music to a great extent. Thus, it may be said that the development or enhancement of a culture is possible mostly through syncretisation of its various dimensions. Syncretism is basic to creativity, development and in multi religious and multi cultures India, adaptability to varying situations for peaceful co-existence and restoration of unity cutting across cultures.

References

Chaitanyadev, B. (1974). *Indian Music.* Indian Council for Cultural Relations. New Delhi.

Sanyal, Amiyanath. (1959). *Raga and Ragini*. Orient Longmans.

Vasant. (1970). *Ragkosh* (*Sangeet Raga Sudha*) 2nd Edition. Sangeet Karyalaya. Hathras.

Wikipedia on Syncretism (http://www.missiology.org.uk/pdf/cotterel-fs/15 ferdinando.pdf and other related works on it.

8

Anthropo-Historic Discussion on Syncretism in Language and Dressing Pattern among People of Central India

— Neha Singh

Introduction

Syncretism is the hot topic in present era, used by anthropologist and sociologist. The concept of syncretism in fact has become the focus of much debate among the anthropologist and scholars. The word syncretism is mostly related with the past and linked with the present, to determine and co-related the things which happened or happening, not only in India but all over worldwide. If we discover the history of the word, from where it originated we could not find the answer. But we if talking about the definition of syncretism is that "Syncretism is the process whereby two or more independent cultural system, or elements there of conjoin to form a new distinct system. Ethnic origins, religions and languages are the major sources of culture diversity. Syncretism is among the most important factors in the evolution of culture in generally but especially in the history of religion. But generally, I have observed that people mainly correlated this word with religious aspects of culture. Syncretism refers to the hybridisation or amalgamation of two or more cultural traditions. However all culture may combine a variety of elements in a diffused or borrowed form. The usefulness of the concept of syncretism involve the intermixing, through converges linkage of different religious tradition at least as a descriptive concept referring to what happens concretely when peoples and culture meet.

In this present paper the researcher has tried to express the role of language and dressing pattern of different societies. That due to many of the factor are responsible to assimilate different forms in amalgamated or synthesized form, which given a new form of synthesized product. India is a country incredible for its diversity, biological and cultural region. The process of synthesis and integration has been extensively at work in most parts of India. The process of synthesis and integration has been extensively at work at the regional level (Das 2003).

India is a country in south Asia; the name etymologically came from ancient civilisation Indus Valley civilisation which was at the bank of river Indus, around 3000 BCE. According to 'Puranas', a religious and historical text written in 5th century CE, The 'Bharata' is used as a sign for the country, which is referring the ancient mythological great emperor Bharata, who had conquered the whole sub-continents of India and ruled this land peace and harmony. Not only this, If we count the discovery of artifacts used by human and its forms including stone tools and so on, both suggest that this country has an extremely early date for Hominid activity, human habitation, and technology.

This paper is an attempt to give a conceptual understanding of historical events in India and its importance in the formation of Indian civilisation from Aryan Invasion 1500 BC to 20th century in brief. And Based on these events, whatever changes had been taken place in the cultural elements specially and later research has focused on syncretic form of language and dressing pattern of people of central India. Whenever we say the Central India which is primarily define as the states of Madhya Pradesh and Chhattisgarh. Madhya Pradesh is the state which is surrounded by land of states. In November 1, 2000 CE, Chhattisgarh was divided from Madhya Pradesh and formed a separate state. Central Indian life and culture and history are exclusively pivoted around these two states. It is described by the urbanity and cosmopolitan lifestyle in cities; even we can say everything is outstanding in technology and advancement nowadays. Madhya Pradesh acted as the 'rocking cradle' of numerous Indian dynasties in the historical events. As a result, this is the place of flock of literatures and languages and also the agent of amalgamation of cultural elements. Central Indian languages revolve around both tribal and non-tribal people, which are entirely belongs to the Indo-Aryan language family. Hindi is the principal and official language of the state, spoken by majority of the population. Apart from Hindi, several other Indian languages and dialects are also rampant all over Madhya Pradesh. Excluding 'standard Hindi', several regional variants also finds its guaranteed place. Some people regard them as localised dialects of the Hindi language. Most of the tribal people and natives speak languages that comprise Bhilodi (Bhili), Gondi and the sequestered Kalto (Nahali). A substantial number of people also speak

Marathi, a legacy of Maratha rule in Madhya Pradesh. Urdu, Sindhi, Punjabi and Gujarati are some other dominant languages in this area. In Chhattisgarh, most of the local people speak Chhattisgarhi language, which is a fraction of the East-Central group of Indo-Aryan languages. People in southern Chhattisgarh, precisely in Bastar, mouth accents derived from Dravidian languages which supports the idea of path of migration of Dravidian might have through this way. Other languages spoken in Chhattishgarh comprise Hindi, Oriya, Marathi and tribal languages. The language in the Northern Sarguja State area mirrors the influence on it of dialects of Vindya Pradesh, Uttar Pradesh and Bihar. As opposed to Chhattisgarhi, the language over there is majestically referred to as "Sargujia" by the population of that region. Similarly, in sections in the Eastern part that followed under Raigarh, Sarangarh and Phuljhar (Saraipali) states, the language possesses a distinctive influence of Oriya on the language (*newworldencyclopedia.org*).

Historical Events from 1500 BC to 20th Centaury

The Vedic Period

The Aryan influence, some scholars claim, gave rise to what is known as the Vedic Period in India (c. 1700- 150 BCE) characterised by a pastoral lifestyle and adherence to the religious texts known as **The Vedas**. Society became divided into four classes (the *Varnas*) popularly known as 'the caste system' which were comprised of the *Brahmana* at the top (priests and scholars), the Kshatriya (the warriors), the Vaishya (farmers & merchants) and the Shudra (labourers). The lowest caste was the *Dalits*, the untouchables, who handled meat and waste, though there is some debate over whether this class existed in antiquity. At first, it seems this caste system was merely a reflection of one's occupation but, in time, it became more rigidly interpreted to be determined by one's birth and one was not allowed to change castes or to marry into a caste other than one's own. This understanding was a reflection of the belief in an eternal order to human life dictated by a supreme deity.

While the religious beliefs which characterised the Vedic Period are considered much older, it was during this time that they became systematized as the **religion** of Sanatan Dharma (which means 'Eternal Order') known today as **Hinduism** (this name deriving from the Indus (or Sindus) River where worshippers were known to gather, hence, 'Sindus', and then 'Hindus'). The underlying tenet of Sanatan Dharma is that there is an order and a purpose to the universe and human life and, by accepting this order and living in accordance with it, one will experience life as it is meant to be properly lived. While Sanatan Dharma is considered by many a polytheistic religion consisting of many gods, it is actually monotheistic in that it holds there is one god, Brahma (the Self), who, because of his greatness, cannot be fully apprehended save through the many aspects which are revealed as the different gods of the **Hindu pantheon**. It is Brahma who decrees the eternal order and maintains the universe through it. This belief in an order to the universe reflects the stability of the society in which it grew and flourished as, during the Vedic Period, governments became centralised and social customs integrated fully into daily life across the region. Besides The Vedas, the great religious and literary works of The **Upanishads**, The Puranas, The Mahabharata, and The Ramayana all come from this period.

In the 6th century BCE, the religious reformers Vardhama Mahavira (549-477 BCE) and **Siddhartha Gautama** (563-483 BCE) broke away from mainstream Sanatan Dharma to eventually create their own religions of Jainism and **Buddhism**. These changes in religion were a part of a wider pattern of social and cultural upheaval which resulted in the formation of city states and the rise of powerful kingdoms (such as the Kingdom of Magadha under the ruler Bimbisara). Increased **urbanisation** and wealth attracted the attention of **Cyrus**, ruler of the Persian **Empire**, who invaded India in 530 BCE and initiated a campaign of **conquest** in the region. Ten years later, under the reign of his son, **Darius I**, northern India was firmly under Persian control (the regions corresponding to Afghanistan and Pakistan today) and the inhabitants of that area subject to Persian laws and customs. One consequence of this, possibly, was an assimilation of Persian and Indian religious beliefs which some scholars point to as an explanation for further religious and cultural reforms.

The Great Empires of Ancient India

Persia held dominance in northern India until the conquest of **Alexander** the Great in 327 BCE. One year later, Alexander had defeated the **Achaemenid Empire** and firmly conquered the Indian subcontinent. Again, foreign influences were brought to bear on the region giving rise to the Greco-Buddhist culture which impacted all areas of culture in northern India from art to religion to dress. Statues and reliefs from this period depict **Buddha**, and other figures, as distinctly **Hellenic** in dress and pose (known as the Gandhara School of Art). Following Alexander's departure from India, the Maurya Empire (322-185 BCE) rose under the reign of **Chandragupta** Maurya (322-298) until, by the end of the third century BCE, it ruled over almost all of northern India.

Chandragupta's son, Bindusara reigned between 298-272 BCE and extended the empire throughout the whole of India. His son was **Ashoka** the Great (lived 304-232, reigned 269-232 BCE) under whose rule the empire flourished at its height. Eight years into his reign, Ashoka conquered the eastern **city-state** of Kalinga which resulted in a death toll numbering over 100,000. Shocked at the destruction and death, Ashoka embraced the teachings of the Buddha and embarked on a systematic programme advocating Buddhist thought and principles. He established many monasteries and gave lavishly to Buddhist communities. His ardent support of Buddhist values eventually caused a strain on the government both financially and politically as even his grandson, Sampadi, heir to the throne, opposed his policies. By the end of Ashoka's reign the government treasury was severely depleted through his regular religious donations and, after his death, the empire declined rapidly.

The country splintered into many small kingdoms and empires (such as the Kushan Empire) in what has come to be called the Middle Period. This era saw the increase of trade with Rome (which had begun c. 130 BCE) following **Augustus Caesar**'s conquest of Egypt in 30 BCE (Egypt had been India's most constant partner in trade in the past). This was a time of individual and cultural development in the various kingdoms which finally flourished in what is considered the Golden Age of India under the reign of the Gupta Empire (320-550 CE).

The Gupta Empire is thought to have been founded by one Sri Gupta ('Sri' means 'Lord') who probably ruled between 240-280 CE. He laid the foundation for the government which would so stabilize India that virtually every aspect of culture reached its height under the reign of the Guptas. Philosophy, literature, science, mathematics, architecture, astronomy, technology, art, engineering, religion, and astronomy, among other fields, all flourished during this period, resulting in some of the greatest of human achievements. The*Puranas of Vyasa* were compiled during this period and the famous caves of Ajanta and Ellora, with their elaborate carvings and vaulted rooms, were also begun. Kalidasa the poet and playwright wrote his masterpiece *Shakuntala*and the *Kamasutra* was also written, or compiled from earlier works, by *Vatsyayana*. *Varahamihira* explored astronomy at the same time as *Aryabhatta*, the mathematician, made his own discoveries in the field and also recognised the importance of the concept of zero, which he is credited with inventing. As the founder of the Gupta Empire defied orthodox Hindu thought, it is not surprising that the Gupta rulers advocated and propagated Buddhism as the national belief and this is the reason for the plentitude of Buddhist works of art, as opposed to Hindu, at sites such as **Ajanta** and **Ellora**.

The Decline of Empire and the Coming of Islam

The empire declined slowly under a succession of weak rulers until it collapsed around 550 CE. The Gupta Empire was then replaced by the rule of **Harshavardhan** (590-647) who ruled the region for 42 years. A literary man of considerable accomplishments (he authored three plays in addition to other works) **Harshavardhan** was a patron of the arts and a devout Buddhist who forbade the killing of animals in his kingdom but recognised the necessity to sometimes kill humans in **battle**. He was a highly skilled military tactician who was only defeated in the field once in his life. Under his reign, the north of India flourished but his kingdom collapsed following his death. The invasion of the Huns had been repeatedly repelled by the Guptas and then by **Harshavardhan** but, with the fall of his kingdom, India fell into chaos and fragmented into small kingdoms lacking the unity necessary to fight off invading forces.

In 712 CE the Muslim general **Muhammed bin Quasim** conquered northern India, establishing himself in the region of modern-day Pakistan. The Muslim invasion saw an end to the indigenous empires of India and, from then on, independent city states or communities under the control of a city would be the standard model of government. The Islamic Sultanates rose in the region of modern-day Pakistan and spread north-west. The disparate world views of the religions which now contested each other for acceptance in the region and the diversity of languages spoken, made the unity and cultural advances, such as were seen in the time of the Guptas, difficult to reproduce. Consequently, the region was easily conquered by the Islamic Mughal Empire. India would then remain subject to various foreign influences and powers (among them the Portuguese, the French, and the British) until finally winning its independence in 1947 CE in 20th century (*www.ancient.eu/india*).

Syncretism and Anthropology

Syncretism is a combination of separate concepts into one new, unique idea. Cultural syncretism is when an aspect of two or more distinct cultures blend together to create a new custom, idea, practice, or philosophy. Cultural syncretism can occur for many reasons, from immigration to military conquest to the marriages between groups, and results in a culture finding ways to blend new customs into their own. The term syncretism belongs in part to anthropology and in part to religious studies. In the latter, it has been a way of describing a phenomenon not unusual in spiritual practice: the process of combining practices taken from different religious traditions (Leopold & Jensen 2004). Syncretism has recently re-emerged as a valuable tool for understanding the complex dynamics of ethnicity, interconnectedness and post-modernism. In the present era of increasing cultural condensation, syncretism is a prevailing event. The sociologists and social anthropologists have thrown much light on the variety of religious forms through their studies of belief systems, rituals, symbols and meaning all over the world but they have not paid adequate attention to the phenomenon of syncretism, though we find a few exceptions (Firth 1970:87). In anthropological literature the Cargo cult has been described as a form of syncretism. Cargo cults are essentially syncretistic, blending the "Christian doctrine" with "aboriginal beliefs" (Worsley 1990). Anthropologists have also included the blend of African, Native American, and Roman Catholic saints and deities in Caribbean "voodoo" cults as instances of syncretism. Though the process of syncretism provides an independent field of study, it was nevertheless ignored by the anthropologists and when discussed it was imperfectly included within "the study of acculturation" (Kottak 1991:407).

Acculturation results when groups of individuals come into continuous firsthand contact, (with) "changes in the original culture patterns" of either or both groups (Redfield *et. al* 1936: 149). In much of anthropological studies these days the acculturation concept is stated to be replete with shortcomings. Indeed in different societies the pre-change culture traits, culture patterns and religious customs survive in greater or lesser degree and therefore "acculturation" persists in such societies only as an incomplete and imperfect process. Shaw and Stewart (1994), have observed that within anthropology, where notions of the 'purity' of traditions have not had much credibility for some time, syncretism has been ascribed a neutral, and often positive, significance. Recently, there has been criticism of concepts such as 'cultural purity', wholeness or 'authenticity'.

In post-modern-anthropology in which syncretic processes are considered basic not only to religion and ritual but to 'the predicament of culture' (Clifford 1988: 14-15) identities no longer presuppose continuous cultures or traditions. Everywhere groups improvise local performances from (re-) collected pasts. Organic culture (is indeed) reconceived as inventive process or creolised 'intercultural' (Clifford 1988: 14-15). Syncretism has always been part of the negotiation of identities and hegemonies in situations such as conquest, trade, migration, religious dissemination and intermarriage. The growth of a western-dominated world economic system, however, was accompanied by the growth of a Western-dominated world cultural system (Hannerz 1987, 1992), in which processes of capitalism and cultural hegemony transformed not only relations of power and production but also experiences of personhood, of the body, gender, time, space and religion. The appropriation of totalizing and globally spread processes such as capitalism, commodity consumption and 'rationalist' models of development is often inseparable from the appropriation of totalizing and globally spread religions... (Shaw and Stewart 1994).Van der Veer argues that there are debates over syncretism in societies in which identities are defined through religion. Since India combines these by being a secular state in which religious affiliation partially defines cultural identity, it makes sense that syncretism and multiculturalism are often equated in Hindu political discourse (1994).

Agents of Syncretism in Language

Ethnic origins, religions and language are the major sources of cultural diversity. India is full of diversity of its culture. From the beginning of Indian civilisation has a pluralistic in character. From the Vedic period of time and rise of Buddhism and Jainism in early medieval period which witnessed the early zenith in the bhakti movement. This composite tradition attained primacy during the late medial period. We have seen that many of the people, kings, and people of different countries entered in India. And given a certain impact through their influences or some time accidently impacted in our country. Mostly these changes of language resulted through the assimilation or synthesis form and results a new form of language, because each group or community has distinct identities of their own. Often interaction, exchange, and integration characterize inter community relation, and bind people together. Language is an important attributes of a population and has great relevance and significance in a multilingual, multiethnic country like India. There is probably more diversity of language and dressing pattern in India than anywhere on the earth. If we given in light upon the history of India.

Indian society has a rich diversity staring from the arrivals of the Aryans; there was an interaction with conflict, co-operation and synthesis of different cultural religious streams. Linguistic evidences demonstrate the incorporation and adoption of regional features into the mainstream of Sanskritic culture distinctly. Certain kind of echo formation, which is characteristics of the Austric family of language, found their way in the Indo- Aryan speeches. As early as 2000 B.C. the people who reside in Indus- valley had migrated to gangetic plains and to particular places in the western side, segregating two chief languages i.e. Indo-Aryan languages and Iranian groups. It needs no special mentioning that Indian languages are a part of this Indo-Aryan family. These four racio- linguistic group have met and flourished in India- i.e. The Austric, the sino-tibetan, the Dravidian, and finally the Aryan. It has been suggested by some that over and above those four groups, there might have been one or more there seems to be some evidences from linguistic for this idea. But nothing definitely has a yet been found out, and we are quite content to look upon these four groups as the basic ones in the Indian scene.Language is an important source of diversity. There are as many as 325 languages and25 scripts use, deriving from various linguistic families- the Indo Aryan, Tibeto-burman, Dravidian, Austro-asiatic, Andamanese, Semitic, Indo-Traian, Sino-Tibetan, and Indo-European apart from thousands of dialects.

In fact, origin and development of Indian languages in generally sectioned into three major phases: Old phase, comprising the Vedic and classical Sanskrit, middle phase developed from about third century B.C. Incorporating specified vernacular Sanskrit dialects namely *prakrit*. Pali had served as major dialects. The third phase had commended from 10th century A.D. modern language structure in India includes languages of North and central provinces of the sub continental.

The language of India primarily belongs to the two linguistic families. First is Indo-Europian which spoken by Indo Aryans which is about 75 % of the population and other one is Dravidian population spoken about 25%. If we look back to our past, that we find that individual mother tongues in Indian are total than more about 1000 including dialects. If we are talking about Hindi language, which is started as Apabhramsha in the 7th century and it became stable by the 10th century. Several dialects of Hindi have been used in literature. Braj was the popular literacy dialects until it was replaced by Khari boli in 19th century. If we are talking about history of India at that time two main languages have played an important role i.e. Persian and English.

The northern Indian languages from the Celestine family evolved from Old- Indo- Aryan such as Sanskrit, by the way of the middle Indo- Aryan and *prakrit* language. There is no consensus on the specific time when the modern north Indian language such as Hindi, Marathi, Punjabi, and Bengali emerged out 1000 C.E. is commonly accepted. The development of each language was influenced by social and political contact with foreign invaders and speakers of other languages. Hindi and Urdu are closely related languages were strongly influenced by Persian and Arabic. The south Indian (Dravidian) languages had a history independent of Sanskrit. The origin of the Dravidian languages, as well as their subsequent development and the period of the differentiation are unclear and adequate comparative linguistic research in to the Dravidian languages are lacking. Since the middle of the second millennium BC, Indian civilisation has drawn several migrant groups of communities to fits fold. The advent of the Indo-aryans, the Tibeto-burman-speaking mongoloid people, *kushanas, sakas,* Greeks, Arabs, Turks, Persian, Afghans and Mongols in ancient and medieval periods and the Portugese, Dutch, French and English people in later times testifies to the pervasive of the migration process in India. In the course of time, most of these migrant groups adopted them to local conditions and were influenced by the languages, beliefs and cultural patterns of the indigenous people. The extensive and protracted process of interaction, exchange and mutual adaptation among various groups and communities brought about India's characteristic diversity and a composite structure culture and civilisation. It is important to shed light upon the fact that both the Dravidian languages and all Indo-Aryan languages complement each other by borrowing words and grammatical tenets from each other. It remains only to be mentioned that origin of Indian languages not only did witness their evolvement in the pre-historic eras, during the supremacy of Hindu rulling in India, the time can be approximately dedicated to the 10th to 14th centuries.

Under the thriving Mughal Empire, Persian became very influential as the language of prestige of the Islamic courts, but, as a matter of fact, the Persian was displaced by Urdu. This Indo- Aryan language is actually a combination with the Persian elements in its vocabulary with the grammar of the local dialects. The two largest languages that formed from Apabhramsa where Hindi and Bengali, others include Oriya, Gujarati, Marathi, and Punjabi. The common Hindi that is spoken in India as actually standard Hindi, which is the sanskrit version of the local Hindustani spoken in Delhi area since the Mughals. In the Hindi-speaking areas the prestige dialects was long Braj-bhasha, but this was replaced in the 19th century by Khariboli based commonly known as Urdu.

In addition, all modern Indo-Aryan languages, Munda languages and Dravidian languages, have borrowed many words either directly from Sanskrit or indirectly via middle Indo-Aryan languages, word originating in Sanskrit are estimated to constitute roughly fifty percent of the vocabulary of Modern Indo-Aryan languages.

Agents of Syncretism in Dressing Pattern

In India, if we talking about dressing pattern of our culture that the pattern of dressing was simple, no use of scissors at that time, and no use of stitched clothes in India in earlier times. Because according to Hindu mythology, that a piece of cloth, has been cut with scissors considered as un-whole (Kshit) as opposed to Akshit. Meaning of Akshit is impure. In Hindu society all the rituals which we perform from birth to death like - *upnayan sanskaar*, which not only performing by Hindus but also some other religion like- Buddhism and Jains are performed and wear clothes which is unstitched. Firstly the use of this tool like scissors firstly brought in India by the Greeks. Even today a very large majority of population mostly like to wear like- Dhoti, Lungi, Sari, etc. Presently, the impact of different societies, cultural impact of dresses we seen here widely in all around, and our present generation inspired by foreign clothes and liked to wear without any hesitation. Our traditional and cultural dress of women is sari and men's wear dhoti that has been our traditional dress. But now women's girls like to wear, pyjama- kurta, salwaar-kameej, jeans-top, kurti mostly wear. And girls like to wear short dresses due to impact of modernisation. And the dresses which use to wear by men's like- shirt, pant, jeans, trousers, waist coat etc. took place of our traditional dress. But somewhere, in some occasions people mostly like to wear our traditional attire in behalf of these foreign dresses, like in rituals, festivals, marriage ceremonies etc. But majority of people, did not know about the origin of these dresses, there where it comes, and what the story behind it.

Now I would like to inform all these original habitat of foreign dresses like- In India there has no use of stitched clothes, even a shock. The shirt, trousers, coat and the waist coat all these dress are came from Europeans, their impact in our country was arises from the establishment of east India company, due to the impact which brought lots of changes, not only in our dress, but in our cultural pattern. If we talking about the other form of dresses like- Pyjama, this word is from Persian in origin, the meaning of Pyjamais a garments which worn over the legs. And the Kurta, it has some confusion because that some says it may originate from Afghanistan and some says from

Persia, both Kurta-Pyjama. And the Salwaar- kameej came to us from Afghanistan but it is not possible that the Kameezis from Portugese or Turkish in origin. The chemise, an undergarment worn by women, is off from French origin, and the blouse is English and so is the petticoat. There is no word for the last three in any Indian language.

In absence of stitched clothing in earlier time people used to wear clothes which they wear as tied all together. Interestingly, sewing and stitching were known and very much in use for other purposes since Indus valley civilisations. Even a few decades back in rural India, we would seen men mostly wearing dhoti in lower parts of body and women still wear sari, both are in unstitched form.

In fact, as recently as the late 19th century, when the Brahmo-Samaj in Bengal started a campaign in Bengal that women should cover the upper part of their body by wearing blouse, there were vociferous protests from organisations of Bengali Brahmins lamenting the fact that the blouse was part of a European conspiracy against our traditions and culture.

Gyanandanandini Devi was invented the form of Drapping sari, she was wife of Satyendra Nath Tagore, who was first Indian ICS officer. He and his wife was invited to socialised with English officers, and she had to refuse to wear western dress and then prevalent way of wearing one piece Sari was not very civil for the Victoria age. For that reason, she started wearing blouse and Sameez with Sari, which become a tradition.

Language and Dressing Pattern in contemporary society

In this present paper, researcher has trying to explaining about the present dressing pattern and the language which we use to communicate with people has been now totally in mixed form, but in some way our traditional dressing pattern we using as in occasional and in daily, are somewhere in amalgamated form. In central part of India, the states are Uttar Pradesh and Madhya Pradesh. In Uttar Pradesh there has 75 districts and the language which spoken as Khariboli, Awadhi, Bundeli, Brijbhasha, Bhojpuri, Puravancha languages are spoken in different parts of Uttar Pradesh. But due to migration, which is related with job or any other way and due to marriage, is the main reasons for transforming and intermixing giving a result of a new form. Today the dialect which we use for speaking in this area are not totally Hindi, it is a mixed form of Urdu and Persian, specially the language which is called as our national language Hindi is now fully a synthesized form of language, where some word mixed up and formed Hinglish, generally present generation using to speak in Hinglish for general communication, it is a mix form of Hindi and some words of English. Nobody which I have ever seen presently who totally speaking in original Hindi language except in rural areas, but in rural areas here people after getting education adopted and uses English very frequently. But during in formal way people totally using English. The Hindi, in which people speaking, in this form of dialect there has full mixing of the words of Urdu, Persian and Sanskrit.

But there has a certain impact of languages in different areas through their way of speaking the words and whole sentence is quite different from other region. Hindi is mutually intelligible with Urdu, both languages being standardized registers of Hindustani. Urdu is generally associated with South Asian Muslims. The main difference between the two is that Hindi is written in the Devanagari script, while Urdu is written in Nastaliq, but when spoken equally both are mutually intelligible. Mutual intelligibility decreases, however, in specialised contexts where Urdu has borrowed words from Persian and Arabic, while Hindi has done from Sanskrit and English. Sanskrit has had a propound impact on the language and literature of India. Hindi, India's most spoken language is a Sanskritised register of the Khariboli dialect.

Awadhi language is an eastern Hindi language which is considered as a dialect of Hindi- Urdu continuum. This language is also spoken majority in Awadh region of Uttar Pradesh. Moreover some speakers can be found in Delhi and Madhya Pradesh. Furthermore a blend of Brij-bhasha, Awadhi, Bundeli is broadly spoken in Vatsa country of south of Awadh region which even in habits Allahabad and Kanpur areas. Also this verbal communication is extensively spoken innumerous Caribbean countries where many residents of Uttar Pradesh have been brought as indentured labours by the British government. As per 2001census, this language is ranked as 29th language in the list of language. This Awadhi language is recognised by number of names such as Abadi, abadhi, abohi, briswari, kosali, and kojali. Also it is considered as the main dialect of Eastern Hindi branch in Indo-aryan group of languages. These are basically spoken in northern parts of the Indian sub continent and also its Diasporas are distributed all across the world. This language is also broadly spoken in lower areas of ganges- Yamuna doab. This language belongs to Indo-european family which further includes few groups such as Indo-Iranian, Indo Aryan group, central zone and east central zone. This language is largely spoken in many dialects Awadh region like- Rae-bareli, Gonad, Balrampur, Pratapgarh, Sultanpurand Lucknow, Agra, Kaushambi, Fatehpur, Sitapur, Mirzapur, Sant Ravidas Nagar, LakhimpurKheri, and Ambedkar Nagar. Bagheli language is a Hindi eastern verbal communication which is orated in the Baghelkhand district of central India. The Bagheli orators are seen chiefly in six areas of Madhya Pradesh (Satna, Rewa, Sindhi, Umaria, Shahdol and Anuppur). The language spoken is Baghelkhand has been known as Bagheli since the 13th century.

Bagheli is a regional language used for intra group and inter group communication. It is also known as Baghelkhandi, Rimahi and Riwai (Rewa district). Some alternatives names of Baghelilanguage are Godwani, Kawathi,

Bhugelkhud, Gangai, Mannadi, kenat, kevati, kevat, boli, kewat, kewani, kewot, Mandal, kumhrai and riwai. Northeast Madhya Pradesh includes satna, rewa, sidhi, umaria, shahdol, anuppur, mandla, dindori, jabalpurand, chhindwara regions of Bagheli idiom. Also in Uttar Pradesh, Mirzapur, Allahabad, and Banda areas of bagheli language. Even Hamirpur district inhabit Bilaspur, Chhattisgarh and Koriya districts. This language is also spoken in some parts of Nepal. According to Dr. George Abraham Grierson in his linguistic survey of India classified Bagheli under Indo-Aryan, Eastern Hindi. The extensive research by Dr. Bhagawati Prasad Shukla also agrees with Dr. Grierson's classification. Ethnologue classifies Bagheli as Indo- Iranian, Indo-Aryan, East-central zone (Grimes 1992: 552).

Conclusion

India is a multiracial, multiracial, multi-religious country. The fully form of this diversity we have seen everywhere in India. If we look at the past of the history this diversity has been shows for the 3000 years a great tendency towards an integration of these diverse elements.

This paper is fully dedicated to a close reflection on syncretism from two distinct, yet interrelated, theoretical perspectives presented by the field of Anthropology in linguistics and dressing pattern. According to the historians that this diversity was starting from the arrivals of Aryan-invaders, there wasan interaction with conflict, co-operation and synthesis of different cultural and religious streams.

Almost everything that we see, taste, hear, smell and touch, the building we have built, the tools we use, the cloths we wear, the languages we speak and even the ideas that we have are products of processes, discoveries, inventions and development that occurred at place far and near, in the distance and not so distant past, and have reached us through very complex and round about routes. We know that Indian society has a rich diversity. Starting from the arrivals of the Aryans, there was an interaction with conflict, co-operation and synthesis of different culture. Let us look at some of the elements of our daily lives that we do not normally consider as part of our culture but as important as our classical traditions in dance and music.

Syncretism is when a culture adopts certain aspects of a foreign culture, and incorporates it or changes it according to their own culture. This assimilation can take many and varied forms, from religion to education, from agriculture to industry. The concept 'syncretism' in fact has become the focus of much debate among anthropologist and scholar such as Mac Gaffey repudiating the concept entirely, given that it has projected conations popularly in the hands of some theologians, and the fact that all religious system are to some degree 'syncretic'.

India is one of the multilingual nations in the world today. Linguistic diversity in the world today, is an issue of growing social importance because a majority of all living languages are threatened in their continued existence. Multilingualism is a common and increasing phenomenon in present day society which can be studied from different perspectives. The purpose of this paper is to focus on language spoken in India. The languages of India belong to several language families; the major one is the Indo-Aryan family languages of this family are spoken by a large number of people in India. Second major language group is Dravidian families. Other groups are Austro-asiatic, Tibeto-burman, and a few minor language families and isolates are other language groups spoken in the country.

Indian clothing has been influenced by centuries of various cultural influences from outside the Indian subcontinent, which India has adopted and made it her own. All the while there has been and is a simultaneous indigenous evolution of clothing, and fashion in India. Indian people have also easily adopted clothing from outside India like western wear. In India this form of cultural and their aspects are fully in synthesized form, from the beginning, after the entry of Aryan- Invaders, Dutches, Portuguese, Francis, Britishers and they brought some changes in the form of export and import of trade, but some way it impacted accidentally in India, This impact in form of behavior, dressing pattern, food, speaking articles and many more things given impact in our tradition and culture. We know our traditional dressing pattern, which worn by the male in form of dhoti and for female it is sari, without blouse and petticoat. All these types of cloths are without the use of scissors. After the impact and collaboration with people of foreign countries makes changes and their form of cultural pattern mixes with our pattern of dressing and given a new form of dresses in Indian tradition. All the form of dresses we wear today, which originated from different areas and synthesized in our pattern as I describe you in above part.

Presently women in India are equally comfortable in jeans and trousers or saris and salwars. Men too are the same with trousers and shorts and the kurtas. These are not fancy dress or special occasion clothing, but natural every day wear.

References

Anita M. Leopold and Jeppe S. Jensen. (2004), eds., *Syncretism in Religion: A Reader*, Sheffield, UK: Equinox.

Clifford, J. (1988). *The Predicament of Culture: Twentieth Century Ethnography, Literature and Art*, Cambridge, MA: Harvard University Press.

Firth, Raymond. (1996). *Religion: A Humanist Interpretation*. London: Rutledge.

Hannerz, U. (1987). The World in Creolisation, *Africa* 57: 546-59.

Hannerz, U. (1992). *Cultural Complexity: Studies in the Social Organisation of Meaning*. New York: Columbia University Press.

http://www.ancient.eu/india Retrieved on 08/08/2015, 22:38:46.

http://www.newworldencyclopedia.org/entry/Languages_of_India Retrieved on 08/08/2015, 23:56:49.

Peter Van der Veer, "Syncretism, Multiculturalism, and the Discourse of Tolerance," in *Syncretism/Anti-Syncretism: The Politics of Religious Synthesis,* eds. Charles Stewart and Rosalind Shaw London: Routledge, 1994.

Redfield, R., R. Linton and M. J. Herskovits. (1936). A Memorandum on Acculturation. *American Anthropologist* 38: 149-152.

Stewart, Charles and Rosalind Shaw (Ed.) (1994). *Syncretism? Anti-Syncretism: The Politics of Religious Synthesis*. London: Rutledge.

Worsley, Peter M. (1990). "Cargo Cults" in *Anthropology: Contemporary Perspective* Ed. Whitten, P. and D.E.K Hunter, New York .USA: Harper Collins Publication.

9

Assam: A Socio-Religious Syncretistic Entity of North East India

—Ankit Kumar Gaur

North East as an Indigenous Socio-Cultural Entity

The North-East India consists of miraculous socio-cultural features in terms of ethnicity, linguistic and socio-cultural practices among its habitants. Numerous indigenous tribal communities inhabit the hill ranges of this region like the Naga Hills, Patkai Hills, Lushai Hills and Shillong Plateau. Each ethnic group has its own distinctive socio-cultural entity (Sharma 2003). The mysterious and unexplored North-East India comprises of seven states commonly known as "Seven Sister States". These states are Arunachal Pradesh, Assam, Manipur, Meghalaya, Mizoram, Nagaland and Tripura. North-east India is the homeland of a large number of tribes that constitutes approximately 300 tribal communities who speak around 400 dialects and estimated 32 million people live, among whom 9.1 million are indigenous people (Jose 2012: 01-07). The North East is a very rich region with great indigenous wealth of flora, fauna and minerals beside a great tribal culture a great social wealth, People of this land having different religious beliefs and practices, primarily based on supernaturalism without any intermixing of their socio-ethical values. In every human society, worship performs with traditional rituals for the well-being of all. Many tribal communities preserve this tradition through folklore. Tribal folklore is rich in magico-religious beliefs and taboos. Their taboos, festivals, rituals and other cultural aspects are closely associated with the surrounding vegetation preserved on religious ground. Among seven sisters and one-brother states, Assam is the geographically good enough for the best habitat among others.

Assam: Socio-Religious Entity

Assam is the gateway to the northeast and an umbrella for all type of ethic group, tribal and non-tribal both. The ethnic origin of the Assamese varies from Mongoloid tribes to those of directly Indian stock. The inhabitants of Assam divided into the indigenous tribal group such as the Kacharis (Bodo, Sonowal, Dimasa, Thengal, Mech, Madahi etc.), the Miris, the Deoris, the Rabhas, the Garos and so on. On other hand, non- tribal groups include the Ahoms, the Kayasthas, the Kalitas and many others that represent the present Assamese culture. Culture of Assam is a rich textile woven with multi-colour yarns of distinct heritage of all the races that inhabit here. Every tribal group has its own unique religious beliefs and they celebrate their respective festivals with joy and happiness.

Historical construction of Culture of Assam

It has been seen that Assam has biologically composite people and from this has stemmed a composite culture. Three distinctive cultural traits can be observed among the people of Assam i.e., The Vedic or Hindu culture, the Tibeto-Burman or Tribal culture and the Tai or Ahom culture. The cultural backdrop of the Assamese people dates back to almost 2000 years when the first cultural assimilation took place with Austrio-Asiatic and Tibeto-Burman as the major components. Assam has a large number of tribes and each tribe is unique in its tradition, culture, dress and way of life. Most tribes have their own languages though Assamese is the principal language of the state. Thus, the culture of Assam is traditionally a hybrid one. The people of the state of Assam are an intermixture of various racial stocks such as Mongoloid, Indo-Burmese, Indo-Iranian and Aryan. The Assamese culture is a rich and exotic tapestry of all these races evolved through a long assimilative process.

In Assam, a number of festivals are celebrated by the different races and groups of people present in the state. The rich cultural heritage of Assam has emerged out of the assimilation of various customs, beliefs, traditions, rituals and customs. Bihu, the major festival of Assam is celebrated thrice a year as Bhogali Bihu, Rangali/Bohag Bihu and Kangali Bihu. Bohag Bihu is observed by the ethnic tribes in their own traditional style. Bihu is celebrated as Baisagu by the Bodos, Baikhu or Khokchi by the Rabhas, Bisu by the Tiwas and Bohagiyo Bihu by the Deoris. Baisagu is the most colourful festival celebrated by the Bodo Kacharis. It is celebrated as a spring festival and the dance form associated with this festival is the Baisagu dance in which any individual can participate irrespective of age or sex. Similarly, the Bohagiyo Bihu of the Deoris is also a spring festival and accompanied by the colourful Deodhani dance. Madahis celebrate Umra Puja and Sarania Kacharis celetrate Ba-gohain (Ba = (Bamboo)-gohai = (god)) in the month of Bohag too. A host of other festivals like Me-Dam-Me-Phi, Ali-Aye-Ligang, Kherai, Rongker, Hachang,

Langkhun are also observed by the ethnic tribes of Assam. The festivals are remarkable for their association with nature and encouraging peace and harmony amongst the different communities.

Ali-Aye-Ligang is an agro-based spring festival of the Mising tribe. The first Wednesday, of the month Gunmur Polo (Feb-Mar) marks the beginning of this festival, which goes around five days. The prime attraction of this festival is the Gumrag dance in which young boys and girls dance with great passion. Rongker celebrated as a spring festival at the beginning of the New Year by the Karbis. The Langkhun celebrate by the Tiwas, it is actually a form of worshipping bamboo. Me-Dam-Me-Phi celebrates by the Tai-Ahom community, which is actually a death rite. In this occasion, the Ahom community worships their ancestors and it held annually on 31 January of every year. The numerous festivals celebrate by the different ethno-cultural groups are characterised by a spirit of accommodation and togetherness. These festivals are colourful, passionate, mesmerizing and reflect the true spirit and tradition of the people of Assam. From ancient times, Assam had a predominantly rural base and culture. Even in the days of Bhaskarvarma and other famous rulers there were very few towns in Assam and people were primly based on agriculture (Chatterji 1970).

The base of Assamese culture lies in Hindu religion and the Vedic civilisation. A majority of the Assamese is the Vaishnavas (A sect of Hinduism). The Vaishnavas do not believe in idol worshipping and perform Namkirtana where the glory of Lord Vishnu being recited. The fifteenth century was the dark phase of Assamese society. During this period, art and culture received a severe setback, society was more involved with material pleasure and even religious practices were perverted. Then like a breath of fresh air came Mahapurusha Srimanta Sankardeva.

In fact it is not possible to discuss the culture and people of Assam without referring to Srimanta Sankardeva and his propagation of the Assamese version of neo-Vaishnavism. Mahapurusha Sankardeva said to be the pioneer of medieval renaissance in Assam. Sankardeva preached the message of Bhakti that is unmotivated love and devotion to the lord. He was indeed a great socio-religious reformer and also responsible for developing a scientific and progressive outlook amongst the Assamese community. Sankardeva created the institution of the 'Naamghars' and the 'Sattras' which welcomed one and all with open doors irrespective of caste, creed, race and religion. Interestingly the first pillar of the Bordua Namghar was erected by Chandsai, a Muslim devotee to the chanting of 'La illallahu Muhammad ur rasula ulla' (Bora 2002: 68).

Sankardeva praised the Sattva guna - "the quality of goodness" – like humility, compliance, restraint, benevolence and non-violence (Bora, 2002, 112). He had a great role to play in the efflorescence of Assamese literature.

He composed the holy book 'Kirtan-ghosa' that contains a large number of religious hymns. In fact, the 'Kirtan-ghosa' was his magnum opus, a collection of vernacular renditions of episodes from the Bhagavata highlighting the glory of Lord Krishna. Sankardeva found solace in Krishna, the character around whom the Bhagavata revolved. He felt that absolute surrender to Lord Krishna without any adherence to ritualism was the greatest religion of man. Thus Sankardeva adopted the medium of congregational prayer called 'kirtan' or 'naamprasanga' which involved chanting of songs along with dramatic performances. Srimanta Sankardeva was responsible for making 'bhakti' an instrument of peace and harmony. Sankardeva was also instrumental in setting up of the 'sattras'. It was through the 'sattras' that he propagated the principle that 'service to God is service to humanity'. These sattras also became centres for the pursuit of art and culture. The sattras performed 'bhaonas', which is a form of theatre meant to arouse devotion using the medium of songs, dances, dialogue and characterisation. Sattras also performed 'Bargeets' which were devotional songs having great literary value.

This great figure was also the initiator of the Satriya style of dance, which evolved towards the end of the 15th century or early in the 16th century. This graceful dance form introduced by Sankardeva in his wonderful composition of 'ankiya bhaona', the Vaishnava theatre. Originally, this dance form performed only in the Sattra, the Vaishnava monastery. Satriya is a classical dance form and have performed in the monasteries for several centuries. However, recently this dance form has emerged from the monastery on to the contemporary scene. Sankardeva preached social equality and he was responsible for shaping the future of a composite Assamese society and culture. He was a philosopher and believed that all men had a common identity and social standing. It is to his credit that even after 500 years of his demise the religion that he preached is still widely followed today. As the Late Prof. Dr. Maheshwar Neog has said "The neo-Vaisnavism inculcated by Sankardeva brought in its train a literary upheaval and the fine arts like music, dancing and painting also came to have their place in the life of the people" (Neog 2004: 24).

The history of Assam went through various phases of formation and fragmentation before it took the shape of the modern one. Modern Assam is a creation of British colonialism. The British entered Assam in 1824. The Burmese war and the Treaty of Yandabo in 1826 brought in the British influence into the state. With the advent of the British, a new age began. After its annexation, the British Empire, in 1826 through the treaty of Yandabo, Assam was made a part of Bengal Presidency (British territories). This age brought great literary and cultural changes in Assam. When Assam came under its rule the British faced great difficulty in administration due to language and cultural barriers. To overcome this crisis the British hired people from Bengal in order to serve as clerks and 'moharis'. They drilled in the fact to the British that Assamese was not a language in its own right but only a branch of Bengali. It was during this period that Assamese language received a huge setback and Assamese language was replaced by Bengali language in schools, colleges and courts. This changeover took place because Assamese was nothing but a dialect of Bengali.

At this point, the Christian Missionaries contributed a great deal towards the development of the Assamese language and literature. The American Baptist Mission published the 'Dharmapustak Antobhag' i.e. the New Testament in Assamese in the year 1813. The complete Bible, or 'Dharmapustak' inclusive of both the Old Testament and the New Testament was published in Assamese by William Carey in 1833. William Carey was helped in his translation work by Atmaram Sharma. The Missionaries with great zeal and gusto mastered the local languages that give them easy accessibility to the locals.

Assamese Culture- a syncretic unit

There is a famous English proverb, which says that 'Rome was not built in a day'. Similarly, the culture of a particular society can never evolve in a single day. It takes hundreds and hundreds of years for any culture to establish itself. However, it is very difficult to pinpoint the exact date as to when a particular culture evolved. In English, the word 'culture 'has been derived from the Latin word Cultura, the root word being 'cult' (Sharma 1987: 26) Understanding culture is trying to understand people. When delving into the historical evolution of Assamese culture it is essential to remember that the rich culture of Assam is composed of different stages and it is a mixture of many diverse elements. Culture is about people. In the words of Malinowski, "culture is a total system of life and includes the entire mental, social and physical means which make life run its course" (Sharma 1987: 6). In order to gain knowledge of Assamese culture, it is very important to look into the history of how Assam became a home to a large population of various ethnic groups. Assam has developed a composite culture resulting out of the assimilation and amalgamation of the cultures of the diverse ethnic groups inhabiting the state. It is traditionally a syncretistic unit, developed due to the cultural assimilation of different ethno-cultural groups under various politico-economic systems in different periods of history. The roots of the culture go back to almost two thousand years B.C. when the first cultural assimilation took place with Austro-Asiatic and Tibeto-Burman as the major components. With reference from the great epics Mahabharata and based on the local folklores, it is also hypnotized that there was probably a strong kingdom of these mixed population (of Austro-Asiatic and Tibeto-Burman origin) in the era before Jesus Christ, which led to an early assimilation at a greater scale. Thereafter, in the course of time western migrations of various branches of

Mediterranean and Nordics came across with the mixed northern Indians such as Magadha. These events enriched the aboriginal culture and under certain stronger politico-economic systems, Sanskritisation and Hinduisation were intensified and became prominent. Such an assimilated culture therefore carries many elements of source cultures, of which, exact roots are difficult to trace and are matter of research. However, in each of the elements of Assamese culture, i.e. language, traditional crafts, performing arts, festivity and beliefs either local elements or the indigenous elements in a Hinduised/ Sanskritised forms are always present. Vaishanavite Movement, the 15th century religio-cultural movements under the leadership of great Saint Srimanta Sankardeva and his disciples have provided a new dimension to Assamese culture. In this way, a renewed Hinduisation in local forms took place, and it was initially greatly supported by the Koch and later by the Ahom Kingdoms. The resultant social institutions such as *Namghar* and *Satra* (the Vaishnavite Monasteries) have become part of Assamese way life. The movement contributed greatly towards language, literature and performing and fine arts. It is also noticed that, Vaishnavite Movement attempted to introduce many cultural attributes and modify the way of life of common people.

With the above arguments, it is not difficult to understand that on one hand, greater cultural assimilations created common attributes of Assamese culture during the strong politico-economic systems under stronger dynasties, while on the other hand Neo-Vaisnavism has given a proper cultural shape and strong platform of religious beliefs in Assamese culture. Here researcher strongly says that the time-factor for such integrations and differentiations has played extremely important role along with the position of individual events in the entire series of historical events. With a strong base of tradition and history, the modern Assamese culture is greatly influenced by various events; those took place in the pre-British Assam and in the Post-British Era.

Assamese culture in its true sense today is a 'cultural system' composed of different sub-systems. It is more interesting to note that even many of the source-cultures of Assamese culture are still surviving either as sub-systems or as sister entities. In broader sense, therefore, the Assamese cultural system incorporates its source-cultures and however, it is also important to keep the broader system closer to its roots. Some of the common cultural traits available across these systems are respect towards areca-nut and betel leaves, traditional silk and cotton garments, forefathers and elderly, great hospitality, Bamboo culture and respect towards particular symbolic cloth types such as Gamosa, Arnai, Saddar-mekkhela and Pat/Munga Saari, *et cetra*.

Religious Beliefs & Festivals

Religion is an integral part of any community or society, necessary for its development. It often considered as an organised approach for leading a fulfilling and happy life. The religious community of Assam mainly comprises of Hinduism, Islam, Christianity, Sikhism and Buddhism. Apart from this, various indigenous groups also follow Animism, Tantricism, Brahminism and Vaishnavism. Despite such vast differences in their religious faiths and beliefs, all the people within the state live in perfect peace and harmony with each other. All the festivals, whether it is Durga Puja, Id-ul-Fitr or Christmas, is celebrated by all with equal zeal.

Hinduism, being the major religion in Assam, comprises about 64.9% of the total population, according to the Census Report of 2011. The immaculate form of this religion started when the Aryans came to this region. Originally, the Assamese were practicing the rituals of Tantricism, before the advent of the Neo-Vaishnavite culture founded by Srimanta Shankardeva (1449-1568). The latter form of worship emerged in the state during the 15th century AD and comprises of a major portion of the religious beliefs of the Assamese people at present.

There are followers of Durga, Kali, Saraswati and the Vaishnavite culture in Assam. Among the various temples present in the state, the Kamakhya Temple needs special mention. The temple is dedicated to Goddess Durga and is an important pilgrimage spot of the state. They celebrate Bihu, Tithis of Sankardeva, Madhabdeva, and their disciples, Ambuvachi festival, Rash leela, Janostami etc. Muslims comprise of the second largest religious group in the state and comprise about 30.95% of the entire population. The Powa Mecca in Hajoan is important pilgrimage centre for the Muslims and is visited by thousands of devotees and followers all round the year. Christians also form a sizeable population of the state (3.75%) and several churches are located here. Assam, initially, had a large number of tribes following the customs and rituals of Animism, along with elements of Hinduism. But, in recent times, many such people have adopted the customs and doctrines of Christianity.

Conclusion

The Socio-religious syncretism stands for the merging or union of different socio-cultural institutions, religious and theological beliefs and Assam is an example of Socio-Religious Syncretism in North East India. It has geographical region that flourished in relative cultural isolation for thousands of years but during the course of time, the kings who came across and ruled this land, made an impact of their existence as colonisation and expansion in this geographical locality. In this way, Assam became one of the most socio-religiously syncretistic regions in North East India. In the contemporary Assam, new religious practices are arising by the interaction between Assamese culture, Neo-Vaishanavism, impact of Christianity and other factors, which are making Assam as a unique syncretistic entity. With this researcher concludes that this unified form is the fruit of historic reconciliation of the incongruent religious and cultural practices through hybridisation or amalgamation of different socio-cultural factors and it is really a matter of research that this syncretistic entity, is it a kind of common cultural identity which is overwhelming the small cultural groups? Alternatively, Hybridisation or amalgamation of these factors is the agent of peace and harmony or agent of violence and unrest.

References

1. Bora, P. (2002). Mahapursha Srimanta Sankardeva : The Apostle of Equality. In *Culture and Religions of Assam*. Omsons Publications. New Delhi. p.112.
2. Bora, U. (2002). Present Day Scenario: Assamese Culture – A Study. In *Culture and Religions of Assam*. Omsons Publications. New Delhi. p. 68.
3. Chatterji, S. K. (1970). The *place of Assam in the history and Civilisation of India.*Gauhati University Press.Guwahati. pp. 9-30.
4. Das, B.M. (1987). *The People of Assam: Origin and Composition*. Gyan Publishing House. New Delhi. p. 26, 32.
5. Jose, K. (2012). *Understanding North East India: Contemporary Cultural Perspectives*. NewDelhi: Omsons Publications.
6. Nath, R.M. In Sen. S. (2009). *Tribes and Castes of Assam*. Gyan Publishing House. New Delhi. p. 145.
7. Neog, M. (2004). *Cultural History of Assam*. Omsons Publications. New Delhi. p.24.
8. Sen. S. (2009). *Tribes and Castes of Assam*. Gyan Publishing House. New Delhi. p. 142.
9. Sharma, H. C. (2003). Prehistoric Archaeology of North-East. In T. B. Subba & G.C. Ghosh (Eds.), *The Anthropology of North-East India A Textbook*.New Delhi : Orients Longman Private Limited. pp. 11-27.
10. Sharma, M. (1987). Culture. In Chittattukalam Kuriala (ed.). *Culture and Religions of Assam*. Omsons Publications. New Delhi. p. 26.
11. Stewart, Charles and Rosalind Shaw (Ed.) (1994). *Syncretism? Anti-Syncretism: The Politics of Religious Synthesis*. London: Rutledge.

10

Syncretism among the Tribes of North East India: A Socio-Historical Perspective

— Kuntala Dowarah

The geophysical position, ethnic composition and cultural heritage of north east India has historically remained as a geo- ethnic region. There are four river valleys of Brahmaputra, Barak, Dibang and Imphal with mixed population of tribes and non tribes. The traditional lifestyles of the hill dwellers survived because of the culture of reciprocity and kin based cohesive solidarity practiced by them, inspite of many challenges. The region came under the colonial rule from 19th century that paved the way for the introduction of transport and communication, trade and commerce, western education, and conversion into Christianity. Post independence period brought into focus the development and political aspirations of local ethnic and linguistic groups and leading to the formation of new identities. The transition from hunting, gathering, fishing, shifting agriculture based economies to cash crop economy, highly literate, consumerist, computer savvy technology driven societies is occurring in a very short time frame.[1]

North East India is rare situation where real synthesis of the old and new is taking place to create an entirely different kind of reality. Traditions are continued, people are aware of their heritage but at the same time they are modern, and they look to the outer world. The process of transition is rather fast.

Religion is an important element in the traditional people's life and existence. It however lacked unifying power among most of the communities of the region. Deity was usually identified with a particular clan and at most it existed at the level of a single petty state. Each clan maintained its own cremating ground for keeping the remains of the deceased members. A member of another clan had no place in it. Even members of the same clan did not share this faith. Hill tribal religions did not have religious books, creeds or hymns books. There was also no common worshipping place for the entire community. Closely related to this was a body of superstitious beliefs. Tribal believes in the existence of spirits which resulted in fear, insecurity and timidity. In order to appease the spirits, people made expensive sacrifices and performed time consuming rituals. Such beliefs made people to perceive common diseases like cholera, small pox, malaria, and other major ailments as impersonated beings and identified each with a spirit. Causes for their outbreak were mostly attributed to human violation of the respective personified spirits. In this respect the process of healing technique was through sacrifices, divination and other primal procedures.[2]

T K Ommen in his article on 'Cultural change among the tribes of North East India, discuss on the changing cultural contours of the region. He refers to the western theories of change that process of displacement is inevitable, but the Indian experience it is different for him. It is partially true that the old cultural patterns are done away, but it is also not true that the new cultural pattern is adopted in totality. Thus accretion occurs in partial. Therefore change is the coexistence of the displacement and accretion. Thus the emergent product is the mutation of both, the old and new tradition. The mutation process of displacement and accretion give birth to another dual process- pluralisation and hybridisation. Pluralisation implies cultural elaboration leading to an increase in cultural choices. The resultant cultural set from which one can choose is confined neither to the traditional stock nor to the modern. Hybridisation is an innovative leap to cope with cultural dead ends. All cultures, if denied of occasional breaths of cultural fresh air from outside will die of cultural claustrophobia. That is why we need acculturation that is cross-fertilisation creating new breeds. This is what cultural hybridisation does and hence its importance.

The three major agents of change among the tribes of north east india are the state, the civil society of which the church is the major element in the market forces. The promulgation of the constitution of India ushered in the state legal system for the whole polity. While there is a uniform criminal justice system, a uniform civil code is yet to be introduced. This means that three legal systems co-exists in the context of the civil codes- the state legal system, the religious legal system and the folk legal system. The state legal system is applicable to those who are the followers of Indic religions- Hinduism, Buddhism, Jainism and Sikhism. Those tribes who do not belong to any of these religious group follows civil codes, which may be designated as the folk legal system or a combination of folk legal system and religious legal system[3].

The British Indian census had a religious category variously designated as animists, naturists, primitive etc. But the first census of free India in 1951 abolished this category an d absorbed them into the category of Hindu, if they were not the converts into one of the world religions- Christianity, Islam or Buddhism. But change in the nomenclature of a religious community does not bring about change in their religious beliefs and rituals. Even conversion to a new religion does not bring about changes in culture instantly. Thus religion of northeast India is an amalgam of their primal vision and the new religions into which they inducted. Nature worship by tribes fostered a cosmocentric view affirms that the sacred is dispersed in the entire universe. This is opposed to the homocentric view proffered by western Christianity. However it cannot be affirmed that those tribes of North east India which embraced Christianity have endorsed homocentricism displacing their pre Christian cosmocentrism; prevailing worldview is the mutation of the two.

Christianity in North East India

The spread of Christianity in the hill districts of Assam followed the British administration. The East India Company was more interested in expanding trade in India than spreading Christianity or civilizing the tribes. In the early days of colonisation the European community in India was bitterly opposed to missionaries, chiefly because they might have a disturbing effect on Indians. The Charter Act of 1813 laid down as a duty of the administration to introduce useful knowledge, help religious and moral improvement, reduce the powers of the East India Company and increase the control of the British Parliament over Indian administration.

Christianity thus came to the hills of the North-east as a consequence of administrative policy. The Welsh Presbyterian Mission introduced the Roman script and showed greater zeal for proselytising, as did the American Baptists, who encouraged the Assamese language and script. The abolition of East India Company's powers in 1833 gave a fillip to mission work. During the British rule, the administration supported the work of missionary and subsidised the cost of education, yet the North east was not open house for missionary work.

Mission work was prohibited in part of Garo Hills, unadministered area of Naga Hills, Arunachal and the plains of Manipur and until 1930 in Tripura. Political and social factors decided the extent to which proselytising was permitted. The administration and the missionary worked hand in glove, one facilitating the work of the other. Interestingly, the spread of Christianity in the hill areas of North-east has been faster after Independence than before it. David Scott, the first Commissioner of Assam, brought some English missionaries to preach Christianity to the Garos. Major Jenkins, who succeeded David Scott as the Commissioner of Assam invited American Baptists to come to Assam. In 1836, Nathan Brown, Miles Bronson and OT Cutter came to

Sadiya to take up proselytising work, but did not make much progress amongst the Hindus and tribals (animists) of the plains. From Sadiya they moved to Sibsagar where they established a mission but here again the missionaries did not meet with much success. Bronson then moved to Tirap, where he concentrated on establishing a mission school to teach the Gospel to the Nagas, but had to leave due to death of his sister. By and large the American Mission remained confined to the Brahmaputra Valley, espousing the cause of assamese language.[4]

It was only after the arrival of Rev EW Clark that proselytising began to have some success. Encouraged by Clark's success in baptising a few Nagas in November/December 1872, he was granted permission to open a permanent mission amongst the Ao Nagas. The first Christian village was founded at Molungyimsen in 1876, which was moved to Impur 10 miles North of Mokokchung in 1894. Clark served in Nagaland for nearly three decades and left Nagaland in 1911. He produced Ao-English dictionary and translated the gospels of Mathew and John in Ao language.

Christianity spread well in Ao area but its progress was slow in the Angami and Lotha areas. In Angami area, Christianity spread much later in the beginning of 20th century. Angami language was reduced to writing in Roman script and Biblical work was translated in Angami. The American Baptist Mission entered Naga Hills only after 1876, when the hills had come under some kind of administration. As late as 1891 AW Davis wrote that Nagas were not inclined towards Christianity. In 1947 only 20 percent of the population was Christian in Nagaland; as against nearly 85 % in 2005.

In Manipur missionary work was started by American Baptist Church in 1894 in Mao area, three years after the administration was taken over by the British. They met with much resistance from the animists; the Meiteis of the valley had already converted to Hinduism and were against missionary work. However, the missionaries found the Tangkhul Nagas in Ukhrul area more amenable. Schools were built primarily to convert the hill Nagas of Manipur. By 1907 a strong foundation was laid in the hills of Manipur for the spread of Christianity. In the beginning of the 20th century, there was not a single Christian in Manipur but the decadal growth of Christians as a whole during 1961-71 was 83.66 percent. The Christian population of Manipur as per 1981 census was 34.11 percent of the total population.

In Mizoram, Christianity came in the closing decade of 19th century close upon the heels of the administration in 1890. Two British missionaries came to Aijwal in 1894 and opened two missions – one by Welsh Presbyterian and the other by London Baptists. The spread of Christianity in Mizoram has been phenomenal. In 1901 census, Lushai Hills recorded only 26 Christians in a population of 82,434. By 1981, more than 80 percent of Mizoram population had converted to Christianity. The Christian population of Mizoram as per 1991 census was 85.73 percent of the total population. The centenary of the coming of Christianity to Mizoram was celebrated with great fervor in 1994.

In Meghalaya, the first Presbyterian Church was established amongst the Khasis in 1841 and the American Baptist Mission in Garo Hills in 1864. Before the coming of Christianity, Khasis and Jaintias worshipped a formless God and referred to their religion as Niamtre, while Garos refer to their traditional religion as Sangrarek.

The first Catholic Mission in the hills was German, which was opened towards the end of the 19th century but remained confined to Shillong. During the World War I, Italians replaced it. In 1933, the Catholic Church was opened in Tura in the Garo Hills. The Christian population of Meghalaya as per 1991 census was 64.58 percent of the total population. Incidentally, the influence of the Church of England in the hills is minimal.

Islam in north east India

North-East India and Assam witnessed the spread of Islam in 13th century. The region came into contact with the Muslims when expeditions were undertaken by a number of Muslim invaders. Between 1206 A.D. and 1662 A.D. several expeditions were made by different Muslim invaders to this region. Every Muslim invasion contributed a little towards the strengthening and propagation of Islamic faith in this region.

Khasis came into contact with Muslims around the 17th century. Muslims paid occasional visits to the Khasi hills as wanderers, traders, fortune tellers, hunters and in other capacities. In the course of time these Muslims adopted Khasi customs. In some places of the Khasi hills, some Muslims were even honoured with chieftainship. The Syiems of Mawiong are believed to have descended from four migrant Muslim families. The Muslims of Sylhet made repeated efforts to invade Khasi hills.

Khasis maintained some trade relationships with the Mughal emperors through their viceroys at Murshidabad. During and after the British rule, a number of Muslims from Kabul, Kashmir, Punjab, Jaipur, Allahabad, Madras, Calicut, Lucknow, Banaras, Chapra, Gauhati, Nagaon, Cachar, Sylhet and Dhaka migrated to Shillong and settled there for trade and commerce. Many of them married Khasi women. Thus, there is the presence of a group of Muslim Khasis within the tribe, which is the result of marriage between Muslim males and Khasi women. It has been observed that children born out of the union between a Muslim father and a Khasi mother are considered Muslims as far as their religion is concerned. But for all practical purposes they are treated as Khasi. Bareh opines that the decorations of the graves of Khasi chiefs have been influenced by the decorations of the taziya of Muslims. [Taziya is a model or representation of the shrines of Hassan and Hussain, sons of Ali, cousin and son-in-law of Prophet Muhammad.] Clan among Garos is known as chatchi and there are five known exogamous clans among them. They are Sangma, Marak, Momin, Shira and Areng. Some scholars are of the opinion that originally Garos had two matri moieties – Sangma and Marak and that at a later stage Momin and other chatchi came into existence. It is generally believed that the Momin chatchi originated from the union of a Muslim man and a Garo woman[5].

Muslims constitute 6.99 per cent of the total population in Manipur. A large number of Muslims from undivided Bengal entered this region through the western boundary at different historical times and settled there. The present day Manipuri Muslims (known as Pangans) are believed to be the descendants of the Bengali immigrants and war captives who had come to this region in the beginning of the 17th century. These Muslims, some of who married Meitei women, in the course of time formed a distinct community. Among the Manipuri Muslims the traditional clans are still in existence. It has been reported that in a village called Prompat in the Imphal valley, the Muslim householders belong to 11 sagaior clans namely, Ipham, Kulaibaum, Koijing, Wang, Bogi, Yumikhaibaum, Mogjai, Chesham, Moinam and Phisubaum[6].

The Bodo Kacharis, who constitute an important plains tribe of Assam, observe various ceremonies and festivals connected with birth, death, marriage and agricultural activities. Baisagu and Kherai are the two important festivals of Bodo Kacharis. Baisagu is a spring time festival and Kherai is a religious annual community festival. During the Kherai festival they worship and offer sacrifice to a number of gods and goddesses. One of these gods is called 'Nawab Badshah' or Muslim God by Bodo Kacharis. At the time of offering sacrifice to this god, the priest wears a dhoti in the fashion of a lungi and the sacrifice is made by facing west. While sacrificing the cock, the priest utters the word Bismillah– in the name of Allah. As in the case of Bodo Kacharis, some influence of Islam is also discernible among Rabhas – another plains tribe of Assam. Rabhas celebrate Baikho and Khoksi festivals annually with the intension of propitiating Baikho, the goddess of wealth and prosperity. The Rabhas of Baida area in south Goalpara sacrifice a cock in the name of 'Sainnas Thakur' – one of the gods of Baikho. During the sacrifice, like Bodo Kacharis, a Rabha priest faces west, wears a dhoti in the fashion of a lungi and utters the word Bismillah.

Matriliny is rare among Muslims and presents an interesting problem of anthropological and sociological studies. Studies on the coexistence and interaction of Islam, which is essentially patrilineal, and various matrilineal societies have been undertaken by a number of scholars. Many of these studies have dealt with the problems of adjustment and accommodation between apparently incompatible principles. It appears that one of the most significant aspects of Islam-tribal contact situations in Northeast India is the contact between Islam and the matrilineal tribal societies. It has already been pointed out earlier that in Northeast India, the matrilineal Garos and Khasis have come into contact with Islam. Of these two groups the influence of Islam is clearly discernible in the latter. The socio-cultural life of the Muslim Khasis exhibits a mixture of the principles of Islam and matriliny. The children born out of marriages between Muslims and Khasi women are of two categories: one follows the Khasi tribal tradition and the other follows tribal Islam. The pattern of family, kinship, marriage, inheritance and residence of the Muslim Khasis clearly indicate a compromise between Islam and matriliny[7].

Among Khasis, the youngest daughter (khadduh) is the custodian of the ancestral house, traditions and religion (ka bat ia ka niam). However, among the Muslim Khasis, the youngest daughter neither enjoys any special rights and privileges nor has any religious duty to perform. With regard to inheritance unlike the tribal and Christian Khasis, the youngest daughter among the Muslim Khasis is treated as equal with her sisters. Contrary to matrilocal Khasi custom, the tendency among the Muslim Khasis is to leave the family of orientation after marriage. A majority of the Muslim Khasis reckons the descent through the female line and use Muslim surnames along with maternal clan titles. The Khasis are exogamous and Muslim–Khasi kinship alliances have not remarkably affected the clan organisation of the Muslim Khasis. The preceding discussion indicates that the introduction of Islamic beliefs into different tribal societies of Northeast India did not result radical socio-cultural changes. The tribals of the region who have embraced Islam have organised their way of life primarily according to the dictates of their tribal traditions. At the same time one also notices that various elements from both tribal and Islamic traditions coexist within the same socio-cultural framework of the tribals. Thus, a kind of 'syncretism' between Islamic and tribal customs and rituals has taken place. The socio-cultural life of many of the tribals who have come under the influence of Islam is guided more by their tribal traditions than by Islamic tradition.

Conclusion

The spread of Islam (since 1206), Sikhism (since 1668) and Christianity (since 1826) along with the people coming from outside the region resulted in acculturation among these religions and the different local societies. In the process, conversion of groups of local peoples to these religions took place and also these religions gradually took over many elements and features of indigenous folk traditions. Christianity has its impact on the socio economic systems such as liberalism (which advocates unrestrained freedom for the individuals), capitalism (that stands for private ownership of capital and organisation of economic activity towards maximum profit), feudalism (that exploited the serfs) and socialism (characterised by the supremacy of the state)[8]. But many aspect of the lifestyle of the tribes of northeast India still hold strong.

End Notes

1. Kulkarni, B. Francis; "Revival of Traditional Institutions Impacted by Christianity: The Challenges Ahead for Missionaries in North East India" in TB Subba, Joseph Puthenpurakal and Shaji Joseph Puykunnel(edts.); *Christianity and Change in North East India*; 2009; New Delhi: Concept Publishing company.
2. Snaitang, Rev.Ol; "Christianity and Change among the hill tribes of North East India" in TB Subba, Joseph Puthenpurakal and Shaji Joseph Puykunnel(edts.); *Christianity and Change in North East India*; 2009; New Delhi: Concept Publishing company.
3. Ommen, TK. (2009). Cultural change among the tribes of North East India; in Subba, TB; Joseph Puthenpurakal & Shaji Joseph Puykunnel(edts.);(2009). *Christianity and Change in North east India.* New Delhi: Concept Publishing Company.
4. http://www.indiandefencereview.com/interviews/ne-insurgency-the-religious-dimension/
5. ALI A.N.M. IRSHAD Islam in the Hill Areas of Northeast India [Second Lecture, XV Dr. Verrier Elwin Endowment Lectures,Department of Anthropology, North-Eastern Hill University, March 29-30, 2011] *The NEHU Journal*, Vol X, No. 1, January 2012.
6. *Ibid.*
7. ALI A.N.M. IRSHAD Islam in the Hill Areas of Northeast India [Second Lecture, XV Dr. Verrier Elwin Endowment Lectures, Department of Anthropology, North-Eastern Hill University, March 29-30, 2011] *The NEHU Journal*, Vol X, No. 1, January 2012.
8. Subba, TB; Joseph Puthenpurakal & Shaji Joseph Puykunnel(edts.);(2009). *Christianity and Change in North east India.* New Delhi: Concept Publishing Company.

11

Syncretism: Religious Dimensions among the Khasi of Meghalaya

— D. Sun

Christianity was sown in the Khasi Hills as early as 1813, with the advent of Krishna Chandra Pal, a Bengali Christian convert of William Carey, the founder of Serampore Baptist Mission. Pal was succeeded by Alexander B Lish who opened three schools at Cherrapunji, Mawmluh and Mawsmai. He also translated the Gospel of St Matthew into Khasi. William Carey himself took the initiative to get the New Testament translated into Khasi (Marak and Das, 1973) but failed to arouse much interest. This mission ran for a period of five years, but came to an end due to vehement protest from the natives. Thomas Jones, a missionary of the Welsh Calvinistic Church Organisation arrived at Cherrapunji in 1841 along with his wife. He took over the mission activities from the Serampore Baptist Mission, and started the first school at Mawsmai. He translated the Bible into the Khasi language by using the Roman script. For this reason, he is known as the father of Khasi literature. Both Jones and his wife worked with great zeal along with a few Khasi converts.

After twenty years of the arrival of the Welsh Calvinistic mission, another denomination, the Roman Catholic Mission, came to the Khasi Hills around 1890. Among the Catholic denominations, it was the Catholic of Salesian Mission Society which first laid its foundation in these hills and then the others followed suit. A number of convents, schools, technical institutions and colleges were established by the Roman Catholics. After the arrival and establishment of these two denominations, missionaries from other denominations started flowing in, example, the All Saints Church, Seventh Day Adventists etc.

The foreign missionaries have departed years ago, but Christianity has established itself in vast areas, and the local missionaries are taking the responsibility of conducting the activities connected with the church.

With the coming of Christianity and western education, transformation in social life became inevitable. The Christian converts abandoned their former religious rites and beliefs to a great extent and accepted Christian teachings, but they continued to revere and preserve their rules of inheritance, household usages and observance of the age-old Khasi cultural and political customs (Natarangan 1977). So, large was the spread of Christianity that some orthodox Khasi saw it as a threat which will erode the social structure. With this view in mind, sixteen non-Christian Khasi formed an association on the 23rd November, 1899, known as Khasi Youngmen Association with an aim to caution the Khasi people and to rejuvenate the moral teachings and tenets passed on from generation to generation. In 1901, the association was renamed '*Seng Khasi*'. The *Seng Khasi* took upon itself the responsibility of defending the Khasi religion. According to them, the main purpose of the organisation was "to defend the faith of the forefathers, to understand the true meaning of conscience and truth as handed down to them by their ancestors, which have been misled by the foreigners".

Seng Khasi also declared itself as an association of those Khasi who adhered to the traditional Khasi religious faith. When the sixteen persons had formed the association, their main aim was only to create awareness among the Khasi, concerning the onslaught of the missionaries, but when the name was changed to *Seng Khasi*, the stress was on religion. The leaders of the *Seng Khasi* tried to revive and to reform the original version of the Khasi religion. Having initiated the process of revivalism and reformation of the Khasi religion, the *Seng Khasi* propagated through this organisation the following principles: to abide by the matrilineal system of descent founded by the ancestors, to love and respect one's kith and kin, both on the maternal and paternal side, to believe in God, and to serve God through service of people. Besides above principles, the leaders of the *Seng Khasi* announced the following aims and objectives: to uphold and strengthen the belief of the Khasi Pnar descendants in their ancestral religion rooted in the womb of time, to hold gatherings for those who follow their matrilineal system, to be conscious about the need for progress, to make an endeavor towards that end, by keeping the body healthy and sound, by improving the mind in the pursuit of knowledge, by involving oneself in an effort to do good and by cultivating a spirit of love for justice and goodwill towards all men, to be courteous, self-respecting and self-disciplined in all matters and to propagate the principles of the *Seng Khasi* (Das 1989).

The *Seng Khasi* started organizing archery competitions and traditional dance performances such as *Ka Shadsuk Mynsiem* and the *Nongkrem* dance.

The Christian Khasi initially were advised not to take part in these events. In the next phase of the cultural history of the Khasi, however, it was found that the Christians too gave their support in the form of participation in the festivities, and contributions of articles in newspapers and development of literature (Nataranjan, 1982). Some individuals worked effortlessly for cultural revivalism. They were the enlightened youth who received their higher education at Kolkata and other centres. They felt that branching the Khasi into two i.e., one under the umbrella of *Seng Khas*i and another under the umbrella of Christianity was not an important agenda, and that the main issue is the survival of their identity, being a minor group in a huge country, India, with all its cultural complexes.

Attempts to break away from the mainstream of Khasi culture were abandoned by the Christians under the impact of changed situations. A sense of tribal heritage developed and was cultivated among the Christian and non-Christian. The ancient customs and manners no longer remained a taboo to the Christian Khasi. The trend is evident from acceptance by the Christian Khasi of the tribal norms like dances and observance of state religious ceremonies. Christian Khasi have started taking pride in their cultural heritage (Mathur 1979).

In course of time, Christianity and the traditional Khasi religion, as revived by the Seng Khasi movement flourished and developed co-operatively. In the process, many indigenous cultural elements and fragments of traditional belief were grafted within the Christian beliefs of the Khasi. We can say that the Khasi who have adopted Christianity have not embraced it in its purest form, as they continue to remain under the clutches of their tribal beliefs and religious convictions. This ongoing trend whereby the Khasi have embraced a new religion but have still not totally abandoned their old religious beliefs is syncretism. In every domains of day-to-day life, the Khasi whether Christian or otherwise, do adhere to tribal customs, beliefs and practices consciously or unconsciously which have religious overtones.

We can understand this concept of syncretic value-system of the Khasi with some examples. Take for example, marriage ceremony, the Christian Khasi will get married in the church, taking Christian vows of marriage, following Christian precepts and wear a western wedding gown with a veil, which is totally different from the customary tribal ways, but apart from this, all other rituals concerning marriage are observed even today in the customary tribal ways. Food items such as rice, pork etc., have to be carried in pots from the bride's house to the groom's house in the morning of the wedding day. Family members of the groom are to take this special food which is cooked without salt. On the wedding day, the groom leaves his house accompanied by his maternal and paternal uncles along with other male relatives and friends, with blessings from all concerned. A group of uncles and friends from the bride's side meets the groom's party half-way and they stop to exchange greetings and betel nuts (*kwai*), and they jointly march to the church, awaiting the arrival of the bride. The only changed seen in observance of these customs among the Christians is that the journey is made first to the church and then after the ceremony, directly to the bride's house. Only male relatives and friends of the groom go to the bride's house from the church after the ceremony. This is one of the old Khasi religious customs which is followed by the Christians till today. After the wedding, and on reaching the bride's house, the mother of the bride blesses the couple on the doorstep and anoints the groom's head with oil, welcoming him to the family.

A few days after the wedding, a day is fixed for the bride and her family members to visit the groom's mother's house and houses of his mother's sisters. This is a very important customary visit known as *leit kai iing kiaw.* The mother of the groom anoints her daughter-in-law's head with oil and blesses her on the doorstep wishing goodwill and joy. The bride takes gifts such as *kwai,* banana, sugar and snacks known as *ki kpu* to her mother-in-law's and her sisters' place. She stays in her in-laws place for a few days and then returns back with her husband to her mother's house. These are universal tribal customs followed by all sections of the Khasi.

Secondly, in the case of a newborn baby, the first stool passing out of its bowels is believed by the Khasi to be ancestral stool (*ka eit iawbei*). When the infant smile on its sleep, the Khasi believed the child is in conversation/playing with the ancestress *(rkhie iawbei*). The stretch marks appearing on the belly of the mother after delivery is known as ancestress scratch (*trud iawbei*) and the hair of an infant who is not one year old, is called ancestress hair (*niuh iawbei)*, and no knife, scissors or blade should touch the infant's head until it has crossed one year. It is also believed that no food item should be denied to a pregnant woman, for during that period, it is the baby in her womb who wants the food, and not the mother. If for some reason, the desired food item is not given, then it is believed that the baby will be born with extra saliva (*jawduid*) coming out from its mouth. Such beliefs are recurrent among the Christian and non-Christian Khasi alike. On the first birthday of the baby, the eldest maternal uncle of the baby is to cut the baby's hair. Christian Khasi continues to observe such customs up till now.

There is also an old practice among the Khasi of applying a black tikka on a baby's forehead or typing a matchstick to the baby's cap or applying lime on the corner of the ear to ward off 'the evil eye'. And if ill-luck still strikes and the baby is supposedly attacked by the 'evil eye', known as *sabuit*, then a woman specialist is called to find the solution. The lady will take some lime on her fingers or on a betel leaf (*tympew*), start chanting to the evil eye by spitting on the lime and rubbing it on her fingers or betel leaf, and then order the evil eye to leave the child alone and go to its own place or else it will be shamed in front of the world. When this is done, the lime is applied to the baby's stomach and feet as a sign of condemning the evil eye. Then the lime is thrown in the direction where the sun sets by saying "*phet shaba sep ka sngi, sep u bnai*" (run to the place where the sun and moon sets). Sun (2003) also explained that to free an individual from the evil eye is not the only duty of this lady specialist. When called upon, she massages women during pregnancy and also after delivery. She advises pregnant women about precautions to be taken and also gives a bath to newborn children. She also prepares a concoction from different herbs along with rice beer which works as a medicine (*dawai niang sohpet*) particularly in destroying the germs present in the navel of the newborn baby. This woman, as a repository of traditional knowledge, emerges as a shaman and medicine woman simultaneously.

Thirdly, with the spread of Christianity, many tribal practices such as cremation rites and preservation of the dead body for several days have been abandoned, but the belief regarding the soul (*mynsiem*), has not been totally given up. In this regard, the two faiths intertwine. Both the religions (tribal Khasi and Christianity) do not believe in reincarnation after death. The Christians believe that good souls will go to heaven and bad ones will go to hell, whereas for traditional Khasi, souls which have led a righteous life go to be one with the predecessors in God's midst, whereas bad souls go to an underground abode of evil spirits known as *khyndai pateng niamra*. The belief that the soul of the deceased comes for the last time to the house on the third night is not repudiated by the Christian sections of the Khasi. It is for this reason that the house of the deceased is kept open until the third day in view of his supposed visit, and hence, all elders generally remain awake during this period.

The custom of collection of funeral subscription, *u synniang u bynhei* for the completion of the religious rites is still being carried out, from all members of the clan of the deceased. Whenever anyone talks about a person who is dead, the people will touch the *shangkwai* (basket for keeping betel-nut, betel-leaf and lime) and repeat the words '*bam kwai ha iing u Blei*' meaning 'partaking betel nut in the house of God'. This old religious-cultural Khasi custom of paying respect to the dead ancestors has survived among the Christian and non-Christian Khasi uniformly.

The respect and reverence for the dead ancestors, despite adoption of Christianity is an important syncretic element, which remains in force. A distinguishing feature of paying respect to the ancestors in an adjusted form is observed in the Christian Khasi family belonging to the Roman Catholic denomination. Once a year, the Catholic Khasi used to place wreaths of flowers and burn candles on the graves of their beloved ones on the 2nd of November every year. This tradition gets fused in a syncretic manner in the still prevalent functional ceremony called '*ban kynmaw ieit ia kiba la leit noh*'(to remember those beloved ones who are gone). Though there would be no such flower-giving ceremony among the members of the Protestant Church, yet they do place floral wreaths on the graves of their loved ones. In their case, it is done on an individual family basis, unlike the Catholics who observe it as a whole by the church. Hence, we can infer that the attachment and respect shown by the Christian Khasi for their ancestors is basically the same as those Khasi who continue to follow their traditional faith, but it is asserted in a moderate capacity among the former.

Another important feature that still prevails among the Khasi (Christian Khasi alike) is their superstition concerning the timing for starting any important work. The month of April or *Iaiong*, as per Khasi calendar year, is regarded as a bad month for beginning any new work such as starting a new business, construction of a new house or a marriage. *Iaiong* is related to a storm (*'eriong)* and it is believed that all the good will of the occasion will be blown away by the storm; hence, no new work should be started during this month. Till date all Khasi, Christians and non-Christians alike, adhere to this age old belief. Here, again we notice survival of the old spiritual order.

Next, according to the Khasi belief, there are different kinds of deities. Different authors have differently named the deities as spirits, deities, gods and demons such as Gordon (1907), Nataranjan (1977) and Mawrie (1981). Some family members keep the devils as their household deities and worship them so that in return the devils will give the keepers wealth and earthly prosperity. These devils are of different types and have different powers. Some of the well-known ones and which are strongly affirmed by the Khasi today are *ka taro, ka shwar, ka bih* and *u thlen* (Mawrie 1981). Just mere mention of any of their names sends shivers to one's spine, for if a person is afflicted by any of them, it is a known fact that his sufferings will be of a very serious nature. *Ka Taro* is well-known amongst the Pnar of Meghalaya. It brings suffering to those persons who have stolen something from its keeper. The thing taken may be as small as a safety pin or betel nut or may even be money. It may even visit the close friends and relatives of its keeper. The suffering brought by it is unbearable and unless the thing taken is given back, the patient will not be cured. It is necessary to offer a prayer to the concerned deity by engaging an expert medicine man. *Ka Shwar* is yet another devil known to the Khasi. It torments its victim by strangling or twisting the neck, it attacks those people who make trouble for its keeper, and only persons who are well versed in the ways of this deity can cast off its evil spell. *Ka Bih* (poison deity) is a common and well-known devil among the Khasi. It is of various types and works in different ways. Some poisons acts very slowly, with chronic pain resulting in death, whereas others act so fast that death takes place almost immediately (Mawrie 1981, Sun, 2003). It is also said that when this deity attacks a person there is no cure. It occurs yearly, at a particular time of the year for a person who is afflicted by it. It cannot be totally cured and efforts of specialists in the field of medicinal herbs almost frequently failed. But the most dangerous deity well-known all over Meghalaya is *U Thlen*. This deity demands human blood and in return it will shower immense wealth on its keeper. If the keeper cannot satisfy the deity, it is said that it will shame him in front of the world by taking the shape of a fish, a cat or snake on the keepers' rooftop.

The traditional belief in the power of *U Thlen* is so strong that it persists in the minds of Christian Khasi, even those residing in the urban areas of Shillong. The fear of such a devil is so strong that the Khasi hesitate to take *kwai* (betel nut) and tea from the hands of an unknown person or unfamiliar neighbours and friends. Their Christian faith still cannot lead them to do away with the fear and belief in what is locally known as *U Nongshohnoh* (a person who works for the *Thlen* keeper). In case of illness suspected to be due to *U Thlen*, even the Christian Khasi in the urban areas resort to the traditional way of curing the patient with the help of a member from the Syiem's family (Sun, 2003). The Khasi and the Pnar are indeed highly superstitious in their mental outlook, and this we may say because of their dependence on divination, despite high level of literacy and Christianity.

The prominent domains of Khasi society where traditional faith still holds its foundation are the matrilineal social structure and the mode of deriving descent through the female line. Another norm of the ancient faith that is strictly adhered to is the rule of clan exogamy. Even today, a Khasi whether a Christian Khasi or otherwise, will not dare to think of offending the rules of clan sanctity, rules prohibiting marriage within the same clan *(Kur)*. Hence, we can conclude that though many Khasi have accepted Christianity, but they are largely under the clutches of their old religious beliefs. We can say with authenticity that the adoption of the new religion is only part adoption. In multiple domains of day to day life, the Khasi whether Christians or not, adhere to tribal customs, beliefs and practices of their ancestors, which have religious overtones. The Khasi have embraced a new religion, nevertheless they have not totally abandoned their old religious and cultural beliefs. This co-existence of dual religious beliefs may be characterised as syncretism, at its best.

References

Das, N.K. (1989). *Ethnic Identity, Ethnicity and Social Stratification in North-East India.* New Delhi: Inter-India Publications

Gordon, P.R.T. 1907[1975]. *The Khasis*. Delhi: Cosmo Publications (First Published 1907).

Mawrie, H.O. (1981). *The Khasi Milieu* (with introduction by Sujata Miri) New Delhi: Concept Publishing Company.

Marak, S.A. and Das, M.M. (1973). A Few Aspects of the Khasis of Shillong. *Bulletin of the Anthropological Survey of India*.XXII (1-2): 86-175.

Mathur, P.R.G. (1979). *The Khasi of Meghalaya*. New Delhi: Cosmo Publications

Natarajan, Nalini. (1977). *The Missionary among the Khasis*. New Delhi: Sterling Publishers.

Natarajan, Nalini. (1982). Impact of Missionary in Khasi Society. In *Tribal Movements in India*. Vol.-I. K.S.Singh (Ed.) New Delhi: Manohar.

Sun, Deimaphishisha. (2003). Matriliny, Tribal Religion and Christianity: Syncretism in Khasi Socitey. In *Culture, Religion and Philosophy*. N.K.Das (Ed.) Jaipur and New Delhi: Rawat Publications.

12

Syncretism: Christianity and Traditional Belief System among the Nagas in Northeast India

— Daili Neli

Introduction

The American Heritage Dictionary (4th edition 2000) defines syncretism as "reconciliation or fusion of differing systems of belief, as in philosophy or religion, especially when success is partial or the result is heterogeneous." Syncretism refers to ways in which people incorporate elements from other religionsmore or less spontaneously, whether consciously or not. Typically this occurs when a less powerful group encounters the religion of a more powerful group (David Lindenfeld).[1]

The various Naga tribes located in Arunachal Pradesh, Assam, Manipur, Nagaland and in western part of Myanmar had an entity social and cultural life so deeply that they were often inseparable from community life as a whole. But one thing all these tribes shared in common was that at some point they faced an encounter with Christianity.

The belief system of the Nagas was animistic in nature and simple. The universe to them was peopled with innumerable spirits, the majority of whom were malignant (Horam 1975: 119). It is interesting to note that the Nagas generally believed in the existence of Supreme Being who is the creator and dispenser of all good things. The supreme God was believed to be "the creator of the universe, dispenser of good and prosperity and who lived in heaven" (Kamei 2004: 148). Although, there are no written dogmas as such, their idea of God and faith in the Supreme God is well expressed in their traditional songs, myths, folktales, names and so on. The Ao Nagas calls him Lijaba, Uri Ura for the Tangkhuls Nagas, Alhou for the Sema Nagas Asapavan for the Anal Nagas, Terhomia for the Angami Nagas (Wati Longchar). According to Gangmumei, Zeliangrong religion is essentially characterised by polytheism with an element of Henotheism and thus "worship of one Supreme God out of many gods" (2006a: 65) is practised. The God worshipped by Zeliangrong people, whether Heraka or Tingkao Ragwang Chapriak is called "Ting Kao Ragwang (the Universal God or the King of the gods of the Universe and Heaven)" (2006a: 66). The Mao Nagas referred to this God as *AmonoPfüpei* (meaning mother who gave birth and caretaker) is used to address this Supreme Being (see Lotsiiro 1990; Neli 2009).

The Nagas believed that God was manifested in nature and they see a number of ghosts or spirits working in their cosmic order. These spirits may appear in different forms: in dreams, by noise or sound, as strange objects, as wind, etc. There are spirits in the forests, in the streams in the bushes in the fields and of course in the village itself (Horam 1975: 119). Thus, often thick forests, big rocks, streams, rivers, brine springs and trees and other natural objects that appear supernatural or unusual are thought to be the abode of the spirits. The spirits are given different names in terms of their characteristics and generally in terms of their abode. These enumerable spirits can be classified into two categories: the benevolent spirits and the malevolent spirits.

The benevolent spirit is believed to be the spirit responsible for the welfare and prosperity of the people, whereas, the malevolent spirit is always thought to be dangerous and destructive to human affairs.

Historically the Nagas and their region remained impermeable to the outsiders prior to British. The first Christian Mission which came into contact with the Nagas was the American Baptist Mission and followed by different Christian denominations. The American Baptist Missionaries came to Assam in 1836. Following their arrival, missionaries were sent to the Naga Hills along with the help and assistance of the British Government. The first missionary to come into contact with the Nagas was Mr. Miles Bronson in 1839 (Lotsiiro 2000: 45). He made a long visit of three weeks to the Namsang Nagas in the present Tirap district of Arunachal Pradesh. The Nagas hardly had any contact with the outside world until this time. Miles Bronson established a mission school in 1845 at Namsang Village, a Konyak Naga village to teach elementary education and the gospel to the Nagas. Later, slowly Christianity spread the gospel to the rest of the other Nagas. When the Nagas embraced a new religion 'Christianity' syncretism begins.

Initially, few Nagas were converted and practicing Christianity while others were violently opposed to any foreign religion. Today, Christianity has a far reaching impact on Nagas culture and tradition. If one travels through the

Naga areas, one will find many external signs of Christianity today. Biblical quotations and captions and other meaningful Christian sayings would be noticed at different places. These quotations and sayings seen would definitely notify a visitor to the Naga area that the Nagas and their land have embraced Christianity. They are the external ways by which the Nagas want to express the influence of Christianity on their society and their land. Apart from the biblical quotations the Bible is loved and respected by the Nagas. They have the Bible translated in their language. They love to read the Bible, quote the bible and discuss about the Bible. Therefore, one can say that these are the signs indicative of Naga Christianity being a Bible conscious, Bible loving and Bible based Christianity (Lotsüro 2000).

The cross is one of the most significant and popular symbols of Christianity among the Nagas. They wear the cross as necklaces and crosses are seen in/on car decals, on the church building, etc. Pictures of Jesus, especially of the Sacred Heart of Jesus, and Jesus praying in the Garden of Gethsemane are often displayed in front of public and private vehicles in the churches, on the walls of the houses etc. Crucifixes and rosaries also are displayed in front of vehicles especially by the Catholics. The adoption of Christian and biblical names for places and people are also popular among the Nagas. There is also the pride of place for churches in every village. Every village, big or small has one or more churches. These churches are constructed in the most prominent location in the villages and they are often the best buildings in the villages. People are generous in contributing towards the building of their churches. The strict observance of Sunday rest is also one of the most visible manifestations of Naga Christianity. On a Sunday, all the mundane activities of life come to a standstill (excepting the Seventh Day Adventists). All shops and business close down usually.

Christianity has taken root in most of the Nagas, but it has by no means eclipsed traditional Religious beliefs. For many people globally, the coming of Christianity meant the end of traditional beliefs. This was not the case of the Nagas. Although, the church has became a centre of different kinds of activities in the Naga villages. Some elements of the traditional society still persist in the present context. It may be noted that there are some cultural traditions that have been revived and preserved. The situation of the coexistence of the tradition and Christianity is apparent in the Nagas society. However, most of the traditions that have been revived and preserved have significantly changed both in form and content. Continuity and change in society or the fusion of Christian culture with traditional culture need to be seen in this way in the context of the Naga society of today.

Conclusion

It should be admitted that the Missionaries had some weakness. They thought every ancient culture was devilish with no exception. This was due to their inability to study the meaning and value system behind native cultural behaviors. This led to undermining of the indigenous cultural features that resulted in misunderstandings. Surprisingly enough, there seems to have been a tendency among the converts to think that anything that was 'Western' was 'good and civilised'. This attitude resulted in the danger of total rejection of the Naga culture and a copying of Western culture in the name of Christianity. Lotha (2013: 81) rightly pointed out that western Christian missionaries brought Christianity and education to the Nagas, but it is also true that they brought along attitudes that were anti to Naga culture. This has resulted in the destruction of Naga culture. Anything western and Christian was considered good and anything Naga was considered pagan and devilish destined for hell. This kind of attitude of the western missionaries went a long way in the destruction and erosion of the Naga traditions.

Besides, some old traditions had been revived in the recent past due to the fear of the loss of the root and hence identity of the people. These revived traditions are by and large those which are not opposed to actual Christian teachings. However the old traditions that are found today exist with modification in forms and change in meaning and they do not carry the significant form and meaning they had in the past. Continuity and change in society or the fusion of Christian culture with traditional culture need to be seen in this way in the context of the Naga society of today. Today, even the enlightened Church-leaders see no harm in singing traditional songs and observing the traditional cultural festivals and dances if there is no pagan revelry and obeisance to anything connected to old religion. In short syncretism thus becomes a means of adaptation and self-identity preservation.

13

Language Shift And Maintenance: A Process of Linguistic Syncretism among the War Khasi of Meghalaya

— ***Supratim Bhattacharya &***
Pushpita Purkayastha

The undivided Khasi Hills district of Meghalaya is chiefly populated by the Khasi tribal group and a number of its sub-groups who are distributed and confined territory wise. The eastern side is the belt of the major Khasi(Synteng) tribe while the southern end is the homeland of the War Khasi, the south-central is the abode of the BhoiKhasi, the north-western side is the abode of the LyngngamKhasi, and so on.Both ecologically and culturally Khasi Hills is the part of the Austro-Asiatic speaking Khasi population who dwell both in the forest clad hilly belt as well as in the plains that were broken up by the different administrative provinces delineated by the British and later on by the rulers of democratic Union of India.

In the entire region there are several identified dialects overlapping the major Khasi language. However, for historical reasons or for other practical purposes there have been both maintenance and shift of their traditional languagein different pockets of the Hills. In addition with the religious proselytisation particularly the Abrahamic religion of Christianity, English has become a dominant languageamong them especially among urbanised and educated masses.

The present study highlights the process of language shift or maintenanceas the case may be of the War Khasi tribe living in the rural set up of southern Meghalaya that is coterminous with the border regions of the neighbouring country of Bangladesh. It also ventures to see under what socio-cultural circumstances a linguistic community shifts its linguistic identity towards another linguistic community dealing there by extra-linguistic factors responsible for either maintenance or shift of language behaviour as a process of syncretic language behaviour. To understand the above situation, empirical study was conducted among the War Khasi inhabiting the village of Shella of Sohra sub-division in the East Khasi Hills District of Meghalaya.

The Village

Shella is a big village accommodating mainly the War Khasias the owner community of the village land along with partial accommodation of other tribal communities like Pnar, Garo, Hajong, Tripuri, Bodo and Koch and non-tribal communities like Bengali and Nepali. All these groups are tenant residents of the village located on the border of Chattak and Sunamganj of Bangladesh, carved out from the erstwhile district of Sylhet of East Pakistan (now Bangladesh).

Shella is one of the nine villages of Shella Confederacyunder a *Wahdadar*, the administrative head, located on the southern border of the War habitation on the elevation across the river Shella between altitudes of 500 feet to 1000 feet.

The Shella Confederacy comprising nine War Khasi villages namely Shella, Mustoh, Nongwar, Nongtrai, Umtalng, Lumnong, Lyngkhom, Tynger and Dewsaw is situated roughly between 25^0 10' and 25^0 16' North latitude and between 91^0 36' and 91^0 42' East longitude. The village Shella is situated between the geographical coordinates of 25^0 10' and 25^0 11' North latitude and between 91^0 41' and 91^0 42' East longitude.

The village accommodates nine *kher* (hamlet)namely Sohlap, Mawryngkhong, Nongnong, Duba, Jasir, Jamew, Disong, Nongrum and Ramsongkatonor, situated all along the hilly terrain flanking the river on one side. However, a part of the ninth *kher* (Ramsongkatonor) is extended on the other side of the river too in the vast plains forming a sub *kher* (sub hamlet) in the name of Pyrkan, which has been carved out especially for administrative reasons for the smooth running of the *dorbarshnong* (village council).

Demographic Features of the studied hamlets

Hamlet	*House holds*	*Total*	*Male*	*Female*
Pyrkan	64	306	167	139
Duba	19	86	47	39
Disong	18	100	44	56
Jamew	16	99	47	52
Total	**117**	**591**	**305**	**286**

Average Literacy Rate of the studied hamlets: 87.88%
(Male= 86.67%; Female= 88.89%)

Historical Backdrop

From the formative period of British expansion in this region the lime quarries of Shella formed one of the principal attractions of Sylhet and drew the Europeans to establish a trade in that mineral. Hence, it is obvious that Shella established a contact with the plains people since that time. Before the partition of the country the people of this village used to export local commodities like limestone, betel leaves, betel nuts, orange, timber, etc. that grew here in abundance, to the plains and received in return the import of rice, egg, fowls and goats, fish, earthenware, brass and bell-metal utensils, etc.

After partition though trade through such import-export has come under government control, still it is running in a limited scale in a controlled manner and the War Khasi of Shella are in continuous contact with the plains people through bordering markets. There are instances of some Hindu families of Sylhet who have settled in and around the Shella*bazar* area and are earning their livelihood from small scale business with the War Khasi. Since weaving is not practiced in this village the people are dependent for their clothing on the Hindu cloth merchants of Shella market, who are basically Bengali refugee settlers in the Kalatek village situated at an approximate distance of five kilometers across the river bordering the international fence with Bangladesh.For ornaments and iron implements they contact the Hindu smiths settled in the Shella*bazar* area.

Methodological Aspect

For the collection of data a schedule was structured on the basis of various variables related to ethnic identity, socio-economic and socio-cultural parameters like education, language affiliation, etc.In total, the data were collected from 117Householdscomprising 591 individuals.

The result reflected the trend of language shift and maintenance. Out of 591 informants 292 informants did not shift from their mother tongue (i. e. War)but 299 informants have shifted from their mother tongue to Bengali and English. It seems that they have been influenced by the migrant population who have come from their original homeland and settled at the present locality along with some other communities since the historical past.

Literacy

Among the War speaking people 87.88%(Male= 86.67%; Female= 88.89%)of the informants are literates. However, the female literacy rate is comparatively more than the male population. The reason that can be substantiated here is that in matrilineal society there is a general propensity to educate the female child in a better way in comparison to the male child.

Migration

Immigration to this part of the soil from the neighbouring country of Bangladesh along with cross border movement and trade is the main reason for language shift among the indigenous settlers here. This process of movement is a regular feature till today and especially on bi-weekly market days people from across the boundary also infiltrate into the *bazaar* area with the objective of economic exchange. It has been found from empirical observation is that there is a two way flow of goods and commodities carried out by both the sexes.

Preference of living

The isolated hamlets (Disong, Duba and Jamew) being uniethnic in nature accommodates only the War population. However, in the fourth hamlet (Pyrkan) there are some instances of accommodation of families who have a different ethnic origin, i. e., Nepali. Hence, it is evident that generally they prefer to live with their own community. The neighbours of other language speakers are very few.

Marriage

Occurrence of marriage outside the community is very negligible among the War speaking people. Where such marriage occurs normally the informants speaks the language of spouse because almost half of the War speaking people including children is monolingual. Bilingualism occurs either in cases of marriage with a partner of different linguistic background or acculturation with other linguistic group. In the present case of Shella the second factor of culture contact with other ethnic group is the deciding factor for language shift.

The other factor is religious. People who subscribe to Christianity have a propensity to speak in English as they consider it as the language of the church. Those who come under the influence of Hinduism prefer to speak in Bengali. Here Bengali plays an important role not only because of immigrant population but also due to the existence of Ramakrishna Mission. The institution of Ramakrishna Mission is the oldest mission in Meghalaya founded in 1924 by Swami Prabhananda, popularly known as KetakiMaharaj.

Language of communication

Bengali is the *lingua franca* of the *bazzar* area when interaction between two different ethnic groups take place. Mother tongue is used in the family and amongkin groups. In some cases where either mother or father is non-native speaker of children's mother tongue Bengali or English is used by them. However, this was found to be of rare occurrence.

Mother tongue

They have acquired their mother tongue (War) at home. Proficiency in other tongues, i.e.,Bengali or English does not differ significantly. They are less comfortable communicating in English. While they feel most comfortable to speak in their mother tongue at home, shift to the other language occurs when they interact with other ethnic groups.

They use their mother tongue to speak with pets and domesticated animals. For language use with pets and domesticated animals most significant is that other language is not used by any one. Mother tongue is also used for their inner speech.

On market days especially War language is used with sellers of their own community and own locality or outside locality. There is a tendency towards bilingualism in Bengali when they speak with the sellers of other communities.

Language in increase

However, the informants feel that other language like English and Benagali is increasing other than their mother tongue of War for the use of communicating language. The other language is increasing because they want their children to be proficient in this language. They also think that the proficiency in English will be helpful for their children to get higher education, to secure a job and for better integration with urban neighbourhood.

Books

The informants feel that there are no books in their languages due to following reasons:

1. The language is not developed;
2. There is no script of the language;
3. There is a lack of good writers; and
4. There is no market for them.

Cultural communication through multimedia programmes

Radio and television broadcast the various programmes in Khasi and English. Some programmes like drama, talks, etc. are broadcastedweekly. The programmes like news, folksongs are broadcast daily in Khasi. In both the cases it is a foreign language for them since Khasi is the language of the bigger Khasi group. However, there is a feeling that programmes in mother tongue in radio and television are helpful for promoting the use of language, for spreading knowledge of mother tongue literature, for transmitting religious beliefs and for promoting a sense of integration.

Dorbar Shnong

Generally mother tongue is exclusively used for interaction at the *DorbarShnong*meetings. Mother Tongue is considered to be most useful mode of communication for unifying own community and for spreading of culture and social value of community.

At the altar of God

At the altar of God like the Ramakrishna Mission and *ChandiMandir* or the church they pray in Bengali and English respectively as the case may be. Since at both the place mother tongue cannot be used they resort to the said languages.

Reasons for language shift

They have expressed the number of views for adopting the other tongue as stated below:

1. Perspective of acculturation for historical reasons;
2. Usefulness;
3. Compulsion; and
4. By adopting the other tongue it is easy to communicate with others and also easy to communicate their views to others.

Discussion

From the analysis of data we may infer at the case of language shift and maintenance.

1. Bengali is the link language of Shella located at the frontier position bordering Bangladesh.
2. The southern side of the village is influenced by Bengali language which happens to be the language of the just immediate neighbouring country having a larger social and cultural canvas. It is so because the other side of the international border bears a larger social and cultural contour than the locale of the study which is just anuniethnic village.
3. The exposed hamlets have more or less shifted their mother tongue from War to Bengali or English.
4. The less exposed hamlet has maintained their mother tongue of War.
5. Ethnically the Warare the speakers of Austro-Asiatic speech family whereas Bengali belongs to the Indo-Aryan language family.
6. There is no language organisation among this group.
7. Though most of them believe that books, newspaper, magazines, radio and television are helpful for the development and spread of the

mother tongue and for the unification of their own community, yet they are equally of the opinion that mother tongue is less useful for spreading education and getting job or for communication with other communities.

8. Under these situations generally the most important factor for adopting the other tongue is historical reason, social pressure, usefulness and advantage of the other tongue. However, very few of them feel that other tongue is comparatively prestigious.
9. Most of them are not very much hopeful about the future of their mother tongue. They feel that it will remain but decrease in due course of time.

14

Syncretism in Kinnaurese Religion, Custom, and belief

— *Sumitabha Chakraborty*

Introduction

Syncretism refers to the hybridisation or amalgamation of two or more cultural traditions. However, all cultures comprise a variety of diffused and borrowed elements. 'Syncretism' loses much of its descriptive precision and many have deprecated the utility of the term. It makes best sense in the context of functionalist theories of integrated social systems, or doctrines of cultural holism, that presupposes unified and bounded social or cultural units that, under certain conditions, can be conceived as merging to produce some novel syncretic formation. Syn-cretistic analysis, however, unavoidably raises problems of history and social change and thus sits uneasily alongside classic functionalist theory.

Melville Herskovits (1941: 184-85) found the term useful to describe the culture of African Americans. He argued that the European and African cultural traditions have blended together for undergoing the acculturative process. Anthropology shares the concept of syncretism with the domain of comparative religion where the term has used since the early 1600s. Because religion is one of the most important aspects of one's culture, theologians continue to apply the term to religious systems (various form of Hinduism, Tibetan Buddhism etc.) that amalgamate several different traditions. Likewise, the blending of different supernatural powers or the blending of magical performances of witchcrafts with beliefs gives birth to the concept of 'syncretism' in religion. Hastings (1980) opined that religious syncretism is the product of contact and interpretation of men's mind, blending of religious ideas and practices by means of which, either one set adopts more or less thoroughly the principles of another or both and are amalgamated in a more cosmopolitan and less polytheistic shape. Religious syncretism exhibits blending of two or more religious belief systems into a new system, or the incorporation into a religious tradition of beliefs from unrelated traditions. The new religion that emerges from syncretism is heterogenous in nature and acquires a new identity. Religion, belief and custom of the local inhabitants of the Kinnaur valley are not an exception of that. From an empirical research among the Kinnaurese of Himachal Pradesh it was found that due to dwelling in an inaccessible and remotest part, confronting uncongenial environment and awe-inspiring nature, the local inhabitants have strong beliefs and faith in spirits, demons, omens which they always akin to amalgamate or blend with the deity worship of Hindu pantheon in a more cosmopolitan shape. To understand the religious syncretism of the Kinnaurese it is essential first, to know more about their beliefs in the supernatural and then, the ritualistic approach. Therefore, an attempt has been made in this article to find out those tenets of the Kinnaurese religion which are amalgamated or blended with the traditional belief system and transformed into a syncretic religion.

Map of the Kinnaur District

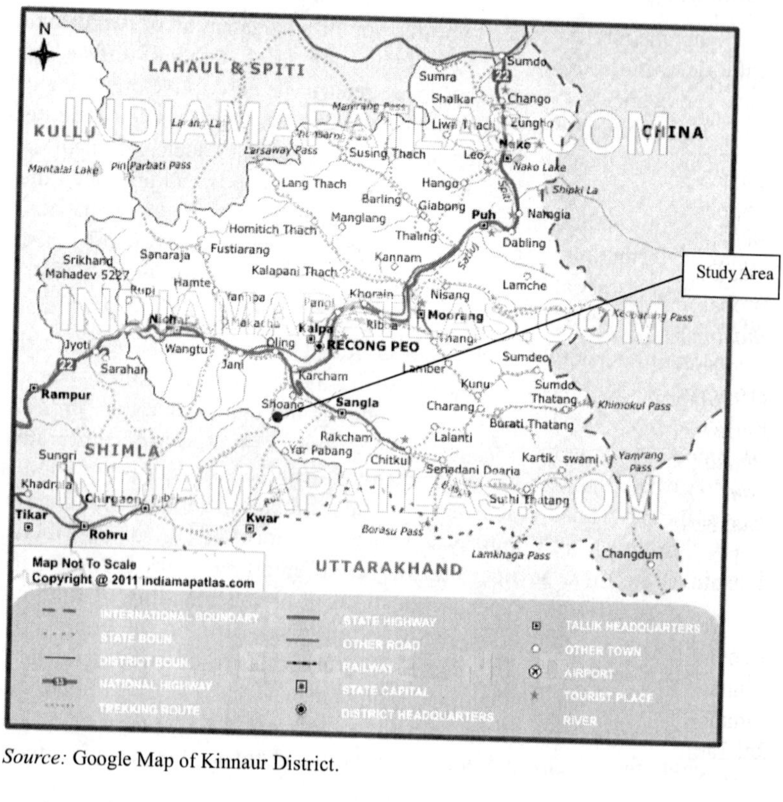

Source: Google Map of Kinnaur District.

Area and Location

The bordering district Kinnaur is spread over the Himalayan mountainous terrain, stretching over about eighty kilometers in length and sixty-four kilometers in breadth. It is situated in the northeastern part of Himachal Pradesh, covering 11.7 per cent of the total state area. Geographically, the district Kinnaur lies between 31°05'55" and 32°05'20" north latitude and between 77°45'0" and 79°00'50" east longitude. The high altitude inhabited area of this district ranges from 2500 meters to 4000 meters. Physiographically, the district is bounded by Spiti in the north, Tibet in the east, Shimla in the west and Tehri Garhwal and Uttarkashi of Uttaranchal in the south and covers both sides of the Sutlej river (District Census Hand Book 1981).

From time immemorial, Kinnaur had been variously referred to as Kunawar, Koonawar, Kinner, Kanawar or even Kanaur in historical records. Whatever the pronunciation is, the Kinnaur valley was an integral part of Rampur Bushahir State until the formation of new district in the year 1960. The state has some legends; one of such was – the state was first ruled by a legendary figure 'banasur', who was believed to be the contemporary of Lord Krishna of Hindu Pantheon (Sankrityayan 1956). But this was contradicted with the view that the ruling family has descended from the Praduman, grandson of Sri Krishna (Census village survey of Nichar and Kothi, 1961). In another legend, it was revealed that after the death of Praduman, the throne was lying vacant. It was then decided by the Estate official that whosoever entered the palace gate at a certain time would become the Raja. Two Brahmin boys happened to wander there at that right moment. Thus the Raj was founded by the emigrant boy from the Deccan (south India) in samvat 472 and his name was Dunber Singh (Bajpai 1981; quoting Kennedy 1824). The reigning dynasty probably first rose to power as the head of a confederacy of petty chiefs or *thakurs* amongst whom most of the Estate of Bushahir appeared to have been originally divided (Chandra 1992). While describing the area, Sankrityayan (1956) mentioned that Kunawar was once *Kimpurush desh* (*kim* means house; *purush* means men; *desh* means area) and were divided into seven different '*thakaras*', later known as *khunds* (equivalent as a pargana) – *khund do-shan*, *pandrah-bis*, *atharah-bis*, *bangpo*, *pagramang*, *shuwang* and *tukpa* on which total Kinnaur is spread up.

People

Very scanty historical information inferred their origin was having a close association with Hindu mythology. According to most of the ancient literature, Kinnaurese are referred to as 'super beings', different and higher than the common man; nearer to the God along with Gandharva, Yaksha, Kirata. In Raj Tarangini, the Kinnaurese are said to have been born from the shadow of Lord Brahma (Sen 1969). In Matsya Purana, they were introduced as the descendants of Arishta and Kashyapa (Matsya Purana, part - VI). Kinnaurese were referred as descendants of Atri by Manu; effeminate race by Vyas (cited in David Neel, 1967). Due to having the quality of a melodious voice and beauty, the Kinnaurese were believed to be the court singers and dancers of Lord Indra. Apart from mythology few scholars have opined their origin as '*ashvamukha*' (Shashi 1971) because of having the appellation of the word 'Kinnaurese', which means half men and half giant (cf. District Hand Book 1961). Sankrityayan (1956) opined that Kinnaurese is a corruption of the name given to the enslaved and defeated Dasas, who at one time lived in the Himalayan region and were gradually accepted in the Aryan fold. Whatever the origin of the Kinnaurese might be, it is a generic term to identify the traditional inhabitant of Kinnaur divided into many ethnic groups, viz., the *Kanet*, the *Domang*, the *Chamang*, and the *Chanala*. The *Kanet* are identical with the *Kunindas* of early Hindu history, and are a mixed race which sprang from the *Khasas* (Cunningham, 1884, cited in District Census Hand Book 1961:2). Atkinson (1882) pointed out that the '*Kanet*' are the members of the *Khasa* group, who have an Aryan descent and followed the path of 'Rajputisation'(.....), settled in various parts of the Himalayas and mixed up with the tribes.

The dry physical environment and inaccessible terrain have greatly influenced the economic pursuit of the people. Moreover, backwardness, inadequacy of knowledge, low literacy and extremely weak infrastructure severely affects the economic development of the Kinnaurese. Inspite of that, since earliest known times, the Kinnaurese have primarily been identified as an agro-pastoral group. A single type of economy could not have been followed throughout the year because of the tremendous cold climate with heavy snowfall; thus they chose animal husbandry and livestock breeding. Sheep, goat, ponies and horses have always played an appreciable role to provide meat, milk, wool, hair, manure, hides and skins for various purposes. This kind of profession further identified them as '*khosia*' (*kho* means sheep/goat; *shia* means possession). Prior to the Chinese aggression (1962), the local production of salt, woolen cloth, dried grapes and the seeds of *chilgoza* (a kind of fruit) were exchanged with different kinds of cereals within the neighbouring countries, mainly Tibet. But after the aggression, the exchange of commodities had stopped. Since then, horticulture gradually became more prominent and they started to produce apple, apricots, almond, walnut, plums, cherry, peaches and hazelnut in huge quantities within a few years. Nowadays, it is considered that the best quality apple is the cash crop of the Kinnaurese.

The social structure of the Kinnaurese is broadly categorised into two divisions – (i) *Khosia*, which includes the Rajput *Kanet* only, stands atop in hierarchical ladder; (ii)*Beru*, the people (*Domang*, *Chamang* and *Chanala*) who stands low in social hierarchy. From the Administrative point of view the

Khosias possess Schedule Tribe status, while the people of *Beru* possess Schedule Caste status. On the basis of hierarchy, the Khosia is grouped into three statuses (*khel*) – Orang, Maorang or Orangmech and Waza (Raha 1995). Each *khel* is divided into a number of lineages (*khandan*), which are of two varieties – (a) original *khandan* (descended through generation); (b) immigrant *khandan* (came on migration as wives or son-in-law [*makpa*]). By the rule of patriliny, a wife accepts her husband's *khandan*. The smallest operational unit of the society is household (*perang*) based on individual house (*kim*). *Kimperang* acts ideally as the basic residential, economic, social and religious unit of the Kinnaurese.

Kinnaurese Religion, Belief and custom

Dwelling in an inaccessible and the remotest part, confronted with uncongenial environment and awe-inspiring manifestation of nature the Kinnaurese in blind acceptance compel to seek the refuge of supernatural powers, which project as a shield against the onslaught of malevolent forces. The defenselessness and unanswerable queries before natural forces (storm, rain, earthquake etc) may perhaps be the root for their religious faith in nature deities, which curiously co-existed both in Hinduism and Buddhism. According to them, belief in malevolent and benevolent spirits is their age-old tradition and to appease those spirits, they undertook propitiation of deities. Atkinson (1882) rightly pointed out that the religion of the *Khasa* was a curious blending of belief with pre-Brahmanical and Buddhist nature of worship.

Belief in Spirits

The *paharias* are spirit owning people; each hill, cave, inaccessible place is tenanted by malevolent spirits and demons as commented by the local inhabitants. It is their belief that those spirits have the power to control winds and storms, falling rocks and the avalanches, which are believed to the weapons of their wrath. While passing a snow clad mountainous pass, the people keep quiet and try to maintain silence lest they offend the spirit. According to them, a cairn with flags represents the deity of the pass. In their faith, many of the big forest trees, especially the *deodar* and *kail* are the abode of *Bansir*, a ghost that usually appears at night and does harm to those who do not appease it. *Bakr-Suna*, another ghost is believed to inhabit in the dense forest and mostly appears in deserted places as a bleating goat. It is supposed to horrify its victims with a hail of pebbles and stones. *Ruksas* is a ghost of an evil person usually residing at the confluences of two streams, on a high boulder or in a cave or on a tree. It has, as they informed us, a frightful appearance with long protruding teeth and scalpel sharp nails. *Khunch*, an evil spirit residing in certain inhabited houses, is credited to migrate with the bride or the cattle to the house of the new master. According to them, these malevolent spirits always have some association with every distress and therefore, the local people have a tendency to appease those spirits by undertaking propitiation of deities (gods/ goddesses). Gangavishmaji, an aged person of Kothi village once opined that 'in Kinnaur there are no gods and goddesses (*devi/deotas*), but all of them are *ruksas'*. The burning place of the dead person is the suitable place for *mashan* (demon), *shyuna* and *khersuna* (two ghosts). They believe that propitiation of spirits, ghosts, and demons can bring happiness, wellbeing and prosperity in every sphere of life. That is why they appease anthropomorphized deities with sacrifice of animals following the Hindu pantheon in one hand and on the other, go to Buddhist monasteries (*Gompha*) and consult the 'lama' to ward off the evil effect by performing magico-religious activities. Here belief in spirits is blended with the tradition of deity worship of Hinduism and magico-religious belief of Lamaism.

Hinduism: Deity worship

The way of Hinduism is practiced by the people of Kinnaur is justifiably identified as 'local Hinduism' (Chandra 1992), where the people neither follow enchanting of Sanskrit mantras and slokas nor perform Brahmanic way of worship of deities. Only the anthropomorphic deities are propitiated with sacrifice of animals and mysterious incantations.

All the deities of the Kinnauri pantheon, irrespective of principal and subordinate, have the structure alike. The deities possess anthropomorphic figure with number of faces – *mukhang*, made of either gold or silver and are fixed on a central wooden pole in a circular manner and adorned with colourful clothes. A bunch of long black fur is put on the top of the central pole to depict the hair of the *devi-deotas* (deities). Moustaches, ear-rings, none-pins are the main depicting features shown clearly on the *mukhang* to differentiate the female and male god. The central pole then rests on a wooden square structure comparable to the palanquin. Two long horizontal wooden poles are fixed with the structure so as to it give the shape of a palanquin. The free ends of both sides are held by two person and they give a jerking motion to swing the body of the *devi-deota*, when they are interrogated and worshipped. It is very interesting to notice that the total adornment may differ, as in the case of a principal or subordinate deity. It is noteworthy to mention that the principal deity of Shuwang pargana Devi Chandika has as many gold faces (*mukhang*) as nine (reported by a pujari) and her clothes are brocade; she is carried on wooden poles covered with silver coverings. On the other hand, the subordinate village gods have silver made *mukhang* (faces) and are adorned with ordinary clothing. This kind of differentiation is perhaps meant to maintain the status among the *devi-deotas* (deities) equivalent to the Kinnaurese social hierarchy.

It has mentioned that the Kinnaurese *devi-deotas* (deities) are enthroned in the temples (*santhang*) and behave like human beings. The subordinate *deota* (gods and goddesses) offer their respect to the principal deities by paying him/her, a regular visit. During the study, it was often noticed that the visit of a subordinate deity to their superior is almost regular, whereas there are only occasional visits of the superior to their subordinates. The principal deity always makes a visit to the subordinate deity either on invitation or on His/ Her own accord at regular intervals. This system is popularly known as *bonning* system (Raha & Mahato 1985; Chandra 1992). In this system, the programme of the visit of the particular principal deity is planned and fixed according to His/ Her wish. The principal deity must visit to each of subordinate deities once in a year, as per schedule. When the principal deity gives his or her consent, the preparations are made by the village host. All the religious functionaries – *groksch* (the oracle of the deities), *mathas* (the spokesperson of the common people to the deities), *kardars* (member of the administration of the deities), *baijantries* (lower caste musician) and the villagers accompany the deity in a procession. The principal deity through this visit usually wishes to converse with the subordinate deities and confirms the welfare of the common village people. During His/ Her stay at the host village, a number of goats and sheeps (*khadu*) are sacrificed and plenty of country liquor (*ghanti*) is offered to the deity. After that, both the items are consumed by all the religious functionaries and the common masses as '*mahaprasad*'.

On the other hand, when a subordinate deity pays his or her visit to the principal deity, the system is popularly known as *boiling* system (Raha & Mahato 1985; Chandra 1992). Here the subordinate deity first expresses his or her wish and purpose of the visit to the principal deity. If the principal deity gives permission or consent, then only can the village deity move. On such an occasion, the village deity is accompanied by his or her functionaries. Besides religious importance, the *bonning* and *boiling* system has social implication to the society and people to help them evade any kind of fear and harmful effect caused by the evil forces. While accompanying the deity in the procession the people usually interact with each other which help them culminate marriage negotiation for their children. Thus, from the above discussion, it is visualised that the anthropomorphic gods and goddesses have a social order with distinct administrative rules and regulations which act as the guiding force to bind up the common people of Kinnaur.

During the study, it was also observed that the deities have relationship. *Vishnu-Narain* deity of Kalpa village is the brother of the *Naranas* deity of Roghi village. The principal deity Chandika is the sister of *Bhima-Kali* deity of Sarahan area and *Ukhi* (Usha) deity of Nichar area. It is also mentioned in the District gazetteer of Shimla state that the Maheshwar deota of Wangpo, Atharabis and Rajagram area is the brother of Chandika, *Bhima-kali* and *Ukhi* as they are the children of king *Banasur* of Bushahr. According to the information of the local people, the *Sheshering deota* of Pangi village has three brothers, namely, *Markaring deota* of Khwangi village; *Naranes deota* of Roghi village; *Pathoro deota* of Rarang village. It is the belief of local people that the *Sheshering deota* comes out from the temple on 15th and 30th day of each month to interact with the villagers and a desire to know their sufferings. During the study, it was also learnt that all the anthropomorphic deities have undergone purificatory rites. Whenever any birth and death occurs in the village, the village deity is believed to be unclean and on the day of purification, the deity is taken out of the temple, bathed well, new clothes and adornment put on, hair done up and the deity is then placed on a newly made palanquin. The religious function goes on with pomp and posh. The interesting matter here is the anthropomorphism in god concept. It has been observed during the study that the temple (*santhang*) of the Kinnaurese *devi-deotas* (deities) is well governed by some hereditary and hierarchical post oriented persons who come from different lineages (*Orang*, *Ma-orang* and *Waza*) of *Khosia* Rajput (*kanet*). The different posts of the temple are mentioned as –

- *pujares* – Priest
- *grokch* – one who speaks to the villagers on behalf of the deity
- *mathas* – one who speak to the deity on behalf of the villagers
- *kaithas* or *khajanchis* – one who keeps the account record of the temple
- *chalia* – one who carries the palanquin of the deity
- *kroshya* – one who guards the temple

Worship pattern and conversation

On the basis of the observation at the Chandika temple of Kothi village there are two types of worship – (i) the daily worship and (ii) occasional worship. Both the patterns of worship are followed in accordance with the conversation of the deity with his/her religious functionaries. The worship pattern is neither exactly similar nor perfectly performed in accordance to the Brahmanic way by enchanting Sanskrit mantras and hymns. In daily worship, the *pujares* performs his duties thrice a day – in the morning at the time of sunrise, in the midday and in the evening at sunset. Every time, before offering worship, the *pujares* washes himself with water from the sacred pond (*pandav talav*). In the Kinnaurese social hierarchy, the position of the *pujares* is placed at the middle level of the Rajput; by a rotation of a one year term, they follow their duties as a priest. As like as a corporeal soul, the deities are offered flower for adornment, fruits and sweets as eatables and country liquor (*ghanti*) after midday meal. This puts forward the incidents of belief in the anthropomorphism god concept.

The occasional worship of Devi Chandika is of much importance to the people of Kothi village. When Devi Chandika wishes and instructs her people or when any villager needs to solve his problem with the help of the Devi's divine intervention, it is only possible through a particular kind of worship. This special worship is preceded by a regular worship of all the deities in the presence of the *pujares*. After that, Devi Chandika is seated in the palanquin and carried out of the temple by the *chalia* (palanquin bearers) to the temple courtyard. The Principal deity is kept in a vertical swinging motion by giving jerks to the *chalia*'s body so as to reflect life in the deity. It is the belief of the common people of the Kinnaur that the deity is made ready to listen to their problems and miseries and subsequently, to inform them of a path to a solution. In this matter the grokch and *mathas* play their roles as mediators of the deity and common people. Nobody is allowed to directly appeal to the deity about his or her problem, rather the common people confess their problem to the deity through the *mathas* and in return the *grokch* gives the answer to the question as the representative of the deity. Here also, the Supreme Being maintains the power of divinity. While jerking, if the palanquin bends towards the left side, it signifies a negative answer and if it bends towards the right side it indicates a positive answer. The common people have to pay a minimum amount of ten rupees for single question to the *kaithas* and which is deposited to the temple fund. Furthermore, it is important to note that the Kinnaurese never felt the need of the service of a Brahman to worship both the principal and subordinate deities because the common people always felt that the *devi-deotas* (deities) are as authoritative as the religious head who perform magico-religious, jural and political functions to govern their societies. In case of any misery and mis-happenings in their society, the deities are believed to be very approachable to mitigate their problems. Thus, the personified deities always create a sense of divinity to the Kinnaurese religion.

Lamaism

The people of Kinnaur follow Lamaism, which is blended with the indigenous demonology of the mountains. In Lamaism, emphasis is given to the propitiation and appeasement of the demons in their fierce aspects, which includes several indigenous sacraments. A lama takes his responsibility after acquiring knowledge on various sects of tantric Buddhism, viz. *Mantrayana*, *Vajrayana*, *Sahayana* and *Kalachakrayana* and blending it with the shamanistic faith of the Bon religion of Tibet. In Kinnaur, a lama performs some magical activities, mystic rituals and lives out the mystic path. By enchanting the hymn – '*Om Ma Ni Pad Me Hum*', a lama generally propitiates the different yoni of the universe. According to the lama '*Om*' stands for *Dev* means God; '*Ma*' stands for *Asur* means non-God; '*Ni*' stands for *Nar* means human being; '*Pad*' stands for *Jeev* means animals other than human; '*Me*' stands for an unworthy place of living and '*Hum*' stands for *Narak* means hell. The lama always performs rituals to ward off evil effects of the spirits on the villagers. During the course of study it was observed that various deities and spirits are worshipped along with Lord Buddha and his other reincarnations (Sakyamuni,

Padmasambhava, Avoalokiteswara). According to them, *Nam-Chhra*, *Langan* or *Chhogdak* (deity for removing the obstacles), *Tarema* or *Chhering-ma*, *Paldan Lamo*, *Ningmet-Chheebe* (deity of health and long life) are appeased in the *Gompha* (monasteries) following the path of Mahayan Buddhiam. It is very important to mention here that the Kinnaurese of Kalpa area try to correlate these deities with Hindu God and Goddesses, like, *Nam-Chhra* is correlated with Narayana; *Chhog-dak* with Ganesha; *Tarema* with Lakshmi; *Paldan Lamo* with Mahakali; *Ganbo-Chhang-Dugba* with Taradevi and so on. Thus it is evident from the early discussion that the belief of the people in spirits is blended with Lamaism based on magico-religious performance. Both mask dance and *chham* dance are performed annually in the *Gompha* premises for the protection of the village as well as the crops against the malevolent spirits, which are believed to roam in their surroundings; it is a belief that by doing so, the evil spirit departs and prosperity returns in every sphere.

Summing up

From the discussion in the foregoing pages, it is evident that due to inhabitation in harsh climatic condition with arduous, rugged mountainous terrain, the people of Kinnaur always have a feeling of insecurity and fear in their life that brings forward a belief in the existence of spirits, ghosts and demons in the surrounding nature, which are believed to create various misfortunes, sorrow and unpleasant situations. The belief in spiritualism has greatly been blended with anthropomorphized deity worship following pre-Brahmanical rituals and shamanistic performance of Lamaism to ward-off the evil effects of spirits, demons and ghosts. Interestingly enough, at the time of our study, we were informed that the principle deity (*Khunt deota*) had made a yearly visit to each and every subordinate deity's (*Ghori and Gaon deota*) place of jurisdiction. Whenever the people of particular pargana (*ghori*) area fall in trouble believed to be caused by the malevolent spirits, demons and ghosts, they make a prayer to the respective subordinate deities as a result of which the subordinate deities pay their routine visit to the Principle deity. It is a kind of ritualistic performance the local deities assimilated due to the belief of the people. Likewise, all the shamanic performance of the lamas is also performed in the Gompha (monasteries) to appease and propitiate the spirits, demons and ghosts.

References

Hastings, James. (1980). *Encyclopaedia of Religion and Ethics*. Vol. 12. Edinburgh: T & T Clark.

Herskovits, Melville. (1941). *The Myth of the Negro Past*. Boston: Beacon Press. pp. 184-85.

Census of India. (1981). District Census Handbook. Kinnaur District.

Sankrityayan, Rahul. (1956). *Kinnaur Desh Mein* (in Hindi), Allahabad.

Census of India. (1961). District village survey. Nichar village.

Census of India. (1961). District village survey. Kothi village.

Bajpai, S.C. (1981). *Kinnaur in the Himalayas: Mythology to modernity*. New Delhi: Concept Publishing Company; quoting Kennedy, 1824

Sen, Biswajit. (1969). Caste, Class and Leadership in a Himalayan Village. In *Proceedings of Seminar of Indian Institute of Advanced Studies*. Simla.

Matsya Purana, part – VI.

David Neel, A. (1967). *Magic and Mystry in Tibet*. London: Oxford University Press.

Shashi, S. (1971). *Himachal: Nature's peaceful paradise*. New Delhi: Cosmo Publication.

Census of India. (1961). District Census Handbook. Kinnaur district.

Cunningham, J.D. (1884). Notes on Moorcroft's Travels in Ladakh. In *Journal of Asiatic Society of Bengal*.vol. XIII, part. I.

Atkinson, Edwin T. 1882 (reprint 1973). *The Himalayan Gazetteer*, Vol. II. part- I & II. Delhi: Cosmo Publication.

Raha, M.K. (1995). *Society and Religion in Kinnaur in the people of the Himalayas* (eds.). Calcutta: Anthropological Survey of India.

Chandra, Ramesh.(1992). *Highlander of North Western Himalayas*, New Delhi: Inter-India Publications.

Raha, M.K. & S.N. Mahato. (1985). *The Kinnaurese of the Himalayas*. Calcutta: Anthropological Survey of India.

Internet Source: www.googlemap.com

15

Regional Variation in Syncretic Cultures across India

— *Avijit Sahay*

Introduction

Syncretism in India is often associated with and equated to the intermingling of Hindu and Muslim cultures across India. This perception of syncretic culture of India is not erroneous, but it definitely is partial. While it is true that Islam has had the most profound impact on every aspect of Indian culture, it is also true that Islam is not the only culture to have influenced and shaped the modern day Indian society. India is an incredibly diverse and plural society. In the last five millenniums, many different races and many different cultures have come and found their home here. This constant influx of new arrivals has given India a syncretism that is reflected in India's art, architecture, literature, language, culture, religion, and tradition.

Indian landmass has continuously been settled since some 30000 years ago. By 3000 B.C.E., settlements in the North Western parts of India developed into an urbanised civilisation along the river Indus. The Indus Valley Civilisation reached its zenith around 2500 B.C.E. after which it began declining. The causes of its decline are still not clear, but in the next 1000 years, the northern and north western parts of India were settled by a completely new type of people-the Aryans. Whether Aryans came into India by conquest of Indus Valley people or not, once they had settled, they began acquiring the cultural traits of the native Indian population. The Aryans were nomadic people who worshipped nature gods like Wind, Fire, and Thunder. The Indus Valley people on the other hand worshipped mother goddess, Pashupati, etc.

The intermixing of these two cultures brought about in India the Shakti cult, the practise of applying vermilion by married Indian women, and probably the worship of Shiva as Pashupati. Thus, the contemporary form of Hindu religion is actually the product of syncretism between the Indus Valley culture and the Vedic culture of Aryans. By 500 B.C.E., a culture very similar to the modern day Hinduism had developed throughout the length and breadth of the Indian sub-continent. If we consider the culture that existed in India at the beginning of the 5th century B.C.E. as a proto-Hindu culture and accept it as the original culture of India, then any new philosophy, thought, or religion that has influenced India since then has been instrumental in shaping modern Indian culture.

India has experienced no dearth of new philosophy, thought, or religion. While some new philosophies like Buddhism and Jainism originated from within the mainstream Hindu culture and over time became separate religions, others like Islam and Christianity were introduced through conquest or missionary activities. All these years of intermingling and intermixing has contributed to the rich pluralism of Indian society.

Scope of the study

Syncretism by definition is "a fusion of different religions, cultures, or philosophies". India, being a melting pot of various cultures since the dawn of history, thus, has in the last more than three millenniums witnessed the fusion of various traditions and philosophies. Whether voluntarily or forcefully, new cultures have been adopted and moulded according to the needs. The scope of the present study is not to find out the meeting points of the various cultures that have influenced India. Nor is it to discuss the finer elements of syncretic culture of contemporary India. The study simply is an attempt to show the spatial distribution of cultures that have influenced the majority culture of any region.

The concept behind this study is that the diversity in Indian culture is because in each region of India, the dominant and majority culture interacted with various other cultures. This interaction was unique for every region and this thus gave the contemporary Indian culture its much acclaimed diversity. To study the different cultures of different regions of India, it is important to know the cultural interplays that have taken place in these regions. The present study, through the help of maps will provide such an information.

The Science of Cartography

Cartography or the science of map making has always been central to the study of Geography. If geography is concerned to provide accurate, orderly, and rational description and interpretation of the variable character of the earth's surface (Hartshorne 1959), then cartography is the most objective and scientific tool which a geographer can apply. All the characteristics of earth, whether anthropogenic or natural can be displayed on maps. In this study too, maps are used to display the influences of various cultures on contemporary Indian Society.

Cultural Realms and Culture Areas in Cartography

Cultural studies in Geography have always tried to map areas of similar cultures to form cultural regions. This is evident in the theories of Cultural Realms and Cultural Regions. However, the zenith in cultural mapping was reached by American Anthropology, when ethnographers prepared a map of Culture Areas of Native American tribes. The present work on the cultural areas of India is inspired from the Culture Area Approach of American Anthropology.

Most of the studies on cultural geography focus on the dominant culture of the region, however, in the present work, a cultural map of India would be prepared based not on the dominant culture but on the culture that most influences the dominant culture of a region.

Methodology

In this study, a cultural map of India, based on the influencing cultures has been prepared. This has been done in two steps. In the first step, a discourse on different cultures in India has been given, and regions where they are dominant identified. In the second step, different regions of India based on the major influencing cultures have been shown. In this way, a final cultural area map of India has been constructed that displays not just the pluralism of the Indian society, but also the regional variations in syncratic cultures across India.

Limitations of the Study

In the preceding paragraphs, Cartography has been introduced as a science in its objectivity and value neutrality. However, this view is partial. Maps are made by humans who are subjective and thus, maps can never be value neutral. The greatest limitation of this study is that culture is a highly sensitive matter and no researcher studying culture or religion can lay claim to complete objectivity specially if the culture being studied is the same as that of the researcher. Not everyone will agree with the choice of dominating culture or the influencing culture that have been adopted in this study. However, the aim of this study is to present a new methodology of studying Indian culture in geography and it is hoped that further research, if any, would add more objectivity in the study of cultural regions of India based on influencing cultures.

Another limitation is the classification of North Eastern region within the narrative of wider cultural regions of India. Not only are the north eastern states except Assam different from the rest of India culturally, there is also no homogeneity within this region, which makes any generalisation error prone. Originally, the hill regions of North East were dominated by various tribes and each tribe had its own language and customs. However, in recent years, Christian Missionary activities have made huge impacts over these regions, and the dominant culture of North East is no longer tribal, but Christian.

Dominant Cultures

Constituting about 80% of the country's population, Hindus form the overwhelming majority in India. However, Hindu religion is neither present in all parts of the country, nor is it totally dominant over large parts of India. In frontier areas of India, many different religions are also dominant. Religions that are in majority locally are as follows:

Islam

In most parts of India, Muslims form the largest minority group, however, in the state of Jammu and Kashmir, and in the Union Territory of Lakshwadeep, Muslims are a majority. Of these, in Jammu and Kashmir, Hindus and Sikhs in Himalayan foothills and Buddhists in Laddakh plateau have influenced the culture of the state.

Christianity

Originally, Christians were in majority in no part of the country. However, in recent years, through conversions, Christians constitute a major portion of the tribal regions of India. In the Hills of North East India, the original tribal religion has now almost completely been replaced by Christian culture.

Sikhism

In Punjab and parts of Haryana, Delhi, and Himachal Pradesh, Sikhs are in a majority and form the dominant culture of the north west of India. In the places where Sikhs are a majority, earlier Muslims, and now Hindus form the second largest group. The Sikh religion itself is considered by many as a product of Syncretism of Hindu and Muslim religions. It tries to amalgam the best practises of both in one universal religion.

Tribal and Animist Religions

Tribal religions form an important mosaic in the religious diversity of India. Most of the tribal groups are found in the hills of North East India and in a belt from Eastern to Central parts of the country. These tribal religions were once dominant cultures in their respective regions, but today, because of migration of non-tribal people from outside, and conversions to other faiths, chiefly Christianity within the tribal society, has left the practitioners of tribal religions in a minority. However, the traditions and customs of these religions still continue to strongly influence the tribal regions of India.

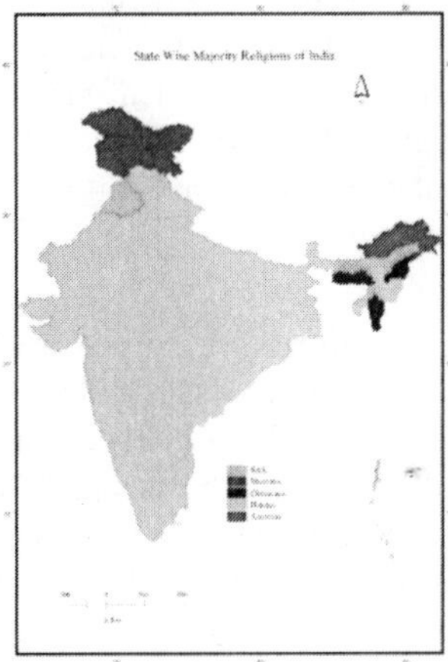

From the map given above, it is clear that Hinduism is dominant and a majority religion in large parts of the country. Apart from the border and frontier areas, the rest of the states of the country have a majority Hindu population. However, this does not translate into a homogenous pan-Indian culture. This is because there are many different cultures and many different religions that have over the years influenced the major Indian culture.

When the Aryans came to India, large parts of the country had already reached an advanced stage of civilisation. Thus, instead of Aryan culture subsuming the native culture of that time, there was an interaction between the two. While North India witnessed rapid Aryanisation of the indigenous culture, the process was slow and only limited in the more interior parts of the country. The next waves of migrants coming to India were the Greeks and many ethnic groups collectively called in ancient Indian literature as Yavanas. The Yavanas made an impact on the North and Western regions of India, but made little contact with South India. Thus, new culture was introduced to some parts of the country while others remained immune to it for long periods of time. This process of cultural diffusion continued till the coming of Europeans through seas. As the major European powers entered into India through the Western coast and made settlements in the Malabar and Coromandel Coast, Christian and Western influence is more visible here.

Thus, different parts of India came into contact with different cultures of the world and as a result, each region progressed culturally in different ways.

Most of the impact of ancient cultures like Yavanas, Sakas, Kushans, cannot be studied individually today because these cultures died down or became totally subsumed within the Indian culture. However, the influence of later religions and philosophies like Islam, Christianity, etc can be studied by comparing the cultural traits of different regions with the religions that have influenced the majority religion of those regions. To do this, it is necessary to first find out what regions have been influenced by which religions. Thus, a spatial distribution of religions that have influenced the majority religion needs to be identified. This is done in the second part of the study.

Influencing Cultures

The cultures that have influenced the original culture of India can be classified as those that originated in India, and those that came to India via conquests or missionary activities. Of all these new cultures, only Islam because of Muslim conquest, and Christianity because of Colonial patronage have a pan-Indian influence. The rest, even though present throughout the length and breadth of the country, are dominant in only few isolated pockets. Thus, every region of India has a unique culture not only because of the diversity present in Hindu culture, but because the influence on Hinduism of various other religions.

In his Presidential Address to the 1940 Ramgarh Session of the Indian National Congress, Maulana Abul Kalam Azad had said "It was India's historic destiny that many human races and cultures and religions should flow to her, finding a home in her hospitable soil. And that many a caravan should find rest here....This vast and fertile land gave welcome to all, and took them to her bosom".

Jews

Of all the carvans that Maulana Abul Kalam Azad mentioned, one of the first was that of Jews. Many Jews claim to have migrated to India during the time of King Solomon, though this claim is debatable. A more plausible date of Jewish migration to India is that of 7th Century B.C., when the First Temple was destroyed. In the next more than 2500 years, successive waves of Jewish migrants came and settled in India. The Jews that came to India are generally divided into three distinct communities and these are:

- The Cochin Jews
- The Bene Israel or the Jews of Mumbai
- The Baghdadis or the Easter Jews

At the time of creation of Israel as the Jewish Homeland, there was a thriving and a highly prosperous community of Jews living in India. With the creation of Israel, a combination of economic and religious factors led to mass migration of Jews from India. Today, less than 500 members of this once thriving community live in India, and of them almost 4000 live in Mumbai alone. However, the community of Jews who have had the most enduring impact on Indian culture are that of Cochin Jews.

Today, there are barely more than a dozen Cochin Jews surviving in India. However, their importance far outstrips their numbers. The Bene Israels of Mumbai may at present be the largest Jewish community in India, but their impact on the culture of Mumbai has at best been limited. On the other hand, the Cochin Jews have profoundly impacted their original home of Malabar.

The Jewish community here developed its own language which was a mix of Hebrew and Malayalam. This new language or more precisely dialect is called Judeo-Malayalam. While it is common for Jewish diasporas that lived in different regions of the world to adopt the local language with their native Hebrew, like the Ladino of Spain and Yiddish of Central Europe, Judeo-Malayalam stand apart because of its use Malayalam script instead of the Hebrew script followed in other Creole languages of Jews.

The Cochin Jews judiciously borrowed symbolic and ritual motifs from the local Hindu culture and enacted them in their own ritual life, within the framework of Judaic law (Katz 2000). The borrowings and assimilations that have led to the peaceful coexistence of Jews with Hindu, Christian, and Muslim neighbours of Cochin have been very well documented and are not within the scope of this study. Suffice it to say that from the Synagogues dotting the Malabar Coast of India to the Jew Town of Cochin, all bear the stamp of, and are a testimony to more than 2500 years of cultural exchanges between the local population and the Jewish settlers.

Parsis

Another ancient community that found a home in India is that of Parsis. Followers of the ancient religion of Zoroastrianism, they first came to India in 7th century A.D. and settled along the Western coast from Surat to Mumbai. Deeply integrated into the Indian society and yet maintaining their own traditional culture, they are the most prosperous community of India. Mumbai being the financial centre of India and the greatest cosmopolitan of the country is home to a wide variety of cultural groups. Almost all the major religions and ethnic groups have a claim to have influenced and contributed to the culture of Mumbai. However, the religious group that can lay greatest claim to have influenced the Hindu narrative of Mumbai is that of Parsis. They have not just helped in building some of the most famous landmarks in the city, but also have played the greatest role in making Mumbai the financial capital of India through their entrepreneurial skills.

Jainism and Buddhism

Once dominant over vast areas of North and Central India, Jains today are concentrated mainly along the Western part of the country in the states of Maharashtra, Gujarat, and Rajasthan as well as in the Southern Indian state of Karnataka. Buddhism, on the other hand though flourished for more than 1500 years now survives only in the Himalayan regions of Laddakh, Sikkim, and Arunachal Pradesh and in pockets of Maharashtra.

Syncretism by definition applies to cultural exchanges between two contrary and completely opposite cultures and beliefs. Thus, Buddhism and Jainism being offshoots of Hinduism are out of the scope of this study. However, the influence of these two religions on Hindu culture can never be overstated. The philosophy of ahimsa, so central to Hindu worldview finds full expression in the teachings of Buddha and Mahavira.

Islam

Islam first arrived in India in the 7th century A.D, as the religion of traders from Arab world who had come to Kerala. However, its true impact on Indian society was felt from the 12thcentury A.D. when Muslim rule was established in Delhi. Over the centuries, the great civilisations of Hinduism and Islam interacted, sometimes voluntarily, sometimes forcefully to evolve a common Hindustani culture of North India. To understand the cultural exchanges between the two cultures, it is best to quote Maulana Abul Kalam Azad again, "Islam has now as great a claim on the soil of India as Hinduism. If Hinduism has been the religion of the people here for several thousands of years, Islam also has been their religion for a thousand years.... Eleven hundred years of common history have enriched India with our common achievement. Our languages, our poetry, our literature, our culture, our art, our dress, our manners and customs, the innumerable happenings of our daily life, everything bears the stamp of our joint endeavour. There is indeed no aspect of our life which has escaped this stamp. Our languages were different, but we grew to use a common language; our manners and customs were dissimilar, but they acted and reacted on each other, and thus produced a new synthesis. Our old dress may be seen only in ancient pictures of bygone days; no one wears it today".

Again it is not within the scope of this study to discuss merits of these arguments, nor is it important to describe the various elements in the contemporary culture of India that are a product of syncretism between Hindus and Muslims. This study simply focuses on the spatial distribution of syncretic cultures across India, and it is Islam that has most influenced the native cultures of India.

The maximum impact of Islam has been felt in North, East, West, and Central India. In between these, the hilly state of Himachal Pradesh has remained relatively untouched by Islamic influences spread over rest of the country. In South India too, Islam has deep roots, but shares space as influencing culture with Christianity, which also has major influence there.

If plotted on a map (see map2), then the impact of Islam will be strongly evident almost in all parts of the country. In the east, in Assam and West Bengal, Muslims constitute more than 33% and 27% respectively of the population. Similarly, in Kerala, they constitute about 26%. Other states with high Muslim population are Uttar Pradesh, Bihar, Jharkhand, Maharashtra, Karnataka, Delhi, and Uttarakhand.

Christianity

Christianity in India was first introduced in A.D. 52 by Saint Thomas. For most of the 1500 years after that, Christians remained a very small minority around the Malabar Coast and extreme south of India. However, with the coming of Europeans, Christianity got a new lease of life. Apart from being in majority in the North Eastern states of Nagaland, Mizoram, and Meghalaya, Christians constitute an important minority in states like Manipur, Arunachal Pradesh, Goa, Andaman and Nicobar, Kerala, and Sikkim. In Tamil Nadu, in the extreme south, Christians are an important minority group. Similarly, in certain tribal districts of Central and Eastern India, sizable minority of Christians can be found.

Sikhism

Sikhs are a majority in Punjab and an important minority in Delhi, Haryana, Himachal Pradesh, and Jammu region of Jammu and Kashmir. In many respects, Sikhism in itself is a product of syncretism between Hindu and Muslim cultures of medieval India.

Tribal and Animist Religions

In large parts of India, even at the time of advent of British, Animistic and Tribal religions were dominant. However, today, these religions have become just an influencing culture in their own land. Only Arunachal Pradesh to some extent still has a majority animistic culture, but this too is being subsumed within the Hindu and Christian cultures. Other areas where tribal religions are important are Madhya Pradesh, Chhatisgarh, Jharkhand, Orissa, and the hill states of North East India that include Manipur, Meghalaya, Mizoram, Nagaland, and Tripura. In the states of Meghalaya, Mizoram, and Nagaland, Christianity has become the majority religion and in the rest, Hindus are in majority. However, in all these states, tribal influence still shapes many aspects of culture like language, customs, traditions, etc.

Cosmopolitan Culture

It must be noted here, that with rising levels of urbanisation and education, certain pockets of India have seen the influx of so many people from all parts of the country that they have become cosmopolitan. In these regions, even though one religion or culture is dominant, no culture can possibly claim to have influence that religion more than others. This phenomenon is clearly visible in Mumbai and Delhi, and now is gaining ground in new IT hubs like Bangalore and Hyderabad.

The findings presented in the preceding paragraphs can be shown in a map as given below:

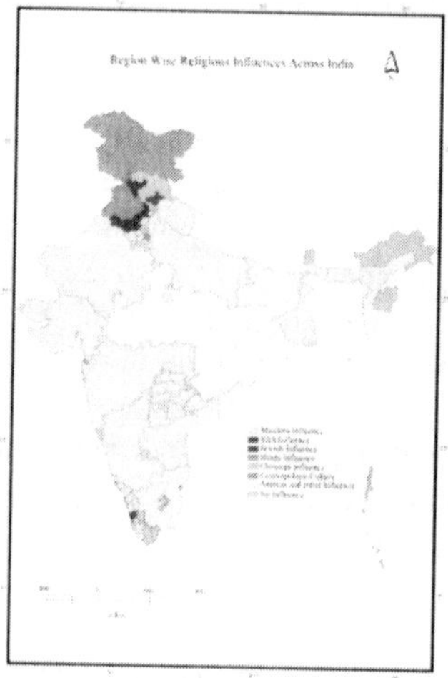

Conclusion

In spite of having a huge majority of Hindu population in almost all the states of the country, the cultural mosaic of India is deeply diverse. The argument presented in this paper is that this is because historically, each region came into contact with different cultures uniquely. However, the purpose of this study is not to present the elements of different cultures from different regions of India, but to find out which contemporary religion has affected which part of the country. This has been done by preparing a cultural area map of India that is been based not on the dominant culture of an area but on the culture that most influences the dominant culture.

References

Ahmad, A (1999). *Social Geography*, Rawat Publications, Jaipur.

Burman, J.R. (1996). 'Hindu-Muslim Syncretism in India' in *Economic and Political Weekly,* 31 (20): 1211-1215.

Census of India. (2001).

Census of India. (2011). Table No. C-01, Population by Religious Communities.

Hartshorne, R (1959). *Perspectives on the Nature of Geography*, Association of American Geographers.

Katz, N (2000). *Who Are the Jews of India?* University of California Press, Oakland, California.

Keay, J (1981). *India Discovered*, William Collins, London.

Thapar, R (1977), *Tribe, Caste and Religion in India*, Macmillan Company of India, Meerut.

16

Religious Syncretism and culture among Amri Karbi of Kamrup District, Assam

— ***Pinky Barua***

Introduction

Northeast India consists of Assam, Arunachal Pradesh, Meghalaya, Nagaland, Manipur, Mizoram, Tripura and now included Sikkim. The region shares international border with China, Bhutan, Myanmar Bangladesh and connected with a narrow channel. North East India has uniqueness from the mainland India for its topography, climate, various ethnic groups, caste people, race and all the groups are having their own customs and culture. Assam state is situated in greater sub- Himalayan province. Assam state lies at 26.14 °N latitude and 91.77°E longitude. Assam comprises of the Brahmaputra valley and Barak river valleys with an area of 30,285 square miles (78,438 km^2). Assam shares international border with Bhutan and Bangladesh. Paddy is the main food crop of the land. Paddy is cultivated in entire Assam. Rice is the staple food in Assam. Assam is having about 22 million people, who are mostly Hindus (Assamese) followed by Muslims, Christians and Buddhists. Assam is inhabited by several distinct tribal groups for example plain tribal groups living are Bodos, Mishing, Kacharis, Rabhas, Lalungs (Tiwa) and Deuri while Karbi, Dimasa and Kuki falls under the Hill tribal group. All these tribes can be categories separately with their Traditional Attire, Ornaments, Songs, Dance, Food habit, Religious belief system and language. Each tribe has their own dialect to communicate with the members of their own society. These tribes follow some peculiar food habits. They take boiled, alkaline and sour preparations alternatively. In Assam, tribes are mainly following Christianity,

Hinduism and Buddhism in recent times. Agriculture and farming is the primary occupation of these tribes; women mainly rear animals, fowls and engage in weaving and fishing too.

Religion is a socio-cultural phenomenon which gives the people/ community an identity of its own and answers to questions, which are mysterious and fall into indefinable areas of experience and expectation (Behera 2000:15). Religion is the most important component of human life and is related to social, cultural, political, economic, spiritual and environmental aspects of human being. Religion has been defined by Theologian, Sociologist, Psychologist, Anthropologist and various others (Behera 2000:15). Definitions of religion have been forwarded by several eminent scholars, some of are depicted below:

Hegel defines religion, as early as 1832 when his comprehensive work on religion. *Lectures on Philosophy of Religion* were published, as consciousness of God in general (Hegel 1984:185) and identifies magic as the earliest type of religion, taking the form of power over nature (Hegel 1987:272). Religion is a synthesis of two elements the object (the divine) and the subject (the consciousness).August Comte (1798-1857) described the same three staged history by the means of theology, Metaphysics and Science or Positivism. Engels, takes a less interactive approach and puts, 'all religion is nothing but the fantastic reflection in men's minds of those external forces which control their daily life, a reflection in which the terrestrial forces assume the form of supernatural forces (Engels 1957:146) and Marx defines religion as 'the opium of the people'. E. B Tylor (1929) in *Primitive Culture* identified religion with Animism, conceived as the beliefs 'in supernatural beings'. Sir James G. Frazer thought that religion grew out of magic. According to him, all early societies believed in magic, with some moving onto religion (1922). Cliffrod Geertz (1973) defines religion as a system of symbols. It is an organised system of beliefs, attitudes, emotions, behavior and a set of beliefs concerning the cause, nature and purpose of the universe. Emile Durkheim (1976:47) defined religion is a unified system of beliefs and practices relative to sacred things, that is to say, things apart and forbidden. His definition continues that religious beliefs and practices are socially integrating, that is, they 'unite into one single moral community' (ibid).

Religious Syncretism

The Encyclopedia Britanica defines the term 'Syncretise' as an 'attempt to combine or unite different opposing principles'. Syncretism refers to connections of a special kind between language, cultures or religions. Religious Syncretism, where religious miscegenation is believed to have taken place, refers to an attempt to bring together and combine as harmoniously as possible or to the situation of coming together diverse religious views. The former signifies the process while the latter to the phenomena (Behera 2000:17). Syncretism takes the form of symbiosis, acculturation, superposition, Harmonisation etc, but not always and these terms are interchangeably used for syncretism. The study of syncretism does not consider the situation as it changed through time, a religious syncretism in itself is a state that reflects both change and continuity.

Study Area: The study is carried out at Sonapur circle Dimoria Block in South Kamrup district which is about 35 km from Guwahati city, situated at National Highway 37 on the river Digaru which flows into the Kalangriver close to the river Brahmaputra. Sonapur lies at 26.12°N latitude 91.98°E longitude. Amrikarbis are presently scattered in South Kamrup (Sonapur, Dimoria, Rani, Chandrapur), Nagaon and they prefer to live in the foothills of above mentioned places. This group follows a distinct culture, customary practice, culinary practice and separates a social organisation which is different from the Hill Karbis of KarbiAnglong district.

Methodology: The study is based on both primary and secondary sources of data. Primary data is collected through Interview Schedule which is the main research tool. Method of Observation, In-depth interviews, key-informant interviews, focus group interview, case study etc. In-depth individual interview is conducted with the use of interview schedule to collect data.

The collection of secondary data are reviews of relevant literatures, books, journals and magazines, newspapers, research and survey conducted by various organisations, e-resources, published and unpublished articles, government records etc were collected from different libraries.

The Tribe: The Karbis mentioned as Mikirs in the Constitution Order, Government of Assam, constitute an important ethnic group in the hill areas of the present Assam (Bordoloi *et al.,* 1987: 52). They are one of the many Tibeto-Burman communities inhabiting Assam (Lyall 1908:1). Racially, the Karbis belong to the Mongoloid group and linguistically to the Tibeto-Burman. The majority of Karbi inhabit the KarbiAnglong district and some pockets of the adjoining North Cachar hills, Sivasagar, Nagaon and Darrang districts of Assam. According to Charles Lyall (1908), the Karbis inhabit in greatest strength in the KarbiAnglong hills named after them, the isolated mountainous block which fills the triangle between the Brahmaputra on the north, the Dhansiri valley on the east and the Kopilli on the west. The Karbis are divided into five clans (*kurs*) which are exogamous. The five *kurs*are Terang, Teron, Timang, Inghy and Ingti.From the point of view of habitation, the Karbis are divided into three groups: Chintong, Rongkhang and Amri. Those who live in the plains are called Amri while the hill Karbis are known as Chintong and Rongkhang. The Karbis follow a patriarchal system. The line of descent is traced through male members only. The common form of marriage is monogamy. However, cross cousin marriage is a preferential one among them.

They have no bride price system. Clan wise the Karbis have different burial ground and they cremate the dead. The Agriculture is the mainstay of the Karbis. They practice both shifting and settled cultivation. Settled cultivation is generally practiced in the plain areas and shifting cultivation in the hilly areas. The traditional village council of the Karbis is known as *Mei*[1]and is consist of all elderly male members of the village. No women are allowed to be member of the Traditional village council. The staple food of Karbis is rice.

The Amris are originally found to be the western most settlers who now largely occupy the hills of Amri Block-the western most part of Hamren sub-division, Ri-bhoi ares of East-khasi Hills, Low hills and foothills of southern Kamrup (from Guwahati eastward) and scattered areas Kamrup district upto Mayang. The Amris came to reach the western most portions in the course of their migration from the east (Phangcho, 2003:30). The Karbis living in the plains are known as Amris constituted a distinct identity calling themselves also as Dumurali. Dumurali Karbis are plain dwellers now inhabiting the southern part of Nagaon district covering mainly from Jamunamukh on the east to Sonapur (in southern Kamrup) on the west. They believed to have some down from the neighboring hills in the south after having lived there for many years (Phangcho 2003:30). The Karbi houses are mainly built with bamboo and timber posts in hilly areas. In the plain areas, the houses are constructed on the ground. The pattern of house of plain (Amri) karbi is similar to that of Boro Kachari, a predominant plains tribe of Assam (Bordoloi *et al* 1987:81).

Discussion: The main house is called "Borghor (Kitchen House)" and is one of the most important parts the house. The Borghor is divided into two parts one is Ingkut and another part is Inkum. Ingkut is the Kitchen of the house and Ingkum is a big room for family. Ingkut is traditionally the most sacred domestic space according to the Amri tradition and the kitchen is a domain of the Amri women. There is wall between the Ingkut and Ingkum with one door and one main wooden post. The wooden post must be of a specific tree named "Gomari Xunaru" and the room is for performing rites and rituals on specific day. This sacred post is named as "Nungpe- Armu" (Main post). This post is a sacred symbol of Amris and the whole family members of the household worship it. This is, whether the poor or rich each Amri family must have a Borghor and Nungpe-Armu in east of the Borghor. They hang newly harvested paddy in the uppar part of the main post, this is regarded as a well sign of Lakshmi Devi (Goddess of Wealth).Thus, and it as a special religious significance among the Amri Karbis.

Karbi worships are performed in varieties of places- the hill karbis have no definite shrine or temples such, while the plains karbis do have shrines called 'Than'. Both the groups also performs worships in places like corner of a house, middle of a house, cross road, bank of a steam, forest area, paddy or any crop field at the time of beginning of cultivation or harvesting, places of hunting or fishing etc (Phangcho 2003:57,58). It is found that, there are several God and Goddess commonly worshiped by the Karbis. But some are not worshiped in some localities and names are also different in different area. For instant- Rasinja, Parkok Arnam are not worshipped in Dimoria-Sonapur Areas of the AmriKarbis. Again, Than Arnam who is equivalent to Lord Sive in Karbi Anglong, is known as Burha Gosain in Dimoria – Sonapur areas (Phangcho 2003:58). The Dehal puja is the most important community worshipping occasion of the Amri Group. This Dehal[2] Puja is called Katsirdom and is observe in every year in month of February. It continues for three days and every Amri has to take part in the puja for all around development of the villagers. Dehal Katsirdom signifies a symbol of unity and togetherness of all AmriKarbis. The term 'Hem' is House while the term 'Arnam' means God. Thus, it regarded as Household God. The House hold God is regularly worshipped by the member of the family and observed by Amri Karbi once in a year.

The Amri Karbis have specific ritual ceremony for purification. The Kathar (belongs to Ingti Clan known as priestly clan) perform these purification rituals in the village. To perform such rituals, some wild herbs are used i.e. Tibong, Arjang, Ingrhi and Suwe. Offences such clan endogamy marriage, inter tribe marriage (apart from Tiwa), hitting cow with a weapon, quarreling between two person and hitting a person of different religion are performed by purification process.

Karbis have been converted into Hinduism and Vaishnavism especially those who reside in the plains of Nagaon. Karbis, some subsequently become Koch a caste of the Hindus. Conversion into Vaishnavism started by Srimanta Sankardeva himself the founder of Vaishnavism movement in Assam. The karbi Christian are to be found mainly in the Karbi Along District and are divided into several denominations, such as (i) American Baptist, (ii) Welsh Mission, (iii) Church of God, (iv) Baptist Fedaration (v) Baptist Mild Mission, (vi) Seventh Day Adventist (vii) Catholic (Phangcho 2003:62). In South Kamrup like Sonapur, Chandrapur and Rani locality also Amris are slowly converted to Christian in recent times. Due to spread of Vaishnavism, Amris perform Bhagabat Path and Naam Kirtan in Naam Ghar according to the Mahapurush Sankar deva. Some beliefs and practices of Assamese Neo-Vaishnavism are also followed by Amris of the place. It is seen that followers of Neo-Vaishnavism religious or other Hindu sects have again converted to Christianity. They were treated as second grade Hindus by other non tribal Hindus, could be a cause for conversion. It is seen that there are some changes taking place in the area like establishment of Church, Christian beliefs, Change in religious performance, change in customary law, Rituals related to Marriage is also affected.

Conclusion

Amri Kabis rituals, religious practices had been already affected by or influence by Hindu Religion, Neo-Vaishnavism, Assamese Community and again Christianity in recent times. Due this conversion process, there is some socio-economic and cultural changes occur, still they are following their traditional practices. With the changing religion, they become a part of new belief and new social system.

Reference

1. Athparia, R.P, (2012). *The Karbi of Assam*, Sanskriti-NEICR Publication, Guwahati.
2. Barua. P, (2010). *Reproductive Health care and Traditional Practices of women: A sociological study of Tiwa community*, An unpublished M.Phil Dissertation, Gauhati University.
3. Bordoloi. G.C, and Saikia, M. (2010). *Tribes of Assam: Part -1*, Tribal Research Institute, Assam.
4. Chakraborty, S. (2014). *Syncretism in Kinnaurese Religion, Custom and Belief* in The Journal of Northeast Indian Cultures (An international Journal of Assam Don Bosco University) Vol. 1, No. 2, Guwahati, Assam.
5. Devi. L. (1968). *Ahom-Tribal Relations*, Lawyer's Book Stall,Guwahati.
6. Gait, E. *A History of Assam*, Lawyers' Book Stall, Guwahati, 1905/1984.
7. Jacob, J.K. (2014).*An Anthropological study of Religion among the Rangdani Rabha of Assam*, An Unpublished Ph.D. Thesis, Assam Don Bosco University, Guwahati.
8. Phangcho, P.C, (2003). *The Karbis: A Spatio-temporal analysis in Tribal Geography*, Angik Publication, Guwahati.
9. Regma, N. (2011). *Cultural Tradition and Customary Laws of Rengma Nagas*, Spectrum Publication.
10. Stack. E and Lyall. C, (1908). *The Mikirs,* United Publishers,Guwahati.
11. Waddell.L, (1908). *The Tribes of Brahmaputra Valley*, Logos Press, New Delhi.
12. Behara, M.C and T. Mibang, (2007) *Marriagein Tribal Societies (Cultural Dynamics and Social Realities),* Bookwell, New Delhi.
13. Singh, N.N, (2015), *Religious Syncretism among the Meiteis of Manipur*, India, IRJSS, Vol. 4(8), 21-26, August 2015.
14. Nath, D. (2011). *Religion and Society in North East India*, DVS Publishers, Guwahati.
15. Sonowal, C.J. (2014). *Religion and Ethnic Reconstruction Among the Tribes of NortheastIndia,* Akansha Publishing House, Guwahati.
16. Behera, M.C. (2000). *Tribal Religion: Change and Continuity*, Commonwealth Printers, Delhi.
17. Sarma, G.C. (1985). *The Lalungs (Tiwas),* Tribal Research Institute, Guwahati, Assam.

Notes

1. *Mei* is the local term used for Village Council among the AmriKarbis of plains (in South Kamrup).
2. 'Dehal' and 'Than' seems to be derived from Assamese 'Deoshal' and 'Than' respectively, meaning the place of God/ Goddesses. The Than usually has a roof in the top without side walls, this type of worshipping God is totally absent among the Karbis of KarbiAnglong and N.C Hills (Phangcho, 2003:60).

17

Cultural Syncretism: An Empirical Study on Hindu-Christian Community of Kalyani

— *Samita Manna, Reshmi Chakraborty, Aritra Ghosh*

The pluralistic and composite ethos of Indian civilisation is celebrated with its variegated religious thoughts, languages, cultural beliefs and philosophies of different cultural groups. Religion is a form of culture having specific beliefs and practices. Cultural and religious diversity are two basic components of India. All the major religions of the world like Hinduism, Buddhism, Jainism and Sikhism have been assimilated in India. Apart from these, some of the oldest religions in the world such as Zoroastrianism, Islam, Judaism, Christianity and Baha'ism also have their followers in India. (http://www.bangladeshsociology.org on 29.08.15).

In the present era of globalisation, an assimilation of these traits can be seen in the form of multiculturalism. There is a wide spread belief that every culturally unitary group has their own territory or own traditional ethos (Gupta 1992: 7).

'Religion' (*religio*) has two distinctive etymological roots (Derrida, 1998). Firstly, *relegere*, from *legere*, means to bring together, to harvest or to gather. Secondly, *religare*, from *ligare*, means to tie or to bind together (cited in Turner, 2005. p. 305). That means religion is something which brings about social harmony and binds individuals authoritatively into the social order. It is the institution that makes the social world intelligible. Therefore, it is a crucial element of sociology (Turner 2011:284).

Sociologists have defined religion from different points of view. It is a form of culture; it involves beliefs and practices; it provides a sense of purpose. Sociologists are not concerned with whether religious beliefs are true or false, but with how religions are organised, whether religious beliefs constitute sources of social solidarity or conflict, and what social forces are at work which keep religions alive or lead to their decline (Giddens 2013).

In fact, the tendency is to look upon these world religions as essential criteria of one's identity - a distinct marker of one's social self that readily marks out the 'other' as different and therefore alien to the worldview of the 'religious self' (access by: www.shodhganga.inflibnet.ac.in on 29.08.15).

Sociological definitions of religion can be divided into three types: 'inclusive definitions', 'exclusive definitions' and 'definitions in use'. Inclusive definitions tend to be functionalist in orientation, viewing religion as functionally necessary for society. Exclusive definitions look to define religions by reference to the substance of their varied beliefs, rooted in the idea that all religions make a distinction between a worldly empirical reality and a 'super-empirical' or transcendent reality. Rather than assuming that there is a real phenomenon called religion and then exploring the varied ways in which it is manifested in the society, 'religion in use' definitions are constructionist and investigate all those situations in which people themselves make reference to 'religion' or 'religious meaning' and engage in self-defined 'religious' practices (Giddens 2013). Their fundamental concern, as sociologists of religion, remains the same, namely, to further the understanding of the role of religion in society, to analyze its significance in and impact upon human history, and to understand its diversity and the social forces and influences that shape it (Hamilton 2001: 2).

It is not surprising that sociology, itself a product of the Enlightenment, should have a long tradition of skepticism toward religion. Karl Marx's (Marx and Engels 1878/1964) popularised idea of religion as an alienating and suppressive force and Sigmund Freud's (1928/1985) emphasis on its illusionary power continue to flicker a dim shadow over the perceived social relevance of religion (cited in Dillon 2003: 6). But in Weber's work religion takes a vital role and it affects on various social aspect.

In a single word, culture is the way of life or the life style pattern. Culture is acquired from birth to death. It is a continuous life long process in the existence of every human. Through socialisation, from childhood to death, cultural traditions are passed on from generation to generation. India has vast cultural diversity, and the existence of many religions is one of the causes behind it. Religion creates some belief patterns, values, norms, taboos etc and these factors generate cultural tradition. For this reason, religion and culture are greatly inter-related.

According to Tylor, culture as a 'complex whole' including "knowledge, belief, art, morals, law, custom and any other capabilities and habits acquired by man as a member of society"(cited in Dasgupta 2007:145). Culture is a product of human minds, the changes and modifications always going on as they are required. Cultural pluralism means there are 'multiplicity of the concept of a common good which accommodates diversities of culture' (Pal 2005).

"The cultural identification in the contemporary world is thus increasing dramatically as compared to other dimensions of identity" (Huntington 1997:29). Defining identity is not an easy task. In this globalised period, identity is constructed and it is fluid, multiple, impermanent and fragmentary (Bendle 2002).

Roy has stated about 'universalisation of culture', that means a multicultural dimension is welcomed in his views. He has several books and essays on Oraons, Mundas, Birhors, Kharias and other tribes of India (cited in: Dasgupta 2007:164).

Syncretism is the practice of balancing two or more separate sets of beliefs to create a new one. It also includes the synthesis of two contradictory thoughts. From the sociological point of view, as Umoh said, 'syncretism is necessary for the smooth functioning of a society with different backgrounds, as its absence can disturb the balance of such a society" (Umoh 2013: 35). Hermann Usener called it as "mishmash of religions" (cited in Eliade 1987:219).

Syncretism has recently re-emerged as a valuable tool for understanding the complex dynamics of ethnicity, interconnectedness and post-modernism. In the present era of increasing cultural condensation, syncretism is a prevailing event. The sociologists and social anthropologists have thrown much light on the variety of religious forms through their studies of belief systems, rituals, symbols and meaning all over the world but they have not paid adequate attention to the phenomenon of syncretism, though we find a few exceptions (Firth 1996:87).

Drawing on the creative ambiguity inherent in Emile Durkheim's (1912/1976) conceptualisation of ritual and the virtual interchangeability of religious and social behavior, Bellah points to many expressions of ritual in everyday life – rituals of dinner, sports, military drill, academia, and of politics. He argues that such diverse rituals may "be seen as disclosing an element of the sacred, and thus of the religious, at the very basis of social action of any kind" (Dillon 2003: 5).

As Richardson (2001) said, that "humans are not only born into a culture, but they are also born into a particular culture. It is this cultural background into which one is born that is internalised and forms the basic collective identity of a people and the ethnic identity of a group". Ethnicity, as pointed out is the differences between insiders and outsiders, between 'us' and 'them'.

We-feelings and homogeneity are the crucial factor for ethnicity (D'Souza 2006). In the context of globalisation, these distinctions are vanishing significantly, yet, there is a distinction line, as when a Tribal-Christian identifies himself as a Tribal-Christian or others as Hindu-Christian and so forth. In this process, the traditional identity currently sustains its value.

As Yogesh Atal says (2008), "we live in one world, but in multiple cultures. Not only is there a continuity of multiplicity of cultures, in each culture there are several layers of subcultures – indigenous and alien; and each one of us lives through several of them". The cultures have become more complex and plural. Atal's vision on cultural pluralism is to a great extent attached with this present study. Marshall Mac Luhan's concept of 'Global Village' is considerably prominent in this context.

Robert Redfield in his book 'The Folk Culture of Yucatan' (1941) deliberates the concept of 'folk – urban continuum'. Prior to that, there was a general thinking that tribal or folk societies are so-called isolated and closed societies. However his study shows, that folk society is small, homogeneous and tradition- bound, yet is not totally closed and that this society is also influenced by the outside world. In this context, he has talked about the concept of great tradition and little tradition. The former is manifested in urban and intellectual elite, whereas the latter is represented in villages and rural communities.

Basically, tribal identity is closely related with the definition of their names and also it is related with their social structure and livelihood (water/ river, forest land etc). These two things preserve their traditional identity with their heritage, language, culture, customs and their ways of life (Gupta 2007). With the changing social structure, their livelihood has been changed creating changes in their whole life-style including their traditional cultural roles. In this context, Nehru argues, 'non-imposition of our culture on them' to preserve their own ethnicity (ibid 2007).

As Gupta views (2007), "the truth is that Adivasis were never Hindus nor they had any religion or God. They always did not have a way of life nor do they have a temple or worshiping place for any deity. If at all they regard or worship anything it is nature, trees or the spirit of their ancestors living in rocks".

This cultural globalisation generates a plural cultural ethos where every little tradition and greater tradition of culture influences each other and this combination produces a multi-culture. Here various cultural traits lay under one roof.

Bindu Puri (2005) in her essay "*Understanding the Right to Culture, Cultural Imperialism and Multiculturalism in the context of the Human Rights Debate*" says that, every culture has its own identity and it has a powerful appearance in individuals' life and 'the notion of a culture is problematic in terms of individual liberty'. Different kinds of experiences of cultural imperialism can be found through Indian tradition. According to her view 'in the Indian experience with the ascendancy of the dominant Brahmanical culture there has been a marginalisation and relegation to the periphery of the less dominant cultures, like the tribal cultures' (Puri 2005: 210).

Again in her own words, "If every human being human being had a basic right to his own culture then how can plurality of cultures co-exist without the ever present dangers of cultural imperialism"? According to her, plurality of culture is a general phenomenon of today's society. But at the same time it generates a marginalised position for the less dominant culture (ibid 2005: 209).

This view is very prominent in Ghurye's work, where he mentioned about the tribal absorption in Hindu culture, in his book titled '*The Aborigines – so-called – and their future*'. He used the term 'acculturation' to define it. There are also many other Indian sociologists, who speak on this issue.

According to M.N.Srinivas (1985:105) 'the unity of India is essentially a religious one. People may worship different deities but the religious scriptures – Puranas, Brahmanas, Epics and the Vedas – knit the numerous heterogeneous groups together into one religious society and give them the sense that their country is sacred'.

Nirmal Kumar Bose in his article '*The Hindu Method of Tribal Absorption*' (1941) told about the Brahminical influence on Mundas and Oraons, which he called Hinduisation. But Srinivas's concept of Sanskritisation can be associated with the above stated Hinduisation. Surajit Sinha also told about 'tribal-peasant continuum'. All of these studies have been illustrated a cosmic cultural aspect (Ahuja 2010; Doshi 2007). Sinha's other important view is about 'vanishing' primitive tribes in India. Globalisation has been creating a uniform culture by absorbing multicultural traits of dominant group and also non-dominant like low caste marginalised groups and the tribal groups. As a result, the concept of a pure ethnic group is now facing tremendous challenges in this century.

Barker in his book '*Cultural Studies: Theory and Practices*', said that 'Cultural studies does not speak with one voice, it cannot be spoken with one voice, and I do not have one voice with which to represent it' (Barker 2008: 4). Culture varies from time to time and space to space. It has a wide range of multiplicity.

Simon During in his book '*Cultural Studies: A Critical Introduction*' tells about cultural globalisation and multiculturalism. In this perspective of cultural globalisation he observed the unique relationship of region-nation-local based cultures. He also analyzed how cultural globalisation with multiculturalism divided the whole world into a new context (During. 2005: 98). Irving Kristol in his essay '*The Tragedy of Multiculturalism*' (Wall Street Journal) also explained the dark side of multiculturalism (Kristol 1995: 50).

Grossberg, Nelson and Treichler in their book '*Cultural Studies*', discuss about the history of cultural studies, various cultural identity like national identity and nationhood, cultural institution and also culture as colonialism, post-colonialism and culture in the global aspect in postmodern era. They critically analyze the views of many thinkers' like Marxists, feminists, structuralists and postmodernists etc (Grossberg 1991: 1-2). Assimilation is a process and popularly it is identified as a 'melting pot' in which different groups come together and form a common culture, - a new unique society by incorporating their cultural traits (Gordon. M. Assimilation and Pluralism. Access by: www.sagepub.com on 27.09.2015).

Cultural studies have also discussed about folk culture, little tradition, great tradition, mass culture, cultural capital, cultural industry, cultural hegemony and many other concepts related to changing cultural aspects. In a book titled '*The Cultural Studies Reader*' many philosophers like Adorno, Horkheimer, Stuart Hall, Foucault, Lyotard, Bennett and many others discuss about the multiple horizons of cultural studies (During 1999: 2).

In this present study, Hinduism, Christianity and Tribalism blend with each other and create a cultural syncretism. At the same time in this syncretism, the traditional aromas of those cultures have been mixed and generate a new cultural fabric.

II

For this present study, Kalyani Raghunathpur area has been purposively selected. This area is dominated by the Hindu-Christian people. Both Tribal – Christian and non – Christian Hindu people live together without religious bigotry between them. This area is under 'Gayaspur' Municipality, Kalyani, Nadia, West Bengal. It is also known as Girja Para'.

According to the Father of the local Church (the Christian priest of the local church) there are total 400 households. According to Father's enumeration, the Tribal Christian population is more than the Hindu- Christian population. Yet in this present field work, it has been observed that there are a total of 160 households; 90 households are Hindu-Christian and 70 householders are Tribal Christian. Except for these, there are some Nepali Christian, Anglo – Christian, Madrasi – Christian, General Hindu, and General Tribal people in this locality. Their number is very meager.

This area was developed as early as the 1970's. Before that, it was dominated by Muslim people. The Church was established after the 1970's and the locality gradually developed. From the 1970's -1980's, this area was known as '*Girja Para*' and since then, the existing families started to settle here with their different cultural identities.

With the passage of time these cultural groups assimilated each other, creating a stream of cultural syncretism. In this wave of transformation, each cultural group is gradually absorbing with the dominant cultural traits of the locality, i.e. Christianity as this area was developed by the Christian priest.

Many Hindu – Christian families live in this locality. There are also converted Tribal assimilated with Hinduism as well as Christianity. Tribal - Christian and Hindu – Christian, both these categories of people perform Christian rituals amidst their own traditional rituals.

For this present study, only Oraon Tribal-Christian peoples have been selected purposively. The 70 Oraon families have been interviewed during the time of field work. This paper has tried to find out the nature of socio-cultural interaction pattern of the Oraon-Christian families with the Hindu families and also the nature of assimilation between the two.

The Oraons are also known as Kurukh peoples, originated from Konkan (their home ground). They are basically forest dwellers and agriculture is the central part of their economic structure. They follow the *Sarnaism* (Sarna religion), mostly related with Hinduism. Oraon peoples believe in naturalistic religion and are divided into many totemistic clans. They are found in different parts of India, also in Bangladesh.

There are a total of twelve types of clans in them. Every clan sustains their clan identity, especially during their marriage. However, due to urbanisation, this converted tribal group does not follow their traditional norms and taboos like their homeland group. Table: 1 depicts the detail information about these twelve types of Oraon clans.

The economic condition of these Oraons is not so good. 32.86% of their income is Rs. 5,000 – Rs. 10,000. Then, the income of 20% respondents lies under Rs. 10,000 – Rs.15, 000 and the income of 17.14% respondents is below Rs. 5,000. A few households have a good economic condition (Table: 2).

The Oraon- Christians (28.57%) are day labourers. There are a good number of Oraons who are engaged in private sector and business. Only 5.71% of Oraons are engaged with farming. Also there are a few Oraons who are engaged in governmental jobs, but this number is very small. Vehicle drivers are another occupation of this tribal group. Economically well settled Oraons have a liking for private jobs outside the India. A few (or very few) of them – (according to what you want to bring across ok) are interested to pursue private job within the country (Table: 3).

The traditional Oraons follow various customs, beliefs, values. They celebrate their age old festivals associated with the worshiping of deities related with their forest and agriculture based life style (Table: 4). They are the followers of nature. But in this present era, these festivals have lost their ethnic ethos because of the changing social condition. Now, the Oraon Tribal-Christians have assimilated the culture amalgamated with Hinduism.

III

This study focuses on the nature of cultural syncretism with multicultural dimensions which are the major characteristics of this area. All sample Oraons tribal population who live in this locality migrated from Jharkhand, Ranchi and Orisha. To understand their cultural diversity, the changing rites and rituals are studied through the rite of passages.

In the Oraon Community, after birth of a child, the priest, a local Church, commonly called Father among Catholics incorporates the child to Christianity through '*Baptism*' i.e., the child is blessed by the Father with 'holy water'. Usually this ritual takes place in the Church at 27th day of the birth of the child or after one and half month. It is a purely Christian ritual.

'*Annaprason*', the rice giving ceremony for the first time is purely a Hindu cultural ritual; the maternal uncle plays the major role in the form of a custom, when a child reaches the 5th or 7th month of age, by giving the first 'feed' of rice into a child's mouth. The Oraon Christians integrate this custom from Hindus and perform this ritual joyfully with the family members of their community along with the other community members.

At the time of a birthday celebration they combine the Hindu and Christian rituals together. They eat Cake as well as *Payes (a sweet is prepared with milk, rice and sugar)*. It is a very common practice among them.

Right from their early years, (13 is mentioned later in the sentences) they learn the beliefs of Christianity from the local Church, where the priest as a teacher teaches the main traits of Christian practices and beliefs. This is one type of oriental course which is continued up to the age of thirteen. Normally at this age (13 yrs.), one has to be examined by the Father/priest, of the local Church on what is learnt and after qualifying successfully, one will be declared ready by the priest to receive '*Khrista-prasad*' (food offered by Jesus). There have no concept of born Christian. Christianity is always a process of learning and professing, which a Christian person maintains throughout his/her life.

Inter religious marriage is a well known practice of this area. From generation to generation this inter-religious marriage practice is continued among the Oraons with social sanctions by maintaining sacred taboos.

This type of inter religious marriage practice has made a bridge of brotherhood to establish cultural pluralism in their day to day life. The Oraon Christians of this area are firstly assimilated with the Hindu culture as the Oraon themselves claim as Hindus. After converting them into Christianity they accept Christianity as a part of their life. In this way a triad culture has been emerged in this Oraons locality: a culture of the Oraons, culture of the Bengali Hindus and the culture of the Christian. With this trio culture, a cultural syncretism is observed. It is a social phenomenon of global society which can be compared with the 'melting pot' of American society (Gordon. M. Assimilation and Pluralism. Access by: www.sagepub.com on 27.09.2015). Here, it can also be stated that the area is dominated by the Christians and a good number of Hindu people also live there along with the Oraons. Marriage is also another important ritual where the Oraons are greatly influenced by the Bengali-Hindu culture along with the Christian religiosity and their marriage ritual is the combination of the three distinctive cultures, which create a new multicultural form.

In general, before marriage the Father/priest, of the local Church, teaches the adult members about the importance of conjugal life which is known as "*Hastarpan*" (act of laying hands on). After that, when the two families propose their willingness for conducting the marriage, they have to follow the other ritual named '*Banprakash*'. Two adult members, that is the ones getting married of those two families have to present themselves before the priest in the Church, on three consecutive Sundays and people are asked to give their opinion about their readiness for marriage. Also, if anyone wishes to withdraw from the proposed marriage, he or she has the liberty to withdraw himself or herself. This procedure being completed, the priest officially announces the Banprakash, the official declaration about the marriage of the two parties.

After the official declaration of *Banprakash* by the Father,/ priest, *Lotapani* is another sacred ritual generally performed by the Oraons. The Oraon-Christian people arrange a social get-together with a social feast in the presence of the *Raiber* > who is this (sic) where the elder members of the bride and bride-groom bless them for their future conjugal life. Formerly, this ritual was executed with on a large scale and it needed a lot of money. Presently, they arrange this ritual only in the presence of the family members of both the parties.

The ritual of '*Aiburovat*' is held on the previous day of the marriage, before the maiden has her food. (What is it???). Now-a-days, the use of '*mehendi*' in the hands and on the feet for decoration is a common practice among them. On the day of the marriage, early in the morning, they go to river to bring some water. However, at the present time, as there is no river in the nearby area, to keep up their custom, they go to the houses of five of their neighbours' to bring some water. Some Oraon Christians perform the Hindu ritual *Gaye Halud* (turmeric paste on their body). Oraons are basically endogamous. So, same clan marriage is restricted in their community. A few of them have performed inter-religious marriage, but in the case of clan identity they consciously preserve the endogamous rule.

In this marriage ceremony, the Father / priest utters the holy words of sealing the marriage in front of all members, and Jesus present in the tabernacle in the Church; the bride and bride-groom respond to the sacred words as directed by the priest to seal the marriage between the man and woman At that sacred moment, the bridegroom puts vermilion on the forehead of the bride and the bride's hands are filled with glittering and different types of bangles, of which the first type of bangles is made by conch shell, the second type of bangles is made with metal known as *red pola* used as 'symbol of marriage' and the third type of bangle (one) made by iron known as *noya*. They also perform the ritual of changing garlands between them.

After completion of the marriage ritual, they usually offer some homemade sweets called *Pitha – Payes* to all of their guests. Finally the marriage ceremony comes to an end with a feast by the bride's family. All the neighbours of the locality, the relatives of the girl's family and the boy's family and sometimes the Father/priest, also attend the ceremonial function.

At the time of 5th or 7th month of pregnancy, the Oraon family members perform the 'Sadh' ritual for the pregnant woman. At that time, they arrange a feast and the pregnant woman is given many items of foods which she likes.

In the case of their death rituals, there is no difference between male-female, old – young and others. The only difference is found in the case of a married woman. When a person dies the family members inform priest of the Church about the incident. He rings the church bell which alerts the community about the incident of death in their locality. After hearing the sound of the bell and getting news about the death, all neighbours from the locality gather in the house of the deceased to show their respect to the deceased person through communal prayer. After about thirty minutes the priest rings the second bell to request them to go to the burial ground. After hearing the second bell is rung, the family members of the dead person take water to complete the bathing of the dead person; then they cover the dead body with a new white dress. Only the married woman after her death has been allowed to be dressed with new clothes like a bride. The favourite belongings of the deceased person also are kept in the coffin with the dead body. The colour of the coffin is always black. After the prayers at the grave everyone present at the burial ground is given some soil to place on the coffin as a reminder that we have come from the soil and to the soil we are returning; as the people throw the soil, they also pray for peace of the soul.

On the third day of the death of the person, the family members altogether pray for the dead person. It is the belief of the Christian that Jesus rose from the dead after three days and for that reason, this ritual has an important role in their cultural life. All Christians of various communities in the locality also pray for the peace of the soul.

Previously the family members of the deceased used to keep 40 days as mourning period. During that period, they did not eat non-vegetarian food; but on the 41st day of the death a ceremonial feast was arranged with all the members of the locality and the mourning period was declared over by eating non-vegetarian food like fish, chicken, mutton etc.

Now, as a result of the busy life-style, the family members of the deceased person perform rituals of mourning period on odd number of days like seven or nine or eleven days. There is no concept of purity or pollution in Christianity but the Oraon-Christians follow some traditional customs related to it. When they come back from the burial ground they first wash their hands with turmeric powder and place their hands over the fire. The use of turmeric powder and placing their hands over the fire are the symbols of purity. Also there are no norms to eat vegetarian food in those 40 days time period, but they maintain the ritual of eating vegetarian food during those 40 days.

Apart from these, the Oraon- Christians perform some other customs in their life. At the time of New Year festival, they offer some foods, fruits and sweets to Jesus. Earlier days they offered those things to their traditional deity named *Dharmesh* at the time of *Sarhul* festival (Table 4). They have various taboos in relation to their clans as well. However, they do not follow those traditional rites except that on Friday, they do not eat meat.

Language

Language is the medium through which peoples inter change their ideas, values, opinions and emotions. Every language has its own cultural component which is carried on from generation to generation. In their daily life, these Oraon-Christian people use the Bengali language, though they cannot read and write Bengali. They also interact with each other in their own traditional *Kurukh* language. They speak their own language when they are at home??. The new generation is also familiar with this language. They understand the *Kurukh* dialects but cannot read and write. Some of the new generation Oraons can speak with this language but there are also a good number of Oraons of the younger generation who cannot speak, yet understand the language.

IV

India has its own plural cultural heritages having the syntheses of multicultural components of different traits of various groups. The groups vary according to its religion, language, caste, locality, ethnic identity, geographical location and also nation-state boundaries. With the passage of time, each group assimilates the other by following the norms, beliefs, mores, customs etc. A good number of anthropological works deal with the various aspects of cultural syncretism. They have studied the various processes of cultural assimilation between Hindu-Tribal, Tribal-Peasant, Hindu-Muslim, Tribal-Christian, Hindu-Christian, Muslim-Christian etc. So the cultural syncretism is not a new concept among social researchers. Society persists with its plurality of culture that is cultural syncretism, since its primordial period.

The Girja Para is dominated by the Hindu population but the influence of Christianity among the Bengali-Hindus and the Tribals is also noticeable. Since 1970s the Oraons have been settling here and adopting Christian culture in their livelihood. But as this area is dominated by the Bengali-Hindus, the Oraons slowly also absorb Hinduism.

This study shows that the Oraon Christian community till today still maintains some of their basic ethnic traits in their everyday life. They preserve their traditional clan name, they use their language, they exchange their ethnic ideas with their fellow men and they sometimes restore?? their tribal religiosity in performing the rite of passages of their life.

At present, due to their 'tribal identity' the Oraons get many governmental facilities and simultaneously, due to their Christian identity they also get many facilities from their Christian community. For this reason, they use two names in a parallel way - one Christian name and other tribal name. They use both these names according to their necessity.

Urbanisation, globalisation, cultural pluralism and modern economic facilities have a great impact on them. These factors make them conscious about their social status. Side by side, the Christian identity provides them a better social status, with educational and economic facilities. Till today, the majority of the tribal are not the part of mainstream society; they are isolated, marginalised and deprived section of our society.

The 21st century has opened a new road for the tribal people. Tribes are no more considered as a segregated community in the global village. Globalisation and global culture has made them aware about their real existence. As a result, different tribal groups come in forward to restore their tribal ethnicity. It is not immoral to say that globalisation of culture or cultural syncretism is directly related with the term 'cultural imperialism' where the dominating powerful cultural groups have a great impact on the less dominated marginalised group. The intrinsic value of every culture has been merged with each other losing one's ethnic identity for raising a universal culture.

The present study shows that the Oraons of this area maintain their tribal identity just for getting the socio-economic benefits as scheduled tribe from the government of India. From this study it is also observed that, they are not (at all)> too strongly put could it be – really> interested to preserve their traditional tribal identity. The Oraons in this area are assimilating the three distinctive cultures: Christianity, Hinduism and Tribalism, for their survival.

References

Access by: www.shodhganga.inflibnet.ac.in on 29.08.15.

Ahuja. R. (2010). Indian Social System. Rawat Publications. New Delhi.

Atal. Y. (2008). Entering the Global Village. Rawat Publication. New Delhi.

Barker. C. (2008). Cultural Studies: Theory and Practices. 3rd edition. SAGE. London.

Bendle. M. F. (2002). The Crisis of 'Identity' in High Modernity. British Journal og Sociology. Vol. 53, No. 1. March.

Dasgupta. S. (2007). Recasting the Oraons and the 'Tribe': Sarat Chandra Roy's Anthropology. (In). Anthropology in the East. (Eds.). Uberoi et. al. Permanent Black. New Delhi.

Dillon. M. (2003). Handbook of the Sociology of Religion. Cambridge University Press. New York. p. 5.

Doshi. S. L. and Jain. P. C. (2007). Rural Sociology. Rawat Publications. New Delhi.

D'Souza. L. (2006). Globalisation, Nationalism and Ethnic Identities: The Future of the Nation – State. (In). Sociology of Globalisation. (Eds). Somayaji. *et.al.* Rawat Publication. New Delhi.

During. S. (2005). Cultural Studies: A Critical Introduction. Routladge. New York.

During. S. (1999). The Cultural Studies Reader. Routladge. New York.

Eliade. M. and Adams. C. J. (1987). The Encyclopedia of Religion. Macmillan. New York. p. 219.

Firth. R. (1996). *Religion: A Humanist Interpretation*. London. Rutledge. p. 87.

Giddens. A. and Sutton. P. W. (2013). Sociology. 7th edition. Polity Press.

Gordon. M. Assimilation and Pluralism. Access by: www.sagepub.com on 27.09.2015.

Grossberg. L., Nelson. C. and Treichler. A. P. (1991). Cultural Studies. Routledge. New York.

Gupta. A. and Ferguson. J. (1992). Beyond "Culture": Space, Identity, and the Politics of Difference. Cultural Anthropology. Vol. 7. Blackwell Publishing. p. 7.

Gupta. R. (2007). Tribal Contemporary Issues. Ramnika Foundation. New Delhi.

Hamilton. M. (2001). The Sociology of Religion. Routledge. London. p. 2.

Huntington. S. P. (1997). The Clash of Civilisations and the Re-making of World Order. Penguin Books India Ltd. New Delhi.

Kristol. I. (1995). Neoconservatism: The Autobiography of an Idea. Free Press. New York. p. 50.

Pal. J. (2005). The Idea of the Culture of Unity in Diversity. (In). Tribal, Culture, Art. (Eds). Vanlalnghak et.al. DVS Publishers. Guwahati.

Puri. B. (2005). Understanding the Right to Culture, Cultural Imperialism and Multiculturalism in the context of the Human Rights Debate. (In). Tribal, Culture, Art. (Eds). Vanlalnghak et.al. DVS Publishers. Guwahati.

Richardson. M. (2001). The Experience of Culture. SAGE. New Delhi.

Srinivas. M. N. (1985). Caste in Modern India and Other Essays. Media Publishers. Bombay.

Srivastava. V. K. Major Contributers to Anthropology. Delhi University. Delhi. Access by: www.bangladeshsociology.org. on 15. 06. 14.

Stewart. C. and Shaw. R. (1994). Syncretism / Anti-Syncretism. Routledge. London. p. 3.

Turner. B. (2011). The Sociology of Religion. SAGE. London. p. 284.

Turner. B. S. (2005). Talcott Parsons's Sociology of Religion and the Expressive Revolution. Journal of Classical Sociology. Vol 5(3). SAGE. London. p. 305.

Umoh. D. (2013). Superstition and Syncretism: Setbacks to Authentic Christian Practice in Africa. International Journal of Humanities and Social Science Invention. p. 35.

18

Syncretism in Religious and Cultural Dimension: A study of the Jaintias of Meghalaya

— *R.P. Athparia*

The People

Passah & Sarma (2002: XI) said that the "name Jaintia could be an Aryanised form of the name *Synteng* by which the people of Jaintia Hills used to be called even today. From the word *Synteng* we get *Syntein, Syntiang, Zontain*, *Zontia* and ultimately *Jaintia*". Again, the name "*Synteng*" could also be an Aryanised form of the name "*Sutong*", the original clan of the *Jaintia* royal dynasty from which was also derived the names "*Suteng*" and "*Sutnga*".

It is wrong to say that the ethnic name "Jaintia" has now been largely replaced by the term "Pnar" (Simon, 1996:1). In fact, the people residing in the central region of Jaintia Hills are called "Pnars" by those living in the southern and northern regions and who are in turn being called as "Wars" and "Bhois" respectively by the Pnars. But all the three are collectively known by a generic name "Jaintia" or "Synteng" (Passah & Sarma 2002: XI).

The Jaintias are believed to have come from South-East Asia. Probably they started their migration from Mongolia via West Asia and along the foothills of the Himalayas to South-east Asia, thence to their present habitat through Burma (Pakem 1977: 1-3). Bareh (1997:9-10) states that "Khasi is a general name given to the various tribes and sub-tribes that inhabit the Khasi and Jaintia Hills. The name includes the following sub-tribes:- (1) *Khynriams* or

Nonglums (Khasis proper) inhabiting the middle ranges of Khasi Hills, comprising the *Khynriams* and their allied tribes in the central plateau; (2) the *Jaintias* are called *Syntengs* but they prefer to be called *Pnars*; (3) the *War* people of the south comprising the *Shella* people and their allied groups of tribes; (4) The *Amwi* people and their allied *War Synteng* in the south of Jainta Hills who appear to form a parent tribe of *Khasi* during earliest period of settlement in the land;(5) The *Bhoi* people both Khasi and Pnar, inhabiting the north of Khasi and Jaintia Hills with their different sub-groups, were also in some cases, a result of diversion of the people from the central plateau forming an intermixing with the Mikirs on the outer fringes of this land".

Chattopadhayaya (1988:3-4) states that the jaintias do not like the term "*Synteng*" because it is associated with "*Sahteng*" which means either the people who were left behind in their westward migration or simply a "backward" community. However, according to Suniti Kumar Chatterjee (1976:26) in his "*Kirata Jana Kriti*", the word Jaintia (*Zantain* or *Zonten*) was derived from the word "*Synteng*". According to Pakem (1972:352), the word *Synteng* has said to be derived from the word "*Sutnga*" (*Suteng*), the ruling dynasty of the Jaintias, or from the word "S*ohkynting*" (*Snynting* or *Synting)*, a village through which the Khasis came to the Jaintia Hills. Tradition has it that "*Teng*" is the ancient mother and therefore *Syntengs* means the children of the ancestral mother. Jaintians seem to have an organisation and the original Khasi word *Synteng* (*Zeintein*) developed into Jaintia (Chattopadhayaya 1988:4). According to Gurdon (1996:1-2) the Khasis inhabit the Khasi Hills proper, and the *Syntengs* or *Pnars*, the Jaintia Hills. The Jaintia Hills take their name from the Rajas of Jaintia, the rulers of this part of the country, who had as their capital Jaintiapur, a place situated at the foot of the Jaintia Hills on the southern side, now falls within the boundaries of the Sylhet district (now Bangladesh).

According to Gemini Paul (1956:151), the Jaintias were the original inhabitants of a State in the Chinese region called *T'Sin-tiang***.** This is an Austric word and the people of this State were called *T'Sin-tiang* or *T'Sin-tien*. In course of time, they came to be known as *Synteng* or *Syntien.* This term got corrupted into *Chyntien* and then as *zyntein* and ultimately as Jaintia which is the present name. Chatterjee (1976:26) writes:

> "*It is the consensus of opinion among indologists that in Sanskrit the term Kirata indicates the wild non- Aryan tribes living in the mountains, particularly in the Himalayas and in the indented Eastern areas of India, who were Mongoloid in origin. These Kiratas were connected with China or the Chinese, the Photas or Tibetans and other Mongoloid peoples. They were distinguished from the wild or primitive tribes of Austric origin who were known specially as Nishadas, Sabaras, Pulindas, Bhillas, Kollas. There are certain amounts of speculation about it.*"

The author further states that:

"*In Burma and in Indo-China, the Mongoloids had largely absorbed the earlier Austric peoples. The history of Burma has been in the main a conflict between the Mran-ma or Burmese Mongoloids from the north and Rman (Rmen) or Mon, Austro- Asiatic living in central and southern Burma, leading finally to the complete subjugation and gradual absorption of the Mons in spite of the latter possessing a superior culture and having been the teachers of the Mongoloid rulers on Burmese art, culture, religion and higher life (ibid:38)".*

Furthermore, the author states that:

"After Negroes, the people that came to India appear to be the Proto-Australoids- a medium sized dolichocephalic race from eastern Mediterranean area, who arrived in India with a Palaeolithic culture who has developed a characteristic culture in India, which included primitive agriculture with the digging stick and hoe (ibid:8)".

The Proto-Australoids of India are known as Nishadas and they are Austric speaking people. Khasi-Jaintias are Nishadas and not Kirata. They use hoe in tilling land. Chatterjee argued that:

"*In Burma and Indo-China lived speakers of Austric languages, who were largely of the Proto-Australoid with Mongoloids in very early times in Burma and Indo-China. This mixture produced the ancient Ramen (Rman) or Mon people of central and southern Burma, Palaungs and wa of upper Burma, the Khmer, the Chams, the Stieng, the Bahnar*

"*Jaintias of Khasi Hills is Mongoloid by race and Austric by speech. Their earlier history was obscure and still remains obscure (ibid:10)".*

According to the author, except the Khasis and the connected Jaintias (Syntengs) of Assam the Mongoloid peoples who are found in India are speakers of languages and dialects belonging to the Sino-Tibetan or Tibeto-Chinese speech family. But Chatterjee's opinion was that the Jaintias are Mongoloid by race and Austric by speech is not correct. It could not be possible for the Khasis and Jaintias to retain the Austric language after being surrounded by the Indo-Mongoloid, by Sino-Tibetan or Tibeto-Chinese and also by Aryan speakers. The Khasi-Jaintias could retain their linguistic and racial characteristics because of their strong foundation and other Austric or Austro-Asiatic speakers of Siam and Indo-China *(ibid:19-22)".*

This absorption of the Mons (Austro-Asiatic) by the Mongoloid might have taken place in Assam and eastern India. And in some cases the Austric speech had triumphed over the Sino-Tibetan; a case in point is the Khasi. The same author stated that:

Again it is difficult to accept the opinion of Chatterjee that the mixture produced completely different races like Mon, Wa, Paloung etc. Then again how could the Khasi- Jaintias be Mongoloid when they have close relation with Mon-Khmer Palaung Wa of Burma and Indo-China and in South Burma and Indo-China Mon- Khmer are an Austric people? According to Bareh (1997:16), Khasi is strictly connected with the Palaung-Wa dialects spoken by the tribes that live along the central and upper reaches of the Mekong River. The close sisters of Khasi appear to have been the Mon and Palaung-Riang-Wa dialects of Burma. It is clear that from the first, Khasi is described as a sub-group of the Mon-Khmer and Palaung. But there exists also some important phonetic relations between Khasi and Vietnamese. Khasi has also shown a few relations with Wanchoo, a tribe in the Tirap district of Arunachal Pradesh.

From the above, it is clear that there is a possibility of the mingling of these Proto-Austroloids with Mongoloids in very early time in Burma and Indo-China, as Chatterjee himself said. Thus, Jaintias are neither Mongoloid by race nor Kirata. Their language is Austric, and by race, it is quite possible that purity of the Austric race could not be maintained because they lived all along with Mongoloid. Chattopadhayaya (1988:6) quoting Bareh said that the Khasis lost a good deal of Austric racial features due to the pressure of strong and sturdy Mongoloid types. The changes in the physical features are more visible in the urban area in recent years due to admixture through matrimonial connections with plains people.

Chttopadhayaya (1988:6) states that the origin of the Khasi is a vexed question. It is still shrouded in mystery and yet to be resolved. Regarding origin of the Jaintias, Gassah (1994:69) states that there are two schools of thought which represents the outer or non-local sources, the Jaintia Kingdom got its name from the southern plains tract which was originally known as Jaintiapur because of the presence of the famous shrine of Jayanti Devi, an incarnation of Goddess Durga or Gouri, as mentioned in the Puranic and Tantric literature. However, the other school of thought did not accept this viewpoint. The local scholars believe that the term 'Jaintia' is entirely local in origin. In support of their contention, they say that the sanskritised term *Jaintia (Zantain)* is derived from the word '*Syntang*'. The word '*Syntang*' in turn is derived from many sources. Another local opinion is that the term has its association with the ancient mother. However, another scholar is of the opinion that the Jaintias call themselves as 'Pnar'. It was after the occupation of the Jaintia paraganas that the *Syiem* of *Sutnga* went to settle in Jaintiapur and the British called the *Syiem* and his people by the name '*Jaintia*'. Such an opinion is, however, still considered debatable.

The Jaintia Identity and Oral Narratives

Needless to say those myths, the oral narratives, originated at a time when man had no valid answers to many or vexed questions of existence. The people then attempted answers, necessarily positive and graphic, conferring powers on god, various deities and semi-divine heroes credited with creation and care. One important issue is the social system and customs that the people would want to survive and continue. There is thus an attempt to relate the mythological system with the kinship system. The stories are told again and again, particularly in the annual festival and ritual event.

For many years, the peoples inhabiting the Khasi and Jaintia Hills of Meghalaya were broadly called Khasis. This generic name was in vogue and these peoples were divided and identified into five sub-groups, namely, *Khynriam, Pnar*, *Synteng,* or *Jaintia, War*, *Bhoi* and *Lyngngam*. But recently an opinion has been generated to establish that the Jaintias have a separate and distinct identity and are divided into six sub-groups: the *Bhoi*, the *Biata,* the *Hadem,* the *Lalung*, the *Pnar* and the *War* (Sen 2002:88).

However, some scholars have maintained that 'there are many proofs in support of the argument that the Khasis and Pnars are descended from the same ancestress' (Simon 1966: 49). This argument is based on oral traditions and a narrative has been quoted:

In the beginning there was only one woman in the Talang clan named *Iawtalang*. She had nine daughters who were all very industrious. So devoted were they to their work that even when the youngest was on the point of child bearing, the eight sisters left her at home with her husband, a man of the Dkhar clan. The youngest sister's husband was so furious that he cooked the after-birth and gave it to the elder sisters on their refura, saying that it was the meat of a sacrificial cook. After they had finished eating he taunted them saying that they were devourers their own kith and kin. In intense shame they fled the village and almost all of them founded other clans in other localities. The clans which they founded are: *Buam, Nongtdu, Pyrtuh*, *Syntung, Suting, Talang, Lyngdoh and Nialang*. It is said that *Syntung and Suting* clans are one and the same (Simon, 1966:49-50).

In support of the ethnic name Synteng, Bareh (1997:10) states that:

> *"According to a tradition Teng was the ancient mother and therefore Synteng means children of an ancestral mother. The word has its significance as Khasi does. The old Khasis were accustomed in naming things after mothers. Even the Syiem, the head of the state, in the male attribute is called U Kmie, literally the mother. Jaintia seems to have been an Aryanisation of the original Khasi word Synteng (Zaintein) which developed into Jaintia."*

Regarding the origin of the ethnic name Jaintias, Sen (2002:89-90) states that:

> *"Whether the progeny of 'seven huts' of the mythic narrative of 'Ki Hynniew Trep' include the Jaintias cannot be said for sure since the*

generic term Khasi is mentioned only. But the versions from both the Khasi and Jaintia Hills narrate the same myth of origin. The most widely spread version mention of a place of habitation of Ki Hynniew Trep called Sophetbneng, a hill top in Khasi Hills. In one version, God initially created sixteen families who stayed with him in heaven and could commute between heaven and earth by means of a ladder in the shape of a tree on a hill top known as Sohpetbneng. Later seven of these families (Ki Hynniew Trep) expressed their desire to remain on earth. God granted them their wish but remarked the ladder (Rymbai 1979:110). In another version, in the golden age after creation, Man had personal relation with god and could continue between heaven and earth but in due course of time Ki Hynniew Trep, the ancestors of the Khasi race, drifted away from God to choose their own way and thus the golden bridge (the tree at Sohpetbneng) collapsed but communication was restored later. It happened when a tall big tree on the top of U Diengiei peak over casting the earth with darkness (signifying man's spiritual crisis) with its overspreading branches and leaves, was ultimately felled down by God(Mawrie1981: 5-6).In yet another version, on one day when only seven women were on earth an evil spirit cut off the tree which served as the ladder for communication between earth and heaven and these seven women were forced to remain on earth and their progeny came to be known as Ki Hynniew Trep settled on earth they were given three commandments by God which form the essence of Khasi religion, Ka Niam Khasi."

Sen (2002:90) further states that there are some new elements in a version of the narrative collected from Jaintia Hills (source: Christobin Rymbai, R.T.Rymbai, and O.P.Lyton of Jowai, Jaintia Hills). The new elements are: the presence of *Syiem U Lakriah*, the semi-divine hero through whom the people received the commandments from God: the presence of a supreme golden, *Ka Blei Synshar* and of the mother earth, *Ka Blei Rimman*. The narrative is as follows:

"There were sixteen families in heaven. Of whom seven were sent to earth. They could visit heaven by a golden ladder. The nine families living with God in heaven could also visit the earth by that ladder. Her and the members of the seven families had divine qualities for which other creatures on earth accepted their leadership. Order was restored. But the seven families soon found that the world was full of stones. There was no soil and they faced difficulties in cultivating. U Lakriah, therefore, went to heaven to ask for soil from God. God directed the supreme goddess, Ka Blei Synshar, to give U Lakriah three basket full of earth (soil) from heaven. U Lakriah came back with these baskets and covered the stones with soil. (In another version, Ka Blei Symshar sent Ka Blei Rimmand, the mother earth, to cover the stones with soil. It is also said that God

could only be approached through Blei Rimmand by libations). When evil spirits made life miserable, people prayed to God and solicited his presence. God came to earth met U Lakriah in some unknown place and conveyed his wishes and advice. These were known as Niamon commandments. God also decreed that He could be approached by prayer, libation and sacrifice. U Lakriah would ascertain the wishes of God by divination."

In all these narratives, one element is common i.e., the seven families of the Khasis (and perhaps including the Jaintias) are the progeny of these seven families and are known as the children of *Ka Hynniew Trep*. The mythic narrative of *Ka Hynniew Trep* is repeatedly referred to enhance the identity consciousness. Indeed, to this day they invariably refer to themselves as *Ki Hynniew Trep* in their prayers and worships, and whenever there is a cause to call the people to combine and unite together as one. They call their religion *KaNiam Tynrai* or *Niam Tre* (Rymbai 1993:68).

The Jaintia Identity from Historical Event

The issue of a separate identity of the Jaintias perhaps got strengthened by a historical event of a political formation, the Jaintia Kingdom, around thirteenth century A.D. The situation prevailing in the hills and the political administrative arrangements made before the establishment of the Kingdom to ensure a sense of unity among the Jaintias has been narrated by Pakem (1990: 80-81) in these words:

"With the increase in population and size of the territory (Raids or Elakas) consisting of a group of villages, secular functions increased. This necessitated the bifurcation of sacred and secular functions. The sacred function was retained by the Lyngdoh, and then the secular function was entrusted to an official called U Doloi. Again, when the number of Doloiships increased there was feeling among the Jaintias to establish unity among them. This gave way to the growth of the institution of the Kingship in Jaintia Hills. To make it more acceptable to the people, the office of Kingship was originally occupied by a person who was supposed to be divinely ordained through a miraculous birth of the royal family out of a mermaid Ka Li Dakha. Since this incident was supposed to have occurred within Sutnga Doloiship, the royal dynasty was then called Ki Syiem Sutnga (the Sutnga dynasty). It was this dynasty which had brought all the political units of Jaintia Hills under one central authority with wider latitude of powers to the units called Raid or Elakas. With the conquest of the Jaintia plains in the thirteen century A.D. the central authority had, for the first time, its own territory where its writs covered every aspect of administration."

This is how, through historical process, a Jaintia identity was perhaps generated. Oral narrative was referred to establish the Jaintia hegemony. It is known that the Jaintias have another name, *Pnar*, which is perhaps their endoethnonym, i.e., the name given to them by an ethnicos for self identification. Jaintia does not seem to be an endoethnonym (Sen 1998: 85-91). This has perhaps been derived from the name of the Jaintia Kingdom. Now the question arises how did the Kingdom get its name?

There are a number of explanations of this question. One view among the historians was that the Kingdom got its name from Jaintiapur, its capital, located in Jaintia Parganas in the plains part of the Kingdom. This explanation was based on the puranic and Tantric texts which suggest that the Kingdom got its name from Jayanti Devi or Jainteswari, an incarnation of Goddess Durga or Gouri, the reigning deity of the Kingdom with her shrine at Jaintiapur. There is also a Hindu myth in justification of this information. Since the Kingdom got its name from Jaintia Parganas or Jaintiapur or from Jayanti Devi, the reigning deity of the kingdom as the myth suggests, and from whom descended the royal family, the hills with many a small divisions with local chiefs, got a new name, Jaintia (Sen1985: 201-04). The people living in the hills also got a new name, Jaintia, an exoethnonym i.e., a name given to them by outsiders. In course of time, however, it became an endoethnonym as well, by acceptance.

There is another version, a linguistic version that the name Jaintia might have been derived from Synteng, another racial name (perhaps an exoethnonym) of the people who now call themselves Jaintia. This version is also based on a fact that the historically known lines of Kings of Jaintiapur were known as Syntengs (Chatterjee 1976: 167).

There is yet another explanation that the word Jaintia has been derived from Sutuga, a place name. It is believed, through oral tradition, that the Jaintia Kingdom was established by a chief (*Doloi)* of a pre-state polity in Jaintia Hills, called Sutuga. Historical evidences also suggest that the Kings of Jaintiapur came from the Hills and they belonged to the Pnar or Synteng community. Oral narratives particularly that of *Ka hih Dakha* and *U Loh Ryndi* also seems to justify this claim (Sen 1985:197-201).

Thus, we can conclude that genetically, linguistically or culturally, the Jaintias are distinguished as or separate ethnic group and not a sub-group of the people given a generic name. It is certain that over a historical period they started claiming for an identity. The claim sought support from narrative, ritual and historical events.

Language

The question of language has an important bearing on the origin of the people. The present linguistic researches show that Jaintia forms a group of the Mon-Khmer language which belongs to an Austro-Asiatic type. Gurdon (1996:xxi-xxii) has mentioned the important work of J.R.Logon, who, in a series of papers published at Singapore between 1850 and 1857 in the Journal of the Indian Archipelago (of which he was the editor), demonstrated the relationship which exists between the Khasis and certain peoples of further India, the chief representatives of whom are the Mons or Talaings of Pegu and Tenasserim, the Khmers of Cambodia, and the majority of the inhabitants of Annam. He discovered an intimate relation between Khasi and Indo-China-Palaung dialects which prevail in Burma and Indo-China and again this group is connected with a larger family which consists of Santal, Munda and Korku. Bareh (1997:15) opines that the present linguistic researches show that Khasi forms a group of the Mon-Khmer language which belongs to an Austro-Asiatic type. J.R.Logon in 1850-57 has brought to light some signifying results of his research. He was able by comparing vocabularies, to discover the nearest kinsmen of the Khasis in the Palaung, a tribe inhabiting one of the Shan States. Logon further remarks that the Khasi and other Mon-Khmer tribes' greatly differ in physical characteristics from Munda. He speaks of Khasi as "a solitary remembrance that the Mon-cambodian linguistic formation once extended much further towards North-West than now.

Grierson (2006: 4) said that the languages of the Mon-Khmer family fall naturally into five groups. These groups are:

(1) A number of closely related forms of speech used by the inhabitants of the hill country of the lower and middle Me-kong.

(2) Mon or Talang in Pegu, Anamese of Anam and a number of minor dialects (including Stieng and Bahnar) spoken in the latter country.

(3) Various dialects of the Khmer spoken in Cambodia.

(4) Palaung – Wa, group includes the Palaung spoken north- east of Mandalay, the language of the Was, and a number of other dialects spoken in the hilly country round the upper middle courses of the Chindwin and the Me-kong.

(5) Various dialects of the Pnars (Synteng) of Jaintia Hills, War dialect of the South, Lyngngam of the far North-Western frontiers of the country and Khasi proper which is represented by the Cherra form of speech.

Bareh (1997:17-18) states that "the Amwi dialect of Khasi group is more Mon-Khmer than Khasi in construction. This dialect prevails in the southern Jaintia Hills, and we suggest that it constitutes a proper link between Khasi and Mon-Khmer. Is it not possible to assign a true parentage of Khasi to Amwi itself? This suggestion finds support when we remember that the first Khasi tribes settled in the Eastern parts of Jaintia Hills."

The Khasis (including Jaintias, War and Lyngngams) were originally a Mon-Khmer language connected with its migration from Burma, and, the Khasis were, therefore, speakers of Mon-Khmer speech which is a branch of the Austro-Asiatic family. Khasi has retained its originality in many ways. There are other isolated members of the Mon-Khmer speaking stock, and in all probability, khasi with its characteristic features seems to have emerged from the latter class which is the Palaung-Riang-Wa-Lemet group.

The jaintia or Pnar or Synteng, like their immediate neighbours, the Khasi, have no recorded history of their own. However, we find such written history about the people in the *Buranjis* (history) of Assam and subsequently with the advent of the British; a more detailed written history could be found. But even the recorded history written by the British officials who had worked among the Khasi and Jaintia, in most of the cases, treated the two together as one people without keeping any clear or separate accounts and references to the Jaintia alone. Of course, in general, the Khasi and the Jaintia cannot be treated separately because they have many things in common. Similarly, the history of the migration of the Jaintia people is shrouded in mystery as they could neither tell us exactly where they first came from, nor enlighten us about the route of migration they took before settling down in the present habitat, the Jaintia Hills. At times, the people narrated the history of their origin and migration in the form of stories and legends. These legends were also not to be found in a written form because the Jaintia do not have their own script. With the absence of any script, it becomes difficult to construct a fair account of their history. With regard to the history of the origin and migration of the people, one of the opinions is that Jaintia entered the present hills in batches and were known by different names. Some of these batches were the Amwi, Changpung, Jowai, Nartia, Raliana, and Sutnga etc.It is therefore envisaged that the Jaintia as a tribe or group did not migrate to their present habitat all at the same time. Later, all the batches formed a single group under the centralised administration of the traditional Chiefs at different levels of administration. This does not mean, however, to say that the various batches belong to different races or groups of people; they are no doubt of the same stock and origin.

Jaintia Village and Houses

Like the Khasis, the Jaintias do not build their houses on the extreme summits of hills, but a little below the tops, generally in small depressions, in order to obtain some protection from the strong winds and storms which prevail in these hills at certain times of the year. It is *Sang* or taboo to the Jaintias to build a house on the last eminence of a range of hills, this custom having perhaps arisen owing to the necessity of locating villages with reference to their defense against an enemy. The Jaintias build their houses fairly close together, but not as close as houses in the Bhoi and Lyngngam villages. Jaintias seldom change the sites of their villages, to which they are very much attached, where, as a rule, the family tombs are standing and *Mawbynna* or memorial stones. In many villages memorial stones are to be seen which from their appearance show that the villages have been there for many generations. During the Jaintia rebellion the village of Jowai was almost entirely destroyed, but as soon as the rebellion was over the people returned to the old site and rebuilt their village. Similarly, after the earthquake, the ancient village sites were not abandoned in many cases. There is no such thing as a especially reserved area in the village for the *Syiem* and the nobility, all the people, rich or poor, living together in one village, their houses being scattered about indiscriminately (Gurdon 1996:33).

Generally, the Jaintias live in homogenous villages and the villages are mostly mono-ethnic. A Jaintia village is a socio-cultural and socio-economic concept rather than a political unit. The household in a village are bound by social and economic bonds. The village headman always occupies an honorable place in the social set-up of the village.

The Jaintia houses were made of hard wood and stone walls. The good quality timber, like the oak, pine, jackfruit etc. was used. They plaster the space in front of the house with red earth and cow dung, the latter indicating an influence of Hinduism. They have comparatively large houses. The house of the *Doloi* of *Sutnga* in Jaintia Hills was more than 80 ft. long in the 1970s (Prakash 2007:1675).

As the hill villages go, the Jaintia villages are fairly big. Nongtalang in the *war* area is the biggest village over 100 houses. In the interior hills, the people live in groups of small villages. 75 percent of the Jaintias live in the villages. The *Lyngdoh* (priest) is highly respected. The villagers are deeply attached to the place of their birth and were reluctant to leave for new avenues which offered jobs and professions away from their houses (Prakash 2007: 1676).

Nongtalang, the summer capital of the Kingdom, came under the influence of the Hinduism when the Jaintia Kings embraced the faith. It still has a Hindu temple with a Brahmin priest, a descended from the Brahmin family from the days of the Jaintia Raj (Prakash 2007:1676).

The position of the ancestral mother is great among the Jaintias, and as the originator of the clan and family occupies an important and responsible position. The married sons and daughters start living separately except the youngest daughter who remains in the ancestral home, to inherit the position, place and importance of her mother.

It is observed that in an Indian society there is always a gender bias in every field or aspects of life, for instance in many religious books like The Holy Bible, the Quran and the Gita, has portrayed only the male figure as the supreme most powerful being. Whereas, on the contrary, women are always portrayed as a weak, gentler sex, submissive to their husbands and family etc, so the questions revolve around us today is that whether it is the society or the customs that have given a particular image or character to the women? If she doesn't fulfilled the above criteria she is considered as unfit mother, wife, sister, etc. Is it the customs or traditions that control the behaviour of particular sexes in a great extend? Customs and traditions have always been a great impact to shape the society of particular communities. It has its own rules. Do's and Don'ts, either approved or disapproved by one's culture. The present study will try to look upon the various customs and practices followed by the Jaintias and how it affects on the status of women? How much women folk have benefited after the intervention of new religion (Christianity) in their respective societies? It is rightly said by Jawaharlal Nehru that, "You can tell the condition of a nation by looking at the status of its women".

Significance of Study

In this paper an attempt has been made to examine the adoption of Hinduism and Christianity in to the traditional religion of *Ki Hynniew Tre* among the Jaintias. They claim that their religion or *Niam* and other ceremonies are pure and follow the tenets of traditional times. At this stage, a proper understanding of the tribal religion is called for. Lamare (2005: 58) states that a tribal religion is only the embryo and the relic of the pre-logistic state of imagination and ideas, upon which much of the organised religions have depended for their spiritual quest". Sema (1980:69) believes that almost all men or groups, were at one time or the other were the followers of the tribal religion. Like many other tribal religions, the Jaintia religion, which has belief in nature, is mainly characterised by people from outside as animism. John Hughes Morris (1996) went a step further and termed it as "a crude form of demonology, its main principle consists in the endeavour to propitiate evil spirits by the offering of sacrifices" (c.f. Lamare, 2005:59). Debroy (1981:89) in his article "*The Dominating Motives in Jaintia Religious Life*" referred to the Pnar or Jaintia religion as animism, or in other words, referring to the Jaintia religion as the attribution of the practice of ancestor-worship. This kind of generalisation does not throw much light on the motives, aspirations and ideology of the people, where the same is being preserved and maintained for generations together. Sten (1974: 100) reported in the "*Report of the Land reforms commission for Khasi Hills*" that the Khasi religion binds the system of inheritance. This is exactly the position with the Jaintias also. The Jaintia religious beliefs, customs and taboos can be traced to three ways: (i) worship of the ancestors, (ii) sacrifice and (iii) recognition of a common life in religious acts, rituals and totems.

The impact of Christianity can also be seen in social hierarchy. When Christianity came it preached an egalitarian value and the first victim of their arrival in the Jaintia Hills was the *Lyngdoh* clan because in the new order the priestly clan had no role to play whatsoever. The growth of cash money and inter-community marriages, which could be considered as subsidiary developments of the spread of Christianity, further diluted the traditional hierarchy.

The whole of the Jaintia life of an individual is very dependent upon the good will of various deities to whom he/she must offer appropriate propitiation in some way or the other in his/her life time. Christianity appears to have an appreciable impact on the traditional religion of the Jaintias in recent years. Since before Independence, Christianity penetrated into the Jaintia land through a process. It was rather a systematic process of acculturation among them especially in cultural and religious field.

Choice of Villages

For the present study ten villages were selected, namely, Shangpung, Amlaren, Tuber, Rymbai, Umkiang, Wahiajer, Jowai, Syndia, Raliang and Nartiang. Out of the ten villages, two villages were selected from urban and two from the semi-urban and six from the rural villages. In the following table it shows that altogether 120 samples were taken from 6 males and 6 females of ten villages for the present study.

Sample Villages

Meghalaya: Jaintia			
Village/Sex	***Male***	***Female***	***Total***
SHANGPUNG	6	6	12
AMLAREM	6	6	12
TUBER	6	6	12
RYMBAI	6	6	12
UMKIANG	6	6	12
WAHIAJER	6	6	12
JOWAI	6	6	12
SYNDIA	6	6	12
RALIANG	6	6	12
NARTIANG	6	6	12
TOTAL	**60**	**60**	**120**

Here, we will try to examine the position in so far as it touches or affects the traditional religion of *Ki Hynniew Trep.* We shall also highlight four points in the present study to understand the impact of Christianity and Hinduism on the tribal religion. The four points are as follows:

(a) The roles that the tribal religions are playing in their at the present day;

(b) The causes of the decline of the tribal religions;

(c) The religious and social syncretism of Christianity and Hinduism on tribal religion.

In other words, we have to examine how far the Jaintia tribal religion has changed as a result of the contact with the neighbouring Hindus and Christian followers for maintaining the tribal identity.

Jaintia Religion

The Jaintias call their traditional religion as *Niam Tre* or the original religion. They claim that their religion or *Niam* and other ceremonies are pure and follow since time immemorial.

The Jaintias worship a number of gods and goddesses. The dead ancestors cannot prevent natural calamities and epidemics. For that, particular gods and goddesses are appeased. Most of these gods and goddesses are propitiated with rituals and sacrifices. In addition to these gods and goddesses, there is also the Almighty god, *U Tre Kirot*. It is this Supreme-Being, who controls all other gods, goddesses and men. According to Jaintia belief, the Supreme Being dwells in a place which is very much different from the dwelling places of gods and goddesses. While gods, goddesses and spirits usually dwell on earth below the sky where human beings are living, the Creator dwells in the high heavens above the Sun, the Moon and the Stars. Similarly, religious sacrifices to the Creator and sacrifices to gods, goddesses and spirits are quite different from each other.

The Jaintias are known to have been addressing and worshipping nature and at the same time different names and attributes have been given and propitiated. Though these things are still prevailing, yet it is very important to note that the Pnar religion has a clear conception of God almighty and refers to him as *U Blai Wa Booh, Wa Thoo*. He in their religion is the creator of the universe, of man and guardian of all things big and small. In their general talk, they refer to him as *U Tre Kirot* as mentioned above. They also address God as *Ki Blai*, i.e. *U Blai Pyrthat* or God of thunder; *Ka Myntdu* or goddess of river; *Ka Ron Chyndi* or goddess of accident.

Ancestor veneration also plays an important part in the religious life of the people. They invoke the blessings of an ancestral spirit before they initiate any work. The Jaintias also have a clear conception of heaven, which they call *Soorkep* and hell *Ka Nurok, Ka Ksaw*. They also believe in the spirit of the dead ancestors and it has its affection and sentiments and should be attached to the parts of its own body, the bones. The bone repositories are the place where the spirits reside. The practice of offering food near the bone repositories are carried out, and the people would observe the same sincerely. These days food is being offered to the ancestors once a year before the community festival, the *Behdeinkhlam* and people pray for the well being and prosperity. Generally, in the dry months between January and March, they collect the bones of the dead kinsfolk in the bone repositories in presence of all. In bone preservation also, the principle of matriarchy operates. The bone of an individual will remain with that of his or her mother.

Lamin (1999:98) has mentioned that the spirits and deities worshipped by the Pnars were numerous but the following were considered as the more important among them:

(a) *Blai Muluk* or god of the state. He was propitiated annually with the sacrifice of a goat or cock.

(b) *Blai Lum Blai* Wah or god of the hill and water, he was also propitiated annually in the similar manner.

(c) *Blai Spah* or the god of wealth. This god was propitiatedwith a view to become richer

(d) *Blai Ryngkaw* wasa or the tutelary deity of the village. This god was propitiated with sacrifices and there was no fixed time or day for this.

In addition to the above the Pnars also had the belief in the God the Creator or *U Blai WaBuh Wathoow* or the god who looked after the well being of men.

In their religious life, the cock plays a very important place and takes the form of a mediator between God and man. They refer the cock as *U Khon Lymboit, U Khon Lymbiang*.The cock is usually sacrificed by the people to invoke or appease the gods. Along with this other animals are also sacrificed, but the cock sacrifice is taken as the original one. Whatever may be the kind of sacrifice and the variation in regard to the supreme God and to the gods and goddesses, it is a fact that common sacrifice is a sign of interest. The *Niam Tre* stands out distinctively from any other religion. In fact subtle differences are seen even between the different Jaintia villages. On the other hand, there are some similarities with other religions and this has to be taken into consideration without any generalisation in order to arrive at the proper understanding of the original religion of the people.

The Jaintias have no temples or any concrete place for worship., but they are monotheistic in their approach and would invoke God by various names as have been mentioned earlier, but when they invoke the name of God in general, they would address him as *U Tre-Kirot, U BlaiWa Booh-U Blai Wa Thoo*. The religion *Niam Tre* for that matter is an intrinsic part of the social existence of the Jaintias of Jaintia Hills. It is important in the life of the people that the religion can be traced right from the time when the baby is conceived in the mother's womb, which is locally known as *U Trop Ksiar Trop Rupa*. The duty of the mother along with the husband and the uncles during this period of time is to stand by their religion, which is again followed by certain customs and duties that are to be performed. They would pay the respect to almighty God and pray for the well being of the mother and child till the time of delivery. The people also believe that God has ordained them to come to the earth to not only multiply, but also to live by means of one's own effort and labour by following the path of righteousness, i.e., *Kamai Hok*, and also to know man and to know God, in other words *Tip Bru Tip Blai.*Their religion also stresses a lot on the maternal and paternal relationship i.e., *Tip Kur Tip Kha* and these are important aspects of their social structure which were integrated as part of their religion. In fact, the Jaintia religion is God given, not founded by man. They say that God gave them their religion when He sent their first forebears, *Ki Ynniaw Wasa* (the seven Inns) from heaven to live on earth. The three commandments in the Jaintia religion are:

(1) *Kamai ia ka Hok*: which means earn righteousness.

(2) *Tipbru Tipblai*: which means to know man and know God.

(3) *Tipkur-Tipkha*: which means to show respect maternal and paternal relatives.

To the Jaintia God can be worshipped anywhere and by anyone, so long he is clean in his heart and takes care not to defile his body and places by evil deeds, where he performs his worship and sacrifices There is still a strong belief among the people the mother earth should not be desecrated and this goes back to the oral tradition about *U Lakriah* who was send by God to this earth along with a commandment where he and his people should not bury anything that would rot and decay as to why the Jaintia people cremate their dead. The people believe that when a person dies, his soul goes to God and the mortal remains need to be purified by fire. Their concept of a living spirit after death is very clear and this spirit remains and carries on living to bless and watch over the family members. This belief is very strong and the people would show their reverence to their ancestors especially during the *Behdeinkhlam* festival, whom they believe to have kept a constant watch on them even if they had departed from the earth.

Among the Jaintia, the most prominent rituals and ceremonies are the birth ceremony which is locally known as *Syip Syin*; *Chong KhaChongman* or marriage; and *Ka Niam lap* or the death ceremony. In fact, the religion does not start or end up with the social life of the people only. It also permeates into the political organisation, law of inheritance and land tenure system etc. In short it is a kind of a total experience for the people where almost every aspect of their life does have a religious sanction behind it. Their religion expects them to live a righteous life, and their dealings with their fellow men should be followed with truth and honesty not only in their thoughts and actions, but in their wishes as well (Lamare 2005: 59-62).

Festivals and Ceremonies

The festivals and ceremonies are closely connected to their religion. Several activities of traditional culture are inextricably intermingled and they are exercised mostly in relation to religion and there is always a hereditary transmission of culture values and skill, which is obvious in a folk culture and that, is its communal aspect (Sen 1985:107-108). In this regard, the *Behdeinkhlam* festival and the *Laho* dance are unique and stands on their own beauty and incomparability, which is again not found in any other parts of the hills.

The *Behdeinkhlam* can be traced back to the earliest period when Jowai, the present headquarter of Jaintia Hills was inhabited by *U Niang Lyngdoh* and his sister *Ka Long Lyngdoh* who had immigrated from their home place to escape the plague that had wiped many. It was *U Niang Lyngdoh* who had given the name Jowai or *Jwai* to this new place. Over the years when people came to know about this new place they came over to stay in Jowai and because of the location and the fertility of the land the population also grew steadily. *U Niang* and *Ka Long* also decided that some form of a ritual and ceremony should be carried out so that they would be free from such kind of calamity as had befallen, prior to their coming to this new place. They decided to call this festival as *Behdeinkhlam. Khlam* means plague and *Behdein* means to drive away with sticks. The festival is generally celebrated during the month of July after the sowing is over. In the oral tradition, *U Niang* and his sister along with her four daughters stayed in a place called *U Lum Soo Lung*. Later on, four daughters of *Ka Long* decided to stay in different localities of Jowai. *Ka Bon* stayed in *Chilliang Raij* or the locality of the children of the *Raij, Ka Tein* stayed at *Dulong, Ka Wet* at *WahSynji*or presently known as *Panaliar*and *Ka Doh* at *Lum Longkjam*. The clan *Soo-kpoh-Khad-Ar-Warnai* also came out from these four sisters who were also known as *Ki Iaw Bei*. From their marriage different clans came out in Jowai. *Ka Bon* through her union with a man from the *Thangkhiew* clan led to the emergence of the clans like *Pasubon, Lipon*, and *Rangad* and their bone repository is near a grove called *Ka Khloo Langdoh*. From *Ka Tein* who got married to the *Shadap Manar*clan and from them came *Pasweth,Lakiang, Mutyen*, *Kma,Kynjin, Katphoh, Seinphoh, Leinphoh, Niangphoh, Lanong, Liwit* and *Litean* clan. Theirrepository is at *Ka Blai. Ka Doh* with her union with a man from the *Dkhar*clan, the clans like *Siangbood, Syngkon, Nangbah* and their repository is known at *Ka Blai.* These clans together they are known as *Ki Soo-Kpoh-Khad-Ar-Warnai*. Strictly speaking they all belong to the same great clan and therefore they cannot get married to one another. The members of this great clan have absolute rights to the important post of offices in Jowai like of a Dalloi, Langdoh or others. After the *Soo Kpoh*, then came subsequently the other clans such as the "*Le-Kyllung'*, the '*San-Syngkong' (Shylla, Pde, Pariat, Blah, etc.),* the *'Iaw-Chibidi' (Laloo,*

Nartiang, Marong, Pyrbot, etc.) and many others (Kyndiah 1998:4). It is through the *Behdeinkhlam* festival original settlers are given importance who carried out the ritual in the premises of the high priestress attributed mainly to the four sisters i.e., *Ka Bon, Ka Wet, Ka Tein*and *Ka Doh* (Lamare 2005:64).

Prakash (2007: 1683) states that tiger killing festival is the biggest in the War areas of the Jaintia Hills, generally observed during January-march. On the fixed day, the villagers move into the jungle in search of a tiger. After the hunt, when the tiger is killed, its flesh and intestines are chopped off, its carcass, including the skull and outer skin, is taken to the Lyngdoh house with the duo ceremony and prayers. On this day, the people offer food and pay homage to their departed ancestors. They go house to house to drive away the epidemics and misfortune in a year of good luck and prosperity.

Sacrifice of a leopard is a part of the *Rong Khli* festival which is observed by the followers of the indigenous *Niam Tre* faith in Jaintia Hills. The animal Rights activitists have protested over this ritual. In reply, the Meghalaya Forest Minister in 2003 expressed in the Meghalaya Assembly that "Being a sacred tribal custom it cannot be stopped...... After all, only one leopard is being sacrificed after a gap of one decade" (*Indian Express*, dated 30-03-2003). This shows that the Jaintias are more adhered to the traditional custom than to the present notion of forest resource.

Another important festival of the Jaintias is the *Laho* dance. It is the traditional dance of the Jaintias which seek to glorify God and to express their gratitude to the creator, who has blessed them with all the comforts and basic needs. In this sense the *Loho* dance is closely associated with the agricultural rites. The dance was referred earlier as *Chad Chipiah*. In this dance, there are three dancers in each group. The female dancers dance in the middle and each is flanked by two male dancers, one on the right and the other on the left. The one on the right symbolizes the uncle, who is the protector of the family, the clan and the community as a whole. The male dancer on the left stands for the husband or the father of the children, who is the progenitor of the clan. The lone female dancer, who dances backward and forward, right and left in the midst of the dancers stand for the priestess or *Ka Langdoh* who is the custodian of religion. The female dancers should be virgins; and married women do not participate in the dance.

Here we have noticed that there is a role of the women in the festivals and ceremonies. The women are also given importance in their community group dances like *Ka Chaad Rawa*, *Ka Chaad Sukra* and *Ka Chaad Pilang.* In the case of the previous two dances which is again performed only by the women folk of the society, it is seen that the dance sequence is in a group of six, eight or ten and sometimes even up to twelve. It is said that these dances were introduced right from the time of the Jaintia Kings. The *Ka Chaad Pliang* is performed by the women folk.

Hinduism in Jaintia Hills

The establishment of Hinduism in the Jaintia Hills especially in Nartiang goes back to the time of the Jaintia rulers. To understand as to why the Jaintia of this region had embraced this new faith is something very interesting. The oral tradition speaks about the time when the Jaintia King used to be his summer capital. It was during his long stay in the hills that the king introduced this new faith to his subjects. Henceforth, it was also decided some of the festivals relating to this religion and the most prominent being the *Durga puja*. In fact the annual summer journey of the king to the hills was done with a large entourage of people including the Brahmin priests. It was through such interactions that the people of Nartiang slowly started to accept this new faith. Acceptance came voluntarily, and no force was applied (Lamare 1994:1).

The influence of this new faith can be traced to the time of Bor Kuhain when the Sutnga and the Jayantia dynasty came under one crown. He was said to be the first Hinduised king of the Jaintias, and Jaintiapur was inherited by him from Jayanti. He was credited to have built a palace at Borkhat and a shrine of *Lord Shiva* near Syndal. He was succeeded by Parbat Roy (A.D. 1500-1516) and then by other two successors, till the coming of Bijoy Manik (A.D.1548-1564). Bijoy Manik was a powerful king of the Jaintias and followed the policy of war and subjugation. He consolidated his rule in the plains and perhaps it was during his time the Brahminical cult made a steady in roads to the hills. Hinduism standing as an organised religion, having clearly defined doctrines and a large number of followers, attracted not only the attention of the king but also the members of his family and his other followers (Lamare 2000: 56-57). Ali (1954: 72) states that "The Raja of Jaintia and the members of his family were converted to Hinduism and they formed a distinct community in the capital of the Kingdom, called "*Suhtnga Samaj*". In the Jaintia hills itself, Hinduism was making deep inroads. In1828 the British authorities observed that 'within the last half a century the Brahmanical doctrines have made such progress that most of the leading men (of the Syntengs) have adopted them and have been classed by their spiritual instructors in the *Khatri* or Military tribe (Dutta 1982:9). It was added further that their principal deity was "*Jayanti Iswara*" (or *Goddess Kali*) but "many worshipped the whole Hindoo Pantheon" and at the same time "modify the revengeful spirits by human sacrifice". In the Jaintia hills, Nartiang was the principal centre of Hindu worship. The Synteng people of Nartiang are still the adherents of Hinduism."

Another important feature of the traditional religion was the worship of Hindu deities often side by side with their tribal counterparts. The Hindu deities who were worshipped were given Jaintia honorifics. Thus the Hindu God of artisans, *Biswakarma* was called *U Biskorom*and *Shiva, Mahadev Khlow*, and Hindu Goddesses *Lakshmi, Durga* and *Chandi*were also given Jaintia honorifics, *Ka Laksmi, ka Parvati and Ka Ran Shandi* respectively. Thus a good deal of syncretism in their religion eas taking place, whose base was 'animism' but its upper layer, was the Sanskrit religion (Dutta 1982: 9).

Thus we find the influence of Hinduism had a significant impact on the Jaintia culture. The life of the people was transformed gradually, but the tradition of the people did not wane out with this kind of assimilation. The degree of its survival depended on its own cultural self-image and identity. Its conception of its self as a group at least is based on deep rooted attitudes and values enshrined in the oral tradition. Since some of the people had taken to Hinduism its influence can be seen in the life of the people. In fact, the Hindu converts form a small section of the community and the larger chunk of the population are still the ardent followers of the indigenous religion called *Niam Tre.*

A common feature of the traditional religion of the Jaintia was the belief in a supreme God, the creator who was designated as *U Blai.* He was an invisible Being to be worshipped not by means of sacrifices but by simple prayer. Although the Jaintia had the conception of a heaven, they had no idea of a hell. They had however clear conception of sin which they called "*Pap*" and belief in the transmigration of souls, which might have been borrowed by them from the Hindus. The worship of ancestors occupied an important place in their religion. They believe that the deceased ancestors might be of assistance in this material world if propitiated and might cause suffering if displease for any reason. They were therefore propitiated by the offering of food periodically, especially in time of trouble. The memorial stones locally called Mawbynna found everywhere in the Jaintia hills were erected to honour the ancestors. Side by side, worship of natural forces was also prevalent. Almost all the rivers and mountain peaks were regarded as sacred abode of the gods. The most sacred river in the Jaintia hills was the Kopili to which human sacrifices were even offered. The nature Gods and Goddesses were believed to possess the power of life and death over mankind, subject only to the control of *U Blai.*

Christianity among the Jaintias

It was in the year 1842 that the Bible was preached for the first time in Jowai by Rev. Thomas Jones. After him, Rev. Daniel Morton Sykes came and started a primary school in 1854. The peole came into proper contact with the missionaries only after 1858, when Francis Jenkins was the commissioner of Assam. Thomas Jones, who by this time had managed to get the support of the ruler of Cherra, where the latter donated a land at a place called Nongsawlia for the construction of the church, soon made Cheerapunji his base for missionary activities. From this year onwards, one can see the fusion of

Christianity amidst the local people and how the same is being anticipated and reciprocated by the people.

The 19th century marked the beginning of a crucial period in the history of this region from the point of view of education and literary activity. Earlier the Jaintias had no script of their own and it was only with the advent of the Baptist Missionaries from Serampore in 1813 that for the first time, Khasi words were compiled in the Bengali script. Later, the Welsh missionaries prepared the first books in the Roman script. It was to this effect that in 1854 a school was started in Jowai and in 1858 a church was established. The idea behind the establishment of the school was to educate the people and to equip the local population with the knowledge sufficient enough to read Bible.

In case of the Catholics, their first contact with the Jaintias started in the year 1891. The interaction that followed between the Jaintias and the English was not at all cordial. They were looked at as intruders, who had manipulated the political reins from the Jaintia King and introduced a new faith to the people. The Jaintias looked at these developments as an attack on their political freedom, religious rituals and beliefs. The Jaintias resented the British and the missionaries to such an extent that they considered everything taught and practiced by them was a taboo. As an example, in this regard, the potato that was introduced by the British was looked as a taboo and was not eaten. This practice was carried out for many generations and till date some Jaintias do not eat the tuber (Lamare 2005:85).

Whatever, casual relationship that was there between the Jaintias and the Christian missionaries, it is an established fact that education came into this part of the hills only with the coming of the missionaries. Earlier, though there were contacts with the plains, yet the impact of the Bengali literature was only on the selected few.

Owing to the influence from the plains at an earlier stage and Christianity at a later stage, the Jaintia society went through a process of change. But the Jaintias did not make a break from their culture; they retain those traditional practices like matriliny, religion etc., which they think is essential to maintain their identity. Prior to the exposition of this culture to other societies, the Jaintia society was treading along with time with very few changes. But once this society was exposed to the other more advanced societies, the Jaintias also had to go for a change not only to maintain its identity but also to survive.

Lamin (1999: 101) has rightly said that many Jaintias believe that Christianity has not done any harm to their own customs and traditions whereas those educated leaders of the traditional religion put the entire blame on Christianity for having lost everything about their customs and traditions. Education and employment are important to everyone but these have often meant forgetting their own culture and customs as if there could be no progress without Christianisation or westernisation which means more or less the same thing to the local people.

The impact of Christianity can also be seen in social hierarchy. When Christianity came it preached an egalitarian value and the first victim of their arrival in the Jaintia Hills was the Lyngdoh clan because in the new order the priestly clan had no role to play whatsoever. The growth of cash money and inter-community marriages, which could be considered as subsidiary developments of the spread of Christianity, further diluted the traditional hierarchy.

From the above discussion we find that they have their own traditional beliefs and practices. These have been in vogue till they came into contact with the Christianity. The whole of the Jaintia life of an individual is very dependent upon the good will of various deities to whom he/she must offer appropriate propitiation in some way or the other in his/her life time. Christianity appears to have an appreciable impact on the Jaintias in recent years. Since before Independence, Christianity penetrated into the Jaintia land through a process. It was rather a systematic involvement among them especially in the field of education by the Christian Missionaries that the faith gained momentum among them after Independence. We shall, therefore, begin with their conversion into the new religion.

Conversion of Religion

As stated above the Jaintias were converted to Christianity before and after Independence. Table 6.1 shows that out of 120 respondents in ten study villages, 74 (62%) said that their parents have converted before their birth, 6 (5%) said that they were converted 10 years ago, 3 (3%) respondents said that they were converted to Christianity some 20 years ago, 5 (4%) said they have converted 30 years ago, 1-female respondent said that she converted 50 years ago and 31 (26%) said that it is not applicable. It means that they have not

Table 6.1: Conversion of Religion

Conversion of Religion	*Male*	*Female*	*Total*
Parents converted before my birth	37(31%)	37(31%)	74(62%)
Less than 10 years ago	3(3%)	2(2%)	6(5%)
20 years ago	3(3%)	0(0%)	3(3%)
30 years ago	3(3%)	2(2%)	5(4%)
50 years ago	0(0%)	1(1%)	1(1%)
Not applicable	13(11%)	18(15%)	31(26%)
Total	**60(50%)**	**60(50%)**	**120(100%)**

converted and pursue the traditional religion of *Niam Tre.* From the table, it is clear that most of the respondents in the study villages have converted to

Christian. While 26 per cent families still follow the traditional religion. The table also shows that most of the families reported that their parents have converted to Christianity before their birth. It shows that the respondents in the study villages have to Christianity after Independence. Now, we shall examine ~~see~~ the impact of the new religion on their traditional religion.

Impact of Modern Religion on Tribal Religion

To understand the impact of religion on traditional religion we have asked 23 questions among 120 respondents as shown in table 6.2. A majority of them, 39 (33%) said that there is no impact due to conversion. 34 (28%) said that due to conversion of Christianity their customs are eradicated from the society, again 15 (13%) respondents said that the inter clan marriage is taboo in the new religion, 8 (7%) said that conversion has made the women status high and 6 (5%) said that they still follow the traditional customs even after conversion. However, 5(4%) said that the conversion has restricted the rituals and sacrifices and another 5(4%) said that the religious customs got influenced from non-tribal customs. On the other hand, 4 (3%) said that the conversion has encouraged the remarriage of widows, 3(3%) said that incest marriage is taboo to the conversion, 2 (2%) said that church marriage encouraged and 1(1%) said that women have become nuns. However, the respondents did not say anything about the impact of women due to conversion like the marriage of the women with outsiders and deprive of all the traditional property rights. It shows that there is no much impact on the traditional rights of the women due to the conversion of Christianity in the study villages.

Table 6.2: Impact of Modern Religion on Tribal Religion

Impact of Religion on Tribal Religion	***Male***	***Female***	***Total***
No Impact	20(17%)	19(16%)	39(33%)
Restriction of Polygamy	6(5%)	7(6%)	13(11%)
Inter-Clan Marriage Taboo	8(7%)	7(6%)	15(13%)
Restrictions on rituals and sacrifices	1(1%)	4(3%)	5(4%)
Eradication of customs	15(13%)	19(16%)	34(28%)
Incest marriage taboo	0(0%)	3(3%)	3(3%)
Higher Women Status (Christianity)	4(3%)	4(3%)	8(7%)
Women become Nuns	0(0%)	1(1%)	1(1%)
Remarry in case of divorce	1(1%)	3(3%)	4(3%)
Customs followed by religion	1(1%)	5(4%)	6(5%)
Religious customs got influenced from non-tribal customs	4(3%)	1(1%)	5(4%)
Church marriage encouraged	1(1%)	1(1%)	2(2%)

Note: Multiple responses: Total Respondents: 120

In regards to conversion, it can be said that the converted Jaintias still maintain their traditional beliefs and practices. Prohibition of marriage within the same clan as provided by their customary law of clan exogamy is an important social code which they strictly adhere even today although some of the customs have lost its sharpness in the face of the developing socio-economic and socio-political forces. It can also be said that even after the conversion they retain some of the traditional religious faiths. It is seen from the table 6.2 that the vital issues like intra- clan marriage and remarriage in case of death of a spouse and divorced rules have not changed much among the converted cases. There are nuns among the converted Christian Jaintias. Thus, we can safely say that even after the conversion they have not discarded their traditional beliefs and practices.

Syncretism of Religious and Cultural Life of the Jaintias

In the beginning, the Christian converts had their own separate colonies. That is why we have relics of localities as Mission compounds in the urban areas and large villages of Jaintia Hills. In these areas only the Christian converts were permitted to reside and the non-Christians were not allowed to reside in these localities (Rymbai 1993:98). This practice is no more now in the Jaintia Hills. At present in the same house members living together professing and practicing the traditional religion called *Niam Tre* and Catholicism or any other denomination of Protestantism. Another healthy sign of syncretism among Christians themselves is that they subtly accepting the eternal truth of the tenets and tolerance of the *Niam Tre*. Christianity follows now some of the aspects and rites of the tribal religion which its followers see as the eternal truth of all religions.

The first band of converts formed the base of Western culture in the Jaintia hills. The converts were preferred to others in the jobs. This created a system which helped to the spread of Christianity. In this context there was a quarrel between the local people and the administrators about ten years before Independence. Even the traditional festival called *Behdeinkhlam* was stopped by the sub-divisional officer of Jowai who happened to be a Christian himself. Persons who protested against this action in the court of law at Shillong were ousted from Jowai. However, the festival was revived again in 1948 (Lamin 1999:100-101).

In the Jaintia hills today, the traditional rituals are not performed properly and even the traditional marital rules are neglected. In Bapung village, it was a rare thing to have a Jaintia girl to marry an outsiders a few years back. But now it is quite common to see the local women marrying men belonging to communities from outside like Nepali, Bengali, and Kachari. If the couples happen to be Christians the church takes over the matter and initially such marriages were encouraged by church leaders themselves. The Hindus did make some protest but many of them ultimately accepted Christianity (*Ibid*:102).

In the village, there is clear cut division in management of the two religions, namely, *Dong Skur* or Christian, and *Poh Shnong* or traditional religion. These two religious councils form two cultural affiliations. Sometimes there emerged tension between the followers of these two affiliations regarding marital alliance. This happens because the church insists that whoever is married to a Christian must also accept Christianity. Such efforts of the church are often opposed by the followers of the traditional religion (*ibid*: 103).

In spite of religious differences, these two religious groups strictly adhere to clan exogamy as a rule for marital alliance. Breach of this rule is considered a serious crime than adultery or murder or a taboo (*chong sang*). Both Christians and non-Christians consider it to be an unredeemable sin. Thus Christianity does not seem to have challenged some of the basic values of the Jaintia society (*ibid*: 103).

Among the Khasi-Pnars the first conscious and visible attempt on the part of the people professing their traditional religion to their countrymen about the truth and worth of their own religion, traditions, institutions, customs and culture was the establishment of the Seng Khasi in 1899 in Shillong by the few educated Khasi-pnar s whom Christianity had not succeeded to draw to its fold. They did this because they saw the veritable danger of the people giving up not only their religion but also such of their sterling customs, culture and institutions which marked their identity and which were bound up with the tenets of their religion.

Both *Seng Khasi* and *Sein Raij* have now branches in the villages in the Khasi and Jaintia Hills districts to wake up their people to a sense of just pride in the eternal values of their own religio, and the institutions, customs, culture, way of life, etc born out of the tenets. The progress is slow but it is working its way silently even among their brethren who are Christians in the way that they who are now no longer averse to the use of certain words and phrases like *U Blei Nongthaw Nongbuh, ka Niam Tipbriew Tipblei* or attending certain festivals or funerals of adherents of the old religion, a thing which was not done in the earlier days (Rymbai 1993:97).

Conclusion

We have found that the majority of them have converted to Christianity in the sample villages after Independence. During the colonial period, the Jaintias were pursuing their traditional religion. Jaintia religion was basically ancestor worship. After conversion to Christianity the traditional beliefs and practices have diminished from the society. However, 26 per cent families have reported they have not converted to Christianity. It shows that these families still follow the traditional religion.

In regards to conversion, it can be said that the converted Jaintias still maintain traditional beliefs and practices. Prohibition of marriage within the same clan as provided by their customary law of clan exogamy is an important social code which they strictly adhere even today although some of the customs have lost its sharpness in the face of the developing socio-economic and socio-political forces. There is no strict adherence of clan exogamy in the Christian followers.

An important feature of the traditional religion of the Jaintias is the worship of Hindu deities side by side with their tribal counterparts. The Hindu deities who are worshipped are given Jaintia honorifics. Thus a good deal of syncretism in their religion has taken place, whose base was 'animism.' Owing to the influence from the plains at an earlier stage and Christianity at a later stage, the Jaintia society went through a process of change. But the Jaintias did not make a break from their culture; they retain those traditional practices like matriliny, religion etc., which they think is essential to maintain their identity. Prior to the exposition of this culture to other societies, the Jaintia society was treading along with time with very few changes. But once this society was exposed to the other more advanced societies, the Jaintias also had to go for a change not only to maintain its identity but also to survive.

The whole of the Jaintia life of an individual is very dependent upon the good will of various deities to whom he/she must offer appropriate propitiation in some way or the other in his/her life time. Christianity appears to have an appreciable impact on the traditional religion of the Jaintias in recent years. Since before Independence, Christianity penetrated into the Jaintia land through a process. It was rather a systematic process of acculturation among them especially in cultural and religious field.

The Jaintias believe that the spirits of the dead, whose funeral ceremonies have not been duly performed, are believed to take the forms of animals and roam on this earth. This idea of transmigration of souls has been probably borrowed from the Hindus or animistic thought. The Jaintias, apparently, do not believe in punishment after death, at least, there is no idea of hell, although the spirits of those who have died under the ban of sin or *Pap* remain uneasy, being obliged to wander about the earth in different forms. The Jaintias not only revere the memories of deceased ancestors but they adore them by means of offerings, which are sometimes periodical, and sometimes made when thought necessary. These offerings take the shape of articles of food which are theoretically partaken of by the shades of the deceased ancestors, the idea of making such offerings being very similar to that of the Hindus when they offer the '*Pinda*' or cake to nine generations of ancestors, i.e. to propitiate the shades of the departed, and to obtain their help thereby. It is observed that the influence of the *Kni*or mother's brother, in the Jaintia family is very great. It is he who is the manager on behalf of the mother. His position in the Jaintia family is similar to that of the *Karta* (head of the family) in the Hindu joint family. It is on this account that he is so much revered and honored in the Jaintia society.

The Jaintias believe that the spirits of the dead ancestors must be propitiated, ritually invoked and therefore defied in order that the living clan members continue to receive their blessings. This belief is so strong that the people show their reverence to their ancestors especially during the *Behdeinkhlam* festival, whom they believe to have kept a constant watch on them even if they had departed from this earth. This festival had helped them to maintain clan-cohesion and preservation of family genealogy among the Jaintias for centuries.

Nartiang, the summer capital of the Jaintia King offers something more with regard to the religion, ceremonies and festivals of the Jaintias. This lies in the fact that this place had been a significant change when most of the people had embraced Hinduism and the Brahmanical influence is very strong and can be still seen till today. Apart from the Hindu festivals like *Durga Puja, Doljatra*, the people still carries out their indigenous rites and ceremonies such as *Ka Knia Khang, Ka knia Blai Langdoh, Ka Knia Kupli, Ka Knia Umtisong, Ka Knia Pyrthat, Ka Knia Pyrdong Chnong, Ka Knia Khlam, Ka Pom Blang Iaw Nartiang.*

References

Ali, Syed Murtaza. (1954). *The History of Jaintia* (Dacca: Govt. Press).

Bareh, H. (1997). *The History and Culture of the Khasi People* (Gauhati: Spectrum Publications).

Chatterjee, S.K. (1976). *Kirata Jana Kriti* (Calcutta: Asiatic Society of Bengal)

Chattopadhayaya, S.K. (1988): *The Jaintia (Socio-Political Institutions of Jaintia Hills)* (New Delhi: Cosmo Publications).

Debroy, H.L (1981). *A Tribe in Transition: The Jaintias of Meghalaya* (New Delhi: Cosmo Publication.

Dutta, P.N (1982). *Impact of the West on Khasi and Jaintias: A Survey of Political Economic and Social Change* (New Delhi: Cosmo Publications.

Gassah, L.S (1994). "The Jaintias" in B. Pakem, Shibani Roy and Arabinda Basu (ed) *People of India, Meghalaya* Vol.XXXII (Calcutta: Seagull Books) 69-89.

Grierson, George, A. (2006). "The Mon-Khmer Family" *Languages of North-eastern India A Survey,* Vol.1 (New Delhi: Gyan PublishingHouse) 1-57.

Gurdon, P.R.T. (1996). *The Khasis* (with an introduction by Sir Charles Lyall, xiii-xxvii Delhi: Low Price Publications).

Kyndiah, Belbin. (1998). "Three Stages of Behdeinkhlam," *The Shillong Times,* Saturday, July 4:4.

Lamare, Shobhan N. (2005): *The Jaintias: Studies in Society and Change* (New Delhi: Regency Publication).

Lamin, Henry. 1999). "Christianisation and Change The Pnars of Meghalaya" in T.B.Subba (ed.) *Wonder that is Culture* (New Delhi: Mittal Publication).

Mawrie, H.O. (1981). *The Khasi Milieu* (New Delhi: Concept Publishing Company.

Pakem, B (1972): "The Socio-Political System of the Jaintia Tribe of Assam; An Analysis of Continuity and Change". in K.S.Singh (ed) *Tribal Situation in India* (Simla: Indian Institute of Advanced Study) 252-263.

Pakem, B. (1977). "The Changing Power Structure of the Political Institutions of Jaintia Chieftainship," *Journal of North East India Council for Social Science Research*. 1:1:1-3.

Passah, P.M and Sarmah, S (2002): "Introduction" in P.M.Passah and S. Sarma (ed) *Jaintia Hills A Meghalaya Trbe-Its Environment, Land and People* (New Delhi: Reliance Publishing House) xi-xv.

Paul, Gemini (1956a): "A myth as to the Origin of States in Khasi Hills" *Vanyajati* 4(1): 38-39.

Paul, Gemini (1956b): "The Place of Khaddu: The Youngest daughter in Khasi and Synteng Society, *Vanyajati* 4(2), April: 82-84.

Prakash, Ved (2007): *Encyclopedia of North East India* Vol.-4(Noida: Atlantic publishers & Distributors) 1671-1684.

Rymbai, R. T (1979): "Some Aspects of the Religion of the Khasi-Pnar" in U.Hipshon Roy (ed). *The Khasi Heritage: A Collection of essays on Khasi religion and Culture* (Shillong: Ri Khasi Press) 123-128.

Rymbai, T (1993): "Christian Missions and the Indigenous Religion of the Khasi-Pnar". In Soumen Sen (ed) *Religion in North East- India* (New Delhi: Uppal Publishing House) 68-102.

Sema, V.C.Kanito (1980): "A Critical assessment of Christian Acculturation in North East India" in Sujata Miri (ed) *Religion and Society in North east India* (New Delhi: Vikas Publishing House) 60-69.

Sen, Soumen (1985): *Social and State Formation in Khasi-Jaintia Hills: A Study of Folklore* (New Delhi: B.R.Publishing Corporation).

Sen, Soumen (1998): "Endoetnonym and Exoethnonym of, and Ethnicos: Identity and Folklore" *South Indian Folklorist*. 2:85-91.

Sen, Soumen (2002): "Narrative, Ritual and Historical Events: The Jaintia Identity" in P.M.Passah & S.Sarma (ed) *Jaintia Hills A Meghalaya Tribe- Its Environment, Land and People* (NewDelhi: Reliance Publishing House) 87-94.

Simon, I.M (1966): *Khasi and Jaintia Tales and Beliefs*. (Guwahati: Gauhati University).

Simon, I. M (1996):*Gazetteer of India, Meghalaya, District Gazetteer, Jaintia Hills* (Shillong: Government of Meghalaya, Arts and Culture Department).

Sten, H.W (1974): *Report of the Land Reforms Commission for Khasi Hills* (Shillong:North East India Press).

19

Cultural Diversity and Religious Syncretism: A Sociological Study on Santal in Kalyani, Nadia, West Bengal

—*Aritra Ghosh, Rimi Sarkar and Samita Manna*

Introduction

India is amongst the most diverse societies in the world. It has people from all the major religions in the world – Hindus, Muslims, Christians, Sikhs, Buddhists, Jains and Zoroastrians. Even though Hindus constitute about 82 percent of the population, there are more than 149 million Muslims in the country, making it the second largest population in the world. Religious diversity is coupled with enormous linguistic and cultural diversity (Mahajan 2006). The bulk of the Indian population represents racial admixture in varying degrees. Unlike several other lands where the dominant human cultures have tended to absorb or eliminate others, in India the tendency has been to nurture diversity, which has been favoured by the diversity of the country's ecological regimes. Powerful kingdoms and enumerable dynasties, contributed to the shaping of India's cultural regions. An important source of diversity among the people of India is the cultural identity of particular communities and regions (Das 2006).

'The pan-Indian, civilisation dimension of cultural pluralism and syncretism encompasses ethnic diversity and admixture, linguistic heterogeneity as well as fusion, and variations as well as synthesis in customs, behavioural patterns, beliefs and rituals. The process of synthesis and integration has been extensively at work at the regional level' (Das 2003).

Syncretism has always been a part of the negotiation of identities and hegemonies in situations such as conquest, trade, migration, religious dissemination and intermarriage. The growth of a western-dominated world economic system, however, was accompanied by the growth of a western-dominated world cultural system (Hannerz 1992).

Veer suggests "Syncretism in India is a trope in the discourse of 'Multiculturalism' and that scholarly discussion of syncretic phenomena such as Hindu worship of sufi saints usually omits consideration of conflict or of the process of expansion and contraction of religious communities (Veer 1994). Multiculturalism is not necessarily anti-syncretic, however, either in the USA or elsewhere. In India, modern Hindu nationalism is, according to Veer based on encompassing claims about the inclusivist syncretism of Hinduism – claims which are now often combined with western ideas of multiculturalism. Since India combines these by being a secular state in which religious affiliation partially defines cultural identity, it makes sense that syncretism and multiculturalism are often equated in Hindu political discourse (Stewart & Shaw 1994).

Religious syncretism exhibits blending of two or more religious belief systems into a new system, or may be due to the incorporation into a religious tradition of beliefs from unrelated traditions. This can occur for many reasons, and the later scenario happens quite commonly in areas where multiple religious traditions exist in proximity and function actively within the culture, or when a culture is conquered, and the conquerors bring their religious beliefs with them, but do not succeed in entirely eradicating the old beliefs or especially practices.

Culture is a form of human activity. Each generation must work to preserve, reproduce and select the necessary values, knowledge and principles and then renew them and modify them according to the changing realities of life. Customs include traditional forms of labour, behavioural pattern, lifestyles and systems of upbringing (Erasov & Singh 2006).

Cultural factors play an important role in the shaping of the ethos. The ethos is a historically evolved community of people with shared, relatively stable cultural and psychological features, a common language, aware of their own unity and their differences from other such communities and having a name for themselves (ibid 2006).

In the anthropological study of religion in India, the major emphasis has been given on the descriptive account of religious customs and their association with ethnic groups, including the tribes, the themes of purity or pollution in relation to caste system, descriptive concepts relating to religious phenomena and the modernisation processes.

Bose in his book *The Hindu Method of Tribal Absorption* clearly mentioned about the Juangs who had started worshipping the Hindu gods and goddesses, although it was done in their own way. Starting with the ceremonial bath in the morning, the offerings of sun dried rice to the gods and goddesses and uttering the sacred terms *satya*, *devata*, *dharma*, it has been proved how strongly religious ceremonies of Juang have been influenced by those of the neighbouring Brahmanical model. There is a clear indication that Hindu religious ideas have penetrated into their culture. The Juangs seem to be losing pride in their own culture and are adopting Hindu culture with a certain amount of avidity (Bose 1975).

Madan described the diversity or plurality of religious in India at two levels. First at the global level, in which the major religions, whether indigenous or foreign origin, were in focus and second, the intra-religious level at which secretarian or quan-secretarian movements took place (Madan 2004).

The tribal people, throughout the country, are now under the process of change. These changes are not homogeneous in nature. The elite Santals of Murshidabad district has got the opportunity to assimilate with the urban people and accepted the urban way of life. On the other hand, within the urban life once again they have formed a new group with some marginal characteristics restoring a few traits of tribal culture with the urbanity (Bhattacharyya 2013).

One research project *Tradition versus Modernity: Mother and Child Health (0 – 5 years) In Two Integrated Tribal Development Blocks of Paschim Midnapore, West Bengal: Problems and Developments* was conducted by Manna on the three dominated tribal groups of the Santals, Mundas and Lodhas of Paschim Midnapore. The study revealed that irrespective of their ethnic identities and geographical locations all of the sample respondents possessed similar characteristics in relation to acceptance of modernity (Manna 2011).

Sanskritisation was a widespread cultural and social process among the Hindus in different parts of India. The tribal people are not an exceptional one as they think themselves a part of the Hindu Society and culture. According to Srinivas (1972), Sanskritisation is the process by which a low Hindu caste or Tribal or other group, changes its customs, rituals, ideology and way of life in the direction of a high, and frequently like the twice born caste.

Srinivas has stated, in his book *Social Change in Modern India*, that Sanskritisation is not confined only to Hindu castes but also seen among tribal and semi tribal groups such as Bhils of western India, Gonds and Oraons of central India etc. This process of change usually impacts the tribe with the undergoing Sanskritisation claiming themselves to be a caste, called as Hindu (ibid 1972).

On the other hand, Kalia (1959) has described the process of tribalisation which is seen among Jaunsar – Bawar in Uttar Pradesh and in the Bastar region of Madhya Pradesh. According to Kalia, the high caste Hindu temporarily borrows tribal customs, mores, rituals and beliefs which are in many respects antithetical to their own. Kalia's example may be illustrated as radical changes which can be seen in the style of life of Hindu people when they move away from their reference group.

On account of various levels of cultural contact, adoption and incorporation, the tribal people have been borrowing many cultural traits and religious practices from various sects and major religious group such as the Hindus, Muslims, Christians and others. Hence the different tribal groups have been assimilating with the different cultural groups by restoring their own cultural ethos from time immemorial without being concerned about nomenclature.

In this paper an attempt is made to understand the cultural change of the Santal tribe through their various cultural practices and religious performances and to find out the cultural syncretism in the ways of life of urban Santals in Kalyani.

II

The major objectives are as follows:

- To explore and understand the phenomenon of syncretism among the urban tribals at different points of socio-cultural and religious levels.
- To study the changing life of Santals in relation to their beliefs, customs, rituals and practices.
- To explore how do they restore their tribalism in their livelihood.

The study has been conducted at Kalyani Urban area, 20 No. ward Rathtala, Sidho Kanho Lane which is known as Adivasi Para. In Kalyani, 20 No. ward has been selected purposively and from this ward thirty six (36) Santal families are surveyed through complete enumeration. All the primary data have been collected through direct interview method. Each and every member in every house has been directly contacted and relevant information is collected according to the objectives of the study. For this study non-participant observation method is followed to know their socio-economic background as well as their cultural practices i.e., the customs, religious beliefs and rituals (marriage, death, birth and others).

The present study shows the changing ways of life of Santal people. These people have migrated from undivided Bihar and Orisha and settled here. Gradually with the passage of time they have been assimilating with the neighbouring urban culture. Santals are one of the major tribes of West Bengal.

They live in the States of Jharkhand, West Bengal, Bihar, Orissa, and Assam. After Independence, due to reservation policy probably they would have been benefitted mostly by getting jobs in various sectors. Kalyani urban settlement is the example of this. During the time of Bidhan Chandra Roy, the then Chief Minister of West Bengal, developed Kalyani Township and brought this Santal community as labourers for the development of this area. Since then they were the citizens of this area. Syncretisation of culture has started from that very time. Mainly they are the agriculturists. Even in rural areas (Bankura, Purulia, Pachim Midnapore) of their homelands they practise agriculture but a good number of Santal tribes have been migrating from their rural areas due to availing more facilities. In many cases, a good number of them have already converted into Christianity.

In this urban area they claim themselves as Hindu in spite of their tribalism. Especially they maintain their tribalism in various parts of their rite of passages and different rituals of their life. These parts of cultural traits lie in the core culture (stated by Linton 1955) of their life.

Clan of the Santal

The Santal are one of the dominant tribes in India. The Santals belong to the Proto-Australoid group. Santals believe in supernatural beings and ancestral spirits. Santali rituals consist mainly of sacrificial offerings and invocations to the spirits, or bongas. The Santals are very conscious about their identity and heritage. They have their own totem and clans. Six types of clan have been found among them in the Kalyani urban area. Some restrictions have existed with their respective clans. In many cases these clan names are attached with the names of animals or plants or some objects. *Table-1* describes in detail the type of clan and their meaning. Till today they are very much conscious regarding maintaining the clan identity through which they restore their tribal identity.

Table 1: Clan of the Respondents of Santal.

Sl No.	*Clan*	*Meaning*	*Frequency*
1.	Hembrom	Supari (Betel – Nut)	07
2.	Murmu	Chapeya (Do not cut the Karam tree)	12
3.	Kisku	Shankhachil – A Species of White breasted Kite. Never eat these.	06
4.	Soren	Saptarshi – Seven great ancient sages of India	02
5.	Mandi	Meroda -One type of grass	04
6.	Hansda	They never eat and kill any duck.	05
Total			**36**

Education of the Santal

Earlier very few Santals are literate. But now with the spread of urbanisation and industrialisation, a good number of Santals are migrating from rural areas. As a result, a major change has been observed with respect to their education. Mainly regarding female education, a significant advancement is noticed. In this study from *Table 2* it has been observed that, considering the level of literacy, all Santals show a well conscious picture regarding their education. Illiteracy rate is not found among them in this locality. In this community, it has been found that 14 women and 17 men are educated up to secondary level, 4 Santal women and 8 men have graduated and also 1 woman and 2 men are holding post graduate degree. It has been seen that they are very much conscious about their future. Many of them are economically affluent and they are admitting their daughters and sons in different residential schools, or English medium schools. On the other hand in Kalyani, till today there is no adivasi school. Nearest school is *Sabuj sangho High School* at Bagmore and *Pannalal Institution* at Kalyani. So, all the children are attending to these schools for education. Gradually, they are becoming conscious regarding changing education.

Table 2: Educational Qualification of all the members of Santal Community

Sl. No.	*Educational level*	*Santal*	
		Male	*Female*
1.	Illiterate	—	04
2.	Age below the school going children	07	04
3.	Just read and write name	03	09
4.	Class I-IV	14	12
5.	Class V-X	19	16
6.	Secondary	17	14
7.	Higher Secondary	14	10
8.	Graduate	08	04
9.	Post Graduation	02	01
	Total	**84**	**74**

So it can be said that in urban area Santals (male and female) are educated and more alert about their future planning and the young generation are not an exception. Sometimes it is very difficult to distinguish them from urban people. In urban area, due to rapid cultural assimilation they are able to understand the importance of education for their overall development.

In Kalyani Urban, Santals are gradually absorbing the urban culture of the dominating Bengali Hindus of Kalyani. As this urban Santals earn a good amount of money so all the children of the Santals are attending different schools like the urban people of kalyani. Many of them are also attending in different English medium schools at Kalyani.

Occupation of the Santal

In general the Santals practise their traditional economy for sustaining their livelihood through subsistence agriculture. Hence, their economy is often called underdeveloped; this economy is also associated with some traditional custom and rituals. The socio-economic life of the Santals also depends on forests. Their basic needs are fulfilled from the trees and plants of the forests. They are also engaged in hunting, fishing and cultivation for their livelihood. Mainly the Santals are agricultural tribe. Beside agriculture, they also domesticate animals like cows, buffaloes and pigs. With the advancement of time, the Santals have accepted different professions in every field. There are good numbers of Santals who are doctors, engineers, govt service holders, teachers, officers and workers in rails etc. Besides, a good number of Santals are engaged in different organised and unorganised sectors.

From Table 3, it is observed that 8 (eight) Santal men are engaged with Central Govt. Services and 5 (five) men and 2 (two) women are Primary School Teachers. 3 (three) men and one woman are high school teachers. On the other hand, 4 (four) men are attached in Kolkata police and 6 (six) men and one woman are W.B. govt employees. These new types of profession change their traditional ways of life and make them urban dwellers. After migration they have shifted from their rural agricultural life and accepted urbanism as their way of life.

Table 3: Occupations of the Santal Families

Occupation of the Santal families	*Number of Person*	
	Men	*Women*
Service Central	08	-
Primary Teacher	05	02
High School Teacher	03	01
Kolkata Police	04	-
RPF	02	-
Railway Service	07	02
Occupation of the Santal families	*Number of Person*	
	Men	*Women*
Private sector	05	-
W.B. Govt service	06	01
Total	**40**	**06**
Total 36 Families		

Income of the Santal Families

From the Table 4, it has been observed that out of 36 families, 47.22% of the Santals' family income lies above Rs.15000.00 per month. Out of 36 families no one family has been found to be earned below Rs. 15000.00 per month. Besides, three (8.33 %) families earn above Rs. 55,000.00 per month. So it is clear that in urban area with getting education and new occupational opportunities, the Santal families maintain their livelihood like the urban mainstream people. It has also been seen that majority of Santal families live in the Pakka houses, with all urban amenities and modern households gadgets for meeting the needs of their daily life. All the Santal families of the society are socio-economically better off. Due to their economic solvency they have the common urges to adopt urban culture quickly. All (36) Santal families of Kalyani Rathtala have Television, refrigerator and motor bike. Out of thirty six families three families have AC machine and two families have their own cars.

Table 4: Income of the Santal Families

Sl. No.	*Monthly Income (Rs.) of families*	*No. of Santal families (%)*
1.	Below 15,000	—
2.	15,001-25,000	17 (47.22)
3.	25,001-35,000	11 (30.56)
4.	35,001-45,000	04 (11.11)
5.	45,001-55,000	01 (2.78)
6.	Above 55,000	03(8.33)
	Total	**36 (100.00)**

III

Customs, Rituals and Religious Practices among the Santal Community

Birth Ceremony

The Santal society is patriarchal and the dominance of the male is found in every affair of life. But the females in the Santals society always play the active role in various matters in familial problems. The new born baby is highly welcomed in Santal society.

Generally, in earlier days a midwife (*Dhai Ma*) along with the help of elderly women relatives attends the woman during the time of child birth. Earlier when the child is born, the umbilical cord is cut by the midwife with an arrow-blade (*Tirer Fola*).Then the first blood is touched in the mouth of the baby. If the baby is a boy then one arrow is kept by the side of the forehead of the male baby and in the case of female baby a glass of water is kept beside left side of the bed of the baby. This ritual is going on during the last six month from the date of the delivery of the baby.

Birth pollution period varies from place to place. Eleven days from birth are considered as unclean period. It has been seen from the study that this period continues for nine days in this area. After nine days Santals observe one ceremony, called *Chetiyar.* This ritual starts with the worshipping of *Marang Buru*. The mixture of turmeric dust with Sunned Rice (*Atop Chal*) has been spreading in every corner of the house. After that, the dust of Neem (Azadirachta indica) leaves is mixed with the hot rice and is served to all the members of the family. It is called '*Nimvat*' which is served first to the Marang Buru then parents of the baby and the neighbours. This ceremony is continued for two days. After the period of pollution the mother is allowed to do every work.

But, nowadays, in urban area, all the deliveries are taken place in nursing home and hospital. So the role of midwife is performed by the senior member of the family. It has been seen from the study that many Santal families are influenced by urbanity along with their traditional culture. But it is noticed *Name giving ceremony or Annaprason ceremony* is not their own traditional ritual but they perform this ceremony like the other urban Hindu dwellers.

Marriage Customs

Monogamy form of marriage is practiced among the Santal. During the time of marriage, it is strictly prohibited for a Santal to marry within his own clan. Santal's marriage started with two names *Pilchu hadam* and *Pilchu bhudi*. It is believed that Santal's world was created by them and they were the first married couple in their society.

Parents of boys or girls will appoint an interlocutor called Raibaar (matchmaker). Raibaar is a person who mediates initial talk about marriage proposal to both the families - bride and groom.

After fixing the marriage date, it is announced to all the members of the family of the locality. Generally the Santals invite the members with a Sal (Shorea robusta) leaf prepared like a plate after stitching. In their society this leaf is very sacred. After preparing the invitation card made of Sal leaf (Shorea robusta), little Sunned Rice (Atop Chal) with grass (cynodon dactylon) is kept on it. This customs is known as *Sarjam Giro* (Sarjam means Sal and Giro means invitation). This is sent first to the bride's family after fixing the wedding date. Before the marriage day, another ritual has to be performed by would be bride and groom which is known as *Sagun Giro* (Sagun means auspicious and Giro means invitation). In this ritual the Manjhi (the Santal Priest) ties the bride and groom together with a yellow coloured clothe as a sign of their oneness.

Next on the marriage day, both the bride and groom are anointed ceremonially with turmeric (Curcuma longa) paste. The wife of elder brother performs the important role to conduct all the rituals. In the courtyard of groom's house one small whole is created by the married women and this whole is filled with water. The groom stands on the hole which is covered by the piece of bamboos (*basher fala* which indicates agriculture) that means from this day he has to be ready to take all responsibilities of the house. Then his brother's wife applies turmeric (Curcuma longa) paste on his forehead and he is taken for ceremonial bath. After taking bath he wears a new dress dhuti and jama. All heads of the families with their wives are invited in their community and they also take major role in the marriage ceremony by wearing yellow coloured dress offered by both bride's and groom's family. This ritual is known as *Sashang Lugri.*

On the wedding day the bridegroom starts from his house with his relatives for the wedding ceremony. Before the journey, he eats *khicuri* (mixture of *rice, dal and lentils*) form his brother's wife. Then bridegroom wears a new dress and put *alta* (lac-dye) in his leg. A betel nut cutter, known as *janti* is with him from the day of application of turmeric paste. Before leaving his house, the mother asks his son,' where are you going,' (*Kadam Chala Kana- In Santali Language*) then his son replies that he is going to bring a *Dasi* (bride) for her (*Amm Lagid Karmi Aghun, chala Kanna.* After that he is allowed to go for marriage. All the women folk of bride's family welcome with dance line by line for receiving the groom. This ritual is known as '*Daram Da'*.

Later on, the elder sister of bride brings a new dress for the groom. Finally bride's mother receives the groom. The groom usually comes to the wedding place on sister's husband's shoulder as well as bride comes on her sister's husband's shoulder.

The groom is made to stand on one side of the alter facing and then bride comes with a new saree, ornaments, garland and *kajallata* in her hand (a receptacle for collyrium), she stands opposite facing the groom and a screen is there where the bride's relatives stand there and on the another side is gathered by the groom's relatives. In this position bride and groom moves round anticlockwise direction for five/seven/nine times. After that the priest ties the turban on groom's head. There is a plate on which paddy, *durba* or bermuda grass (cynodon dactylon), vermilion, iron bangles etc have been kept. At first groom applies vermilion to the forehead of bride thrice and after that the 'wearing iron bangle' marriage ritual is done. Couple then sits on a mat and guests or relatives come and bless them.

On the next morning the newly married couple starts their journey for groom's house after completion of the formal ritual. There the groom's mother welcomes them through the same process (*Daram da*). After that the bridegroom's sister demands some amount of money from the couple before entering into the house. This ritual is known as *Duyar Sinch* (Bloking the door). After that in the evening a reception is organised for the newly married couple where all the members and relatives come and wish them. In this way this ceremony is over.

Marriage is a social institution and the two adult members of opposite sex unite them through marriage by social sanction and rituals. Like other Hindu people Santals follow the patriarchal norms of the society. By norm the adult male as a groom comes to bride's house and through marriage they form the union and finally the bride is taken to groom's family. The main rituals and various procedures of religious performances are same like the Hindus. Only they use their local language and follow dances in each and every part. They drink *hadia* (country liquor) ceremonially apart from their aristocracy. They also use vermilion, lac dye (Alta), turmeric paste, iron bangle, bangle with conch sail, red *pola* another type of bangle (marriage symbol). All these are used as the symbols of married women. Finally they settle their life in husband's family. Now the Santals are far from their traditional forest based livelihood. Just like urban Hindus they perform their marriage ceremony.

Death Rituals

The Santals believe that when a person dies, his soul or spirit is not extinguished but rather transformed. After the death incident in the locality, the head of the family of the deceased informs all the villagers with a stick. It is the symbolic behaviour of the member of the deceased family which helps to understand others about the death incident of the locality. The relatives of the deceased person who live in a reasonable distance are also informed. They all gather in the house of the deceased. On the death of a person his house and his village become polluted. No marriage or festival or worship occurs during that time. The body is then prepared for cremation or burial. In their society some rituals is connected with death. In case of a woman whose husband is still alive vermillion is put on her forehead and also *lac- dye* (Alta) is put on her legs by female relatives. Besides in case of the dead person – man, woman or children- the body is anointed with oil and turmeric paste, dressed in new clothes and laid in a *Khatiya* (death bed) which is brought out in the courtyard. The dead body is carried thereafter by four relatives or friends on their shoulders to the junction of roads at the end of the locality. In that time the *khatiya* is kept on the courtyard but previously one Dom used to go to the end of the locality or *para* with one hen, branch of paddy, paddy seeds, mud etc and did some rituals with these things centring around the dead body, but now these rituals are no more. So the dead body is taken to the crematorium from this junction, no woman is allowed to accompany the dead body. The male folk carry the dead body on their shoulder. After reaching the cremation ground, every favourite item of the deceased are also kept in front of the dead body. After performing the last death ritual the body is prepared for cremation. After cremation all the family members and relatives return their home. An earthenware pot filled with water is kept in courtyard and then some Neem (Azadirachta indica) leaves and cow dung is placed beside it for purification. All the members are purified by sprinkling of Neem water mixed with cow dung. After that, the touched Neem (Azadirachta indica) leaves are burned and turned into asses which are again taken by all family members of house. Then all the relatives and villagers go to bath. The Dom takes a little assess of the burnt material of dead person and digs the matter in one corner of the house.

Generally after eleven or nine days *Shradhya* ceremony is held. In that day all the male members of the family shave their head and do the *Shradhya* ritual. The male member of the family who puts fires in the deceased's mouth goes for the *Shudhikaran* Process. He anoints with the oil and turmeric. Then he takes bath and is dressed with new clothes. After putting the new dress he sits beside the pond side (Ghat) where all male members come and the priest is also present there. There they arrange a puja for peace of the soul and worshiped the Maran Buru. Sunned Rice (atap chaal), grass (cynodon dactylon) and Banana (Musa acuminata) are the important things which are offered to the soul there. In this way the rituals come to an end. In that day completely veg food is prepared by the women and before serving the cooked food, the chief male offers some food to the deceased soul and pray to accept it. The next day chicken and rice with rice beer is served to all the members those who were associated with the death rites and rituals.

Now-a-days some changes are noticed regarding the death rituals. In urban area, many tribals now follow the Hindu rituals and side by side they also perform their own rituals. Right now they wear *Kacha and* carry the *Ason* (the sitting material) like the Hindu rituals. Now, they cremated the dead body to the electric chulli instead of wood. So some traditional death rituals are always missed by them.

Language

The young people generally speak in Bengali language. The adult men those who have been engaged with different govt or railway services they can also speak fluently in Hindi. Many of them can speak in English language. Particularly the young children are getting education in English medium school. So they can speak fluently in English. Their tradition *alchiki* language is only limited among the older generation. With this language (*Alchiki*) the elder members can speak and understand among themselves.

The young generation people are only able to understand properly instead of reading and writing. Language is a major part of cultural syncretism. Considering the language they have adopted Bengali language from urban Hindu culture for maintaining their interaction with the larger society.

Festivals of Santal

Santals are nature loving people; they love singing and dancing with nature. It is within their blood. Dancing is the important rituals of the Santals when they are in fairs and festivals. After a long day of hard work, Santals relax themselves with the light music and dance. Throughout the year they have been engaged with different types of festivals and religious activities for keeping themselves well. The **Karam** festival is very much popular among the Santals, which is celebrated in the month of September and October. They celebrate this festival and worship the deity to increase their wealth and make free their society from the enemies. **Baha** is the Sal blossom annual festival, celebrated in the month of *Falgun* that means February-March. Baha festival stands for purity, softness and artistic thoughts.

In the month of August and September they observe the festivals **'Ma-More'** every four years of interval. They celebrate this festival to overcome the social hindrances which are very common in their day to day life.

Dasai Parab is another important festival of their life. This festival takes place in the month of October, but before that in the day of *Panchami of Durga Puja*, male female both are engaged with dancing taking with Dhol, Madol, kortal etc. and they round the village visiting door to door of the neighbours. **Khunto Sarhai** is one of the festivals which occur in the month of November during Kali puja. Generally in this festival the two bulls have been engaged with fighting in the field of their community. People come and enjoy their fighting which encourages getting strength in their life.

Santals have a rich cultural heritage. But now with the spread of urbanisation they do not follow their own festivals properly. Being the residence of urban sector they do not celebrate Dasai Parab and Khunto Sarhai. Now they celebrate some festivals of Hindu like Saraswati Puja and Kali Puja. They participate in Durga Puja like other Bengali people. They wear new clothes, enjoy the festivals and worship the goddess Durga like Bengali people. Besides that, all students celebrate Saraswati Puja with great satisfaction. Worshiping of Goddesses like Sitala, Manasa, Kali and Saraswati etc. are very popular among the Santals as a part of the Hindu culture. They are much closed to Hindu groups. Now-a-days, they also worship Ganesh and Laxmi in their daily life.

Dress and Food

Regarding their dress and food they try to maintain their lifestyle following the Hindu culture. Generally Santals women's dress is traditional sari with red or green border and men wear dhoti. But now being residents of urban area they wear urban costumes like the urban dwellers. New types of western dresses have been found particularly among the youngsters. Now-a-days, young girls wear salwars, jeans, tops and kurtis like other urban girls. The boys use mostly shirts, branded T-shirt, jeans and formal pants etc., but during the time of their traditional customary functions all men wear their conventional dress like dhotis and women are dressed up with sarees named f*utagacha* with their traditional ornaments and flowers in their head.

Generally Santals peoples' regular food is pupped rice (muri), Rice with water, boiled rice, pot-herb and rice (*Shak vat*) different type of vegetables etc. The urban impact can be seen in the field of their culture, language, traditions, occupation, customs and so on. Interestingly, the Santal people acknowledge the impact of urbanisation on them and they also agree that with this changing process it is very difficult for them to sustain with their age old beliefs and practices. On the one hand, this urbanisation process has made them aware to realise their actual existence in the midst of other urban communities of the locality. The Urbanisation has made direct impact on them and forced them to accept certain traits of Bengali culture. In this area of such change is cooking style and ingredients. Gradually many changes have been taken place in their cooking style by applying different ingredients which are mostly use by the Bengali dominated women. The Bengali dishes like fish curry, mutton curry and vegetable curry with spices are very popular in their day to day item.

Now a day in rural areas the economically affluent people also use gas for cooking purpose. In urban area for cooking gas is very common and easily available fuel used by the people for cooking purposes. The Santals with changing economic conditions automatically adopt the urban culture. The children are also taking fast food like egg roll, chowmin, burger, vegetable patties, cold drinks, cake, cadburry, different types of sandwiches etc. for their preferable food items. They also visit with their parents to different restaurants for their recreation.

Political Participation

The Santals are governed by their customary laws and have their own method of treating different kinds of offences. The offices of the political organisation are generally hereditary. The political organisation and administrative unit of the Santal village are mostly governed by the council of elders who regulates the life of the people within the village and beyond. In this urban locality they have also their traditional political head known as *Manjhi* who controls the local political unit. Till today in their community *Manjhi* plays important role for maintaining the solidarity of the group. In this area the name of the *Manjhi* is Panchanon Soren. He is working as a head of their locality. This position is selected according to inheritance. Without his presence no social ceremony (Marriage, Death, Naming ceremony, festival etc.) could be possible in their community.

The impact of urbanisation influences them to become aware about their political rights and thereby franchise their votes during the elections. The Santals of the present day have also been starting to join in to the local political parties with a hope to challenge their various socio-economic problems during their crises. It has been observed form the study that no Santal is directly attached with any political party. Women are not much interested in joining different political parties. One new phenomenon has been noticed in this area that before going to casting their votes all the members of the community have to present in a common place. They all sit together and discuss the matter and decide the person whom they cast their votes for selection of the political man.

From the discussion, it is clear that cultural syncretism has several direct and indirect impacts on the traditional culture, tradition and social norms of the Santals. The impact is observed in their day to day activities. The processes of migration and urbanisation have helped them to learn about changing ways of life.

This process of cultural syncretism has brought many changes in their day to day activities. The age old customs and traditions are no more attached in their daily life and they have been influenced by the urban people and adopted new cultural and new religious traits from the locality.

This paper has taken an attempt to find out the linkages between urbanisation and the traditional ways of the Santals. The special attention is given to find out the impact of modernity on Adivasi society as a whole. How do the Santals accept the new form of their life? This is the major question raised by the social scientist. This paper has tried to locate the various processes of cultural syncretism by which the traditional Santal people are identified as Urban Santals in the locality.

Their traditional forest based life style is not visible as they are now the urban dwellers and Bengali Hindus are the major dominant group of the locality. As a result slowly and gradually they absorb with the Hindu urban culture. Cultural syncretism is the spontaneous normal process of assimilation. Different groups with the passage of time adopt many new traits and absorb themselves with it. With this process of assimilation one day will come when this Santal group will be marginalised in consideration to their own ethnic group.

Earlier Santals associate them with forest which provides them fuel, fruits, leaves, flowers and raw material for fulfilling the needs of their daily life. But Urban Santals of this area use flowers customarily as availability of those wild flowers are less and their traditional forest based festivals are less in number. So automatically they adopt new urban culture for their survival.

References

Bhattacharyya, S. (2013). *Changing Status of a Marginalised Group in Murshidabad District : The Santals*. Unpublished Doctoral Thesis.

Bose, N.K. (1975). *The Structure of Hindu Society.* New Delhi: Orient Longman.

Das, N. K. 2003. *Culture, Religion and philosophy: Critical Studies in Syncretism and Inter Faith Harmony*. Jaipur : Rawat Publication.

Das, N. K. (2006). *Cultural Diversity, Religious Syncretism and People of India : An Anthropological Interpretation. Bangladesh e-journal of Sociology.* Vol. 3 (2)

Gadgil, M and Guha, R. (1992). *This Fissured Land: An Ecological History of India*. Berkeley: University of California Press.

Kalia, S.C. (1959). *Sanskritisation and Tribalisation*. Bulletin of the Tribal Research Institute. Chindwara (M.P). Vol. 2 (4)

Linton, R. (1955). *The Tree of Culture*. New York: Alfred A. Knopf Inc.

Madan, T.N. 2004. *Religions of India*. (In) Handbook of Indian Sociology, Veena Das (Eds.). New Delhi: Oxford University Press.

Mahajan, G. (2006). *Negotiating Cultural Diversity and Minority in India*. In *Democracy, Conflict and Human Security*. Vol. 2. Sweden: IDEA.

Manna, S. (2000). *The Fair Sex in Tribal Cultures – Problems and Development*. New Delhi : Gyan Books Pvt. Ltd.

Manna, S. (2011). *Tradition versus Modernity: Mother and Child Health (0 – 5 years) In Two Integrated Tribal Development Blocks of Paschim Midnapore, West Bengal:*

Problems and Developments. Unpublished Dissertation.

Srinivas, M.N. (1972). *Social Change in modern India.* New Delhi: Orient Blackswan Pvt.Limited.

Stewart, C. And Shaw, R. (1994). *Syncretism/Anti-syncretism – The Politics of Religious Synthesis.* London: Routledge.

Veer, P. (1994). *Syncretism, Multiculturalism and the Discourse of Tolerance*. In C. Stewart and R. Shaw eds. *Syncretism/Anti-syncretism – The Politics of Religious Synthesis.* London : Routledge.

20

Syncretism in Early Indian Society: A Case Study of Buddhism

—*Agnik Bhattacharya*

I

The ideas and theories of syncretism couldn't be traced in the broader historical paradigm. However we do have some evidences of cultural homogeneity and harmonisation. It may avoid the presence of such syncretic culture. The theory experienced in medieval India was actually a gradual process or flow of events. It owes to the earlier society.

In this context, what could syncretism justify? Although, different definitions survive on theories, debates and controversies, a symbol of flexibility allows people of various communities, class and gender to coexist within the society. The ideas were often used to describe the friendly relations of Hindus and Muslims in medieval India. According to Gaborieau, the cult of saints owe to religious steps, which have promoted Hindu-Muslim syncretism in India.[1] Many scholars feel the *bhakti* movement prompted eclectic faiths and lessened the religious orthodoxy.[2]

The theories were often put forward by Asim Roy, J.J.Roy Burman et al, with the help of different historical, anthropological and archaeological data unfound in the context to early Indian society. We see or rather notice smaller evidence of cultural unity and social equality; which may be absent within the society, but was felt within the *Order* of a particular religious community. So, the root of syncretism within the Indian culture can be felt from the 6^{c} BCE, although many scholars differ with this idea.[3] Differences on the basis of class and caste did have a huge impact on the compositions of early Indian society, but the impact was hugely influenced by the prevalent political ethics. The rise of fundamentalism in recent years in India has obliterated the deep rooted syncretism in Indian culture.[4] The influence of political ideas behind promoting the notions of syncretism can be noticed in early and medieval India.

In an interview carried on Ananda Bazaar Pratika on February 18, 2015, Sheldon Pollock argued no Muslim ruler to have forcefully converted Hindus; had they done so, there could have been no Hindus left in the country.[5] So, if we consider Pollock facts true, we come across the huge political influence behind the promotion of syncretic culture in the medieval period; mainly by the Muslim rulers. Similarly, we find evidences of certain rulers who made a vague effort to maintain religious harmony in bringing them on one common platform through common faith. Asoka, for example promoted the idea of 'Dhamma', that was his on the understandings and through it, he not only wanted to rule, but also he wanted to maintain an equilibrium of different religious sentiments within his empire. However, his attempt was criticized, failed, but was reiterated by later historians, as an obvious attempt to bring homogeneity; at least among different religious beliefs.

II

The early India social structure however did not experience cultural homogeneity. On the other hand, it had a society based on certain divisions mainly on the basis of class and caste, and discriminations on the varna and jati basis. The society owed to the four-fold varna system, the highest ritual position provided to the Brahmanas. The second position went to the Kshatriyas, the third to the Vaisyas and the fourth belonged to the Sudras. The Sudras were the most poverty stricken and badly affected class, who always faced the atrocities of the other three upper classes. By the time of the Gupta Empire, the Sudras were considered untouchables. They were forced to live away the living areas of other three upper classes.[6] Early Indian society starting from the prehistoric to the Harappan period was a complex structure with every permutation and combination. In the beginning, i.e., the Stone Age and later in the Mesolithic age; the society was a collective commune, where there're no such economic transactions with political influence. So, the idea of a syncretic culture altogether can be traced, keeping in mind over the proper definition of society. However, some historians argue the Paleolithic and Mesolithic period did not have the society structure, as they were mostly 'barbaric'. Social history does not mean '*a backward projection of sociology*', nor economic history an application of economic theory with '*retrospective effect*'. Sociological generalisations transcending time and place and deliberately attempting to prepare unchangeable character of Indian society posed a real danger to historians.[7]

The idea of society or a common habitat developed mainly from the Vedic period, although some evidences of society were found in the Harappan civilisation. However, the exact nature of the society is still unknown, as the key to the mysteries of civilisation unfound, i.e., the Harappan script is still undeciphered replete answers to different questions, yet to be answered.[8] The early Indian society since the Vedic and later Vedic period was based on certain rigid rituals, norms and customs expected to be emulated by everyone. A heterogeneous society was created through the modus operandi, where no signs of syncretism were noticed. Signs of demarcation, religious atrocities, and cultural differences were visible, when the sources were studied, that were important in context to early India.[9]Demarcations survived in the trade and commerce, as the two main law books *Dhramasastras* and *Dharmasutras* restricted the *Brahmanas* to partake in trading activities. Certain areas were earmarked as '*mlechchas*', as the people living in those areas practiced trade.

So, the process of dividing the society on the basis of caste, gender, creed and race; things that people do not have the option of choosing during the birth, the people who belonged to the highest strata of the society created a social habitat that become rather impossible to live in. The social compositions of early India was challenged, as it wanted a change as the common people desired to express their voice and ambitioned to stop the phenomenon, in the name of religion and other affinities related to it. Hence in the 6[c] BCE, a new religious group emerged to change the complexion of the society, by bringing a cultural uniformity among the mosaic of several cultures and traditions. The new religious group, many considered it not only as a religiously active community rather it could in all sense also be considered as an alternative philosophical order. It preached the ideas of *'Nibbana'*, through proper and correct deeds. The notions of syncretism were not directly found in the different activities practiced by the Buddhist community, but the trends of their activities certainly prove that Buddhist have tried to bring cultural homogeneity at least within the Sangha (*Order*).

III

Buddhism was a religious organisation. It also had a huge and rich philosophical merit hidden deep within the constraints of the Sangha *(Order*). But, on that being considered as a counter or protestant movement against the Brahmanical dominance, was not only the single social and religious group that contained religious ideas to guide people. The Brahmanical group that had a lot of texts, which was used as weapon to sustain supremacy; did contain a lot of philosophical and social ideas that were formulated for the guiding purpose for everyone, irrespective of anything[10]. Inspite of being a highly material and philosophical group, the people mainly commoners along with the people belonging to elite closer got attracted towards the new culture or religious group, that started spreading like a rage. The main reasons or the hypothetical way of answering why Buddhism did become popular, was the first reason was definitely '*the language,* despite the coexistence of brahminism.

The language did play a vital role in making Buddhism, what it stood out to be in early Indian society. The language through which the Brahmanical texts or Brahmanical dominance was spread was '*Sanskrit*', which was unknown and understood by everyone among the society. Often, people failed to understand what was being said and done through Vedic rituals, although they did have the desire to know, but failed as the language was quite rigid, tough and clustered with heterodox nature of Brahmanical elites. The Sanskrit cosmopolis did not come into being simultaneously with the appearance of the Sanskrit language. Its development was slow and tentative, and for it come about at all the very self understanding of the nature and function of the '*language of the gods*', as Sanskrit was known, had to be transformed.[11] So, to understand the rituals and above all, to reach the Almighty, people started searching a language or a proper medium. Buddha used this opportunity and started using '*Pali*', a very common language for spreading his comparatively new religious belief. It is not that people got attracted to Buddhism within a blink of an eye; it did face a lot of restraint from every sphere of the society. But after people started understanding what Lord Buddha wanted to say and the philosophical merits hidden inside it, people finally got what they had asked for.

Translating the religious belief into Pali and teaching people the way to '*nibbana*' inspired from the *Upanishads* and other texts, Buddhism grew rapidly. But the use of a common language was not the sole reason for its growth. Lord Buddha always wanted to make the Sangha in such a way that it would be open to all without any discrimination. He framed laws that were complied later after his '*mahaparinibbana*' and decided the *Vinaya* rules to run the Sangha and not any individual.[12] However, in the beginning, Lord Buddha did not allow women to be a part of the Sangha, but later after several requests and firm devotion by *Ananda* and *Mahaprajati Gautami*, he agreed for the entry of women within the Sangha.[13] The phenomenon that originating in India, Buddhism should expect for a few remaining in Bengal, Orissa, and Assam, have given place to Hinduism, which is now the dominant religion of the country. Unlike the religion of the Vedas allowed animal sacrifice to please the gods, Buddhism sets it face against sacrifice; on the contrary, it waged a merciless campaign against the practice. In this connection, it may legitimately be asked how the Buddha preached the principle of *ahimsa* and *daya* to living animals, as he himself could eat meat and all his followers obliged to do so. The explanation was simple, in a society, where meat was commonly used as a daily food; he and his followers had to depend upon public alms; so that if they had refused to eat meat, they could have possibly starve to death.

Though, Gautama Buddha belonged to an aristocratic family, his life and work were those of a democrat. He served the interests of the masses and concerned with their happiness, he travelled widely for 45 years, protecting them and carrying his life's mission out; he founded the Sangha, the order of the Buddha fraternity of monks and nuns. All the members therein were parish, required to be present at a formal meeting of the community. The leader of the Sangha was generally elected among the *Theras* or senior monks and he was being respected by all. As Buddhist monks had no private property of their own, all furniture or things in the monastery, for the use of the monks, belonged to the whole community or the Sangha. In short, no official act of the Sangha was valid, unless it was decided at a meeting, where all members and visiting monks in a parish were either present or could communicate their wishes.

Buddhism arose and flourished in eastern Uttar Pradesh and Bihar, in the kingdoms of Magadha and Kosala. The Buddha spent his time in Bihar, and after his death the three councils were held successively at **Rajgir, Vaisali, and Pataliputra**. But, the real key to the understanding of the rise of new religious movements lied in certain significant developments in the material life of the people[14]. The Buddhist emphasis on non-injury to animals assumes a new significance in the contest of the needs of new agriculture. *Pali* canons do not stress so much on the need for non- violence towards animals. The earliest Buddhist text, the *Sutta- nipata* states that cattle should be protected, because they were givers of food, beauty and happiness[15]. Some urban centers identified in the *Pali* text practiced trade, by the use of punch mark coins, which are stratigraphically ascribed to the fifth century BCE and may have been appeared earlier. The Brahmana attitude towards the trade was unhelpful; the earliest law book prescribed the trade and agriculture for the Vaisyas but assigns them the third place in the society, the first two places reserved by the Brahmanas and Kshatriyas. The inhabitations of Bihar, Magadha, and Anga were held in contempt, because they traded in certain articles. In contrast to this the early Buddhist text records several instances of sea voyages with a sense of approval[16].

But the new religious belief that gained so much popularity started losing its feet after the '*maha parinibbana*' of Lord Buddha; the reason may be due to proper guidance. Although after his death, it gained a lot of patronage from kings and royal elites but these patronages dismantled the stability among the Sangha. A lot of fake monks entered the Sanghas, in the hope of occupying the wealth donated by several kings and rich merchants to the Sangha[17]. Due to this the 3 councils or *Sangitis* were organised to solve the problems among the members of the Sangha and to compile the teachings of Lord Buddha. These councils did solve the problems but not entirely and for a long time it lost its place of prominence, until the 7th century when it again started gaining in the eastern region of India, once again under royal patronage, i.e. '*The Palas'*. Viharas like *Nalanda, Vikramsila and Odantapuri* became new centers of Buddhist learning but with the introduction of the Islamic rule in India, Buddhism declined rapidly along with these centers of learning. However, there are certain debates regarding the decline of the group after the 13^{c} onwards.

IV

In spite of Buddha's attempt of equalizing the differences within the society, certain questions still remain unanswered. Did Buddha do something to stop the divisions within the society? Did the ideas of syncretism existed outside the Sangha? Was Buddha trying to bring a social and religious and not political? To make out a hypothesis of these obligations put forward by different historians is really difficult. We do see rather notice that the notions of untouchability did exist within the society, when Buddha and his religious mandarins were at its peak and it was not really abolished from the society. Similarly, after the '*maha parinibbana*', we do find traces of a heterogeneous social order due to the influx of economic resources. At the same time, if examined from the political diaspora, Buddha never challenged the existing political order, nor tried to change, rather his struggle was on to bring a social reform by making everyone feel the truism in properly performing the routine works (*which he believed to be the best way to attain moksha*). So, Buddha's revival was more of a religious one than a social and political, which can be proved as in early Buddhist texts like *Diggha nikaya* and *Majhima nikkaya*, we find Buddha speaking about the *Ucca Kula* and the *Nicca- Kula*. He also followed the *varna* hierarchy order, but due to his differences with the existing Brahmanic supremacy, he choose to give the Ksatriya the first position in the order and not the Brahmanas. The patterns of syncretism that we notice in the medieval India was to assimilate with two religious belief, that was absent in Buddha when he was expanding the Sangha. Buddhism thus can be considered as an alternative and parallel belief that had no intensions of mixing or collaborating with the Brahmanical and other religious belief. Later in the Buddhist Sangha we find certain factions due to which certain sects arrive in the forefront, which further criticizes the presence or existence of syncretism in early India with Buddhism as its example. Differences and sectarian divisions were also noticed among the Sufis, who claimed to promote the syncretic culture, but instead of the opinions all *the Silsilas*campaigned the thought of religious equality and cultural homogeneity. These notions later became the main ideologies of bhakti movement, considered to be a pioneer in promulgating syncretism.

Buddhism on the other cannot be considered as a subaltern revolution as Buddha in no way was trying to provide economic and political supremacy to the have not's, rather he was trying to save them from the atrocities of Brahmanical religion. On the other hand, his attitude towards women and certain regulations set up for them do not really show that he was a man, who completely disbanded the ideas of gender inequality. However, some activities of Buddha through which he tried to maintain equal status at least within the men of the Sangha, shows that although he was not preaching syncretism, yet he was trying to bring social, political, cultural and economical homogeneity.

The concepts of syncretism that were strongly experienced in spite of different debates are hence absent in early Indian society, what is thus visible and present is a conscious attempt to bring equality within a specific group of men and women; to provide them a common platform to solve and discuss problems and to believe in '*Karma*' and not rituals to reach the Almighty.

So, the roots of syncretism if not completely was present, but some traces of it were definitely available in the society of early India, which may or may not have inspired the later campaigners of syncretism in medieval India is not clear; answers of which were yet to be found. But, the debates and questions that surfaced, no way tried to lower the gallant effort of the Buddhist order; rather it acknowledged the brave effort of Buddhist order, who have cherished the notions of equality that has now achieved global appreciation and which may have paved the path of syncretic culture within the broader dimensions of Indian civilisations.

Notes

1. (Roy Burman 1996).
2. *Ibid,* p. 1211.
3. Lord Buddha did try to abolish the differences within the *Sangha*, but still the concept of untouchability and other social demarcations did continue to exist within the society, outside the *Sangha*.
4. *Ibid,* p. 121.
5. Sheldon Pollock brought out references of the establishment of two '*Nayacharya*' at *Nagadeep* and *Mithila*, to prove the authentication of his statement.
6. The untouchables were considered impure and forced to menial jobs to survive in the society. They were ordered to wear metal ornaments and eat in broken bowls, while entering the living areas of the Brahmanas and Ksatriyas they had to clap a stick. So that people could be made aware in advance as coming in touch with them, would pollute the other classes of the four fold varna system. See Basham, A.L. "*The Wonder That was India*" (2004) and Kane P.V. "*History of Dharmasastras*" (1956).
7. (Sharma 1983).
8. Although the exact nature and composition of society is not known, yet by the pattern of construction and design of the buildings, we can assume that some sort of differences and demarcations did exist within the society.
9. In context to early India, the sources are divided into two halves mainly: (i) *Archaeological Sources*, (ii) *Literary Sources.* Literary sources are further divided into *Religious* and *Non Religious* respectively.
10. Early Vedic texts and also later Vedic texts did have a lot of philosophical teachings and guidance. In fact Buddhism did borrow a lot of Upanishadic and Vedic principles and ideologies while spreading and forming their Sangha (Order).
11. (Pollock 2011).

12. Due to transparency among the community, we find rich merchants like *Anathapindaka d*onating lands for the building of *viharas* and at the same point of time we find courtesans like *Amrapali* becoming a part of the Sangha.
13. With the permission of Lord Buddha, the Bhikkhuni Sangha was formed and **Mahaprajapati Gautami** (*the fostermother of Buddha*), was elected to be the head of the Sangha. Buddha formed laws and the nuns were asked to follow it strictly and at the same time Buddha too predicted that it would be one of the main reasons for the Sangha to dismantle.
14. The Neolithic people of the east aborigines and non Aryans cultivated small patches of land in the upland by burning the forest and then cutting the trees. They domesticated cattle not for dairy products and agriculture but for non-vegetarian food.
15. (ed Sahu 2006).
16. Trade also included the use of money, which led to money lending and usury. But the existing social order did not favor lending at interest.
17. However due to royal patronage and royal interest Buddhism started spreading outside the Indian sub continent. Kings like Asoka, Kanishka and later Merander helped Buddhism, to spread too far off countries like Sri Lanka, South East Asia, Far East Asia, China and even Africa.

References

Altekar, A.S. *The Position of Women in Hindu Civilisation: From Prehistoric Times to Present Day.* Delhi: Motilal Banarasidas Pvt. Ltd., 2009.

Badyopadhyaya, Jayantanuja. *Class, Caste and Religion in Medieval India: Social History of Transition Failure.* Kolkata: Mitram Publishers Pvt. Ltd., 2013.

Bailey, Greg And Mabbett, Ian. *The Socilogy of Early Buddhism.* Cambridge: Cambridge University Press, 2003.

Basham, A.L. *The Wonder that was India.* London: Picador(an imprint of Pan Macmillian Publishers Pvt. Ltd.), 2004.

Bhattacharya, Sukumari. "Prostitution in Ancient India." In *Women in Early Indian Socities*, by General Editor, Chattopadhyaya, B.D. ed. Kukum Roy, 196-198. New Delhi: Manohar Publishers & Distributors, 2011.

Chakravarti, Ranabir. *Exploring Early India: upto c.AD 1300.* New Delhi: Macmillian Publishers India, 2010.

Chakravarti, Uma. *Beyond the Kings and Brahmanas of 'Ancient' India.* New Delhi: Tulika Books, 2012.

Chandra, Satish. *History of Medieval India* . New Delhi : Orient Black Swan, 2014.

Chattopadhay, B.D. "Images of Raiders and Rulers." In *Rethinking Early Medieval India*, by Upinder ed. Singh, 325-340. New Delhi: Oxford University Press, 2011.

-*Representing the Other? Sanskrit Sources and the Muslims (8th- 14th century).* New Delhi: Manohar Publications Pvt. Ltd., 1998.

Dahlquist, A. *Megasthenes & Indian Religion.* Delhi: Motilal Banarasidas Publishers

Private Limited, 1977.

Desai, P.B. "Kalyana Inscription of Sultan Mohammad, Saka 1298." *Ephigrphia Inidica 32*, 1957-58: 165-68.

Dr. Sachau, Edward. C. *Alberuni's India.* New Delhi: Rupa . Co, 2009.

Eaton, Richard.M. "Temple Desecration in Indo- Muslim States." *Frontline*, January 5th , 2001: 70-77.

Sahu, Bhairabi Prasad. ed.*Iron and Social Chnage in Early India.* New Delhi: Oxford University Press, 2006.

Basham, A.L. ed. *A Cultural History Of India.* Delhi: Oxford University Press, 1985.

General Editor, Majumdar , R.C. *The History and Culture Of The Indian People: Vol- III - The Classical Age.* Mumbai: Bharatiya Vidya Bhavan, 1997.

The History and Culture of the Indian People:vol-V- The Struggle For Empire. Mumbai: Bharatiya Vidya Bhavan, 2001.

Majumdar, R.C. *Ancient India.* Delhi: Motilal BAnarasidass Publishers Pvt. Ltd., 1977.

Pollock, Sheldon. "The Sanskrit Cosmopolis and the Vernacular Revolution." In *Rethinking Early Medieval India: A Reader*, by Upinder ed. Singh, 271-272. New Delhi: Oxford University Press, 2011.

Roy Burman, J.J. "Hindu Muslim Syncretism in India." *Economic and Political Weekly*, 1996: 1211-1215.

Sharma, R. S. *India's Ancient Past.* New Delhi: Oxford University Press, 2012.

Material Culture and Social Formations in Ancient India. New Delhi: Macmillian India Limited, 1983.

Singh, Upinder. *A History of Ancient and Early Medieval India: From the Stone Age to the 12th Century.* New Delhi: Pearson Longman Pvt. Ltd., 2009.

Sircar, D.C. *Studies in the Religious Life of Ancient and Medieval India.* New Delhi: Motilal Banarasidass Publishers Private Limited, 2013.

Tiwari, K. N. *Comparative Religion* . New Delhi: Motilal Banarasidass Publishers Private Limited, 2009.

21

An Empirical Study on the Syncretistic Values among the Indian Population

—*Anupma Bharadwaj*

Introduction

Syncretism is the process by which two or more independent cultural systems, or elements thereof, conjoin together at a given time and space to form altogether a new and distinct system. The process of syncretism occurs largely due to long time and continued interaction of different cultural systems; howsoever they may be opposed to each other, theoretically and conceptually. In India, due to age-old interaction of the Hindus with the Muslims and the Christians, a number of syncretistic phenomena can be observed in the cultural systems of the respective populations. It should be very clearly noted that syncretism is much more than merely borrowing of cultural traits among two groups, which often takes place when two cultural systems meet together. In syncretism, the elements of a culture, by virtue of circumstances, is so deeply imbibed in another culture that it appears to be its integral part. There are innumerable numbers of *Dargah* (a Muslim Shrine) in India, where the Hindus pay reverence and propitiate before the shrine to achieve their desired goals. Similarly, a number of Hindu beliefs, rituals, and observances have moved into the Christian and Muslim cultural systems in India, and vice versa. The paper furnishes a number of significant instances of beliefs, rituals, and observances that are observed among the Hindus, Muslims, and Christians that manifest syncretistic values.

Indian society has a rich diversity. Ever since the arrival of the Aryans, there has been an interaction between different cultural and religious streams.

While Brahmanism imposed an exclusionist caste hierarchy on society, other streams like Jainism, Buddhism, Sikhism, etc. contributed to the synthesis of local cultures. Indian culture is a plural one, encompassing the diversity of the country, incorporating and drawing heavily from all those people who came and settled here. Even amongst Hindus there are multiple sects, and Hindu culture is not uniform.

Islam first came to India through Arab traders[1]. The arrival of the Mughals on the political arena was marked by multiple changes. Like any other ruler the Mughals were ruthless exploiters and applied coercion as well as ideological maneuvers to rule. The impact of Islam and the culture of the Mughals led to development of a synthesis, popularly called Hindustani culture, reflected in all fields, such as, music, sculpture, architecture, literature, fine arts and so on. At the religious level Islam and local Hindu traditions interacted and strengthened Sufi tradition and *Bhakti* cults, both of which were very popular and had a large subaltern following. Sufis were more tilted towards the spiritual side of Islam. They opposed to some extent the orthodox Ulemas of Islam, who were close to the elite and power centers of the society. Their doctrine promoted spiritual universalism and demolished the barriers of caste and creed.

For example, **Baba Farid** of Punjab wrote his poetry in Punjabi, and his verses have been quoted in the Granth Saheb[2]. Baba Farid has his poetry included in the Guru Granth Sahib, the most sacred scripture of the Sikh community, which includes a number of hymns composed by Farid. Guru Arjan, the 5th guru of Sikhism, included these hymns himself in the Adi Granth, which is the predecessor of the Guru Granth Sahib.

Mir Miyan, another Sufi saint, was requested to lay the foundation stone of Harmandir in the Golden Temple[3]. Guru Arjan planned to build a temple in the centre of the holy tank called *Amritsar* or *the pool of the nectar of immortality*. As the temple was to be thrown open to people of all religions, castes, creeds and climes, he invited Mian Mir to lay the foundation stone of the Harmandar Sahib. He came to the city of Amritsar. Mian Mir was given one of the warm welcomes for which Guru Arjan was famous. The two holy men embraced each other in sincere love and regard. The purpose of the temple was disclosed to the Sufi saint. Mian Mir was delighted at the fine objectives the Guru had in mind. The foundation-stone was laid in January 1588.

Sayyid Waris Shah wrote Heer Ranzha, the greatest classic of medieval Punjabi literature. It is based on a traditional folk tale of Heer and her lover Ranjha. *Heer Ranjha* is considered one of the quintessential works of classical Punjabi literature.

Nizamuddin Auliya, another major Sufi saint said that there are as many ways of worshipping God as there are particles of sand.' Nizamuddin Auliya stressed love as a means of realizing God. For him his love of God implied a love of humanity. His vision of the world was marked by a highly evolved sense of secularity and kindness

Sheikh Moinuddin Chishti was a great Sufi saint with a large following. While Ulemas and Brahmins looked down upon other people's modes of worship, Sufi and Bhakti saints modified and integrated these modes into a new synthetic stream. They respected other people's spiritual practices, and kept away from power centers.

Dara Shikoh was a great scholar and he wrote a book called *Majama-ul-Baharayn* (meeting of two great oceans, i.e., Hinduism and Islam). Dara Shikoh is widely renowned as an enlightened paragon of the harmonious coexistence of heterodox traditions on the Indian subcontinent. He was a champion of mystical religious speculation and a poetic diviner of syncretic cultural interaction among people of all faiths. This made him a heretic in the eyes of his orthodox brother, and a suspect eccentric in the view of many of the worldly power brokers swarming around the Mughal throne. He was also a patron of fine arts, music and dancing, a trait frowned upon by his sibling Aurangzeb. The 'Dara Shikoh album' is a collection of paintings and calligraphy assembled from the 1630s until his death[4].

Hava Mahal at Jaipur is a mix of Hindu and Mughal architecture. Many Muslims celebrated Diwali and Holi and Hindus participated in Id and Moharrum, *Phoolwalon ki Sair* was one Delhi festival in which Hindus and Muslims participated alike.

During the reign of Akbar Shah, Bahadur Shah Zafar's younger brother, **Mirza Jahangir**, once happened to insult the British Resident Sir Archibald Seton[5]. The Resident had the prince arrested and sent to Allahabad. It was feared that Mirza Jahangir might not come back alive. His mother, Nawab Mumtaz Mahal prayed at the *Dargah* of Khwaja Qutubuddin Bakhteyar Kaki, that if her son got released she would offer a *chaparkhat* (bed of flowers) to the tomb. A few days later Seton himself issued order to free the prince. When Badshah Begum, Mumtaz Mahal went to present her offerings at the Dargah, almost all Hindus and Muslims participated in the procession. Since then it was decided that every year Muslim should offer a *pankha* at the Dargah and, to the Hindus too at the *Jog Maya Mandir*. Thus, both Hindus and Muslims participated in the two ceremonies with great enthusiasm.

Let us examine some facts from the field of literature.

Malik Mohammad Jaysi was a great poet of Avadhi and wrote the classic *Padmavat*. Jaysi was a poet who wrote in the Awadhi dialect. He hailed from Jais, presently in the Rae Barely District in U.P. His most famous work is *Padmavat* (1540), a poem describing the story of the historic siege of Chittor by Allaudin Khilji, who attacked Chittor in 1303, after hearing of the beauty of Queen Rani Padmavati[6].

Abdur Rahim Khan-e-Khana was a Hindi poet was in the court of Akbar. In one of his poems Rahim says, 'I have transformed my soul into a bird (*chako*r) who keeps looking at Lord Krishna out of devotion. In this world we should meet all the people with love, you never know in whose form you we come across *Narayan* (God).' A Muslim by birth, Rahim was also a devotee of Lord Krishna and wrote poetry dedicated to him. Abdul Rahim was known for his strange manner of giving alms to the poor. He never looked at the person he was giving alms to, keeping his gaze downwards in all humility. When **Tulsidas** heard about Rahim's behaviour when giving alms, he promptly wrote a couplet and sent it to Rahim, as such:[1]

"Why give alms like this? Where did you learn that? Your hands are as high as your eyes are low"

Realizing that Tulsidas was well aware of the reasons behind his actions, and was merely giving him an opportunity to say a few lines in reply, he wrote to Tulsidas saying:-

"The Giver is someone else, giving day and night. But the world gives me the credit, so I lower my eyes."

Ras Khan made great contributions to Hindi poetry and wrote songs in praise of Lord Krishna. Ras khan was a poet who was both a Muslim and a follower of Lord Krishna. His real name was Sayyad Ibrahim and is known to have lived in Amroha in India. Ras khan was his pen name. In his early years, he became a follower of Lord Krishna and learned the religion from Goswami Vitthalnath, and began living in *Vrindavan* and spent his whole life there. According to him lord Krishna was the most powerful and the greatest. Sadly, he died in 1628 A.D. His *Samadhi* is at Mahavan, which is situated about six miles east of Mathura. Ras khan spoke both Hindi and Persian languages; he translated "*Bhagwata Purana*" into Persian. It is a very peaceful place. Many Krishna devotees come there to pay their respects and meditate here. The poetry of Ras khan focuses on various "*Lilas*" of Lord Krishna, such as *Bal Lila*, *Chir Haran Lila*, *Kunj Lila*, *Ras Lila*, *Panghat Lila*, and *Dan Lila.* These were his favorite subjects. Apart from Lilas, Ras khan has also created poems on Lord Shankar, Goddess Ganga, and the Holi Festival.

Mazhar Jan-i-Jana was a renowned poet of Delhi, distinguished as one the "four pillars of Urdu poetry. He said that the Vedas were the revealed book of God, and Ram and Krishna must have been prophets of God.

Ramanand founded the Bhakti movement, propounded devotion to Ram and threw open the doors of his circle to all low-caste men and women and also to Muslims. His ideas also influenced the founding of Sikhism in 15th century, and his verse and he are mentioned in the Sikh scripture *Adi Granth*.

Tulsidas was an ardent Ram bhakta, in fact the greatest Ram bhakta of all the times. He wrote his literature not in Sanskrit but in popular Awadhi language, so that it could be accessible to all the people. He is said to have lived in Ajodhya in a Mosque.

In the city of Allahabad, two instances of syncretistic phenomena would not be out of place to refer here. First, it is the assembly of 'Yesu Durbar." Every Sunday, one can see the poor and gullible tribal and non-tribal men and women of varying sects and communities, coming on foot, or by horse cart, or tractor, or bus, or by train, and heading towards a ground near Naini. In one corner of the ground, a stage would be set, where devotional songs relating to Christianity are played by audio system. After the ground gets full of audience, a man, who is no less qualified than a Vice Chancellor of a Deemed University, appears in a priest's uniform, and starts blessing the crowed. And the crowed believes that all their miseries would be cured by the blessings of the priest; because it not the priest but the Lord Jesus himself has blessed them through the learned man.

Secondly, at Sohbatiabagh Mohalla of the city of Allahabad, right along the G.T. Road, there is a *Dargah*, called *Gazi Miya Ka Dargah*. Every Thursday morning, hundreds and thousands of people, men and women from all sects (Hindu women being more in number) flock to the Dargah to seek blessings for the cure of their miseries.

From the above instances, it is clear to conclude that it is a myth to say that Hindus and Muslims keep themselves aloof from each other, and are always hostile to each other. The fact is contrary to the truth. It is true that the elites of both the communities for their vested interests look down upon other communities and other religions. But the poor of both the communities flock to the holy seers irrespective of their caste, creed, and religion

Notes

1. *Rizvi, Saiyid Athar Abbas (1983). A History of Sufism in India. New Delhi: Munshiram Manoharlal.*
2. Anand, Balwant Singh. *(1975),* Baba *Farid: Makers of Indian literature*, New Delhi.
3. Chopra, R. M. (1999) Great Sufi Poets of The Punjab", New Delhi.
4. Sarkar, Jadunath (1984). *A History of Jaipur*. New Delhi: Orient Longman.
5. Husain, MS (2006) *Bahadur Shah Zafar; And the War of 1857 in Delhi*, Aakar Books, Delhi.
6. https://en.wikipedia.org/wiki/Abdul_Rahim_Khan-I-Khana.
7. http://www.outlookindia.com/article/ras-khan-a-medieval-krishnaite-sufi/215243

22

Syncretism- A Religious Harmony in India

— *Srija Mandal*

India is incredible for its biological and cultural diversity. It is the natural resources that attracted to many streams of people at different times, from different directions; bringing together a great diversity of human genes and human cultures. Thus the bulk of the Indian population represents cultural admixture in varying degrees. Unlike several other lands where the dominant human cultures have tended to absorb or eliminate others, in India the tendency has been to nurture diversity, which has been favoured by the diversity of the country's ecological regimes [Gadgil and Guha 1992]. An important source of diversity among the people of India is the cultural identity of particular communities and regions. Despite maintaining distinct identities several jatis, sects, and communities have organic links with other segments of the population of the region, which develops a cultural identity over time.

The purpose of this paper is to understand such dynamics of the social and the religious self through the process of 'syncretisation'. In doing so, the paper has been divided into two major sections. Part I revolves around religion in everyday life practices and delineates the concepts of syncretism. This section examines a wide gamut of scholarly writing that has been produced to explain the significance of the concept of syncretism. Part II deals with ritual practices, literary and cultural traditions and the significance of religious places that validate the syncretistic nature of religious traditions across all societies. This section essentially draws from instances of rituals relating to everyday well-being, agricultural cycles, fertility cults and traditional cures. The idea is to visit religious syncretism in all its various manifestations in human lifestyle and coexistence patterns.

Part I - Understanding Concepts

To understand relevant concept and the way they might have been shaped, one needs to go through perspectives that have been developed by scholars who have been involved in long term research through experiences gathered from people and their contexts. The key concepts that have been dealt with here is syncretism.

In its most common form in the study of South Asian cultures, 'syncretism' denotes the combination or alliance of opposing religious or philosophical doctrines, often with political undertones, that results in public and private rituals and commonly accepted local practices which appear to the observer to link orientations that are normally disparate, if not disjunctive (Claus and Margaret 2003).

The Ancient Greek prefix 'syn' means 'with' and the word 'krasis' means 'mixture'. Thus, the term "synkrasis" meant 'a mixture or compound'. The history of the usage of syncretism goes back a long way to the times of Plutarch (AD 45-125). Plutarch used a political meaning of the term in an essay titled "On Brotherly Love"(*Peri* P*hiladelphias*), which appeared as a chapter in his Moralia. In searching for the origin of the word "syncretism", Plutarch claimed to have found an example of syncretism in the Cretans, who reconciled their differences and came together in an alliance whenever they were faced with an external threat. He labeled this coming together as "their so called 'syncretism'". For Plutarch, syncretism was not only a testament to political expediency but also fostered peace and brotherly love. For explaining syncretism within the framework of permeability of religious phenomena, Eliade (1987) retains that no definition of syncretism is possible without a specific context and that the term cannot serve as an adequate description of homogeneous sets of phenomena.

The Dictionary of Sociology [Fairchild 1944 cited in Roy Burman 1993: 70] defines syncretism as, "The process of amalgamation of conflicting, or at least different, parties or principles of cultures - more specifically assimilation of foreign groups. The foreign elements disappear as psychological and cultural entities into the majority, and the majority adopts both the individual and a selection and adoption of their cultural traits". Generally speaking, syncretism has been associated with folk religion with reference to practices of primitive societies only and Wuthnow [1988 cited in Roy Burman 1993: 70] states that, "These kind of beliefs and practices also suggest some clues about the relations between popular religion and social environment. Popular religion has been most evident in relatively non-modern societies".

Syncretism essentially focuses on the permeability and fluidity of religious situations. It has been rightly said by Peter van der Veer (1994: 208) that "This can be seen as such a broad process that indeed every religion is syncretistic, since it constantly draws upon heterogeneous elements to the extent that it is often impossible for the historian to unravel what comes from where". This is where Eliade (1987) says that a social presupposition for the rise of syncretism can be the co-existence of various groups.

The co-existence of various groups in society can never be devoid of power dimensions and this readily gets reflected in the different forms of syncretism as explained by Roy Burman (1993). He has classified syncretism into five categories based on the political situation under which it operates: (a) Defensive syncretism that relates to two or more ethnic entities when threatened by an external power; (b) Aggressive syncretism emerges when two or more ethnic groups come together as a strategy of social mobilisation to attain political control over an alien territory or group; (c) Recessive syncretism involves a process of borrowing religious traits by one or more ethnic groups from the external oppressive power so as to mobilise people to overthrow the oppressor; (d) Adaptive syncretism occurs when minority groups and majority groups coexist without any political subjugation or clashes and in fact the minority groups borrow some of the majority religious faiths; (e) Pragmatic syncretism involves a multi-ethnic situation where two or more equally powerful groups share political power and consciously or otherwise syncretise their religions in a selective manner.

Veer suggests that "syncretism in India is a trope in the discourse of 'multiculturalism"' and that scholarly discussion of "syncretic" phenomena such as Hindu worship of Sufi saints usually omits consideration of conflict or of the processes of expansion and contraction of religious communities.

Part II - Syncretism as Lived Experience

I realised that we do not make efforts to mark out the syncretic elements of our society since it is very much present in our consciousness and are an integral part of our lives and seem quite natural and obvious. What made me sit up and look at this 'obvious' phenomenon is the description of a ritual that takes place in the *Shiva* temple of Tarakeshwar, which is one of the most important pilgrimage for Hindus in West Bengal. Roy Burman (1999: 46-47) narrates:

> The *Charak* puja is an annual feature of the shrine when thousands of devotees from all over the state assemble there. During the puja, the first *'niler bati'*-lamp for *Nil* puja is kindled in the name of the Muslims. Both the Hindus and the Muslims pour milk on the *'Shivalinga'*. Interestingly at the *Brahmanpara* (hamlet of the Brahmins) there are two pir shrines-those of *Bare pir* and *Chhote pir* (elder and younger pir respectively). On every Tuesday and Saturday in the Bengali month of'*Baisakh*, the Hindu villagers offer fruits at the shrines and they take a collective lunch at the shrine of the *Bare pir*. These pirs are incidentally

known locally as *Tarak Baba's pirs*. Apart from these the Hindus also offer the milk of a milching cow after 21 days of its delivery of the calf. These apart there is also an interesting myth which is popular in the area and is associated with a Muslim devotee to the shrine ofTarakeshwar. It is believed that long back when a Muslim devotee carrying milk as offering was refused entry into the temple by the attendants, he was confronted by Baba disguised in the form of an old man under a tree. After hearing his woes Baba accepted his bowl of milk and miraculously the attendant found it lying within the precincts of the temple which was locked at night. It is also commonly known that many Muslims of Ramnagar and adjoining villages occasionally visit Tarakeshwar temple for asking boons. Often young Muslim boys too join their Hindu friends carrying pots from far-flung places of their residence on foot.

This is an instance among numerous that bear testimony to the patterns of coexistence that are found across the world. In fact syncretic traditions can be classified according to their significance with regards to various rituals among religious communities. Sila Khan (1997:21-22) proposes an interesting classification of these phenomena of interactions between communities through worship of deities and saints:

- Divine power or charisma (*Sakti* in the Hindu tradition, *barakat* in the Islamic one) may attract devotees regardless of their origin, around a particular religious figure. For example the worship of a Sufi saint like *Muinuddin Chishti* by Hindus and the cult of a goddess perfonned by Muslims, with the hope of securing a boon.
- There is in some situations a tendency to cling to one's former beliefs. For instance, some Muslims continue to worship a Hindu deity as they did before their conversion while 'delslamized' Hindus (a much lesser known phenomenon) still perform a cull at the dargah of the *Pir* who converted them.
- All over the subcontinent a number of Muslim saints are still regarded as the guardians and protectors of a Hindu or Jain shrine. For example, Sila Khan cites the following instances from different parts of India: *Vavar* is the guardian-deity or the god *Ayyappa* at the shrine of *Sabarimalai* in Kerala, some Draupadi temples of Tamil Nadu are protected by Muttal Ravuttan, *Bar Shah* is worshipped at *Saundatti* (Kamataka) near the shrine of the Goddess, *Angar Shah* at the entrance of the Jain sacred complex of *Shatrunjaya*, near Palitana in Gujarat. In all these cases the Hindu devotees generally bow before the Muslim saint before making their offerings to the deity, whereas Muslims occasionally come to revere the god or goddess at the site.
- The last phenomenon described in the above classification would include the so called 'syncretistic cults', i.e. where Hindu and Muslim

elements seem to co-exist within one single tradition and where the saints have a dual identity. Sila Khan illustrates this phenomenon through practices recorded by scholars in different places. For example, the legend of *Satya Pir* in Bengal recorded by Roy (1983: 214-17) and the celebrated cult of the *Panch Pir* (ibid. 213-15), the *Imamshahi sect* (Ivanow 1938: 19-70) or *Ramdev Pir* [Sila Khan 1997].

Based on this classification, syncretic traditions can be described under deities that are propitiated for physical well-being through votive offerings and thus include border deities who are worshipped for protection from evil; cults related to agricultural cycles; and sacred spaces like Sufi shrines that are the most popular symbols of Hindu-Muslim syncretism in India. Another most significant contribution to such processes has emerged through cultural interaction between communities in the realm of literature, arts, music etc. Such interactions are certainly not restricted to Hindu and Muslim communities in India. Such practices abound all over the world and among innumerable groups that live together.

Well-being and Votive Offerings

Human actions tend to be guided by their beliefs and vice versa. This occurs especially when we faced with everyday problems of diseases, injuries and other crises related to physical, social or economic well-being. Speaking particularly about Hindu religion, self-maximizing aspect in the form of seeking out gods to solve practical problems of life, involves both Hindus and non-Hindus alike. This makes religious activities a domain in which conventional communal boundaries may be crossed. It is therefore a key zone in which social interaction and mutual understanding may occur across communities. Examples from the state of West Bengal in India abound in such syncretic practices.

Syncretic elements are most prominent in the villages of Sunderban where the vagaries of nature take a heavy toll over the lives of the people in the form of getting killed by wild animals while going into the dense forests to collect honey etc. The local ecological factors forced them to adopt the local or folk cultural behaviours in order to maintain livelihood, which ultimately led to the process of religious synthesis as well as syncretism. However, there have been a differential rate of the degree of acceptence in different societies, if observed individually, but the uniqueness of this mythical spread is that lies at the cognitive dimension of the people [Bera, Mukhopadhyay and Sarkar, 2010].

The religious factors at Sunderban centering around *Bon Bibi- Dakshinrai- Gaji Shaheb -Na*i *bibi* and others make cohesive agent between caste, creed and religious sect. At villages like Gobindokati, both Muslims and Hindus assemble at the shrine of *Ghazi Shaheb* during *Ghazi mela* and worship both *Ghazi Shaheb* and *Bon Bibi* at a shrine. Hindu priests and Muslim *maulana* (Muslim priest) both propitiate the deities and conduct the ritual where boons are asked for [Roy Burman 1999].

In the districts of North Bengal, often Hindu and Muslim boatmen are found to perform*'Ganga puja'* (worshipping river Ganga). This again is a manifestation of the unity of human efforts to control the fury of nature. In a village called *Majhergram* in Burdwan district of West Bengal, the *Manasatala* (shrine of the snake goddess), for Hindus is also the *pirerthan* (seat of the pir) for the Muslims. Women from both communities worship at the shrine to ward off small pox from the village.

Another instance on syncretistic traditions in Bengal is the pirification of a tree-spirit. In the village of *Girisgangasagar* in the Medinipur district, a banyan tree was held sacred as the supposed abode of *Nekursanipir*. As it was situated on the way to the local court of justice, both Hindu and Muslim litigants resorted to it in the belief that the *pir* would favour their law-suits. Votive offerings to the pir consisted of pieces of red rags tied to the branch or clay horses kept at the bottom of the tree. Such examples reflect a highly pragmatic approach to religion, which comes as a ready recourse in times of emergency and such pragmatism clearly cuts across dogmatic religious identities.

Cults related to Fertility and Agricultural Cycles

Another area where syncretic elements have been found to exist in abundance in India is related to agriculture. Food has certainly been the fundamental basis of human existence since the beginning of the human society. Along with this necessity came the human capabilities to negotiate with nature and the cosmos with regard to hunting, gathering and consumption of food. This inevitability also led to ways of appeasing spirits and other natural beings so as to retain the balance between humans and the universe for a harmonious coexistence. Most of such elements are reflected through agricultural rites. For instance, at some places like *Anushkura* village in Kolhapur district of Maharashtra, India, the Hindu and Muslim peasants celebrate the pre-sowing and post-harvest ceremony around a sacred grove placed within the agricultural fields.

Roy (1983) describes one of the syncretic fertility rites of Bengal in India. Bengali Muslims made pirs of local non-Muslim gods and in many of the district, Manai-pirs appeared as the pirified Hindu god, *Kartik*, and the rites and fertility beliefs pertaining to his adoration were almost identical with those of local *Kartik* celebrations (*Kartik-vrata).* Unmarried women propitiated the pir for good husbands and married women worshipped him felr pregnancy. On the day of *Manai pir's shirni*, the women sang about the *pir* and the ceremony was concluded by the village *mullah* reading out the *sura fatiha* from the Quran.

Sacred Spaces

It is argued that Sufi shrines have long been one of the arenas in India where Hindus interact with Muslims religiously depicting pattems of intercommunal cooperation toward the worship of local saints and deities. The shrines will continue to remain decisive meeting points of religious communities in the Indian landscape. These shrines determine the importance of sacred spaces as well as religious syncretism and continue to be centres of interactions in the realm of the lived religious experiences of people.

The *dargah* of Khwaja Muinuddin Chishti situated in Ajmer district of Rajasthan in India, is probably one of the most famous shrines venerated by people from all communities. Illustrating the immensely syncretic appeal of Ajmer and looking upon it as a paradigm for the South Asian city, Mayaram (2005) writes that Ajmer-Merwara, as it was called in the colonial period, is a terrain that is highly meaningful for a plurality of religious sects. It houses Pushkar, which has the only *Brahma* temple in the country and is one of the 'centres' of the Hindu sacred world. The pilgrimage also witnesses one of the largest animal fairs. The United Presbyterian mission at Beawar was the first Christian Mission to be established in Rajputana and controlled operations in western and central India from Ajmer. The city also presently has the only Parsi (Zoroastrian) temple in Rajasthan, three Sikh *gurudwaras* and Pushkar also has an all-India centre of the *Saivite-Sakta Nath* ascetics. Ajmer also has Jain and Buddhist (and before Independence, Jewish) populations. It is a seat of the plurality of god and goddess cults and ancestor shrines, the *Ramdev* cult of the Dalit and erstwhile untouchable castes as also Hindu and Islamic tantrik practices.

All such practices establish the space that is invaded by people from different communities who continue to celebrate the essence of living together till eternity.

Discussion

In this paper an attempt is made to comprehend the syncretistic religious and cultural traditions of India. Syncretism refers to the synthesis of different religious forms.In Indian context religious syncretism has had a positive implication as a foundation and form of resistance to cultural dominance. The case studies show how religious ideas and rituals mediate between diverse ethnic communities, religious communities, sects, and cultural regions and give rise to a complex unity. The complex cultural unity of India is built up through protracted inter-relationship of the diverse cultural traditions, both literate and pre-literate.

Syncretism comes across as a process that is ongoing and very much a part of all religious traditions. It is, as Veer (1994) says, an aspect of religious interaction over time. Every religious tradition goes through certain adaptations and accommodations; it originates, takes root and develops through exchanges of belief systems over a period of history and while moving from one region to the other. It needs to be driven home that despite efforts at homogenizing religious beliefs, what has sustained is the syncretic appeal of religious experiences that bring people of different faiths together in a celebration of their mass consciousness that surpasses non-native dogmas usually laid down in scriptural texts or orthodox directives. One feels closer to the spirituality of the divine and seeks comfort in what Rabindranath Tagore calls the religion of man.

References

Bera, Gautam Kumar, Asok Kumar Mukhopadhyay & Amitava Sarkar. (2010). *'Syncretism at Sunderbans:Anthropological and Linguistic Dimensions'*. New Delhi:Mittal Publications.

Claus, Peter., and Margaret A. Mills, eds. (2003). South Asian Folklore: An Encyclopedia. Garland Publishing, Inc.

Gadgil, M. and Guha, R. (1992). *'This Fissured Land: An Ecological History of India'*. London: Oxford University Press.

Mayaram, Shail. (1997). "Rethinking Meo Identity: Cultural Faultline, Syncretism, Hybridity or Liminality?" in Comparative Studies of South Asia, Africa and the Middle East, Vol. XVII No 2.

Roy Burman, J.J. (1999).*'Hindu-Muslim Syncretic Trends in West Bengal'*. Indian Journal of Secularism, VoL3, No.1, April-June.

Veer, Peter Van der. (1994). "*Syncretism, Multiculturalism and the Discourse of Tolerance*," in Syncretism/Anti-Syncretism: The Politics of Religious Synthesis, eds. Charles Stewart and Rosalind Shaw London: Routledge.

23

Syncretic Cultural Practices among the Halam of Tripura

– *Shajymon M.L,*
Gautam Kumar Bera

I. Introduction

Tripura is one of the North Eastern states of India having rich traditions of as many as 19 tribes and non tribal people as well. The non-tribal people are basically Bengalese, Assamese and Nepalese. The population of Tripura is blessed with a unique social scenario and multifaceted expressions of religious, social, cultural and linguistic blends. It is a land of forest and envious natural resources. The flora and fauna of the state is conducive for human habitation, agriculture, Rubber Plantations and blessed with natural wealth such as Natural Gas. Rice is one of the major crops of the state.

The Geographical area of Tripura is 10,491.69sq.km. The total population according to 2011 Population Census data is 36,71,032. This population is spread through 8 districts such as West-Tripura, Sepahijala, Khowai, South Tripura, Gomati, North Tripura, Unakoti and Dalai. It has one Tribal Autonomous District Council, 23 -subdivisions, 45 blocks, 32 Revenue circles, 187 Tehsils, 886 Revenue Moujas, 64-Police stations, Three member of Parliaments including 1(one) Rajya Sabha, 60 Members of Legislative Assembly and 30 Members for Tripura Tribal Autonomous District Council including 2 nominated members. (***Tripura at a Glance, 2011-12, 28th Issue, Directorate of Economics & Statistics, Planning (Statistics) Department, Government of Tripura, Agartala.***

One of the major tribes of Tripura is **Halam** and there are as many as 11 sub-groups/clans in this community. According to the Census of India 2001 the Halam population is 47,245 and is in the fifth position in terms of number according to published by the Tripura Directorate of Census Operation, Tripura. District census hand Book of 1951. Tripura. Bibarani of 1031. Tripura. Samendra Chandra Deb Barman. (***Tripura Tribe: A status analysis. Manoshi Das, jayanta Choudhury, Rebati Tripura,Published by Tripura Tribal Research and Cultural Institute. November 2011. Print Best, Colonel Chowmuhani, Agartala.)***

The population has risen to 53,549 in 2008. According to a field study/ survey conducted by the Tribal research and cultural institute, government of Tripura in 2008 records that Halams were followers of only two religions such as Hinduism and Christianity. 52% are Hindus and 48% are Christians. **(Das & Choudhury, 2011).** It show that Erstwhile immigration during the sovereign and democratic period to this state and the influence of Christian Missionaries, the Halam community welcomed and embraced different cultures and religions without losing some of its value system, traditions and practices. The strong sense of their affinity to a common culture and their rootedness enhanced them to maintain status quo in a few areas in spite of external influence and inspiration.

The Indian society in general and tribal society of the nineteenth century in particular confronted socio-economic and political challenges. The value of traditions and customs were also undergoing radical revision and transformation during that period (Bera & Jose, 2010). The tribal community in Tripura were also very much a part of this phenomenon. However there are many aspects which are an integral part of any community irrespective of tribe, non-tribe, caste and creed. Therefore it is inspiring and knowledgeable to make an attempt to identify and portray such common elements sustained and nurtured by the respective communities in spite of all external forces or enticing influences.

The endeavour over here is to identify such syncretic cultural practices among the Halam of Tripura; in other words an attempt to elucidate the commonality among the different groups of **Halam** practicing different religions. Religions as we know, certainly give a unique and universal identity and different social status to its adherents. However it is significant to admit that in spite of the attractions of the new or foreign/local religions and cultures and their influence, there are a few sociological and anthropological elements which are unique and equally powerful in terms of identity and commonality considered with esteem by the **Halam** community of Tripura.

II. Meaning of Halam, Origin and Location in the State of Tripura

It is important to observe that there is not enough literature regarding the origin etymological root, meaning and development of the word Halam. However an attempt to get some light in this situation has got some result.

According to Dr. Bera, a leading anthropologist, the meaning of Halam is **'Killer of the Humans'**. It shows that there are different legends regarding the name and origin but not many are written down therefore it is not available for reference. According to this they had been reputed for Killing Strangers. This was labelled to them by the neighbours. During the erstwhile princely state they were recruited in large numbers in the army of the King. They were basically ***Jhum*** cultivators and they roamed around for this purpose from one hillock to the next in search of suitable land for ***Jhum*** cultivation (Bera & Bera, 2009).

Another Legend found by researchers is that Halams migrated to Tripura from Khurpuitabhum, belonged to the Hill region of North Manipur. The meaning of the place is **'*Khur ' means'* source', *' Pui' means'* river'** ***and ' ta ' means'*** **from'**. This interpretation is according to the language of the Kukis. The scholars believe that they would have preferred to stay near the river side for practical and agricultural reason. A dispute occurred between the Tripuri and Manipuri over the possession of a village Thanghum situated to the west of **Surma** and Barak. According to some scholars, this village was the original home of the Halams. The river **'PUI'** by which they would have lived is **SURMA. (Tribal Research and Cultural Institute, Govt. of Tripura, 2010).** We hardly come across more literature regarding historical, etymological and demographic legacy of Halam than what is presented here.

The Halam community is spread in eight districts in Tripura; however maximum concentration is in the south Tripura Districts. They speak the HALAM language. These days they speak the state language Bengali, for all domestic and administrative matters. This is the common medium of instruction in almost all Government schools across the state. This has made them bi-lingual. This has helped and enhanced the net work of relationships with non-tribal population and by getting into the government service sector, entry to the urban area and to the mainstream society. Thus it has enhanced greater socialisation and social mobility which strengthened their financial or economic profile.

III. Halam and their Sub-groups/Clans

Traditionally believed or opined is that the umbrella term Halam consisted of 12 groups or clans. However different scholars have different presentations of the sub groups regarding their title and the numbers. I would like present three opinions with regards to this number twelve. According to Das and Choudhury (2011). The following are the names and the number of sub-groups.

1. Ranglong/Langlong,
2. Molsom
3. Kaipeng
4. Koloi
5. Korbonng-Only Teliamura Area Of West Tripura
6. Hrangkhawl
7. Bongcher
8. Rupini
9. Chorei
10. Lankai
11. Bong
12. Sak-Achep- In Kamalpur- Dhalai District-

According to **Bera and Bera** there are 12 sub-tribes such as 1. Boncher, 2. Charai, 3. Hrangkhol, 4. Kaipeng, 5. Kaljang, 6. Kalai, 7. Lankai, 8. Machaphang, 9. Migli, 10. Mitahar, 11. Molsom and the 12th Rupini. (Bera & Bera.2009)

The record of the finding of the **Tribal Research & Cultural Institute, Govt. of Tripura**, divide Halams into 12 clans, but later the number of their branches rose to 16. They are: 1. Kalai, 2. Kulu, 3. Korbong, 4. Kaipang 5. Kaireng. 6. Chadai 7. Dab. 8. Sakachef. 9. Thangachep 10. Nabeen 11. Bongsher. 12. Morchhum, 13. Rangkhwl 14. Rupini 15. Langai 16. Lanlung. (2010).

IV. Religious Groups and their Population in General

According to the record of the finding of the Tribal Research & Cultural Institute , Govt. of Tripura, Halam were the followers of only two religions. They are Christians and Hindus. The percentage of each religion is almost equal i.e. Hindus 52% and Christians 48%. The attraction towards Christianity was due to the various facilities provided by the Christian Missionaries. The Christian community has different sub-groups such as Catholics, Presbyterians, Baptists, Believers' Church, KCC- Kuki Christian Church, EAC-Evangelical Assembly Church, EFCI: Evangelical Fundamental Church of India among the Halams of Tripura. These communities are currently active among the Halam community. They have their regular worship and spiritual activities especially on Sundays and other auspicious days. (Das & Choudhury, 2011).

IV. Normal Cultural Practices and Commonality among Different Groups Practicing Different Religions

IV.a. Language - Halam

The ***Halam language*** is a very powerful and vital agent of keeping alive the culture, tradition and unity among the Halams. The common nomenclature of Kuki-Halam is called ***RIAM-CHONG*** The Halam language is spoken by all, meaning the different clans of the community/tribe with slight nuances here and there in their colloquial expressions. Generally every clan of the Halam community speak the same language and now a days they are bi-lingual. For education and for the service sector Bengali is essential. The people of this tribe are open to such situations and there is a growing affinity or passion seen for English especially in the educational institutions. During their interactions in the villages, they still prefer to communicate in the Halam language.

IV.b. Dress/Cultural Dress

The following are the common traditional dress of the Halam community. The name and type of garments they make and use continue to be the same. It is continued with much loyalty and passion. It is a matter of sustaining and bequeathing great identity, tradition and affinity to their culture in a tangible and empirical way. In spite of the exposure and influence of modern culture and the development of 21st century, this type of traditional dress pattern has not lost momentum. It is a great surprise to see some of these traditional manifestations of culture valued and maintained with esteem.

Riam Kultai and Puantsen (Shirt- Dhoti for men)

Khemachi Kulthai- Upper cloth for women -

Nikni/Puanbom- (Down cloth) and ***Risa***- Breast Cover

Khamsa / Lukom. (Head Gear: Women and Men)The ***Unakoti*** sculpture is symbol of Halam Kuki tradition in Unakoti-District of Tripura. Unakoti is one of the most attractive tourist places of Tripura.

Borki is the traditional Blanket and this blanket is very big as well as very heavy.

MULRI is also a Traditional Blanket: - very big- heavy, very expensive used for winter season. It is very difficult to weave, is hand weaved and the average price is above 5000/-.

Kongkhit., Puante' for women to tie around the waist (Light blanket/ cloth for women)

Jani:- light Blanket for men

IV.c. Food

Halam are basically non-vegetarians. They are dependent on nature and whatever herbs, animals, birds, vegetable, etc is available in the jungle/forest or in the vicinity of their habitation is consumed for food. They are basically rice eaters. They do use a lot of dry fish and fermented fish in their delicacies. The following are some of the food items and their nomenclature in their Halam language.

Main Rice dish in Halam language is called ***Bu.***

Side-dish: *Mach-ial* is made with **dry fish** mashed with any of the following vegetables such as Pumpkin, Ash gourd, Brinjal, Bitter guard, Snake guard, Tapioca, Potato, Chilli, or Garlic

Majuar: A particular leaf of a big tree in the Jungle known for its fragrance and used as Curry leaves.

Chang-al= A dish with dry fish with sodium water-

They eat almost all types of meat; however the following are commonly used due to their availability.

1. ***Sele-sechang*** - Sieal / Yak-/ Jungle buffalo / cow
2. ***Vokme***: Pork
3. ***Kel / Bera-te: -*** Goat/Mutton/Sheep
4. ***Ar-me*** (Chicken- Cock and Hen)
5. ***Pharvali-me*** (pigeon)- Kaboothar
6. ***Kang-dal*** (Frog)- Big-size
7. ***Vasu***: (Dove)-
8. ***Arrati/arrtui*** (eggs: Chicken and ducks)

IV.d. Common Tune

The following words are used as a tone during Jhum Cultivation by both men & women.

Hoi-Ha. This particular Tune is used during the Jhum Cultivation as well as harvest time. Sometimes some tunes are used to alert people in times of danger as well as when help is sought. But there is a variation in the tune according to the situation and gravity of the situations.

Naite- an-in-la / Vai-eng Uai-na-La : It is the name of the song in their language sung to make children sleep:

These are two basic and common traditional practices used by all. However, due to the influence of modernity some of these systems and tunes gave way to modern devices. Traditional villages and senior people are very much part of these practices.

IV. e. Customary Law/Traditional Social Judicial System

When an accidental murder or unintentional murder happens the following system is followed. Intentional murderers were punished by killing them on the cross. This is known as BOLPHORA PHUN / ON THE CROSS in Halam Language. The accused will be tied with a chain to the cross and will be pierced till death. This practice has stopped since the Independence of India.

There is another interesting legal procedure among the Halam community that prevailed earlier. For those above 15 years the following system was maintained. If the court found no other witness for the incident, then the court would make the accuser and the accused to remain under deep water and the one who resisted more would be set free. The other one either died in the water or lost in the prosecution. There was no difference between man or woman in this situation. This is no more practiced these days. It is said that this gave way under Christian influence and values.

I. Khun Rui/Mithat Lei (Murder Case)

If someone is murdered by mistake or by intention a normal penalty is levied upon admitting the mistake. The penalty amounts to Rs.1201/-. This amount is distributed among the following with the amount against it.

(a) KHO SA'K/The villagers of the victim: Rs 200-(**"Sa'k"** means revenue or income)

(b) HALAMASA SA'K/Head of the Halam Community: Rs. 30

(c) SRIZUOR SA'K /Assistant Head of the Halam community. It could be a male or female: Rs. 10/-

(d) KALIM SA'K(/Head man of the village of the victim: Rs.15/-

(e) BING SA'K/ Family of the victim: Rs.10/-

(f) MUKTIAR LE SUKTIAR SA'K/ Head Lawyer and Assistant Lawyer of the village of the victim: Rs.10/-

(g) MITRATHI HUINA/(Removal of tears of the family of the victim) The life partner of the victim or parents of the victim or immediate beneficiary. Rs.15/-

The balance amount of Rs. 911/- will be given to the family of the victims.

II. Mi Nu Anpotna Lei/Taking Away Someone's Wife

The following amount is a fine imposed on the person who took away the wife of someone. The amount is Rs.1010/-. This amount is distributed the following manner.

(a) KHO SA'K = 200/-

(b) HALAMASA SA'K =Rs. 10/-

(c) PANCHI THEIPHANG SA' K /For the removal of humiliation of the husband of the woman taken away. = Rs. 15/-

(d) PALAI SA'K (MESANGER OF THE COURT) = Rs. 20/-

(e) SEMUR HIPNA / To mask the humiliation of the man whose wife is taken away Rs. 15/-

(f) KALIM SA'K ......Rs. 5/- (see the earlier explanation)

(g) MUKTIAR LE SUKTIAR SA'K/ Head Lawyer and Assistant Lawyer of the village of the victim: Rs. 10/-

The balance amount of Rs. 735/- will be given to family of the victim.

III. Zuor Maruk Rui/Elopping = Rs. 1000/-

(a) KHO SA'K = Rs. 200/-

(b) PALAI SA'K = Rs. 20/-

The balance Rs. 781/- will be given to the family of the girl by the boy.

IV. Mi Nu Machai Lei (Adultry)

A fine of Rs. 500/- is levied upon the accused.

(a) KHO SA'K = Rs. 100/-

(b) PALAI SA'K = Rs. 20/-

The balance Rs. 380 will be given to the wife of the accused/ husband who had the illicit affair with another's wife.

V. Anru Lei (Stealing/Theft of Materials) Rs. 150/-

(a) The whole amount or the complete materials should be returned

(b) KHO SA'K = Rs. 50/-(Head of the village)

(c) SATAN MAIMOK- The family of the victim: 75/-

The balance amount of Rs. 25/- also will be given to the family of the victim

VI. An Ze'm A' Ntahat Ko'k Lei/Injury During Fight = Rs. 600/-

KHO SA'K = Rs. 100/-(Head of the village).

The balance amount of Rs. 500/- will be given to the victim who is innocent in this incident.

VII. Ma'ktha Sum/Divorce = Rs. 200/-

KHO SA'K = Rs. 50/-(Head of the village).

The balance amount of Rs. 150/- will be given to the partner of the victim.

VIII. MAN TUON RUI / BRIDE MONEY Rs. 300/- This amount is given by the Bridegroom to the family of the bride.

(a) TANG TE ZO'L LEI / FATHER OF THE BRIDE: 30/-

(b) PUNTE PHA LO / Mother of the Bride: Rs. 7/-

(c) DELTHA / FAMILY OF THE BRIDE = RS. 30/-

(d) ZU -MATKOLAKAHT/ONE POT RICE BEER WILL BE GIVEN TO THE BRIDE BY THE BRIDE GROOM

The rest of the money will go to the family of the bride.

IX. ***Su-sem-sial/Dispute Regarding Wrong Promises to Boys or Men Regarding Consent for Marriage***

A girl is not expected to give consent for marriage for more than one person. In case a woman or young girl fails in this case, there will be confusion and dispute among the boys or men. During the prosecution the judge has to decide upon one of the boys and the girl or girl's father will have to pay a fine of 100.

KHO SA'K = Rs. /-(Village Judges).

The rejected boy will get 70 rupees.

X. Sutmun Anthuina Lei = 60/-

If any one violates the judgement of the court then he or she will be levied a fine of Rs. 60/- . This will be also applicable to any sort of malpractice regarding the formalities/custom/practices of any formal celebration of the village or the Halam tribe.

XI. Kristian Achang Ngai Sutmun Anthui Na Lei. Rs. 30/- Readmission charge from Christianity.

From 18th century the following was practised. If anyone becomes Christian and then later on comes back to the earlier religion then he or she has to pay a fine of Rs. 30 for readmission to the old religion.

XII. Mi In Alut Sara Mi Zem Na Lei - 150/-. Trespassing

If anyone trespasses the area/houses of others and creates trouble and man handles or attacks the family members or owner of the property, the village judges will fine him Rs. 150/- Out of this amount Rs. 30 will go to the village judges and the rest will go to the victim.

XIII. ***Khua Khel Lei*** **= Rs. 200/-**

If anyone wants a change of prosecution place other than the place of the incident then a fine of Rs. 200 needs to be paid to the concerned village judges.

IV.f. Monogamy

Halams basically follow monogamy. They generally prefer to marry from their own clan. They don't choose partners from close relatives. It is neither preferred nor appreciated. Marriage by service is a traditional practice but these days situations occur where marriage is conducted by payment of bride-price. Both these are common and the marriageable age for boys is conventionally understood as 24-28 and 20-22 for girls. The period of voluntary service rendered by the bridegroom in the bride's house is called ***Jamai Utha.*** (Tribal Research & Cultural Institue-2010).

IV.g. Entertainments

1. Besut Ankai

It is game similar to tug of war but is conducted between two persons; either two men or two women, hold on to a round ring shaped bamboo. It looks like the ring that is used to keep the mud pots.

2. Sumtum Andom

This is a game to show one's muscle power. A person who is in a semi-seated position needs to be raised up, raising him up by keeping the hand around the other below the waist level. The one who makes the other straighten in short time will be the winner.

3. Rotuan Anson

It is a game with a long bamboo similar to Tug of War. The long bamboo will be held by two groups of an equal number of persons who push each other back ward> correct??? Or pull each other forward over a boundary>>? by holding the same bamboo. It is a very common game among the Halams.

4. Reisong Anher

It is a game of two persons with an axe with handle. The game is that one person can remove the handle of the axe by twisting while the other will hold the axe. This is also to prove physical power.

5. Kek Andai

It is game with a hard jungle fruit seed collected from a reed- like plant. The name of the fruit seed in Halam is called KEK. It is a group game or a team can composed of more than 10 persons in each team. The seed is thrown at the opposite team placing the seed in different joints of the body, angles and different parts of the body. The seed is like a small round shaped biscuits> and then??? Incomplete

IV. h. Traditional Ornaments

The following main traditional ornaments are still available or used on various occasions. Ornaments are basically connected more with women than with men.

The following are the ornaments used by women:

- **THEISEP/THEIBUANGRI**: Chain around the neck up to the chest made out of the dry fruits of the tree called ***Theibuang Kung.***
- **OLKHIT:** It is also like a chain tightly around the neck thin in size made with the pieces of the *Theibuang Kung* fruit. It is joined with a homemade cotton thread.
- **DANGKARI**: It is a chain made with coins.
- **MOHON MALA:** It is a long chain made of silver
- **KUARBET:** It is an ear loop made of silver.
- **BENCHI:** It is a like a small mike horn>? in the upper part of the ear and made of silver and connected with the lower ear loop with a thin chain.
- **BOMJUY:** It is a ***hair-band*** made of silver or gold or bronze.
- **ZAKSER**: It is a bangle or bracelet long in size starting from wrist to almost close up to the elbow. It is made of silver and used on the leg also.
- **ZAKETAM/LOSI**: It is a ring made of silver/gold/bronze and used by men and women.
- **KUAR BET**: It is an ear ring used by men made of silver, gold, copper or bronze.

IV. i. Traditional Tools And Equipments

The following are the traditional tools used by the Halam tribe

- There are basically three types of Bamboo Baskets. One is called **LONGKHAI** the second is called SENGKONG and the third is SALONG.
- **BAIENG**: it is a basket used to keep the babies like cradle.
- **REL**: It is a bamboo made cylinder shaped basket almost six feet in size to keep the food grains
- **TOBONG**: It is a small round shaped bamboo tray to keep small articles
- **SUMDUK:** It is made up of wooden box to keep any type of precious documents, ornaments, money etc.
- **CHEM** is the knife
- **CHEMTAK** is a flat knife used to cut wood and bamboos

- **CHEMRAZUM** is a instrument used to plough the land for jhum cultivation
- **BAKHEP** is a type of big spade for preparing the soil for cultivation
- **RAI** is the axe.
- **THAL SAILI**: It is the bow and arrow
- **SUMPUK** is the pounding wooden container and the stick is called **SARAL**
- **BUBEL:** is the general name for cooking utensils.
- **SEILUNG** is the wooden stick to grind any spices to make dishes and the container is called **HATA.**
- **BUKOI**: is the wooden or bamboo spoon to mix the rice or gravy.
- **MAKHE**: It is a big spoon to serve the food made with wood or metal.
- **KHUNG** is the drum made of animal skin around a wooden frame.
- **DEGREE** the name of the stick used to beat the drum.

IV. j. Shifting Cultivation/ Jhum

Jhum cultivation is indeed a common characteristic of any tribal community. Likewise the practice of Jhum cultivation is still maintained with great passion among the Halam community. In spite of the exposure or influence of Modern technology as of now the Halam community dearly maintain the practice of Jhum Cultivation and would like maintain as a mark of identity of the Halam community.

IV. k. Myths/Stories

The following epic song bequeathed from generation through oral tradition will give a fresh look at the origin of the name Halam. As of now, there is no written version of it in the following manner. The content of this epic song is the origin of the Halam people, significance of the tribe, as well as the traditional understanding of the forefathers or ancestors of Halam. It will give a rather meaningful understanding of the Halam. As of now, there is hardly any generally accepted and ratified explanation of the meaning, evolution and advent of Halam to Tripura. What is available through oral tradition by a senior epic-lyrist has some historical as well as legendry value. The evolution story is rather popular among the Halam community; however this epic is not known to the new generation. The lyric of the epic is as follows:

1. ***Ooo, Lenpur, na - Zua. Tanchaksa ati, nachun Lengteinu ati, Lengteinu nainei ati, Lenlur ati, Rangvung -ati, Lenpur o khomual o.***

(The Halam and Kuki community originated from the first father named **Tanchaksa and his wife named Lengteinu. They lived in a place called**

Lenpur believed to be present Syria. Then comes Lenlur to succeed Tanchak Sa and then Rangvung. There is no unanimous opinion whether they are the sons of Tanchaksa. These are their leaders)

2. ***Ooo, Lenpur, Khuisama, Sarona ati,***
   Tiana khochuichim ati, tiana khochui ralung o.

(The **descendants of Rangvung are Khuisama and Sarona respectively. The leaders were always male members.)**

3. ***Ooo, Lenpur, Sazukma, Luangthaima, Huluma, Radoia ati,***
   Lenglur a Lengsial, Rangvung-in, Masar tualim ei manleng ati.

In the stage during the succession, different duties were assigned to different leaders, symbolic of the village growing. At this stage, the leaders are *Sazukma, Luangthaima, Huluma, Radoia* respectively. During Lenlur's regime, he assigned an in-charge caretaker of Masar (name of the area) to Rangvung as an independent charge and believed to have handed over all the Yaks of that area.

4. ***Ooo, Lenpur, Sianlek-in a Siel eivalo ati***
   Rangvung-in Sianlek a maming Tonnianga a ti.

It is believed to have happened that the youth leader named **Sianlek** from Lenpur village was sent to **Rangvung** of **Masar** village to ask for a Yak for meat for the village festival called "***SETHAT***", feast of the sacrifice of the yak. The animal sacrifice is done in the following manner. First they make a huge pit, keep the animal in the huge pit and pierce the animal with various sharp instruments as a ritual for the forgiveness of sins. During this process, the animal could die. Later they cook the meat and share it among the entire village families. They make sure that every family in the village gets a share of it. The first youth coordinator was believed to be Huluma. He functioned as a teacher of all art, music, dance and crafts. The present name Halam is believed to be associated with the name of this Youth Leader Huluma. In short, the name Halam originated/derived from HULUMA, the name of the Youth Coordinator cum Teacher of Lenpur. It shows that this youth leader cum teacher was given more importance than all other leaders; he was valued with esteem as he probably had much to offer the people. In connection with the festival of the sacrifice of the YAK there were other activities organised and were coordinated and materialised in and through the leadership and wisdom of Huluma. Therefore, it is quite meaningful and rational to think that the name Halam is attributed to or derived from the name of the leader and teacher HULUMA. (**Interview with Mr. Joshua Halam**)

IV. l. Proverbs

The following proverbs will definitely throw some light into the value system they believe in. One may not find these proverbs in written form but senior or elderly people are familiar with the following proverbs in the colloquial expressions. These are commonly used in the day to day events of life and activities. There can be and there are many more to be identified and be added. An analysis would reveal the truth that any proverb is very practical, simple in its meaning and self explanatory. In fact this is the wisdom of the tribe and its culture. Therefore values are universal but with local application as far as the Halam community is concerned, these proverbs are highly relational and it is overwhelming to see the importance attached to relationship in terms of hierarchy in the family and in society.

1. ***Nupahe telloi thamoka seil alo.***
   (He who does not obey parents falls in dark).
2. ***Pansak nai anchukar panthangnai asing asuak.***
   (Invested for self, but profited by another)
3. ***Loko chong hi pakirituan , pakirituan hi marul anchang*:**
   (The majority opinion has the weight of truth)
4. ***Akung adep-in mai son ro -***
   (Those who are in front should respond/act to the need promptly/ instantly.)
5. ***Sara sanai machithal andu:***
   (Poverty stricken children eat more salt.)
6. ***Napa namro, chandal sanro:***
   (Leave the strong, help the weak.)
7. ***Ranglong le chong anrual noro, Dap le mal anchang noro.***
   (Unity among Ranglong and friendship with Dap is impractical)
8. ***Akung tin Am achaiten, arel tabor' ansunglui.***
   (Fault at the beginning leads to fault all along)
9. ***Andi le Taito rabo senna bui.***
   (Among true lovers, No separation)
10. ***Chun chong an-ngai zola phunchong.***
    (Obedience to mother leads to success in life)
11. ***Zuo chong an-ngai- Tura lenbuang.***
    (Obedience to father lead to growth like banyan tree)
12. ***Rual chong an-ngai, rapapam Thing.***
    (Evil advice is like broken/fallen plants/trees)

To a great extent, we can observe and conclude that sociological and anthropological concerns are vital for those who coin these proverbs. The above proverbs manifest the said observation in an explicit manner.

IV. m. Patriarchal (Panam/ Pa' Nchi) System, Status of Women and the Role of Men and Women

As far as the Halam community is concerned, women are respected and valued with esteem. The community is patriarchal and women do not generally have property rights. This is a tradition followed by the community till date, irrespective of any religion to which they belong. The main role of the women is house hold activities and work in the field or Jhum. Child-bearing and bringing the children up are considered as major responsibilities. The head of the family is always a man. In the Jhum both men and women work. This system is maintained till date.

IV. n. Rite of Passage

After death: A memorial celebration is expected to be conducted. Commonly it is done within one year: A memorial is known as ***Da'n-atho***. This is organised for the salvation of the soul. It is also a thanksgiving-rite for the soul to Rest in Peace: Basically, the Hindu Halam cremates the dead bodies and Christians continue their tradition of burying the dead body in the mud.

V. Impacts of Bengali-Immigrants on Halam Tribe of Tripura

Immigration and its impacts: The following are some of the perspectives or feelings expressed by the Halam people in connection with the phenomenon of Bengali Immigration to Tripura from Bangladesh.

- Due to the influence of Bengali Immigration the Halam learned to read and write through the script of the Bengali Immigrant.
- Dress habit has changed into Bengali Immigrant style like Kurtha Pyjaba and Dothi-i.e from Riampultai to Bengali Dress
- Food habits have changed and many styles of immigrant Bengalis have been adopted.
- Compulsory use of Sarees in the schools and educational institutions for girls were imposed but due to the agitation of -Tribal Students Federation (TSF) in and after 1980 this was relaxed. It was published in the gazette notification by the government.
- Bengali Hindu Religions spread rapidly among the tribal.
- System of worship was influenced by Bengali Immigrants- Shiva worship was prominent and then Durga pooja, Kali pooja and Lakhi pooja became popular among the Halams.
- 300 years before the Dharmanagar Office thilla and District Magistrate office areas were the habitation of Halams, but now it has come under the possession of Immigrant Bengalis.
- Since 100 years, the Halams have left the Office thilla and now Immigrant Bengalis have settled there.

- Halams were there in Syllet since BC 210-300 especially in the Syllet district TAO'T, HOMRU, SAKORNAL. etc. KOJOBAK (NOLDORI), KHOPUI, of Bangladesh.
- Before the influence of Immigrant Bengalis, the Halams buried their dead. Now due to Bengali Hindu influence, they have started to cremate. . However there are exceptions. But there was a thinking that if they cremated the person who died of a contagious disease it would spread rapidly. So they would not cremate the bodies of people who died of contagious diseases.
- Use of mustard oil for cooking was learned from Immigrant -Bengalis
- Uses of Bengali spices: Like black pepper, jeera , onion, garlic, Dal, etc is the impact of immigration.
- Low land cultivation or settled cultivation of cash crops is to some extent the impact of immigration.
- Domesticating animals and using Bulls for ploughing the paddy fields is learned from immigrants.
- Drinking milk is yet another impact.
- Immigrants started schools in their areas and the tribal were welcomed.
- They started schools in Bengali areas first and slowly progressed to Tribal areas.
- Syllet was part of Jurisdiction of the Tripura King -i.e. one of the districts of Tripura during the rule of Tripura King. Geographically the area got redesigned.
- Bengali Religious songs and folk songs attracted the Halams. The Rabindra Sangeeth did not exert an attraction.
- Greater socialisation and social interaction happened by learning Bengali.
- Learning of Bengali Language facilitated great social mobility, greater political involvement and participation and greater interactions with other tribal communities.
- Learning Bengali language was a blessing for improving or rising up from a fallen state and status.
- Some type of disregard for the immigrant population was felt due to the loss of property in the plains or present urban areas and also due to loss of political, social, cultural and economic superiority.
- Halams became bi-lingual and it helped them to interact with almost as many as 19 tribes of Tripura and the non tribal.
- Learning the Bengali language helped or facilitated greater social mobility; however it is evaluated as an outcome of a helpless situation.

- The Halams felt they were badly cheated while selling farm produces through maladjustments and malpractices or cheating with faulty weighing machines especially while selling the produces like Jute, cotton, roofing grass by attaching extra weight in one side of the weighing balancer.
- Learned more about plantation of cash crops; sugar cane was one of the first items to be planted in the tribal areas.
- Complete market/business was controlled and owned by the Immigrant Bengalis.
- Language, Food, Dress, culture. etc were influenced.
- The Immigrants became the super power in the so called tribal land.
- Bengali, the Immigrant language became the state language.
- Immigrant Bengalis were labourers in Tribal Houses and farm in the early days and it is not the case now a days.
- Hardly any Halam people got well established in the Urban areas.
- According to the Halam community, the Bengali Immigrants were a big obstacle in Halam getting settled or established in Urban areas. They had to run away to Hills due to demographic pressures.
- Though Halam prefer to be in Hills yet valleys are important for them. Tripura has numerous tiny hills. These were occupied by Tribal people. But now the urban scenario is changed totally.
- Forest department officers used to torture the Tribal in the beginning, due to majority of employees being Bengalis in the Forest Department, therefore they arrested and put many Halams in the jail and tortured them. It is a grievance often expressed by the members of the Halam community. Heavy Fines were levied for cutting trees, bamboos and even shone>?/roofing grass. Some expressed that these were treated more fatal than murdering a human being. Now though, things are different.
- Hardly any musical instruments of Bengali Immigrant culture influenced the Halam tribal community.
- They strongly felt that they lost their precious land; urban - land resettlement needs to be done in order to provide land security.
- Destroyed the rich tradition, culture , life style of the Halam

VI. Unique Uncommon Practice

The following is a very uncommon practice to probably all other cultures or tribes. This is basically a Hindu Practice. According to a Hindu practice among the Halam, if there are no sons or elders in the family to do the funeral rites and subsequent rituals after the death performed by the elder or the son for the purification of the soul then the male/the head of the family does it for himself/herself, when he /she is alive. This is known as ARINGDA'N-ANTHO in Halam language.

References & Bibliography

1. Interview with the Resource Person: **Mr. Joshua Halam.**

   Noagang Village & Post office, Police Station Dharamanagar, Block: Panisagar, Sub Division: Dharmanagar, North Tripura District.

   Educational qualification: SSLC Passed.

   Profession; Government Service in the Agriculture Department of Tripura.

   (Lyricist& Singer, Music Composer- Tribal Music and Non-tribal Music)

2. Gautam Kumar Bera and Nishi Bera, *(2009).* ***Echoes from the Hillocks; A compendium on the Tribes of Tripura****. Tripura Bbani Prakashani, Agartala. 2009.*

3. Gautam Kumar Bera (Chief Editor) B.K. Medhi, R.P. Athparia, K. Jose SVD (Ed), 2009. ***Tribal Development in Tripura.*** EBH publishers (India), Guwahati. ISBN: 978-93-80261-03-4. 2009.

4. ***A Land of Rich Ethnic Tapestry: Tripura, A Pictorial Monograph on Tribes of Tripura.*** Tribal Research and Cultural Institute, Government of Tripura. Adland Publicity (P) Ltd. Kolkata, 2010.

5. Gautam Kumar Bera & K.Jose SVD (Ed*)* ***Ethno-Social Mobility in North East India.*** Abhijeet Publication, Delhi. 2010.

6. Manoshi Das, Jayanta Choudhury & Rebati. ***Tripura Tribe, A Status analysis.*** Tribal Research & Cultural Institute, Government of Tripura. Print Best, Agartala. 2011.

7. Manoshi Das, Jayanta Choudhury. ***Halam Tribes of Tripura; A Status Analysis.*** Tribal Research and Cultural Institute, Government of Tripura. Print Best, Agartala. 2011.

24

Influence of Different Religions on a Particularly Vulnerable Tribal Group: An Anthropological Exploration

— *Geetika Ranjan*

Introduction

Tribal people have always had relationships with other religious streams, as well as with local cults and sects, not only borrowing from them but also, in some cases, influencing them (Srivastava 2010). Anthropologists of religion have begun to recognize that religion is not just a cultural system. It is the interpenetration of cultural systems. All religions- even tribal ones- are best understood as products of 'syncretism" and /or multiple contacts with outside cultures (Clarke and Beyer 2009). The tribal population of India, as per 2011 census, is 10.43 crore, constituting 8.6% of the total population. The present paper is an exploration of the influences which different religions have on the tribe – Bhoksa. There are five scheduled tribes in the state of Uttaranchal – Jaunsari, Tharu, Bhoksa, Bhotia and Raji. The Bhoksa inhabit Nainital, Bijnor, Pauri Garhwal and Dehradun districts of the sub Himalayan Bhabhar Tarai area of Uttar Pradesh\Uttaranchal. Bhoksa is Particularly Vulnerable Tribal Group (PVTG). Particularly Vulnerable Tribal Groups (PVTGs), who are those characterised by:- a) pre-agriculture level of technology; b) stagnant or declining population; c) extremely low literacy; and d) subsistence level of economy.

"Hardly a central theory in Anthropology, syncretism has recently re-emerged as a valuable tool for understanding the complex dynamics of ethnicity, interconnectedness and post modernism" (Das, 2006).In the same vein the present study focuses on the several reasons as to why Bhoksas have adopted various beliefs and practices of other religions. The study is based on fieldwork as well as on the secondary information available in different public records, government's reports, books and journals.

Van der Veer opines that there are debates over syncretism in societies in which identities are defined through religion (1994). India is one such country where several religions are flourishing. It has a large number of cultures within cultures. Apart from the major religions such as Hinduism, Islam, Sikhism, Buddhism, Jainism and Christianity the various tribes have their indigenous tribal religions.

In order to understand the process of syncretism among the Bhoksa , it is pertinent to understand their history. According to H.R. Nevill, the Tharu and Buksas are an aboriginal race who claims royal descent (Srivastav 1958). The Bhoksa claim their roots to royal family on the female side. They believe that the ruler of Tarai was defeated by some invader in the ancient past. After the defeat, the women of the royal family in order to save their honour from the invaders took shelter in the forests. They were accompanied by their attendants who were 'chamars' and 'sais' (low castes in the Hindu caste hierarchy). Intermarriage between royal women with the 'chamars' and the 'sais' gave rise to two distinct groups/tribes – Tharu and Bhoksa. The Tharu are the descendents of the 'chamars' and the Bhoksas descended from the 'sais' (Hasan 1979.21).

Thus the Bhoksas have been residing in the Tarai area since the ancient past. Because of high incidence of Malaria, the tract was considered uninhabitable by the outsiders till the fourth decade of the twentieth century. Only Bhoksas inhabited the Tarai and faced its deadly climate and wild animals.

Fieldwork among the Bhoksa living in selected villages falling under the Ramnagar block of Uttarakhand, reveals that the Bhoksa are influenced by several religions such as Hinduism, Islam and Sikhism. While on one hand they revere their own *tribal deities* and follow their religious beliefs and practices, culture contact with the non-tribal groups has religions. The Bhoksa remained almost isolated from the outside world till the beginning of the twentieth century. The Tarai being a very inhospitable area, it did not attract the outsiders to settle here and hence, the Bhoksa had monopoly over the habitat. However as the colonial rule over India saw to the development of the means of transport and communication the Tarai no longer remained the preserve of the Bhoksas. Even before 1947 i.e. the year when India gained independence from the British rule, people from other communities like Hindus, Muslims and government officials were entering the Bhoksa populated areas of the Terai. The Hindu and the Muslim merchants used to frequent these tribal areas and sell their goods. The real threat came in the form of the Rai

Sikhs and the Punjabis who entered the Tarai when the State Government, in order to develop agriculture on a large scale invited the former to settle in the area. The Bhoksa no longer remained the masters of the land in the Tarai. The Rai Sikhs and the Punjabis usurped their land. 'They literally came saw and conquered" (Hasan 1982.38), ultimately leading to serious problems of land alienation and law and order. Culture contact with the non-tribals influenced the lives of the Bhoksas in many ways than one.

The Religion of the Bhoksas

The Bhoksa have taken to the beliefs and practices of other religions. An in – depth study of the tribes brings forth a picture that conveys that they have taken to the worship of the Hindu deities, Sikh Gurus and Muslim saints out of choice with the common hope of receiving good fortune and benefits from the adopted religious practices. Their dedication, loyalty and obedience to these are self motivated. Religion has direct access to the psyche of a people. It is the mystery, the aura of the divine or the supernatural that brings within its fold many holistic dedicated followers. The Bhoksa are no exception to this. Yet adhering to the approach and viewing the Bhoksa religion against the backdrop of the totality of their lives and culture, one understands the working of several factors which have played a major role in determining the inclination of these tribes towards non – tribal religions.

It is rather interesting to note that the Bhoksa claim to have an independent identity taking pride in their age old tribal religion and call themselves Kshatriya using 'Singh' as their title. While there is a distinct impact of Hinduism on their religious beliefs, they continue to have deep faith in the essential ingredients of their exclusive pantheon of their tribal Gods and goddesses. The Bhoksa worship a large number of indigenous local gods and goddesses. The Bhoksa claim that their tribal deities were later adopted by the neighboring Hindus. The Goddess called Sunderi Devi or Basunderi Devi is most important among them. Her adherents are known as Deviwares and constitute one of the two sects into which the Bhoksas are divided. There are some deities which can be said to be typical Bhoksa deities which are not worshipped by the Hindus. These are the village deity - Bhumia, the protector of the village- Bhumsen, Budhraja and Purab Baro. As a result of the influence of Hinduism the Bhoksas worship most of the Hindu gods popular among the Hindus of Tarai.They are, Shiva Parwati, Ganesh, Lakshmi, and Mahadeva, Rama, his wife Sita and his brother Lakshaman. The pivots of Hinduism in north India are household words among the Bhoksas (Hasan 1979).

Influence of Hindus on the Bhoksas

The Bhoksa is a 'hinduised tribe'. Hinduisation does not necessarily mean total conversion to Hinduism as such (Pegu 2012). Anthropologists like

Majumdar (1944), Hu (1955, 1957), Srivastava (1958) and L.R.Singh (1998) have focused on the effects of Hinduism on religions. Hindu religion has strongly influenced the Bhoksa. Till the Tarai remained an area of the jungles and marshes, it was seldom frequented by outsiders. However with the beginning of the twentieth century the clearing of the dense jungles and gradual development of the network of roads in the colonial period, saw to the frequenting of the Hindus such as the Brahmins and the Banias in the Tarai. The Banias settled in the Tarai for mainly trading with these tribes. They provided them with requirements of daily use against cash or under barter. Brahmins too have a strong hold over the Bhoksa. They play a vital role in the socio-religious affairs of this tribe. In the caste hierarchy the Brahmins are considered to be on the highest strata. The Bhoksa's exposure to the Hindu castes and their continuous contact with the latter resulted in Bhoksa becoming influenced to the Hindu high caste way of life. The contact of the Bhoksa with the Hindus opened before them the life style of a people whose worldview was dominated by the ideas of purity and pollution, of superiority and inferiority of castes and the like. They were people who in every way belonged to the larger whole of the society, the so-called mainstream Indian society. Being part of the larger world they were more in rhythm with its pace. The Bhoksas till then were a world in themselves. Less smart, lesser known, they were made to realize that in the ways of the world they are lagging behind the fast pacing outside world. The Brahmins and the Banias (the high castes among the Hindus) looked down upon the Bhoksas. The census of India makes a clear distinction between the tribes and the castes. The Bhoksas report that the high caste Hindus consider them to be of a lesser origin despite the fact that they claim to be the descendents of the Rajputs (high caste Hindus) from the female side. The Kshatriyas also do not consider them to be their equals as they belong to the low castes from the male side.

Bhoksa is a Scheduled Tribe. The title 'Scheduled Tribe' is an administrative term under the Constitution of India so that the goal of the overall development of the tribes can be achieved. Development of the weaker sections of India was the main goal of the makers of the Constitution of independent India. In this vein it specifies the provisions made for the tribes for their development. On being asked why are they called a scheduled tribe (*Anusuchit Janjati* in Hindi) the Bhoksa say '*Hume anusuchit janjati isliye kaha jata hai kyunki hum junglee hain, ganwar hain, hume akal nahin hai'* (We are called a scheduled tribe because we are uncivilised, unmannered and foolish).Similar views about themselves throw light on the psyche, the mindset of the people of these tribes. Among the people of the older generation one does not find bitterness against the belittling attitude of the high caste Hindus towards them. To accept that they are actually 'inferior' to the Brahmins, the Kshatriyas and the Baniyas because they are a 'tribe' comes quite naturally to them. The fact that they are a tribe and not a part of the Hindu social fold has been driven home to them by their non – tribal neighbours. The internalisation of the etic concept of Bhoksa as a 'tribe' by the Bhoksa themselves, further fuelled in them a sense of relative inferiority of the Bhoksa vi-i-vis the relative superiority of the caste Hindus. The latter have been the reference groups for the Bhoksa. The process of Sanskritisation is seen in the Tarai. In search of better treatment by the high caste Hindus and as a step to boost up their self esteem the Bhoksa have been adopting the high caste Hindu ways of life. The caste Hindus, particularly the Brakhmins are looked up by the Bhoksa with much awe and respect. The Brahmins are called 'Pundits'. They come to the Bhoksa inhabited villages to negotiate marriages as it is customary among the Bhoksa that only the 'Pundit' can negotiate marriage between two parties and decide the date of wedding. As among the Hindus, the marriage ritual among the Bhoksa is conducted under the guidance and ritual performance of the Pundit. The presence of the Brahmin is considered auspicious and a must during life cycle rituals. The Brahmin is required to perform various religious rituals like *Havan*, *Nama Karan sanskar*(name giving ceremony for the new born), birth and death rites *et al*. Many Bhoksas also like to invite the Brahmins to their houses as a matter of prestige and status symbol. They worship Hindu deities and observe the religious rituals associated with their reverence. Thus the deities and scriptures of the 'great tradition' (Redfield 1956) of the Hindus has found a prominent place in the 'little tradition' of the Bhoksa.

Hendry (1999:12) has observed that in complex society's people have come to live with apparently conflicting worldviews increasingly. In Japan a sick person simultaneously consults a diviner as well as a doctor and may also visit a shrine or a temple to pray for recovery (Ohnuki-Tierney 1984). However not only in complex societies, this can be seen in the case of a PVTG such as the Bhoksa. In the Bhoksa tribe the Brahmins have come to occupy a parallel position with the Bharraras, the traditional medicine men and diviners. The Bharraa or Sayana is the 'wise', 'knowledgeable' expert among the Bhoksa , seen as a link between the mortal and the ethereal. The Bhoksas of the younger generation believe that the Bharraras are no longer effective and their mantras do not have any written or literary base unlike the Brahmins who recite from the Hindu religious scriptures like the Vedas. However, the majority of the Bhoksa continue to hold their traditional Bharrara in great regard and seek his counsel in times of distress and when 'caught' by a spirit.

Influence of the Muslims and the Sikhs on the Bhoksa

The Bhoksas have been highly influenced by the Muslims and the Sikhs apart from the Hindus. Recollecting the remnants of their long antiquity most of which seems to be shrouded in ambiguity, the Bhoksa claim to be the descendents of the ruler popularly called Raja Jagatdeo who lived in the time of the Mughal rule in India. There are Bhoksas of Muswani gotra (clan) in

Garhwal, who unlike the Bhoksa of Kumaon do not eat pork. Crooke (1892) has mentioned about a legend that the Muswanis were originally Muswans or Mussalmans (muslims), working for Rajput ranis (queens) who later migrated to the Tarai in the ancient past.

With the development of communication and transport in the terai, muslim traders also entered the Bhoksa living in the Kumaon area, thus exposing the latter to yet another community and its line of faith. Hasan (1971) writes that the Bhoksa offer prayers to Prophet Mohammad and his daughter ,Bibi Fatima and include their names in their mantras(religious recitations) to cure diseases and to ward off evil spirits.

Example:

I begin in the name of Allah
Who is great and merciful
By accepting godhood of God,
By accepting kingdom of Mohammad,
By accepting Fatima Bibi,*
By accepting Dul Dul, the Horse,
Let mantras prove effective,
For my master's word is true (Hasan 1971).

* Daughter of Prophet Mohammad

** Horse used by Imam Hussain, the Prophet's grandson, during his martyrdom in Karbala.

Crooke mentions two Muslim saints, Sarwar Lakhi and Kalu Sayeed among the deities worshipped by the Bhoksa (1892).

The Bhoksas are greatly influenced by the Sikh religion. They are devotees of Guru Nanak, the founder of Sikhism, who look upon him not only as a saint but as their deity. The Bhoksas are divided in two sects based on their two main deities – Basundari Devi or just Devi of Kolhapur in Nainital district, is the goddess of one sect. She is also deeply revered by the neighbouring Hindus. The main god of the other sect is Guru Nanak. The worshippers of the 'Devi' are known as 'Devivare' and those of the Guru are known as 'Guruware'. The 'Guruwares' consider themselves to be superior to the 'Deviwares' on the ground that the 'Devi' is only a disciple (cheli) of the Guru but the latter refute this. Numerically the Deviwares are much greater in number than the Guruwares and being a dominant group are able to establish their social superiority over the other sect. It is important to mention here that the Bhoksas have been worshiping Guru Nanak since much long before the Sikhs entered the Tarai and started ocuupying the Bhoksa land. The Bhoksas owe their attachment to Gurunanak to the old Sikh shrine of Nanakmata in Khatima tehsil of Nainital district. The Sikhs who entered the Tarai and usurped the Bhoksa land followed by many of their kind have not been able to influence the Bhoksas' religious beliefs in any manner. The shrine at Nanakmata is frequented by not only the Bhoksa but also by the non – tribal population of the area since the ancient past. However the Bhoksa do not attribute their faith in Guru Nanak to the influence of Sikhs on them. They consider the latter to be the cause of their poverty and misery. A major change that has been seen is that as the Bhoksa learnt more and more about the fact that Guru Nanak, the founder of Sikh religion is deeply worshipped by the Sikhs; the popularity of Guru Nanak has started decreasing among them because of their dislike for the Sikhs. The association of their Master (Guru Nanak) with their exploiters came as a rude shock to the tribal people and has consequently weakened the position of the Guruwares among the Bhoksa as a whole. Among the Bhoksa the worshippers of Guru Nanak, the Guruwares has gradually been declining. As a tradition the intermarriage between the two sects has been permissible but the Guru worshippers are finding it increasingly difficult to find eligible boys and girls from the Deviware sect to marry their sons and daughters. Thus when we analyze the process of syncretism among the Bhoksas we see that it has been more as a way to survive. Although they have been willing to adopt the practices of the Hindus as they themselves wish to be recognised as one by the latter, they have quite consciously not adopted the practices of the Sikh religion due to their animosity and fear of the Rai Sikhs. The latter are considered as hardy and shrewd men with sharp business acumen. Muscle power coupled with money power has made them form a strong nexus with the local police, the Government officials and the like. They all look down upon the Bhoksas. For them the word 'Adivasi' (tribal) or 'Janjati' (tribe) smacks of a people of a lesser order, lacking in etiquettes ('tameez') and 'culture'. The Rai Sikhs and the Punjabis ridicule these tribes of being incapable of making the most out of the fertile tracts of the Tarai prior to the entry of the former in the area. No wonder the State Government had invited the sturdy Sikhs and the Punjabis to settle in the Tarai and cultivate the land so that the State could get more revenue from the area. Despite being much lesser in number than the Bhoksa, the Rai Sikhs and the Punjabis call the shots in the area. Due to their omnipotence, the Bhoksas' dislike for them remains quite latent as they dare not manifest it out of fear. They do not make effort to emulate the beliefs and the practices of the Sikhs as firstly they are not Hindus and secondly the anguish towards the usurpers of their land is so deep rooted that the question of conscious emulation of their culture does not arise.

Conclusion

The present paper focuses mainly on the influence of different religions on the Bhoksa. However as a result of contact between cultures the mutual give and take can be seen in other areas as well such as language, music, dress et al. In the district gazetteer of Nainital it is mentioned that the Bhoksas of the Tarai speak Hindustani with some admixture of Kumauni (Hasan 1979). However one clearly notices that in their conversation there is a large proportion of Persian and Urdu words. This is the result of their long contact with the Muslims not only as rulers in the past but also through the Muslim saints. They also use several Punjabi words which show Sikh influence on them. They are fond of Punjabi songs and dances and one normally finds them dancing to the Punjabi numbers and perform the 'Bhangra' (folk dance of Punjab, the main state of the Sikhs and the Punjabis).

Thus in the case of the Bhoksas syncretism has been out of a need to survive as well as with the spirit of deriving maximum benefit from the gods and the beliefs of the other lines of faith. It is rather interesting to note that the Bhoksas are very clear about the *place* which *their* deities hold for them. Their own tribal deities are their *own*, who have been taking take care of them since the ancient past, whereas the deities of the other religions have started *listening to them* ever since the Bhoksa started worshipping them. They believe that there is no conflict between the deities.

The present research emphasizes that religious notion of a people can be adequately garnered when understood against their historical backdrop. Further it also reiterates the human tendency, to adopt what nourishes its psychology and leave out what doesn't. A major contribution of anthropologists has been to demonstrate that syncretism is not inevitable (Stewart and Shaw 1994). Allegiance to diverse religious beliefs is also determined by the kind of relationship a group shares with the adherents of those beliefs. Adoption of the religious beliefs of the 'other' takes place not only when the relation between the two groups concerned is amicable but also when it is quite the opposite, and in the latter case it acts as a tool which help a people find acceptability with those whose claim to superiority is unanimously recognised by the tradition of the land.

References

Crooke, W. (1892). *The Tribes and Castes of Bengal*. Calcutta: Bengal Secretariat Press, Volume 2.

Clarke, Peter,B. and Peter Beyer. (2009). *The World Religions: Continuities and Transformations*. (ed). London : Routledge.

Das, N.K. (2006).Cultural Diversity, Religious Syncretism and People of India: An Anthropological Interpretation. In *Bangladesh e-journal of Sociology*. Volume 3. Number 2.

Hasan, Amir.(1971). *A Bunch of Wild Flowers and Other Articles*. Lucknow: .Ethnographic and Folk Culture Society.

Hasan, Amir. (1979). *The Buxas of Tarai*. Delhi. B.R.Publishing Corporations.

Hasan, Amir. (1982). *Meet the U.P. Tribes*. , Gurgaon: Academic Press.

Hendry, Joy. (1999). *An Introduction to Social Anthropology*. London. Macmillan Press.

Hu, C.T. (1955). Demographic Study of Village Chandanpur. In *The Eastern Anthropologist.* Volume 1X, 1, pp. 1-20.

Hu, C.T. (1957). Marriage by Exchange Among the Tharu. In *The Eastern Anthropologist*. Volume X, 2, pp. 116-129.

Majumdar, D.N. (1944).*The Fortunes of Primitive Tribes*. Lucknow: Lucknow University Publications.

Ohnuki-Turney, Emiko.(1984). *Illness and Culture in Contemporary Japan*. London. Cambridge University Press.

Pegu, Ruhini Kumar. (2012). Hinduisation and Identity Conflict: The Mising Case. *In IJCAES Special Issue on Basic, Applied & Social Sciences*, Volume II, October.

Rawat, Ajay S. (1998). *Forests on Fire-Ecology and Politics in the Himalayan Tarai*. New Delhi: Cosmo Publications.

Redfield, Robert. (1956). The little community. Chicago: University of Chicago Press.

Srivastava, S.K. (1958). *The Tharus: A study in Culture Dynamics*. Agra:Agra University Press.

Srivastava, V.K. (2010). Socio and Economic Characteristics of the Tribal Communities that call Themselves Hindu. *Religions and Development, India. Working Paper Series*, Volume 01, No. 03.Indian Institute of Dalit Studies.

Stewart, Charles and Rosalind Shaw. (1994). *Syncretism/Anti syncretism: The Politics of Religious Synthesis* (ed). London: Routledge.

25

Synthesis of Cultural Modernisation with Western Impact – A Sociological Review on India Society

— *Surojit Sen Gupta*

Modernisation has many dimensions. It may be perceived at society level, group level, or individual level. It may also be perceived as economic modernisation, political modernisation, social modernisation, cultural modernisation, educational modernisation, administrative modernisation, and so forth. The concept has thus been employed in a diffused manner.

Modernisation is the most overwhelming feature of the contemporary scene, in the sense that most nations are nowadays caught in its web. The characteristics and the processes of modernisation in different countries are in some respect common and in some respect different. Historically, modernisation (as the process of change in social, economic and political systems) has developed from a great variety of different traditional societies in different regions of the world. Eisenstadt (1969) submits that the different starting points of the process of modernisation of these societies have greatly influenced the specific contours of their development and the problems encountered in the course of it.

Conceptualizing Modernisation

Modernisation is not a philosophy or a movement with a clearly articulated value-system. It is a process of change (Gore 1982). Earlier, the term 'modernisation' was used to refer only to change in economy and its related effect on social values and social practices. It was described as a process that changed the society from primarily agricultural to primarily industrial economy. As a consequence of this change in economy, the society simultaneously underwent changes in values, beliefs and norms (Gore 1982). Today, the term 'modernisation' is given a broader meaning. It is described as "social change involving the elements of science and technology." It involves change based on rationality. According to (Alatas 1972) modernisation is a process by which modern scientific knowledge is introduced in the society with the ultimate purpose of achieving a better and more satisfactory life in the broadest sense of the term, as accepted by the society concerned.

To Eisenstadt (1969), modernisation refers to both (a) structural aspects of social organisation, and (b) socio-demographic aspects of societies. Karl Deutsch (1961) has coined the term 'social mobilisation' to denote most of the socio-demographic aspects of modernisation. He has defined social mobilisation as "the process in which major clusters of old social, economic and psychological commitments are eroded and broken and people become available for new patterns of socialisation and behaviour".

Rustow and Ward (1964) have maintained that the basic process in modernisation is the application of modern science to human affairs. According to Pye (1969) modernisation is the development of an inquiring and inventive attitude of mind, individual and social, that lies behind the use of techniques and machines and inspires new forms of social relations. Toynbee (1962) feels that there is no difference between modernisation and westernisation.

Modernisation and its Features

Karl Deutsch (1961) referring to one aspect of modernisation (that is, socio-demographic aspect, or what he calls 'social mobilisation') has indicated some of its indices as: exposure to modern life through machinery, response to mass media, urbanisation, change from agricultural occupations, literacy and growth of per capita income. To Eisenstadt (1969), some of the indices pertaining to the structural aspects of social organisation (or modernisation) are: specialised roles are 'free-floating' (that is, admission to them is not determined by ascribed, properties of the individual), and wealth and power are not inscriptively allocated (as in traditional societies). This is associated with institutions like markets (in economic life) and voting and party activities in politics.

Moore (1961) has suggested that a modern society has specific economic, political and cultural characteristics. In the economic sphere, a modern society is characterised by - (a) the development of a very high level of technology, fostered by the systematic application of knowledge, the pursuit of which became the province of the secondary (industrial, commercial) and tertiary (service) occupations, as against the primary (agricultural) ones; (b) growing specialisation of economic roles; and (c) the growth of the scope and complexity of the major markets, the markets for goods, labour, and money.

In the political sphere, a modern society is in some sense democratic or at least populist. It is characterised by - (a) the decline of traditional legitimation of the rulers with reference to powers outside their own society; (b) the establishment of some sort of ideological accountability of the rulers to the ruled, who are alleged to be the holders of the potential political power; (c) growing extension of the territorial scope of power of the central, legal, administrative and political agencies of the society; (d) continual spread of potential power to wider groups in the society-ultimately to all adult citizens and to moral orders; and (e) total disappearance on weakening of ascriptive political commitment to any given ruler or group.

In the cultural sphere, a modern society is characterised by - (a) a growing differentiation of the major elements of the major cultural and value systems, that is, religion, philosophy and science; (b) the spread of literacy and secular education; (c) a more complex institutional system for the advancement of specialised roles based on intellectual disciplines; (d) expansion of the media of communication; and (e) development of a new cultural outlook, characterised by an emphasis on progress and improvement, on happiness and expression of abilities, on individuality as a moral value and stress on dignity of the individual and on efficiency.

Western Cultural Impact and Indian Society

The mode of the Western cultural impact on the Indian tradition had distinctive features. Historically, the distinctive element was in its gradual expansion through succession and replacement of various forms of Western traditions differing in political and cultural orientation and influence. The earliest contact was with the Portuguese and their impact was proselytizing and predatory (O'Malley 1941) which brought with them pre-modern values and religious prejudices. They were followed by the Dutch and the French in the 17th and 18th century. Neither the Dutch nor the French had Christianisation as their main objective. The Dutch were mainly interested in commerce. The French had political goals, but their influence was marginal. Only the British (Spear 1961) finally emerged as a dominant power in India. The Western impact on the Indian culture has, therefore, been primarily of the British (Srinivas 1966).

The consolidation of the British power in India, which started in the early seventeenth century, was complete only towards the end of the nineteenth century. Behind this political power was the cultural tradition of the West. The cultural tradition of the 19th century West which overwhelmed the Indian scene was in its ethos and structure fundamentally different from the traditional cultural patterns of Indian society. Its basic tenets were in contradiction with most of the essential attributes of the contemporary Indian tradition.

The impact of western culture has also been described by Alatas (1972) in terms of four types of changes in the culture and social system in terms of eliminative changes, additive changes, supportive changes and synthetic changes. The eliminative changes are those which cause the disappearance of culture traits, behaviour patterns, values, beliefs, institutions, etc. The additive changes refer to the adoption of new cultural traits, institutions, behaviour patterns and belief systems covering diverse aspects of life. The supportive changes are those which strengthen the values, beliefs or behaviour patterns present in society before contact with the West. The synthetic changes result in the creation of new forms from existing elements plus adopted ones.

The Western impact has led to acculturative and innovatory changes in the cultural pattern of India. Its processes, therefore, bring to light not only how far modernizing acculturation has taken place in the Indian tradition, but also the extent to which such acculturation reinforces the endogenous tendencies for change and modernisation, and how far these changes do or do not pose a threat to the cultural identity of the Indian tradition. The two aspects of the problem are in a way interrelated - the first relates to the process of cultural synthesis and the second to the phenomenon of cultural identity.

Generally there are two types of changes brought by the western impact. The first is the emergence of a westernised sub-cultural pattern through a minority section of Indians who first came into contact with Western culture. This also includes the sub-culture represented by those Indian intellectuals and scholars who not only adopted many Western cognitive patterns and styles of life, but also supported its rapid expansion. As the influence of this westernised sub-culture was localised, it may also be treated as a part of the primary stage of Westernisation. This process forms part of the Little and not the Great-tradition, because its mode of expansion and adaptation did not develop a systematic world-view. It was primarily sub-cultural. The second type of primary Westernisation in the Little tradition which refers to the process of general diffusion of western cultural traits, such as the use of new technology, dress, food, and changes in the habits and styles of life of people in general, resulting from the cultural contact with the British.

Besides primary Westernisation, there has also been going on in India another form of Westernisation, which is not confined to the Little tradition alone. This form of Westernisation has a pan-Indian character and has contributed to the growth of various forms of cultural structures which out-cross the local or regional boundaries and extend to the country as a whole. These cultural structures are representative of a coherent normative system and have their basis in an organisational structure which is far different from the normative system of the Little tradition. Some examples of such cultural structures are - education, law, science and technology, new forms of politicisation, urbanisation, industrialisation and finally new media of cultural transmission through press, printing and facilities of transport and communication. The emergence of these institutional foci is called the process of cultural modernisation.

Westernisation and its Process – A Glimpse on Indian Society

In global context, Westernisation refers to the process of change brought about in non-western countries as a result of the adoption of Western cultural elements on their part. It refers to the process of diffusion of western values and ideologies like liberalism, equalitarianism, humanism, rationalism and individual freedom. The process of Westernisation has spread like a socio-cultural movement to the different parts of the world and has brought about wide spectrum of changes in economy and polity of the human society.

In the Indian context, the process of Westernisation refers to the series of changes brought about in Indian culture and Institutions as a result of long period of western contact in course of its history. It is under the influence of the Britishers that the real process of Westernisation started in India. They have left such long lasting influences on Indian culture that even after six decades of the end of British rule Indian culture still is under the heavy influence of the western culture of the British. M.N. Srinivas (1966) rightly speaks Westernisation refers to "the changes brought about in Indian Society and culture as a result of over 150 years of British rule". In his opinion the term Westernisation subsumes a number of changes occurring at different levels - technology, institutions, values and ideology. Establishment of 'Pax - Britanica' - science, technology, industry and military organisations, all created conditions for a new modern India. He goes on to add that Westernisation results not only in introduction of new institutions but also in fundamental changes in old institutions. The most important value preference of the process of Westernisation is the humanitarianism, which means, "an active concern for the welfare of all human beings irrespective of caste, economic position, religion, age and sex" (Srinivas 1966). He includes both equalitarianism and secularisation within the broad term of humanitarianism.

The western culture is spread in India mainly as a politico administrative culture. The progressive rationalism and humanism of western culture added to its pace. Of course, all the changes which become visible during the process of westernisation do not owe their origin to western culture. Max Weber (1958) argues that many of the cultural traits of western culture such as, rationalism, codification, experimentation, utilitarian orientation in thought and action etc., also existed in Indian and Chinese culture. But these cultural elements were in isolated forms and could not become universally popular due to lack of other supporting infrastructural cultural traits which later on was added by the western culture. Similarly all that is called western, did not originate in western society itself. Some important components of western technological superiority in the 18th and 19th centuries were derived from ancient Far East and from medieval India (Srinivas 1966). For instance the paper, printing types and gunpowder were invented in China. The search for the sources of natural energy and their utilisation for human purposes had originated in 12th century India. The ideas of 'Hindu numeral', 'positional reckoning' and 'perpetual motion' were passed on to Europeans through Arabians. The main point of distinction between medieval Indians and Europeans was that the later had keen interest in the ideas of 'perpetual motion' and to put it in meeting human needs. Even the religion of Europeans that is Christianity had its origin in Asia sub-continent.

By the time when Britishers started influencing Indian culture, economy and polity, the western culture had enriched itself with various progressive and scientific traits. Its own structure had undergone radical internal metamorphoses, its traditional hierarchical and holistic character had broken down and its value structure was rendered more open, liberal, equalitarian and humanistic. It was enriched with rationalism, a high degree of technological and industrial culture along with the cardinal values of equality and freedom. It shriveled the Indian culture and polity at its root. The whole social structure was thrilled and stimulated to a considerable extent. The process of Westernisation has had its influence on both the Little and Great traditions. Its influence on Little traditions has been termed as "Primary Westernisation" and on Great traditions as "Secondary Westernisation" (Singh 1986).

Changes in Little Tradition – Primary Westernisation

Primary Westernisation means changes induced by the western impact on the Indian little traditions. At the initial phases, western culture made its impact on peripheral aspects of Indian culture. It created a sub-cultural pattern limited to a specific group of people within a particular geographical area. In other words, during the early periods of British rule, the western impact was peripheral and localised. Among the various impacts of western culture on Indian traditions two were most sticking ones which in later time grew into Great traditions of Westernisation (Singh 1986).

At first, in the British trade centres like Calcutta, Bombay and Madras, there emerged a new commercial middle class. The social composition of this middle class differed from region to region. For instance, in Calcutta region most of these commercial classes were *Baniya* (Merchant) by caste. In Madras mostly, the Brahmins emerged as commercial class; whereas in Bombay, they were mostly Parsis. These commercial-middle-classes served as middle-men between natives and British traders. This class was not westernised to any significant extent. Though they adopted western dress, language and way of living, in their basic psychological dispositions they were quite eastern. They have been termed as quasi-westernised "middle men" (Singh 1986). However, their importance in the process of cultural change lies in the fact that they served as forerunners of westernisation in Indian society. The impact of west throughout 18th century was mostly confined to middle-class businessmen in trading centres.

Towards early part of 19th century, another group of English educated professional class and social reformers emerged, who in later period, took up a major role in the process of Westernisation. The introduction of English education resulted in the emergence of this class. These classes took up the values and ideologies of western culture. The rational humanism, equalitarianism and 'ethical positivism' which were dominant cultural traits of western culture appealed many patriotic English educated people. They thought the inculcation of these values as the only way to Indian freedom.

Here, one point needs to be emphasized that, many of the western cultural traits, such as 'ethical positivism', humanism etc., were not in contradiction to Indian culture. They were only subsumed under the excessive dogmatic beliefs, ritualism and lack of real Vedic knowledge. Different socio-cultural reform movements that grew up with western education contributed to Indian Renaissance. Raja Rammohan Roy founded Brahmo Samaj through which he propagated western ethical system and spirits of positivism. After him, Keshab Chandra Sen led the Bramho Samaj, who had a more strong admiration of Christina ethics. Like Bramho Samaj in Calcutta other reform movements were also started in Bombay and Madras. In Madras, the Veda Samaj and in Bombay, the Prathana Samaj were established to bring about reformation in Hindu religion in the direction of western culture.

In this way, throughout nineteenth century the sub-cultural patterns of Westernisation grew up in specific localities. The people who headed the movements were moved by the noble nationalistic spirit of bringing about national reawakening. The nationalistic leaders appreciated western values so far those contributed towards national reawakening. They advocated for modernity but not at the cost of traditional cultural identity. But after them new violent generations of English educated youths emerged who hated everything of Hinduism. In their vain search for material pleasure and so called status positions they went against Indian culture and discarded all the ethical doctrines of Hindu Philosophy.

But all these reformist movements as well as "Protestant sub-culture" of the later generation were mostly localised and could not take an all India character. "The protestant sub-culture" of the de-nationalised and hyper-westernised youths could not make any substantial impact. These groups had no ground in either of the cultures, Indian or Western. But the reform movements, though were 'localised and elitist' had a force of their own. They could influence the British administration. Many progressive laws were passed, prohibiting the practice of 'sati', child marriage, ban on widow remarriage and untouchability. With the growth of British rule, lawlessness, banditry, private armies and thugee which were common in the 18th and 19th century India were abolished and controlled (O'Malley 1941). The expansion of education, transportation and communication served as prelude to the greater Westernisation in the basic structural patterns of Indian society. The western cultural traits of humanism, nationality, equality started stimulating Indian minds which later on brought about changes in Great traditions of Indian culture.

Changes in Great Tradition – Secondary Westernisation

Gradually towards the end of nineteenth century and beginning of the twentieth century, the process of Westernisation started taking firm roots in Indian social structure. Western culture emerged as an ideology. Many social reformers justified the adoption of western cultural spirit in order to make the Indian's feel, the necessity for liberty, freedom and equality. This had a great effect on Indian minds. On the other side, the cumulative effects on the changes in Little traditions and many other economic, political as well as administrative policies also effected the Great traditions of India. Gradually a new structural pattern with many new institutions started replacing many of the old institutions.

In traditional and medieval India the law was based on the social hierarchy. Punishment for violation was being sentenced on the basis of one's caste position. Generally, it was in favour of higher castes. For the same violation the punishment for a 'sudra' was more than that of a 'Brahmin'. But there also have been some recorded instances where it has been noted that Hindu legal system did not always work in favour of Brahmins. In either case, law in the favour of Brahmins, or law against Brahmins, the principles of hierarchy was being maintained in the administration of the legal justice. This was true for both the Hindus and Muslims in India. On the whole, the legal system in the country, before the .establishment of the British rule was hierarchical, particularistic and non-equalitarian.

With the consolidation of the British power, the legal system was given a historical boost. A common judiciary system was established in the country. The progressive modern laws were enacted which were based on the principles of universalism, rationalism and individualism. A universalistic law was codified with the enactment of Indian penal code, codes of civil and criminal procedure. The legal system was made a three tier structure. There were lower courts in each province and above these lower courts was a provincial High Court. At the highest level, there was the judicial committee of His Majesty's Privy Council. This Court was the ultimate court of appeal having the highest power in the judicial structure. Thereafter, many progressive laws were enacted against the inhuman customs to ensure personal security and to uphold humanistic values. All these Acts brought about revolutionary changes in the fields of marriage, family, social customs, the property inheritance and the status of women in Indian society with introduction of new liberal institutions based on western cultural patterns.

There were different regional laws regulating economic, political and industrial systems. It was during the British period that such diversified laws were codified and universally administered throughout the country. "By the first quarter of twentieth century a uniform all India pattern was established in the form of judicial administration based on a homogeneous normative structure of law. Sociologically, the content of new legislation was as important as its pan-Indian character which created an institutional base for a new national identity and process of cultural modernisation" (Singh 1986).

The modern scientific and universal education was introduced by the British Government. The historical milestones in the education policy of British Government were Macaulay's policy of European learning through English (1835), and Sir Charles Wood's recommendation to impart education through private and voluntary organisation (1854). The Indian Education Commission set up by British Government in 1882 also recommended for involving private agencies in expansion of education. Gradually, an educational system evolved with a three tier structure. At all lower level there was primary vernacular schools; at the secondary level there were high schools and other secondary institutions; and finally at the higher level there were colleges and universities.

The modern education was scientific and liberal in spirit. The courses of study on literature and humanities carried the basic spirits of European Renaissance, Reformation and Enlightenment. Social Sciences focused too much on day to day realities of social life. There was emphasis on science, technology, medicine and biology. The education was made open to all irrespective of caste, creed and religion. The educational system began to become secular. All these developments in the field of education were a clear break with the past.

The modern scientific and technological education helped in the process of the growth of industrial centres. The British policy of Trade and Commerce added impetus to it. Many industrial units were created for the processing of the raw materials which were to be used by the British companies. The concentration of trade, commerce and industry around the port areas led to the growth of urbanisation. But the modern industrial urban centres under the influence of western culture have been organised on the basis of secularistic principle. Achievement orientation has replaced ascription orientation, personal quality, wealth, industrial success, administrative position etc., which have become the basis of social stratification in urban centres. The influences of urban culture have been spreading to rural centres with a net result of increasing modernisation.

It is during the British rule that a nation-wide network of transportation and communication came to be established. The Railway, Posts and Telegraphs, the Printing Press, News Papers etc., broke all the regional barriers. As a result of nation-wide transportation and communication people became both physically as well as psychologically mobile. Phenomenal increases in newspapers, periodicals and other easy means of communication have made a double edged impact on Indian society. On one side, it has modernising effects and on the other side, it has traditionalizing effects. Modern means of transportation and communication has helped in the diffusion of modern secular means. It has accelerated the process of industrialisation and urbanisation. At the same time, it has strengthened intra-solidarity of many divisive forces like caste, religion, race etc.

Traditional and medieval India fell divided into many feudal enclaves. The people were divided among themselves in the name of caste, religion, region, race etc. Caste, religion and regional loyalties superseded the national loyalty. Indians during the medieval age could not see their whole motherland and fell divided under many regional feudal masters. Indian nationalism was lost in the feudal worship, caste and religious loyalty. The establishments of British Empire unified the country under one rule. Apart from political and administrative unification of the country, the western culture also injected the spirits of freedom, equality and humanism into Indian mind. All these made the Indians to rise-up from centuries slumber, and the western values of modern democracy showed the Indians the new light. Thus, for India, the growth of the spirit of nationalism, modern democratic socio-political structure and the growing mass politicisation are the blessings of the British rule in disguise.

The process of Westernisation has not stopped with the departure of British rulers from Indian soil. True, that British rules are no more there, but British influence is very much present in all aspects of our socio-political life. The new constitution of India carries many of the humanistic values which were thought to be written during British rule. The values of 'welfare state', 'parliamentary-democracy' 'universal franchise', 'individual right' and 'liberty' which have become cardinal principles of Indian constitution have a western origin. In the judicial and civil administration, the western trends are distinctly present. The judicial system in independent India is mostly the system which was introduced by the British educational system which is still dominated by western values.

During the British rule, the western culture was being adopted with a social suspicion. There was a general rejection rather than appreciation of western cultural and behavioural patterns. The adoption was mostly backed by professional necessity to serve under British Government. The few spiritualistic leaders like Ramakrishna, Vivekananda and nationalistic leaders like Gandhi, Nehru, Tilak, advocated for progressive and humanistic values of western culture but they did not accept the proposition of replacing Indian culture by western culture. But after independence, the western habits seem to have gained a sort of social sanction in India. In contemporary India, English language, western food and dress habits are being considered as status symbols. The Coat-Suit, Dining Table, Spoon-Eating, Watch-Dog-Culture are rapidly becoming Indian way of life. Even where these western habits are not practiced, they have begun to constitute the ideals or desirable things for them who do not yet have them (Singh 1986).

Conclusion

To conclude, after independence the western values are rapidly being absorbed into Indian culture and life-style with emphasis on secularism, democracy, small family norm, achievement orientation, individualistic contractual relationship etc., to mention some. Of course, the process of adoption is not free from stress and strains. Indian values of holism, hierarchy, traditionalism, ascription orientation, collectivism etc., often clash with western values creating a lot of structural stresses, social disturbances and personal disappointments. The future of India's modernisation depends on the extent to which these stresses and strains are resolved. For a happier and prosperous life, east and west have to melt together.

Thus, the influence of west on the Indian society and culture is rapidly increasing. Many persons are so dazzled by the western culture that they are mock-full about their own culture and traditions. The leadership of independent India rightly wants to encourage the Indian culture. This is a laudable step. But as we should not be blind worshippers of the west, we should not at the same time worship Indian culture blindly. There should be a synthesis of the two.

Note: *We have heavily depended for secondary sources required for this article on M.N. Srinivas's social change in Modern India (1966), Yogendra Singh's Modernisation of Indian Tradition (1986), Yogendra Singh's Culture Change in India (2000) and Ram Ahuja's Indian Social System (2005).*

References

Ahuja, Ram, (2005). *Indian Social System*, Rawat Publications, New Delhi.

Alatas, Syed Hussain, (1972). *Modernisation and Social Change*, Angus and Roberstson, Cremorne, Sydney.

Deutsch, K., (1961). *American Political Science Review*, September.

Dube, S. C., (1988). *Modernisation and Development*, Vistaar Publications, New Delhi.

Eisenstadt, S. N., (1969). *Modernisation: Protest and Change*, Prentice-Hall of India, New Delhi.

Gore, M.S., (1982). *Education and Modernisation in India*, Rawat Publications, Jaipur.

O'Malley, L.S.S., (1941). *The Impact of European Civilisation, Modern India and the West: A Study of the Interaction of their Civilisation*, Oxford University Press, London.

Pye, A. E., (1969). *Towards a Communication Theory of Modernisation*, Bombay.

Rustow, D.A. and Ward, R. E., (1964). (Eds.), *Political Modernisation in Japan and Turkey*, Princeton University Press, New Jersey.

Singh, Amar Kumar, (1969). (Eds.), *Modernisation in India: Studies in Socio-Cultural Aspects*, Asia Publishing House, Bombay.

Singh, Yogendra, (1986). *Modernisation of Indian Tradition*, Rawat Publications, New Delhi.

Singh, Yogendra, (2000). *Culture Change in India*, Rawat Publications, New Delhi.

Spear, Percival, (1961). *A Modern History*, The University of Michigan Press.

Srinivas, M. N., (1966). *Social Change in Modern India*, California Press, Los Angles.

Weber, M., (1958). *The Protestant Ethic and the Spirit of Capitalism*, Charles Scribner's Sons, New York.

Weiner, M., (1967). *Modernisation: The Dynamics of Growth*, Higginbotham's, Madras.

26

Indigenous Beliefs and Practices of theDeoris of Assam

— *Arifur Zaman*

I

The term religion is generally used to denote a man's relation to supernatural powers and various organised system of beliefs and worships in which these relation have been expressed. Religion as a social force exerted influence in both literate and preliterate societies. It provides the vital force for making up the foundation of society through ages. Religion has been marked as a dominant concern of mankind because it can only be realised, conceptualised and even feel the essence. Due to the dynamic and elemental characteristics, the word religion is very hard to define in an appropriate and concise manner. It comes from the Latin word 'religare' which means to bind together or from the word 'religere' which means to rehearse, to execute painstakingly, suggesting both group identity and ritual(Yinger 1957). Thus literally, religion is a principle of unification and harmonisation. It is a universal institution which is deeply rooted in man's social and biological world.

Anthropologist Wallace (1966) defined religion as 'a set of rituals, rationalised by myth, which mobilizes supernatural powers for the purpose of achieving or preventing, transformations of state in man and nature'. Behind this definition it is recognised that when people cannot solve serious problems through technological or organisational means that cause them anxiety, try to solve by the manipulation of supernatural powers or beings. This requires rituals, which according to Wallace is the primary phenomena of religion, or 'religion in action'. Its major function is to reduce anxiety and keep confidence high, which serve to keep people in some sort of shape to cope with reality (Haviland 1990). Religion specially Tribal religion is a topic,on which there have been dozens of monumental works done by various stalwart Anthropologists and Sociologists like Tylor(1871) Frazer(1911), Durkheim (1912), Karsten (1935), Srinivas (1952), Malinowski (1954), Redfield (1965), Vidyarthi (1968), Spencher (2002), Zaman(2010), Medhi(2012), and others.

Assam is a confluence of diverse ethnic community. Each and every ethnic communityhas its own distinctive cultural and religious beliefs and practices which are often associated with their day to day activities like festivals, birth, initiation, marriage, death and so on. Here tribal religion basically is a community religion that involves active participation in the religious beliefs,ceremonies, rituals and festivals of the community. However in contemporary times the tribal groups of Assam have been found in transition from primitive to modern stage of social development. Some tribe lost their culture and the original beliefs and rituals had also undergone changes due to the impact of other religion like Hinduism, Christianity, Islam, Buddhism etc. Yet there are some tribes who are found to retain their own pristine traditional customs and practices. The Deori a plain tribe of Assam is one such community.This paper attempts to study the indigenous belief system practiced by the Dibangiyas, a sect of Deori tribe inhabiting in the plains of Assam. For the present discussion a study was made on a village, Bahgora Deori Gaon of Lakhimpur District, Assam. The materials for the present discussions were collected during month of Decemberand January,2014. The study village is a homogenous one,inhabited by the Dibangiya Deoris only.

II

The Deoris are one of the major scheduled tribe inhabiting in the plains of Assam. The word 'Deori' is originated from the Sanskrit word 'Deva Grihika' meaning in charge of a temple or a priest. The original habitat of the Deoris was on the bank of the river Kundil and in Sadiya. From there they gradually spread over to the different parts of Assam. At present the Deoris are mainly found in Lakhimpur, Dibrugarh, Sibsagar, Jorhat, Sonitpur and in the Sadiya region of Tinsukia district of Assam. They are also found in two districts of Arunachal Pradesh,i.e., Lohit and Changlang.Racially the Deoris are Mongoloid and Mongoloid characteristics are still visible among them.

The entire Deori tribe is divided into four divisions or *khels* on the basis of the places of origin. The Deoris who were believed to reside near the bank of the river Dibang are known as Dibangiya, those near Tengapani and Borpani or Borgang are known as Tengapania and Borgoya respectively. The people who inhabited in Pat Sadia were named as Patargonya.Of all the four divisions of the Deoris, the Dibangiya Deoris have preserved their traditional socio religious organisation almost along with their indigenous dialect known as *duan*. The Dibangiya's have twelve exogamous clans (*jaku*). They are *Sundariya, Patriya, Kumataya, Airiya, Chitigaya, Chugrangaya, Charia, Dupia, Murangya, Lagachiya, Teliya* and *Kalia-Chakuya*. The *Jakus* plays an important role in selecting the functionaries of the priestly council. Among the different functionary of the Dibangiyas, the chief priest is called the *Bardeori* who is invariably selected from *Sundariyo* clan only. Next to him, who assists the *Bardeori* is known as the *Sarudeori* who only comes from *Patriyo* clan. Again there are other assistant priests, viz., *Barbhorali* and*Sarubhorali* who are selected from *Airiyo* clan. A typical Dibangiya residential house consists of a structure built on piles. The family of the Dibangiya society is mostly a joint one. Rice is their staple food, along with the rice they take locally produced vegetables, creepers and edible roots, meat, fish, etc.They also prepared *suje* (locally brewed rice beer) which is considered to be a prestigious item for entertaining the guests. Their society is patrilineal in nature and monogamy is the ideal form of marriage prevalent among them. They are mainly agriculturalists. They are also found to be engaged in other subsistence economy like fishing, weaving, wage earning etc.

III

Religion plays an important role in the socio cultural life of the Deoris of the village. Religion may be termed as any set of attitudes, beliefs and practices, rites and rituals related to supernatural powers, that power may be force, spirits, ghosts, god, demons and others. Religion is considered as the beliefs and patterns of behaviour by which human try to deal with the important problems that cannot be solved by known technology or organisational techniques. To overcome these limitation people turn to the manipulation of supernatural beings or powers. Supernatural powers or forces are those powers which are believed to be not human or not subjected to the laws of nature.

The exact nature of supernatural differs from people to people and society to society. For some supernatural may be constituted of ghosts and spirits,for others it may be manifested through a pantheon of anthropomorphic God and Goddesses, or a single high God, or soon. The religion of the Dibangiya Deori of Bahgora Deori Gaon according to them is known as 'kundi' as they believe *Kundi Mama* as the chief parochial deities. They believe *Kundi Mama* also known as *Burha Burhi* or *Gira Girachi* as also the creator of the entire universe. The word *Kundi Mama* is related to God and Goddesses or *Purush* and *Prakriti* where *Kundi* and *Mama*represent*Purush* and *Prakriti* respectively. They also worship Balia Baba or Pichadema and Tamreshwari or Pichachidema, who are believed to be the eldest son and daughter of the same supreme God. All the deities are worshipped for the well being of the masses and also for agricultural improvement. They do not worship any idol or image.

IV

Religious rites and rituals are performed in a place of worship where people offer prayer to appease the supernatural for the benefit of the self as well as for the whole community (Zaman 2010). The place of worship plays a significant role in the socio religious life of a community. The Dibangiyas of the village also have a common and permanent worshipping place for the deities, known as *Kundiku* or *Midiku*which means the abode of deity. The people show great devotion and respect to the *Midiku*. The site of the *Midiku*is always located on the eastern side of the village or in the centre of the village. The *Midiku* consists of four structured houses. The house which is erected at the centre of the *Midiku* is the main house, which is the abode of Kundi Mama. On the left side of the main house is the abode of Goddess Tamreshwari and on the right side of the main house it is the abode of BoliaBaba. There is another house which is situated in the compound of the *Midiku*but separated from the main house known as *Morong*. *Morong* is a hall of congregation, where members of village meets for prayer and celebrate religious functions. It is the place where birds and animals are sacrificed and foods are cooked and consumed by the members after the performance of community rituals. The *Dao*(weapon by which animals and birds are sacrificed by the priest during rituals) is kept at the main house of the shrine. The *Dao* is considered to be a sacred object and have great power and religious value.

The propitiation system at the shrine is performed by the priest. In all societies, there exist individuals,whose job is to guide and supplement the religious practices of others. Such individuals are highly skilled at contacting and influencing supernatural beings and manipulating supernatural forces. Among the Deoris of the village the religious duties, rites and rituals are conducted by a set of religious functionaries, namely*Bardeori, Sarudeori, Barbhorali* and *Sarubhorali*,invariably selected from four different clans. It has been already mentioned that the *Bordeori* is selected from *Sundariyo* clan only, *Sarudeori* from *Patriyio,Borbhorali* and *Sarubhorali* from *Airiyo* clan respectively.The priests among the Deoris are always a male person and each priest is entitled with different duties to carry out. *Bardeori* is the chief priest and also the most respected person of the village. He is a full time ritual specialist as well as custodian of the *Midiku*. For the selection of *Bardeori* the person concern should be healthy,honest and a man of good character. He should not be a person mauled by a tiger or bitten by snake earlier, nor excreta of a vulture or crow should have fallen upon him. The *Bardeori* alone can enter into the main house of the shrine and worship the deities by singing hymns and reciting incantations .He is also entitled to perform sacrifices of birds and animals related to different rituals.The second in the hierarchy of priests among the four is *Sarudeori*. He assists the *Bardeori* during the performances of rituals and sacrifices. He is also entitled to perform all the rituals in *Midiku* in the absence of the *Bardeori*. The duty of *Barbhorali* is to collect dues of the temple and to provide animals for sacrifice. After sacrificing animals or birds it is the duty of the *Barbhorali* to collect the blood of the sacrificed animals for offering to the deities. The last in the hierarchy of priest is *Sarubhorali* who act as an assistant of *Barbhorali* for management of assets of the shrine.

In addition to the four priests there are some other officials to look after the activities of the *Midiku.* They are *Bora*, *Barik*, *Pariya,*etc. These office bearers are needed in all the rituals held in the shrine. The duty of *Bora* is to employ special workers to clean the premises of the shrine and to arrange the objects for rituals. *Barik* announces the news about the ritual date to the villagers a day before it is to take place and he also assist the priest on the occasions of the rituals. The duty of the Pariya is also to assist the priest in conducting rituals at *Midiku* as the probationary pupil of the priest.

The Deori priests are conferred with highest honour in the society. Rigid taboos and restrictions are observed by them in their day to day life. As for example they should be devoted to serve the community as a whole. They should keep themselves pure by abstaining from having food from others and debarred from cutting hair or shaving beard in the outside.

V

Observances of religious rites and rituals are integral part of every community. Rituals are the means through which a person can relate to the supernatural. Ritual practices are often an expression of the belief that supernatural powers can be made to act in certain ways through prayers, sacrifice and various ritualistic activities. The Dibangiya Deoris of the village also observe various rituals throughout the year. In every rites and rituals which are performed in the village shrine, the deities are worshipped by the *Bardeori* by reciting incantations. The incantations and the spells are in oral form and they carry special meaning which is difficult for the common people to understand. The incantations can never be published or brought into written form as they believed that anyone trying to do so will face ill consequences.

While performing puja or rituals in the *Midiku* offerings are made to the deities which consist of different items. Generally three types of propitiation system are followed while performing rituals in the shrine. They are *Sattiki*, *Rajashiki* and *Tamshiki.*In the first phase known as *Sattiki* , uncooked food and other items like soaked gram, banana, sugarcane, betel nuts, betel leaves, incense stick ,earthen lamp etc are used for puja offerings. To appease the God and Goddesses different sacred incantations are recited by the *Bardeori* inside the shrine. After the completion of the first phase, the second phase *Rajashiki* starts. In this phase after presenting the wishes of all the villagers attending the rituals, the priests take a mark in their forehead with spot prepared from paste of *chandan* (sandal wood) and give similar mark to all the people and after that they starts the decapitation of the birds and animals offered to sacrifice. Generally Goats (black or white in colour), Duck, Pigeons (in pair), etc., are sacrificed. In the third phase i.e., *Tamshiki*, the meat of the sacrificed animals or birds are cooked along with other dishes in the *Morong*. After offering to the deities, a community feast is arranged where all the villagers take part.The Dibangiyas of the village observe various rituals like *Bohag Bisu, Magh Bisu, Chai-Labiruba, Makan Chiban, Saonia puja,* etc. Wednesday is considered as the most auspicious day among the Deoris for starting religious activity or any good work.

Bihu is the main festival of the Deoris of the village, which they called *Bisu* and it has close association with their agricultural activities. The *Bisu* festivals are observed before starting the agricultural operation with unrestricted joy and merry making.They observe both *Bohag Bisu and Magh Bisu* every year which falls in the month of *Bohag* (April -May) and *Magh* (January-February) of Assamese calendar. *Bisu* is a community festival and a ritual called *Bisu Puja* is performed during *Bisu* in the village shrine.During *Bohag Bisu* puja all villagers irrespective of age and sex gather at the *Midiku.* The *Bardeori* with the three assistant priests offer prayer inside the *Midiku* and no one is allowed to enter the *Midiku* when the prayer is in progress. In the *Bisu Puja* sacrificing of goats, ducks, fowls etc., are made and after the ritual all the villagers take part in the community feast.The villagers also offer prayers to their ancestral spirits. They believed that the spirit of the ancestors never depart from the family but continue to live with the family in the form of a spirit. Therefore to appease the spirits they perform rituals for the welfare of the family members. During the day of *Bohag Bisu*, in the morning each family performs a puja called *Mora Leruba* to worship their ancestors. The puja is performed at the backside of the house where *Suje* (rice beer) and *Kaji* (a special curry prepared out of vegetables and flesh of fowls) are offered to the ancestors.

Another central aspect of *Bohag Bisu puja* among the Dibangiyas is the appearance of *Deodhani* where a particular man or woman is possessed by a supernatural power or spirit. That particular man or woman is considered as the personal communicator from a supernatural being who is directed to foretell about the future happenings of the village people and that is why all villagers respect this situation with awe and respect. In Deori society it is commonly known as *Deo Utha.* During the period when a person is embodied by a deity, offerings are made in the *Midiku* to propitiate them. The deities indicate their presence by entering inside the body and soul of some males or females. Under the influence of the deity some sort of extraordinary power and euphoria is generated which lifts that particular person to miraculous states of exaltation. The particular man or women even drinks the raw blood of fowls and goes into the state of trance and starts dancing with the tune of drum and cymbals. They generally predict ensuing events in the coming year in the village. Animal sacrifices are made to them and people worship them, offers prayer and sacrifices to gain favour.

Like *Bohag Bisu,* during *Magh Bisu* also a grand feast is arranged on the first Wednesday of Magh month, in the premises of *Morong* attached to the temple. The chief priest offers puja to the deities of the shrine and sacrifice of cocks and goats are also performed.*Metua Puja* is one of the rituals observed by the Deories of the village during three times a year. It is performed during *Bohag*(April-May), *Ahin*(September-October) and *Phagun* (February-March) at the *Midiku.* In this ritual a goat either black or white in colour is required for sacrifice. The chief priest along with the assistant priests offer sacrifice and prays for the well being of the villagers and to get relief from physical calamities.

Another ritual called *Sat Labiruba* which is performed during the month of *Ahar* (June-July). This ritual is performed for purification purpose of mother earth. There is a believe that the earth attains menstruation during this period which is known as *Sat* that is observed for seven days and during that period no ritual can be performed at the shrine. As such *Sat Labiruba*is performed to purify the shrine which is polluted due to *Sat.* The priests offer prayer to Ai Basumati (goddess earth) and sacrifice red coloured cocks. *Chua Labiruba* ritual is an annual purification ritual of the *Midiku.* Before performing any other kind of ritual at the shrine this ritual is performed. It is generally performed during the month of *Saon* (July- August) where the chief priest sacrifices chicken and pigeons and prays to the deities for the well being of the villagers.

Saonia puja is observed during the month of *Saon* (July- August). This ritual is performed for paying tribute to God and Goddesses for better agricultural yield. During this ritual also the *Bardeori* of the village offers bananas, betel nuts, betel leaves, incenses, etc., to the deities and sacrifices fowls and pray for successful harvesting of paddy.*Achira Puja* is another ritual which is generally held during the month of *Ahin* (September- October) and Kati (October-November) for better agricultural yield and also to get relief from natural calamities, diseases, etc. The main important items required for this ritual are black coloured cocks, powdered rice, milk, rice, black gram, *suje*(rice beer), betel nuts,etc.The *Bakat Makan* ritual is organised during the month of *Aghun*(November –December) before starting consumption of *Sali* rice. This ritual is performed in the *Midiku* where the chief priest *Bardeori* sacrifices fowls and offer their blood and decapitated heads to the supreme deity, *Kundi Mama* and prays for the well being of the village and community. This ritual is meant for offering the first fruits of harvest to the chief deities.

VI

The rites and ceremonies that mark the occasions such as birth, marriage, death etc., are often been called as rites of passage or crisis rite of an individual. Van Gennep (1960) defined the rites of passage which usher individuals through the crucial crisis of their lives, such as birth, puberty, marriage, parenthood, advancement to a higher class, occupational specialisation and death. Among most of the societies of the world, the performance of rituals on these occasions are found and all these are concerned with changes of status like at birth when a new person enters the society, at marriage when two persons unite and at death when a person leaves. Like any other community the Dibangiya Deoris of the village also perform certain kind of religious activities at the time of birth, marriage and death.

Among the Deoris a good number of beliefs and taboos are associated with the pregnant mother and new born baby. A pregnant mother has to follow certain restrictions like she is not allowed to carry heavy objects, cannot take part in husking and grinding works, etc. After the birth of the baby, a *sarai* (disc on stand) containing uncooked rice, egg, betel nut, betel vine leaf, coins, etc., is placed as an offering near the bed of the mother by a women of the house for the well being of the new born baby. Till the period of releasing of the umbilical cord from the baby's body, the mother is thought to be unclean. This period is regarded as polluted period and the mother neither can enter the kitchen nor can she cook meal for any person during this period. Only after performing *Chua Labiruba* which is a purificatory ritual, the household along with the new born baby and the mother breaks the impurity. To perform this ritual old men and women of the village and the priestly council are invited. A pig is generally sacrificed to mark the occasion.

Marriage is considered as an indispensible part of life of the Deori people. Clan exogamy is strictly followed in case of marriage. They have four different forms of marriage, namely *Bar Biya, Maju Biya, Saru Biya* and *Gandharva Biya.Bar Biya* is an expensive affair as all types of customs, traditions of Deori marriage are observed in this type. This type of marriage is arranged by parents and it is continued for three days. *Maju Biya* is quite less expensive than *Bar Biya*, which is also arranged by the parents of the prospective couple and continued for two days. *Saru Biya* is a popular form of marriage among the Deori which is completed in a day and the expenditure of such marriage is quite low. The most widely prevalent type of marriage among the people of the village is *Gandharva Biya* or marriage by elopement, where the couple concerned take initiatives. In this type of marriage the boy with the help of some of his friends elope the girl on an appointed date. No formal ceremony is observed in this type of marriage. However a simple feast is arranged by the bridegroom family on the same day or on the following day of elopement. The important items of required in the marriage feast constitute fish, pork, rice beer, rice, vegetables, betel nuts and betel vine leaf. Suje (rice beer) is the most inevitable item for Deori marriage ceremony.

A series of rites and ritual are observed by the Dibangiya Deoris for the death of an individual as well as for the salvation of the disposed corpse. There are two primary ways of disposal of the dead body. Generally men and women dying natural death are cremated. But the dead bodies of children, pregnant women and epidemic cases are buried. The dead body is duly honoured by them. Before carrying the corpse to the cremation ground, the dead body is washed with water and is adorned with a new dress. An egg is broken in the forehead of the deceased by the eldest son. The significance of this ritual is to detach all kinship relationship with the deceased. Usually the eldest son puts fire in the pyre but in absence of the eldest son any male member of the family can perform his duty. A social taboo is observed by the members of the deceased family for four days. On the fourth day a funeral ceremony is held followed by a feast. The final mortuary ritual among the Dibangiya Deori is known as *Daha* where all the villagers and the priests are invited. The priests and the elderly persons perform *Suje Luguruba* ritual to satisfy the soul of the deceased. After the end of the ritual a feast is organised where large number of chickens, pigs, rice beer is required.

VII

The social structure of the Dibangiya Deoris are interwoven and interrelated with their religion and every sphere of life of the Deori people is guided by rites and rituals of their religion. The Dibangiyas are still found to be maintaining their tradition of aboriginal practices. Kundi- Mama is the supreme God of this group of people, who is worshipped at household as well as in community level. Besides the supreme deity they also worship Balia Baba and Goddess Tamreswari. The deities are propitiated at the *Midiku* , which occupies a central place in their socio religious life. The propitiation system at the *Midiku* can only be performed by the priests.There are a set of priestly council for conducting the rites and rituals in the village shrine. The priests are considered as the chief intermediaries between God and human. Only the priests could offer prayers and sacrifices in the shrine to appease the deities. The cult of sacrifice is a dominant feature of indigenous religious practices of the people in the village. They offer sacrifices to the deities to ward off sickness, sufferings and afflictions and also for the well-being of the village and community.*Suje* (rice beer) is a part and parcel of the socio ritual life of the Deoris of the village, which is offered to all the deities, ancestors and other supernatural beings. Without these offerings no ritual can be performed, nor do any socio cultural functions become complete. The main occupation of the community is agriculture and every harvesting activity of the village starts with appeasing of deities of the *Midiku*. Bohag Bisu is the main festival among the Dibangiyas which has relation with agricultural activities. The most considerable aspect of *Bisu* is that it must be started by a puja which they termed as *Bisu Puja*. The *Bisu Puja* is generallyperformed at the village shrine. Besides *Bihu,* there are host of rituals which have been performed by the villagers in their respective households or at the shrine during different time of a year. They also observe various rites and rituals in connection with the principle events of life. As for example, when a child is born certain rites are performed to ensure strength, good fortune and to protect the baby from the influence of evil spirits. There are other rites when someone gets married and funeral rites are performed to ensure safe passage into the immortal world. The Dibangiya Deoris have been maintaining their pristine traditional socio- religious practices intact. However they are found to be influenced by the beliefs and rituals of the neighbouring Hindu population of Assam, as a result of which some of the customary rules, values, norms of Assamese society have glued to their social life. They propitiate deities like, Laksmi, Saraswati, Krishna, etc., of Hindu pantheon. They are also the followers of Sakta cult of Hindu religion, as a result of which animal sacrifices figures prominently in their religious performances. Although the influence of Hinduism is slightly visible among them yet the trend towards traditional indigenous beliefs and practices are still prominent.

References

Deori, N and Karabi Deori, (2009). *Deori Loka Sanskritir Ruprekha*, Kiran Prakashn, Dhemaji.

Durkheim, E., (1912). *The Elementary Forms of Religious Life*, Free Press, New York.

Frazer, J.G., (1911). *The Golden Bough- A Study in Magic and Religion*, The Macmillan Press, London.

Haviland, W.A., (1990). *Cultural Anthropology* (9th Edition), Harcourt Brace CollegePublishers, U.S.A.

Karsten, R., (1935). *The Origin of Worship: A Study in Primitive Religion,* Kegan Paul, London.

Malinowski, B., (1954). *Magic, Science and Religion*, The Free Press, New York.

Medhi, B.K., (2012). Religious life of the Assamese Sikhs, in K. Jose SVD, Gautam K. Bera,BirinchiK. Medhi,R.P. Athparia (Eds) *Concept of God and Religion*, Abhijeet Publication, New Delhi: 3-23.

Redfield, R., (1965). *Peasent Society and Culture,* Chicago University Press, Chicago.

Spencher, K.M., (2002). *Religion in Life*, Indian Publishers Distributors, Delhi.

Srinivas, M.N., (1952). *Religion and Society among the Coorgs of South India,* Clarendon Press, Oxford.

Tylor, E.B., (1871). *Primitive Culture*, J Murray, London.

Van Gennep, Arnold, (1960). *The Rites of Passage*, University of Chicago Press, Chicago.

Vidhyarthi, L.P., (1968).*Applied Anthropology in India,* Kitab Mahal, Allahabad.

Wallace, A.F.C., 1966, *Religion: An Anthropological View*, Random House, New York.

Yinger, M.J., (1957). *Religion, Society and the Individual: An Introduction to the Sociology of Religion,* Macmillan Publishing, New York.

Zaman, A., (2010). The Balia Baba Than: aspect of sacred complex in a Tengapania Deori village of Assam, *Bulletin of the Department of Anthropology,* Dibrugarh University. Vol- 38:17-32.

27

Culture, Religious Change and Identity: A Case Study of the Muklom (Tangsa) of Arunachal Pradesh

— *Sunumi Changmi*

Introduction

The Mukloms are a small sub-tribe of the Tangsa Naga group living in Changlang district of Arunachal Pradesh. There is hardly any literature on them. The Muklom family structure is patriarchal and patrilineal. They practise Christianity, Rangfraism and old traditional practices (that includes sacrifices of animals). This study uses whatever secondary material that is available, but it is based mainly on primary data collected through interviews and observation. The author, being a member of the Muklom community, also uses personal experience and observation. The data used is drawn from fieldwork done in the months of October 2015. The objective of this study is to discover the impact of various religious practices on the cultural practices of theMuklom.

This paper is divided into four sections. The first section provides basic information on the Mukloms; the second section deals with thedefinition of religion; the third section deals with religion and its influence on Muklom cultural and social identity, and the fourth section gives some suggestions and remedies to sustain traditional practices.

Muklom is the name of a sub-tribe of the Tangsa. Tangsa is an umbrella term for about 35 different trans-Patkai ethnic groups, arguably related to the Naga[1]. Different etymologies have been proposed for the name Muklom

(Matcha 2005:55). Some say the syllable 'Mok' means 'oblivion' and 'Lom' means 'warmness'. The meaning of Muklomwould be 'oblivious in warmness', becausethis group of people used to crave for living together and become oblivious in warmness in the process of migrations in the early period. They did not break or scatter. Ever since they lived or settled in togetherness. According to another explanation, the Muklom have migrated from a hill in Burma (Myanmar) called 'Mokloom', and therefore they becameknown as 'Moklum'.Yet another source said that the name of the place of origin was called 'Molom-Solom' from which the term Muklom was derived.Some outsiders pronounced it 'Moklum' or 'Moklom', butthe Muklom themselves preferred to be known as 'Muklom'.

The Mukloms: Basic Features

As mentioned at the outset, the Mukloms are a small sub-tribe of the Tangsa Naga group. They have a distinct identity, which will be discussed in the following sections.

(a) Identity, Habitat and Population

The Mukloms came from Burma across the Patkai hills to settle in Tirap, now Changlang district of Arunachal Pradesh a few centuries ago (Maitra 1995). According to Muklom oral tradition, they migrated to their present habitat about three or four generations ago. They came from the east in search of food and suitable agricultural land. The Mukloms call themselves Tangsa as a means of projecting a regional or broader identity. In fact, the name Tangsa is a broad term that embraces several communities living in the mountainous terrain of Changlang District, for example the Havi, Muklom, Jugli, Kimsing, Longchang and Sangwa. The Mukloms are today recognised as a distinct Scheduled Tribe under the generic name of Tangsa (Naga).

The Mukloms live in twenty-one villages in the mountainous terrain of Changlang district in Arunachal Pradesh. This district lies between latitudes 26°40' - 27°40' N and longitudes 95°11' - 97°10' E (Sarkar 2002). Muklom villages are located in the Changlang, Khimyong and Kharsang circles of the Changalng Sub-Division of the district (Kri 2010). The Muklom villages cover an area of approximately 4,662 sq km. Changlang, which is the district headquarters and Kharsang, a small town, are the two main commercial and socio-cultural centers.

According to the Census of India, in 1981, the Mukloms numbered 1,917. In 2011, the Census of India lists them as MoglumTangsa. The total population in 2011 was 2,606 of which 2,312 were in rural areas and only 294 were in urban areas, indicating that they were mainly rural people. Of the 2,606 Mukloms, 1,275 were males and 1,331 were females, with a sex ratio of 1,044, which is favourable to women.

(b) Economy

Agriculture is the main source of livelihood. Settled agriculture is a common practice in the plain areas of Kharsang circle and jhum (shifting) cultivation in the hill areas. At present, many Mukloms have adopted another kind of agricultural practice, that is, the plantation of tea and cardamom in both the plains and the hill areas. In the case of settled agriculture, they employ labourers from outside, viz., Nepali, Bengali, Kachari, Santhali and others. But for jhum cultivation they follow the traditional methods and villagers help one another during the whole agricultural cycle. Agricultural products are mainly food items for self consumption. If there is any surplus, it is sold in the market for cash.

Handicrafts are another source of income, though not on a large scale. Sometimes women weave clothes and men weave bamboo mats and baskets. They sell some of these items in the local markets. Domestication of animals like pigs, cows, and poultry is usually handled by women which includes bringing home fodder for the animals.

Selling of surplus agricultural products like vegetables, tubers, etc. is done by women, but selling of meat is done by men. The money earned from selling goods is often handed over to women. Buying grocery items is the task of the mothers. They have the freedom to spend money as needed, though they require the consent of men when they have to purchase big assets or property. Thus, in general, women have freedom of buying or selling products.

At present several Mukloms are employed in various government services and in other private jobs. Therefore dependence on agriculture is slowly decreasing in favour of other jobs in the service sectors. Education is given increasingly more importance in the present time.

(c) Literacy and Education

According to the Census of 2011, the total literacy rate for Muklom tribe is 68.98% with 76.87% for males and 60.51% for females. These rates compare favourably with the literacy rates for all the Scheduled Tribes in Arunachal Pradesh, which are 64.58% for persons, 71.48% for males and 57.95% for females. These rates indicate that the Mukloms have begun to take modern education seriously. It is not surprising, therefore, that some Mukloms are now employed in non-agricultural occupations.

(d) Political Organisations

The traditional village council is known as *Khaa-phung him* and is led by village elders or male members called *pho-khowano*. All kinds of disputes related to land, property, marriage, divorce, etc., are settled by village council. However, women do not have any role in the council and its deliberations. It is said that women are meant to look after the household and to perform domestic chores. However, with the introduction of Panchayati Raj Institutions after the 73rd amendment of the Constitution of India, women have started to take part in politics. Thus, modern institutions give more space to women and their participation is active and visible.

1. Definition of Religion

To define religion is a complicated task, as the ideas and the kind of beliefs and practices denoted by religions are too diverse to fit into a single rule. However, the basic function of religion is seen in two parts, the first being the manifest; often not explicit as its manifest function but, nevertheless, an important component of the role of salvation and to provide them with appropriate guidance of salvation and to provide them with appropriate guidance for its attainment. Religion to some extent provides solace and reassurance from the many uncertainties that engulf a person day to day existence (Kamie 2014:231).

According to Kamei, tribal religions are not static entity; they evolve and change in response to varied factors which alters the socio-political, cultural and economic conditions from which they have arisen. Religious syncretism is one of the most frequently observed and well documented phenomena among tribal religious practices in the wake of prolonged exposure to other religious practices (Ibid: 234-235). Religious conversion presents perhaps the most persistent threat towards the survival and continuation of many tribal religions. Against the onslaught of increasing religious conversion, in some of these tribal religions there has been a conscious shift towards a centralised organisational structure to strengthen and preserve the indigenous faith. Such adaptive measures have been documented in some of the tribal communities; for example the Adis of Arunachal Pradesh and the Khasis in Meghalaya have adopted Donyi polo and Seng Khasi respectively to preserve their indigenous cultures.

Sonowal(2014) has studied the religion, ethnicity and revivalism among the tribes of Arunachal Pradesh. He discussed on the religious revivalisms ofAdis, Nyishis and Apatanis. He stated:

> The Government of Arunachal Pradesh enacted a Bill "The Arunachal Pradesh Freedom of Indigenous Faith Bill, 1978 (Bill No.4 of 1978) to provide prohibition of conversion from indigenous faith of Arunachal Pradesh to any other faith or religion by use of force of inducement or by fraudulent means and for such matters connected therewith. However, the Bill couldn't stop conversion among Arunachal Tribes. The Christian Missionaries adapted a middle path. They declared their non hostility components (good) of local culture in Christianity (Sonowal 2014:80).

He further says, in tribal society, religion and cultural identity are synonymous terms. For instance, the nomenclature Donyi-Polo religion, has been derived from the recognition of Donyi Polo-the combined divine figure of Donyi (the Sun) and (the moon) as Adi's popular Gods. It is evident that in tribal religion and faith the inherent philosophy is always not clear. Rather it is the ritual part that is regarded as more important, especially among the commons. To compete with rational religion like Christianity, the Adi intellectuals have constructed the belief system, religious ethics and philosophy of Donyi Polo, and published these in a booklet. The beliefs and principles which were presented in this booklet have been adopted by thc people and practiced in their day to day life (Ibid: pp 86-87).

Often religious communities tend to claim that they have retained their separate identities rather than melted and coalesced with the present trend and practices of outsiders' influence. However, in-depth study is needed to determine whether religious communities resist to the present change or that change is in fact occurring without being noticed.

The Tribal Value System Lost its Grip on Religion

Tribal Christians have been criticized for losing their very cultural aspects. They are accused of practicing an alien or outsider's religion that seems to destroy every ounce of the indigenous cultural practices. We may quote from a book written by Khimhun:

> In the same way the Rangfraism practiced by the Nagas of Arunachal Pradesh of Northeast India believed that most of the ethnic groups of Tangnu and Shangnu Nagas of Myanmar and Nagaland also belonged to this Faith; but unfortunately most of them got converted into Christianity and now they are feeling a sense of identity crisis (Khimhun 2010:3).

This feeling is also shared by some of the Muklom Christians, as a youth female expressed her views:

> By looking at the Pangwa sub-tribe of Tangsas, it can be said that Muklom may eventually have to revive their old cultural practice that is not popular in the present context. In the olden times, traditionally, parents would invite for a meal their daughters, who were married off. It was a kind of small family feast that took place. This occasion was marked by killing a pig in honour and love of their daughters and son-in-laws. But this practice is hardly found now. I think such practices should not be stopped because there is no harm in following the original practices, if they do not harm anybody's faith. This practice was more about recreation or re-bonding the family ties and I feel this basic practice needs to be revived again.

It shows the Some of the traditional Muklom informants also mentioned the recent change among theMuklom Christians:

> In Muklom society, the maternal uncle holds a very important place. For instance, when a child is possessed by malevolent spirit or if the child

happens to lose his way home while playing around in the jungle,then the maternal uncle plays important role. It is believed that even if any child is possessed by malevolent spirits the maternal uncle has the power to rescue his nieces or nephews by chanting mantras in his own dialect. He is considered to be powerful and he can drive away the malevolent spirits. Even in the time of festivals likeMoh-mol, thematernal uncletied a thread around the wrists of his nieces and nephews by chanting a mantra, *ngabahouhom e anggo, ulom e anggo, upang e anggo* meaning 'your maternal uncle is there to protect and guide you, not even a common cold should touch you'. This shows that the maternal uncle has an important role to play; spiritually he acts asshield to his nieces and nephews.

Unfortunately, this practice is confined to the traditional Muklom and Rangfra followers. As an elderly Christian female says, "Christianity does not belief in a mortal man to be a protector of human welfare, but only god can ensure such promises".

Muklom Christians are criticized by their fellow counterparts' viz., Rangfra followers and Traditional Mukloms for abandoning their valuable religious-cultural practices. Consequently, in this case it is seen that cultural values that were followed in the past have lost theirgrip; some have even been replaced by new practices that were not known to the Mukloms previously.

In the same manner this kind of instances can be seen in Rangfraism. The Rangfra followersclaimed to embrace all the best of world's religion as mentioned by Barkataki-Ruscheweyh (2015). However, it is clearly seen that Hinduimsalso have a strong hold on the Rangfraism as mentioned byBarkataki-Ruscheweyh:

> It is not surprising that many Rangfraa Society activities are supported by Hindu nationalist groups, like the RSS (Rashtriya Swayamsewak Sangh) and the VHP (Vishwa Hindu Parishad). Rangfraa is shown in many calendars and publications of the Vivekananda Kendra as the God of the Tangsa and Tutsa communities in Arunachal Pradesh. Hindu organisations played an active role in having the Rangfraa statue made in Jodhpur in Rajasthan (located thousands of kilometres away in western India) and transported by train and road across India so that it could be installed in the prayer-house at New Changlang. Mr. Khimhun and other Rangfraa Society office bearers maintain close links with the Vivekananda Kendra and the Arunjyoti officials and often take their advice and use their facilities.

This clearly shows how Rangraism is directly influenced by the Hindu elements of worship system. In addition to what is mentioned above, they use flowers to offer to god, they practice lighting of *diyas* in their temples and offer incense sticks to the god 'Rangfra'. All these practices have become a part of the worship circular.

With relations to the change in worship system of Rangfra, Mr. L. Khimhun, the Secretary of General Rangfra Faith Promotional Society, says:

> Our ancestors used to eat rice and we also use to eat rice. Our ancestors cooked their rice in bamboo poles. Now tell me, is it necessary that we should also cook our rice in bamboo pole in this scientific age? Is there any harm to anybody if I cook my rice in a pressure cooker? If there is no harm, why one should criticize me? Similar is the case in our system of worship and prayer. Our ancestors worshipped and prayed to Rangfraa and we also worship and pray to Rangfraa. We have changed only the method of cooking and not the rice. To change the Religion is as good as substitute the rice with bread by saying that the rice eaten by our ancestors is not good let us eat bread instead (Khimhun 2006:12).

As per the food habits of Rangfra followers,one of the Muklom youths says:

> It is not compulsory to abstain from meat, it depends on individuals. If your wife is on a fast, then the family prefers not to take/ eat meat on that particular day. The *Rang-samal* (priest) too encourages the followers not to consume meat on the day of worship/service day because it has to be a holy day.

This clearly shows how religious practices have their share of influence on the food habits of Rangfra followers. There is an old saying, *ngamya* when a person chokes up or accidently bite their lips while eating. In fact, such a happening signalsthat this person will receive meat in the future. There is a radical change at the present context among the Rangfras because they abstain from eating meat during worship days.

In a similarly way, a Rangfraites (Ming kechu considered to be holy) says:

> The believers of Rangfrah have changed manifold in their practices. For instance, in both marriage and death rituals the secretary of 'rang-shum-him' or the temple is in charge of performing rituals and practices which were earlier done by their clan members. Much more change is likely to take place in the near future because Rangfraism is also known as *thong-naal* meaning replacing old with new cultural-beliefs. Thus, new is incorporated and old is abandoned.

He further states that many changes have taken place in the new belief system. Earlier animal sacrifices took placeevery six months or year to ward off sicknesses.As it is believed that it was a waste of money, it has now been replaced by mass prayers or fasting. No animal sacrifice is encouraged at present. Rearing of animals is basically for their economy assistance. Rangfraism is almost akin to Christianity, where animal sacrifices and propitiation of evil spirit is not observed anymore.

However, the crux of the matter in this discussion is to what extent a change should be welcomed and how one should draw the boundaries between a healthy change and a change that may cause the loss of the basic identity of a community. It is true that old aged customs that were part and parcel of the Mukloms in the past may not be relevant in today's context. For example, the killing of twin babies in the Muklom society was not considered as crime in the past due to strong beliefs attached to its practices. This same practice is no longer accepted. Therefore, change or reformation in cultural practices is essential and sometime it is inevitable. Nevertheless, a rampant change of cultural practices may raise concern aboutMuklom'sidentity. Likewise, a male believer of traditional Muklom practice says:

> No matter what religion you profess, your origin should not be forgotten. Even if you are Christian Muklom or Rangfraa followers; you need to maintain and preserve your culture. Religion and culture should not be mixed up. Christian Muklom should not forget their legendry songs and language because someday it may look like a lost community, if they do not know their root. We do not know what the rituals in marriage are or what the stories of our grandparents are.

In addition that what have been mentioned above, a traditional religious male politician says:

> A very strange thing that I have observed among the Rangfra followers is that people abstain from eating meat on particular days or month and keep a different kitchen to cook meat. This kitchen is detached from the main house. In the main house they do not cook as every Rangfra worshipper has an individual temple.

Further, one of the traditional followers also made a point by saying this:

> There seems to be confusion among Rangfra followers as some are trying to discard the old practices and some are trying not to give away the entire set of rituals. For instance, recently, in a nearby village a disagreement took place over death rituals. The deceased family wanted to send off the dead in traditional ways but since they had accepted new beliefs-Rangfraism, some said they have to observe Rangfraa norms. Eventually, the secretary was not allowed to lead the rituals since the clan members did not agree to do so. The same is seen while observing the harvest festival.

Another traditional believer shares her views:

> Christian Mukloms have totally abandoned their festivals and culture and it is same with Rangfraism. We thought that it would be something to do with indigenous culture but no, it is again totally different from the traditional practices.

As is evident from the interviews, culture and traditional practices are very dear to the Mukloms. At the same time it cannot be denied that no culture is static, as it keeps evolving over time.It is very important to note the tremendous change in the lives of the Muklom(Tangsas) especially in the area of socio-religious and cultural practices.At times there seems to be confusion as to how much originality is being retained by the Muklom in true sense. Both Christianity and Rangfraism in some way disdainthe old traditional and cultural practices saying it is out dated and out of touch with modern practices.

Conclusion

Rapid changes in religious practices are seen in the Muklom society. It can be said thathad religion existed unaided it could have been a void in itself. But we know that cultural and social practices have their own share of influence on religion and vice-versa that keep all elements intertwined. This can affect what believers persistently reject as well as what they may absorb into their patterns of belief and practices. And such influence is continuous, since the inception of religion. It is clear from the discussion that both Christian and RangfraaMukloms have accepted new practices due to outside influence. The transition period is very visible in the Muklom society. Some seem to be confused by the change in their religious practices. Syncretismof old traditional practices with Rangfraism ways of worship is also witnessed among the Mukloms. Some have embraced Christianity, while others continue the ancestral ways of worship. It shows that change is an ongoing process and it may continue to take place. Nevertheless, some traditional cultural practices are seen at the present context among both Christian and RangfraMukloms. However,it is important to draw the boundaries ofchange as to what extent it can be permitted without losingthe Muklom cultural identity.

There are some suggestions put forward by informants, that say that Christian Muklomshouldrevive the traditional moh-mol festival without religious differences and Rangfra followers should not be encouraged to practicethe notion of purity and impurity by abstaining meat because the Muklomsfeel it is not traditional practice.As far the views of informant, in spite of the internal differences in religion, Muklom identity must be preserved.

References

C.J.Sonowal. (2014). Dynamics of Religion, Ethic Identity and Changes in North East India. In C.J.Sonowal, *Religion and Ethnic Identity and Changes in North East India* (pp. 58-116). New Delhi: Akansha Publishing House.

Kamie, A. L. (2014). Religion, Revivalism and Ethnic Assertion: A case study among the Rongmei Tribe of Manipur . In C.J.Sonowal, *Religion and Ethnic Reconstruction among the Tribes of Northeast India* (pp. 230-255). New Delhi: Akansha Publishing House.

Karotemprel, S. (1996). The Impact of Christiaity on the Tribes of North East India. In J. Puthenpurakal, *Impact of Christinaity on North East India* (pp. 16-48). Shillong: Vendame Institute Publications.

Khimhun, L. (2006). *The Second Coming of Rangfraa.* Tinsukia: Rangfraa Faith Promotion Society (RFPS).

Khimhun, L. (2010). *Uniqueness of Rangfraism.* Tinsukia: Rangfraa Faith Promotion Society.

Khimun, L. (2011). Philosophy and Sprituality of Rangfraism. In K. Borang, *Socio-Cultural and Spritual Traditions of Arunachal Pradesh* (p. 24). Guwahati: Heritage Foundation.

Matcha, H. (2005). Traditional Healing System of the Muklom: Its Change and Continuity . In *Traditional Systems of the Tangsa and the Tutsa* (p. 62). Guwahati: Vivekananda Kendra Institute of Culture .

Syiemlieh, D. (1996). Socio- Cultural Background of the Peoples of North East India (19-20 Centuries). In J. Puthenpurakal, *Impact of Christinaity on North East India* (pp. 191-201). Shillong: Vendrame Institute Publications.

28

Syncretism in an Urban Context of Assam: Cultural and Religious Dimensions

— *Ranga Ranjan Das*

I

The growing 'intolerance' has become one of the major issues in recent days but a contradiction of Indian culture and civilisation. Pluralism and secularism are important aspects of Indian society since the very beginning. Flood (2004: 5) cited ' in India's population of approximately 900 million people, 700 million are Hindus, the remainder are Muslims, Sikhs, Christians, Jains, Buddhists, Parsees, Jews and followers of 'tribal' religions. There are 120 million Muslims and 45 million tribal peoples or adivasis, with 14 million Sikhs and an estimated 14 million Christians'. India is one of the most complex countries in the world from an ethnic standpoint. Managing religious relations in India is a complex endeavour. The government's approach to religious freedom has been a constitutional one, stressing the individual right to freedom of conscience but most importantly the right of religious groups to preserve control of their religious institution. Constitution prohibits discrimination on grounds of religion, race, caste, sex or place of birth (Bajpai 2010: 21-29).

Pluralism is the keystone of Indian culture and religious tolerance is the bedrock of Indian secularism. It is based on the belief that all religions are equally good and efficacious pathways to perfection of God realisation; Valsamma Paul v Cochin University, AIR 1996 SC 1011, paragraph 25 (cited in Bakshi 1991:2). The people of the country are of diverse ethnic origin, speak different languages, there are many cultural variations, tribal groupings, different religions, etc., but the nation has successfully endeavoured to discover a common thread of unity through these diversity. On the whole, there has been conscious stress on the oneness of the nation against regionalism and ethnic and religious separatism. The people as a whole are the repository of the sovereignty. Despite India being a secular country, its secularism has been tested by many ugly communal strife and violence. Religious fundamentalism, borrowing foreign doctrine of Islamism as well as intolerance subtly promoted by some organisations seeking to represent the majority population by allowing fringe outfits to promote intolerance through violence are acting as disruptive forces weakening secular nationalism of the people (Deka 2015).

Syncretism is a term used in Christian theology since at least the 17th century. According to Oxford English Dictionary, it denotes an 'attempt to sink differences and affect union between sects or philosophical schools'. In comparative religion the term refers to a process of religious amalgamation, of blending heterogeneous beliefs and practices. As such it is an aspect of religious interaction over time. This can be seen as such a broad process that indeed every religion is syncretistic, since it constantly draws upon heterogenous elements to the extent that it is often impossible for historians to unravel what comes from where. One could therefore argue that it is a useless concept.Syncretism can be seen, negatively, as a corruption of the absolute truth. It can be seen positively, as a sign of tolerance. Multiculturalism appears to have replaced the term 'syncretism' in discourse about modern, secular society (Van der Veer 2003: 185-196). The term 'multiculturalism' gathers a number of interrelated themes; it underscores the need to have a stable identity, emphasizes the contribution of cultural communities to the fulfillment of this need and brings out the link between identity and recognition. It stresses the importance of cultural belonging and legitimizes the desire to maintain difference (Bhargava 1999: 1). However the term syncretism has more applicability in the current context. As Parel (1957) finds syncretism is a natural temptation for exceptional men of higher perception, men who see and experience the transcendent unity of mankind based on purely natural foundation-metaphysics, natural theology, natural mysticism-men, it may be added, who do not seem to be aware of the true meaning of the supernatural and of its infinite superiority over the natural, however sublime. In anthropology and history as if it were a transparent, descriptive term, referring to the 'borrowing, affirmation or integration of concepts, symbols, or practices of one religious tradition into another by a process of selection and reconciliation (Berlin cited in Van der Veer *ibid*, p 185]

The Indian civilisation has always accorded a place of honour to syncretism or *samanvay*. The great pioneer of Sufi Islam in India is Khawaja Moinuddin Chisti of Ajmer. He had instructed his followers to cook vegetarian food for the communal dinner (langar) at the time of his annual Urs, so that Hindus and Muslims can equally partake. This meal is not only vegetarian; it is strictly devoid of onion and garlic for the benefit of Hindu devotees. This wonderful tradition of fraternity continues to this day, that is to say, seven and a half centuries after the great Sufi (Ghosh and Kumar 2008: 15).

Language is an important attribute of a population, and has great relevance and significance in a multi-lingual and multi-ethnic country like India. The pan-Indian, civilisational dimension of cultural pluralism and syncretism encompasses ethnic diversity and admixture, linguistic heterogeneity as well as fusion, and variations as well as synthesis in customs, behavioural patterns, beliefs and rituals. The process of synthesis and integration has been extensively at work at the regional level (Das 2003a). Though each group or community has a distinctive identity and ethos of its own, it does not exist in a social vacuum. Rather, it forms part of an extended and dynamic network. Often, interaction, exchange and integration characterize inter-community relations. The sharing of space, regional ethos and cultural traits cut across religions and sectarian differences and bind the local people together. It is now revealed and established more vividly those cultural and religious practices in diverse eco-cultural zones of India have historically converged and people shared common traditions extensively. Thus, we witness a fine balancing between pluralism and syncretism pervading the base of Indian culture (Das 2003b)

In a multi-ethnic situation the process of maintaining the ethnic boundary is somewhat different from that of uni-ethnic situation. In a multi-ethnic situation connubium, commensality and language are three major attributes by which ethnic groups maintain their ethnic boundary. No single ethnic group enjoys a decisive numeral dominance and spatial and socio-cultural hold for nurturing and sustaining its ethnic boundary. Each group has to communicate and interact face to face with a number of other groups involved in the same economic activities. Even in the spheres of connubium, commensality and language they have to evolve a compromising formula and an attitude of tolerance (Rizvi 2006: 18). In Assam, the major sources of cultural diversity is ethnic origins, diverse religion, indigenous beliefs and practices, languages and large number of dialects as well as various migrant groups come from within and outside India at different times and phases, following different routes and directions (Das 2003 c).

II

Study on modern city is marked by disagreements. Social scientists not only employ a variety of theoretical orientations when interpreting the city's ecological and social structure but utilize diverse research procedures as well. The study of the city, notably urban ecology, has been the focus of considerable debate between those scholars who believe that impersonal or 'materialistic' forces shape its destiny and those who contend that socio-cultural factors are the prime sources of change. In another view, it is stated that [early Chicago school, Wirth (1938) and Redfield (1941)], the city-generally contrasted with the folk society is seen as generating secularisation, secondary group relations, tenuous social norms and the like. One group of sociologists emphasizes the 'cultural homogenisation' of (or dedifferentiation') in city life, while another group focuses on the increased differentiation in the industrial city-particularly along occupational lines. The assimilation of ethnic groups also gives rise to contradictory patterns. The sociologist's traditional theoretical model of this process was constructed upon the premise of continued assimilation of ethnic groups and the homogenisation of urban life. Although this may occur over decades or centuries, it is not likely to happen in the immediate future. Indeed, the very process of assimilation leads to a heightened form of social identity. For one thing, a group must have a well-defined concept of its past if it is to formulate a clear conception of its future (Cited in Sjoberg 1972: 455-459). Nevertheless, urban populations are usually very heterogeneous, consisting of many different religious and ethnic groups, as well as representatives of many different socioeconomic status levels. Within a country, individual cities grow primarily as a result of migration. Cities increase rapidly in size when many people are attracted to them, and they decline in size when many people already in them decide to live elsewhere (Cited in Anderson 1972: 466-473).

Assam, and for that matter all the North eastern states have been by tradition basically rural. But the rural character has substantially changed in the recent decades, particularly since Independence. Old towns have expanded in area, population and in terms of economic activities. New towns and industrial centres have come into existence during this period. All these developments have triggered impressive population movements from the villages to the towns (Das 2004: 138-139). The internal and external migration of population as well as rural urban migration to avail suitable livelihood option has exerted enormous pressure mainly in Guwahati. As stated Guwahati is a fastly growing city within north east due to geo-strategic location. The rapid increase of commercial centres, business and employment opportunities, growing educational and technical institutions, displacement due to flood, erosion, intercommunity conflict are some of the push and pull factors for many people's not only within Assam but from other parts of India. The expanding employment opportunities and higher wages in urban centres, and the shrinking employment and comparatively lower earnings in the villages, complement and reinforce each-other, causing the 'pull' and 'push' that result in the migration from the villages to urban centres (Sarmah 1994: 15). As stated besides immigration of people from the other parts of India, there has been practically unabated migration of people from villages within the state and its neighbourhood. A pertinent question always rise: what happens in the realm of religion and community life in general when people of diverse origin and background, belonging to different cultural traditions and experiences come and settle down in the new urban habitat, namely, an urban neighbourhood? Whether the term 'syncretism' is applicable or not in the present context?

III

An urban neighbourhood is quite different from a traditional village from which the migrants originally came. Under such circumstances, a question would naturally arise whether the urban inhabitants live in a kind of social vacuum and whether there are elements of anomie and atrophy in social life. After all the urban setting is not merely diffuse and vast, it is also in a way over-bearing. The question therefore is how the migrants fit into the changed circumstances of life and how do they cope with the so-called urban pressures impinging on their life. Birubari has emerged over the years as a heterogeneous neighbourhood inhabited by people belonging to different ethnic, cultural, linguistic and religious communities.

The Birubari is located under 53 No East Guwahati Constituency of Guwahati, Assam. It is situated in Ulubari and partly of Beltola mouzaand under the jurisdiction of Paltan Bazar Police station. Territorially, the Birubari area is located in the southern middle part of Guwahati. Earlier, Birubari was regarded as a fringe and outskirt area of Guwahati proper. There was no proper communication and road connection. People are mostly unaware of this area. Various sources reveal that earlier there are tribal settlements. They are mostly from Rabha (a scheduled plain tribe of Assam) and Bodo-Kachari (a few) community. It was better known as 'Rabha Goan'. It is mentioned in some of the published souvenirs associated with Bihu and Birubari Sakha Sahitya Sabha. However, regarding the name of Birubari, it lacks authentic information. In this connection, I met some of the respected residents of Birubari during my University days. One of my school teacher Late Girish Chandra Nath (retired as an Assistant Teacher from Arya Vidyapith H.S and MP school) wrote a popular article on historical background of Birubari and published in a souvenir of Sakha Sahitya Sabha. Regarding place name legend, he cited two illustrations: one he mentioned about legendary hero 'Biru Veer' who was supposed to be earliest settler and second, about abundance of a variety of bamboo grooves locally known as '*birubah*'. Both these version of place lore provide us the root of the term 'Birubari'. As we know place lore is one the interesting area of folklore studies. Place lore denote local legends, beliefs and descriptions of customs that are connected with places, and oral histories, memories, natural and cultural surroundings, such as hills, valleys, forests, wetlands, lakes, rivers, fields, stones, old trees, graveyards, chapels, churches and other objects . Place lore is a shared folkloric tradition that needs a long time to emerge and develop. Generally a rich and lively place-lore characterizes the narrative traditions of those regions where people have settled for decades

(Valk 2008: 10). However, the remnant of tribal village is still found in the population structure, economy and habitat, traditional beliefs and practices, as well. So far Rabha village is concerned, there is ample evidence. The existence of Sri Sri Manasa temple by the side of Gopinath Bordoloi Lower Primary School, at the heart of Birubari since the very beginning trace back to 'Rabha Village'. Besides Late Latish Rabha (holding post of Deputy Mayor of Gauhati Municipal Corporation) trace back to his origin from those early Rabha families. Nevertheless, earlier the area was a remote one within Gauhati. It is evident from the presence of specialised government hospitals for infectious diseases. Lokapriya Gopinath Bordoloi Chest Hospital (Tuberculosis) and Cholera Hospital are situated at the centre of Birubari. Further, B.Barooah Cancer Hospital is located adjacent to Birubari.

At present, the greater Birubari area comprises both hills (Narakashur *pahar*) and plain areas. It is reported that a few families from indigenous Muslim community from rural Kamrup settled over here during the early post-Independence period. Most of them are from Dampur area of Hajo, Kamrup Rural. Prior to that a sizeable number of families from Rabha as well as Bodo Kachari tribe have settled here. The addition of other families from their community help them clustering into separate group. As stated earlier, the manasa temple epitomizes Rabha community where worship of Ai Manasa (traditional Snake goddess) is held annually and provide an opportunity of cultural as well as religious syncretism among Rabhas and Bodos of the locality. It cut accross beyond boundaries of traditional beliefs and practices where participation of other communities Assamese Hindus, Bengali Hindus, Hindi speaking people (Bihar and UP) are found in contemporary times.

The post 1960s and early 70s are the beginning of expansion of Birubari. Peoples from various parts of Assam started settling in Birubari. Many of them come to Guwahati to fulfill economic needs. Some of them are government servants. Involvement in schools, colleges, health care institutions, pitty trade and commerce compel them to settle here. New areas, hemlets, colonies started growing and there are rapid expansion of Birubari area occupying all the vacant land of the plains and hills at a cheap rate. A large holding of land is under possession among a few families with an origin from Bihar during post-Independence period before introduction of Ceiling Act. After its introduction they had to handover those lands to new migrants at a cheap rate. Late 70s and early 80s showed newly structured Birubari. Meanwhile Arya Vidyapith College and Arya Vidyapith School (located within the same boundary) in Sarab-Bhati has started functioning with full-enrollment. A section of college staff developed Professors' colony by settling over there. Now the greater Birubari area has a well recognised boundary: to its north Sarabhati, west- Kalapahar, south-Rupnagar and east-Ulubari. Various hamlets have developed over the years and signified by ethnic composition. The

Birubari proper is the nerve centre for commercial activities. Settlement started here with migrant indigenous muslim families and identified as Mazjid area with the growth and development of Birubari Majzid. The entire area and surrounding vicinity is occupied by indigenous Muslim, a few settlements of Assamese Hindus and of Burmese origin. They have always been maintaining inter-ethnic cohesion and brotherhood since the very beginning. Sankarpur, Pragatipur, Jayanagar, Kailashpur, Nizarapar, Baikunthapur are hilly areas. Sankarpur is an area mostly of Assamese Hindu settlers where two *namghars* (prayer house-a creation of Srimanta Sankardeva) are established. Jayanagar and Kailashpur area is inhabitated by heterogenous groups: Assamese Hindus, Bodo-Kachari, Rabha, people of origin from Bihar and U.P. *Bathou puja* is a part of cultural heritage of Bodos. The religious philosophy among the Bodo-Kacharis is centred around the super power of *bathou barai* or *khoria barai maharaja* which is analogous to *Sibrai* or Lord Shiva of the Hindu trinity. The *sizu* plant (Euphorbia splendens) is regarded as the representation of bathou, the supreme deity of adoration. In Birubari, there is a *bathou* temple where Bodos worshop *bathou* (Lord Shiva as principal deity) annually. Most of the Bodo families assemble during *bathou puja* and celebrate it (during Bohag, first month of Assamese calendar) traditionally. Some of the Rabha families also participate in the *puja* symbolizing religious syncretism in an urban context. Besides, there is a Baptist church in the Jayanagar area. A few Garo families are settled surrounding the church. It is observed that church provide an opportunity to share a common platform for Christians belonging to Assamese, Bodo-Kachari and Garo as well. The Bengali Hindus are mainly settled in the hamlets like Udaypur, Sadhupatti and Kalimandir area. A kali mandap (Permanent seat for goddess Kali) is located in Udaypur where Durga puja and Kali puja is held. Nearby Udaypur, a small pockets of Sikh population has given rise a Sikh temple. However, a small section of Sikh community is settled in Birubari. They are successful businessman. Further Jonakpur hamlet is adjacent to Professor Colony. Most of the residents of Jonakpur area are of Assamese Hindus. They are mostly from lower Assam. Surrouding the bathou temple area which is in plain area, upto the hills, a settlement of Meitei people is found. They are mostly from Silchar, Karimganj as well as Manipur valley. They congregate in the open field of *Bathou* temple premises during their traditional festivals.

After 1990s, a new wave of new migrants was observed in Birubari. People from Bihar have started growing rapidly. They have occupied majority of the rented shops by trade. They are owners of tea stall, groceries, cloth and sandal shops, saloons, etc. They are not permanent land holders but carried on economic pursuits staying on rented premises. Besides, other groups of people are from Dhubri, Goalpara, Boko, Chhaigaon, Barpeta, Salmara, etc. They are migrant Muslims (Bengali Muslim). They came here as a wage earner. Some of them are specialised as mason, tile worker, electrician, plumber, painter and others. A few of them are shop owners for spices and vegetable in the Birubari market. The number of these people is growing in a rapid speed in recent days. However, the ethnic composition of Birubari and religious structure provide an interesting picture pertaining to cultural and religious dimensions.

IV

Various studies reveal that urban localities are mostly heterogeneous. A mixed population is always found in terms of ethnic, socio-cultural as well as religious affiliation as well. People used to come from different places, areas with their distinct socio-cultural background. Initially, they face adjustment problem in the new localities. Slowly but gradually they developed the art of social adjustment in the new environment. They know that their new abode is not for amusement rather it is purely economic needs. It is their part of survival mechanism. The inhabitants of Birubari have nicely learned the art of socio-cultural adjustment in the midst of heterogeneous ethnic composition. Sociologists and Anthropologists have showed marked differences between an urban and rural way of life. Robert Redfield had formulated the theory of rural-urban continuum. In his theory, he clearly showed the complexity of urban life.

A new migrant not only carry his physical existence but his identity and culture moves along with him. In a new environment he always search for new companion and establish relationship with their neighbour irrespective own community and religion. No doubt social and economic status plays an important role in every locality. In Birubari, I have observed the syncretism in real sense which cut across all the boundaries of ethnic identity. It is perhaps sharing a common space by different groups of people over the years. In these days, urban life is out and out influenced by globalisation and modernisation. Birubari, though an urban neighbourhood exhibits features of folk life during traditional religious festivals and ceremonies. The Bodo-Kacharis and Rabhas are grouped separately under different '*giate*'. It is informed that families belonging to both are included under both the '*giate*'. It means a few families from Bodo community voluntarily associated with Rabha *gaite* and vice-versa. The concept of giate in the context of Birubari is significant. It is one of the unique feature of group solidarity of tribal folk life. In an urban locality such grouping is essential in order to maintain ethnic identity. For them the term 'giate' is equivalent to '*raiz*' or '*samaj*'. There is a selected *gaonbura* in every *giate*, followed by chairman, secretary, treasurer, *ghai deuri* (chief priest), *pani deuri* (associate priest) and members. They retain their traditional beliefs and practices through '*giate*'. They assemble prior to celebration of their traditional religion, mainly during *manasa* puja and *bathou* puja. Noted linguist and folklorist, Pramod Chandra Bhattacharya (1966) mentioned "the Boros of the northern bank of Brahmaputra valley narrate their origin of creation in relation to the worship of bathow. Bathou represents the five basic elements of creation. He is known as *Sibray* (Siva). *Bathou* or *Sibray* with his wife (Sibury) created this universe and the first man, Monsinsin. As Monsinsin remained a lifelong celibate, Sibray and his wife created Darimoba, the male and Siring Dowba, the female in order to propagate the human population (*mansoy*). Bathou created the *sizu* plant, the first tree which stands as an emblem of the supreme God at the altar….the *sizu* tree is planted on the north-eastern corner of the courtyard parallel to the easternmost portion of the main house. The altars of Khamaikha (Kamakhya or the mother Goddess), mainaw (the goddess of fortune or Lakshmi) and *bathou* (great father) are placed inside the easternmost portion of the main house". A sizu plant is there nearby *bathou* temple. Contributions are collected from the members of the *giate* during ritual time. Traditional liquor is offered in order to appease principal deity. Often friend circles outside Bodo community used to visit in order taste local rice beer in its purest form. It is also observed that a section of Bodos and Rabhas earn their bread and butter by selling homemade traditional liquor. They are cheap in comparison western liquor. A section of lower economic class pay regular visit to these centres and bind under relationship, sometimes marital bonding is seen. Marital ties strengthen the bonding of inter-community relationship between two groups. I have seen one of the Assamese boy of my locality, had developed love affair with a Rabha girl while visiting for consuming local beer. His marriage was arranged. Unfortunately he became too alcoholic and died untimely leaving his wife and a daughter.

In Assam, the Rabhas are recognised as one of the plain tribes of Assam (*supra*). However, they are divided into various groups: Pati, Rongdani, Maitory, Dahuri, Totla, Bitlia, Kocha and others and distributed in various districts like Kamrup, Goalpara, etc. The pati groups are found inhabiting adjacent to Assamese society since the very beginning. They are in the midst of a gross impact of their own socio-cultural practices by Assamese community. Cultural trait percolates to them from neighbouring Assamese society. The term 'acculturation' is more suitable in anthropological parlance. Even Pati Rabhas have forgotten their own dialect. They now speak Assamese language. In Birubari, majority of the Rabhas are from Pati group. They use Assamese language within and outside. Even the Bodos of Birubari also face the same situation. New generation communicate through Assamese at all levels with a flavour of rural lower Assam. Ranjit Bodo (school class mate) said '*moi Bodo kaba noru, ma-deutais alop kaba pare*' [I can't speak Bodo rather father and mother can speak]. This is the real situation. The new generation accepted Assamese as their mother tongue. Languages in most of the cases pave the way for building syncretism in a multiethnic setting in urban context. People prefer to adept in dominant language. It is not only a situation for indigenous groups for Assam. But other groups like both Bengali muslim and Hindu, people from Bihar, Nepalis, Garos, Meitei adopted Assamese language for inter-ethnic communication. It has made the process of synthesis and assimilation faster.

Manasa is a folk deity among various tribes of Assam including caste Hindus. Among the Rabhas, manasa occupy a significant place in their religious life. *Manasa puja* is being organised by Rabha giate in the temple (*supra*). Sacrifices of pigeon are made by traditional priest. I have seen drinking blood of pigeon by the priest during purification of temple on the early hours of the day of *puja*. *Xorai* (offerings include gram seed, piece coconut, seasonal fruits) are offered to get rid of snake bites, fatel diseases and seek blessings for the members of *giate* as well as for the general welfare of all residents. It is also observed that on the eve of *puja*, the prices of pigeon increases thrice from their actual rate and it became scarce. People from other communities like Assamese, Bengalis, Bihar origin; Bodos has a deep faith on the *manasa*. As it is reported many of their desires are fulfilled. They are waiting to reciprocate through offering a pair of pigeon (*paro*). Some of it is being sacrificed while other are set free. As Doshi and Jain (2001: 285-286) observes: "Religion has been the core of India's tradition.....not only been a tradition of worship, it also controlled the entire community life....rituals are related to religion.... religion is a belief and rituals are mechanisms through which beliefs are fulfilled. If a community has a belief that floods can be controlled by worshipping evil spirits, that belief is religion and the sacrifice of a goat is ritual". In greater Birubari, the clustering of families, sharing a common space over the years make it happen so that every group possess particular space for socio-religious activities. At various hamlets, some religious establishment has emerged over the years (See Table).

Sl. No	***Religious Establishment***	***Community Affiliation***	***Hamlets/Locality***
1.	Bathou temple	Bodo-Kachari	Nizarapar
2.	Church	Assamese/Garo/Bodo-Kachari	Jayanagar
3.	Gurudwara	Sikh	Udaipur
4.	Kali temple	Bengali Hindu	Udaipur
5.	Manasa temple	Rabha	Birubari proper
6.	Mosque	Assamese/ Bengali	Birubari proper
7.	Namghar	Assamese Hindus	Sankarpur, Kailashpur, Pragatipur, Jonakpur
8.	Shiva temple	Assamese/Bengali/Bihari/Bodo-Kacharis/ Nepali	Joyanagar, Sankarpur (hill top)

Whether, it is church, mosque, *namghar*, guru-dwara, temple, all of them follows their prescribe rules and regulations, code of religious conduct. Hindu religion provides more scope for inter-ethnic integration. People may belong to different communities: Assamese, Bengali, people from Bihar and U.P (hindi speaking people), Nepali, Rabha, Bodo-Kachari and others. Though they have different sects, beliefs and practices, influence of Hinduism is prominent among them in their day to life. Vermillion in the forehead of married woman, participation in Durga puja, celebrating Deepawali, appeasing lord Biswakarma and Ganesh, goddess Saraswati, Lakshi, Kali by following rituals are impact of Hinduism.

The different *namghars* are the hallmark of Assamese Hindu households of different hamlets in Birubari. *Namghar* is regarded as village level religious institution, result of new-vaishnavite movement initiated by Sankardeva in Assam. *Nam-prasanga* (singing of devotional songs and prayer accompanying traditional musical instrument) during anniversaries of Sankardeva, Madhabdeva, Harideva, Gopaldeva and Damodardev, also during *janmastami* (birthday of lord Krishna) are held in various *namghars* of Birubari in one way or other. *Namghars* in a locality always attracts Assamese woman. It is not necessary that they may belong to the sect initiated by Sankardeva, which denies idol worship. However, in urban context there is trend for following dual religious norms. They participate in *namghar* activities and also offer idol worship held during different cylindrical years. There are different worship at household (Lakhi puja, Narayan puja, Bishu puja) and public levels (Saraswati puja, Biswakarma puja). Saraswati is worshipped as a deity of knowledge while Biswakarma is worshipped as a deity of creation in Hindu pantheon. In an urban context, within mixed population structure, individuals participate in it irrespective of religious boundary. For example, two youth (Islam) has the responsibility to manage local water distribution system nearby area of Birubari O.P. They have seen worshipping Lord Biswakarma which has become a popular puja. Some popular religious worship and festival has played the role of assimilation in recent times.

There is a common space for Durga puja and Kali puja held annually (courtyard of Gopinath Nagar L.P. School) organised under two different banners: *Brihattar* Birubari *Durga Puja Udjapan* Committee (Greater Birubari Durga Puja Celebration Committee) and BYMA (Birubari Young Men's Association). The Durga puja is not only a widely celebrated festival in Assam but it unites and strengthens the bond of fraternity among various communities under Hinduism. *Durga puja* provide a wonderful platform for conglomeration of diverse ethnic groups (Assamese Hindu, Bengali Hindu, Bihari Hindu, Rabha, Bodo-Kachari, and Nepali) in Birubari. The member of organizing committee reflects the people from different groups. Further, it is expanded during *Rongali Bihu* where people irrespective of religion contribute for a successful cultural night. There are various clubs (Young Boys' Association, Panchajainna Club), Birubari Development Committee (Birubari Unnayan Samitee) and members may from any religious groups. At public level, people have always in touch beyond own community. Such association led to interaction at family level. The socio-religious get- together, birth day parties, marriage ceremonies passes beyond community jurisdiction in a heterogeneous urban context. My immediate neighborhoods' ethnic composition: north: LGB Chest Hospital Complex, east: Manipuri Hindu, west: Bengali Hindu, south: indigenous muslim and Bengali muslim. Being only Assamese Hindu family, it is observed that inter-community relationship at family and personal level. Assamese Hindu invites during 2 *bihus* (*bohag* and *rongali*) and even in *Satya-Narayan puja* and they invite us during Idd (Id-ul-fitr). However, they don't invite during Idd-uj-Zoha (*Korbani* Idd). They always ready to help in any distress. It is evident from various personal experiences. In 2012 my father had a tragic accident where he survives (huge sum involve) only by grace of almighty. In the days of our economic hardship, our neighbours came forward than our own relatives. In an urban context, sharing a common space make people come closer. Rodman (2003: 205) observes 'Places are not inert containers. They are politicized, culturally relative, historically specific, local and multiple constructions. The physical, emotional and experimental realities places hold for their inhabitants at particular times need to be understood apart from their creation as the locales of ethnography'.

Sharing space over the years has helped in developing cohesion. In Birubari, I have never experience any kind of communal feelings pertaining to religion. I still remember, though I am young, there was a tense situation over the destruction of Babri Maszid. There was a close vigil of police personnel. Not a single kind of instance was recorded so far in Birubari. A large number of Hindi speaking people are become resident of Birubari. Some of them are permanently settled while some settled in rented premises. *Chhat puja* (worship of sun god) during the month of November is celebrated with pomp and gaity. They assemble in the large ponds of the Department of Fisheries, Government of Assam. Now gradually, it is seen that people from Assamese and Bengali communities also followed the rituals associated with worship. The rituals associated with *Chhat puja* have it own charm to catch the eye of an outsider. Continuous sharing of ritual ideology and significance has an overall effect in a neighbourhood context, enhancing syncretism in a greater meaning.

In the age of modernisation and smart phones, there are changes at the attitudes of the new generations. They go beyond their community in terms of friendship. Their food habits and dress patterns are influenced not by their own community rather latest professional brand. The aged woman folk use their traditional dresses during festive and ritualistic occasion. Rabha women use mekhela chadar (Assamese traditional dresses) during *manasa puja* while Bodos use *dokhona* and *aronai* (Bodo garments) during *bathoupuja*. The cultural syncretism is observed in terms of food habits. Pork is one of items of delicacy among the tribal people. The taste of pork passes to other non-tribal Hindu people in Birubari. There is famous area (rather point/stoppage) known as *gahori kata chuk* (pork cutting point). The English term 'syncretism' is tested in the context of Birubari. Though the tribal people are influenced by elements of Hinduism, they retain their traditional beliefs and practices. The Garo are Christians from since the early times. All the communities are adhered to own religious beliefs and practices in a harmonious way. There is no problem at all. Even the new families nicely adjusted to the existing own groups. In this way they maintain a separate identity within a greater identity. But all comes together in organisation like 'Greater Birubari Unnayan Samity', 'Greater Birubari Rongali Bihu Celebration Committee' and Durga puja committees (Hindu and Tribal). In this regard, the term '*Samanvay*' is more appropriate and equivalent in the context of an urban setting.

V

Definitions of religion are undoubtedly controversial. While most people define religion based on their own perception of it, most of these definitions have diverse elements and religion emerge as a multifaceted phenomenon. The presence of religion is seen in all the social spaces. It has become an issue in socio-political context. Religious conversions, Shah Bano case, Ram temple movement, Babri Maszid demolition, Islamic terrorism, and growing intolerance depicts a picture of India different from the one in the earlier decades of the republic (Puniyani 2005: 27). It is contradictory from the sociological view. Religion needs to be located squarely within human society and culture; there is no privileged discourse of religion outside of particular cultures and societies. Emile Durkheim rightly defined religion as 'a unified set of beliefs and practices relative to sacred things' which create a social bond between people (*ibid* Flood). In Indian context Hazarika (2015) view is significant and said 'Indian nation building owes its integration to our forefathers who sacrificed narrow identities for creation of an Indian identity that could over-shadow all others. True citizens of India still believe in that….we should emphasize the term worldview rather than religion, because the nation's engagement should not be with Hinduism and its dogmatic religious diktats, but rather with the rational consciousness underlying the worldview that is contemporary and relevant, irrespective of caste, creed, religion and region…'

In such a multi-cultural neighbourhood 'Birubari', religious life is also characterised by diversity. The residents subscribe to different faith: Hinduism, Islam, Christianity, Sikhism and tribal religions. It is popularly assumed that migrants to urban area are under considerable pressure of socio-economic adjustments. However, a close examination of the domain of religion in Birubari shows that people are strongly committed to religious activities. In fact, it becomes an important rallying point for organizing activities and finding new meaning and satisfaction in the urban context. The basic assumption is that in the context of rapid urbanisation in Assam compelling or encouraging people to move from villages to towns and cities, the hold of tradition in religious life remains quite strong. At one level, in their day to day activities and economic pursuits, the people may be part of an atomistic urban context, while at another level, in the context of the neighbourhood, they may retain and develop many of the attributes of social relations. No doubt urban context also provides numerous opportunities for fulfillment of discrete religious activities and in no way poses as a threat to religio-cultural autonomy of different migrant groups. In Birubari every group become successful in maintaining their identity by forming separate societies. They nicely inhabit adhering to own faith, beliefs, practices and religion. In an urban setting, people are aware of their own aims and objectives. Their main aim is economic rather than other. They know the present situation is completely different from their native place. An urban context generally provides all the avenues for income. Outsiders focus generating income resources by doing any trade. They do not hanker after government job. The smooth functioning of trade will be possible after cordial relations with the new people. They adjust quickly and help forming solidarity in a new locality. Sharing a common space over the years provide 'syncretism' a new meaning in an urban context.

Bibliography

Anderson, Theodore R (1968).(1972). 'Comparative Urban Structure' in David L. Sills edited *International Encyclopedia of the Social Sciences*. Vol. 1. New York and London: The Macmillan Company & The Free Press, and Collier-Macmillan Publishers.

Bajpai, Kanti. (2010). 'Diversity, Demography and Devolution in India' in Sanjib Baruah edited *Ethno nationalism in India – A Reader*. New Delhi: Oxford University Press.

Bakshi, P.M. (1991). *The Constitution of India*. Delhi: Universal Law Publishing Co. Pvt. Ltd.

Bhargava, Rajeev. (1999). ' Introducing Multiculturalism' in Rajeeb Bhargava, Amiya Kumar Bagchi and R. Sudarshan edited *Multiculturalism, Liberalism and Democracy*. New Delhi: Oxford University Press.

Bhattacharya, Pramod Chandra (1966) 'Introduction' to Bhabendra Narzi's *Boro-Kacharir Samaj aru Sanskriti*. Guwahati and Kokrajhar: Bina Library.

Das, Ranga Ranjan (2004-2005). 'Birubari: Religious Life in an Urban Neighbourhood' in*Bull. Dept.of Folklore Research*. Vol. VI. Guwahati: Gauhati University

Deka, Harekrishna. (2015). 'This nation: on the cusp of history' . *The Assam Tribune*, 4th November.

Das, NK.(1989). *Ethnic Identity, Ethnicity and Social Stratification in North East India*. New Delhi: Inter-India Publication.

.....(ed) (2003a). *Culture, Religion and Philosophy: Critical Studies in Syncretism and Inter-Faith Harmony*. Jaipur: Rawat Publications.

......(2003 b). 'Introduction: An outline of Syncretism' in *Culture, Religion and Philosophy: Critical Studies in Syncretism and Inter-Faith Harmony*, pp. 11-36, Jaipur: Rawat Publications.

……(2003 c). 'Religious syncretism and cultural Homogenisation in North East India' in *Culture, Religion and Philosophy: Critical Studies in Syncretism and Inter-Faith Harmony*, pp 295-324, Jaipur: Rawat Publications.

Doshi, S.L. and PC Jain, (2001). 2011. *Social Anthropology*. New Delhi: Rawat Publications.

Flood, Gavin. (2004). *An Introduction to Hinduism*. New Delhi: Foundation Books.

Ghosh, Kunal and Vikas Kumar, (2008). *Separation in North-East India- Role of Religion, Language*. New Delhi: Suruchi Prakashan.

Hazarika, Sujata Dutta. (2015). 'Idiosyncrasies in the name of religion'. *The Assam Tribune*, 13 November.

Parel, Anthony J, (1957). 'Religious Syncretism in India'. *Thought*. Vol 32, Issue 2, pp 261-279, Philosophy Documentation Centre.

Puniyani, Ram. (2005). 'Religion: Opium of the Masses or..' in Ram Puniyani edited *Religion, Power and Violence-Expression of Politics in Contemporary Times*. New Delhi: Sage Publication India Pvt. Ltd.

Rizvi, BR. (2006). 'Ethnicity and Ethnic Movements in North-East India' in Bimal J. Deb edited *Ethnic Issues- Secularism and Conflict Resolution in North East India.* Shillong and New Delhi: NEICSSR and Concept Publishing Company.

Rodman, Margaret C. (2003).'Empowering Place: Multilocality and Multivocality' in Setha M. Low and Denise Lawrense-Zuniga edited *The Anthropology of Space and Place*. Blackwell Publishing

Sarmah, Mrinal. (1994). 'Housing Problem among the Rural migrants of Lower income category: A brief study in an encroacher's colony in Guwahati city'. *Bull.Dept. Anth*. Gauhati University, VIII, 14-19.

Sjoberg, Gideon. (1968), (1972).'The Modern City' in David L. Sills edited *International Encyclopedia of the Social Sciences*. Vol. 1. New York and London: The Macmillan Company & The Free Press, and Collier-Macmillan Publishers.

Valk, Ulo. (2008). 'Notes on Assamese Place-Lore' in *Indian Folklife*- A quarterly Newsletter, Serial No 31, Chennai: National Folklore Support Centre.

Van der Veer, Peter, (2003). 'Syncretism, Multiculturalism and the Discourse of Tolerance' in Rosaland Shaw and Charles Stewart edited Syncretism/*Anti-Syncretism: The Politics of Religious Synthesis*. Routledge.

Web Source

www.bangladeshsociology. org, 'Cultural Diversity, Religious Syncretism and People of India: An Anthropological Interpretation' by NK Das, Former Superintending Anthropologist (Cultural), Anthropological Survey of India.

29

Looking into Indian Civilization through religious syncretism: A study on the process of blending religious belief of the Savar and Hinduism

— *Sampa Basu*

India is a country known for its unity among diversity. There are various religions, languages, cultural diversities. However each group or community has anidiosyncratic identity and philosophy, but some common criteria likethe sharing of space, regional cultural traits and local ethos cut across ethnic and sectarian differences and unite the people together.In a nutshell, it can be said that syncretism has been going on. Thus equilibrium between cultural diversity and syncretism is the foundation of Indian civilization. Srivastava(2010) has rightly suggested that tribal communities have been Hinduised from time immemorial. In our country, actually, most of their interactions have been with themajority Hindu community, the structural principle of which is the caste system(Srinivas, 1952). It is worth mentioning here that Hinduism is a non-proselytisingreligion (Srinivas and Shah, 1968). Many Scholars (Braden, 1967; Biardeau, 1989; Srinivas and Shah, 1968) suggested that Hinduism is pluralistic, allowing different beliefs and practices to coexist.

Such an assemble of little tradition and great tradition and vice versa has been observed among the religion of the tribe Savar. The Savarsare very ancient tribe of India andin the ancient Hindu mythologies they have been placed prominently under various references.

The Cult of Lord Jagannath and the Tribe Savar

O'Malley (1911), referred that 'the Savarawere associated with the worship of Jagannath of Puri and it is said that the original image of the deity was discovered in the land of Savaras where its priest was a Savar, named Besu or Vishwabasu'. Such impact of tribal culture on the epitome of Hindu religion or on the culture of Hindu community has also been described by the eminent researchers.Himangsu Mohan Ray in his book 'Savara: The Snake Charmer' (1986) has referred that the Savar tribe of West Bengal claim that the community has been originated from Viswavasu who is the priest of 'Nil Madhava' or 'Jagannath of Nilachal'. Same history of origin of the tribe Savar has been reported from theethnographic studies of theSavars of the villages Naihati and Asanpur and Jhaokhali of the district Paschim Medinipur, Batdanga, Ledhashal and Katium villages of Bankura, Pargora, Bandudabor, Amjharna and Ghatiuli villages of Puruliya.AnncharlottEschmann(1978) has pointed out that the 'Nabakalevara' ritual is the ceremony of periodical renewal of the body of the deity, is a tribal custom.Such practices of renewal of wooden deity are found among the primitive tribes like Savaras and Khonds.On the occasion of 'Nabakalevara' ritual,the process of the renewal of the oldpost indicates a great similarity between theJagannathtenet and the tribal ritual. Accordingly,after the carving of new imagesthe mysterious life substances (Brahma) is transferred from old to thenew images and the old images areconsidered dead. The old images are taken to thecemetery in the manner of corpses. The burialground, known as KoiliBaikuntha, is locatedwithin the area of the temple of LordJagannath. Thereafter the Daitas startweeping. They keep mourning for 10 days.They place claim onthe articles used by the deity as they believe that are the heirs of the deceased. **Verrier Elwin**in his book ***Religion of an Indian Tribe (1955)*** has also traced tribal origin of the lord Jagannath of Puri temple. He has referred in his book that "The god Jagannatha had appeared in Seori-Narayana and an old Savar used to worship him. The king of Odisha had built the great temple at Puri and wished to install Jagannatha in it, and he found a Brahmin to fetch it from Seori-Narayan, but nobody knew where it was except the old hermit, Savar. The Brahmin besought him in vain to be allowed to see the god and even went so far as to marry his daughter, and finally the old man consented to take him blindfolded to the place. The Brahmin, however, tied some mustard seeds on a corner of his cloth and made a hole in it so that they dropped out one by one on the way. After sometime they grew up and served to guide him to the spot. The Brahmin then went to the Seori-Narayana alone and begged the god to go to Puri. Jagannatha consented and assuming the form of a log of wood, floated down the Mahanadi to Puri, where he was taken out and placed in the temple."

As per Elwin there is an alternative Savara legend, according to which there are three most important and prominent Kitungs (Gods) - two brothers and a sister, Ramma, Bimma and Sitaboi. Ramma is always coupled with the brother Bimma. The legend maintains that it was from them that the Savara tribe was born. Such a set up has significant resemblance to the Jagannath triad.

Etymologically, the word 'Jagannath' means 'Master' or 'Lord'. But Padhi (1964), has suggested that Jagannath was aresultant from the name "Jagant" which was another name of "Kitung" the Chief Savara deity.Kitung is said to have 10 incarnations like LordVishnu and the Jagant incarnation of Kitung is oneof them. But accordind to Pattanaik (2013), It is indeed difficult to say anything definiteon the etymology of the term Jagannath. The nameof the deity Jagannath came into use since ancienttime. Literary sources like the Ramayana refersto a deity, (Jagannath), Vishnu Purana 7th centuryA.D., Janasiddhi (8th Century A.D) andTrikandeswar (9th century A.D.) mention thename of Jagannath. It was only from the beginningof the 14th Century A.D. exclusive use of the nameJagannath relating Puri deity has been known.

During the 15th. and 16 th. Centuries A.D. when the debate on the subject of evolution of Jagannath Cult reached its zenith, the literary work of Sarala das, Nilambar Das and Jagannath Das depicted the Savara tribe in an overstated manner as the early worshipper of Lord Jagannath.

As the tribal people do not possess stratified society, all ofthem belong to same strata. At the Puri temple also it is seen that the tribal priests and non-tribal priests occupy equally important positionsin the worship of Lord Jagannath. Moreover,offerings to Lord Jagannath popularly known as 'Mahaprasad'bears indication to a classless and casteless society. It is through 'Mahaprasad,that comradeship is created among all castes- high and low. Each and everybody can take 'Mahaprasad' from the same plate without any hesitation. The other name of this 'Mahaprasad ' is 'Kaivalya'. It is general belief that 'Mokshya' or salvation can be achieved by taking 'Mahaprasad'.

The factors responsible for the acceptance of tribal origin theories are as under:

1. The structure and shape of Jagannath deity is commensurate with a pillar. The Savaras, the earliest tribal inhabitants of Odisha, were tree worshipers, and their rituals involved dancing and singing before the*Kitung* or *Jaganata* or God. It has been argued that when the Vedic Aryans migrated to Odisha, they adopted the local tribal tradition of*Jaganata* worship, and effected the transformation of the tribal wooden pillar *Jaganata* to aryanized *Jagannath*. In fact, among tribals of Vindhya region, tree or khamba (pillar or post) worship is prevalent.
2. A deep association of a class of non-Brahmin, tribal origin servitors, called Daitas(descendants) or Daitapatis, exist with the worship of the Jagannath deities. These Daitas are the hereditary servitors of Jagannath. They are exclusively connected with the funeral rites of

Jagannath during the 'Nabakalevara' ritual and some other important responsibilities. The instances of worship of Jagannath by Savaras is also mentioned in Mahabharata written by Sarala Das,Darubrahma Gita written by Jagannath Das in the 16th century and in DeulaTola written by Nilambara Das in the 17th century.

3. The images of the Jagannath triad are built out of neem wood, as opposed to universal use of stone for construction of images of all brahminical Hindu deities.
4. There is no caste distinction in the cult of Jagannath which is akin to the practices of tribals and significantly different from classical Vaishnavism.

Therefore, it can be assumed that in course of time, the cult of Jagannath gradually emerged intoAryanised form and various major faiths like Saivism, Saktism, Vaishnavism, Jainism and Buddhism have been assimilated into this Jagannath Cult.

Gaajon festival and the Tribe Savar

Gaajon is a festival of the Hindus. In this festival, the supreme god Shiva is worshipped with great zeal in West Bengal, specially in south Bengal. It is actually the celebration of Lord Shiva's wedding with Parvoti. In North Bengal same festival is known as *Gambhira*. It is also called *Neel Puja* in East Bengal The god Shiva is worshipped by a Brahmin priest. *Gaajon* is generally celebrated by the lower class people and it is a folk culture with a scent of great tradition. The process of worshipping the god and the typical customs associated with the festival is rooted in indigenous culture and spirituality. Lord Shiva is not only the part of literary Hindu tradition, but he is also a concomitant part of folk tradition. It is interesting that the term *Gaajon* point out towards the folk theme of participation in the village wedding as Gaa means village in Bengali and Jon means people. That means people from the villages gather to celebrate Lord's wedding. It is said that Lord Shiva got married in the month of Chaitra and *Gaajon* is generally celebrated during last three days of *Chaitra* (March-April). A major part of *Gaajon* is *Charak*. The term *Charak* is derived from *Chakra*. It is symbolized by the action of the performers who tie themselves with a rope and hand on to a long bamboo pole and then spin around. Such a painstaking self-restraint tradition could only be found among the indigenous people and their magical performances.SubalSavar of the village Batdanga under the district Bankura, has narrated a folktale about this festival which her grandmother told him. He has said that the LOrd Shiva is the deity of the tribe Savar. Because, during *Dakhyajogya* (Hindu legend about lord Shiva), the Savarsconciliated the god by providing their blood and since then they have been observing Charak and offering blood to appease Shiva.

Experiencing *Charak* in a tribal dominated area like Purulia could be cited as an example of the festival. Pargora is a remote village of Bundwan block under Purulia district, West Bengal. Many Savar families are living here from many generations. The neighbouring villages are inhabited by the non-tribal Hindu people, specially belonging to the Scheduled Caste or other communities. Every year in the month of *Baisakh* (April-May) people belonging to different communities celebrate *Gaajon* together.

In the village temple Lord Shiva is worshipped. Here he is symbolized not by Shiva Linga which is the most common form, but by a totem pole made up of wood having a head, two hands, and two legs with a body. Brahmin priest worshipped Lord Shiva with conventional materials like Bel (*Aeglemarmelos*) pata, betel leaves, flowers, milk, sweets, vermillion etc. *Jagya* is performed at night. The pattern of performance is truly Hinduised, but the essence of performance is truly indigenous. Ambuj Savar, a middle aged man of Pargora is one of the Savar men who perform at *Gaajonutsava*nd *Charak* every year. During field work in Purulia on the eve of *Gaajon*Ambuj was found to perform the ritual spinning around a long bamboo shaft. Before doing this he drank *Haria* a lot and he was in trance with the beat of music played by the other tribal and non – tribal people. For doing this he had to pierce with an iron hanger at his back and tied with a thick rope through which he can hang. The technique of piercing is very unique as it never causes deep injury. This could be related to a sense of sorcery, a typical tribal practice. According to the villagers Savars mainly perform in *Charak*. They believe that taking pain in such a way may fulfill their wish. This is the way of appeasing god in *Charak*. The performer like AmbujSavar never feels pain during *Charak* performance. Usually after removing from the hanger he bows his head to the god in the ground and another person put his big toe on the injury and rubs with soil taken as the *Ashirbad*(blessing) of god. Even if a small stain of blood comes out it is rubbed with the soil and pain vanishes. When a man performs this ritual, others present at the location beat drums and play music. The women dance with the song. Thus the occasion becomes a carnival. Fare is organized at the same place with small impermanent stalls of food, toys, cosmetics etc. providing the backward people a space for amusement. In such way it becomes a folk festival with a Hindu divinity at the Centre.

Conclusion

A peculiar blending of Hinduism and tribal religion, an instance of syncretism has been found in the religion of the tribe Savar. Tribal origin of the lord Jagannathcult and the Hindu festival of Charak or Gajan, observed by the tribe Savar shows the assembling of great and little tradition in their religion. Thus their religion exhibits the processof universalization and parochialization (Marriott 1955).

But the equilibrium between cultural diversity (between the said tribe and the neighbouring Hindus) and syncretism is possible as Hinduism is a non-proselytising religion, as Hinduism is pluralistic, allowing different beliefs and practices to coexist. This characteristics of Hinduism can be explained by the concept of ' Nilkantha Syndrome' of Indian Civilization (Saraswati 1979). As Saraswati explained that like the lord Shiva (Nilkantha), India represents a civilization where she accommodates an element, which others are unable to digest. She has borne the onslaughts of various waves of cultures since the beginning of her history, and whenever, some agreeable elements come, she duly absorb them.

Saraswati'scocept (1979)of Sacred -Secular Continuum of Indian civilization has also been traced at the sacred place of Puri temple. At Puri temple, it is seen that the tribal priests and non-tribal priests occupy equally important positionsin the worship of Lord Jagannath. Moreover, 'Mahaprasad' of Lord Jagannath bears indication to a classless and casteless society as anybody can take 'Mahaprasad' of the lord Jagannathfrom the same plate without any hesitation. The other name of this 'Mahaprasad' is 'Kaivalya'. It is general belief that 'Mokshya' or salvation can be achieved by taking 'Mahaprasad'.

References

Abraham, Priya, (2008). "125th brother of Jagannath". *The Telegraph*. Retrieved 21 October 2012.

Appadurai, A., 1990, "Disjuncture and difference in the global cultural economy" in M. Featherstone, ed. GlobalCulture, London: Sage.

Biardeau, Madeleine (1989) Hinduism, the Anthropology of a Civilization. Delhi:Oxford University Press.

Bose, Nirmal Kumar (1975) The Structure of Hindu Society. Delhi: Orient Longman.

Braden, C.S. (1967) The World's Religions, A Short History. Nashville: Abingdon.

Das, N.K.(1985) "Cultural Diversity, Religious Syncretism and People of India: An Anthropological Interpretation" atwww.bangladeshsociology.org/BEJS% 203.2%20Das.pdf

Elwin, Verrier (1955). The Religion of an Indian Tribe, Oxford University Press.

Eschman, Anncharlott (1978). The Cult of Jagannath and the regional tradition of Orissa,Manohar.

Hall, S. 1987 'Minimal selves' in L. Appignanesi, Ed. Postmodernism and the Question of Identity, London: Institute of Contemporary Arts.

Marriott, Mc. Kim (1955),Village India, Chicago: Chicago University Press.

O' Malley, (1911), C-I, Vol. V, Part-I.

Pattanaik, S (2013), "The Cult of Lord Jagannath" in Odisha Review, October.

Padhi, B.N. (1964), Daru Devata (Oriya), Cuttack.

Ray, H.M. (1986) Savara the Snake Charmer,Midnapur: Samaj Sevak Sangha Press Srinivas, M.N. (1952) Religion and Society among the Coorgs of South India. Oxford: Clarendon Press.

Srinivas, M.N. and A.M. Shah (1968) "Hinduism" in International Encyclopaedia of Social Sciences, 6.

Srivastava, V.K. (2010) 'Socio-Economic Characteristics of Tribal Communities That Call Themselves Hindu', Indian Institute Of Dalit Studies and Religious and Development Research Programme, Working Paper Series, Vol-1, No. 3.

Vidyarthi,L.P., Saraswati, B.N. and MakhanJha(1979), The Sacred Complex of Kashi: A microcosm of Indian Civilization, Delhi: Concept Publishing Company.

Index

I

L

M

S